Frontiers of Finance: The Political Economy of Public Debt in the Dutch Republic

Library of Economic History

VOLUME 20

The titles published in this series are listed at *brill.com/lehi*

Frontiers of Finance: The Political Economy of Public Debt in the Dutch Republic

By

H. Alberto Feenstra

BRILL

LEIDEN | BOSTON

Cover illustration: *Allegorie op de Republiek der Zeven Verenigde Nederlanden*, by Jan Caspar Philips, 1739. Print. Titlepage of J. Wagenaar, *Hedendaagsche historie, of Tegenwoordige staat der Vereenigde Nederlanden*, 1739. © Rijksmuseum, Amsterdam. Object number RP-P-1909-1661. https://id.rijksmuseum.nl/200243504.

The copy editing of this book has been supported by Stichting Unger-Van Brero Fonds.

The Library of Congress Cataloging-in-Publication Data is available online at https://catalog.loc.gov
LC record available at https://lccn.loc.gov/2025048259

Typeface for the Latin, Greek, and Cyrillic scripts: "Brill". See and download: brill.com/brill-typeface.

ISSN 1877-3206
ISBN 978-90-04-43320-5 (hardback)
ISBN 978-90-04-74525-4 (e-book)
DOI 10.1163/9789004745254

This book is printed on acid-free paper and produced in a sustainable manner.

Contents

Preface

This book is the result of a thorough revision of the Ph.D. thesis that I defended at the University of Amsterdam, on 22 June 2018 (*Between Shared and Conflicting Interests. The Political Economy of the Markets for Public Debt in the Dutch Republic, 1600–1795*). I cannot emphasise enough the value of the guidance and inspiration in that process offered to me by my supervisors Joost Jonker and Marjolein 't Hart. The aim of the revised version was to make it more accessible to a wider audience than the Ph.D. thesis. To that end, I reduced its size in a hopefully more readable style. I also added a completely new chapter on the position of the province of Holland within the Dutch Republic. Within that chapter 2, I gave an overview of the most important developments in political economy and analysed the Dutch figures. I also added an international comparison for more perspective on the Dutch situation and figures. Furthermore, I processed and added more archival material in the various chapters. For example, I expanded the analysis of the domestic private capital market with more data from Holland and the rural district (*nedergerecht*) Wagenborgen in Groningen. Furthermore, I almost doubled the number of observations in the analysis of the Frisian newspaper advertisements. For the case of the province of Groningen, I completed the reconstruction of the provincial debt by starting the series around 1625. I also made a novel reconstruction of the interest payments by this province, which is missing in the archival overviews and thus in the *Gewestelijke Financiën* series. Furthermore, I added observations of daily wages in Zeeland and Groningen. In the latter case, this meant an extension of the existing analysis back in time to the 1610s and improved quality of the analysis with better data in the period 1630–1680. For Zeeland, I improved the analysis of the effect of the tax on bonds. This allowed an improved comparison with Holland. A similar analysis for Holland subsequently improved the comparative analysis with Friesland. In several other cases, I made minor corrections by re-examining the archive materials or by processing archive material that I had already collected but not or insufficiently analysed.

I am grateful for the support and help I received in the revision process. In general, I thank Maarten Prak and Wijnand Mijnhardt for their encouragement to present my Ph.D. thesis to a wider audience and in a more accessible way, after reading the original manuscript. I would like to thank the editors from Brill publishers for their patience and support, Wendel Scholma, Alessandra Giliberto and Melissa Allieri. The same goes for the LEHI series editors Jeroen Touwen and Peer Vries (former). I am also obliged to the two anonymous referees for multiple valuable suggestions and feedback on the original Ph.D. manuscript. I am grateful to Oscar Gelderblom, Joost Jonker and Christiaan van Bochove who shared their work in progress on auctions and the former for the underlying data on *Weesmeesterkennissen*, VOC bonds and private merchant credit. Clare Wilkinson copy-edited the final manuscript and improved my language. Gerhard de Kok confirmed my impression about the importance of English funds based on his data about the portfolio of the Zeeland regent Daniël Rademacher. I thank Victor Enthoven for suggesting to make the case of Holland more explicit and Evelien Walhout, Christiaan van Bochove and Wietse Veenstra for feedback on the progress of rewritten chapters.

Other colleagues, family and friends have been supportive along the process by either listing to or discussing ideas about the book, including the people from *Stichting Geschiedenis van de Overheidsfinanciën*, *Werkgroep de Achttiende Eeuw*, and Samuel Kruizinga, Lodewijk Petram, Reinier van Langevelden, Roeland Scherff, Judith Manni, Maarten Pansier, Lucas van Braam van Vloten and Suze Zijlstra. Last and the most I thank my wife Mirjam and our children for their unconditional love.

List of Main Events

1548	Unification of the Seventeen Low Countries into the Burgundian Circle, within the Holy Roman Empire, under Emperor Charles V
1568–1648	Dutch Revolt or Eighty Years' War
1572	First independent meeting of the States of Holland; William the Silent (or William I of Orange) becomes Stadholder of Holland and Zeeland
1576	Mutiny of Spanish troops; Pacification of Ghent
1576–1577	Friesland joins the Dutch Revolt
1578	Amsterdam joins the rest of the rebellious province of Holland (the Alteration of Amsterdam)
1579	Union of Arras; Union of Utrecht
1580	Rennenberg's defection (Stadholder of the northern provinces, George of Lailang, count of Rennenberg, returning to the Spanish side)
1584	Death of William the Silent
1585	Fall of Antwerp
1594	Treaty of Reduction (of Groningen), joining City and Hinterlands of Groningen into one province
1602	Founding of the Dutch East India Company (VOC)
1609–1621	Twelve Years Truce
1616	Fixation of the distribution key of the contribution to the common expenses of the Dutch Republic
1617–1619	Conflict between Maurice of Nassau and the States of Holland; ends with the execution of Holland Pensionary Van Oldebarnevelt
1621	Founding of the First Dutch West India Company (WIC)
1648	Peace of Münster; end of the Eighty Years' War; formal recognition of the Dutch Republic as an independent state
1650	Attack on Amsterdam, by Stadholders William II and William Frederick; death of William II
1651	(First) Great Assembly; Start of the First Stadholderless Period in Holland, Zeeland, Utrecht, Overijssel and Gelderland
1652–1654	First Anglo-Dutch War
1665–1667	Second Anglo-Dutch War; First War with Münster; Dutch support Denmark during the Second Northern War
1672–1713	Forty Years' War with France: cluster of wars with France
1672	Year of Disaster; death of Johan and Cornelis de Witt; First restoration of the Stadholderate: William III become Stadholder
1672–1674	Third Anglo-Dutch War; Second War with Münster and war with Cologne
1672–1678	War with France of Franco-Dutch War

1678	Treaties of Nijmegen or Peace of Nijmegen
1688	Glorious Revolution; Dutch invasion in Britain; Stadholder William III and Mary become king and queen of Britain, Scotland and Ireland; start of a Dutch-British alliance
1688–1697	Nine Years' War
1697	Peace of Ryswick, or Peace of Rijswijk, ending the Nine Years' War
1702–1713	War of the Spanish Succession
1702	Death of Stadholder-King William III: Start of the Second Stadholderless Period in Holland, Zeeland, Utrecht, Overijssel and Gelderland
1711	Death of Frisian Stadholder Johan Willem Friso (1687–1711): Start of the Second Stadholderless Period in all provinces
1713	Peace of Utrecht, ending the War of the Spanish Succession
1715	First default by the States General
1716–1717	Second Great Assembly
1718–1720	War of the Quadruple Alliance
1720	Treaty of The Hague, ends the War of the Quadruple Alliance; bursting of financial bubbles in France (Mississippi bubble) and Britain (South Sea bubble)
1726–1732	Alliance of Hanover (or Herrenhausen); start in 1725, Dutch joined 1726
1732	Treaty of Vienna
1740–1748	War of the Austrian Succession
1747	Fall of Bergen op Zoom; second restoration of the Stadholderate; William IV becomes hereditary Stadholder
1748	Treaty of Aix-la-Chapelle, ending the War of the Austrian Succession; the civil militia movement (*doelistenbeweging*) called for democratic reforms; Reform Statute (*Reglement Reformatior*) in Friesland
1749	Reform Statute (*Reglement Reformatior*) in Groningen
1751	Death of Stadholder William IV
1754	Second default by the States General
1756–1763	Seven Years' War; Dutch Republic remains neutral
1763	Financial crisis in the aftermath of the Seven Years' War
1766	Coming of age of William V (1748–1806)
1773	Financial crisis related to Caribbean plantation loans
1780–1784	Fourth Anglo-Dutch War
1785–1787	Patriot Revolution / Patriot movement
1787	Prussian invasion suppressed the Patriot Revolution and restored William V as Stadholder
1792–1797	War of the First Coalition against in Revolutionary France
1792	Revision of the 1616 distribution key of the contribution to the common expenses of the Dutch Republic

1795	French invasion; end of the Dutch Republic; start of the Batavian Republic
1797	Merger of public debts into one national debt

Graphs

Figures

Tables

Map

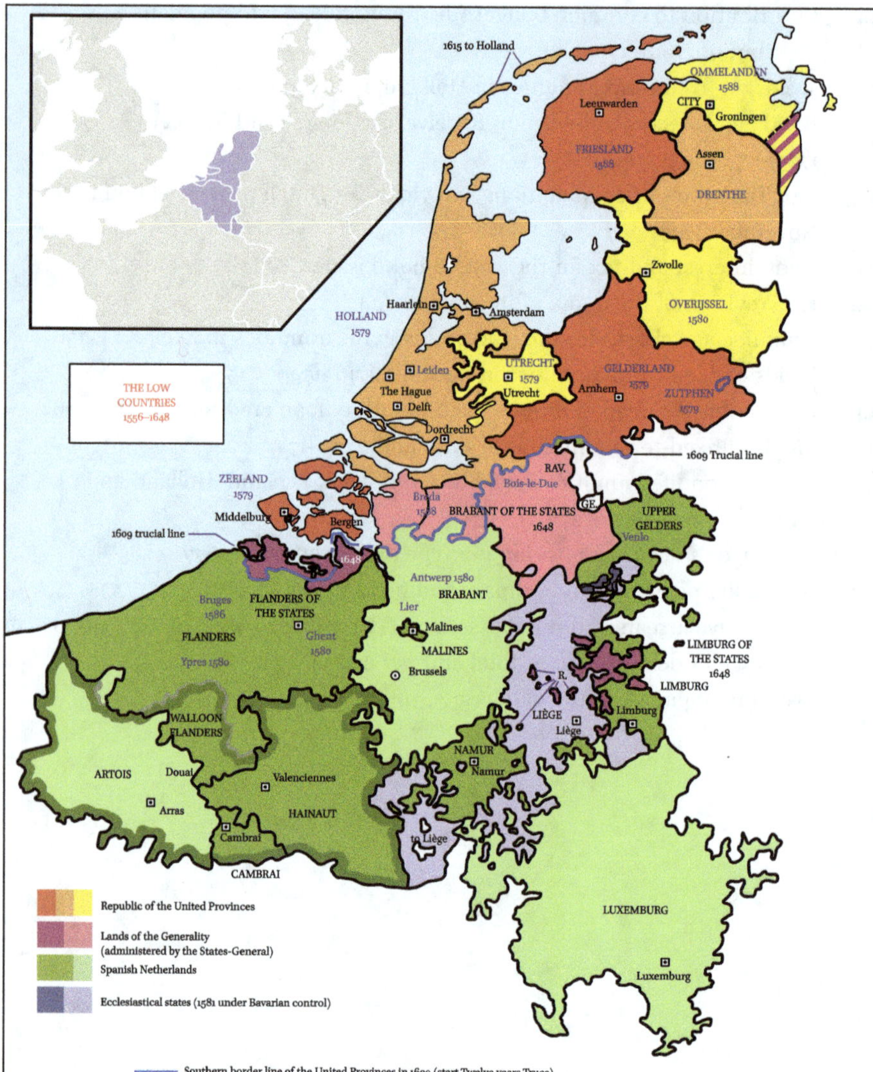

MAP 0.1 The Low Countries in the Early Modern Period

CHAPTER 1

Introduction

In mid-1726, the Friesland tax receiver Gulbartus Knock had to deliver an unpleasant message to his principals, the States of Friesland. They governed one of the seven autonomous provinces that together formed the Dutch Republic. Knock's mission to borrow 50,000 guilders in Amsterdam had failed. He returned empty-handed. Before he was sent on his mission, the States of Friesland had already borrowed 100,000 guilders from lenders within the province, but it needed more. It had hoped to raise the money in the province of Holland. Knock offered identical conditions to those he had offered within Friesland, yet he could not find willing investors in Holland. Disappointed, the States of Friesland proposed a more expensive loan, a life annuity, within the provincial borders.[1]

This episode casts doubt on the image of Dutch financial prowess and fiscal strength in the early modern period.[2] The seventeenth-century Dutch Republic's finances are often considered superior, part of its Golden Age.[3] So far, scholarly attention has concentrated on two aspects: firstly, the financing of the Dutch Revolt against the Habsburg overlords, which is often linked to a financial revolution;[4] secondly, the rise of Amsterdam as a leading interna-

1 Tresoar, Histories Sintrum Fryslan, Secrete resoluties, inv.no 267, f. 215, 217.

2 Augustus J. Veenendaal jr, "Fiscal Crises and Constitutional Freedom in the Netherlands, 1450–1795," in *Fiscal Crises, Liberty, and Representative Government, 1450–1789*, ed. Philip T. Hoffman and Kathryn Norberg, The Making of Modern Freedom (Stanford, Calif.: Stanford University Press, 1994), 133; Philip T. Hoffman and Kathryn Norberg, "Conclusion," in *Fiscal Crises, Liberty, and Representative Government, 1450–1789*, ed. Philip T. Hoffman and Kathryn Norberg, The Making of Modern Freedom (Stanford, Calif.: Stanford University Press, 1994), 309–10.

3 Maarten Prak, *The Dutch Republic in the Seventeenth Century: The Golden Age*, trans. Diane L. Webb (Cambridge etc.: Cambridge University Press, 2005), 75–84.

4 James D. Tracy, *A Financial Revolution in the Habsburg Netherlands: "Renten" and "Renteniers" in the County of Holland, 1515–1565* (Berkeley etc.: University of California Press, 1985); Marjolein C. 't Hart, *The Dutch Wars of Independence: Warfare and Commerce in the Netherlands 1570–1680*, Modern Wars in Perspective (London: Routledge, 2014); Marjolein C. 't Hart, *The Making of a Bourgeois State: War, Politics and Finance during the Dutch Revolt* (Manchester etc.: Manchester University Press, 1993); Wantje Fritschy, "A 'financial Revolution' Reconsidered: Public Finance in Holland during the Dutch Revolt, 1568–1648," *The Economic History Review* 56, no. 1 (2003): 57–89; Wantje Fritschy, Marjolein 't Hart, and Edwin Horlings, "Long-Term Trends in the Fiscal History of the Netherlands, 1515–1913," in *The Rise of Fiscal States: A Global History, 1500–1914*, ed. Bartolomé Yun-Casalilla and Patrick

 | DOI:10.1163/9789004745254_002

tional financial centre in the eighteenth century.[5] Foreign sovereigns benefitted from the capital surplus that had accumulated in Holland since the late Middle Ages.[6] These studies focus on the central province of Holland, and Amsterdam as the main city. Little attention is paid to fiscal and financial developments outside the province of Holland.

The story of Friesland suggests that access to the Amsterdam capital market was neither self-evident nor frictionless. Yet our knowledge of markets for

---

Karl O'Brien (Cambridge etc.: Cambridge University Press, 2012), 44, 64; Marjolein 't Hart, "Mobilising Resources for War. The Dutch and British Financial Revolutions Compared," in *War, State and Development: Fiscal-Military States in the Eighteenth Century*, ed. Rafael Torres Sánchez (Pamplona: Ediciones Universidad de Navarra, 2007), 189–200.

5 James C. Riley, *International Government Finance and the Amsterdam Capital Market, 1740–1815* (Cambridge etc.: Cambridge University Press, 1980); Ann M. Carlos and Larry Neal, "Amsterdam and London as Financial Centers in the Eighteenth Century," *Financial History Review* 18, no. 1 (April 2011): 21–46, https://doi.org/10.1017/S0968565010000338; Larry Neal, "How It All Began: The Monetary and Financial Architecture of Europe during the First Global Capital Markets, 1648–1815," *Financial History Review* 7, no. 2 (2000): 117–40; Alice Clare Carter, *Getting, Spending and Investing in Early Modern Times: Essays on Dutch, English and Huguenot Economic History*, Aspects of Economic History: The Low Countries 1 (Assen: Van Gorcum, 1975); Youssef Cassis, *Capitals of Capital: A History of International Financial Centres, 1780–2005*, ed. Jacqueline Collier Jespersen (Cambridge etc.: Cambridge University Press, 2006), 9–16; Michael Tomz, *Reputation and International Cooperation: Sovereign Debt across Three Centuries* (Princeton, NJ etc.: Princeton University Press, 2007); Marten Gerbertus Buist, *At Spes Non Fracta : Hope and Co. 1770–1815, Merchant Bankers and Diplomats at Work* (Den Haag: Nijhoff, 1974); Peter George Muir Dickson, *Finance and Government under Maria Theresia 1740–1780* (Oxford: Clarendon Press, 1987); Ch Wilson, *Anglo-Dutch Commerce and Finance in the Eighteenth Century*, Cambridge Studies in Economic History 84261320X (Cambridge [etc.]: Cambridge University Press, 1941).

6 Oscar Gelderblom and Joost Jonker, "Public Finance and Economic Growth," *The Journal of Economic History* 71, no. 1 (2011): 1–40; C.J. Van Bochove, *The Economic Consequences of the Dutch: Economic Integration around the North Sea, 1500–1800* (Amsterdam: Aksant, 2008); Christiaan Van Bochove, "External Debt and Commitment Mechanisms: Danish Borrowing in Holland, 1763–1825," *The Economic History Review* 67, no. 3 (August 1, 2014): 652–77, https://doi.org/10.1111/1468-0289.12050; Bas Van Bavel and Jan Luiten Van Zanden, "The Jump-Start of the Holland Economy during the Late-Medieval Crisis, c.1350–c.1500," *The Economic History Review* 57, no. 3 (2004): 503–32; Jan Luiten Van Zanden, Jaco Zuijderduijn, and Tine De Moor, "Small Is Beautiful: The Efficiency of Credit Markets in the Late Medieval Holland," *European Review of Economic History* 16, no. 1 (January 2, 2012): 3–22, https://doi.org/10.1093/ereh/her007; Jaco Zuijderduijn, "The Emergence of Provincial Debt in the County of Holland (Thirteenth–Sixteenth Centuries)," *European Review of Economic History* 14, no. 3 (January 12, 2010): 335–59, https://doi.org/10.1017/S1361491610000055; C.J. Zuijderduijn, *Medieval Capital Markets: Markets for Renten, State Formation and Private Investment in Holland (1300–1550)* (Leiden etc.: Brill, 2009); Maarten Prak and Jan Luiten van Van Zanden, *Pioneers of Capitalism the Netherlands 1000–1800* (Princeton: Princeton University Press, 2022), 58–89.

provincial public debt is remarkably limited considering the praise lavished on the Dutch financial achievements during its Golden Age.[7] The few available secondary market prices for provincial loans display notable differences, albeit in extraordinary situations in the eighteenth century.[8] Similarly, the coupon rates for issuances of other provincial debt remained higher than Holland's.[9] This book seeks to explain the persistent interest-rate differentials in markets for public debt within the Dutch Republic.

The present book addresses the question from a comparative political economy perspective.[10] Shared interests, mutual advantages and common goals and grounds had to be found to make this federation function. Yet various forms of self-interest prevailed regularly, a phenomenon known as provincial particularism.[11] The story of Knock illustrates two related debates about the effects of the decentralised structure of the Dutch Republic, one economic and one political. The first is about whether institutional fragmentation hindered

7 Prak, *The Dutch Republic*; Oscar Gelderblom, Joost Jonker, and Clemens Kool, "Direct Finance in the Dutch Golden Age," *The Economic History Review* 69, no. 4 (November 2016): 1178–98, https://doi.org/10.1111/ehr.12285; Jan De Vries, *The Dutch Rural Economy in the Golden Age, 1500–1700*, Yale Series in Economic History (London: Yale University Press, 1974); Arthur Weststeijn, *Commercial Republicanism in the Dutch Golden Age: The Political Thought of Johan & Pieter De La Court* (Leiden: BRILL, 2011).

8 J. G. Van Dillen, "Effectenkoersen aan de Amsterdamsche Beurs 1723–1794," *Economisch-Historisch Jaarboek. Bijdragen tot de Economische Geschiedenis van Nederland* 17 (1931): 13–14; Riley, *International Government Finance*, 49–55, 276.

9 W. Fritschy, ed., *Gewestelijke financiën ten tijde van de Republiek der Verenigde Nederlanden. Deel I. Overijssel (1604–1795), (Den Haag 1996); Deel II. Drenthe (1602–1795) (1998); Deel III. Groningen (1594–1795) (2001); Deel IV. Holland (1572–1795) (2004); Deel V. Utrecht (1579–1798) (2006); Deel VI. Friesland (1587–1795) (2007); Deel VII. Zeeland (1573–1795)* (2009), Rijks geschiedkundige publicatiën. Kleine serie (Den Haag: Instituut voor Nederlandse Geschiedenis, 1996).

10 O. C. Gelderblom, "Introduction," in *The Political Economy of the Dutch Republic*, ed. O.C. Gelderblom (Farnham etc.: Ashgate, 2009), 2: Gelderblom starts from Adam Smith's definition. O. C. Gelderblom, ed., *The Political Economy of the Dutch Republic* (Farnham etc.: Ashgate, 2009).

11 John Leslie Price, *Dutch Society, 1588–1713* (Harlow etc.: Longman, 2000); Maarten Prak, "Republiek En Vorst. De Stadhouders En Het Staatsvormingsproces in de Noordelijke Nederlanden, 16e-18e Eeuw," *Amsterdams Sociologisch Tijdschrift* 16 (1989): 28–52; Thomas Poell, "Local Particularism Challenged, 1795–1813," in *The Political Economy of the Dutch Republic*, ed. O.C. Gelderblom (Farnham etc.: Ashgate, 2009), 223–54; Pepijn Brandon, *Masters of War: State, Capital, and Military Enterprise in the Dutch Cycle of Accumulation (1600–1795)* (Amsterdam: [s.n.], 2013), 26; Olaf Van Nimwegen, *De Nederlandse burgeroorlog, 1748–1815* (Amsterdam: Prometheus, 2017).

capital flows within the Dutch Republic.[12] The second debate is whether fiscal fragmentation hindered effective public finance and taxation.[13] Consequently, this study explores the limits of political and economic integration within the Dutch Republic and adds nuance to the positive account of the Dutch Republic's public finances. Events like Knock's failed mission imply that the Dutch Republic's internal borders mattered for markets for public debt. This book explains how, when and why.

1 Historiography

In Holland, public interest rates declined from 12 per cent in the 1590s to 2.5 per cent in the early eighteenth century, while its provincial debt rose spectacularly.[14] The question is whether the factors that explain Holland's declining interest rates also applied to the other provinces within the Dutch Republic. Three proximate factors determine the interest rate: supply and demand, risk level, and transaction costs. The first factor – supply and demand – is also interpreted as the opportunity cost: the compensation for the missed income from not investing in an alternative.[15] It forms a base rate that a risk-

12 Jan De Vries and Ad Van der Woude, *The First Modern Economy: Success, Failure, and Perseverance of the Dutch Economy, 1500–1815* (Cambridge etc.: Cambridge University Press, 1997); Jan Luiten Van Zanden and Arthur Van Riel, *The Strictures of Inheritance: The Dutch Economy in the Nineteenth Century*, The Princeton Economic History of the Western World (Princeton, NJ etc.: Princeton University Press, 2004).

13 W. Fritschy, "Binnenlandse Constituties of Buitenlandse Omstandigheden?," *BMGN – Low Countries Historical Review* 117, no. 3 (January 1, 2002): 344–51, https://doi.org/10.18352/bmgn-lchr.5713; J. L. Van Zanden and Arthur Van Riel, "Economische Geschiedenis Met Een Menselijk Gezicht," *BMGN – Low Countries Historical Review* 117, no. 3 (January 1, 2002): 364–69, https://doi.org/10.18352/bmgn-lchr.5715; Wantje Fritschy, *De patriotten en de financiën van de Bataafse Republiek: Hollands krediet en de smalle marges voor een nieuw beleid (1795–1801)* ('s-Gravenhage: Stichting Hollandse Historische Reeks, 1988); Van Zanden and Van Riel, *The Strictures of Inheritance*.

14 Wantje Fritschy, *Public Finance of the Dutch Republic in Comparative Perspective: The Viability of an Early Modern Federal State (1570s–1795)*, Library of Economic History, ISSN 1877-3206 9 (Leiden: Brill, 2017), 68.

15 This is not the same as the risk-free rate. For Amsterdam, Flandreau et al. developed an ingenious method to gauge this from bills of exchange on London and Paris: Marc Flandreau et al., "The Bell Jar: Commercial Interest Rates between Two Revolutions, 1688–1789," in *The Origins and Development of Financial Markets and Institutions: From the Seventeenth Century to the Present*, ed. Jeremy Atack and Larry Neal (Cambridge etc.: Cambridge University Press, 2009), 168, 186–88, 190–91: They found that in eighteenth-century Amsterdam the commercial rates fluctuated between 3 per cent and 4.5 per cent.

free asset – the safest assumed investment opportunity – would yield.[16] The second factor – additional risk – increases interest rates through the risk premium. The third factor – transaction costs – indicates the efficiency of the market and serves as a proxy for the degree of capital market integration.[17] This, in turn, depends on the capital markets' economic, political and legal environment.

In explanations of Holland's declining interest rates, the financial revolution figures prominently. Tracy adapted Dickson's concept of eighteenth-century British public finance to fit sixteenth-century Holland.[18] In his classic study, Dickson analysed the improvements in British public finance after the Glorious Revolution brought William III to the English throne in 1688. He described the financial revolution as a massive increase in British public debt, decreasing interest rates, and a transition from short-term to long-term debt. Parliamentary control over fiscal matters proved vital to the ability to issue cheap loans, as were good relations between the Treasury and financiers in the City of London.[19] The cheap loans allowed Britain to spend out of all proportion to its tax revenues. In his adaptation, Tracy emphasised two institutional innovations: firstly, the collective liability of Holland's six major towns for the loans of the Habsburg state and secondly, provincial rather than urban taxes to fund the debt. This caused a transition to voluntary loans, declining interest rates, expanding public debt and economic growth. Just as Britain could finance its eighteenth-century wars against France, the Dutch financial revolution provided the Dutch Republic with the funds to win independence from the Habsburg Empire during its Revolt (1568–1648).[20]

16 David Hirshleifer and Guo Ying Luo, "On the Survival of Overconfident Traders in a Competitive Securities Market," *Journal of Financial Markets* 4, no. 1 (January 1, 2001): 73–84, https://doi.org/10.1016/S1386-4181(00)00014-8; Van Bochove, *The Economic Consequences of the Dutch*, 106–23.

17 Van Bochove, *The Economic Consequences of the Dutch*, 106–25.

18 Tracy, *A Financial Revolution in the Habsburg Netherlands*; P.G.M. Dickson, *The Financial Revolution in England: A Study in the Development of Public Credit, 1688–1756* (London etc.: MacMillan, 1967).

19 Dickson, *Financial Revolution.*

20 Tracy, *A Financial Revolution in the Habsburg Netherlands*, 1–5, 17, 45, 213–14, 221; Zuijderduijn, "The Emergence of Provincial Debt in the County of Holland (Thirteenth–Sixteenth Centuries)," 338; Marjolein C. 't Hart, "The Merits of a Financial Revolution: Public Finance, 1550–1700," in *A Financial History of the Netherlands*, ed. Marjolein 't Hart, Joost Jonker, and Jan Luiten Van Zanden (Cambridge: Cambridge University Press, 1997), 11; 't Hart, "Mobilising Resources," 180–81; Fritschy, "Financial Revolution," 57–58; Henry Roseveare, *The Financial Revolution, 1660–1760*, Seminar Studies in History (London [etc]: Longman, 1991), 1–2.

Fritschy, however, argues that tax increases proved to be more important resources than loans in the early years of the Dutch Revolt. She called the dramatic increases in taxation a 'tax revolution' or the 'first financial revolution'. Loans only became important after 1600.[21] Neal argues that Holland's financial revolution was incomplete: it lacked a liquid secondary market for public securities.[22] Gelderblom and Jonker disagree. They maintain that, on the one hand, the trade in shares in the Dutch East India Company (VOC) stimulated the emergence of a secondary market. On the other hand, they show that Holland's district receivers provided liquidity since the bonds matured every six months. Only after 1672 did a secondary market for public debt take off.[23]

By then, interest rates in Holland had declined. In explaining the decline, Gelderblom and Jonker highlight the importance of the capital supply. They indicate that a sufficient pool of capital forms a necessary condition for borrowing. In sixteenth- and seventeenth-century Holland, economic growth simultaneously expanded the tax base and private savings. Diminishing economic growth reduced demand for capital during the late seventeenth century, further lowering interest rates. An abundant capital supply fostered declining interest rates in Holland and offered a pool the authorities could tap.[24]

---

21 Fritschy, *Public Finance*, 85–101, 190; Fritschy, "Financial Revolution," 70, 79–80.

22 Neal, "How It All Began," 123.

23 Gelderblom and Jonker, "Public Finance"; Oscar Gelderblom and Joost Jonker, "Completing a Financial Revolution: The Finance of the Dutch East India Trade and the Rise of the Amsterdam Capital Market, 1595–1612," *The Journal of Economic History* 64, no. 3 (2004): 641–72; Lodewijk Petram, *The World's First Stock Exchange: How the Amsterdam Market for Dutch East India Company Shares Became a Modern Securities Market, 1602–1700* (Amsterdam: unpublished PhD-thesis Universiteit van Amsterdam, 2011); Lodewijk Otto Petram, *De bakermat van de beurs: hoe in zeventiende-eeuws Amsterdam de moderne aandelenhandel ontstond* (Amsterdam etc.: Atlas, 2011).

24 Gelderblom and Jonker, "Completing a Financial Revolution"; Gelderblom and Jonker, "Public Finance"; Anne L. Murphy, *The Origins of English Financial Markets: Investment and Speculation before the South Sea Bubble*, Cambridge Studies in Economic History. Second Series (Cambridge etc.: Cambridge University Press, 2009); Riley, *International Government Finance*, 226, 232–35, 329; Joost Jonker, *Merchants, Bankers, Middlemen: The Amsterdam Money Market during the First Half of the 19th Century*, NEHA-Series III 24 (Amsterdam: NEHA, 1996), 96–99; Van Zanden and Van Riel question Jonker's interpretation by arguing that the yield on public debt increased first, pushing private rates up, as it had pushed them down in the eighteenth century: Van Zanden and Van Riel, *The Strictures of Inheritance*: The difference in interpretation may relate to the geographical location. Jonker studied Amsterdam, Van Zanden and Van Riel more remote arreas. E. H. M. Dormans, *Het tekort: staatsschuld in de tijd der Republiek*, NEHA-series III 14

Yet Holland was not Britain, and the Provincial States was not the British Parliament. Holland was but one member of the federal Dutch Republic. It had to deal with other member provinces in the States General, when determining foreign policy and financing warfare. In turn, the provincial governments, the Provincial States, consisted of representatives of the nobility and the cities.[25] The question is what impact the decentralisation of the state had and whether it was advantageous or disadvantageous.

There are two related discussions about the effects of the Dutch Republic's decentralisation. One is economic, about borrowing, the capital market and market integration. The other is political, about contributing to the common expenses and sharing the burden of taxation. Together they are about paying for warfare, as this was the early modern state's main activity.

Regarding the first discussion, in their monumental study De Vries and Van der Woude argue that a single integrated market emerged in the Dutch Republic. They deduce the integration of factor markets from the correlation of grain prices.[26] Van Zanden and Van Riel, however, contend that capital markets did not become integrated until the mid-nineteenth century. At the same time, they concede that capital market integration is empirically understudied.[27] So far, no systematic study has been carried out into capital flows within the Dutch Republic.[28] There are six studies of local private capital mar-

(Amsterdam: NEHA, 1991), 241; Peter Wolfgang Klein, "Kapitaal en stagnatie tijdens het Hollands vroegkapitalisme," in *Kapitaal, ondernemerschap en beleid: studies over economie en politiek in Nederland, Europa en Azië van 1500 tot heden*, ed. C.A. Davids, W. Fritschy, and L.A. Van der Valk, NEHA-series III 25 (Amsterdam: NEHA, 1996), 40.

25 Robert J. Fruin, *Geschiedenis der staatsinstellingen in Nederland tot den val der Republiek*, ed. H. Th. Colenbrander ('s-Gravenhage: Nijhoff, 1901); Prak, *The Dutch Republic*.

26 Jan De Vries and Ad Van der Woude, *Nederland 1500–1815: de eerste ronde van moderne economische groei* (Amsterdam: Balans, 1995), 152, 157; De Vries and Van der Woude, *The First Modern Economy*, 176–77, 179, 693.

27 Van Zanden and Van Riel, *The Strictures of Inheritance*, 210–11, 213, 215, 217: In this respect, Van Zanden and Van Riel attribute an important role to the introduction of the telegraph.

28 The focus is generally on what private capital markets brought to the local economy and whether the cost price of capital hampered local development. For instance: Willy Niessen, *De Nijmeegse onroerend goedmarkt 1570–1630: een onderzoek naar de bewegingen op en de deelnemers aan de Nijmeegse onroerend goed- en kredietmarkt* (s.n.], 2005); Although there are notable exceptions, most of these studies tend to consider these markets as local phenomena, with little attention being paid to the options of cross-border capital flows. Exceptions include: Cornelis Trompetter, "Burgers en boeren – geld en grond," *NEHA-jaarboek voor economische, bedrijfs- en techniekgeschiedenis* 60 (1997): 7–35; Christiaan Van Bochove, "Configuring Financial Markets in Preindustrial Europe," *The Journal of Economic History* 73, no. 1 (2013): 247–78; Jord Hanus, "Een efficiënte pre-

kets. Four concentrate on regional rural credit markets, in Holland, Overijssel, Groningen and Zeeland.[29] Two studies are urban: one concerns Friesland's capital city Leeuwarden, and the other merchant credit in seventeenth-century Amsterdam.[30] Insofar as they overlap, the studies show persistent interest-rate differentials.[31] However, the limited overlap between the studies prevents a systematic comparative analysis of private capital markets, let alone capital flows. Meanwhile, De Vries and Van der Woude have noted persistent wage differences within the Dutch Republic.[32] Real wages converged, implying persistent local price differences as well.[33] Hence, it is not clear

industriële kapitaalmarkt? Het vroeg zestiende-eeuwse 's-Hertogenbosch als voorbeeld," *Tijdschrift voor Sociale en Economische Geschiedenis* 6, no. 3 (2009): 82–113; Christiaan Van Bochove and Heleen Kole, "Uncovering Private Credit Markets: Amsterdam, 1660–1809," *Tijdschrift Voor Sociale En Economische Geschiedenis* 11, no. 3 (2014): 39–72; Christiaan Van Bochove and Ton van Velzen, "Loans to Salaried Employees: The Case of the Dutch East India Company, 1602–1794," *European Review of Economic History* 18 (2014): 19–38, https://doi.org/10.1093/ereh/het021; This worthwhile study groups interest rates from six cities together from 1500 to 1780 to assess various parameters of risk and focusses on the role of notaries and aldermen, and to a lesser extent on geographical differences: Oscar Gelderblom, Mark Hup, and Joost Jonker, "Public Functions, Private Markets: Credit Registration by Aldermen and Notaries in the Low Countries, 1500–1800," in *Financing in Europe: Evolution, Coexistence and Complementarity of Lending Practices from the Middle Ages to Modern Times*, ed. Marcella Lorenzini, Cinzia Lorandini, and D'Maris Coffman, Palgrave Studies in the History of Finance (Cham: Springer International Publishing, 2018), 163–94, https://doi.org/10.1007/978-3-319-58493-5_7.

29 Cornelis Baars, *De geschiedenis van de landbouw in de Beijerlanden* (Wageningen: Centrum voor landbouwpublikaties en landbouwdocumentaties Pudoc, 1973); Richardus F.J. Paping, *"Voor een handvol stuivers": werken, verdienen en besteden* (Groningen: Nederlands Agronomisch-Historisch Instituut, 1995); Trompetter, "Burgers en boeren"; P. J. Van Cruyningen, *Behoudend maar buigzaam: boeren in West-Zeeuws-Vlaanderen, 1650–1850* (s.n.], 2000).

30 Gelderblom, Jonker, and Kool, "Direct Finance"; Harm Tjeerd Nijboer, *De fatsoenering van het bestaan: consumptie in Leeuwarden tijdens de Gouden Eeuw* (s.n.], 2007).

31 Piet Van Cruyningen, "Credit and Agriculture in the Netherlands, Eighteenth-Nineteenth Centuries," in *Credit and the Rural Economy in North-Western Europe, c.1200–c.1850*, ed. Phillipp R. Schofield and Thijs Lambrecht, Corn Publication Series 12 (Turnhout: Brepols, 2009), 101–2, 106.

32 De Vries and Van der Woude, *The First Modern Economy*, 289–93, 559–60; J. De Vries, "An Inquiry into the Behaviour of Wages in the Dutch Republic and the Southern Netherlands, 1580–1800," *Acta Historiae Neerlandicae : Studies on the History of the Netherlands* 10 (1978): 94–97.

33 Jan Luiten Van Zanden, "Kosten van levensonderhoud en loonvorming in Holland en Oost-Nederland 1600–1850. De voorbeelden van Kampen en Alkmaar," *Tijdschrift voor sociale geschiedenis* 11 (1985): 309–23; Van Zanden and Van Riel, *The Strictures of Inheritance*, 37, 145–46. The authors maintain that the lower tax rates in Overijssel caused

whether capital flowed freely within the Dutch Republic or whether there were border effects.[34]

Regarding the second discussion, the debate about the fiscal implications mainly concerns the negative effects of decentralisation in the eighteenth century. Van Zanden and Prak argue that the Dutch Republic's federal multi-stage form of representation fostered trust and boosted tax morale.[35] The preservation of local autonomy, with the Dutch Revolt, helped the Dutch Republic secure a leading economic position.[36] The question is whether its sixteenth- and seventeenth-century institutions were still adequate in the eighteenth century. More specifically, it is debatable whether the existing decentralised institutions yielded sufficient funds to pay for the Republic's defences. This has been labelled the eighteenth-century 'institutional impotence'.[37] It thus bears resemblances to Olson's concept of institutional sclero-

lower nominal prices and nominal wages there. It is questionable whether this was really the causal direction. It might also have been the case that the provincial government adjusted the tax rates to the local wage levels and not the other way around. Van Zanden, "Kosten," 317–18; De Vries refuted Van Zanden's argument that the "broodzetting" evolved from protection of the poor into a device to assure the bakers' income. Jan De Vries, "The Political Economy of Bread in the Dutch Republic," in *The Political Economy of the Dutch Republic*, ed. O.C. Gelderblom (Farnham etc.: Ashgate, 2009), 103, 108, 111–13: Instead, De Vries argues that the poor had other options, such as substituting rye for wheat and charity.

34 John F. Helliwell, *How Much Do National Borders Matter?*, Integrating National Economies (Washington, D.C: Brookings Institution, 1998), 63–64, 72–77; Martin Feldstein and Charles Horioka, "Domestic Saving and International Capital Flows," *The Economic Journal* 90, no. 358 (June 1, 1980): 314–29, https://doi.org/10.2307/2231790.

35 Jan Luiten Van Zanden and Maarten Prak, "Towards an Economic Interpretation of Citizenship," *European Review of Economic History* 10, no. 2 (2006): 111–46. Still, they also consider the limits as a consequence of the decentralised Dutch state. Free riding, so they argue, was a problem among the provinces, for the Republic lacked strong institutions as Holland possessed at its provincial level – a matter we will return to later. Maarten Prak and Jan Luiten Van Zanden, "Tax Morale and Citizenship in the Dutch Republic," in *The Political Economy of the Dutch Republic*, ed. O.C. Gelderblom (Farnham etc.: Ashgate, 2009), 143–66; 't Hart, *The Dutch Wars of Independence*, 158–59; Marjolein C. 't Hart, *Waarom belastingen goed zijn voor democratie: staatsvorming en politieke cultuur in wereldhistorisch perspectief* (Vrije Universiteit, Amsterdam. Faculteit der Letteren: VU, Vrije Universiteit Amsterdam, Faculteit der Letteren, 2014), 14.

36 Prak and Van Zanden, *Pioneers of Capitalism*, 209.

37 Johannes Hovy, "Institutioneel onvermogen in de 18de eeuw," in *Algemene geschiedenis der Nederlanden. Nieuwe tijd : politieke- en religiegeschiedenis 18de eeuw, socioculturele geschiedenis 1500–1800, overzeese geschiedenis 17de en 18de eeuw*, ed. D.P. Blok et al., vol. 9, Algemene geschiedenis der Nederlanden (Haarlem, 1980), 126–38; Van Zanden and Van Riel, "Economische Geschiedenis Met Een Menselijk Gezicht"; Fritschy, "Binnenlandse Constituties of Buitenlandse Omstandigheden?"; Fritschy, *De patriotten*; Wantje Frit-

sis.[38] The Dutch Republic appears to have missed out on the general trend of centralisation and bureaucratisation. Following Tilly's chronology of state formation, it did not transition from brokerage state to national state.[39] Hence, it could be argued that holding on to these early structures became disadvantageous in new circumstances because the institutions were no longer fit for purpose.

Taxation is a central element in the discussion. Fritschy argues that per capita taxes were higher in Holland than in Britain, and for that matter in most of Europe. However, Van Zanden and Van Riel highlight free riding by the individual provinces except for Holland.[40] For example, based on Fritschy's work, they point out that the province of Overijssel tried to keep its contribution as low as possible. They argue that Holland contributed disproportionately and was the only province that felt responsible for the common good.[41] Dincecco confirmed this and indicated that overall taxation increased after unification in 1795.[42] Fritschy maintains that net tax increases were marginal after 1795. Rather than being too rigid, she argues, the Dutch Republic was too small.[43] This is in line with Tilly's argument that sheer size eventually

---

schy, "Overheidsfinanciën als uiting van het 'institutioneel onvermogen' van de achttiende eeuwse Republiek?," *Economisch- en sociaal-historisch jaarboek* 48 (1985): 19–47; Fritschy, *Public Finance*, 196–201.

38 Mancur Olson, *Rise and Decline of Nations: Economic Growth, Stagflation, and Social Rigidities*. (Yale University Press, 2008), https://www.degruyter.com/document/cover/isbn/9780300157673/original; Peer Vries, "Does Wealth Entirely Depend on Inclusive Institutions and Pluralist Politics? A Review of Daron Acemoglu and James A. Robinson, Why Nations Fail. The Origins of Power, Prosperity and Poverty," TSEG – *The Low Countries Journal of Social and Economic History* 9, no. 3 (September 15, 2012): 90, https://doi.org/10.18352/tseg.278.

39 Charles Tilly, *Coercion, Capital, and European States, AD 990–1992*, Studies in Social Discontinuity (Cambridge, MA etc.: Blackwell, 1992), 29; Brandon follows Tilly and explains why brokerage continued to exist: Brandon, *Masters of War*.

40 Van Zanden and Van Riel, *The Strictures of Inheritance*, 34–38, 145–46; Hovy, "Institutioneel onvermogen"; Marjolein 't Hart, "De Nederlandse Republiek en de betekenis van de steden," in *Een wonder weerspiegeld : de Nederlandse Republiek in Europees perspectief*, ed. Karel Davids and Jan Lucassen (Amsterdam: Aksant, 2005), 76.

41 Van Zanden and Van Riel, "Economische Geschiedenis Met Een Menselijk Gezicht," 368; Wantje Fritschy, "Taxation in Britain, France and the Netherlands in the Eighteenth Century," *Economic and Social History in the Netherlands* 2 (1990): 59–62.

42 Mark Dincecco, "Fiscal Centralization, Limited Government, and Public Revenues in Europe, 1650–1913," *The Journal of Economic History* 69, no. 1 (2009): 63–64.

43 Fritschy, *De patriotten*; Fritschy, "Overheidsfinanciën"; Fritschy, "Binnenlandse Constituties of Buitenlandse Omstandigheden?," 348; Fritschy, *Public Finance*, 203–4.

enabled larger national states to extract more revenue in total and consequently win wars.[44]

If this is the case, the question is when and how the decentralised state lost its relative advantage and the higher per capita tax incomes and borrowing capacity could no longer compensate for the Republic's relatively small size. Brandon indicates that the Dutch Republic's demise was gradual. Brokerage persisted because it continued to serve the state and local businesses and powerholders well into the eighteenth century.[45] He argues that strategic considerations within the long-standing military alliance with Great Britain form a better explanation of the defeat in the Fourth Anglo-Dutch War than a lack of funds.[46] Fritschy, 't Hart and Horlings suggest that Britain caught up during the eighteenth century; this follows an older interpretation as eighteenth-

44 Tilly, *Coercion, Capital, and European States, AD 990–1992*, 190; Alberto F. Alesina, *The Size of Nations* (Cambridge, Mass., [etc.]: The MIT Press, 2003), 3: Alesina argued that states face a trade-off between size and homogeneity; and larger states benefit from economies of scale. But this is perhaps only true in a modern technological setting. Marjolein 't Hart, "Coercion and Capital Revisited. Recent Trends in the Historiography of State-Formation.," in *Economies, Public Finances, and the Impact of Institutional Changes in Interregional Perspective: The Low Countries and Neighbouring German Territories (14th–17th Centuries)*, ed. Remi Schaïk, Studies in European Urban History (1100–1800) (SEUH) 36 (Turnhout: Brepols, 2015), 23–32: 't Hart provides a challenging reflection on this thesis, partly from a global and a local perspective, to move beyond the dichotomy of strong large states and weak small states. Spain offers a good example of the more complex forms of state formation, as 't Hart suggests, considering local urban power and money versus an "absolutist" monarch: Carlos Álvarez-Nogal and Christophe Chamley, "Debt Policy under Constraints: Philip II, the Cortes, and Genoese Bankers," *The Economic History Review* 67, no. 1 (2014): 192–213, https://doi.org/10.1111/1468-0289.12010.

45 Brandon, *Masters of War*, 10; Wantje Fritschy, "Schulden als leerschool?: de Unie der Zeven Verenigde Provinciën en de Europese Unie," *Tijdschrift voor Sociale en Economische Geschiedenis* 9, no. 2 (2012): 3–28; Fritschy, *Public Finance*, 153, 194, 204, 309, 376, 381.

46 Brandon, *Masters of War*, 282; Brandon's argument is similar to that of Jan Glete, who argued that the Republic's decline was caused by the inability to reform itself in the eighteenth century, although his analysis was limited to the seventeenth century. In this respect, Glete is representative of the study of the Dutch Republic, which is skewed towards the seventeenth century rather than the eighteenth century. Jan Glete, *War and the State in Early Modern Europe: Spain, the Dutch Republic and Sweden as Fiscal-Military States, 1500–1660*, Warfare and History (London etc.: Routledge, 2002), 173: How and why the "interest aggregation" that fostered the Dutch fiscal-military state in the seventeenth century could not be adjusted to yield similar results in the eighteenth century remains unclear, however.

century decline relative to others rather than absolute.[47] In a recent study, Prak and Van Zanden even more provocatively state that the Golden Age was a temporary acceleration in an ongoing process of growth.[48] Only in the years up to 1795 did British credit fare better than Holland's.[49] After 1688, it took a century before Britain matched Dutch per capita tax revenues. Until the 1780s, the more centralised British state extracted less revenue per capita than the federal Dutch Republic.[50] Still, the question remains whether the Dutch Republic could have extracted more from its population if it had been centralised.[51] Similarly, high tax revenue in Holland does not rule out other provinces' free riding behaviour on Holland's fiscal strength.

The root of that problem lies in the distribution of the fiscal burden. Holland paid more than half of the Dutch Republic's shared expenses, according to the distributive key that was fixed in 1616.[52] But this was not necessarily excessive since Holland was also the most populous, the most urbanised and probably the most prosperous province.[53] Yet its debt was the highest of all the provincial debts by the end of the eighteenth century.[54] Hence, it is not clear how fair the fixed allocation key was in reflecting the fiscal capacities of the provinces, both in 1616 and subsequently over time.

Another question is the extent to which the other provinces mirrored Holland's fiscal development. Fritschy suggests that other provincial interest rates

---

47 Fritschy, 't Hart, and Horlings, "Long-Term Trends," 66. Although De Vries also attributed the relative decline to the Republic's decentralisation: Johannes De Vries, *De economische achteruitgang der Republiek in de achttiende eeuw* (Leiden: Stenfert Kroese, 1968), 177.

48 Prak and Van Zanden, *Pioneers of Capitalism.*

49 Mark Dincecco, "Political Regimes and Sovereign Credit Risk in Europe, 1750–1913," *European Review of Economic History* 13, no. 1 (2009): 39. The yield spreads on Holland's bonds compared with the British consols turned from negative to around par.

50 Fritschy, *Public Finance*, 270.

51 't Hart, "Mobilising Resources."

52 Fritschy, *De patriotten*, 159; Fritschy, *Public Finance*, 122; Tom Pfeil, *"Tot redding van het vaderland": het primaat van de Nederlandse overheidsfinanciën in de Bataafs-Franse tijd 1795–1810*, NEHA-series III 28 (Amsterdam: NEHA, 1998), 553; Hans. L. Zwitzer, "Het quotenstelsel onder de Republiek der Verenigde Nederlanden alsmede enkele beschouwingen over de generale petitie, de staat van oorlog en de repartitie," *Mededelingen van de Sectie Militaire Geschiedenis, Landmachtstaf* 5 (1982): 5–57.

53 Jan Luiten Van Zanden and Bas Van Leeuwen, "Persistent but Not Consistent: The Growth of National Income in Holland 1347–1807," *Explorations in Economic History* 49, no. 2 (2012): 120, https://doi.org/10.1016/j.eeh.2011.11.002.

54 The per capita estimates presented here for Zeeland deviate slightly from the calculated estimates in this thesis. Dormans, *Het tekort*, 165; Fritschy, *De patriotten*, 165; Pfeil, *"Tot redding,"* 122–23.

decreased as they underwent their own financial revolutions, albeit with a certain time lag.[55] Whether they could match Holland's fiscal system and tax income is unclear.[56] Fritschy argues that in Holland, economic growth and an 'urban system' expanded the tax base. She contrasts this to the simpler indicator of a high degree of urbanisation. Within the urban system, town magistrates monitored each other so that each complied with their fiscal obligations. This caused the tax revolution that preceded Holland's classic financial revolution.[57] Moreover, the public character of the annual auctions meant investors were well informed about Holland's current income and consequently its ability to fund the debt.[58] However, the other provinces were less urbanised and the towns possessed less political power than in Holland.[59] This raises the question of how representative Holland was for the rest of the Dutch Republic.

The implicit assumption is that disunity in the eighteenth-century Dutch Republic ran along provincial borders. However, internal discord emerged along ideological lines as well. From the 1770s there was political unrest due to the threat of civil war, defeat in the Fourth Anglo-Dutch War (1780–1784), followed by the Patriot Revolt and a Prussia-engineered Orangist counterrevolution.[60] Hopelessly divided among themselves, the Dutch could not repel the French in 1795, who moreover enjoyed the support of the Dutch Patriots. This and its comparatively small size, Fritschy argues, better explains the Republic's downfall than its fiscal federalism.[61]

The questions about the consequences of financial revolutions and state formation have relevance beyond the history of the Dutch Republic. First, the Dutch Republic provides a historical example of the cooperation between autonomous states in public finance and debt management.[62] Moreover, Weingast contends that for the last three centuries, the world's richest states

55 Fritschy, *Public Finance*, 160–61.

56 Fritschy, 155, 190–91, 376.

57 Fritschy, 61, 85–101, 190; Fritschy, "Financial Revolution," 70, 79–80.

58 Fritschy, *Public Finance*, 76, 95.

59 Fritschy, 17–20, 61–62, 105, 111, 115–19, 202–3; Fruin, *Geschiedenis der Staatsinstellingen*, 222–23; De Vries and Van der Woude, *The First Modern Economy*, 57–71.

60 Van Nimwegen, *Nederlandse burgeroorlog*; Jonathan I. Israel, *The Dutch Republic: Its Rise, Greatness, and Fall 1477–1806*, The Oxford History of Early Modern Europe (Oxford: Clarendon Press, 1995), 1107–1108.

61 Fritschy, *Public Finance*, 194–95, 203–4.

62 In her farewell address, Wantje Fritschy provided an inspiring exploration of the possible lessons the history of the Dutch Republic could have for the European Union today: Fritschy, "Schulden als leerschool?"

have been federal states.[63] Second, European states' fiscal and military strengthening forms one explanation of Europe's rise, militarily and economically.[64] Warfare became more expensive and monetised in the early modern period, which stimulated various paths of state formation. Tilly famously claimed that states made war and vice versa.[65] Fiscal-military states increased their revenue, dependent on their context. This ties in with debates about financial revolutions.[66] Third, financial revolutions are assumed to precede economic growth and leadership, as in the examples of the Dutch Golden Age, the British Industrial Revolution and the nineteenth-century United States.[67]

Building on Dickson, North and Weingast argued in a seminal article that parliamentary control over public finance lowered default risk as it secured property rights, in Britain after 1688. A sovereign subjected to rules could no longer arbitrarily renege on promises to service the debt or otherwise confiscate property. This credible commitment to the debt and upholding property

---

63 Barry R. Weingast, "Second Generation Fiscal Federalism: The Implications of Fiscal Incentives," *Journal of Urban Economics* 65, no. 3 (May 1, 2009): 280, https://doi.org/10.1016/j.jue.2008.12.005.

64 P. H. H Vries, *State, Economy and the Great Divergence Great Britain and China, 1680s-1850s* (London etc.: Bloomsbury, 2015); Philip T. Hoffman, *Why Did Europe Conquer the World?*, The Princeton Economic History of the Western World (Princeton: University Press, 2015); Bartolomé Yun-Casalilla, Patrick Karl O'Brien, and Francisco Comín Comín, eds., *The Rise of Fiscal States: A Global History, 1500–1914* (Cambridge etc.: Cambridge University Press, 2012).

65 Tilly, *Coercion, Capital, and European States, AD 990–1992*.

66 John Brewer, *The Sinews of Power: War, Money and the English State, 1688–1783* (London etc.: Hyman, 1989); Glete, *War and the State in Early Modern Europe*; Rafael Torres Sánchez, ed., *War, State and Development: Fiscal-Military States in the Eighteenth Century* (Pamplona: Ediciones Universidad de Navarra, 2007); Yun-Casalilla, O'Brien, and Comín, *The Rise of Fiscal States*; N. A. M. Rodger, "From the 'Military Revolution' to the 'Fiscal-Naval State,'" *Journal for Maritime Research* 13, no. 2 (November 1, 2011): 119–28, https://doi.org/10.1080/21533369.2011.622886; Richard Bonney, ed., *The Rise of the Fiscal State in Europe, c.1200–1815* (Oxford etc.: Oxford University Press, 1999); William Mark Ormrod, Margaret Bonney, and Richard Bonney, eds., *Crises Revolutions and Self-Sustained Growth: Essays in European Fiscal History, 1130–1830* (Stamford: Shaun Tyas, 1999); Marjolein 't Hart, "How Did States Further the Rise of the Great Divergence?," *TSEG – The Low Countries Journal of Social and Economic History* 12, no. 2 (June 15, 2015): 51–62, https://doi.org/10.18352/tseg.56; Brandon, *Masters of War*, 17–18; Van Zanden and Prak, "Towards," 112.

67 Richard Sylla, "Financial Systems and Economic Modernization," *The Journal of Economic History* 62, no. 02 (2002): 281, https://doi.org/10.1017/S0022050702000505; Gelderblom and Jonker, "Public Finance," 2; Prak and Van Zanden, *Pioneers of Capitalism*, 90, 98–104, 200.

rights spread to the private market. It was not so much the existence of the laws as their enforcement that encouraged impersonal capital markets to develop. This lowered transaction costs, which fostered economic growth.[68] The impersonal and impartial enforcement of the law is therefore a crucial consequence, and not only the parliamentary restrictions on the sovereign.

Hence, according to New Institutional Economics (NIE) to which North and Weingast belong, low interest rates reflect low transaction costs, well-protected property rights and a high degree of trust.[69] Therefore, if representative assemblies constrained the monarch, that state enjoyed a 'democratic advantage' over other states.[70] Building on these studies, Acemoglu and Robinson distinguish between 'extractive' institutions and 'inclusive' institutions that foster market-oriented economic growth.[71]

This narrative has increasingly been challenged.[72] The three issues most relevant for the Dutch context are discussed here. Firstly, various studies cast doubt on the assumption that representative assemblies cause lower interest rates. Sussman and Yafeh find that British interest rates increased in

68 Douglass C. North and Barry R. Weingast, "Constitutions and Commitment: The Evolution of Institutions Governing Public Choice in Seventeenth-Century England," *The Journal of Economic History* 49, no. 4 (1989): 803–32.

69 Bas Van Bavel, Tine De Moor, and Jan Luiten Van Zanden, "Introduction," *Continuity and Change* 24, no. 1 (2009): 14–15; Peter L. Rousseau and Richard Sylla, "Financial Revolutions and Economic Growth: Introducing This EEH Symposium," *Explorations in Economic History*, Financial Revolutions and Economic Growth, 43, no. 1 (January 2006): 1–12, https://doi.org/10.1016/j.eeh.2005.10.002; Peter L. Rousseau and Richard Sylla, "Financial Systems, Economic Growth, and Globalization," in *Globalization in Historical Perspective*, ed. Michael D. Bordo, Alan M. Taylor, and Jeffrey G. Williamson, National Bureau of Economic Research Conference Report (Chicago, IL etc.: University of Chicago Press, 2003), 373–415; Prak and Van Zanden, *Pioneers of Capitalism*, 4,5, 200–201.

70 Kenneth A. Schultz and Barry R. Weingast, "The Democratic Advantage: Institutional Foundations of Financial Power in International Competition," *International Organization* 57, no. 1 (January 2003): 3–42, https://doi.org/10.1017/S0020818303571065; Kenneth A. Schultz and Barry R. Weingast, *The Democratic Advantage: The Institutional Sources of State Power in International Competition*, Essays in Public Policy (Stanford, Calif.: Hoover Institution on War, Revolution, and Peace, Stanford University, 1996).

71 Daron Acemoglu and James A. Robinson, *Why Nations Fail: The Origins of Power, Prosperity, and Poverty* (London etc.: Profile Books, 2012); Vries, "Does Wealth Entirely Depend on Inclusive Institutions and Pluralist Politics?"; Prak and Van Zanden, *Pioneers of Capitalism*, 4.

72 D'Maris Coffman, Adrian Leonard, and Larry Neal, eds., *Questioning Credible Commitment: Perspectives on the Rise of Financial Capitalism*, Macroeconomic Policy Making (Cambridge: Cambridge University Press, 2013); Anne L. Murphy, "Demanding 'Credible Commitment': Public Reactions to the Failures of the Early Financial Revolution," *The Economic History Review* 66, no. 1 (2013): 178–97.

the decades following the Glorious Revolution.[73] Murphy demonstrates that credible commitment was not given spontaneously but hard-fought, not just in Parliament but also in the public media and on the streets.[74] This is line with Stasavage's 'distributive' interpretation of the credible commitment thesis. He argues that default risk and interest rates only decline if investors can protect their investment in the public debt. If taxpayers control the assembly, they may prefer lower taxes over paying interest.[75] Oosterlinck highlights an opposite mechanism: reducing interest rates diminished creditors' incomes, so they objected to such rate reductions.[76]

This latter argument ties in with the image of the passive eighteenth-century Dutch rentier as the personification of economic decline. In contrast to the enterprising seventeenth-century merchant, the rentier lived off income from public offices and interest, and exported capital abroad.[77] This

73 Nathan Sussman and Yishay Yafeh, "Institutional Reforms, Financial Development and Sovereign Debt: Britain 1690–1790," *The Journal of Economic History* 66, no. 04 (2006): 906–35, https://doi.org/10.1017/S0022050706000374.

74 Murphy, "Demanding 'Credible Commitment.'"

75 David Stasavage, "What We Can Learn from the Early History of Sovereign Debt," *Explorations in Economic History* 59 (January 2016): 1–16, https://doi.org/10.1016/j.eeh.2015.09.005: In this regard he emphasised the importance of indirect taxes in the Dutch Republic, which were paid by the whole of the population, while only the more well-to-do possessed government bonds.

76 Kim Oosterlinck, Loredana Ureche-Rangau, and Jacques-Marie Vaslin, "Aristocratic Privilege. Exploiting 'Good' Institutions'.," *CEPR Discussion Paper Series* DP 140771 (v.2) (October 2019), https://cepr.org/active/publications/discussion_papers/dp.php?dpno=14071.

77 Julia Adams, *The Familial State: Ruling Families and Merchant Capitalism in Early Modern Europe*, The Wilder House Series in Politics, History, and Culture (Ithaca, NY etc.: Cornell University Press, 2005), 62, 70–71; Prak and Van Zanden, *Pioneers of Capitalism*, 170; Jan Luiten Van Zanden and Arthur Van Riel, *Nederland 1780–1914: staat, instituties en economische ontwikkeling* (Amsterdam: Balans, 2000), 194–95; Klein, "Kapitaal en stagnatie," 37, 40; M. 't Hart, "Gewetenloze kapitalisten, handige fiscalisten, strategische huisvaders of gedisciplineerde calvinisten? De Nederlandse Republiek als casestudy," *BMGN – Low Countries Historical Review* 121, no. 3 (January 1, 2006): 420–21, https://doi.org/10.18352/bmgn-lchr.6450; M. C. 't Hart, "'The Devil or the Dutch'. Holland's Impact on the Financial Revolution in England, 1643–1694," *Parliaments, Estates & Representation = Parlements, États & Représentation* 11 (1991): 49; 't Hart, "De Nederlandse Republiek," 72–76; Prak, *The Dutch Republic*, 125, 264. Prak concludes that the government loans were draining capital from the productive sector, because the low returns on government debt were risk-free. Hence, he surmises that crowding out explains part of the eighteenth-century decline. Marjolein 't Hart, Joost Jonker, and Jan Luiten Van Zanden, "Introduction," in *A Financial History of the Netherlands*, ed. Marjolein 't Hart, Joost Jonker, and Jan Luiten Van Zanden (Cambridge: Cambridge University Press, 1997), 5–6; Price, *Dutch Society*, 234; Joel Mokyr, *Industrialization in the Low*

also fits Van Bavel's cyclical view of market economies, of which the Dutch Republic is one of his three examples. He argues that initially productive market forces eventually lead to the concentration of power and wealth, followed by rent-seeking which ultimately causes stagnation and inequality.[78] In reality, active merchants and entrepreneurs retained an equal share in public offices in the seventeenth and eighteenth centuries.[79] And even though creditors were saddened being repaid, because it robbed them of a steady income, the States of Holland repaid investors whenever possible.[80]

Moreover, in the Dutch Republic taxpayers and debtholders were not mutually exclusive groups. There were hardly any tax-exempt groups, unlike in France where tax exemptions favoured the rich.[81] Investment by urban magistrates fostered trust in provincial public debt, while direct taxes paid by the rich became increasingly important.[82] In a similar vein, building on Tilly's insights and typology of states, Stasavage argues that small city-states could borrow more efficiently than large states: the capital-intensive trajectory.[83] As such, the Dutch Republic retained this city-state advantage. 't Hart agrees that local support fostered trust in domestic loans, and powerholders were prominent among the investors but formed only one group among the creditors.[84] Hence, in Holland taxpayers and creditors were both partially

Countries, 1795–1850, Yale Series in Economic History (New Haven, Conn., etc.: Yale University Press, 1976).

78 Bas van Bavel, *The Invisible Hand? How Market Economies have Emerged and Declined Since AD 500* (Oxford University Press, 2016); Peer Vries, "Inevitable Decline? A Review of Bas van Bavel, The Invisible Hand? How Market Economies Have Emerged and Declined since Ad 500 (Oxford, 2016)," *International Review of Social History* 62, no. 1 (April 2017): 131–47, https://doi.org/10.1017/S0020859017000025.

79 Prak and Van Zanden, *Pioneers of Capitalism*, 185–86.

80 Fritschy, *Public Finance*, 289.

81 't Hart, *The Dutch Wars of Independence*, 159.

82 Van Zanden and Prak, "Towards"; Prak and Van Zanden, "Tax Morale."

83 Tilly, *Coercion, Capital, and European States, AD 990–1992*, 17–19, 43, 47–51, 99–103, 188; David Stasavage, *States of Credit: Size, Power, and the Development of European Polities*, The Princeton Economic History of the Western World (Princeton, NJ etc.: Princeton University Press, 2011), 22, 132, 150–54; David Chilosi, "Risky Institutions: Political Regimes and the Cost of Public Borrowing in Early Modern Italy," *The Journal of Economic History* 74, no. 03 (2014): 887–915, https://doi.org/10.1017/S0022050714000631: Chilosi critisizes Stasavage for not recognising that official interest rates on forced loans issued by Italian city-states in the Middle Ages were often much lower than the yields on the secondary market. Hence, the market valuation of the cities' creditworthiness was much lower than the forced loan suggested.

84 't Hart, *The Making of a Bourgeois State*, 179.

represented in assemblies, which leaves the question of which group's interests would prevail – and how this played out in the other provinces.

The second issue concerns the causal relationship between economic growth and declining interest rates. Buchinsky and Polak conclude that London's financial market was only marginally connected to England's industrialising north and that capital markets only became integrated after 1750; this therefore casts doubts on the importance of the financial sector as a precondition for economic growth.[85] Gelderblom and Jonker highlight, as mentioned earlier, the necessity of private wealth and savings for governments to borrow from. They emphasise that Holland's expanding economy offered the Dutch just that. In their view, a state's credible commitment or efficient fiscal institutions are insufficient explanation for lower interest rates. As a result, they suggest economic growth was a necessary condition preceding a financial revolution, and the causal direction is from growth to finance.[86]

The third issue relates to the capital supply and concerns the origins of money and the implications for the protection of property rights. Money could be imported. This involves three related yet distinct aspects, with possibly opposite effects. First, a motive for capital imports could be that capital was relatively scarce domestically and it was cheaper to borrow abroad. For instance, after 1688 Dutch capital exports drove down the interest rate on British public debt in London, until around 1780.[87] Therefore, Epstein argued that English public interest rates declined because of a catch-up effect compared to the wider European trend of declining interest rates – as described by Homer and Sylla[88] – irrespective of the political system.[89] Similarly, two-thirds

85 Moshe Buchinsky and Ben Polak, "The Emergence of a National Capital Market in England, 1710–1880," *The Journal of Economic History* 53, no. 1 (1993): 1–24; Ann M. Carlos and Larry Neal, "The Micro-Foundations of the Early London Capital Market: Bank of England Shareholders during and after the South Sea Bubble, 1720–251," *The Economic History Review* 59, no. 3 (August 1, 2006): 531–32, https://doi.org/10.1111/j.1468-0289.2005.00332.x; they argue that there was a significant connection between the financial and real economy.

86 Gelderblom and Jonker, "Public Finance."

87 Stefan E. Oppers, "The Interest Rate Effect of Dutch Money in Eighteenth-Century Britain," *The Journal of Economic History* 53, no. 1 (1993): 25–43.

88 Sidney Homer and Richard Eugene Sylla, *A History of Interest Rates*, 4th edition, 1st edition 1963 (Hoboken, NJ: Wiley, 2005).

89 Stephan R. Epstein, *Freedom and Growth: The Rise of States and Markets in Europe, 1300–1750*, Routledge Explorations in Economic History 17 (London etc.: Routledge, 2000), 7, 17–21, 61–62, 70–71; Sussman and Yafeh, "Institutional Reforms, Financial Development and Sovereign Debt," 908, 922–23. Conversely, these authors emphasised the relatively high rates in Britain.

of Holland's sixteenth-century debt was issued elsewhere in the Low Countries.[90] Hence, borrowing outside their jurisdiction may lower coupon rates for public borrowers because of the price and relative supply.

Secondly, importing capital has implications for property rights protection. Non-domestic creditors were not represented in the borrowers' assemblies and could not constrain the monarch politically. On the contrary, Flores and Flandreau show that in the nineteenth century more autocratic states avoided parliamentary control by borrowing in London, outside their jurisdiction.[91] Similarly, it is questionable whether external creditors could rely on impartial rulings by courts in the debtor state. The Dutch Republic lacked an overarching legal structure; the individual provincial courts formed the highest legal authorities.[92] Before the Revolt, disgruntled creditors of the various Habsburg

---

90 Zuijderduijn, *Medieval Capital Markets*, 157, 178–81: This issuance of provincial debt in the southern Low Countries built on the experience of the sale of urban debt by Holland cities in the fifteenth century, when most of the annuities were paid to non-residents who largely lived outside the province. Zuijderduijn, "The Emergence of Provincial Debt in the County of Holland (Thirteenth–Sixteenth Centuries)"; C. Jaco Zuijderduijn, "De laatmiddeleeuwse crisis van de overheidsfinanciën en de financiële revolutie in Holland," *Bijdragen en mededelingen betreffende de geschiedenis der Nederlanden* 125, no. 4 (2010): 3–24. This phenomenon was not limited to Holland; in towns like Nijmegen and Groningen, most of the urban debt was held by investors other than its own residents around the middle of the sixteenth century: C. Jaco Zuijderduijn, "Foreign Investment in Public Debt. Investors in Urban Public Debt in the Northern Low Countries, Fifteenth to Sixteenth Centuries," *Academia – Working Paper*, June 13, 2016, 6, 11; Tracy, *A Financial Revolution in the Habsburg Netherlands*, 28–29, 115, 117, 223–51.

91 Marc Flandreau and Juan H. Flores, "Bonds and Brands," *The Journal of Economic History* 69, no. 3 (2009): 650.

92 Barendina Sijtje Hempenius-van Dijk, *Hof van Friesland: de hoofdlijnen van het procederen in civiele zaken voor het Hof van Friesland zowel in eerste instantie als in appel*, Procesgidsen 2 (Hilversum: Verloren, 2004), 11–12: Only in Friesland was appeal impossible. In 1524, when Friesland formally accepted the Habsburg rule, it achieved the "ius de non appellando". This meant that no appeal was possible against rulings by the Court of Friesland, which thus gave it supreme authority. This was a deviation from the legislative system in the other Habsburg lands, which granted access to the Great Council of Malines. Fruin, *Geschiedenis der Staatsinstellingen*, 254; Christel M.O. Verhas, *De beginjaren van de Hoge Raad van Holland, Zeeland en West-Friesland: ... tot onderhoudinge van de Politique ordre ende staet der Landen van Hollandt, Zeelandt, Vrieslant ...*, 5 The Hague: Algemeen Rijksarchief, 1997), 68 Instituting legal action against someone could be undertaken by both Hollanders and non-Hollanders. The sole condition was that either the matter at hand or the people in question were present in Holland. Individuals who were not inhabitants of Holland were regarded as 'foreign', (Dutch: *uitheems* or *buitenlands*). According to this legal definition, any inhabitant of the other provinces within the Dutch Republic was considered 'foreign', for they lived outside the Holland jurisdiction and could not be prosecuted before the Supreme Court of Holland. Court cases

lands could appeal to the Great Council of Malines and summon debtors.[93] So the opportunity to enforce commitment through either the law courts or representative assemblies was lacking or was lost within the Dutch Republic.

Thirdly, non-domestic investors require alternative means to force the debtor to service and repay the debt. Without an international enforcer, there is little to prevent borrowers from reneging on their debts once the money is obtained. Two types of explanations stand out as to why cross-border lending nevertheless exists. The first consists of future-oriented reputation-based theories. The second emphasises sanctions, including military intervention or 'gunboat diplomacy'. A less violent sanction is credit rationing, where investors refuse new loans regardless of the offered interest rate.[94]

The Law of Reprisal was one such sanction. It implied that citizens of one city could be held liable for the city's unpaid debt by creditors living in another.[95] The views on the effectiveness differ. Greif considers the mecha-

---

against foreigners consequently depended on their cooperation. Once a foreigner had committed himself or herself to the court, he or she remained committed, even if the ruling was dissatisfactory.

93 Zuijderduijn, *Medieval Capital Markets*, 44–45; Prak and Van Zanden, *Pioneers of Capitalism*, 80.

94 Peter Temin and Hans-Joachim Voth, "Credit Rationing and Crowding out during the Industrial Revolution: Evidence from Hoare's Bank, 1702–1862," *Explorations in Economic History* 42, no. 3 (2005): 328, https://doi.org/10.1016/j.eeh.2004.10.004.; Drelichman and Voth argue that Philip II remained solvent because: "The ultimate test of the sustainability of his debts was that he managed to sustain access to debt markets." Mauricio Drelichman and Hans-Joachim Voth, *Lending to the Borrower from Hell: Debt, Taxes, and Default in the Age of Philip II*, The Princeton Economic History of the Western World (Princeton: Princeton University Press, 2014), 137–42, 247; Tomz, *Reputation and International Cooperation*, 24–25; Flandreau and Flores, "Bonds and Brands"; Kris James Mitchener and Marc D. Weidenmier, "Supersanctions and Sovereign Debt Repayment," *Journal of International Money and Finance* 29, no. 1 (February 2010): 19–36, https://doi.org/10.1016/j.jimonfin.2008.12.011; Alejandra Irigoin and Regina Grafe, "Bounded Leviathan: Fiscal Constraints and Financial Development in the Early Modern Hispanic World," in *Questioning Credible Commitment: Perspectives on the Rise of Financial Capitalism*, ed. D'Maris Coffman, Adrian Leonard, and Larry Neal, Macroeconomic Policy Making (Cambridge: Cambridge University Press, 2013), 199–227; Ugo Panizza, "4 Is Domestic Debt the Answer to Debt Crises?," in *Overcoming Developing Country Debt Crises*, ed. Barry Herman, José Antonio Ocampo, and Shari Spiegel (Oxford University Press, 2010), 91–108, https://doi.org/10.1093/acprof:oso/9780199578788.003.0004; Jonathan Eaton and Mark Gersovitz, "Debt with Potential Repudiation: Theoretical and Empirical Analysis," *Review of Economic Studies* 48, no. 2 (1981): 289–309; Van Bochove, "External Debt and Commitment Mechanisms."

95 Zuijderduijn, "De laatmiddeleeuwse crisis van de overheidsfinanciën en de financiële revolutie in Holland"; Jaco Zuijderduijn, "Wining and dining of water en brood? Het fundamental problem of exchange in middeleeuws Dordrecht (ca. 1300)," in *Publieke*

nism important for impersonal exchange among merchants in late medieval Europe.[96] Boerner and Ritschl argue that communal liability originated from a public debt problem, and was a widespread European commitment mechanism that persisted until the end of the sixteenth century.[97] Epstein considered collective liability a shortcoming of the legal system, disruptive to trade and ineffective. Legal fragmentation may cause friction and hinder capital flows and interest rate convergence.[98] Centralisation explains the overall decline in interest rates, he argued, and made taxation more efficient, consequently reducing default risk.[99] Chilosi shows for early modern Italy that supply and demand were only aligned when they were not hampered by legal fragmentation, which increases transaction costs.[100] Grafe, similarly, argues that limited market integration caused economic stagnation in early modern

financiën in de Lage Landen (1300–1800), ed. Jaco Zuijderduijn and Dries Raeymaekers, Publicaties van de Vlaams-Nederlandse Vereniging Voor Nieuwe Geschiedenis 14 (Maastricht: Shaker Publishing, 2015), 27–48; Manon Van der Heijden, *Geldschieters van de stad: financiële relaties tussen stad, burgers en overheden 1550–1650* (Amsterdam: Bakker, 2006); Zuijderduijn, "Foreign Investment."

96 Avner Greif, "The Fundamental Problem of Exchange: A Research Agenda in Historical Institutional Analysis," *European Review of Economic History* 4, no. 3 (January 12, 2000): 251–84, https://doi.org/10.1017/S136149160000071.

97 Lars Boerner and Albrecht Ritschl, "Individual Enforcement of Collective Liability in Premodern Europe: Comment," *Journal of Institutional and Theoretical Economics (JITE) / Zeitschrift Für Die Gesamte Staatswissenschaft* 158, no. 1 (March 1, 2002): 205–13, https://doi.org/10.2307/40753064; Zuijderduijn, "Wining and dining"; Van der Heijden, *Geldschieters*, 129–31; Zuijderduijn, *Medieval Capital Markets*, passim; Zuijderduijn, "Foreign Investment," 8; Avner Greif, *Institutions and the Path to the Modern Economy: Lessons from Medieval Trade*, Political Economy of Institutions and Decisions (Cambridge etc.: Cambridge University Press, 2006), 309–13; Avner Greif, "Institutions and Impersonal Exchange: From Communal to Individual Responsibility," *Journal of Institutional and Theoretical Economics (JITE) / Zeitschrift Für Die Gesamte Staatswissenschaft* 158, no. 1 (2002): 168–204.

98 Epstein, *Freedom and Growth*, 61.

99 Epstein, 8; Recently, rather than blaming absolutism, a number of scholars have pointed at the lack of centralisation in Spain in explaining its decline in the seventeenth and eighteenth centuries: Rafael Torres Sánchez, "Absolutism and Fiscal Transparency in Eighteenth-Century Spain," *Histoire & Mesure* XXX, no. 2 (2015): 189–214; Irigoin and Grafe, "Bounded Leviathan"; Drelichman and Voth, *Lending to the Borrower from Hell*.

100 Adrian Leonard, "Contingent Commitment: The Development of English Marine Insurance in the Context of New Institutional Economics, 1577–1720," in *Questioning Credible Commitment: Perspectives on the Rise of Financial Capitalism*, ed. D'Maris Coffman, Adrian Leonard, and Larry Neal, Macroeconomic Policy Making (Cambridge: Cambridge University Press, 2013), 49; Chilosi, "Risky Institutions."

Spain.[101] The Law of Reprisal is considered to have become extinct with the formation of larger national states and the state's greater legal capacity from the fifteenth century.[102]

But in the Dutch Republic, this process was halted due to the Revolt and indeed partly reversed.[103] Yet the historiography about contract enforcement mechanisms for public debt focuses on the late medieval period through to the late sixteenth century.[104] In fifteenth- and sixteenth-century Holland, the threat of reprisals had a disciplining and preventive effect. Foreign investors spurred changes that improved the debt service. After the default of 1494, Amsterdam repaid its foreign debt to prevent future threats of hostage-taking and confiscation.[105] The sixteenth-century States of Holland further prioritised interest payments to foreign debtholders over domestic ones.[106] Holland's medieval experience in fiscal intermediation and default thus

101 Regina Grafe, *Distant Tyranny: Markets, Power, and Backwardness in Spain, 1650–1800*, The Princeton Economic History of the Western World (Princeton, N.J, 2012), 146–62, 225–26.

102 Epstein, *Freedom and Growth*, 60–61.

103 Zuijderduijn, *Medieval Capital Markets*, 44–45; Gelderblom, *Cities of Commerce: The Institutional Foundations of International Trade in the Low Countries, 1250–1650*, The Princeton Economic History of the Western World ([s.n.], 2013), 129–31, 129–31: For the transition period from Habsburg rule to independent Republic, Gelderblom found that the probability that an Antwerp merchant would appeal to the Court of Holland depended on the political and military situation. Prior to the fall of Antwerp in 1585, no merchants from that city appeared before this Court. The incidences increased during the Truce (1609–1612) and decreased markedly when the Truce expired and the war resumed. Petram, *The World's First Stock Exchange*, 92–114: Petram also examined court cases in Holland in the early seventeenth-century. He described the conflicts that arose from the new share trade in Amsterdam. The subsequent jurisprudence determined henceforth the legal practices in Holland. Yet all the court cases in his study were brought before the Court in Amsterdam or the Court of Holland. In other words, the cases were held within the jurisdiction of the province of Holland. No mention is made of interprovincial law suits or other practices of cross-border contract enforcement.

104 Zuijderduijn, "Foreign Investment"; Manon Van der Heijden, *Geldschieters van de Stad: Financiële Relaties Tussen Stad, Burgers En Overheden 1550–1650* (Amsterdam: Bakker, 2006).

105 Zuijderduijn, *Medieval Capital Markets*, 130–37; Izak Prins, *Het faillissement der Hollandsche steden: Amsterdam, Dordrecht, Leiden en Haarlem in het jaar 1494, uit de wordingsgeschiedenis van den Nederlandschen Staat* (Amsterdam: Van Looy, 1922); Zuijderduijn, "De laatmiddeleeuwse crisis van de overheidsfinanciën en de financiële revolutie in Holland"; Dirk Houtzager, *Hollands lijf- en losrenteleningen vóór 1672* (Schiedam: HAV Bank, 1950), 48–49. Persons from Holland were taken hostage in Zeeland on various occasions during the sixteenth century. Therefore, the receiver of Amsterdam was called upon to redeem debt outside of the province as soon as there was some financial space.

106 Tracy, *A Financial Revolution in the Habsburg Netherlands*, 9, 95, 109.

showed the risks of external debt and fostered a preference for domestic debt. This makes external commitment mechanisms relevant because the legal and representative institutions remained provincial in the Dutch Republic.

It is thus not obvious that the capital surplus in Holland would have spread out towards the other Dutch provinces. Neal argues that the fragmentation of the capital market disadvantaged the Dutch financial system compared to the British system after 1694.[107] Van Bochove confirms Neals' argument about the local character of Dutch financial markets, yet maintains that this functioned well.[108] The question is whether the other Dutch provinces benefitted from Holland's capital surplus.

The historiographical overview suggests interest rates differed due to differences in risk and the money supply. Without capital, borrowing is impossible. Capital can either be found domestically or imported. Cities form the chief source of capital as it is generally accumulated there. Therefore, rulers turned to urban centres to obtain capital. To supply capital to the state, investors must first be assured that their money will be returned and the opportunity cost compensated. The first factor in servicing public debt is sound public finance, especially a steady income from taxation to fund the debt. This in turn depends on the state of the economy. An expanding economy will both accumulate capital in the hands of the population and increase revenue for the state. Yet even if a state is able to service the debt, the question is whether it is committed to do so and hence willing to pay the bondholders. Representative assemblies could offer such additional security, as North and Weingast emphasised. This is however a political and domestic solution, which also depends on the interests of the representatives. If capital was imported, this enforcement mechanism was useless, since foreign bondholders were not represented in the assembly, while domestic taxpayers were. This has implications for the incentives to honour the debt, and investors would have to find alternative means for contract enforcement, such as sanctions, reprisals or diplomacy. The opposition between bondholders and taxpayers is not restricted to imported capital: it matters in general who controls the assemblies and what their interests are. Default risk presumably increased if the representatives in the assemblies feared tax riots more than dissatisfied creditors.

It is precisely these issues that are central to this book, which examines the effects of borders on political and financial power. Therefore this book adds to

---

107 Neal, "How It All Began"; See, in this respect also: Van Bochove, "Configuring Financial Markets."

108 Van Bochove, "Configuring Financial Markets."

debates about the relationship between state formation, finance and economic growth.

2 Research Questions and Methodology

The literature review leads to several research questions that need to be answered in order to better understand interest rate differentials within the federal Dutch Republic. It addresses those questions by comparing four case studies: the provinces of Holland, Zeeland, Friesland and Groningen. The selected provinces account for the lion's share of the Union's common budget and the quality of the archival source materials is also relatively high. Holland, Zeeland, Friesland, Groningen and Utrecht contributed the most to the budget, but source materials for Utrecht are poor.[109] Overijssel and Drenthe have solid sources, but made small contributions. Gelderland scores poorly on both counts.[110] Hence, the selected cases are feasible in terms of the available sources and include the largest financial contributors.

Each case study analyses the provincial public finances in the local context of the provincial economy, political structure and the province's relation to capital markets. Holland serves as the point of reference. Comparisons with Holland allow evaluation of Holland's representativeness because that province regularly serves as a proxy for the entire Dutch Republic in international comparisons.[111] Therefore, the first chapter focuses on Holland to create a benchmark.

---

109 S.W. Verstegen, *Gewestelijke financiën ten tijde van de Republiek der Verenigde Nederlanden. Deel v. Utrecht (1579–1798)*, Rijks geschiedkundige publicatiën. Kleine serie 105 (Den Haag: Instituut voor Nederlandse Geschiedenis, 2006).

110 Fritschy, *Gewestelijke financiën: vol. I–VII*: This internal federal structure, complex public finance and scanty sources exactly form the reason that no volume about Gelderland was included in the series of Gewestelijke Financiën. Fruin, *Geschiedenis der Staatsinstellingen*, 223; 't Hart, "Merits," 15.

111 Dan Bogart et al., "State and Private Institutions," in *The Cambridge Economic History of Modern Europe*, ed. S. N. Broadberry and Kevin H. O'Rourke, vol. 1: 1700–1870 (Cambridge: Cambridge University Press, 2010), 78–80; Dincecco, "Political Regimes"; Dincecco; Stasavage, "What We Can Learn from the Early History of Sovereign Debt"; Marjolein 't Hart, "The United Provinces, 1579–1806," in *The Rise of the Fiscal State in Europe, c.1200–1815*, ed. Richard Bonney (Oxford etc.: Oxford University Press, 1999), 309–25; Robert C. Allen et al., "Wages, Prices, and Living Standards in China, 1738–1925: In Comparison with Europe, Japan, and India," *The Economic History Review* 64 (February 1, 2011): 8–38, https://doi.org/10.1111/j.1468-0289.2010.00515.x; Richard W. Unger, "Beer and

In Holland, economic growth increased the savings pool and expanded the tax base. This allowed Holland to fund war expenses from growing tax receipts and loans at relatively low costs – its financial revolution. Three questions stand out. First, did the other provinces spend as much relative to their capacity or were they free riding on Holland's solid fiscal basis? Second, to what extent did they cover deficits from taxes or loans? Third, how did they manage their respective debts? More specifically, did the debt burden develop akin to Holland's? When, where and at what interest rates did they borrow? What explains whether a province was committed to servicing its debt or not? To sum up, how did other provinces' fiscal management compare to Holland's?

To enable proper comparisons, this study corrects for population and income differences. That requires information on how wages and populations developed in the four provinces. To this end, I compiled novel reconstructions of the population developments.[112] Similarly, the available wage data link fiscal parameters to the tax-bearing capacity and income levels, which differed geographically. Population and income developments enable us to deepen the analysis of public finances, adjusted to take account of the local economic circumstances.[113]

Two periods stand out in Holland's fiscal and debt history. First, during the Revolt, Holland experienced a tax revolution and a classic financial revolution. Second, by the time of the Treaty of Utrecht in 1713, even though Holland escaped fiscal crises of the kind that afflicted France and Britain, it was so indebted that it wished to avoid involvement in international conflicts.[114]

Taxes: The Fiscal Significance for Holland and England in the Seventeenth and Eighteenth Centuries," *TSEG – The Low Countries Journal of Social and Economic History* 19, no. 1 (April 20, 2022): 61–86, https://doi.org/10.52024/tseg.11492.

112 H.A. Feenstra, *Between Shared and Conflicting Interests. The Political Economy of the Markets for Public Debt in the Dutch Republic, 1600–1795* (unpublished PhD- thesis Universiteit van Amsterdam, Amsterdam, 22 June 2018).

113 This method has been explored for international comparisons, for instance: Hoffman and Norberg, "Conclusion," 301; Prak and Van Zanden, "Tax Morale," 148–49; Van Zanden and Prak, "Towards," 130–31: All of the above concern comparisons were made with the province of Holland, as well.

114 J. Aalbers, *De Republiek en de vrede van Europa: de buitenlandse politiek van de Republiek der verenigde Nederlanden na de vrede van Utrecht (1713), voornamelijk gedurende de jaren 1720–1733. Dl. 1. Achtergronden en algemene aspecten*, Historische studies 39 (Groningen: Wolters-Noordhoff enz, 1980); R. Liesker, "Tot zinkens toe bezwaard. De schuldenlast van het Zuiderkwartier van Holland 1672–1794," in *Bestuurders en geleerden: opstellen over onderwerpen uit de Nederlandse geschiedenis van de zestiende, zeventiende en achttiende eeuw, aangeboden aan Prof. Dr. J.J. Woltjer bij zijn afscheid als hoogleraar van de Rijksuniversiteit te Leiden*, ed. Jan Juliaan Woltjer, Simon Groenveld, and Marianne Elisabeth Henriette Nicolette Mout (Amsterdam etc.: De Bataafsche Leeuw,

Neutrality was only achieved during the Seven Years' War (1756–1763), thanks to the *renversement des alliances*.[115] Regarding the first period, the first question is whether the other provinces similarly experienced a tax revolution, and secondly, whether they experienced a financial revolution. A 'tax revolution' is defined as a dramatic increase in tax revenues. We therefore need to determine whether, when and how much taxes increased. The 'financial revolution' is characterised by a massive increase in debt, declining interest rates, a shift from short-term to long-term borrowing and credible commitment to the debt on the part of the borrower. To assess this, it is necessary to consider how the debt, instruments and coupons evolved and whether the provinces remained committed.

For the second period, De Vries and Van der Woude presumed that the other provinces followed Holland's development and argued that Zeeland and Friesland withdrew from the markets for public debt after 1713.[116] In this period, Amsterdam rose as an international centre for sovereign lending. If De Vries and Van der Woude are correct, this explains why other Dutch provinces did not borrow when other states did. But did the provinces indeed borrow less?

The next question is whether the other provinces could benefit to the same extent from economic growth as Holland did to pay for the Dutch Revolt. This is also important to assess debt sustainability. As long as the economy expands at similar rates to the public debt, then the debt is considered sustainable. In the modern literature, public debt is often considered relative to the size of the

1985), 151–60; Dormans, *Het tekort*; William N. Goetzmann et al., eds., *The Great Mirror of Folly: Finance, Culture, and the Crash of 1720*, Yale Series in Economic and Financial History (New Haven: Yale University Press, 2013); Julian Hoppit, "The Myths of the South Sea Bubble," *Transactions of the Royal Historical Society* 12 (2002): 141–65; Richard Kleer, "'The Folly of Particulars': The Political Economy of the South Sea Bubble," *Financial History Review* 19, no. 02 (August 2012): 175–97, https://doi.org/10.1017/S0968565012000078; Gelderblom and Jonker, "Mirroring Different Follies. The Character of the 1720 Bubble in the Dutch Republic," in *The Great Mirror of Folly: Finance, Culture, and the Crash of 1720*, ed. William N. Goetzmann et al., Yale Series in Economic and Financial History (New Haven: Yale University Press, 2013), 121–39; W. Fritschy and R. Liesker, "Overheidsfinanciën, kapitaalmarkten en 'institutionele context' in Holland en Overijssel tijdens en na de Spaanse Successie-oorlog," in *Kapitaal, ondernemerschap en beleid: studies over economie en politiek in Nederland, Europa en Azië van 1500 tot heden*, ed. C. A. Davids, W. Fritschy, and L.A. Van der Valk, NEHA-series III 25 (Amsterdam: NEHA, 1996), 187–88.

115 Van Nimwegen, *Nederlandse burgeroorlog*, 30–32.

116 De Vries and Van der Woude, *The First Modern Economy*; Price, *Dutch Society*; Prak, *The Dutch Republic*: Both these thematically comprehensive studies concern themselves with the seventeenth century, while no equivalent exists for the eighteenth century.

economy, the Gross Domestic Product (GDP). The debt-to-GDP ratio is deemed a major parameter for assessing debt sustainability.[117] At present, GDP estimates are only available for the province of Holland.[118] Without provincial GDP estimates, I employ four alternative parameters to assess economic performance. Firstly, I offer a qualitative assessment of the development of their main economic sectors. This is because of the uncertain and often incomplete nature of the available statistical materials and the need to identify potential sources of public revenue, which differed per province. Secondly, I quantitatively assess demographic developments as a first rough indication, and the degree of urbanisation as a more advanced indicator.[119] Urbanisation serves as a proxy for urban economic power. The relative share of urban representation within the provincial States is a proxy for urban political power. This differed per case. In Holland and Zeeland, the urban representatives had the majority vote, in Friesland the rural representatives had a majority and in Groningen the two groups were balanced. This method lets me determine whether economic structure or urban political power was decisive for credible commitment. This includes testing Fritschy's claim about the importance of cities monitoring one another within urban systems. This book focuses on the people subject to taxation, the legal jurisdiction, to determine the development of per capita debt and revenue. Thirdly, I assess wage developments as an indication of income levels and inflation. Finally, I use the debt-to-tax ratio to express the years of public tax revenue required to redeem the public debt.[120] An advantage of this method is that it compares ratios without requiring adjustments for dissimilar welfare levels. Yet a state with a modest debt mildly taxing its population returns a similar ratio to a heavily indebted state extracting large amounts from its population. Therefore the four methods are complementary and jointly offer a viable alternative to debt-to-GDP ratios.

The sustainability of the debt depends on the fiscal health and especially public revenues, which are related to the development of the tax burden. The development of the public balances, the primary and fiscal government bud-

---

117 Carmen M. Reinhart and Kenneth S. Rogoff, "Growth in a Time of Debt," *The American Economic Review* 100, no. 2 (May 1, 2010): 573–78; Drelichman and Voth, *Lending to the Borrower from Hell*, 119–22.

118 Van Zanden and Van Leeuwen, "Persistent but Not Consistent."

119 Remi Jedwab and Dietrich Vollrath, "Urbanization without Growth in Historical Perspective," *Explorations in Economic History* 58 (October 1, 2015): 1–21, https://doi.org/10.1016/j.eeh.2015.09.002: This study confirms the correlation between urbanisation and growth for the period 1500 until the mid-twentieth century in richer countries.

120 Drelichman and Voth, *Lending to the Borrower from Hell*, 120–24.

get balances, is a gauge of fiscal health. Distinguishing between different primary fiscal expense items provides insight into the causes of a state's deficits. The primary balance expresses a state's ability to pay for its current expenses from its current income. A positive primary balance means the government can run its normal affairs without borrowing. The fiscal balance includes debt service. Fiscal deficits indicate a need for borrowing. Temporary primary deficits, or liquidity problems, may cause temporary difficulties with creditors, but do not imply long-term unsustainable debts. Together, these balances allow the assessment of the debt's long-run sustainability, the identification of the causes of possible deficits and evaluation of the risk.

When considering the tax burden, I correct for population and income levels. The tax burden is expressed as the per capita equivalent of the number of days an unskilled male labourer had to work to pay these taxes, based on nominal summer-day wages.[121] I purposely use nominal rather than real wages because the main taxes were incorporated into the price of daily necessities. This method thus prevents double counting and simultaneously corrects for geographical differences in the purchasing power of silver. This uniform indicator enables comparisons of the tax burden adjusted for local economic circumstances – it does not reflect the labour market.[122] The analysis of the tax burden further distinguishes between direct and indirect taxes; the latter burdened the entire population, the former exclusively the more well-to-do.[123] From these comparisons, we can dynamically assess how evenly the fiscal burden was distributed and whether there were good grounds for the provincial claims of overburdening.

Comparisons with private market interest rates and secondary market rates give more insight into the coupons. Private capital markets indicate the going rate for alternative investments and the local capital supply – however, the presence of private interest rates does not prove there was an impersonal capital market, because private networks remained important in the eigh-

121 There is debate about the representativeness of day wages compared to annual wages as a gauge for growth; this will be tentatively applied. Jane Humphries and Jacob Weisdorf, "Unreal Wages? Real Income and Economic Growth in England, 1260–1850," *The Economic Journal* 129, no. 623 (October 1, 2019): 2867–87, https://doi.org/10.1093/ej/uez017.

122 This method has been explored for international comparisons, for instance: Hoffman and Norberg, "Conclusion," 301; Prak and Van Zanden, "Tax Morale," 148–49; Van Zanden and Prak, "Towards," 130–31: All of the above concern comparisons with the province of Holland, as well. Vries, *State, Economy and the Great Divergence*, 103–22: Recently, Vries performed a similar comparison between China and Great Britain.

123 't Hart, *The Making of a Bourgeois State*, 122: 't Hart concluded that only a few groups enjoyed tax exemptions within the Dutch Republic.

teenth and nineteenth centuries.[124] Public borrowing may, however, cause a scarcity of capital, as happened in eighteenth- and nineteenth-century Britain. This crowding out effect decreased the volume of private investments, but did not increase private interest rates.[125] The difference between public and private interest rates thus reflects the risk premium. Furthermore, the degree of private interest rate convergence is an indicator of the level of market integration of the various local capital markets across the Dutch Republic.

Secondary market prices provide a more dynamic and accurate indication of default risk than coupons, which may have been subject to usury laws or discounts given upon subscription.[126] A secondary market offers liquidity to investors if the issuer does not refund the investment directly and instantly. Therefore, this market is a vital element in financial revolutions.[127]

Finally, it is necessary to look at the provincial governments' choices in managing their public debt. To explain the provincial States' decisions, a qual-

---

124 To be more precise, we do not know whether a capital market – defined as the free play of price-making forces based upon impersonal exchange in supply and demand – was present. We only know of transactions that inform us about prices, not the factors behind price formation: Gelderblom, Jonker, and Kool, "Direct Finance:" In this article, the private transactions of some notable Amsterdam merchants was analysed. It is often the best we have. Jonker, *Merchants, Bankers, Middlemen*; Joost Jonker, "Lachspiegel van de Vooruitgang. Het Historiografisch Beeld van de Nederlandse Industriefinanciering in de Negentiende Eeuw," *NEHA-Bulletin: Orgaan Ten Behoeve van de Economische Geschiedenis in Nederland* 5 (1991): 5–23.

125 Temin and Voth, "Credit Rationing"; Gregory Clark, "Debt, Deficits, and Crowding out: England, 1727–1840," *European Review of Economic History* 5, no. 3 (2001): 403; Gelderblom, Hup, and Jonker, "Public Functions, Private Markets," 181: The authors tentatively suggest that this happened in Holland as well in 1700, during the War of the Spanish Succession.

126 Kim Oosterlinck, Loredana Ureche-Rangau, and Jacques-Marie Vaslin, "Baring, Wellington and the Resurrection of French Public Finances Following Waterloo," *The Journal of Economic History* 74, no. 04 (December 2014): 1072–1102, https://doi.org/10.1017/S0022050714000862; Filippo Occhino, Kim Oosterlinck, and Eugene N. White, "How Much Can a Victor Force the Vanquished to Pay? France under the Nazi Boot," *The Journal of Economic History* 68, no. 01 (March 2008): 1–45, https://doi.org/10.1017/S0022050708000016; David Le Bris, "Wars, Inflation and Stock Market Returns in France, 1870–1945," *Financial History Review* 19, no. 03 (December 2012): 337–61, https://doi.org/10.1017/S0968565012000170; Van Bochove, "External Debt and Commitment Mechanisms"; 't Hart, *The Making of a Bourgeois State*, 179–80; Marc Boone, Carolus Augustinus Davids, and Paul J. J. G. Janssens, eds., *Urban Public Debts: Urban Government and the Market for Annuities in Western Europe (14th-18th Centuries)*, Studies in European Urban History (1100–1800) 3 (Turnhout: Brepols, 2003), 3; Flandreau and Flores, "Bonds and Brands."

127 Rousseau and Sylla, "Financial Revolutions and Economic Growth"; Neal, "How It All Began."

itative analysis supplements the other, more quantitative approaches. The provincial States faced several dilemmas. The first dilemma was whether or not borrowing was necessary to cover expenses. Warfare could have a sudden and dramatic effect on borrowing requirements. Or was borrowing a convenient alternative to tax increases, as was suggested at the end of the eighteenth century?[128] The second dilemma was where to issue loans: inside or outside the province. Thirdly, the province had to decide on the debt instrument and the coupon. The fourth dilemma was the relative priority to be assigned to the interest payments compared to other expenses and taxes. If the interest was not paid in full, the fifth dilemma was whom to pay first: internal or external debtholders. Defaulting on internal debtholders meant shooting yourself in the foot. A selective external default, however, could provoke sanctions such as credit rationing or trade disruptions.

In analysing the prioritisation in the debt service, Tomz's typology of debtor states is helpful. He distinguishes three types of commitment: stalwarts, fair-weather types, and lemons. Stalwarts are committed to debt service in good and bad times. Fair-weather types pay in good times but tend to default under more difficult circumstances. Lemons are least committed to the debt and may default under any circumstance.[129] North and Weingast indicated that defaulting could become the most attractive choice if the state's survival was at risk.[130] It is useful in this regard to follow the contemporaries' logic to distinguish between default and arrears. Creditors were used to late payments, yet feared the repudiation of the debt.[131]

Commitment to the debt could increase taxes and consequently cause tension between taxpayers and debtholders. An increase in debt service may thus lead to unrest and turmoil among the population. Taxpayers' resistance potentially reduces the commitment to the debt and increases default risk. This, in turn, depended on the relative power in the provincial States of taxpayers with respect to debtholders. Hence, this study analyses the interaction between investors, provincial and federal authorities, and taxpayers to explain variations in yields for provincial public debt.

---

128 Fritschy, *De patriotten*, 158: "'het effect van geen behoorlijke finantieele voorzorg.'"

129 Tomz, *Reputation and International Cooperation*, 17.

130 North and Weingast, "Constitutions," 807.

131 Dormans, *Het tekort*, 147; Nobel shows that much of the success in village debt management depended on the quality of the administrators, and that bankruptcies occurred regularly in seventeenth- and eighteenth-century Holland. Arjen Nobel, *Besturen op het Hollandse platteland. Cromstrijen 1550–1780* (Zutphen: Walburg Pers, 2012), 78–81.

2.1 *A Note on the Sources*

The analysis relies on various types of sources about public finance, public debt, capital markets and the economy. The series *Gewestelijk Financiën* (Provincial Finances) is the main source for all fiscal data. It offers detailed accounts of income and expenses through an online database. The volumes per province accompanying the digital data provide necessary instructive information about the background and interpretation of the data.[132] Yet the series focuses primarily on provincial public income and expenditure, and less on public debt. The information on debt largely consists of loan issues, reimbursements and debt service. Moreover, only the actual expenditure is reported and not the financial obligations. Consequently, defaults or arrears, for instance, are not shown directly. A decline in interest payments could, for example, reflect either default or voluntary conversions.[133] Hardly anything is known about the composition of the debt. Provinces employed a variety of debt instruments simultaneously. Some contained elements of interest and reimbursement, but it remains unclear how the transfers to creditors were classified. This prevents a simple reconstruction of the debt developments based on interest payments and coupons. Hence, we remain largely in the dark about the actual development of the size and composition of the debts.

The second type of source consists of quantitative material about provincial debts. At present, there are only public debt estimates for the province of Holland and the States General.[134] This book reconstructs public debts for the three other provinces based on newly collected materials from various provincial archives and types of source, depending on the available materials. Although far from complete, the reconstructions improve the knowledge of the development of public debt outside Holland.

The third type of source material is the qualitative sources about debt management. These consist of correspondence, reports and resolutions of the provincial governments. The book uses them to assess the considerations in the decision-making processes about debt-related matters. A potential drawback is that they contain rhetorical elements, for instance, if provinces were behind

132 Fritschy, *Gewestelijke financiën: vol. I–VII*.

133 Holland is in this regard the notable exception: R. Liesker and W. Fritschy, *Gewestelijke financiën ten tijde van de Republiek der Verenigde Nederlanden. Deel IV. Holland (1572–1795)*, Rijks geschiedkundige publicatiën. Kleine serie, ISSN 0921–9064 100 (Den Haag: Instituut voor Nederlandse Geschiedenis, 2004).

134 Dormans, *Het tekort*; Gelderblom and Jonker, "Public Finance"; Liesker and Fritschy, *Gewestelijke financiën: vol. 4. Holland.*

with their Union contributions. The more quantitative evidence allows an assessment of these arguments, putting them into perspective.

The fourth source type consists of quantitative materials for the analysis of the private and secondary capital markets. Data collection in these capital market segments is a prerequisite for further comparisons. This is, however, not a straightforward exercise. First, secondary market rates for public debt remain scarce. This was partly because local district tax receivers provided the necessary liquidity.[135] Private archives, probate inventories, auction data and incidental transfers recorded in notarial archives were consulted to fill this gap.[136]

The fifth type of source concerns private market rates. So far, the available studies only partially overlap in the period under consideration. To remedy these omissions and enable comparisons, I collected new local material from mortgage registers, similar to Nijboer's work for Leeuwarden.[137] This is again supplemented with materials from probate inventories and other private archives.

The final source type consists of newspapers, and especially newspaper advertisements. These were used in the present study for various purposes, yet primarily to have an impression of the public knowledge about interest payments, bond yields and prices.

3 Set-Up of the Book

This book is structured as follows. Chapter 2 sets the context of the Dutch Republic in three related ways. Firstly, it offers an introduction to the institutional characteristics of the Dutch federal state. Secondly, it provides a historical analysis of the major developments in the Dutch Republic, from the Revolt (1568–1648) to the Republic's dissolution in 1795. Thirdly, it analyses the fiscal developments in Holland to create a benchmark for the other case

135 Gelderblom and Jonker, "Public Finance"; The secondary market for shares emerged much earlier in Amsterdam: Gelderblom and Jonker, "Completing a Financial Revolution"; Petram, *The World's First Stock Exchange*; Petram, *Bakermat*.

136 Friesland did not have any notaries prior to 1809: Pieter Nieuwland, *Friezen gezocht: gids voor stamboomonderzoek in Friesland* (Leeuwarden: TresoarDen Haag : Centraal Bureau voor Genealogie, 2005), 93–94; For Zeeland, the notary's archives were burned during the second world war: Zeeuws Archief, "Notariële Archieven Zeeland 1796–1842, 1796–1842 Okt. 15," accessed July 27, 2015, http://www.archieven.nl/nl/zoeken?mivast=0&mizig=210&miadt=239&micode=13.1&milang=nl&miview=inv2.

137 Nijboer, *Fatsoenering*.

studies. Chapters 3, 4 and 5 each present a case study of one province, namely Zeeland, Friesland and Groningen respectively. For a uniform comparison, each chapter has the same structure. It starts with an analysis of the state formation process since the sixteenth century. This is relevant for understanding the division of power within the provinces, and it sheds light on the provincial experience with public debt before the Revolt. Thus it becomes possible to assess the importance of the medieval experience with funded public debt and whether it mattered for the commitment to honour the debt.[138] Next, each chapter discusses the economic developments in order to assess the provincial tax base; this includes discussion of the population, urbanisation and wage estimates. Thirdly, an analysis is given of the interest rate developments in the private market. This indicates the local capital supply and gives a benchmark for public borrowing. An analysis of public finances and debt management follows, in the context of the Dutch Republic's institutional structures and economic developments. Chapter 6 concludes by reflecting on the effects of the Republic's decentralisation on public finance and the integration of markets for public debt. Together, these analyses for the four case-study provinces ultimately create a perspective on how representative Knock's failed mission was for public borrowing within the Dutch Republic.

138 Following Zuijderduijn's observation for Holland that its late medieval experience of defaults was a necessary condition for its financial revolution a century later: Zuijderduijn, "De laatmiddeleeuwse crisis van de overheidsfinanciën en de financiële revolutie in Holland"; Zuijderduijn, "The Emergence of Provincial Debt in the County of Holland (Thirteenth–Sixteenth Centuries)"; James Tracy, "The Age of Fiscal Intermediation in Europe, 1300–1800," in *Publieke financiën in de Lage Landen (1300–1800)*, ed. Jaco Zuijderduijn and Dries Raeymaekers, Publicaties van de Vlaams-Nederlandse Vereniging Voor Nieuwe Geschiedenis 14 (Maastricht: Shaker Publishing, 2015), 13–26.

CHAPTER 2

Holland's Central Place within the Dutch Republic

To understand how public finance functioned within the Dutch Republic, this chapter outlines its origins and main characteristics. The Dutch Republic emerged from a struggle for independence against the mightiest state of its time, Habsburg Spain. Not only did the Dutch win their freedom, they also became rich. They were so wealthy that the seventeenth century came to be known as the Dutch Golden Age, which was reflected in the achievements in painting and science.[1] Economic growth had already begun in the late Middle Ages and continued during the sixteenth, seventeenth and eighteenth centuries.[2] Paradoxically, the Dutch Revolt, or Eighty Years' War (1568–1648), fostered economic growth due to investments in the military. After 1648 and again after the Peace of Utrecht in 1713, economic growth faltered due to a decrease in public spending on defences.[3] The link between economic growth and public finance is not limited to this apparent Keynesian effect or the Dutch case alone. The most well-known debate is about the causal direction between financial development and economic growth in financial revolutions.[4]

The history of the Dutch Republic is often assessed from the perspective of its largest province, Holland. For instance, in international comparisons figures for that province's taxation and economic growth are considered representative of the whole of the Dutch Republic.[5] But the story of the province of Holland is only part of the Dutch Republic's story – and probably the most impressive part because Holland was the wealthiest and most populous prov-

1 Prak, *The Dutch Republic*, 222–33, 234–49.

2 Van Zanden and Van Leeuwen, "Persistent but Not Consistent"; Van Bavel and Van Zanden, "Jump-Start"; Prak and Van Zanden, *Pioneers of Capitalism.*

3 Van Zanden and Van Leeuwen, "Persistent but Not Consistent," 123–24; 't Hart, *The Dutch Wars of Independence*; Marjolein 't Hart, *Oorlog en ongelijkheid: een inclusieve geschiedenis van de Gouden Eeuw* (Amsterdam: Boom, 2022).

4 Peter L. Rousseau and Richard Sylla, "Emerging Financial Markets and Early US Growth," *Explorations in Economic History* 42, no. 1 (2005): 1–26; Rousseau and Sylla, "Financial Revolutions and Economic Growth."

5 Bogart et al., "State and Private Institutions"; Stasavage, "What We Can Learn from the Early History of Sovereign Debt"; Stasavage, *States of Credit*; Dincecco, "Political Regimes"; Dincecco, "Fiscal Centralization"; Allen et al., "Wages, Prices, and Living Standards in China, 1738–1925"; Unger, "Beer and Taxes"; Sussman and Yafeh, "Institutional Reforms, Financial Development and Sovereign Debt."

 | DOI:10.1163/9789004745254_003

ince.[6] In a recent study, 't Hart outlined the uneven distribution of the fruits of Dutch economic growth, which benefitted Holland's urban elites the most.[7] These aspects make the assumption that Holland can be taken as representative of the whole of the Dutch Republic questionable. Claims about free riding by the other provinces cast further doubt on the assumption that Holland was typical of the rest. The question then is how representative Holland was and what its position was within the Dutch federal state. To answer those questions, this chapter analyses how Holland developed under the Dutch Republic. This creates a benchmark against which developments in the other provinces are measured, hence assessing Holland's representativeness.

The chapter proceeds as follows. Firstly, it highlights the historical context of the Dutch Republic, from its inception until its dissolution. Secondly, in doing so, it discusses the main characteristics of the Dutch fiscal system, as these developed during the Dutch Revolt. Thirdly, it analyses the effects on the provincial finances of Holland. This includes public income and spending and the public debt in relation to the economy. Unlike the other case-study chapters, this chapter does not contain a separate section about the economy. Others have studied Holland's economic development, prime among them being the monumental study by De Vries and Van der Woude and more recently, Prak and Van Zanden from a *long durée* perspective.[8] Further, Van Zanden and Van Leeuwen reconstructed the development of Holland's GDP under the Dutch Republic.[9] This chapter builds on those studies and further focuses on the two elements of demographic changes and wage levels. This lets per capita figures be calculated and the fiscal capacity be assessed. Finally, the chapter focuses on the role of borrowing in public finance in Holland and compares this to eighteenth-century Britain for a better perspective on the Dutch figures.

1 The Dutch Federal State Formation Process

1.1 *The Birth of the Dutch Republic*

The Dutch fiscal system was formed to finance the Dutch Revolt against the lawful Habsburg overlord, Philip II of Spain (1527–1598). His father, Emperor

6 Van Zanden and Van Leeuwen, "Persistent but Not Consistent," 120; Gelderblom and Jonker, "Public Finance," 2; De Vries and Van der Woude, *The First Modern Economy*, 100.

7 't Hart, *Oorlog en ongelijkheid.*

8 De Vries and Van der Woude, *The First Modern Economy*; De Vries and Van der Woude, *Nederland 1500–1815;* Prak and Van Zanden, *Pioneers of Capitalism.*

9 Van Zanden and Van Leeuwen, "Persistent but Not Consistent."

Charles V (1500–1558), had united the Seventeen Netherlands as a separate entity within the Holy Roman Empire in 1548. This was the first step towards the centralisation of the polities that he ruled in a personal union. The Revolt began as opposition to the religious oppression of the Calvinists, the infringement of local privileges, and resistance to a 10 per cent central tax on commercial transactions.[10] It ended with the Dutch Republic's independence in 1648, at the expense of much heavier taxes with which the Dutch burdened themselves.[11]

The term 'Dutch Revolt' is mostly reserved for the early stages of the conflict, whereas the designation 'Eighty Years' War' is more often used by historians who concentrate on the later stages. Like the terminology, the Dutch operations gradually evolved from rebellion into regular warfare. The first significant change in this respect was the first independent meeting of the States of Holland in Dordrecht in 1572. The main fiscal consequence was that the States backed the Revolt financially. This offered a more sound foundation than the private finances of Prince William of Orange (William the Silent, 1533–1584) and the privateering and looting by the Beggars (*Geuzen*). William of Orange was also reinstalled as Stadholder (*Stadhouder*), or steward, in Holland and Zeeland. The financial and military support given by the towns in Holland strengthened the rebels' case, while desertion, mutiny and a lack of funds weakened the Habsburg army.[12]

That lack of money led to a mutiny by unpaid Spanish troops in 1576 and subsequently the independent meeting of the States General, consisting of the representatives of the provinces. The fifteen loyal provinces invited rebellious Holland and Zeeland to discuss how to restore order and raise a joint army of their own, independent of the Spanish crown. Going back to the system under Charles V, a committee drafted the provincial contributions to the total expenses in a Statement of War (*Staat van Oorlog*). The autonomous, common budgeting clearly foreshadowed the Dutch Republic's fiscal system for the period until 1795, although this would only be for the seven northern provinces.[13]

The Pacification of Ghent (1576) only briefly restored the unity of the Seventeen Netherlands. With the Union of Arras on 6 January 1579, some provinces in the South reconciled themselves with King Philip II. A few days later, the rebellious provinces in the north signed the Union of Utrecht. After 1576,

10 't Hart, *The Dutch Wars of Independence*, 2–3, 12–14, 149; Fritschy, *Public Finance*, 32, 37.

11 Fritschy, *Public Finance*, 63–145.

12 't Hart, *The Dutch Wars of Independence*, 3, 14–18; Fritschy, *Public Finance*, 30, 32.

13 Fritschy, *Public Finance*, 34–38, 112–13; 't Hart, *The Dutch Wars of Independence*, 17–18.

Holland and Zeeland were mostly spared further warfare. Amsterdam joined the rest of the province in the Revolt in 1578. Yet in the South, the Spanish troops gradually reconquered large territories, culminating in the capture of Antwerp in 1585. The Fall of Antwerp implied a limitation of the loan options from that important financial market for the rebels. Meanwhile, George of Lalaing, count of Rennenberg and the Stadholder of the northern provinces of Friesland, Groningen, Overijssel and Drenthe, switched sides. The Provincial States of Friesland did not follow suit. The poor prospects of the 1580s changed for the better in the 1590s when the Dutch conquered the northern and eastern territories of the Netherlands. The subsequent stalemate resulted in the establishment of a truce in 1609. The Twelve Years' Truce (1609–1621) implied the acknowledgement of the Dutch Republic as an independent state. It would nevertheless take until 1648 before this was formally reconfirmed.[14]

The Union of Utrecht bound the Seven United Provinces together until the Batavian Revolution of 1795. Although it was not intended as a constitution, it was more than a temporary coalition. So how should the mutual relations between the provinces that jointly fought against the Habsburg rule be understood? Fritschy questions whether the Union of Utrecht can be seen as the birth of a new state. Even though she eventually concludes that it should, even raising this question suggests that there are good arguments for the opposite case. One interpretation is that the Dutch Republic functioned as a military alliance, akin to the North Atlantic Treaty Organisation (NATO) today.[15] But the Seven Provinces were more closely united than that. Perhaps a more difficult question is whether the Dutch Republic functioned more as a *federation* or as a *confederation* (*statenbond*).[16] Whatever the precise definition, the provinces cherished their autonomy. Each considered itself sovereign in all matters except for foreign policy.[17]

Despite the States General's motto 'Unity makes strength' (*Concordia res parvae crescent*), internal discord and conflicting interests hampered swift decision-making in the Dutch Republic, as William of Orange complained in the early phases of the Dutch Revolt.[18] Therefore, the States failed to create a

14 't Hart, *The Dutch Wars of Independence*, 17–25; Fritschy, *Public Finance*, 29–34, 114–15.

15 Fritschy, *Public Finance*, 29–31.

16 Fruin, *Geschiedenis der Staatsinstellingen*, 184.

17 Prak, *The Dutch Republic*, 173–74.

18 James D. Tracy, "Holland's New Fiscal Regime, 1572–1576," in *The Political Economy of the Dutch Republic*, ed. O.C. Gelderblom (Farnham etc.: Ashgate, 2009), 54; Suzanne van de Meerendonk et al., "Striving for Unity: The Significance and Original Context of Political Allegories by Theodoor van Thulden for 's-Hertogenbosch Town Hall," *Early Modern Low Countries* 1, no. 2 (December 22, 2017): 231–72, https://doi.org/10.18352/emlc.26: A fine

single internal market, with one external tariff, no internal tariff barriers and a common tax on an equal footing everywhere.[19] Centrally imposed taxes yielded barely 1 per cent of the budget. Even after adding the customs and revenues from the occupied territories administered by the States General, the 'Generality lands', the central funds accounted for less than 20 per cent of the total.[20] The navy's income was also decentralised from an early stage. Five separate admiralties derived their income from customs levies in their own districts, three in Holland, one in Zeeland and one in Friesland. This facilitated tax evasion and fraud.[21] Yet the provinces had not thrown off the Habsburg yoke of central taxes only to yield these fiscal powers to the States General. Consequently, for ideological reasons centralisation was deemed problematic as a measure for redistributing the fiscal burden.

1.2 *Fiscal System of the Dutch Republic*

How did the loose association of autonomous provinces amass the funds necessary to wage war and how did it commit the constituent members and prevent free riding behaviour? The first step was to budget for the expenses, primarily for the military. The Council of State drafted an annual budget, the Statement of War, on which the States General had to decide.[22] The Council of State functioned as the executive committee of the States General. Both institutions consisted of provincial representatives of the Seven Provinces. In the meetings of the States General, each province held one vote. A unanimous vote in favour was required for important decisions. Approval of the proposed budgets, the 'consents', was only given if the individual provincial assemblies, the provincial States, agreed. Approval was usually conditional, which lengthened the discussions.[23] Yet without approval, the companies on each province's payroll would remain unpaid, which was undesirable for a state at war.[24]

---

paper studying from an arts perspective uncovers how such rhetorics worked in Brabant's attempts to join the Union as a full member.

19 Fritschy, *Public Finance*, 29–30, 42; Fritschy, *De patriotten*, 34; 't Hart, *The Making of a Bourgeois State*, 74–78; De Vries and Van der Woude, *Nederland 1500–1815*, 123–25.

20 't Hart, *The Making of a Bourgeois State*, 86.

21 't Hart, *The Dutch Wars of Independence*, 127–28; Wietse Veenstra, *Tussen gewest en Generaliteit: staatsvorming en financiering van de oorlog te water in de Republiek der Verenigde Nederlanden, in het bijzonder Zeeland (1586–1795)* (Nederland, 2014).

22 't Hart, *The Making of a Bourgeois State*, 43.

23 Fritschy, *Public Finance*, 39–40; 't Hart, *The Making of a Bourgeois State*, 19–21, 43, 74; Dormans, *Het tekort*, 30–31.

24 't Hart, *The Making of a Bourgeois State*, 34–35, 169; Dormans, *Het tekort*, 29–31; Fritschy, *Public Finance*, 123.

If agreeing on the budget was difficult, agreeing on the individual contributions was almost impossible. The aim was to distribute the burden evenly; without demographic or economic parameters to guide them, the result was often prolonged disagreement, recurring every year. To put an end to at least that source of the disagreements, in 1616 each province's share was fixed according to a distribution key. This book concentrates on the period after that year; others, most notably and recently Fritschy, have analysed the period up to 1616.[25] Altering the distribution key proved difficult because if some paid less, the others had to pay more. As a result, the distribution key remained in force until 1792, when it no longer distributed the fiscal burden fairly across the provinces.[26]

Holland's contribution dwarfed that of the others (Table 2.1). Of the 10 million guilders the war cost per year around 1620, Holland paid 577,000 guilders.[27] Even when expressed per capita, Holland contributed significantly. However, after correcting for population size, Zeeland's contribution was the largest. It exceeded Holland's and Friesland's contributions by one-third. Inhabitants of Utrecht and Groningen also paid significant amounts. Those in Overijssel, Gelderland and Drenthe paid half of the average.[28] There was a clear division between the coastal provinces and inland provinces, in both absolute and per capita contributions, with Utrecht and Groningen somewhat in between.[29]

The direct effects of warfare form part of the explanation for the uneven distribution. There was no fighting in Zeeland or Holland after 1576. Friesland

25 Fritschy, *Public Finance*; Wantje Fritschy, "A 'financial Revolution' Reconsidered: Public Finance in Holland during the Dutch Revolt, 1568–1648," *The Economic History Review* 56, no. 1 (2003): 57–89; 't Hart, *The Making of a Bourgeois State*, 78–80; 't Hart, *The Dutch Wars of Independence*; Marjolein C. 't Hart, "The Merits of a Financial Revolution: Public Finance, 1550–1700," in *A Financial History of the Netherlands*, ed. Marjolein 't Hart, Joost Jonker, and Jan Luiten Van Zanden (Cambridge: Cambridge University Press, 1997), 15–16; Hart, *Oorlog en ongelijkheid*; Maarten Prak, *The Dutch Republic in the Seventeenth Century: The Golden Age*, trans. Diane L. Webb (Cambridge etc.: Cambridge University Press, 2005), 76–77.

26 Riley, *International Government Finance*, 69.

27 't Hart, *The Making of a Bourgeois State*, 59–61.

28 Zwitzer, "Quotenstelsel," 17; Richard Paping, "General Dutch Population Development 1400–1850: Cities and Countryside," *Paper Presented at 1st ESHD Conference, Alghero, Italy.*, 2014; Verstegen, *Gewestelijke financiën: vol. 5. Utrecht*, 14; Jan Luiten Van Zanden, "De demografische ontwikkeling van Overijssel 1475–1795," *Overijsselse historische bijdragen : verslagen en mededelingen van de Vereeniging tot Beoefening van Overijsselsch Regt en Geschiedenis* 109 (1994): 39–49.

29 't Hart, *The Making of a Bourgeois State*, 132–37: 't Hart makes a slightly different distinction, naming Holland the core, Zeeland and Utrecht the semi-periphery and the rest periphery. .

TABLE 2.1 Contribution to common budget (distribution key) and population distribution, 1616–1792.

	Share	Population in 1616	Per capita in guilders (per 10 mln. Gld.)	Per capita contribution (as % of Holland's contribution)
Zeeland	9.1%	74,000	12.29	136%
Holland	57.7%	639,000	9.04	100%
Friesland	11.5%	129,500	8.92	99%
Utrecht	5.8%	72,500	7.97	88%
Groningen	5.8%	81,500	7.11	79%
Drenthe	1.0%	20,000	4.90	54%
Overijssel	3.5%	81,000	4.37	48%
Gelderland	5.6%	138,500	4.01	44%
Total (and population-weighted average)	100.0%	1.236.000	8.09	90%

SOURCES: H.L. ZWITZER, 'HET QUOTENSTELSEL ONDER DE REPUBLIEK DER VERENIGDE NEDERLANDEN ALSMEDE ENKELE BESCHOUWINGEN OVER DE GENERALE PETITIE, DE STAAT VAN OORLOG EN DE REPARTITIE', *MEDEDELINGEN VAN DE SECTIE MILITAIRE GESCHIEDENIS VAN DE LANDMACHTSTAF* 5 (1982) 5–57, P. 17; POPULATIONS HOLLAND, ZEELAND, GRONINGEN AND FRIESLAND: FEENSTRA, *BETWEEN SHARED*, APPENDICES; UTRECHT: S.W. VERSTEGEN, *GEWESTELIJK FINANCIËN TEN TIJDE VAN DE REPUBLIEK DER VERENIGDE NEDERLANDEN, DEEL V, UTRECHT* (*1579–1798*), P. 14; OVERIJSSEL: J.L. VAN ZANDEN, 'DE DEMOGRAFISCHE ONTWIKKELING VAN OVERIJSSEL', IN: *OVERIJSSELS HISTORISCHE BIJDRAGEN* (1994) 39–51; DRENTHE AND GELDERLAND: RICHARD PAPING, *GENERAL DUTCH POPULATION DEVELOPMENT 1400–1850: CITIES AND COUNTRYSIDE. PAPER PRESENTED AT 1ST ESHD CONFERENCE, ALGHERO, ITALY.* (2014).

was less secure than Holland and Zeeland; Spanish troops raided the countryside from bases in Overijssel and Groningen in the 1580s.[30] This ended when the States Army gained control over Groningen and the eastern provinces in the 1590s. After the Twelve Years' Truce (1609–1621) expired, Overijssel and Gelderland again suffered from the hostilities.[31] These provinces also remained

30 Israel, *The Dutch Republic*, 212, 233.

31 't Hart, *The Making of a Bourgeois State*, 79.

vulnerable to enemy attacks after 1648, such as by France and Münster in 1665 and 1672.[32] The eastern provinces essentially served as a buffer zone for Holland and Zeeland.[33]

The direct impact of warfare was far-reaching yet temporary, while the distribution key was permanent. What effect differences in wealth and income had will be discussed in more detail in the various case studies. It is nevertheless clear that the war caused a long-term decline in the inland economy. Meanwhile, the economies of the western provinces recovered quickly and powerfully.[34] This is also true for urban population growth; the urban population stagnated in Overijssel and Gelderland, grew in Utrecht and Groningen, and expanded enormously in the three western provinces, namely Zeeland, Holland and Friesland.[35]

Amsterdam became the largest economic centre within Holland, replacing Antwerp as the central market. Amsterdam grew from 30,000 inhabitants before the Dutch Revolt to 100,000 around 1600, 200,000 in 1670 and even 240,000 in the 1720s.[36] This meant that a quarter of Holland's population lived in Amsterdam. Holland's spectacular growth stimulated the development of an extensive canal network for passenger barges (*trekschuiten*) and ferries (*beurtvaart*).[37] The Exchange Banks facilitated long-distance payments.[38] With charters issued by the States General, the Dutch East India

32 'the Hart, *The Dutch Wars of Independence*, 28–32.

33 't Hart, 173; 't Hart, *Oorlog en ongelijkheid*, 28; Brandon, *Masters of War*, 75.

34 't Hart, *The Dutch Wars of Independence*, 172–78.

35 Prak, *The Dutch Republic*, 250–51, 300.

36 Piet Lourens and Jan Lucassen, *Inwoneraantallen van Nederlandse steden ca. 1300–1800* (Amsterdam: NEHA, 1997). Prak, *The Dutch Republic*, 28, 96–97, 171; De Vries and Van der Woude, *The First Modern Economy*, 406–7; Gelderblom, *Cities of Commerce*; O. C. Gelderblom, *Zuid-Nederlandse kooplieden en de opkomst van de Amsterdamse stapelmarkt (1578–1630)* (Hilversum: Verloren, 2000); Clé Lesger, *Handel in Amsterdam ten tijde van de Opstand: kooplieden, commerciële expansie en verandering in de ruimtelijke economie van de Nederlanden ca. 1550-ca. 1630*, Amsterdamse historische reeks : Grote serie dl. 27 (Hilversum: Verloren, 2001); Clé Lesger, *The Rise of the Amsterdam Market and Information Exchange: Merchants, Commercial Expansion and Change in the Spatial Economy of the Low Countries, c.1550–1630*, trans. John Christopher Grayson (Aldershot etc.: Ashgate, 2006); Clé Lesger, "Intraregional Trade and the Port System in Holland, 1400–1700," ed. Karel Davids and Leo Noordegraaf, *Dutch Economy in the Golden Age*, Economic and Social history in the Netherlands, 1993, 186–217.

37 De Vries and Van der Woude, *The First Modern Economy*, 179–91; Prak, *The Dutch Republic*, 252–54.

38 Prak, *The Dutch Republic*, 106: Amsterdam (1609); Middelburg (1616), Delft (1621), Rotterdam (1635). J.G. Van Dillen, ed., *Bronnen tot de geschiedenis der wisselbanken: (Amsterdam, Middelburg, Delft, Rotterdam)*, Rijks geschiedkundige publicatiën 60 ('s-Gravenhage: Nijhoff, 1925).

Company (VOC, 1602) and the West India Company (WIC, 1621) participated in colonial trade and waged wars far beyond the Republic's territories. This sometimes conflicted with their shareholders' interests, most of whom lived in Holland and Zeeland.[39] Hence, the heavier burden borne by the maritime provinces appeared justified by the relatively peaceful conditions they enjoyed and the economic shift towards the west.

1.3 *Development of the Central Institutions*

The political centre of gravity also shifted to the west of the Netherlands. Power was concentrated in The Hague, formally a village, due to rivalry between Holland's towns. The States General and the States of Holland held their meetings there and the Stadholders their court. The Stadholder was no longer a representative of the monarch, but an official in the service of the provincial States, who now considered themselves sovereigns. He also often served as a Union army commander, thus in the service of the States General. The Stadholders were mainly members of the House of Orange-Nassau. They derived additional prestige from the Principality of Orange in France, where they were sovereign. Within the Dutch Republic, they could act as mediators in domestic conflicts, nominate military officers and select nominated members of the city councils. Despite these options for patronage, they remained servants of either the provincial States or the States General.[40] On the other hand, the lesser provinces also regarded the Stadholder as a protector against Holland's dominance.[41] Throughout the history of the Dutch Republic, con-

---

39 Femme S. Gaastra, *De geschiedenis van de VOC* (Zutphen: Walburg Pers, 2007): More than half of the 6.4 million guilders invested in the VOC came from Amsterdam, as did 8 out of its 17directors . Prak, *The Dutch Republic*, 28, 105–6; 't Hart, *The Making of a Bourgeois State*, 23–24; Henk Den Heijer, *De geoctrooieerde compagnie: de VOC en de WIC als voorlopers van de naamloze vennootschap* (Amsterdam: Stichting tot Bevordering der Notariële WetenschapDeventer : Kluwer, 2005); Henk Den Heijer, *De geschiedenis van de WIC* (Zutphen: Walburg Pers, 2002).

40 't Hart, *The Making of a Bourgeois State*, 18–21; Israel, *The Dutch Republic*, 37, 96; Adrianus Johannes Cornelis Maria Gabriëls, *De Heren Als Dienaren En de Dienaar Als Heer: Het Stadhouderlijk Stelsel in de Tweede Helft van de Achttiende Eeuw*, Hollandse Historische Reeks 14 ('s-Gravenhage: Stichting Hollandse Historische Reeks, 1990); Geert H. Janssen, *Creaturen van de macht: patronage bij Willem Frederik van Nassau (1613–1664)* (Amsterdam: Amsterdam University Press, 2005).

41 Arno Neele, *De ontdekking van het Zeeuwse platteland: culturele verhoudingen tussen stad en platteland in Zeeland 1750–1850*, Balans tussen stad en platteland 3 (Zwolle: Waanders : Universiteit Utrecht, 2011), 105; A. Th. van Deursen, "De plaats van de noordelijke gewesten in de Republiek," in *Nederland en het Noorden. Opstellen aangeboden aan prof.dr. M.G. Buist ter gelegenheid van zijn afscheid als hoogleraar in de Moderne Geschiedenis van Financiën en Bestuur en in de Contemporaine Geschiedenis aan de Rijksuniversiteit te*

flicts about the exercise of power regularly arose between these three focal points: the States of Holland, the central or Union institutions including the Stadholder, and the provincial States. This resulted from ill-defined competencies.[42] The root of the conflicts was the interpretation of the provincial autonomy and the protection of the province's privileges.[43]

Conflicts regularly arose with regard to the army, be it about the payments, the size of the army or appointments of officers and commanders. The troops were in the service of the States General.[44] This made the Receiver-General of the Union and the Council of State responsible for the payment of soldiers. In practice, the provinces paid the companies directly. They could subsequently deduct the amounts spent on wages and other military expenses from the agreed amounts for the budget and only the remainder was paid via the office of the Receiver-General of the Union.[45] As a result, the provinces acted as paymasters. At times, provinces reduced the companies on their payroll unilaterally. The Council of State objected to such practices, arguing that the troops were in the service of the Union and not of the individual provinces.[46]

The first major, open conflict arose during the Twelve Years' Truce, as part of a religious dispute. The States of Holland and Maurice of Nassau (1567–1625) were on opposite sides of the dispute. Invoking provincial autonomy in religious matters, the States of Holland adopted the 'Sharp Resolution' in 1617. This allowed the towns to recruit special soldiers (*waardgelders*) to keep order, under urban authority and not that of Maurice as the army commander. Furthermore, the States of Holland took the position that the regular troops on Holland's payroll fell primarily under its provincial authority. Moreover, the States threatened to spend the money for regular troops on the *waardgelders*. Altogether, this was an unacceptable attack on Maurice's position. Before facing Holland, Maurice secured support from the other provinces. He first marched to the Gelderland town of Nijmegen to install a favourable city council. Next, he dismissed *waardgelders* in the province of Utrecht. Finally, with the support of the States General, he had Holland's main functionary and

Groningen op 25 september 1990, ed. K. van Berkel, H. Boels, and M. G. Buist (Assen etc: Van Gorcum, 1991), 21–22.

42 't Hart, *The Making of a Bourgeois State*, 203.

43 Prak and Van Zanden, *Pioneers of Capitalism*, 94, 147–48.

44 't Hart, *The Making of a Bourgeois State*, 48.

45 't Hart, 192–93; 't Hart, *The Dutch Wars of Independence*, 154–55.

46 't Hart, *The Making of a Bourgeois State*, 47–48.

political leader, the Grand Pensionary (*raadspensionaris*) Van Oldenbarneveldt, arrested and executed in The Hague in 1619.[47]

Such disputes about hiring and dismissing troops continued, even as late payments and incomplete agreement on the Statement of War increased the risk of mutiny. Troop payments and other military expenses were urgent, while raising taxes and issuing loans took time. One remedy to smooth payments was to use 'military solicitors' (*solliciteurs-militair*), who advanced money to the companies' captains. These financial entrepreneurs later collected the payments from the provinces to which the companies were allocated.[48] Another solution was borrowing by the Receiver-General of the Union. The interest burden of these loans was subsequently divided among the provinces. Provinces could also borrow money on behalf of the Union and they were then allowed to deduct the interest burden from their allotted share of the contribution. The Generality's relatively small direct income from taxes limited its credit. That is why Holland guaranteed the Generality's punctual debt service until 1648. In addition, the Union Receiver could also issue loans for specific provinces to cover inadequate troop payments, funded by future revenues from that province.[49] Borrowing by the provinces under the guarantee of the States General appears to be a later phenomenon that built on this second practice.[50] While these loans and short-term credit solved the immediate problem of unpaid soldiers, obtaining payments from the provinces remained problematic without any means of coercion.

Returning to the second question of how to prevent free riding, what means did the central institutions have to enforce provincial contributions? If a province failed to pay the agreed amount, the States General would send an emissary or embassy to urge the province to pay. If a province still refused to pay, the Council of State had the right of execution. The execution could consist of taking hostages or billeting soldiers, as happened in Drenthe in 1604 and again in 1622. But this option ceased to be used after 1639.[51]

---

47 Prak, *The Dutch Republic*, 31–36; 't Hart, *Oorlog en ongelijkheid*, 30; Israel, *The Dutch Republic*, 441–49.

48 't Hart, *The Making of a Bourgeois State*, 38; Pepijn Brandon, "'The Whole Art of War Is Reduced to Money': Remittances, Short-Term Credit and Financial Intermediation in Anglo-Dutch Military Finance, 1688–1713," *Financial History Review* 25, no. 1 (April 2018): 19–41, https://doi.org/10.1017/S0968565017000282.

49 't Hart, *The Making of a Bourgeois State*, 80–81, 165–72; 't Hart, *The Dutch Wars of Independence*, 154–55; Fritschy, *Public Finance*, 135–36; Dormans, *Het tekort*, 135–41, 147.

50 Alberto Feenstra, "Hiding in a Twilight Zone: Credible Commitment in the Dutch Republic and Groningen's 1680s Default," *Histoire & Mesure* XXX, no. 2 (2015): 79–116.

51 't Hart, *The Making of a Bourgeois State*, 82; Fruin, *Geschiedenis der Staatsinstellingen*, 196, 378–79; Dormans, *Het tekort*, 31; Fritschy, "Schulden als leerschool?," 13.

Perhaps the provincial regents became wary of using violence to settle disputes within the federal state after the Stadholders Prince William II (1626–1650) and Count William Frederick (1613–1664) attacked Amsterdam in 1650. Now that peace had arrived with the end of the Eighty Years' War in 1648, Holland wished to reduce the size of the army. But this would mean a loss of power and prestige for the Stadholder. Amsterdam was targeted for a reason, as it tended to act as an independent city-state in its own right.[52] Already in 1640, Amsterdam had refused to pay several companies. The Generality took over that payment. The States of Holland backed Amsterdam in reducing the army expenses in 1641–1642. Again, in 1647, the States of Holland began to reduce pensions for military officers. With the peace in 1648, the army was reduced in size. In 1649, further proposals to reduce the size of the army met with resistance in the States General by supporters of the Stadholder and the army.[53] The States of Holland nevertheless disbanded various companies paid for by the province in June 1650. The States General and William II, as the army commander, would not accept such infringement of their authority. The States General sent delegations to various towns, to no avail. William II secretly sent the army to Amsterdam, but he failed to take it, although he replaced some magistrates. The conflict ended with William's unexpected death from smallpox, in November of the same year. Meanwhile, representatives of other provinces too had disapproved of William's violent actions.[54]

After William II's death, the Dutch Republic entered the First Stadholderless Period. His son William III (1650–1702), born shortly after his father's death, was not appointed as the new Stadholder. In 1651, the delegates of all the provinces met, at the invitation of the States of Holland, to discuss the new situation now the Republic had won its freedom and was without a Stadholder. In this special meeting, the Great Assembly, the States of Holland and four other provinces decided not to appoint a new Stadholder. Besides the Stadholderate and the matter of religion, control over the army was the third main theme in 1651. Each ultimately revolved around the question of power and whether decisions should be taken centrally or at the provincial level. The balance of power shifted towards the provinces and civic control

52 Prak, *The Dutch Republic*, 171: The British Ambassador William Temple considered Amsterdam's behaviour as that of a sovereign state, although it did not formally have that status.

53 't Hart, *The Making of a Bourgeois State*, 47–48; Dormans, *Het tekort*, 82; 't Hart, *The Dutch Wars of Independence*, 161–62; Israel, *The Dutch Republic*, 541–45.

54 Prak, *The Dutch Republic*, 42–44; Janssen, *Creaturen van de macht*, 176–81; 't Hart, *The Dutch Wars of Independence*, 28–29, 48; 't Hart, *The Making of a Bourgeois State*, 47–48; Fritschy, *Public Finance*, 150, 225.

regarding promotions, legal authority and troop movements. The focus on preventing the use of military force for domestic purposes undermined the effectiveness of the army in protecting the Republic against foreign threats, as would be shown in 1665 and 1672.[55] Ironically, William II's attempt to maintain central control over a large army had eroded the Stadholderate, impaired the ability of the Republic's central institutions to exert control and weakened the army.

The Dutch navy was not in good shape either. During the First Anglo-Dutch War (1652–1654), the armoured Dutch merchantmen proved no match for the British specially-built war vessels. Yet as a result of a new shipbuilding programme, the Dutch were able to withstand the British during the Second Anglo-Dutch War (1665–1667) and at the same time support Denmark during the Second Northern War (1665–1670) against Sweden.[56]

Whereas the navy had been strengthened, the army remained in poor condition. In 1665, the prince-bishop of Münster conquered large parts of the eastern provinces and only withdrew because Münster's English subsidies ran out and French troops came to the Republic's aid. The army's dismal performance harmed the position of Holland's anti-Orangist leaders, the pro-Republican States faction, most notably the De Witt brothers, Johan and Cornelis.[57]

In the Year of Disaster, 1672, the Republic was under attack by Britain, France, Münster and Cologne. Despite preparations that had been made for a major war in 1670, the army suffered defeats. Only at sea were Admiral De Ruyter and Deputy Cornelis de Witt able to deal a blow to the British navy. Yet the losses on land caused riots and a call for the restoration of the Stadholderate under the Prince of Orange, William III. The De Witt brothers were scapegoated and murdered by an enraged crowd in The Hague. Following William's restoration, Orangist factions claimed control over city councils. Their inexperience paradoxically hampered the levying of new taxes, necessary for the war efforts. Victories at sea and support from German allies eventually saved the Dutch Republic. The Third Anglo-Dutch War ended in 1674, and the Franco-Dutch War in 1678. The latter peace was only a temporary suspension in a

---

55 Fruin, *Geschiedenis der Staatsinstellingen*, 271–73; Israel, *The Dutch Republic*, 706–9; Prak, *The Dutch Republic*, 45; Dormans, *Het tekort*, 135; 't Hart, *The Dutch Wars of Independence*, 29: Holland, Zeeland, Utrecht, Gelderland, and Overijssel did not appoint a Stadholder, while Groningen appointed William Frederick, the Frisian Stadholder. Janssen, *Creaturen van de macht*, 181; Brandon, *Masters of War*, 41–43, 217, 219.

56 't Hart, *The Dutch Wars of Independence*, 29.

57 Israel, *The Dutch Republic*, 770–71; Prak, *The Dutch Republic*, 50.

series of wars with France that would last until 1713. By the end of the period, the Dutch Republic was exhausted. The Peace of Utrecht (1713) is considered to mark the end of the Republic's position as a power of the first rank.[58]

By 1713, the Second Stadholderless Period had begun, except in Friesland.[59] William III's Stadholderate ended with his unexpected death in 1702. By then, he had also become King of Britain, after the invasion of 1688. His accession to the throne also marked the start of the next war with France, the Nine Years' War (1688–1697). The regime change of the Glorious Revolution transformed Britain from foe to friend for almost a century, until the Fourth Anglo-Dutch War (1780–1784). William III died without heirs. In 1711, his intended successor, the Frisian Stadholder Johan Willem Friso (1687–1711), died as well.[60] The Second Stadholderless Period ended when Zeeland appointed William IV (1711–1751) as its Stadholder in 1747, following new military defeats.[61]

After the War of the Spanish Succession (1702–1713), a Second Great Assembly was called in 1716–1717. Little came from this series of meetings. The secretary of the Council of State, Simon van Slingelandt, presented numerous proposals that reinforced the central institutions.[62] During the war, the provinces accumulated arrears in their contributions to the States General, amounting to enormous sums. Yet the Council of State lacked adequate means of enforc-

58 Israel, *The Dutch Republic*, 796–806; 't Hart, *The Dutch Wars of Independence*, 30–33; Dormans, *Het tekort*, 67–68; Fritschy, *Public Finance*, 150; David Onnekink, *Reinterpreting the Dutch Forty Years War, 1672–1713* (London: Palgrave Macmillan, 2016); Prak, *The Dutch Republic*, 50–60; Gelderblom and Jonker, "Public Finance," 18; Dormans, *Het tekort*, 67; Ida Nijenhuis J.A., "'Shining Comet, Falling Meteor': Reflections on the Dutch Republic as a Commercial Power during the Second Stadholderless Era," in *Anthonie Heinsius and the Dutch Republic 1688–1720: Politics, War, and Finance*, ed. Jan Arie Frederik de Jongste and Augustus Johannes Veenendaal jr, ING-Workshop Series; RGP (The Hague: Institute of Netherlands History, 2002), 117; Olaf van Nimwegen rather views the War of the Austrian Succession as the moment the Republic lost this status as Great Power: G. de Bruin, "O. van Nimwegen, De Republiek Der Verenigde Nederlanden Als Grote Mogendheid. Buitenlandse Politiek En Oorlogvoering in de Eerste Helft van de Achttiende Eeuw En in Het Bijzonder Tijdens de Oostenrijkse Successieoorlog (1740–1748)," *BMGN – Low Countries Historical Review* 118, no. 3 (January 1, 2003): 390–92, https://doi.org/10.18352/bmgn-lchr.5905; O. van Nimwegen, "The Dutch Barrier: Its Origins, Creation, and Importance for the Dutch Republic, 1697–1718," in *Anthonie Heinsius and the Dutch Republic 1688–1720: Politics, War, and Finance*, ed. Jan Arie Frederik de Jongste and Augustus Johannes Veenendaal jr, ING-Workshop Series; RGP (The Hague: Institute of Netherlands History, 2002), 147–76.

59 Israel, *The Dutch Republic*, 989: Groningen appointed William IV as future Stadtholder in 1719, and in Gelderland and Drenthe in 1722.

60 Prak, *The Dutch Republic*, 60; Israel, *The Dutch Republic*, 959–97.

61 Israel, *The Dutch Republic*, 1067.

62 Israel, 986–89.

ing their contributions and even embassies were out of fashion.[63] The result was the Union's official suspension of interest payments for nine months in 1715, followed by a forced reduction of the coupon from 4 per cent to 3 per cent.[64] The main long-term outcomes of the Second Great Assembly were reductions in the military and the adoption of a policy of neutrality.[65]

The Republic was only moderately successful in this endeavour. As early as 1718 it participated in the War of the Quadruple Alliance (1718–1720), to quell Spain's opposition to the Peace of Utrecht. And in 1726 it joined Britain, France and Prussia in the Alliance of Hanover (or Herrenhausen) against Austria. This time there was no war, but the army was enlarged. Amsterdam's representatives objected because of the costs, demanding instant dismissal of the troops. Immediately after the Treaty of Vienna in 1732, Holland single-handedly dismissed those extra troops, against the wishes of the Council of State and the eastern provinces of Gelderland and Overijssel.[66]

The setbacks in the next major war, the War of the Austrian Succession (1740–1748), triggered the second restoration of the Stadholderate throughout the Dutch Republic, starting in Zeeland in 1747. As in 1672, the Stadholder's case benefitted from local unrest and threats by rioters. His position was now made hereditary. In 1748, Count Bentinck warned William IV that promises of change by the new Stadholder had only temporarily appeased the rioting populace. The civic militia movement (*doelistenbeweging*) in particular expected fundamental reforms of the oligarchic institutions – more than the rioters in the *pachtersoproer*, which was a tax riot. Bentinck made proposals to reinforce the central institutions under the leadership of the new Stadholder. William, however, died relatively unexpectedly as well, in 1751, leaving an infant son.[67] Shortly after, in 1754, the Receiver-General of the Union defaulted for the sec-

63 Dormans, *Het tekort*, 147–48; Fruin, *Geschiedenis der Staatsinstellingen*, 304.

64 Dormans, *Het tekort*, 147–48; Aalbers, *De Republiek*, 4 Utrecht prioritsed its provincial debt service over that of the Generality.

65 Aalbers, *De Republiek*; Israel, *The Dutch Republic*, 988.

66 Israel, *The Dutch Republic*, 988, 990, 993–94: The latter alliance was aimed at protecting the Republic's barrier in the Southern Low Countries and suppressing the ambitions of the Imperial East India Company or Ostend Company. Prak, *The Dutch Republic*, 265–66; Dormans, *Het tekort*, 88, 93; Doohwan Ahn, "From 'jealous Emulation' to 'Cautious Politics': British Foreign Policy and Public Discourse in the Mirror of Ancient Athens (ca. 1730-ca. 1750)," in *Ideology and Foreign Policy in Early Modern Europe (1650–1750)*, ed. David Onnekink and Gijs Rommelse, Politics and Culture in Europe (Farnham, Surrey: Ashgate, 2011), 108, 112–13.

67 Israel, *The Dutch Republic*, 1067–78; Isidore Leonard Leeb, *The Ideological Origins of the Batavian Revolution: History and Politics in the Dutch Republic 1747–1800* (The Hague: Nijhoff, 1973), 58–59, 70.

ond time due to provinces' failure to pay their contributions, signalling the weakness of the central institutions and their consequent inability to ensure sufficient income.[68] Like the propositions by Van Slingelandt before and Van der Spiegel later (1792), Bentinck's proposals to reinforce the central institutions were never implemented.[69]

When William v (1748–1806) came of age in 1766, the sentiment surrounding the Stadholderate had turned negative. His hesitant attitude did little to change that. Although the Orangists and States' factions agreed that the army and navy should be strengthened, they could not decide on the division of the funds. So nothing changed.[70] This reinforced anti-Orangist sentiments, most prominently among the Patriot movement, which aimed for a fundamental institutional reform of the Dutch Republic.[71]

The time seemed ripe for reform after the Republic's defeat in the Fourth Anglo-Dutch War. Attempts by the Patriot Revolution in 1785 to introduce thorough reforms were stifled by a Prussian invasion of 1787, which restored, Stadholder William v to his position.[72] A States General committee was set up to re-establish the distribution key for contributions to the common budget according to the provinces' current ability to pay. A survey analysed the distribution of the financial burden over the provinces in 1789. Only Zeeland achieved a significant reduction in the budget. The other major claimants calling for a reduction, Friesland and Groningen, did not. Holland's contribution was increased slightly, which suggests that even its large share since 1616 was nevertheless too small. The implementation took three years, until 1792.[73] The percentages changed, the distribution system remained intact.

By the time the new distribution key was in place, the Dutch Republic was already on its last legs. The Fourth Anglo-Dutch War had, among other things, brought the once-powerful Dutch East India Company (VOC) to the brink of bankruptcy. It could only survive with government loans. Also, the Republic

---

68 Dormans, *Het tekort*, 165; 't Hart, "United Provinces," 313; Fritschy, *Public Finance*, 159.

69 't Hart, "United Provinces," 322–23; 't Hart, "De Nederlandse Republiek," 76; Hovy, "Institutioneel onvermogen," 128–36; Frederik Pieter Wagenaar, "Achttiende-eeuwse overheidsfinanciën: kleine veranderingen met grote gevolgen," in *Overheidsfinanciën tijdens de Republiek en het Koninkrijk, 1600–1850*, ed. Hendrik Boels (Hilversum: Verloren, 2012), 119–35; Pfeil, *"Tot redding,"* 61–65.

70 Fruin, *Geschiedenis der Staatsinstellingen*, 331–33; Israel, *The Dutch Republic*, 1090–95.

71 Fruin, *Geschiedenis der Staatsinstellingen*, 334; Israel, *The Dutch Republic*, 1100.

72 Van Nimwegen, *Nederlandse burgeroorlog*; Fritschy, *De patriotten*; Fritschy, *Public Finance*, 194; Israel, *The Dutch Republic*, 1100–1115.

73 Fritschy, *De patriotten*, 159; Fritschy, "Schulden als leerschool?," 22; Dormans, *Het tekort*, 160–61: from 9.2 per cent to 3.8 per cent. Pfeil, *"Tot redding,"* 112.

was at war with revolutionary France in the War of the First Coalition (1792–1797). Although the Prussians had brought a temporary end to the internal discord, it had hardly disappeared beneath the surface. The French invasion, supported by Dutch Patriots and aided by frozen rivers, marked the end of the 'old' Republic in 1795.[74] As part of the reforms in the new Batavian Republic, in 1797 the public debts were merged into one national debt, which included the debts of the provinces, the Generality and the VOC.[75]

So a lot happened after 1651, but the Dutch Republic's fundamental fiscal and institutional arrangements did not change. After the Great Assembly, control over the military shifted decisively towards the provinces, even though this reduced the army's effectiveness. The Stadholders' personal qualities could temporarily help to overcome that problem, as was the case with William III. Yet the fear of absolutist monarchic aspirations, either from the Habsburgs or the House of Orange-Nassau, caused proposals for more centralisation to be met with sustained opposition. This was voiced by regents and political writers, such as Pieter de la Court from Holland in the seventeenth century and Lieven de Beaufort from Zeeland in the eighteenth century. They and other contemporaries believed that tackling the discord, luxury and corruption of the political elites who withdrew from the merchant elites was more pressing than decentralisation.[76] In general, the eighteenth-century discourse of decline appears to have been more of a political tool than recognition of an economic problem, since the Dutch Republic remained Europe's most prosperous state until the early nineteenth century.[77] If decentralisation was not the problem, centralisation would not remedy the decline.

As long as weak central institutions are supported by strong constituent members, the state's capacity may benefit from the distribution of power. On the other hand, the state's fiscal capacity may be hampered by free riding

---

74 Fritschy, *Public Finance*, 189, 192, 194, 201; Israel, *The Dutch Republic*, 1119–21.

75 Fritschy, *De patriotten*; Pfeil, *"Tot redding."*

76 Joris van Eijnatten, *Liberty and Concord in the United Provinces: Religious Toleration and the Public in the Eighteenth-Century Netherlands*, Brill's Studies in Intellectual History, ISSN 0920-8607 111 (Leiden etc.: Brill, 2003), 208; Wyger R. E. Velema, *Republicans: Essays on Eighteenth-Century Dutch Political Thought*, Brill's Studies in Intellectual History, ISSN 0920-8607 155 (Leiden etc.: Brill, 2007), 45–49, 58–64; Hans Blom, "Decay and the Political Gestalt of Decline in Bernard Mandeville and His Dutch Contemporaries," *History of European Ideas* 36, no. 2 (June 1, 2010): 153–66, https://doi.org/10.1016/j.histeuroideas.2010.01.002; Nijenhuis, "'Shining Commet, Falling Meteor,'" 117, 120.

77 Joris Oddens, Mart Rutjes, and Arthur Westeijn, eds., *Discourses of Decline: Essays on Republicanism in the Honor of Wyger R.E. Velema* (Leiden: Brill, 2021), https://doi.org/10.1163/9789004470651_006; Van Zanden and Van Leeuwen, "Persistent but Not Consistent"; Van Zanden and Van Riel, *The Strictures of Inheritance*; Brandon, *Masters of War*, 10.

attempts by some of its members.[78] Hence, the question remains: how did the loose association of autonomous provinces prevent free riding behaviour, especially after the Great Assembly of 1651 eroded central power and the Council of State therefore no longer applied the right of execution? According to Fruin, honour was the only reason driving the provinces to pay, yet all provinces fell significantly behind with their payments during wartime.[79] The Dutch Republic nevertheless maintained its independence until the end of the eighteenth century and had in the two centuries up to that moment played an important role in European politics. This could only be achieved by maintaining a substantial military force that depended on its revenue-raising capabilities. So how did the provinces raise these funds?

2 Holland's Public Finance

Holland's contribution of roughly 60 per cent thus formed the backbone of the Dutch Republic's public finances. Since 1616, Holland's financial power had probably increased rather than decreased, as evidenced by the increase in its share in 1792. This section analyses how Holland's fiscal health developed, what funds it raised, and how much of a burden this was on its population. More specifically, it examines the relative importance of tax income compared to loans on the income side, to assess the significance of the tax revolution relative to the 'classic' financial revolution.

Taxes were a precondition for issuing loans. Without tax revenues to fund the debt, investors would not lend money. A tax revolution was therefore a precondition for the later classical financial revolution, as Fritschy argues.[80] Therefore, the analysis consists of two main inquiries, one about tax income and expenditure, and the other about Holland's debt management. The first section divides into three parts. Firstly, it analyses the government budget balances or public balances to determine the ability to cover costs from revenue. Then it breaks down the expenditure into its main components. Finally, it analyses the means the States of Holland employed to cover the costs and the burden this imposed on Holland's population. The second section analyses the growth of the debt, the borrowing conditions and the relation to the market.

78 Van Zanden and Prak, "Towards."

79 Fruin, *Geschiedenis der Staatsinstellingen*, 304.

80 Fritschy, *Public Finance*, 85–101, 190; Fritschy, "Financial Revolution," 70, 79–80.

To make valid comparisons with the other provinces, it is first necessary to define what constitutes a tax revolution. While it is more or less clear what the classical financial revolution consists of, that is much less clear for the tax revolution. Fritschy dates Holland's tax revolution to 1574–1609.[81] Holland's development creates a yardstick by which the other provinces are measured, all the more so, since there are voices in the historiography that claim that Holland was overburdened and that its population had to cough up more than the inhabitants of the other provinces. This section creates a point of reference for the tax burden against which those claims about free riding can be tested.

From an international perspective, the residents of Holland were indeed heavily taxed.[82] But was that also the case compared to the rest of the Republic? Because in 1792 Holland's contribution was increased, not reduced. This suggests that Holland's high contribution had still been too low. Similar questions were raised after 1795 concerning the provincial public debts. Representatives of the inland provinces of Overijssel and Gelderland, De Vos van Steenwijk and Vitringa, questioned the causes of Holland's disproportionally large debt. The suggestion was that the debt resulted from either financial mismanagement or a preference for borrowing over tax increases.[83] The preference for debts over taxation has recently been proven empirically for early modern Italy.[84] The underlying question is whether borrowing was an alternative to taxation, or whether high taxes allowed the province to borrow more.

Holland's high public debt has primarily been given as evidence of the latter. However, Holland's share of the total tax revenues from 1788 to 1794 amounted to 81 per cent and its debt accounted for 75 per cent of total debt.[85] This in turn suggests that increased borrowing was conditional on sufficient tax revenues. Borrowing thus yielded Holland an additional option to fulfil its financial obligations towards the Union. The question is whether the other provinces had similar options when paying their share of the common budget.

81 Fritschy, *Public Finance*, 63, 85–88.

82 Bogart et al., "State and Private Institutions," 78–80; Drelichman and Voth, *Lending to the Borrower from Hell*, 28; 't Hart, "Gewetenloze kapitalisten"; Wantje Fritschy, "Geld en oorlog : financieel beleid in Holland en Overijssel vergeleken met Groot-Brittanië en Oostenrijk (1740–1785)," in *De Republiek tussen zee en vasteland: buitenlandse invloeden op cultuur, economie en politiek in Nederland 1580–1800*, ed. Carolus Augustinus Davids (Leuven/Apeldoorn: Garant, 1995), 207–25; Fritschy, "Taxation"; Fritschy, *Public Finance*, 229–30.

83 Fritschy, *De patriotten*, 158: "'het effect van geen behoorlijke finantieele voorzorg.'" .

84 Chilosi, "Risky Institutions," 911.

85 Riley, *International Government Finance*, 80.

Holland's contribution determined the Dutch Republic's options in the international arena, which depended on Holland's willingness to tax and borrow. The States of Holland decided how it raised its contribution. After the Revolt, eighteen towns held one vote each, and the nobility also had one vote. The Grand Pensionary presided over the meetings of the nobility and the provincial States. He also acted as Holland's spokesman within the States General. From this position, he had access to abundant information and influence in many matters, including public finance.[86] From this position, the famous Grand Pensionary Johan de Witt actively concerned himself with reducing the debt burden.[87] Foreign envoys treated him as the main Dutch representative, not unlike the position of Prime Minister, especially during times when the Stadholder was weak or the position vacant.[88] The power was thus concentrated in the hands of the civilian urban representatives, chief among them the Grand Pensionary.

2.1 *Government Budget Balances*

The first step in understanding Holland's fiscal policy is analysing the development of its public balances during the seventeenth and eighteenth centuries.[89] The analysis reflects the development in the order of magnitude, in three-year moving averages, of Holland's primary and fiscal balances.

A complicating factor in assessing Holland's fiscal performance is the effect of the withholding tax on bonds. From 1673 onwards, Holland had a tax on bonds. This was a convenient and easy way to diminish the borrowing costs and free up the money necessary for warfare. The combined French, British and German attacks in 1672 made this urgent. The tax functioned as an interest-rate reduction, even though it was officially a wealth tax. Each interpretation has a different effect on the primary budget balances. When interpreting the withholding tax on bonds as income, the primary surplus increases; the state now has more means to cover the interest charges. On the other hand,

86 Liesker and Fritschy, *Gewestelijke financiën: vol. 4. Holland*, 10–11; Fruin, *Geschiedenis der Staatsinstellingen*, 229; Israel, *The Dutch Republic*, 278–79.

87 Fritschy, *Public Finance*, 163, 241, 243.

88 't Hart, *The Making of a Bourgeois State*, 21.

89 Fritschy, "Financial Revolution," 63; Fritschy, *Public Finance*, 44–46; Liesker and Fritschy, *Gewestelijke financiën: vol. 4. Holland*, 78–133: The data underlying this analysis stem from a variety of sources that differ in their nature. Due to a lack of storage space, the archives of Holland's Chamber of Audit were burned in 1725, while other archives were turned into wrapping paper in 1738. Hence, the data are most reliable for the remainder of the eighteenth century. Despite the varietiation between the sources on a year-to-year basis, the overall differences over a longer period appear relatively modest.

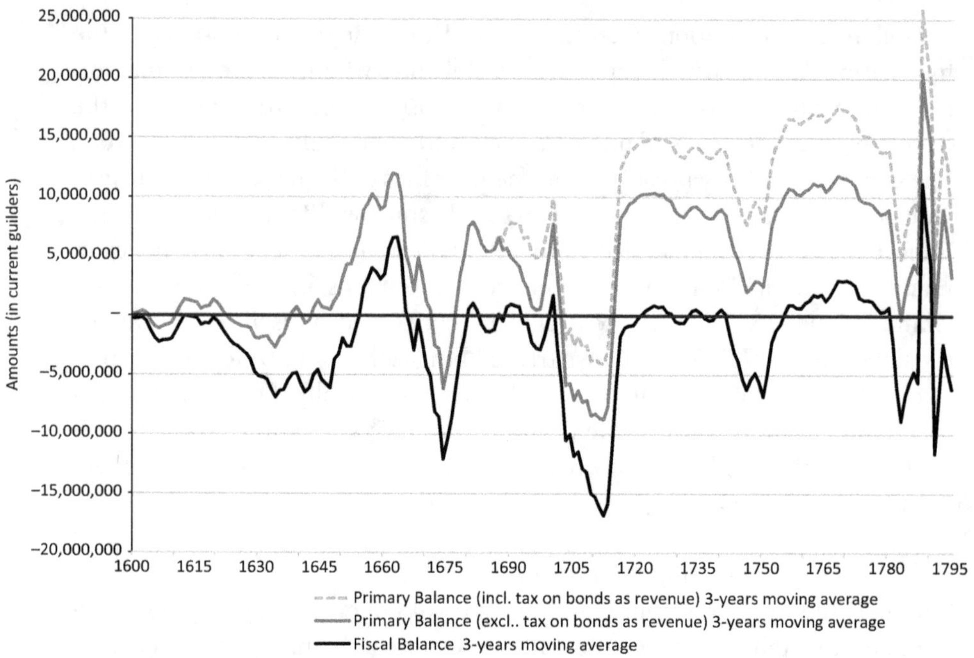

GRAPH 2.1 Holland's government budget balances, 1600–1795.
SOURCE: LIESKER AND FRITSCHY, *GEWESTELIJKE FINANCIËN: VOL. 4. HOLLAND.*

the primary surplus is smaller when treating the tax on bonds as a reduction in fiscal expenses. There is no effect on the fiscal balance. The tax on bonds did of course improve the fiscal balance compared to the situation without the tax. As a result, Graph 2.1 shows one fiscal balance and two primary balances, one including the tax on bonds as revenue, the other subtracting this from the income, to demonstrate the effect on Holland's budgets.

Holland enjoyed a primary surplus for most of the period, with few exceptions. After 1609, wars caused primary deficits on four occasions.[90] The first occasion was in 1621 when the Twelve Years' Truce expired and warfare resumed. Yet even before the end of the Eighty Years' War in 1648, Holland achieved a primary surplus. The short-lived First Anglo-Dutch War had little visible effect; the Second Anglo-Dutch War diminished the primary surplus, yet did not lead to a deficit. The second time Holland experienced primary deficits was during and after the Year of Disaster in 1672. The third instance was during the entire War of the Spanish Succession. Finally, in the dying

90 Following Fritschy's timing, Holland's tax revolution lasted until 1609. Fritschy, *Public Finance*, 63, 85–88.

years of the Dutch Republic, a primary deficit arose. For the rest of the period, the province covered its current expenses from tax revenues.

The fiscal balance also indicates healthy finances in the long run, although it tells a slightly less optimistic story. Fiscal income and expenditure were as a rule balanced in between conflicts. Fiscal surpluses obtained in those periods remained relatively small. As a result, the room to reduce the provincial public debt was limited. Only in two instances did Holland achieve fiscal surpluses more consistently, over longer periods. The first period was between the First and Second Anglo-Dutch Wars when fiscal surpluses amounted to more than five million guilders per year. The second period was between the War of the Austrian Succession and the Fourth Anglo-Dutch War. In the second period, surpluses remained smaller, at less than three million guilders per year, yet were sustained over a longer period. The limited surpluses were offset by larger fiscal deficits during various conflicts, of which the Second and Third Anglo-Dutch Wars and the War of the Spanish Succession stand out, while the War of the Austrian Succession, the Fourth Anglo-Dutch War, and the War of the First Coalition against Revolutionary France caused substantial deficits. Holland thus managed to balance fiscal income and expenditure in peacetime but created little room for debt redemptions.

The larger fiscal deficits in wartime, however, must have resulted in a gradual increase in public debt. The question remains whether borrowing was an alternative to taxation for Holland, or whether the inability to raise sufficient taxes forced Holland to borrow. To answer that question, the next sub-sections offer a closer examination of the expenses, income and tax burden.

2.2 *Expenses*

Warfare unmistakably caused temporary peaks in expenditure, while total expenses grew persistently over time. Three things stand out from the analysis of Holland's expenses. First, the almost constant increases in total expenditure led to a large difference in expenses between the beginning and the end of the period. Second, the increases were due to the rise in interest payments. Third, the periods of war became more expensive and less frequent.

Total expenses increased from around 5 million guilders around 1600 to over 40 million by the end of the eighteenth century. By 1600, expenditure had already increased fivefold since 1575, from 1 to 5 million guilders per year. While the Truce brought a temporary halt to the increments, the resumption of warfare led to a new increase from around 10 million in 1621 to over 17 million in 1648. Up to the second Anglo-Dutch War, expenses declined again to around 6 million – the First Anglo-Dutch War had little effect. From then on, expenses rose to a much higher level, hardly ever dipping below 15 million guilders

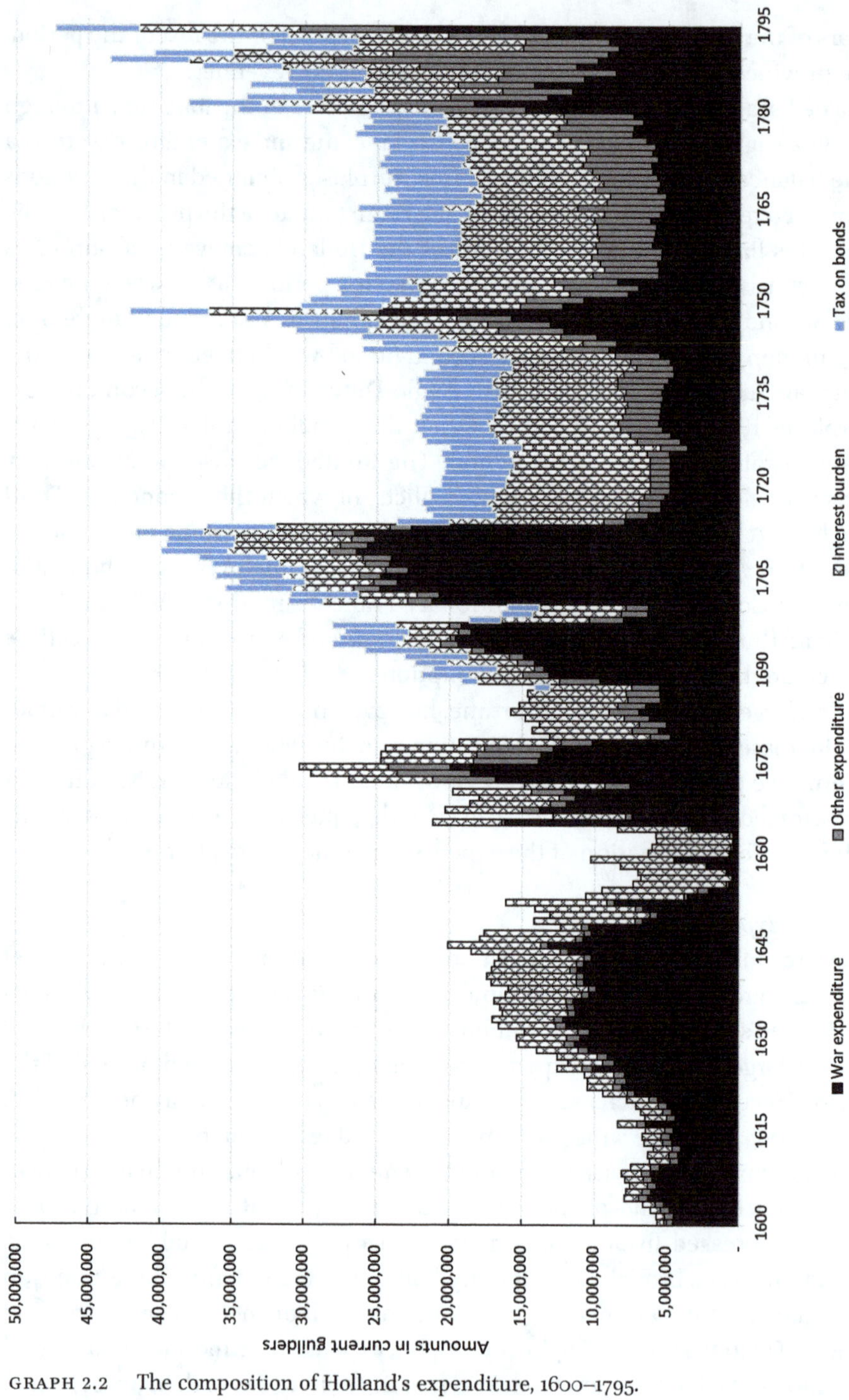

GRAPH 2.2 The composition of Holland's expenditure, 1600–1795.
SOURCE: LIESKER AND FRITSCHY, *GEWESTELIJKE FINANCIËN: VOL. 4. HOLLAND*.

per year. Considering that the tax on bonds was not actually paid, real expenditure amounted to between 20 and 25 million guilders per year during the eighteenth century (Graph 2.2).

War constituted the main primary expense. For Holland, annual military expenditure amounted to almost 10 million guilders. This amount remained largely the same throughout the seventeenth and eighteenth centuries. These averages, however, obscure the fact that warfare became more expensive. Between 1621 and 1648, war expenses amounted to 10 million guilders per year. The Franco-Dutch War (1672–1678) cost 15 million per year, and the War of the Spanish Succession 25 million. In the peacetime that followed, military expenditure decreased to 5 million guilders per year – participation in the War of the Quadruple Alliance and the Alliance of Hanover prevented an earlier or further decline. The War of the Austrian Succession had less of an impact because the Republic remained uninvolved for a long time. But when the French threat became real in 1747, expenditure rose again to 25 million guilders. Hence, warfare became much more expensive, resulting in a fivefold difference between war and peace years in the eighteenth century. Since the Dutch Republic spent fewer years at war during the eighteenth century, the total expenditure on warfare over the course of the century was similar to that in the seventeenth.

For a long time, administrative expenses remained limited to less than 2 million guilders per year. After 1750, they rose to 4 million, largely due to the costs of collecting taxes after the abolition of tax farming. Towards the end of the century, subsidies for the VOC further increased these expenses from 4 to 6 million guilders.[91] Still, the total costs of the administrative apparatus constituted a relatively small proportion of the overall expenditure, accounting for less than 20 per cent.

Over time, interest payments became the most important expense item. On paper, interest expenses constituted 50 per cent of total expenses in the eighteenth century. In practice, the tax on bonds reduced this proportion to one-third. Since 1673, this tax had proved a convenient instrument for lowering the effective coupon and hence reducing the interest burden. Until 1655, Holland relied on voluntary reductions and conversions to reduce the interest rate to 4 per cent. First introduced as a component of the personal wealth tax, the 'revenue' from the tax on bonds was recorded separately from the other tax components from 1687. The tax was not levied continuously and tax rates fluctuated until 1714. Afterwards, the tax was levied constantly at a tax rate

91 Fritschy, 165–66.

of 1.5 per cent, reducing the effective nominal coupon to 2.5 per cent, except for 1746 and 1747 when a tax rate of 2 per cent applied.[92] The withholding tax reduced the actual interest payments to just under 10 million guilders per year after 1714.

The tax on bonds thus kept the growth in interest payments in check. Around 1650, Holland paid almost 7 million guilders annually. Interest rate reductions and debt retirement reduced this amount to less than 5 million on the eve of the Second Anglo-Dutch War, in 1665. In 1672, the interest payments again reached 7 million guilders. Without the tax on bonds, the three consecutive wars with France would have doubled that amount to over 14 million guilders. In practice, debt redemptions decreased the effective amount in interest payments to 8 million in 1740. The reimbursements between 1751 and 1777 similarly reduced the interest payments from 10 to 8 million by 1780, which was only 1 million more than in 1650. After 1780, the relative stability in total expenses came to an end.

All expenses increased in the late eighteenth century, pushed up by the Fourth Anglo-Dutch War, the Patriot Revolution and the Prussian-aided restoration of the House of Orange. Furthermore, the unrest throughout Europe increased the demand for capital abroad, which competed with domestic demand. As a result, the States of Holland could no longer borrow at the usual 2.5 per cent.[93] How Holland covered its expenses is the subject of the next sub-section.

2.3 *Income*

To cover the rising expenses, Holland developed a new fiscal system for raising provincial taxes. Yet it began by providing credit in the form of a bond worth 500,000 guilders in 1572 to William of Orange to pay troops. It was a practical expression of Holland's political commitment. The amount was unprecedented.[94] In fact, in the last years before the Revolt, Holland's annual tax income amounted to 550,000 guilders.[95] Providing such large amounts (90 per cent of its income under the old system) required the States of Holland to increase its tax revenues substantially.

Indeed, a new tax system resulted in a more than tenfold revenue increase after 1574, to almost 6 million guilders in 1609. The key aspect of Holland's tax

92 Fritschy, 158; Liesker and Fritschy, *Gewestelijke financiën: vol. 4. Holland*, 369–75; Gelderblom and Jonker, "Public Finance," 21–25.

93 Dormans, *Het tekort*, 124–31.

94 Fritschy, *Public Finance*, 56–57.

95 Fritschy, 91.

revolution was the introduction of the 'common means' (*gemeene middelen*), which yielded more than 4 million guilders in 1608.[96] These mainly indirect taxes were introduced in 1570, yet levying was temporarily stopped because of the Revolt, to be reintroduced in 1574.[97] Institutionally, the main reform was the uniform province-wide levying of what had previously been local urban excises. The province eventually appointed eighteen district tax receivers as provincial officials – one for each town represented in the States of Holland – responsible for a town and its surroundings. On the one hand, this robbed the towns of their *de facto* fiscal autonomy. On the other hand, the countryside now shared the fiscal burden.[98] The district receivers became key players in the deep penetration of the fiscal state into the provincial economy.

In addition to the expansion in scope, the tax revolution also expanded the number of taxes and led to higher tariffs. Many daily necessities were taxed, not only beer and grain, but also cloth, candles, soap, fuel, cattle, fish and building materials.[99] As a result of this diversification of taxes, end products were taxed multiple times along the supply chain. For instance, for the production of bread, grain was taxed while still in the field and again at the mill, while other ingredients such as salt were taxed separately – and even the peat used as fuel to bake the bread. On top of that, there were almost no tax exemptions.[100] Holland's tax revolution was inclusive in terms of geography, class and commodities.

Impressive as the tenfold revenue increase was during the tax revolution up to 1609, it was still only a quarter of the eventual level of tax revenue under the Republic. The fourfold increase in tax revenues after 1609 took place in three stages. The first was a doubling to about 11 million in 1650. The second was an increase to 17 million guilders during the Forty Years' War with France (1672–1713). Finally, after 1750, Holland's income rose further to around 23 million guilders. This was around forty times as much tax revenue as before the Revolt.

The changing composition of the revenue and the means used to increase tax income inform us about the effects of the tax revolution (Graph 2.3). Until the end of the Eighty Years' War, the income from the common means grew almost constantly. By then, tax revenues amounted to some 12 million guilders,

96 Fritschy, 63, 85–88.

97 Fritschy, 84.

98 Fritschy, 60–62; Liesker and Fritschy, *Gewestelijke financiën: vol. 4. Holland*, 33–34.

99 Fritschy, *Public Finance*, 87.

100 Fritschy, 85, 91; Jan de Vries, *The Price of Bread: Regulating the Market in the Dutch Republic*, Cambridge Studies in Economic History – Second Series (Cambridge: Cambridge University Press, 2019), https://doi.org/10.1017/9781108639590; 't Hart, *The Making of a Bourgeois State*, 122–24, 137.

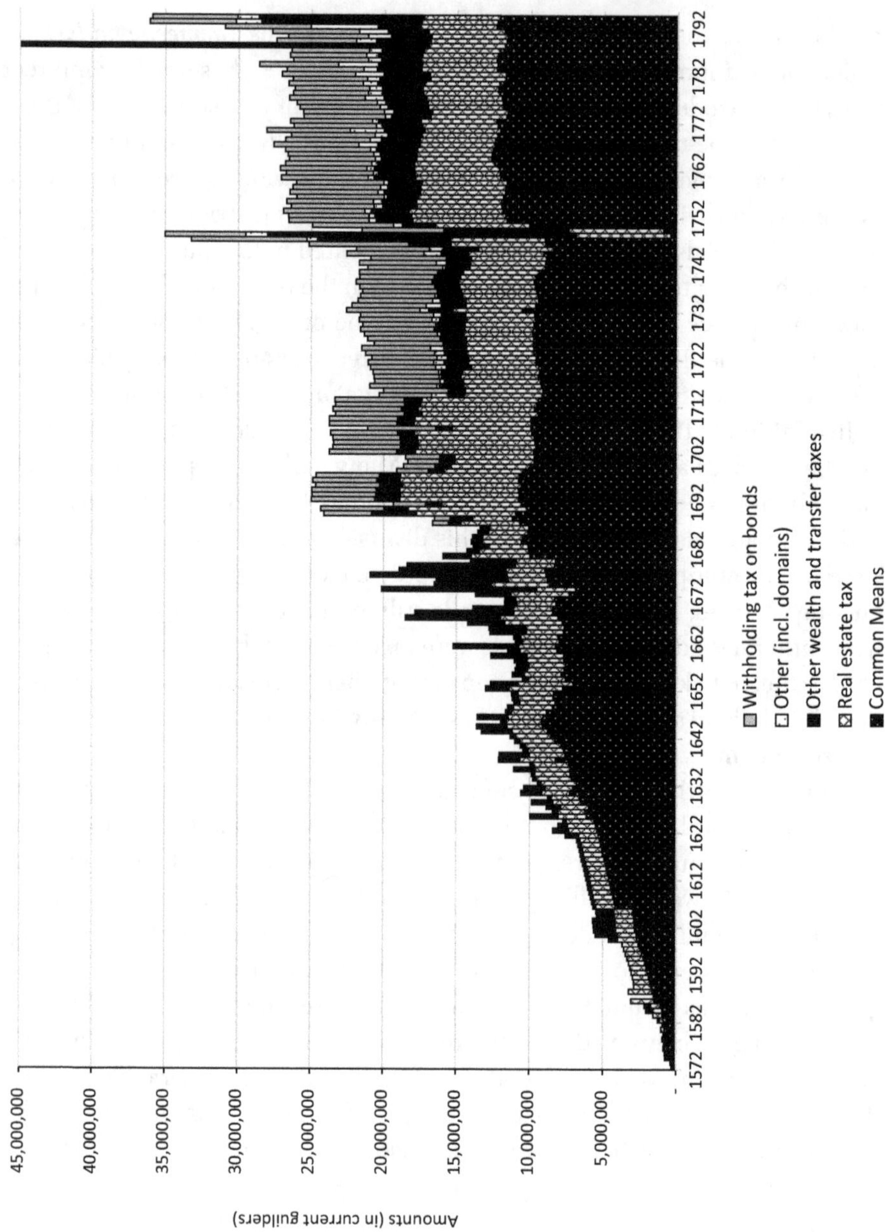

GRAPH 2.3 The composition of Holland's revenue, 1572–1794.
SOURCE: LIESKER AND FRITSCHY, *GEWESTELIJKE FINANCIËN: VOL. 4. HOLLAND*.

three-quarters of which consisted of the common means. Between the 1640s and 1750, the common means accounted for around 10 million guilders, and afterwards around 12 million. This latter increase was mainly due to tariff increases and to a lesser degree the transition from tax farming to tax collection.[101] The common means thus provided a stable and solid base for Holland's income.

From the 1680s, most increases in tax income stemmed from direct taxes on wealth and property on a structural basis.[102] Emergency levies led to huge ad hoc increases in revenue, with the *Liberale Gift* or Voluntary Gift of 1747–1748 and the forced loan of 1788 standing out. The first was a 2 per cent levy on wealth in response to the French invasion and the restoration of the Stadholderate, yielding more than 20 million guilders. The second was a 4 per cent wealth levy to help the VOC after the losses from the Fourth Anglo-Dutch War, generating revenue of 50 million guilders.[103] These amounts suggest that wealth had become a major source of potential tax revenues in the eighteenth century.

Holland's economic development explains the increasing relative importance of direct taxes. The common means were related to economic activity because they were levied on purchases of daily necessities, and there was also direct taxation of property. Every member of society paid excises. As a result, excises absorbed a larger portion of the income of the ordinary people, which made the common means a regressive form of taxation. Holland's rapid economic expansion and population growth made the increasing tax burden easier to bear because it widened the tax base. The increase in revenues from the common means more or less coincided with this economic expansion.[104] The slower pace of economic growth after 1670 corresponded with the stagnation of these indirect taxes. On the other hand, the direct taxes targeted wealth and property, which had accumulated during the expansion phase. This mirrors Holland's economy during that later period, when capital had been accumulated, the level of economic activity was still high but growth was minimal.[105]

Holland met the increasing expenses by increasing taxation. In peacetime, public revenues even exceeded expenditure slightly. This is most noticeable in

101 Fritschy, *Public Finance*, 166.

102 Liesker and Fritschy, *Gewestelijke financiën: vol. 4. Holland*, 224–26; Fritschy, 't Hart, and Horlings, "Long-Term Trends," 42; Fritschy, *Public Finance*, 183–87.

103 Fritschy, *Public Finance*, 172–73, 175, 188–89, 192; Liesker and Fritschy, *Gewestelijke financiën: vol. 4. Holland*, 118.

104 Fritschy, "Financial Revolution," 70, 79–80; Gelderblom and Jonker, "Public Finance."

105 Van Zanden and Van Leeuwen, "Persistent but Not Consistent," 126–28.

the periods 1650–1671, 1715–1740 and 1750–1780. During wartime, however, expenses could easily be double the peacetime amount for several consecutive years, a rise that temporary tax increases could not cover. From around 1670, the excises, so central to Holland's tax revolution, no longer sufficed to cover the expenses. Direct taxes on wealth and property became more important to maintain fiscal health, which implied that Holland's urban elites increasingly taxed themselves. However, the 5 to 7 million guilders they paid in direct taxes was still less than the interest payments of 8 to 10 million guilders earned largely by those same elites for most of the eighteenth century. This indicates a transfer of income from poor to rich.

2.3.1 Tax Burden

The next question is how much of a burden the taxes were for Holland's population and how the burden was distributed within its society. As said, economic developments determined the options for taxation. Yet how much ordinary people paid compared to the richer stratum of society is a difficult question to answer. Not all taxes of the common means were actual excises, levied on end-products. Therefore, Fritschy suggests subtracting some taxes from the common means, such as those on cattle.[106] Indirectly, however, these taxes were paid by ordinary people too. When the cattle were slaughtered, a tax was levied on them again and the meat was sold for consumption. So these taxes were eventually included in the retail price. Therefore, we may still assume that the common means tax burden was largely borne by the whole population and the direct taxes by the upper middle class and the rich.

The essence of Holland's tax revolution was the wide spread of taxes across the economy, with hardly any tax exemptions. Consumer goods were, at least until 1660, at the core of the increase in tax revenues, which burdened the common people most. Thanks to demographic growth and wage increases, those increased taxes were spread over more people, who earned higher incomes. However, both the population growth and wage increases slowed down in the course of the seventeenth century. The effect of each of these two factors was as follows.

Unskilled day wages tripled initially from around 0.30 guilders in 1575 to 0.90 guilders around 1640. Already by 1600, the wage level had doubled to 0.60 guilders. The upward trend then continued more gradually to about 0.75 guilders in 1630 and 0.90 guilders in 1640. From then on, wage levels fluctuated somewhat, but there were no further sustained changes until the early nine-

106 Fritschy, *Public Finance*, 90–91.

teenth century.[107] Hence, after 1640, tax increases were no longer absorbed by rising incomes.

Population growth mitigated the per capita tax burden for longer. Holland's demographic and economic growth was primarily urban; the degree of urbanisation rose from less than 40 per cent before the Revolt to more than 60 per cent between the 1660s and 1730s. The demographic expansion lasted until around the 1670s. In this period Holland's population more than doubled, from around 427,500 in 1575 to around 883,000 in 1670. A period of decline followed, lasting until the early eighteenth century, which resulted in a population of around 840,000 residents. Renewed growth then increased Holland's population to its maximum under the Republic, about 900,000 inhabitants in the 1730s. This was followed by a period of decline, in which the population shrank to around 811,000 inhabitants by 1750. Such growth as there was in the second half of the eighteenth century was rural. Urbanisation declined to around 55 per cent. In 1795, Holland was home to some 830,000 people. This was less than in 1670 or the 1730s. As a result, demographic growth no longer compensated for tax increases after 1670, and especially not after the 1730s.

The picture of economic development that emerges here is roughly the same as the one presented by Van Zanden and Van Leeuwen, based on the reconstruction of Holland's GDP. Both methods indicate growth until about 1670, followed by a period of stagnation. The decreasing rate of urbanisation even points to prolonged economic decline after the 1730s. However, where the combination of demographic analysis and wage level suggests that Holland became poorer mainly after 1730, the GDP analysis shows more positive results. GDP and GDP per capita not only recovered, during the 1760s and 1770s these measures exceeded the levels seen in the seventeenth century.[108] The implication of the combination of stagnant wages and the increase in GDP per capita is that wage workers did not benefit from the rising GDP while the rich became richer.[109]

107 De Vries and Van der Woude, *The First Modern Economy*, 610–11; Van Zanden, "Kosten"; Leo Noordegraaf and Jan Luiten Van Zanden, "Vroegmoderne economische groei en levensstandaard in de Gouden Eeuw," in *Een wonder weerspiegeld: de Nederlandse Republiek in Europees perspectief*, ed. Karel Davids and Jan Lucassen (Amsterdam: Aksant, 2005), 381–408.

108 Van Zanden and Van Leeuwen, "Persistent but Not Consistent," 123: The GDP per capita also increases when applying my higher population estimates, whereas Van Zanden and Van Leeuwen follow De Vries and Van der Woude's lower estimates for the eighteenth century.

109 This result shows striking similarities with the diverging development of GDP and day wages as indicators for growth in eighteenth-century Britain: Humphries and Weisdorf,

From this perspective, the increasing importance of direct taxes on wealth and property seems reasonable. Nevertheless, Fritschy suspects that the well-to-do in Holland contributed less than the rich in the province of Overijssel.[110] Therefore Fritschy, like 't Hart, questions Prak and Van Zanden's argument that the high tax morale was one explanation for the high levels of taxation.[111] Rather, we know of at least ninety-one tax riots in Holland during the seventeenth and eighteenth centuries.[112] The tax riots were, as a rule, an urban phenomenon and directed against indirect taxes, not direct taxes, while the protesters came from lower-ranked and middling groups.[113] These characteristics are not surprising, since the excises hit the ordinary people hardest, a group who were not represented in the urban governments. The tax riots show that the social and economic ceiling of indirect taxation could not be raised indefinitely, and the urban elites may have felt forced to increase direct taxes instead.

This raises the question of how hard the indirect taxes pressed on the general population and what the elites contributed. The impact of Holland's tax revolution becomes immediately clear when comparing the tax burden just before the Revolt to the increase following the introduction of the common means. Holland's tax revenue of 550,000 guilders in 1570 implied a per capita amount of 1.29 guilders, or 4.75 days' wages for an unskilled worker.[114] This figure rose to sixteen days in 1600 and then decreased slightly to fifteen days in 1609 (Graph 2.4). The burden from the indirect taxes increased almost continuously, from four days in 1575 to almost nine in 1600 and nearly twelve in 1609. The tax revolution had thus more than tripled the tax burden from less than five days' wages to over fifteen day between 1575 and 1609. Yet the more than tenfold increase in total revenues would have been impossible without the doubling of wages and a population increase of around one-third in the period to 1609.

"Unreal Wages?," 2877. A systematic analysis of annual wages in the Dutch Republic should become part of future research.

110 Fritschy, *Public Finance*, 191, 376.

111 Fritschy, 187–91; 't Hart, *The Dutch Wars of Independence*, 158, 168; Prak and Van Zanden, "Tax Morale"; Van Zanden and Prak, "Towards."

112 Rudolf Dekker, "Holland in beroering: oproeren in de 17de en 18de eeuw" (S.l.] ;, Ambo, 1982), 28–29, 177–78: 40 during the seventeenth century, 51 during the eighteenth century.

113 Dekker, 37–38.

114 This is, as explained in the book's introduction, a uniform gauge, which avoids debates about the labour market and household composition and the relative contribution of women, children and the elderly.

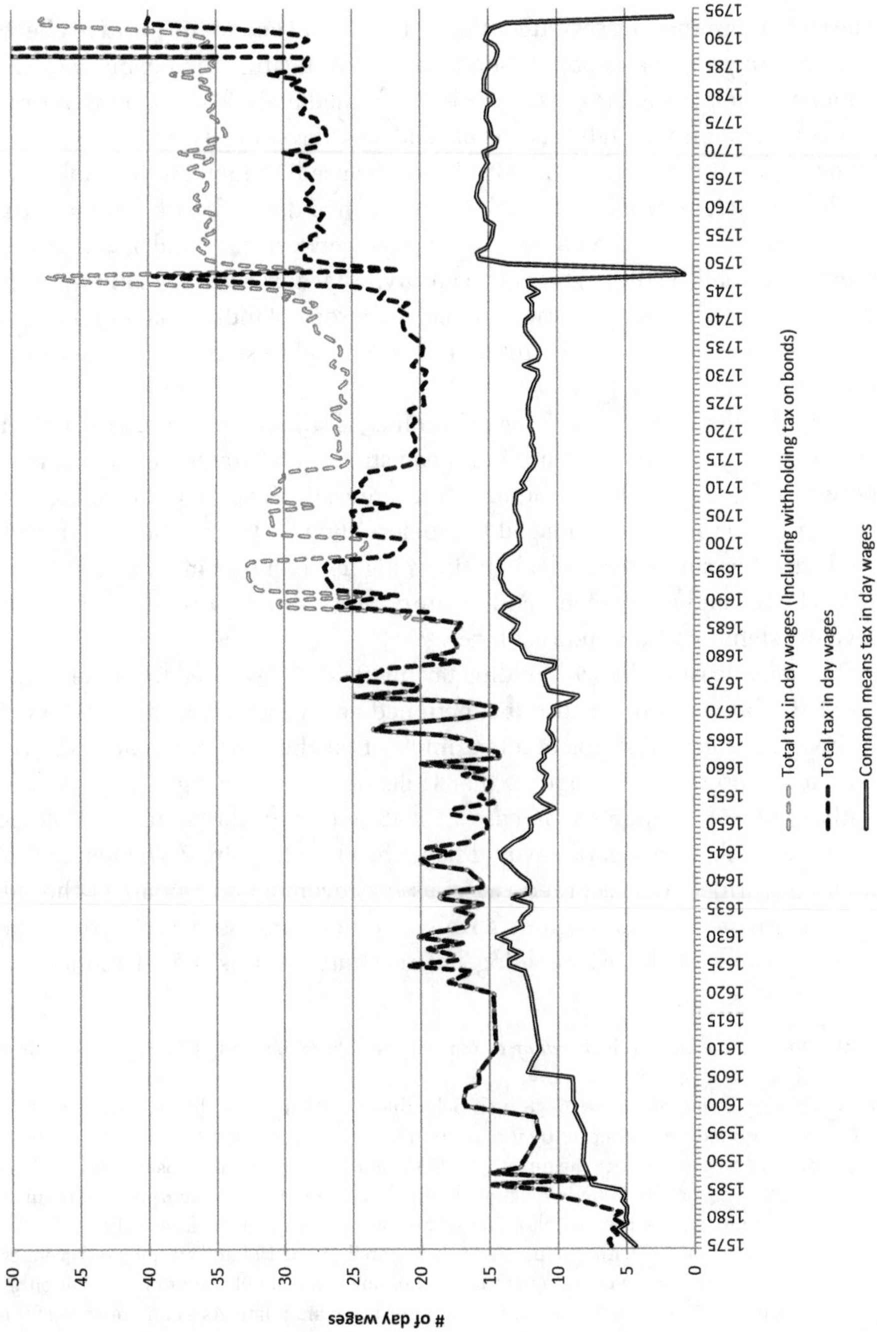

GRAPH 2.4 Per capita tax burden in day wages, 1575–1794.

SOURCE: FEENSTRA, *BETWEEN SHARED* AND LIESKER AND FRITSCHY, *GEWESTELIJKE FINANCIËN: VOL. 4. HOLLAND* AND TEXT.

The third quarter of the seventeenth century saw an end to the positive effects of increasing wages and population growth in mitigating the tax burden. The population felt the effects of tax increases immediately. The tax burden from the common means stabilised at around 12.5 days' wages for an unskilled labourer, until 1750. The wars with France caused an increase in total taxes to the equivalent of about twenty to twenty-five days of work around 1700. This figure decreased to some twenty days between 1715 and 1740. During the second half of the eighteenth century, total tax revenues amounted to the equivalent of 27.5 days' wages. Since the burden of indirect taxes no longer increased, the increase in the total tax burden had to stem from increases in direct taxes.

The number of 27.5 days' wages becomes all the more impressive from a comparative perspective. Other European states only attained the equivalent of twelve days' wages in per capita tax revenues by the end of the eighteenth century, while Holland managed this before 1600.[115] The tax burden in Holland was thus some two and a half times higher than that in other European states by the end of the eighteenth century, and around 60 per cent of the tax revenue stemmed from indirect taxes.

The income from the withholding tax on bonds is excluded from the analysis of the tax burden because it functioned as an interest rate reduction.[116] Although the formal status of a tax implies that the state could alter the tax rate at its discretion, it appears that Holland seldom changed the tax rate. Rather, after a temporary increase in 1746 and 1747, the States of Holland emphasised that the tax rate would never be altered again.[117] The taxation of public securities was recorded twice, as tax revenue and as part of the full interest payment. At some point, a Holland official proposed ending the separate recording of the withholding tax revenues, as this would reduce the

115 Drelichman and Voth, *Lending to the Borrower from Hell*, 28; 't Hart, "Gewetenloze kapitalisten," 435–36.

116 Fritschy, *Public Finance*, 156–58, 250; Gelderblom and Jonker, "Public Finance," 21: "Holland also reduced expenses by forcing an interest rate cut in the form of a withholding tax."; Dincecco, "Political Regimes," 58. On the one hand, Dincecco considers the Holland bonds as 2.5 per cent bonds, a figure obtained as the outcome of the 4 per cent nominal rate minus 1.5 per cent withholding tax; on the other hand, he also includes the tax revenue from the withholding taxes in his analysis of Holland's total tax revenues. That means a double-counting of the withholding tax. It should be interpreted as either a tax or a reduction in the expenses: not both at the same time. As a consequence of this inconsistency he draws a questionable conclusion about the positive effect of Holland's centralisation for high taxes, causing its low interest rates.

117 Liesker and Fritschy, *Gewestelijke financiën: vol. 4. Holland*, 371–75; Fritschy, *Public Finance*, 158.

administrative burden.[118] The separate administration was meaningless. It was a paper reality that artificially inflated Holland's income and expenditure by some 25 per cent. Also, only the bondholders suffered from the reduction and benefitted from the interest payments; no other taxpayers or beneficiaries were involved. Rather, income from the tax on bonds was conditional on the existence of the public debt; without public debt, the tax could not have been levied. Furthermore, the tax on bonds was levied irrespective of the subjecthood of the bondholder; in the case of bondholders who lived outside of Holland, Holland was taxing subjects of other jurisdictions. Hence, when estimating the tax burden, the yield from the withholding tax on bonds must first be subtracted from the total revenues.

The present analysis confirms that Holland's inhabitants were indeed among the most heavily taxed people of their time.[119] Even taking into account the fact that Dutch wages were high internationally, Holland extracted large amounts of public revenue.[120] Until the 1670s, tax increases were spread over a growing population with rising income levels, so that the tax burden rose more slowly than public income. After that, every tax increase meant an increase in the tax burden on the population. That pressure was so high that the income from common means barely increased between the 1670s and 1750, and any increases in revenue mainly came from direct taxes. The fact that the rich began to tax themselves mainly reflected the impossibility of increasing the common means. Tax riots in 1702 and 1748, for example, suggest that the excise revenues had probably reached a social ceiling. Moreover, in the years following 1748, the abolition of tax farming increased the collection costs, which made the net increase in revenue meagre in Holland.[121] This implies that tax farming had been relatively efficient. Furthermore, the relative increase in direct taxes after 1750 indicates that Holland's urban elites were making an increasingly large contribution. However, Holland's regents were aware that the rich and their capital could easily move out of the Dutch Republic. Capital flight proved to be a real danger in 1672, when people moved their money from Amsterdam to London. Arguably, that illustration of capital being a movable

---

118 Liesker and Fritschy, *Gewestelijke financiën: vol. 4. Holland*, 43.

119 Fritschy, "Overheidsfinanciën"; Fritschy, "Taxation," 65,70 1988; Fritschy, *De patriotten*, 66–67; Fritschy, "Financial Revolution."

120 De Vries and Van der Woude, *Nederland 1500–1815*, 707, 742; Robert C. Allen, "The High Wage Economy and the Industrial Revolution: A Restatement," *The Economic History Review* 68, no. 1 (2015): 1–22, https://doi.org/10.1111/ehr.12079.

121 De Vries and Van der Woude, *The First Modern Economy*, 123–24; Israel, *The Dutch Republic*, 1072–74; Dormans, *Het tekort*, 98–99.

asset made the States of Holland hesitant to increase wealth taxes.[122] Whether or not the accusation of insufficient taxation of the elites holds water, it is clear that Holland's population was heavily taxed from an international perspective.

3 Holland's Public Debt

The question of whether Holland's elite paid its fair share was posed by the Overijssel and Gelderland representatives Vitringa and De Vos van Steenwijk, mentioned above, in relation to borrowing. They suggested that borrowing formed a convenient alternative to tax increases and that this reluctance to tax had caused Holland's sizeable public debt. Fritschy corroborates that view by arguing that elites in Overijssel contributed more in direct taxes than Holland's elites. This section examines how important borrowing was for Holland's public finances, in order to assess the relative significance of its 'classic' financial revolution compared to its tax revolution.

The timing of Holland's financial revolution is a subject of debate. Tracy places it in the sixteenth century. The first important step was the collective liability for a loan involving five of Holland's six major cities in 1515. New provincial taxes further increased the States' borrowing capacity.[123] Holland, however, built on medieval experiences when towns borrowed money for their Burgundy and Habsburg overlords, who lacked credit.[124] Tracy finds that these institutional innovations benefitted the States of Holland only after the Revolt had begun.[125] Fritschy, on the other hand, argues that a financial revolution occurred later, after 1600.[126] Their difference in timing is relevant because it implies different causes for the method used to finance the Dutch Revolt. Whereas Tracy emphasises continuity from the Habsburg period in raising loans funded by provincial taxation, Fritschy highlights the

---

122 Prak, *The Dutch Republic*, 79.

123 Tracy, *A Financial Revolution in the Habsburg Netherlands*, 58–63, 89–90,94; Zuijderduijn, *Medieval Capital Markets*, 81; Zuijderduijn, "De laatmiddeleeuwse crisis van de overheidsfinanciën en de financiële revolutie in Holland."

124 Tracy, *A Financial Revolution in the Habsburg Netherlands*, 58–63, 89–90,94; Zuijderduijn, *Medieval Capital Markets*, 80–81 The interest paid over the ensuing funded debt amounted to 7.6 per cent on average, which was much lower than the 26 per cent Charles v paid on average over his personal unfunded debts. Zuijderduijn, "De laatmiddeleeuwse crisis van de overheidsfinanciën en de financiële revolutie in Holland."

125 Tracy, *A Financial Revolution in the Habsburg Netherlands*, 213–14.

126 Fritschy, "Financial Revolution"; Fritschy, *Public Finance*, 23–24, 63–72, 98–101.

loss of credit during the early phases of the Revolt, which necessitated tax increases.

The loss of credit was the result of Holland's suspension of interest payments and prioritisation of war expenses between 1572 and 1576. The Revolt caused a steep rise in borrowing costs; the interest rates on short-term bonds were as high as 30 per cent or 40 per cent in 1575.[127] To settle the most urgent debts, the States confiscated Catholic *émigré* and church property.[128] The combination of default and subsequent confiscation was a flagrant violation of property rights, which are considered essential to a financial revolution. Holland's credit was gradually restored from the 1590s when the revenue streams from the common means could fund the debt. Only after the Twelve Year's Truce (1609–1621) did long-term borrowing constitute a significant proportion of Holland's income.[129] While decreasing, interest rates took even longer to fall below pre-Revolt levels. Hence, the groundwork of the financial revolution was laid in the sixteenth century but it only took effect after 1609.

3.1 *Size of the Debt*

How did Holland's debt develop in terms of size and composition? How much did Holland borrow, when, how, and subject to what conditions? Before the start of the Revolt, Holland's debt was estimated at around 1.4 million guilders. Although that amount may have increased somewhat during the 1560s, it cannot have been more than 2 million and probably barely exceeded 1.5 million guilders.[130] From this perspective, the 500,000 guilders that the free States of Holland promised the Prince of Orange for troop payments in 1572 was a huge amount. Holland's suspension of interest payments in the same year ruined its creditworthiness, which was not easily restored. Arrears were added to the debt in the 1570s and some overdue interest was paid in the 1580s. Meanwhile, the province depended on the credit of army commanders and the individual towns. In 1588, the province took over the debt of 1.5 million guilders that the

127 Fritschy, *Public Finance*, 61.

128 James D. Tracy, "Emigré and Ecclesiastical Property as the Sheet-Anchor of Holland's Finance, 1572–1584," in *Reformation, Revolt and Civil War in France and the Netherlands 1555–1585*, ed. Philip Benedict, Guido Marnef, and Henk van Nierop, Verhandelingen Der Koninklijke Nederlandse Akademie van Wetenschappen. Afd. Letterkunde: Nieuwe Reeks 176 (Amsterdam: Royal Netherlands Academy of Arts and Sciences, 1999), 257–59, 262–63; 't Hart, *The Making of a Bourgeois State*, 80; Fritschy, *Public Finance*, 131.

129 Fritschy, "Financial Revolution," 66, 76, 79–80, 84–85; 't Hart, *The Making of a Bourgeois State*, 161–64: 't Hart notes that the decline in interest rates on public debt started from around 1592.

130 Dormans, *Het tekort*, 19–20.

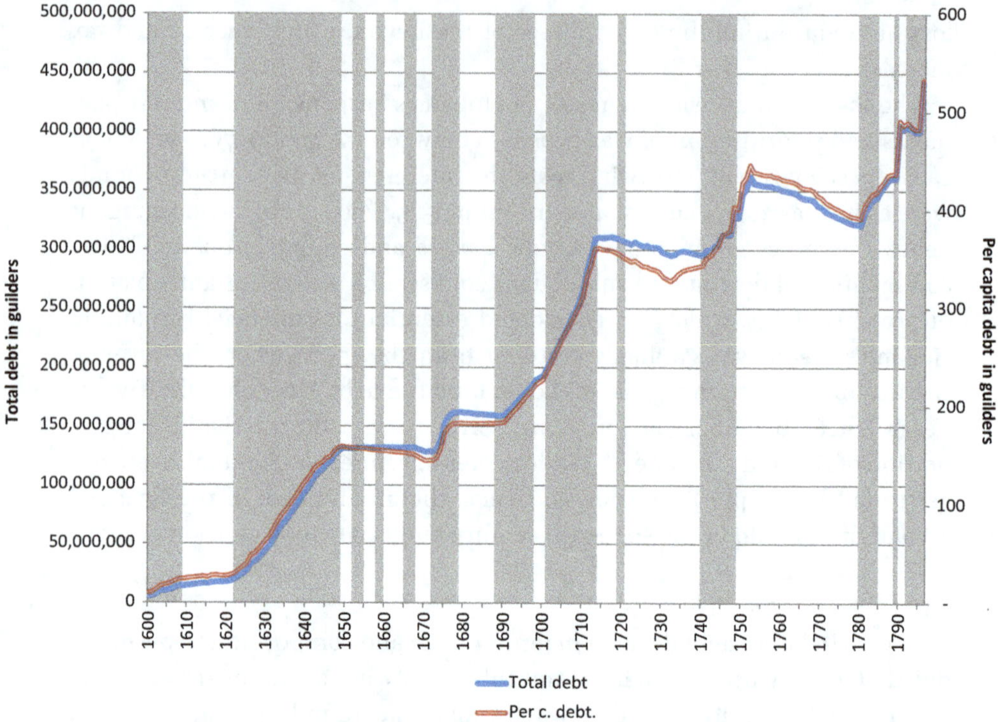

GRAPH 2.5 Holland's debt, total and per capita, 1600–1795.
SOURCES: DEBT: UNTIL 1720, GELDERBLOM AND JONKER, "PUBLIC FINANCE"; AFTER 1720, DORMANS, *HET TEKORT*, POPULATION ESTIMATES HOLLAND, SEE: H.A. FEENSTRA, *BETWEEN SHARED*, APPENDIX.

individual towns had issued based on their own creditworthiness. That year, Holland paid 362,500 guilders in interest. The debt amounted to some 2.1 to 3.2 million guilders, depending on the presumed going rate of 12 or 18 per cent on the short-term bonds or bills (*obligaties*) (Graph 2.8).[131] This bandwidth then offers a point of departure to assess the growth in Holland's debt.

In 1594, Holland issued provincial debt for the first time since the outbreak of the Revolt.[132] The debt gradually expanded to around 5.5 million guilders in 1600.[133] Massively increased taxation levels probably helped restore confi-

131 Fritschy, "Financial Revolution," 61–62, 68, 74–77. Gelderblom and Jonker gave a more conservative estimate of the debt of around 1.7 million guilders in 1591, based on 1588. Gelderblom and Jonker, "Public Finance," 5, 28–29.

132 Fritschy, "Financial Revolution," 75.

133 Gelderblom and Jonker, "Public Finance," 29.

dence in Holland's ability to sustain its debt.[134] Economic growth also boosted savings, which could be invested in public debt.[135]

However large compared to the sums borrowed before the outbreak of the Revolt, the debt in 1600 was only a fraction of the size of Holland's debt at the end of the eighteenth century (Graph 2.5). In 1796, the province's debt amounted to 441 million guilders, or 533 guilders per capita. At the same time, Holland collected some 3.1 billion guilders in taxes in 1600–1795. This makes Holland's tax revenue seven times as large as its net income from loans. Put another way, Holland increased its spending capacity by 14 per cent by issuing loans. More importantly, borrowing expanded wartime spending capacity by around 46 per cent during the seventeenth century and over 100 per cent during the eighteenth century.[136] The increasing relative importance of debt financing reflects the costlier war years, the modest tax increases and the abundant capital supply.

Why did the debt grow, when and by how much? The growth in Holland's debt was concentrated in three periods. First, there was a more than sevenfold increase from less than 20 million guilders in 1621 to almost 130 million guilders in 1648. That increase was equal to a quarter of the province's debt in 1796. Second, Holland's debt almost doubled from just under 160 million in 1688 to over 310 million in 1715. That difference of 150 million was equal to more than one-third of the debt in 1796. Third, the debts incurred during the last fifteen years of the Republic's existence amounted to a quarter of Holland's debt in 1796. Of course, interwar redemptions reduced the debt, most notably after the War of the Spanish Succession and after the War of the Austrian Succession, when the Republic managed to stay out of the Seven Years' War. However, the amounts reimbursed in these periods, respectively 15 million and 40 million guilders, proved relatively small compared to the increases that followed. Hence, around 80 per cent of Holland's debt was incurred in three periods: during the second quarter of the seventeenth century, around the turn of the eighteenth century, and towards the end of the eighteenth century.

The increased tax revenues improved Holland's ability to service the debt. In 1600, revenues and debt had both increased to 5.5 million guilders. Repaying the debt would thus require one year of revenues, in other words, a debt-to -tax ratio of 1. Although both revenues and debt expanded, the debt-to-tax ratio increased over time. It thus required increasingly more years of revenue

134 Fritschy, "Financial Revolution," 76.

135 Gelderblom and Jonker, "Public Finance."

136 Fritschy, *Public Finance*, 191–93.

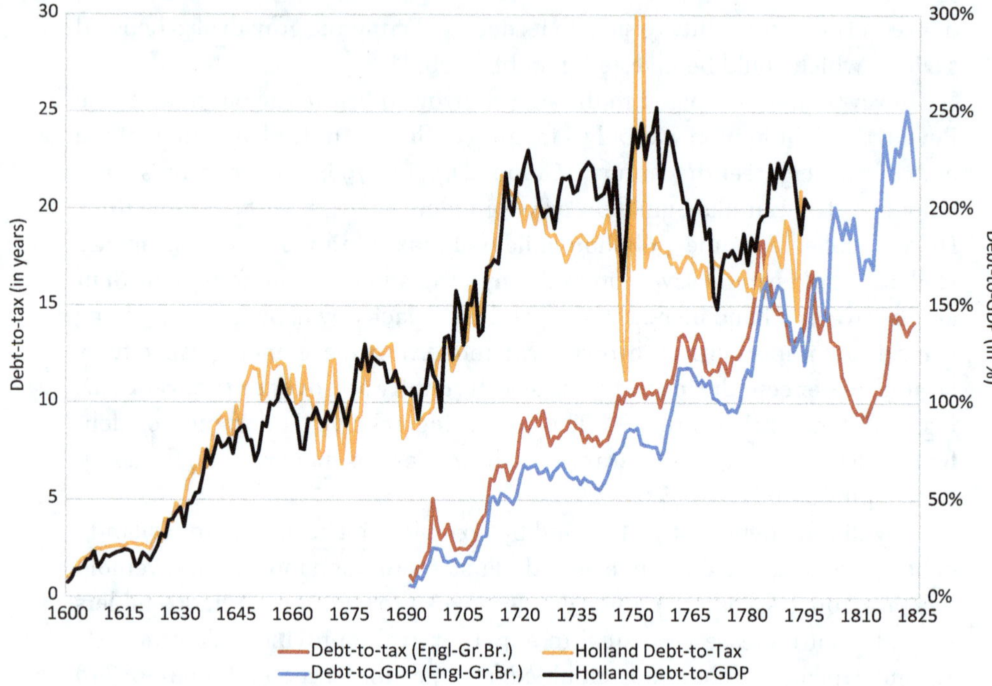

GRAPH 2.6 Debt-to-tax and debt-to-GDP ratios in Holland and Britain, 1600–1825.
SOURCES: HOLLAND: UNTIL 1720, GELDERBLOM AND JONKER, "PUBLIC FINANCE"; AFTER 1720, DORMANS, *HET TEKORT*; GDP: VAN ZANDEN AND VAN LEEUWEN, "PERSISTENT BUT NOT CONSISTENT."; BRITAIN: B. R. MITCHELL, *BRITISH HISTORICAL STATISTICS* (CUP ARCHIVE, 1988).

to repay the debt. The increases are concentrated in two periods. Firstly, between 1621 and 1648, the debt-to-tax ratio shot up from less than 3 to 12. Secondly, the debt-to-tax ratio increased again from around 9 in 1690 to 22 in 1715. Debt retirement and, after 1750, tax increases led to a gradual decline in the debt-to-tax ratio until the 1780s to around 16. The late eighteenth-century turmoil caused a final increase in the debt-to-tax ratio to 21, which was still below the level attained in 1715. Hence, the eighteenth-century debt increases were accompanied by rising tax revenues meaning that the debt-to-tax ratio did not get out of hand. Nevertheless, if so many years of revenue were required to repay the debt, this raises questions about the sustainability of the debt.

To evaluate the significance of the debt-to-tax ratio for the sustainability of Holland's debt, the ratio's values are compared to other metrics and other cases. Firstly, sixteenth-century Spain's debt-to-tax ratio hovered around 5.5, with a maximum of 8. Although Drelichmann and Voth deemed this sustainable in the long run, Spain defaulted four times between 1557 and 1596.[137] Secondly, eighteenth-century Britain witnessed a period of increases in both debt and taxes after 1688. In both Holland and Britain, the debt-to-tax ratio and the debt-to-GDP ratio moved in step with one another (Graph 2.6). In the case of Britain, this simultaneous movement lasted until 1800. While the debt-to-GDP ratio continued to increase, to 250 per cent around 1820, tax increases caused a declining debt-to-tax ratio. In the mid-1780s, Britain's debt-to-tax ratio had reached its zenith of around 18, when debt was around 160 per cent of GDP. Between 1797 and 1815, the share of direct taxes in total revenues increased from a quarter to one-third.[138] The initially lower taxation per capita in Britain allowed the British government to increase taxes.[139] Direct taxes in Holland amounted to around 40 per cent of all taxes after 1750, which exceeded the British increases in 1797–1815. Britain's debt thus increased faster than its economy expanded, yet the growth in public revenue outpaced both in this period.

In Holland, a less pronounced divergence is seen from around 1725 to the mid-1750s. During this period, the debt-to-GDP ratio continued to rise, reaching approximately 250 per cent of GDP, while the debt-to-tax ratio decreased. In this instance, the faltering economy led to an increase in the debt-to-GDP ratio despite debt repayments lowering the debt-to-tax ratio. In other words, the economy contracted faster than the debt diminished. Conversely, the opposite was true for the period leading up to the mid-1770s. After 1760, both metrics began to trend similarly once again. The largely comparable movement indicates that the debt-to-tax ratio serves as a viable alternative to the debt-to-GDP ratio when assessing debt sustainability. In both the Holland and British cases, the debt-to-tax ratio was significantly higher than that of sixteenth-century Spain. Neither entity defaulted despite the high debt-to-tax and debt-to-GDP ratios. This implies that these debt ratios were sustainable in the long run, although this, of course, also depends on the interest rates.

An alternative way of gauging the debt burden is to express it as the per capita equivalent of the number of day wages. As with the debt-to-tax ratio, this indicator moved rather similarly to the debt-to-GDP ratio until around 1715 (Graph 2.7). By then, the per capita debt expressed as wages had risen to over 390

137 Drelichman and Voth, *Lending to the Borrower from Hell*, 18, 119–26, 129–30: in 1557, 1560, 1575 and 1596.

138 B. R. Mitchell, *British Historical Statistics* (CUP Archive, 1988), 575–93.

139 Fritschy, "Taxation," 64; R. D. Lee and R. S. Schofield, "British Population in the Eighteenth Century," in *Economic History of Britain Since 1700, Vol. 1: 1700–1860*, ed. Roderick Floud and Donald McCloskey (Cambridge: Cambridge University Press, 1981), 21. The British population increased from around 5.18 million in 1695 to 9.18 million in 1801.

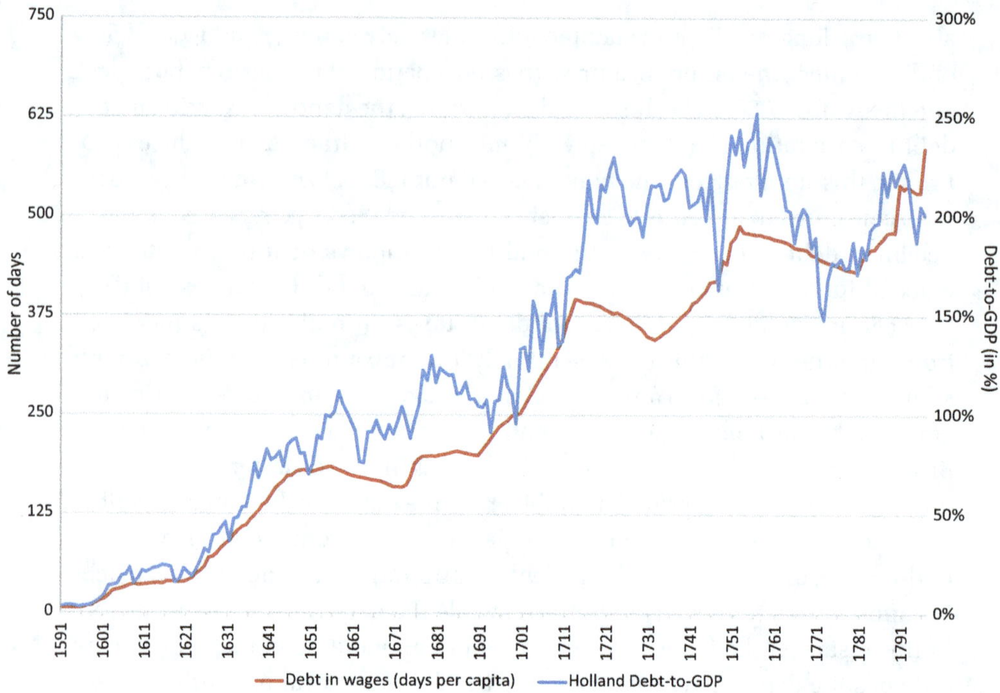

GRAPH 2.7 Holland's debt in day wages and debt-to-GDP ratio, 1591–1796.
SOURCES: DEBT: UNTIL 1720, GELDERBLOM AND JONKER, "PUBLIC FINANCE"; AFTER 1720, DORMANS, *HET TEKORT*; GDP: VAN ZANDEN AND VAN LEEUWEN, "PERSISTENT BUT NOT CONSISTENT."; WAGES: DE VRIES AND VAN DER WOUDE, *THE FIRST MODERN ECONOMY*; POPULATION: FEENSTRA, *BETWEEN SHARED*, APPENDIX.

days, whereas the debt-to-GDP ratio reached 190 per cent. In 1650, these figures had been respectively 178 day wages and 75 per cent of GDP. Wage earners worked around 250 to 300 days per year.[140] The gap that opened up between the debt in working days and debt-to-GDP ratio shows that during the first half of the eighteenth century, the economy slackened faster than the income of wage earners. By the mid-1760s, the gap had closed and the two moved in step again. Although the similarity in the movement is clear, the

140 De Vries and Van der Woude, *The First Modern Economy*, 616–17; Robert C Allen, "The Great Divergence in European Wages and Prices from the Middle Ages to the First World War," *Explorations in Economic History* 38, no. 4 (October 2001): 411–47, https://doi.org/10.1006/exeh.2001.0775; Peter R. Priester, *Geschiedenis van de Zeeuwse landbouw, circa 1600–1910*, A.A.G. bijdragen, ISSN 0511–0726 37 (Wageningen: Afdeling Agrarische Geschiedenis, Landbouwuniversiteit, 1998), 104. Priester assummed a number of 240 working days per year.

correspondence appears weaker than that with the debt-to-tax ratio. This is perhaps best explained by the development of Holland's economy. Both population and income levels stagnated in the 1640s and the 1730s, respectively; as a result, the current method does not incorporate the impact on wage workers of the economic slowdown. It is, for instance, possible that they suffered from unemployment, even when the nominal wages remained stable. Also, wage workers appear not to have benefitted from the little growth that occurred during the eighteenth century. Overall, this method underestimates the burden the debt placed on the economy by 20 to 33 per cent, depending on whether 250 or 300 working days are assumed. Even though the correlation with the debt-to-GDP ratio is weaker, it still indicates that repaying the public debt had become increasingly difficult.

The comparison with Britain suggests that Holland's elite lacked the financial commitment to maintain the Dutch Republic's status as a great power. When Holland's debt levels rose to over 200 per cent of GDP, after 1715, the States of Holland adopted a strategy of neutrality.[141] The States of Holland reduced the debt and hardly increased taxation. When Britain reached similarly high debt-to-GDP levels around 1800, it could increase direct taxes. In Holland, this proved difficult because taxes were already high. This brings into question the notion of an elite in Holland that preferred to supply money in the form of loans if necessary, yet refused to increase its contribution in the form of taxation.

3.2 *Composition and Coupons*

Debt sustainability also depends on the interest rate. Whereas the debt expanded, the coupon rates declined. The coupon rates on bonds fell from around 12 per cent in the 1590s to 2.5 per cent for most of the eighteenth century. This was not self-evident. The default of 1572 ruined Holland's credit and restoring it took time.[142] When Holland resumed borrowing on its provincial account, in 1594, it had to accommodate the investors and convince them that their money was no longer at risk. One option was to offer sufficiently high interest as compensation for the perceived risk, yet other conditions and the type of instrument mattered too. So what did the States of Holland offer investors?

141 Aalbers, *De Repobliek*; Israel, *The Dutch Republic*, 988; Liesker and Fritschy, *Gewestelijke financiën: vol. 4. Holland*; Vries, *State, Economy and the Great Divergence*, 210.

142 Fritschy, *Public Finance*, 68.

Before the Revolt, the debt consisted of annuities, sometimes temporarily supplemented with short-term bonds or bills (*obligaties*).[143] In the 1550s, Holland issued redeemable annuities at 6.25 per cent interest.[144] After the Revolt broke out, it was not until the Truce that Holland succeeded again in issuing redeemable annuities and bonds at that rate. The States of Holland preferred redeemable annuities. If the loans were not fully subscribed, it allowed its eighteen district tax receivers to issue life annuities or bonds, which investors preferred to redeemable annuities.[145] The district tax receivers' autonomy and dual role as debt issuers and interest payers from the tax receipts gave them leverage in local tax management, with the provincial authorities only interested in the results.

Life annuities typically yielded twice as much as redeemable annuities. The investor paid a sum in exchange for a life-long annual payment over the lifetime of a nominee. After the nominee died, the contract ended and the principal was not repaid to the annuity holder. The high interest rate made it attractive for investors, yet expensive for the government. The alternative, redeemable or heritable annuities, returned a lower annual sum but required repayment of the principal to terminate the contract. Redemption was at the discretion of the debtor. Moreover, annuities were liable to a transfer tax. Bonds, however, were made out to the bearer free of charge when they changed hands. In addition, a bondholder could demand redemption at the end of the term, usually six to twelve months. Finally, bonds yielded a slightly higher return than redeemable annuities. Taken together, bonds offered investors more liquidity, compensation and convenience.[146]

Interest rates declined from around 1600 for all of these instruments (Graph 2.8). The gradual decline in coupon rates in 1594–1609 was difficult and uneven. District receivers had trouble issuing voluntary loans. They required a mix of forced loans, bonds and life annuities. Between 1604 and 1609, more than half of the money was raised in forced loans. Until 1607, a fluctuating withholding tax decreased the effective interest rates. But in 1599 the States had stipulated that earlier tax exemptions should be honoured. The decline in interest rates

143 Fritschy, 68; Gelderblom and Jonker, "Public Finance," 4.

144 Fritschy, *Public Finance*, 68, 99; Dormans, *Het tekort*, 26.

145 Gelderblom and Jonker, "Public Finance," 6; Fritschy, *Public Finance*, 95–96.

146 Fritschy, *Public Finance*, 68, 94, 99–100, 161–63; Fritschy, "Financial Revolution," 79; Dormans, *Het tekort*, 59–60; Gelderblom and Jonker, "Public Finance," 4, 8–9, 14; Marjolein 't Hart, "Mutual Advantages: State Bankers as Brokers between the City of Amsterdam and the Dutch Republic," in *The Political Economy of the Dutch Republic*, ed. O.C. Gelderblom (Farnham etc.: Ashgate, 2009), 118–19.

superficially signalled a restoration of Holland's credit, but this was only partially true.[147]

Nevertheless, creditors increasingly accepted lower coupons. In 1597, the bond coupon was reduced from 12 per cent to 8 per cent, and again to 7.1 per cent in 1607. Following the signing of the Truce in 1609, the States reduced the interest rate to 6.25 per cent for bonds rolled over. Investors also had the option to either convert the bonds into redeemable annuities or be reimbursed.[148] In two steps, in 1609 and 1611, all bills and redeemable annuities were reduced to 6.25 per cent. Debtholders accepted the conversion and interest rate cut because the alternative of reimbursement was less attractive.[149] In little over a decade, Holland's coupon rates had been cut in half and had returned to the pre-Revolt level.

The second half of the Eighty Years' War, after 1621, proved much more expensive than the first. Money was urgently needed. In 1623, Prince Maurice warned the States of the risk of mutiny. Borrowing by way of annuities was difficult as investors preferred bonds. Loan issues at 6.25 per cent yielded insufficient funds. In 1625, the States of Holland proposed a forced loan either as a redeemable annuity or as a life annuity.[150] In 1629, the States explicitly allowed the receivers to supplement the annuities with bonds if the loans were not fully subscribed.[151] From then on, the absolute and relative importance of bonds grew sharply, from 0.5 million guilders (or 1.5 per cent) in 1628 to 78.4 million guilders (or almost 60 per cent) in 1649.[152] In the meantime, the States of Holland introduced a voluntary interest rate reduction to 5 per cent in 1640. While some district tax receivers feared large terminations, the Rotterdam tax receiver Berckel reported that his share had already been fully subscribed at the new interest rate.[153] Again, investors deemed a lower coupon the lesser evil than repayment, as this would rob them of a steady income.

147 Gelderblom and Jonker, "Public Finance," 6; Liesker and Fritschy, *Gewestelijke financiën: vol. 4. Holland*, 363; Fritschy, *Public Finance*, 97–99; Houtzager, *Hollands lijf- en losrenterekeningen*, 124.

148 Houtzager, *Hollands lijf- en losrenterekeningen*, 132.

149 Gelderblom and Jonker, "Public Finance," 9; Houtzager, *Hollands lijf- en losrenterekeningen*, 132–33; Fritschy, "Financial Revolution," 77–78.

150 Houtzager, *Hollands lijf- en losrenterekeningen*, 138–39; Gelderblom and Jonker, "Public Finance," 10–11.

151 Houtzager, *Hollands lijf- en losrenterekeningen*, 141.

152 Gelderblom and Jonker, "Public Finance," 29, 33.

153 Houtzager, *Hollands lijf- en losrenterekeningen*, 148–51. Simultaneously with the reduction, a new loan was issued to finance reimbursements following the reduction, worth 800,000 guilders.

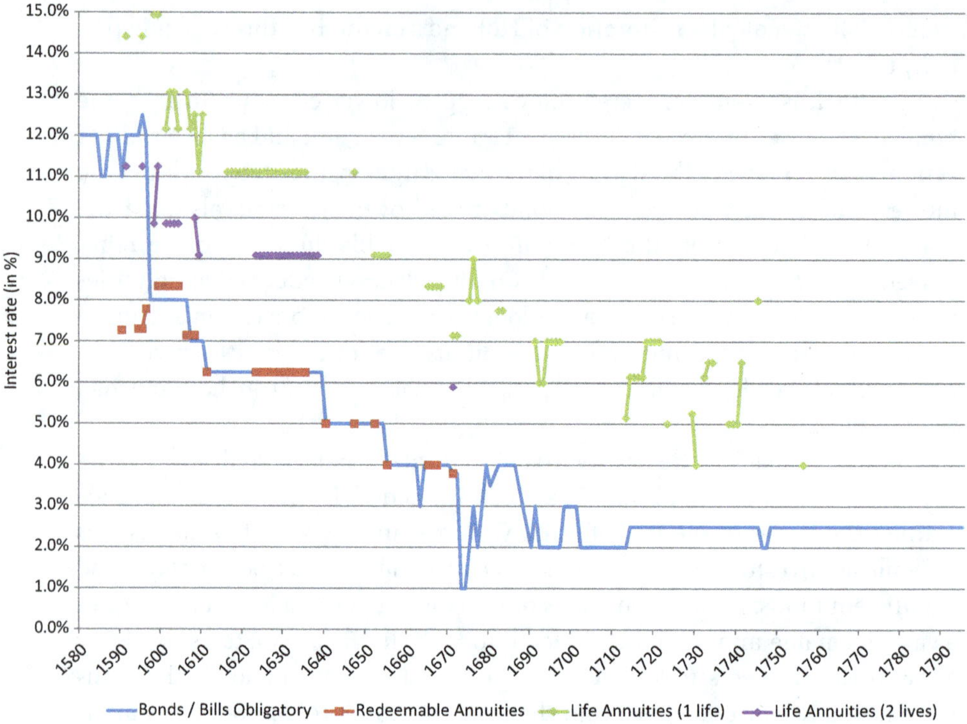

GRAPH 2.8 Coupons in Holland, per instrument, 1580–1795 (after adjusting for tax).
SOURCES: LIESKER AND FRITSCHY, *GEWESTELIJKE FINANCIËN: VOL. 4. HOLLAND*, PP. 369–371, 381–382; GELDERBLOM AND JONKER, 'PUBLIC FINANCE', P. 17; DORMANS, *HET TEKORT*, P. 47, 55, 70–77 HOUTZAGER, *HOLLANDS LIJF- EN LOSRENTEREKENINGEN*, 124, 169, 173.

As a result, Holland's long-term debt was financed with a short-term instrument and at one of the lowest coupon rates in Europe.[154]

Given the investors' preference for bonds, it is hardly surprising that Holland's debt came to consist largely of bonds (Graph 2.9). Yet it is puzzling why life annuities did not make up more of Holland's debt. Although life annuities lacked the liquidity of bonds, it appears both investors and the States of Holland had a certain liking for these instruments; the investors because of the high return compared to bonds and redeemable annuities, the States of Holland for not having to repay the principal.[155] That the compensation was probably too generous was known at the time. Holland's Grand Pensionary Johan de Witt explained in 1671 that, despite the expiry of life annuities, they were

154 Gelderblom and Jonker, "Public Finance," 13–14.
155 Dormans, *Het tekort*, 58–59.

more costly than bonds or redeemable annuities. Presumably, others before De Witt must have realised this too.[156] The States offered 7.1 per cent life annuities in 1671, which the market did not absorb.[157] Hence, life annuities constituted an even smaller portion of Holland's debt in the eighteenth century.

That Holland's long-term debt largely consisted of a short-term instrument was potentially dangerous if bondholders gave notice suddenly, and in great numbers, to the receivers to be reimbursed. This was what happened during the First Anglo-Dutch War. In 1653, several district receivers reported that bondholders had given notice, but that they lacked the means to reimburse them. Receivers had to persuade bondholders to reconsider their requests by promising to pay overdue interest and promptly doing so.[158] After the war, Holland's creditworthiness was restored quickly. Even though it was known there were plans for an interest rate reduction, bonds were issued at 5 to 7 per cent above par. Strengthened by the ease of this interest rate reduction, the States of Holland pursued Grand Pensionary De Witt's proposal to further reduce the coupon rate to 4 per cent in August 1655. This was the last voluntary reduction of the nominal interest rate in Holland under the Republic.[159] The money saved from the reduction was intended for a sinking fund to reimburse firstly foreigners, secondly bondholders who had given notice during the war, thirdly Dutch people resident outside of Holland and finally Holland residents.[160] It is not clear whether the prioritisation of those who had given notice was a favour or a penalty.[161] The liquidity squeeze in 1653 showed the risk associated with bonds withdrawable at notice, yet it was only a taste of what was in store during 1672, the Year of Disaster.

In the meantime, investors willingly put their money in the hands of the tax receivers. The yields of the 5 per cent bonds that sold above par in 1655 were

---

156 Johan de Witt had already calculated the costs of life annuities versus redeemable annuities in 1671, in his Waerdye. Houtzager, *Hollands lijf- en losrenterekeningen*, 92, 96–99, 105–6; Zuijderduijn, *Medieval Capital Markets*, 98; Fritschy, *Public Finance*, 161.

157 Dormans, *Het tekort*, 59–60, 67.

158 Houtzager, *Hollands lijf- en losrenterekeningen*, 159; Dormans, *Het tekort*, 50–51; Gelderblom and Jonker, "Public Finance," 15.

159 Houtzager, *Hollands lijf- en losrenterekeningen*, 76–77, 81, 164–65; Dormans, *Het tekort*, 53; Gelderblom and Jonker, "Public Finance," 16; Fritschy, *Public Finance*, 157, 160; Liesker and Fritschy, *Gewestelijke financiën: vol. 4. Holland*, 374.

160 In 1662, when this order was repeated, the dividing line between domestic and foreign was between residents and non-residents of the province of Holland, not of the Dutch Republic.

161 Houtzager, *Hollands lijf- en losrenterekeningen*, 80–81, 167, 172–73.

GRAPH 2.9 Holland's debt composition, 1591–1795.

SOURCES: GELDERBLOM AND JONKER, 'PUBLIC FINANCE', DORMANS, *HET TEKORT*, 1991, 65–66, 81–81, 110–111.

4.67 to 4.76 per cent just before the interest rate cut. The reduced bonds generally sold at par and occasionally slightly below.[162] Nevertheless, even those yields of 4.1 to 4.3 per cent were still close to the 4 per cent level.[163] The relative strength of Holland's credit is illustrated by a loan that Holland took over from Friesland's admiralty in 1662. Holland paid off the admiralty's old 7 per cent loan and provided a new one at 4 per cent. Friesland's admiralty was supposed to earmark the difference in interest for repaying the loan.[164] In 1664, Holland managed to issue a loan at 3 per cent. Expenditure on the fleet due to the Second Anglo-Dutch War forced the States of Holland to increase this interest again to 4 per cent a year later.[165] Furthermore, the money from the sinking fund was also used to cover war costs.[166] Still, Holland's financial position was strong by the late 1660s.

The Franco-Dutch War that began in 1672 caused the largest financial crisis since the default a century before. From 1670, in preparation for France's imminent attack, Holland issued large amounts of debt and increased taxes.[167] The States also imposed an interest rate reduction of 5 per cent, lowering the effective coupon to 3.8 per cent, in 1671 and 1672. Then the French invasion began; the provinces of Overijssel, Gelderland and Utrecht surrendered. This placed Louis XIV's army on Holland's border. Voluntary loans were no longer an option. Rather, creditors gave notice to district tax receivers. Despite various measures to prevent or stop the run on the receivers, all of them fell behind on payments. Bond prices dropped to 30 per cent of their nominal value in mid-1672, if buyers could even be found at all.[168] A moratorium prevented reimbursements, but it did not solve the problem. In 1675, the interest over 1672 was still unpaid. In addition, the tax yields of wealth levies proved disappointing. Strapped for cash, the States of Holland resorted to forced loans and interest rate reductions using the withholding tax on bonds. The 3 per cent withholding tax on bonds in 1673 and 1674 reduced the effective interest rate to

162 Gelderblom and Jonker, "Public Finance," 15 (Graph 5).

163 Gelderblom and Jonker, 17 The sales prices were 93–98 per cent of the nominal value, or 2–7 per cent below par.

164 Houtzager, *Hollands lijf- en losrenterekeningen*, 172.

165 Dormans, *Het tekort*, 55; Houtzager, *Hollands lijf- en losrenterekeningen*, 172.

166 Gelderblom and Jonker, "Public Finance," 17.

167 Dormans, *Het tekort*, 68: Dormans estimated the amount in loans at 4 million guilders in 1671 and another 7 million guilders in 1762, before the invasion. Gelderblom and Jonker mention 9 million guilders of loans between October 1671 and March 1672. Gelderblom and Jonker, "Public Finance," 18.

168 Gelderblom and Jonker, "Public Finance," 20; Dormans, *Het tekort*, 68.

1 per cent, marking the first forced reduction since 1609.[169] Prices dropped to 70 per cent of the nominal value, resulting in a yield of 1.43 per cent. The limited fall in prices of just 30 per cent was presumably because investors expected the tax would only be temporarily levied at this rate.[170] Given this massive interest rate cut, it is not surprising that the States of Holland resorted to forced loans. By the Peace of Nijmegen in 1678, Holland had raised almost 25 million guilders in forced loans, and only 3 million in voluntary loans.[171]

The withholding tax on bonds eventually became the means by which the States of Holland managed the effective coupon until the end of the eighteenth century. During the Franco-Dutch War, tax rates fluctuated between 0.5 and 2 per cent.[172] In 1678, the Rotterdam receiver issued bonds at 5 per cent. Applying the then-applicable tax rate of 1 per cent, this was equivalent to an effective interest rate of 4 per cent.[173] Then again, the tax was discontinued after 1680, presumably because it impeded the recovery of Holland's creditworthiness.[174] But after 1687, the tax was applied constantly, albeit with varying rates until 1714. After 1714, the interest rate was reduced to 2.5 per cent, except for 1746 and 1747, when the withholding tax reduced the effective rate to 2 per cent. Then the States of Holland promised to leave the tax rate untouched, fixing the effective coupon at 2.5 per cent.[175]

But first Holland had to finance the largest debt increase in its existence, following William III's ascendency to the English throne in 1688. To this end, it pursued a different strategy than it had in 1672–1678: rather than resorting to forced loans, Holland consistently relied on the capital market for voluntary loan subscriptions. From 1687 onwards, the States of Holland increased the tax on bonds by half a percentage point every year, to 2 per cent in 1690. The result was a drop in nominal prices to 80 per cent in 1695, or a yield of 2.5 per cent.

169 Liesker and Fritschy, *Gewestelijke financiën: vol. 4. Holland*, 370; Fritschy, *Public Finance*, 157–58; Gelderblom and Jonker, "Public Finance," 19. Gelderblom and Jonker assumed that an effective interest rate cut of 1 per cent applied, which reduced the effective interest rate to 3 per cent.

170 Gelderblom and Jonker, "Public Finance," 15; Fritschy, *Public Finance*, 246: Fritschy posits that this resulted in a yield of 2.86 per cent. This is only true if the effective coupon had been 2 per cent.

171 Gelderblom and Jonker, "Public Finance," 18–19; Dormans, *Het tekort*, 67–70: Of the 14 million guilders in voluntary loans issued between 1671 and 1675, some 11 million were issued before the invasion. Fritschy, *Public Finance*, 150–51, 158–59, 181, 192.

172 Fritschy, *Public Finance*, 157–58.

173 Gelderblom and Jonker, "Public Finance," 20; Liesker and Fritschy, *Gewestelijke financiën: vol. 4. Holland*, 369–71.

174 Gelderblom and Jonker, "Public Finance," 21–22.

175 Fritschy, *Public Finance*, 158–59.

After the 1697 Peace of Rijswijk, the States reduced the tax to 1 per cent, resulting in the restoration of prices to the nominal value. Conversely, the War of the Spanish Succession led to another tax increase to 2 per cent. As a result, prices fell again, to 75 per cent in 1712, equal to a yield of 3 per cent. Therefore, the States of Holland had to offer investors something more attractive, which they did in the form of tax-free 4 per cent bonds. At first, the exemption applied for the duration of the war; later issues were tax-exempt until ten years after the war had ended. In 1709 or 1710, the States of Holland borrowed 1.5 million guilders from the Swiss canton or city of Bern.[176] Still, this was not enough.

New instruments were needed to provide a solution. In 1710 and 1711 the States issued twenty-year annuities at 9 per cent, consisting of 4 per cent interest and 5 per cent repayment (Table 2.2). The States of Holland also issued lottery loans in 1711, 1712 and 1713, worth 24 million guilders. Two factors played a role. On the one hand, there was the success of the Generality's lottery loans in 1709 and 1710.[177] On the other hand, in 1711 Dutchmen had invested some 2 million guilders in an English lottery loan. When Holland offered more generous compensation, some district receivers issued more than their allotted shares.[178] Hence, it was not a scarcity of capital in the market, but competition that posed a challenge in Holland's efforts to raise funds. Holland's reputation in the market as a creditworthy debtor was therefore essential if it was to continue to rely on voluntary loans.

To raise additional funds without damaging its credit reputation, Holland used Generality loans. As of 1691, the Generality issued loans on behalf of the provinces, mainly to cover defective or belated provincial contributions for warfare. The Generality's debt increased fourfold from 15.5 million guilders in 1691 to 61.2 million guilders in 1715. Almost half of the Generality loans were taken out for Holland: 17.5 million out of 36.6 million. In 1715, the provinces owed 3.8 million in interest arrears to the Generality, with Holland accounting for one-third of this amount. Holland had thus increased its borrowing capacity by more than 10 per cent without risking its credit as a province. However, the burden was too heavy for the Union, which subsequently had to close the payment office for nine months. Upon reopening, the Generality reduced the

176 Gelderblom and Jonker, "Public Finance," 21–24; Liesker and Fritschy, *Gewestelijke financiën: vol. 4. Holland*, 369–71; Dormans, *Het tekort*, 77.

177 Dormans, *Het tekort*, 77; Gelderblom and Jonker, "Public Finance," 24.

178 Fritschy, *Public Finance*, 305; Wantje Fritschy, "The Poor, the Rich and the Taxes in Heinsius' Times," in *Anthonie Heinsius and the Dutch Republic 1688–1720: Politics, War, and Finance*, ed. Jan Arie Frederik de Jongste and Augustus Johannes Veenendaal jr, ING-Workshop Series; RGP (The Hague: Institute of Netherlands History, 2002), 250–51.

TABLE 2.2 Yields on fixed-term-annuities in Holland, 1710–1790.

Year of issuance	Coupon	Term (years)	Effective yield
1710	9.0%	20	6.39%
1745	8.0%	16	3.06%
1745	7.0%	19	3.03%
1745	6.0%	24	3.15%
1745	5.0%	31	3.00%
1747	6.0%	25	3.40%
1747	5.0%	30	2.84%
1790	5.0%	30	2.84%

SOURCE: LIESKER AND FRITSCHY, *GEWESTELIJKE FINANCIËN: VOL. 4. HOLLAND*, P. 383.

coupon rate from 4 per cent to 3 per cent. Thus, the expansion of the provinces' financial resources led to the default of the Generality and damage to its reputation as creditworthy, while Holland's creditors dodged the bullet.[179]

The debt incurred during this period remained important for financial and political policy through the remainder of the eighteenth century. Remaining neutral in international conflicts proved difficult in practice and was only successful after 1730 and especially after 1750. Therefore, improving government finances increasingly depended on lowering interest payments. The States of Holland took three actions. Firstly, Holland sought to redeem the debt.[180] Secondly, expensive lottery loans were converted into regular 2.5 per cent bonds. Third, life annuities were cut. Yet payment problems persisted until the early 1730s. In 1729, interest payments were even suspended temporarily. Holland's credit was not fully restored until 1731, when a large number of investors subscribed to a new loan.[181] Meanwhile, the tax exemption for bonds ended in 1723, which further reduced interest payments.[182] In the 1740s and

179 Dormans, *Het tekort*, 145–48.

180 Fritschy, *Public Finance*, 163–64.

181 Dormans, *Het tekort*, 87–88, 92–93; Fritschy, *Public Finance*.

182 Fritschy argues that investors in Holland (and Zeeland) suffered from the tax on bonds in spite of explicit promises of tax exemption. Fritschy, *Public Finance*, 159; Liesker and Fritschy, *Gewestelijke financiën: vol. 4. Holland*, 381: Also Liesker and Fritschy suggest that

early 1750s, Holland mainly issued ordinary bonds to finance the War of the Austrian Succession. This was supplemented with lottery loans and to a limited extent with fixed-term annuities, probably to enlarge the scope of the market now life annuities were out of favour. After the war, the expensive lottery loans were again converted into regular bonds. Furthermore, the expiration of fixed-term annuities and consistent reimbursements reduced the debt by some 40 million guilders, until 1780.[183] A roughly similar amount was borrowed again in the 1780s, largely in 2.5 per cent bonds. From the late 1780s, the States of Holland found it increasingly difficult to issue bonds at the usual 2.5 per cent interest rate.[184] Hence, after the War of the Spanish Succession, Holland's standard instrument, the bond, also had an effective standard coupon. Furthermore, Holland's debt diversified, with lottery loans and fixed-term annuities now supplementing the bonds instead of life annuities. What made this truly remarkable is that the massive increase in debt was largely financed by voluntary loans with an effective coupon of 2.5 per cent. Even internationally, this rate was very low; only Genoa borrowed at slightly lower interest rates, of just over 2.25 per cent during the eighteenth century.[185]

3.3 *The Private Capital Market*

The accumulation of private wealth during the economic expansion created the opportunity to finance Holland's ballooning debt at low interest rates. This was not the case from the outset. Only gradually did Holland's debt become funded domestically at low costs. When Holland first issued debt in the sixteenth century, a substantial part of the money was imported from outside the province. In the eighteenth century, Holland exported capital abroad. In the process of switching from capital-importing to capital-exporting, Holland's

---

the States actively ended the tax exemption. Gelderblom and Jonker, "Public Finance" Gelderblom and Jonker argue that investors were promised ten years of tax exemption after the war had ended, which thus expired in 1723. Dormans, *Het tekort*, 108, 112–13: Dormans' figures imply that the tax exemption was known to be time-limited and only to apply up to 1723.

183 Dormans, *Het tekort*, 97–98, 105–6.

184 Dormans, 124–31.

185 Chilosi, "Risky Institutions," 899–901; Homer and Sylla, *History*, 129–31; G. Felloni, "Italy," in *An Introduction to the Sources of European Economic History, 1500–1800*, ed. Charles Henry Wilson and Geoffrey Parker, World Economic History (London: Weidenfeld and Nicolson, 1977), 22; Epstein, *Freedom and Growth*, 23, 25 Epstein maintains that the Duchy of Tuscany could borrow much more cheaply than anyone else around 1750, as it could borrow at 0.4–0.5 per cent. Yet I fear that this is based on a misreading of Felloni's article (1977). Epstein seems to have misread the amounts of 0.4 and 0.5 million ducats, paid as interest, as interest rates. The actual percentages are 2.91 per cent and 3.2 per cent.

debt became financed domestically. Within the gradual shift over time, there were three consecutive sources of capital for Holland's public debt.

First, non-domestic funds retained some importance at least until the mid-seventeenth century. They were important enough to be explicitly named as a separate category and prioritised for redemption after the payment problems of 1653. This is reminiscent of sixteenth-century prioritising of interest payments to foreign debtholders that followed after suffering the effects of the Law of Reprisal.[186]

Secondly, economic growth had driven up savings since the sixteenth century. During the second half of the seventeenth century, economic growth slowed, which restricted alternative investment opportunities for investors. Meanwhile, returns from earlier growth and previous investments had increased savings. In short, the supply of capital had grown and private financing needs had decreased. This is reflected by the overall decline in interest rates on the private market.[187]

Thirdly, the flow of money from the States of Holland to investors became increasingly relevant. As indicated above, the debt increase in the 1780s was equal to the repayment in 1750–1780. This leaves the interest payments out of the equation. Adding this means a net transfer from the States of Holland to investors even after the increase in the debt in the 1780s. Hence, the growing public debt and the poor state of the public finances increased private wealth.

The phenomenon that the States of Holland paid more to investors than it borrowed from them goes back to the second half of the seventeenth century.[188] Graph 2.10 displays the additional financing requirements of the States of Holland in the long term. The additional financing requirement is calculated as follows: per year the part that investors wish to reinvest – calculated as the product of the net interest payments and the reinvestment rate – is subtracted from the net amount borrowed, which is in turn defined as the

186 Zuijderduijn, *Medieval Capital Markets*, 130–37; Prins, *Het faillissement der Hollandsche steden*; Zuijderduijn, "De laatmiddeleeuwse crisis van de overheidsfinanciën en de financiële revolutie in Holland"; Tracy, *A Financial Revolution in the Habsburg Netherlands*, 9, 95, 109; Houtzager, *Hollands lijf- en losrenterekeningen*, 48–49. Hostages from Holland were taken in Zeeland on various occasions during the sixteenth century. Therefore, the receiver of Amsterdam was called upon to redeem debt outside of the province as soon as there was some financial space.

187 Gelderblom and Jonker, "Public Finance," 7, 9; Fritschy, "Financial Revolution," 64; Gelderblom, Jonker, and Kool, "Direct Finance"; Fritschy, "Financial Revolution," 79–80.

188 De Vries and Van der Woude, *The First Modern Economy*, 118; De Vries and Van der Woude, *Nederland 1500–1815*, 149.

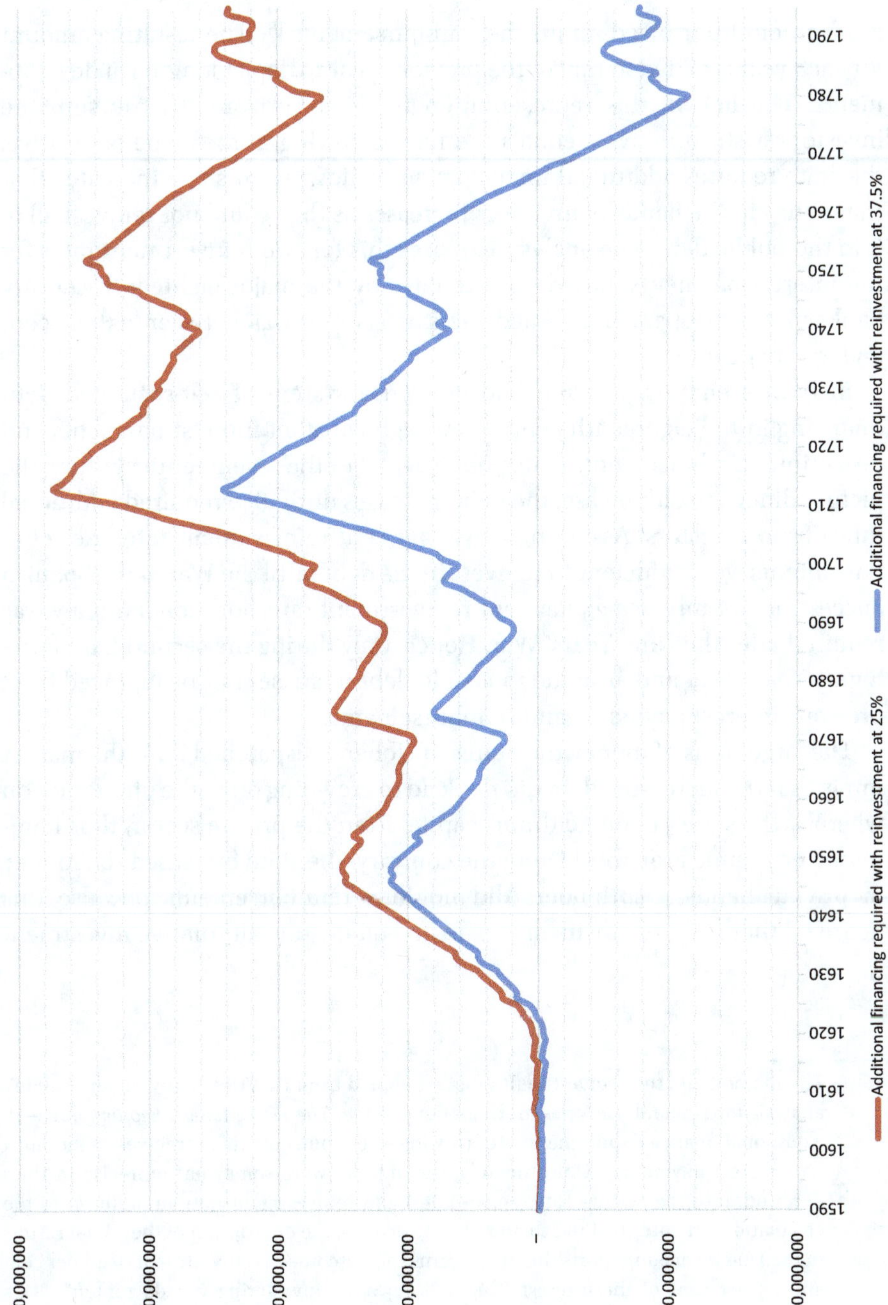

GRAPH 2.10 Reinvestment and financing requirement in Holland, 1590–1795.
SOURCE: LIESKER AND FRITSCHY, *GEWESTELIJKE FINANCIËN: VOL. 4. HOLLAND*.

gross amount borrowed minus the reimbursements.[189] The resulting amount for each year is added to that of the previous year to depict long-term developments. The line in this representation remains horizontal if the sum the investors wish to reinvest equals the net borrowing; if the slope is positive, the state requires additional financing; and a downward slope indicates that the money in the hands of investors increases as they could not reinvest all of it in the public debt. The analysis explores this for two reinvestment rates for the interest payments, based on estimates by the major eighteenth-century banker Henry Hope. He assumed the savings rate was between 25 per cent and 37.5 per cent.[190]

In both scenarios, Holland had created a system of self-sustained debt financing in the eighteenth century through constant interest payments and peacetime reimbursements of its public debt. For the seventeenth century, the picture differs. In either case, the debt increases until 1650 required additional funds from investors. Assuming a 37.5 per cent reinvestment rate, the reimbursements were sufficient to reinvest in the debt until the War of the Spanish Succession. Assuming a 25 per cent reinvestment rate, additional money was required after the Nine Years' War. Hence, only during the second half of the Eighty Years' War and around 1700 could debt increases not be financed from previous interest payments and reimbursements.

The large sums of money the States of Holland dispatched onto the market imply that the increasing debt did not lead to crowding out – the phenomenon whereby the state's demand drains capital from the private sector, thus hampering economic growth.[191] Quite the contrary: the state increased the money in private hands. Debtholders did not like reimbursements because this deprived them of a steady income, and an equally safe alternative investment

189 The method and the reinvestment rates are copied from De Vries' and Van der Woude's analysis for Holland: De Vries and Van der Woude, *The First Modern Economy*, 120–21: Additional finance requirement = (borrowing – reimbursements) – (reinvestment rate x net interest payments). Unfortunately, the authors were somewhat inprecise in their description of the savings rate (spaarquote) and reinvestment rate. In addition to the calculations in both the English and Dutch versions, the description of their final results in the Dutch version reports that it concerns the outcome of reinvestment of 40 per cent and 25 per cent of the interest ("bij 40% /25% herinvestering van de renten"). This precise information is lacking in the English version of the book: De Vries and Van der Woude, *Nederland 1500–1815*, 150–51.

190 De Vries and Van der Woude, *The First Modern Economy*, 124; De Vries and Van der Woude, *Nederland 1500–1815*, 156.

191 Temin and Voth, "Credit Rationing"; Clark, "Debt, Deficits, and Crowding Out."

for their money was hard to find.[192] Domestic demand for capital declined when the economy slackened.[193] What is more, the international capital market was one of Holland's growth sectors in the eighteenth century.[194] The problem was a lack of demand for capital, rather than a lack of supply.

The increasing money supply and decreasing investment opportunities exerted downward pressure on the interest rates.[195] The money paid back was concentrated in Amsterdam and The Hague. In the eighteenth century, 60 per cent of the interest was paid there.[196] The large capital supply fostered Amsterdam's rise as an international capital market in the eighteenth century. Bondholders mainly held on to Holland bonds, even though European sovereign loans yielded more (3.5–5 per cent).[197] This was also because foreign loans could not absorb all the money that flowed into the market after 1752, including extensive loans to plantations in the West Indies.[198] Until around 1780, Dutch capital exports drove down the interest rates on British public

---

192 't Hart, "Devil or the Dutch," 49; Dormans, *Het tekort*, 55; Fritschy, *Public Finance*, 286; Van Bochove, "Configuring Financial Markets," 260; De Vries and Van der Woude, *The First Modern Economy*, 125; De Vries and Van der Woude, *Nederland 1500–1815*, 157–58.

193 Riley, *International Government Finance*, 226, 232–35, 329; Jonker, *Merchants, Bankers, Middlemen*, 96–99. Jonker's interpretation was questioned by Van Zanden and Van Riel, who argue that the yields on public debt increased first and thus took the lead similar to the downward trend in the eighteenth century: Van Zanden and Van Riel, *The Strictures of Inheritance*. Yet, as the present study will show, their interpretation of higher private interest rates rests upon the analysis of some peripheral regions, where money was dearer than in Amsterdam, which Jonker studied. Dormans, *Het tekort*, 241; Klein, "Kapitaal en stagnatie," 40.

194 Van Zanden and Van Leeuwen, "Persistent but Not Consistent," 126.

195 Wantje Fritschy and René Van der Voort, "From Fragmentation to Unification: Public Finance, 1700–1914," in *A Financial History of the Netherlands*, ed. Marjolein 't Hart, Joost Jonker, and Jan Luiten Van Zanden (Cambridge: Cambridge University Press, 1997), 72–73; Dormans, *Het tekort*, 110–11; De Vries and Van der Woude, *Nederland 1500–1815*, 157–58, 189; Pit Dehing and Marjolein 't Hart, "Linking the Fortunes: Currency and Banking, 1550–1800," in *A Financial History of The Netherlands*, ed. Marjolein 't Hart, Joost Jonker, and Jan Luiten Van Zanden (Cambridge: Cambridge University Press, 1997), 53, 57 The Amsterdam interest rates in Table 3.4 seem high compared to merchant credit, the IOU s from The Hague and the rural Beijerlanden. Why this is so remains to be researched. Gelderblom and Jonker, "Public Finance"; Gelderblom, Jonker, and Kool, "Direct Finance."

196 Van Bochove, "Configuring Financial Markets," 259.

197 Fritschy and Van der Voort, "From Fragmentation to Unification," 72; Jan Van de Voort, *De Westindische plantages van 1720–1795 : financiën en handel / Johannes Petrus van de Voort* (Sl: sn Eindhoven:, 1973).

198 De Vries and Van der Woude, *The First Modern Economy*, 124–25; De Vries and Van der Woude, *Nederland 1500–1815*, 157–58; Fritschy, *De patriotten*, 42, 72.

debt in London.[199] The surplus money could have exerted downward pressure on interest rates within the Dutch Republic after subtracting outgoing international capital flows. The question is where this money flowed to, whether it lessened the interest rate differentials within the province or did it even cause the interest rate differentials beyond Holland's borders to decrease.

To grasp its effects, we now look at the development of private interest rates in the Dutch Republic. If De Vries and Van der Woude were correct in assuming that the capital markets were integrated, there would be hardly any geographical interest rate differentials in the private market. From the beginning of the seventeenth century, interest rates began to fall in all cases for which we have data. At the end of the period, the interest rates were between 3 and 4 per cent for each province in the Dutch Republic.[200] This trend is also evident from the aggregated data on six cities in the Northern and Southern Low Countries, which also report average interest rates of 3 to 4 per cent towards the end of the eighteenth century.[201]

Interest rate differentials however persisted, even within Holland (Graph 2.11). This is shown from the comparison below of the series from Amsterdam and the Beijerlanden in Holland's rural south. In the period for which the best data exist, the 1660s–1680s, Amsterdam merchants consistently borrowed at rates 1.5 percentage points or more lower than in the Beijerlanden.[202] This represents a considerable relative advantage. For example, in the peace years 1679–1685, interest rates in the Beijerlanden and Amsterdam were 4.8 per cent and 3.1 per cent respectively, resulting in Amsterdam merchants borrowing at rates one-third cheaper. The loans that the Amsterdam Orphan Masters (*weesmeesters*) issued to manage the orphans' estates usually had a slightly higher interest rate than commercial merchant credit, but were also cheaper than those in the Beijerlanden. This type of loan was limited in size and declined in importance in the third quarter of the seventeenth century when the Orphan Masters preferred other investments such as real estate and public debt. The interest rates paid by the VOC, in turn, moved between that of the

---

199 Oppers, "The Interest Rate Effect of Dutch Money in Eighteenth-Century Britain."

200 Baars, *De geschiedenis van de landbouw in de Beijerlanden*, 118; Paping, *"Voor een handvol stuivers":* The long-term development is subject of this book and presented later on in this study. Trompetter, "Burgers en boeren"; Nijboer, *Fatsoenering*: The results for the latter part of the eighteenth century are based on new archival research, presented elsewhere in this study. Van Cruyningen, *Behoudend maar buigzaam*, 300.

201 Gelderblom, Hup, and Jonker, "Public Functions, Private Markets," 186.

202 Baars, *De geschiedenis van de landbouw in de Beijerlanden*, 118; Gelderblom and Jonker, "Public Finance," 7; Oscar Gelderblom kindly shared the data on the Weesmeesterkennissen, VOC bonds and private merchant credit, for which I am grateful.

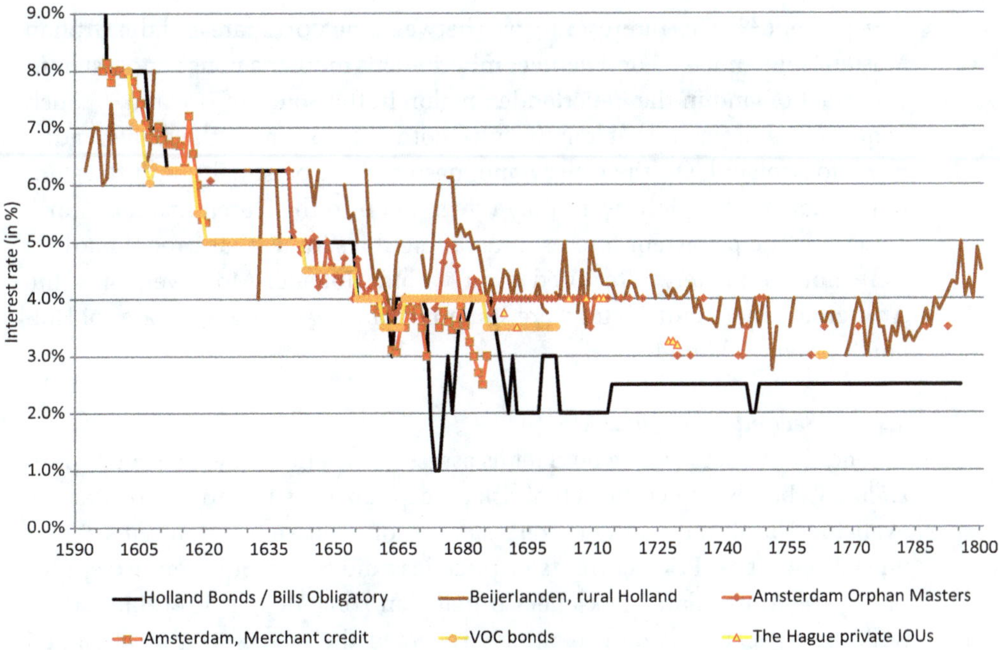

GRAPH 2.11 Public and private interest rates in Holland, 1590–1800.
SOURCES: BAARS, *DE GESCHIEDENIS VAN DE LANDBOUW IN DE BEIJERLANDEN*, 118; VOC AND AMSTERDAM: GELDERBLOM AND JONKER, 'PUBLIC FINANCE'; GELDERBLOM, JONKER, AND KOOL, 'DIRECT FINANCE'; VOC 1760S: VAN DILLEN, *BRONNEN TOT DE GESCHIEDENIS DER WISSELBANKEN*, P. 1376; THE HAGUE: DE MUINCK, *EEN REGENTENHUISHOUDING OMSTREEKS 1700*, P. 100–101; PUBLIC BONDS: LIESKER AND FRITSCHY, *GEWESTELIJKE FINANCIËN, VOL. 4: HOLLAND*.

Orphan Masters and the merchants' credit.[203] In general, the interest rates in Amsterdam were lower than in the Beijerlanden, although the type of credit made a difference as well.

A little closer to the Beijerlanden was The Hague, where we have some interest rates of IOUs of Cornelis de Jonge van Ellemeet, Receiver-General of the Union, over the period 1689–1729. He lent money to relatives with interest rates ranging between 2.75 per cent and 4.00 per cent, with an average of

203 Baars, *De geschiedenis van de landbouw in de Beijerlanden*, 118; Gelderblom, Jonker, and Kool, "Direct Finance:" Among wealthy Amsterdam merchants, interest charges differed per transaction, due to the variation in the risk assessment per creditor, debtor or transaction. Gelderblom and Jonker, "Public Finance," 7; Liesker and Fritschy, *Gewestelijke financiën: vol. 4. Holland*; Van Dillen, *Bronnen tot de geschiedenis der wisselbanken*, 1376; 't Hart, "Mobilising Resources," 186–87, 198: The participation of institutional investors in the total debt was limited and restricted to redeemable annuities, it was less important than in Britain's financial revolution.

3.57 per cent.[204] This interest rate was between the VOC's rate and the Orphan Masters' rate. In 1685, Van Ellemeet inherited his mother's house and a significant tract of land in the Beijerlanden region in the South of Holland.[205] Such connections indicate that relatively remote areas such as the Beijerlanden were not isolated. On the other hand, despite such personal ties, it does not imply that these regions were fully integrated into the Dutch financial infrastructure. The persistent interest rate differentials imply that capital markets were not completely integrated even within Holland. Moreover, only the Amsterdam merchants' rates were sometimes below the interest rates of Holland's provincial bonds.

3.4 *Secondary Capital Market*

Secondary market prices would let us assess whether the effective coupons of Holland's bonds reflect the actual risk perception, yet such prices are scarcely available. Hardly any contemporary publications contained quotations of provincial securities. Price currents or price lists did not quote them except for one by the Amsterdam bookseller Cornelis van Tongerlo in 1747 (Table 2.4).[206] Still, the 2.5 per cent rate seemingly reflected the effects of a large capital supply and investor preferences. Insofar as prices are known, these bonds traded on or above par on the secondary market during most of the eighteenth century after 1714. In the historiography, the late 1740s and 1780s are considered the exceptions to this rule.[207] Also, the careful considerations by the States of Holland discussed above suggest that market developments determined the acceptance of a proposed coupon.

The functioning of the secondary market for public securities in Holland must be understood in the context of the organisation of interest payments by the district tax receivers. Their inability to reimburse bondholders in 1672 sparked the emergence of a liquid secondary market in Holland, which until

204 B.E. De Muinck, *Een regentenhuishouding omstreeks 1700: gegevens uit de privé-boekhouding van Mr. Cornelis de Jonge van Ellemeet, ontvanger-generaal der Verenigde Nederlanden (1646–1721)* ('s-Gravenhage: Martinus Nijhoff, 1965), 100–101.

205 De Muinck, 145: The land had an area of 34 morgen and 189 rods, with a value of 14,400 guilders. This is approximately equal to 28 hectares and 167,909 euros today. (for the currency: https://iisg.amsterdam/nl/onderzoek/projecten/hpw/calculate.php).

206 Van Dillen, "Effectenkoersen," 1–2, 4, 13–14.

207 Gelderblom and Jonker, "Public Finance," 15; Van Bochove, "Configuring Financial Markets," 260, 279: Joost Jonker, Christiaan van Bochove and Oscar Gelderblom also kindly shared their data on Amsterdam auctions during the eighteenth century with me, for which I am grateful. Dormans, *Het tekort*, 77, 193, 204, 210, 230.

then had been rudimentary.[208] At least in the mid-1650s, the States of Holland took market prices into account when considering an interest rate reduction. Bonds sold at 5 to 7 per cent above par, even though investors knew of the intended interest rate reduction to 4 per cent.[209] The relatively late emergence of a more liquid secondary market was due to the role of the eighteen district receivers, who provided liquidity to investors at regular intervals. Their role allowed for a deep penetration into Holland's society, yet also implied that Holland's capital market was dispersed. Neal considered this a disadvantage compared to Britain after 1694 and a reason for the slow emergence of a secondary market in the Dutch Republic.[210] Yet Holland was not completely without a secondary market; a secondary market in VOC shares developed soon after the company's establishment in 1602.[211] Securities, such as VOC shares, could be offered as collateral when taking out loans, a form of pawning. Together with the liquidity provided by the district receivers, this provided the bondholders with sufficient liquidity.[212] The geographic fragmentation of the market encouraged the phenomenon whereby bonds were traded back to their places of origin. Eighteenth-century investors preferred to collect their interest locally and, consequently, used the secondary market to repatriate securities to the place of issuance, where the interest was paid. Hence, secondary markets followed the structure of the primary market, which was local and geographically dispersed.[213]

Arguably, the more puzzling question is why the secondary market persisted after 1672–1678. Why did the pre-1672 system not return, functioning in the same fashion as before? And, why was there no run on the district receivers for reimbursements during the following Nine Years' War and the War of the Spanish Succession, which were more expensive? The market prices in 1687–1720 remained mostly under par and did not allow for voluntary conversions or reductions.[214] The declining prices suggest that bondholders were not reimbursed at par, if at all. Gelderblom and Jonker speculate that the reason for the simultaneous sale of old lower-yielding bonds on the secondary market and the absence of a rush on Holland's district receivers lies in invest-

208 Gelderblom and Jonker, "Public Finance," 19.

209 Dormans, *Het tekort*, 53, 60.

210 Neal, "How It All Began"; See, in this respect also: Van Bochove, "Configuring Financial Markets."

211 Petram, *The World's First Stock Exchange*; Gelderblom and Jonker, "Completing a Financial Revolution"; Van Bochove, "Configuring Financial Markets," 257.

212 Gelderblom and Jonker, "Public Finance," 19.

213 Van Bochove, "Configuring Financial Markets."

214 Gelderblom and Jonker, "Public Finance," 23.

ors' fear of being excluded from lucrative future loan issues.[215] Yet investors had other options. Cash was in high demand by all warring parties, who increasingly turned to Amsterdam for loans.[216] Regardless of the exact reasons for its continued existence, prices from that secondary market remain fragmentary until the end of the eighteenth century.

The records of the Union's Receiver-General, Cornelis de Jonge van Ellemeet, provide insight into prices and yields in the 1720s. By then, Holland's 2.5 per cent bond traded around par, mostly just below.[217] The yields, however, differed per district office. Even nearby towns show differences. For instance, the difference in yields between Rotterdam and Den Briel (some 25 kilometers to the west) in 1730 was 10 basis points, or a relative difference of 3.76 per cent. Nevertheless, the market prices and yields remained close to the official coupon values.

De Jonge van Ellemeet also purchased Generality bonds. What may be surprising is that he bought Generality bonds on the secondary market and not just at issue. More surprisingly still, he sometimes purchased these securities above par, for example, a 2.5 per cent bond in 1729. Why De Jonge van Ellemeet, as the original issuer, did not reimburse creditors at par and resell them at a premium remains puzzling. We may speculate that Generality bondholders were not entitled to reimbursement at their own request. Even more remarkably, market prices did not automatically correct for differences in coupons, for example in 1727. Both 2.5 per cent and 3 per cent bonds sold under par, resulting in yields of 2.58 per cent and 3.15 per cent respectively. Yet considering that the 1715 default was followed by a forced interest rate reduction to 3 per cent, these yields were relatively low. Regardless of the inadequate correction on various coupons, yields fell for both coupons during this period. The little data from the secondary market for Generality bonds suggest it was still flawed, immature and presumably thin.

What the data does consistently show is that the yields for Holland bonds were lower than those for the Generality. Nevertheless, the Generality had provided loans to the provinces during the War of the Spanish Succession, including Holland. The provision of loans implied a reversal of the situation in the first half of the seventeenth century when the States General had

215 Gelderblom and Jonker, 24–25.

216 Riley, *International Government Finance*, 42, 83–86; Tomz, *Reputation and International Cooperation*, 41; Dickson, *Finance and Government under Maria Theresia 1740–1780*, 402–403 (vol. 2).

217 De Muinck, *Een regentenhuishouding omstreeks 1700*, 94–97.

TABLE 2.3 Bond yields recorded by Union Receiver De Jonge van Ellemeet, 1725–1731.

Issuer	Generality			Holland	Groningen
Year and office\coupon	**2.5%**	**3%**	**Average**	**2.5%**	**3%**
1725				2.63%	
The Hague				2.63%	
1726					3.21%
1727	2.58%	3.15%	2.86%		
Union Central Office, The Hague	2.58%	3.15%	2.86%		
1728		3.04%	3.04%	2.57%	
Delft				2.57%	
Union Central Office, The Hague		3.04%	3.04%		
1729	2.48%	3.03%	2.89%	2.48%	
Delft				2.48%	
Union Central Office, The Hague	2.48%	3.03%	2.89%		
1730		3.00%	3.00%	2.64%	
Den Briel				2.69%	
Rotterdam				2.59%	
Union Central Office, The Hague		3.00%	3.00%		
1731		2.97%	2.97%	2.51%	
Delft				2.51%	
The Hague				2.52%	
Union Central Office, The Hague		2.97%	2.97%		

SOURCES: DE MUINCK, *EEN REGENTENHUISHOUDING OMSTREEKS 1700*, PP. 94–97.

required Holland's provincial guarantees to be able to borrow at all.[218] Although the Generality loans offered an extension of the provincial borrowing capacity, the provinces were still responsible for interest payments, albeit indirectly, and the Generality depended on provincial revenue streams. Inadequate payments from the provinces resulted in Generality defaults in 1715 and 1754.[219] For Holland, the Generality did not offer more favourable terms; both

218 Dormans, *Het tekort*, 151: Dormans quotes from the Council of State's petition of 1753.

219 't Hart, *The Making of a Bourgeois State*, 167–68, 177–78; M. C. 't Hart, "Public Loans and Moneylenders in the Seventeenth Century Netherlands," *Economic and Social History in the Netherlands* 1 (1989): 122; Dormans, *Het tekort*; Alberto Feenstra, "De Lange Schaduw van de Spaanse Successieoorlog (1701–1713) in Friesland," in *Nederland in Last. Vijfhon-*

Holland and the Generality borrowed at 4 per cent by the end of the War of the Spanish Succession. Whether this was the case for the provinces outside of Holland is the subject of the next three chapters. Insofar as known, differences in coupons persisted well into the eighteenth century.[220] This also appears to have been the case for Groningen in 1726 (Table 2.3) and the other provinces in 1747. Firmer conclusions require further analysis and more insight into the secondary market prices for the debts of the provinces outside of Holland.

The year 1747, when Van Tongerloo published his price list, is not representative when evaluating the general perception of Dutch provincial bonds: after the fortified towns of Bergen op Zoom and Maastricht fell to the French, riots broke out throughout the Dutch Republic. However, since all prices suffered from similar conditions, the comparison is still informative about the yields. Except for the Amsterdam 4 per cent receipt slips (Dutch: *recepissen*), all provincial securities were quoted under par. The Zeeland 2 per cent bonds and the Friesland 3.5 per cent bonds sold for as little as 50 per cent under par, but with different yields.[221] Friesland's bond equalled a current yield of 7 per cent and Zeeland's 4 per cent was equal to the coupon it issued that year. The Groningen 3 per cent and 3.5 per cent bonds yielded 4.41 per cent and 4.49 per cent respectively, despite the States General's guarantee. Bonds of the Generality itself with a coupon of 3 per cent traded at 72 to 75 per cent of their nominal value and thus yielded 4 to 4.17 per cent. Bonds issued by the same province circulated simultaneously with various coupons. Remarkably, the spread of the yield differed markedly.[222] On average, the Holland bonds yielded 3.2 per cent, the non-Holland provincial bonds about 4.23 per cent; only Friesland's provincial bonds yielded more. So even in this crisis year the yields were modest in general and Holland's bond quotations compared favourably to the other provinces. For the rest of the period, Holland's 2.5 per cent effective coupon reflected what the market deemed fair.

---

derd Jaar Overheidsfinanciën in de Lage Landen, 1500–2000, by Victor Enthoven (Leiden: Primavera Pers, 2021), 89–109.

220 Fritschy, *Gewestelijke financiën: vol. I–VII*; Fritschy, *De patriotten*, 156; Pfeil, *"Tot redding,"* 122–23; Dormans, *Het tekort*, 165.

221 Van Dillen, "Effectenkoersen," 4, 13. These 2 per cent bonds were probably the nominal 4 per cent minus the 2 per cent withholding tax, as for Holland. The quotation list also records 2 per cent Holland bonds, which is also equal to the 4 per cent nominal bonds minus the 2 per cent withholding tax levied in Holland that year. Hence, the withholding tax appears to have been factored in. Liesker and Fritschy, *Gewestelijke financiën: vol. 4. Holland*, 273–373.

222 This might have been because of other unobservable factors, like discounts or personal guarantees by officials.

TABLE 2.4 Van Tongerlo's price quotations and yields for Dutch provincial bonds, 6 November 1747.

Issuer	Specification	Coupon	Low	High	Current yield
Holland	The Hague	2%	72%	73%	2.76%
Holland	Dordrecht	2%	68%	70%	2.90%
Holland	Haarlem	2%		70%	2.86%
Holland	Leiden	2%	68%	70%	2.90%
Holland	Amsterdam	2%	73%	75%	2.70%
Holland	Gouda	2%	68%	70%	2.90%
Holland	Rotterdam	2%	68%	70%	2.90%
Holland	Gorinchem	2%	66%	68%	2.99%
Holland	Den Briel	2%	65%	68%	3.01%
Holland	The Hague	3%		78%	3.85%
Holland	The Hague	3.5%		88%	3.98%
Holland	The Hague	3.25%		84%	3.87%
Holland	Amsterdam	3.5%		90%	3.89%
Holland	Amsterdam	3.25%		85%	3.82%
Generality	General Office, The Hague	3%	72%	75%	4.08%
Gelderland	Nijmegen	3%		95%	3.16%
Gelderland	Zutphen	4%		95%	4.21%
Gelderland	Veluwe	4%		95%	4.21%
Zeeland		2%		50%	4.00%
Zeeland		2.5%		60%	4.17%
Zeeland		3%		70%	4.29%
Zeeland		4%		85%	4.71%
Utrecht		2.5%		68%	3.68%
Utrecht		2.25%		72%	3.13%
Utrecht		3%		78%	3.85%
Utrecht		3.5%		84%	4.17%
Overijssel		3%		75%	4.00%
Groningen	Generality-guaranteed	3%		68%	4.41%
Groningen	Generality-guaranteed	3.5%		78%	4.49%
Friesland		3.5%		50%	7.00%

SOURCE: VAN DILLEN, 'EFFECTENKOERSEN', P. 13.

4 Conclusion

Once the Dutch won their independence, the federal institutions guaranteed provincial autonomy. Nevertheless, Holland's financial clout made the province difficult to disagree with. When Holland and the Stadholders' interests were aligned, Holland's position was undisputed and the Republic's situation was strong. This was the case until the 1640s and under the Stadholderate of William III. The Republic was then able to fend off the mightiest European powers of the time: first the Spanish Habsburg Empire, then Louis XIV's France, while arranging a favourable regime change in Britain. Yet when the interests of Holland and the Stadholder were in conflict, this could bring the Republic to the brink of civil war, as happened in 1618, 1650 and the 1780s.

Fighting wars required increasing large sums of money. Raising those sums first necessitated a tax revolution. This is understood as the tenfold increase in tax revenue in the period to 1609. Holland's tax revolution rested on three pillars. First, the number of taxes increased dramatically, mainly on daily necessities, and tax rates went up too. Second, the economy expanded, which also led to a tripling of nominal wages while the population doubled. Thirdly, taxation was broad-based, almost without tax exemptions, and therefore encompassed all strata of society. The eighteen district tax receivers allowed deep penetration into Holland's society. Yet the economic and demographic growth petered out in the second half of the seventeenth century. This curbed the growth of tax income from indirect taxes, the common means, which had reached its social ceiling. Later tax increases tended to be directed toward wealth and property. As a result, the tax pressure on the more-well-to-do increased in the eighteenth century. But direct taxes could only be increased to a limited extent; capital could easily be exported abroad, as happened in 1672 and during the War of the Spanish Succession. In eighteenth-century Holland direct taxes had reached a ceiling, while Great Britain, with similarly high debt ratios around 1800, still had room to increase them.

Although warfare became increasingly expensive, the number of years at war declined during the eighteenth century. As a consequence, Holland spent relatively similar amounts on warfare during the seventeenth and eighteenth centuries. Nevertheless, total expenditure rose, largely due to rising interest payments. As a result, the richer groups in society received part of the increased direct taxes back in the form of interest payments.

Borrowing was of secondary importance in the financing of the early stages of the Revolt. Hampered by the consequences of the 1572 default, Holland did not issue provincial loans until the 1590s. Borrowing in Holland was characterised by its voluntary nature; after 1610 there were hardly any forced loans, except for in the 1670s. Even more unusual was the way in which long-term debt was financed using a short-term instrument: the bond. In the seventeenth century, bond interest rates declined from 8 per cent to 2.5 per cent, which remained the going rate in the eighteenth century.

Holland's dependence on short-term bonds made it vulnerable to bondholders wishing to be reimbursed, as happened in 1653 and 1672. The subsequent default of 1672 sparked the emergence of a secondary market. The reasons for its persistence afterwards remain obscured and would require further research.

Holland's dependence on voluntary loans on the capital market benefitted its bondholders after the Nine Years' War. Although they suffered from interest rate cuts on existing loans, they enjoyed tax exemption on new bonds for more than ten years. Yet Holland did not impose forced loans and the risk of default shifted towards the creditors of the States General. Arguably, Holland's real financial revolution was an eighteenth-century phenomenon. Until the 1670s, Holland resorted to forced loans in times of need and squeezed bondholders' interests. The largest increase in debt was from 1690 onwards. It was financed voluntarily, by various instruments supplementing the 2.5 per cent bonds, a coupon that was among the lowest in Europe. As a result, financing costs remained relatively low, barely higher than in 1650. Hence, the sixteenth-century institutional innovations of collective debt and provincial taxation benefitted the States of Holland for a long time, after the initial problems of the early stages of the Revolt.

Holland became wealthy, with an abundant supply of capital. The money invested in the debt came from three sources. First, capital imports retained importance until the mid-seventeenth century. Second, economic growth increased private savings and stimulated a shift to domestically held debt. Then when growth slowed from around 1670, the States could benefit from slackening private domestic investment opportunities, which reduced investors' alternatives. Third, the States of Holland flooded the market with money in the eighteenth century. The debt issuance was not just a self-financing system, it also increased the money in investors' hands. In turn, they had ever greater difficulties in finding profitable domestic investments. The combination pushed down interest rates, which attracted foreign borrowers. Domestic differences in interest rates nevertheless persisted. The district tax receivers had considerable leeway to adjust rates to local circumstances and to benefit from local conditions and interest rates. That the lowest interest rates were to be found in Amsterdam may not come as a surprise, as it was an economic and demographic giant within the Dutch Republic. As a result, public debt and private wealth grew hand in hand in the eighteenth century. That suggests

Holland's elites were insufficiently taxed, but this was perhaps the lesser evil compared to the risk of them voting with their feet and moving their capital out of the province.

Holland's case also sheds light on the relationship between financial revolutions and economic growth. The main point of discussion is the causal direction. Both financial innovation and economic growth had medieval roots. As far as public debt is concerned, Holland was a capital-importing region during the late Middle Ages, into the sixteenth century and possibly until the mid-seventeenth century. This coincided with the period of strongest economic growth. Defaults, such as those in 1494, 1572 and 1653, meanwhile showed the risks of external debt, especially that of the Law of Reprisal. This had a deterrent and disciplining effect, causing foreign debt payments to be prioritised; Holland had learned its lesson the hard way since the late Middle Ages. Only after 1672–1678 does domestic debt seem to have become a safe investment, with Holland credibly committed to servicing the debt. By then, economic growth had declined. Capital imports and financial innovation appear to be expressions of economic growth, rather than causes.

From around 1690, low coupon rates were voluntarily accepted, despite the growing debt. This required, however, the outsourcing of part of the risk to the Generality at the time of the War of the Spanish Succession. Holland's history shows a progression from economic growth coupled with capital imports, slowing economic growth and rising domestic wealth, and ultimately capital exports with little economic growth. Capital was a catalyst of rudimentary growth, but it contributed little to the average prosperity of a developed economy and therefore promoted inequality. The question is whether and how the other provinces benefitted from Holland's financial strength and economic growth. The discussion starts with Zeeland, which resembled Holland institutionally and economically, but was on a smaller scale.

CHAPTER 3

Zeeland's Borrowing beyond Frontiers

By the end of the eighteenth century, little was left of Zeeland's initial position as a fiscal stronghold of the Dutch Republic. Zeeland had formed the fiscal core of the Dutch Revolt, together with Holland.[1] Yet in 1792, the rearrangement of the distribution key for the common expenses resulted in a reduction of more than 50 per cent in Zeeland's contribution.[2] Since 1616, Zeeland had been the third largest contributor to the Union, exceeded only by Holland and (by a slight margin) by Friesland, both of which had larger populations.[3] The revision was no overnight decision. Rather, the States of Zeeland had first requested a reduction in the 1760s. Back then, the other provinces had reacted with suspicion and disbelief. For instance, the States of Groningen questioned the claims of impoverishment, emphasising Zeeland's trade and shipping, and its citizens' private wealth and suggesting that Groningen would refuse to cover for an undertaxed Zeeland population.[4] The approval of Zeeland's reduced contribution implies that the other provinces eventually considered Zeeland's plea justified, and were willing to make up for the hole in the budget. This raises the question of what caused the deterioration in Zeeland's fiscal condition.

Economic decline appears to be a plausible explanation for the fiscal difficulties. By the turn of the nineteenth century, Zeeland had become economically peripheral.[5] This picture differs from that in the sixteenth and seven-

1 As late as the second half of the eighteenth century, the States of Zeeland identified itself as such: Nationaal Archief, The Hague (NA), Provinciale Resoluties. Inv.no. 309, Letter from the States of Zeeland to William V, prince of Orange, d.d 31 December 1766, p. 3: "… *and Zeeland, who helped to help the Union's first foundations …*" ["*… en Zeeland, die de eerste gronden van de Unie heeft helpen leggen, …*"].

2 Fritschy, *De patriotten*, 128.

3 Zwitzer, "Quotenstelsel" Holland paid 58%, Friesland 11.5% and Zeeland 9%. Johannes Alle Faber, *Drie eeuwen Friesland: economische en sociale ontwikkelingen van 1500 tot 1800*, vol. II, A.A.G. bijdragen 17 (Wageningen: Landbouwhogeschool, Afd. Agrarische Geschiedenis, 1972), 413–15. Friesland's population amounted to 129,000 people, compared with only 74,000 people in Zeeland, in 1616.

4 NA, Provinciale resoluties, inv.no. 309, "Advis van Stad en Lande", 23 December 1767. "Dat boven dien overwegende de Rykdom der ingezetenen van Zeeland, in tegenoverstelling van die in deze provincie, alsmede de aanzienelijke scheepvaart en koophandel …"

5 Paul Brusse and Willem van den Broeke, *Provincie in de periferie: de economische geschiedenis van Zeeland, 1800–2000* (Utrecht: Matrijs, 2005); Paul Brusse, *Gevallen stad: stedelijke*

 | DOI:10.1163/9789004745254_004

teenth centuries, when it enjoyed a period of economic expansion, in close association with Holland.[6] Yet recent research into Zeeland's development over the eighteenth century has indicated the resilience of its economy, although the balance shifted towards the rural economy. The authors argue that the shift from the towns to the countryside initially stemmed from the revival of the latter rather than from urban decline. For most of the eighteenth century, the major towns maintained their size.[7] This suggests internal changes in the economic sectors, but not outright economic decline. The subsequent question is whether the economy still formed a solid financial basis for Zeeland's public finances, specifically tax incomes.

If the economy was not behind the problems in public finance, perhaps the issue was expenditure, not income. Yet De Vries and Van der Woude argue that Zeeland had little need for additional loans during the eighteenth century.[8] This implies that Zeeland could balance income and expenditure. Therefore, it is necessary to determine when deficits led to a need to increase borrowing, and when or whether this involved a 'real' financial revolution.[9] Moreover, the question remains what caused the financial troubles that ultimately justified Zeeland's lower contribution.

In searching for the causes of Zeeland's deterioration, this chapter addresses political, economic and fiscal factors. The political aspect is only considered insofar as it concerns fiscal aspects and decisions about debt management. The critical examination of Zeeland's economic and fiscal development is aimed at determining whether free riding on the other provinces' accounts can be ruled

---

netwerken en het platteland, Zeeland 1750–1850, Balans tussen stad en platteland 1 (Zwolle: Waanders : Universiteit Utrecht, 2011); Neele, *De ontdekking van het Zeeuwse platteland*; Jeannine Dekker, *Onderdanig en opstandig: desurbanisatie en de politieke verhoudingen op het platteland in Zeeland, 1750–1850*, Balans tussen stad en platteland 2 (Zwolle: Waanders : Universiteit Utrecht, 2011); Wietse Veenstra, *Gewestelijke financiën ten tijde van de Republiek der Verenigde Nederlanden. Deel VII. Zeeland (1573–1795)*, Rijks geschiedkundige publicatiën. Kleine serie 110 (Den Haag: Instituut voor Nederlandse Geschiedenis, 2009); Veenstra, *Tussen gewest en Generaliteit.*

6 Fritschy, *Public Finance*, 104–12; Price, *Dutch Society*, 12, 85; Noordegraaf and Van Zanden, "Vroegmoderne economische groei," 401–2; Veenstra, *Gewestelijke financiën: vol. 7. Zeeland*, 18–19; 't Hart, *The Dutch Wars of Independence*, 17–18.

7 Brusse, *Gevallen stad*; Neele, *De ontdekking van het Zeeuwse platteland*; Dekker, *Onderdanig en opstandig*; Paul Brusse and Wijnand Mijnhardt, *Towards a New Template for Dutch History: De-Urbanization and the Balance between City and Countryside*, trans. Beverley R. Jackson (Zwolle: Waanders : Universiteit Utrecht, 2011).

8 De Vries and Van der Woude, *The First Modern Economy*, 121; De Vries and Van der Woude, *Nederland 1500–1815*, 152.

9 Fritschy, *Public Finance*, 23, 110, 112, 141, 373; Fritschy, "Financial Revolution."

out.[10] To this end, the chapter focuses on the tax burden, the costs and origins of the public debt, and Zeeland's debt management in particular.

In this chapter, I argue that Zeeland's capacity to shoulder the burden of its allocated share in contributions to the Republic's public finances had indeed deteriorated relative to the other provinces, especially compared to Holland, whose share was increased in 1792.[11] The 1616 quota did not accurately represent Zeeland's economic position within the Dutch Republic, in the seventeenth and eighteenth centuries. Zeeland's relevance lies in its initial resemblance to Holland, economically and institutionally, combined with their divergent outcomes. What caused Zeeland's public finances to wane compared to Holland's?

1 Zeeland's State Formation Processes

The first years of the Dutch Revolt shaped Zeeland's future under the Dutch Republic institutionally, economically, demographically and fiscally.[12] This section discusses the institutional changes in Zeeland's state formation process in transitioning from a Habsburg possession to an independent member of the rebellious Dutch Republic. Military action in Zeeland was limited to the first years of the Dutch Revolt. After the Pacification of Ghent in 1576, Zeeland remained freed from warfare.[13]

The main change in the composition of the States of Zeeland under the Dutch Republic was the dominant position of Zeeland's towns. Prior to the Revolt, only one of Zeeland's three members in the provincial States represented its towns. The nobility and the abbot-bishop of Middelburg held the other two votes. After the Pacification of Ghent in 1576, the power of nobility and church was usurped by the urban elites. The Protestants removed the Catholic abbot-bishop from power and turned the abbey in Middelburg into the meeting place and administrative centre of the States of Zeeland. The

10 Van Zanden and Van Riel, *The Strictures of Inheritance*.

11 Riley, *International Government Finance*, 69; Fritschy, "Schulden als leerschool?," 22: evident in the more than 50 per cent reduction in the contribution to the Republic's expenses in 1792.

12 The fiscal changes will be discussed extensively in the next section.

13 Price, *Dutch Society*, 85 The same was true for the other coastal provinces, namely Holland and most of Friesland. 't Hart, *The Dutch Wars of Independence*, 17–18.

nobility retained its single vote, yet with less weight in total.[14] The States of Zeeland henceforth consisted of seven members: the First Nobleman, as representative of the nobility, and six members representing the six towns, Middelburg, Zierikzee, Tholen, Goes, Vlissingen and Veere. The latter two towns were admitted to the provincial States for the first time as a reward for their early support of the Revolt, while Reimerswaal lost its position after repeated flooding caused depopulation and impoverishment.[15] The towns no longer held a joint vote; each held one individual vote, expressing the urban dominance in the States of Zeeland.

The Revolt accelerated the strengthening of the urban position, yet this process had started early in the fifteenth and sixteenth centuries. The towns' increased political influence was related to their economic growth. Zeeland benefitted from its pivotal geographical position in between the existing economic centres in Brabant and Flanders in the south and Holland with its growing economy in the north.[16] The sixteenth-century economic expansion allowed Zeeland to shoulder a heavy tax burden, which even exceeded that of the neighbouring economic centres. Land taxes formed the main source of income, yet the towns increasingly contributed to tax revenues. The influence of the towns grew apace with their contributions. By the 1560s, they opposed centralisation and especially the imposition of new taxes that burdened the urban economy. The rebellious towns eventually won the struggle and gained control over the Provincial States of Zeeland as an independent representative assembly.[17]

The urban control over the provincial assembly implied control over the composition of the delegations to the Generalities and subordinate provincial

14 The waning of the nobility's power had already set in prior to the Revolt: Fredericus Hermanus Jacobus Lemmink, *Het ontstaan van de Staten van Zeeland en hun geschiedenis tot het jaar 1555* (Roosendaal: Van Poll Suykerbuyk, 1951), 155.

15 Jan Hendrik Kluiver, *De souvereine en independente staat Zeeland: de politiek van de provincie Zeeland inzake vredesonderhandelingen met Spanje tijdens de Tachtigjarige Oorlog tegen de achtergrond van de positie van Zeeland in de Republiek* (Middelburg: De Zwarte Arend, 1998), 15–19. The population increasingly abandoned Reimerswaal, until it was officially closed in 1636.

16 Simon Groenveld, "Politieke verhoudingen," in *Geschiedenis van Zeeland. Dl. II: 1550–1700*, ed. Paul Brusse and Wijnand Mijnhardt (Zwolle: WBOOKS, 2012), 147–49.

17 Groenveld, 150–54; Veenstra, *Gewestelijke financiën: vol. 7. Zeeland*, 10–11; Louis Sicking, "Politieke geschiedenis, gewestelijke en bovengewestelijke bestuursinstellingen," in *Geschiedenis van Zeeland. Dl. I: Prehistorie-1550*, ed. Paul Brusse, Pieter Arij Henderikx, and Frans Beekman (Zwolle: WBOOKS, 2012), 235, 240–42; Tracy, *A Financial Revolution in the Habsburg Netherlands*, 15–16, 32–38.

institutions.[18] In legal matters, Zeeland shared a High Court with Holland until the end of the Dutch Republic.[19] One important institution, including financially, was the Zeeland admiralty.[20] Consequently, economic and political power were concentrated in the hands of a few urban families of merchants and investors, which Enthoven has labelled a symbiosis between merchants and regents.[21] The shared political interests of the merchants and urban regents mirrored what was seen in Holland.[22] For instance, in 1651, riots brought the pro-Republican States faction to power in Middelburg's magistrate.[23] Wealth alone was not enough for those with new fortunes to gain access to political power and the highest social classes in the eighteenth century.[24] The intimate connections of the elitist urban cliques were reinforced throughout the history of the Dutch Republic. The Orangist revolution of 1747 did not alter this, partly due to the death of the new Stadholder William IV of Orange. He had annulled the practice of the contracts of correspondence, which the urban elites used to smoothly distribute the available offices among the various factions without squabbling. However, the year after he died, in 1751, the contracts of correspondence were swiftly reinstalled. The clique around his infant son William V was largely occupied with protecting and strengthening the families' position now that the Stadholderate was

18 Dekker, *Onderdanig en opstandig*, 11: In the Stadholderless periods of 1650–1668 and 1702–1747 there was no representive for the nobility.

19 Veenstra, *Gewestelijke financiën: vol. 7. Zeeland*, 9–10; Sicking, "Politieke geschiedenis," 240–42.

20 This is especially clear from the admiralty's budgets. See: Veenstra, *Tussen gewest en Generaliteit*, 237–329. The immediate effect on employment was limited. At its height, in the 1650s and 1660s, it employed only a few dozens of labourers at its shipyards. Brandon, *Masters of War*, 174.

21 Victor Enthoven, "Een symbiose tussen koopman en regent," in *Ondernemers & bestuurders: economie en politiek in de Noordelijke Nederlanden in de late Middeleeuwen en vroegmoderne tijd*, ed. Clé Lesger and Leo Noordegraaf, Neha-series III (Amsterdam: NEHA, 1999), 203–36; Piet Van Cruyningen, "Bevolking en sociale verhoudingen," in *Geschiedenis van Zeeland. Dl. II: 1550–1700*, ed. Paul Brusse and Wijnand Mijnhardt (Zwolle: WBOOKS, 2012), 135. The family Van Tuyll van Serooskerke was one of the very few noble "ambachtsheren" that retained some political power under the Dutch Republic.

22 De Vries and Van der Woude, *The First Modern Economy*, 164–164, 230, 350–67, 403; Enthoven, "Symbiose"; Israel, *The Dutch Republic*, 14–38, 178–88, 197–235; Prak, *The Dutch Republic*, 134, 251; Stasavage, "What We Can Learn from the Early History of Sovereign Debt."

23 Marjolein 't Hart, "Autonoom maar kwetsbaar. De Middelburgse regenten en de opstand van 1651," *De zeventiende eeuw* 9 (1993): 56–57.

24 Riley, *International Government Finance*, 10, 253–54.

hereditary.[25] Consequently, the once-new merchants' families that had entered the urban magistrates became sitting elites who used the contracts of correspondence as instruments that protected the vested family interests in order to retain political power.

2 Economic Developments

As a result of the Revolt and especially the Fall of Antwerp in 1585, Zeeland lost its pivotal economic role between Holland in the north and Flanders and Brabant in the south. This had been one of the strengths of its late medieval and sixteenth-century economic expansion. In line with its political orientation, Zeeland's economic focus largely shifted to Holland, yet not entirely.[26] Until the Revolt, the Zeeland towns functioned as an outport for Antwerp, the largest metropolis in north-western Europe.[27] After the Spanish recaptured Antwerp, the rebels in Zeeland controlled and blocked the passage through the Scheldt estuary. The physical blockade lasted only two years, from 1585 to 1587. Afterwards, the States General preferred to tax trade destined for Antwerp heavily over physically blocking shipments and obliging merchants to tranship cargo in Zeeland, which generated work and income for the province.[28]

The trade between Zeeland and the hinterlands of Brabant and Flanders continued nevertheless; until the end of the eighteenth century, they remained

25 Jeannine Dekker, "Politieke verhoudingen," in *Geschiedenis van Zeeland Dl. III: 1700–1850*, ed. Paul Brusse and Jeannine Dekker (Zwolle: WBOOKS, 2013), 176–77; Van Nimwegen, *Nederlandse burgeroorlog*. Adams described a similar promising start by William IV to enable his supporters to break into the governement circles in Holland, but found that even before his death, the ruling elites had reached an understanding with the new Stadholder. Adams, *The Familial State*, 156–59.

26 Groenveld, "Politieke verhoudingen," 147–49.

27 Victor Enthoven, *Zeeland en de opkomst van de Republiek: handel en strijd in de Scheldedelta, c. 1550–1621* (s.n., 1996), 10–16, 18–32, 67; In 1522, it took over the Scottish staple from Bruges, first in Middelburg, then a few years later in Veere: a visible manifestation of Zeeland's sixteenth-century economic expansion: Gelderblom, *Cities of Commerce*, 30; P. J. Van Cruyningen, "Economie," in *Geschiedenis van Zeeland. Dl. II: 1550–1700*, ed. Paul Brusse and Wijnand Mijnhardt (Zwolle: WBOOKS, 2012), 82, 84: Veere cherished this right until 1799, as it was not viable without it. Brusse, *Gevallen stad*, 1.

28 Enthoven, *Zeeland en de opkomst van de Republiek*, 109–10; Van Cruyningen, "Economie," 101; These revenues are generally named together with the convoy levies (Dutch: convooien en licenten). Veenstra, *Tussen gewest en Generaliteit*, 80: The States General also intended the revenues from these levies to pay for the navy.

important markets for Zeeland's towns, especially for Middelburg.[29] Only between 1750 and 1850 did the economic balance gradually shift from the towns towards the countryside. Given the commercial character of Zeeland's agricultural sector, this was not necessarily an economic degradation.[30] A closer examination of Zeeland's economic developments from the late sixteenth to the eighteenth century is needed to understand this apparent stability in economic performance, despite changes in economic structure. To this end, this section examines the main economic activities, demographic developments and urbanisation, wage levels, and the private capital market.

2.1 *Demographic Developments*

During the late sixteenth and early seventeenth centuries, Zeeland underwent a period of rapid demographic growth, which then petered out around 1660. In about 1600, Zeeland's population numbered less than 70,000 inhabitants, one eighth of Holland's 550,000. In this period, the towns grew faster than the countryside. Especially Middelburg benefitted from the merchants and craftsmen relocating there, mainly from Antwerp after 1585.[31] Zeeland's urban population more than doubled in this period.[32] As a result, the degree of urbani-

---

29 Brusse, *Gevallen stad*, 59–60.

30 Van Cruyningen, "Economie," 100–101; Paul Brusse, "Economie," in *Geschiedenis van Zeeland Dl. III: 1700–1850*, ed. Paul Brusse and Jeannine Dekker (Zwolle: WBOOKS, 2013), 49–115; Brusse, *Gevallen stad*; Neele, *De ontdekking van het Zeeuwse platteland*; Brusse and Mijnhardt, *Towards*; Dekker, *Onderdanig en opstandig*.

31 In analysing the degree of urbanisation, these six vote holding towns are considered to form the urban population. This analysis consequently excludes Staats-Vlaanderen, which is part of the current province of Zeeland, but was not part of Zeeland during the early-modern period. This is mainly done to allow comparisons with other provinces. Brusse used a different definition of a city, which excludes Veere, Goes and Tholen. Brusse, *Gevallen stad*, 25–27, 31, 33; Prak labelled the concentration of urban demographic growth in the coastal towns as "[t]he Republic's 'two-speed' economy." Prak, *The Dutch Republic*, 251; Van Cruyningen, "Bevolking," 105; Brusse, *Gevallen stad*, 36; Priester, *Geschiedenis*, 481; Enthoven, *Zeeland en de opkomst van de Republiek*, 112; Van Cruyningen, "Economie," 83.

32 A few recent studies have greatly improved previous estimates about Zeeland's demographic developments: Brusse, *Gevallen stad*; Paul Brusse and Wijnand Mijnhardt, eds., *Geschiedenis van Zeeland. Dl. II: 1550–1700* (Zwolle: WBOOKS, 2012); Paul Brusse and Jeannine Dekker, eds., *Geschiedenis van Zeeland Dl. III: 1700–1850* (Zwolle: WBOOKS, 2013); Van Cruyningen, "Bevolking," 103–9; Paul Brusse, "Bevolking en sociale verhoudingen," in *Geschiedenis van Zeeland Dl. III: 1700–1850*, ed. Paul Brusse and Jeannine Dekker (Zwolle: WBOOKS, 2013), 118; Although older, this book still sets the standard for the rural areas: Priester, *Geschiedenis*.

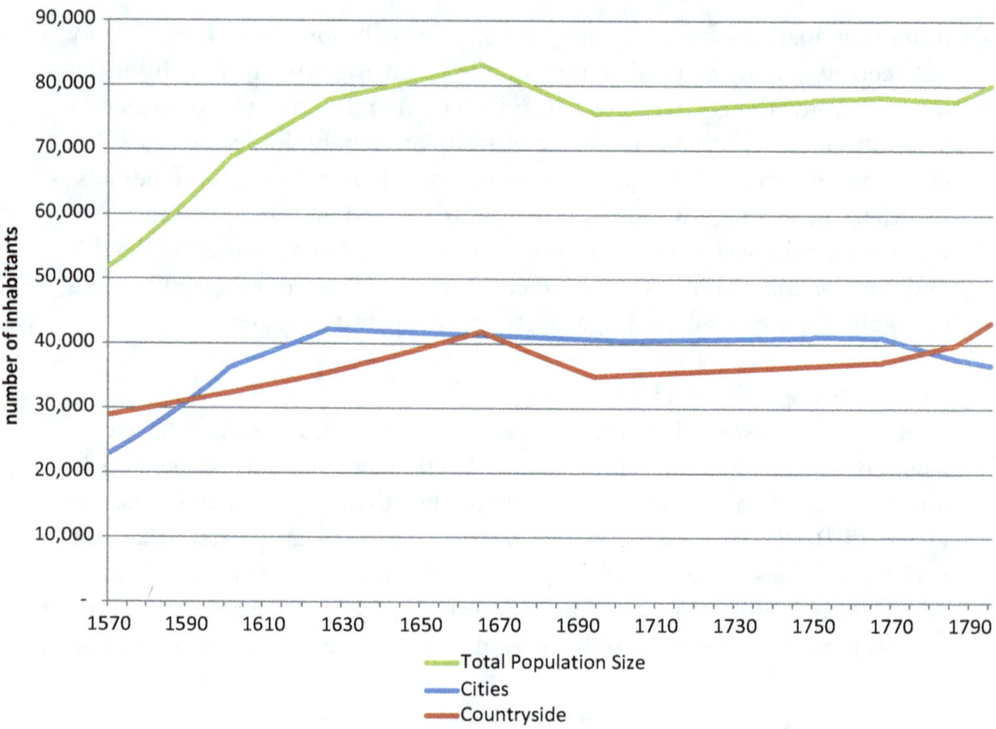

GRAPH 3.1 Zeeland's urban and rural population trends, 1570–1800.
SOURCES: FEENSTRA, *BETWEEN SHARED*, APPENDIX.

sation increased from around 45 per cent in the 1570s to 55 per cent in 1625. But then urban growth stagnated. The rural population increased more slowly, to approximately 35,000 people in 1625 and 40,000 in the 1660s.[33] As a consequence, Zeeland's total population increased to about 75,000 inhabitants in the first quarter of the seventeenth century. The slow but persistent growth in the rural areas increased its population further to just over 80,000 in the 1660s. Meanwhile, Holland's population increased faster, to more than 700,000 in 1630 and 850,000 in 1660. To summarise, Zeeland experienced less population growth than Holland in the period to 1660.

Between the 1660s and 1700, Zeeland experienced a demographic decline, predominantly in the countryside (see: graph 3.1). The towns remained attractive for people seeking employment. Without migration, pre-modern urban towns tended to decline in size, as happened to several towns in Holland.[34]

33 Priester, *Geschiedenis*, 475, 477, 480, 481, 483, 485, 486.
34 De Vries and Van der Woude, *Nederland 1500–1815*, 88–90.

FIGURE 3.1 Allegory on the province Zeeland, by Jan Caspar Philips, 1753.
RIJKSMUSEUM, OBJECT NR. RP-P-1964-3547

The resilience of the urban population figures therefore indicates a strong and stable urban economy.

After 1700, Zeeland entered a period of deurbanisation from around 55 per cent to 45 per cent in 1795. Until 1750, the degree of urbanisation fluctuated between 50 and 55 per cent. The deurbanisation was a gradual process, arising mainly because the rural population grew (albeit slowly) while the urban population did not. The rural population increased from 34,000 around 1700 to 43,000 in 1795.[35] Zeeland's total population increased from approximately 75,000 people to 80,000 in 1795.[36] The urban population remained largely stable until the latter part of the eighteenth century. The exception was Zierikzee: after 1750, its population declined from over 10,000 to about 6,000 inhabitants in 1795.[37] As a result, Zeeland's degree of urbanisation returned to around 45 per cent, the same as it had been in the 1570s.

Even though Holland's population declined in the eighteenth century, Zeeland's demographic growth lagged behind that of Holland over the two centuries as a whole.[38] Numbering 850,000 around 1700 and 828,000 in 1795, Holland's population was more than ten times as large as Zeeland's in 1795, whereas it had been eight times as large around 1600. This meant a relative deterioration in the population ratios.

2.2 *Economic Trends in Zeeland*

Zeeland's economy was advanced around 1600 and fared well throughout the seventeenth and eighteenth centuries. Its economy resembled Holland's on a smaller scale and came second among the seven provinces in several respects.[39] It could build on late medieval developments like urbanisation, the rise in shipping and colonial trade, commercial agricultural production, wheat exports, fishing and a market for wage labour (as represented in Figure 3.1). With the Revolt, privateering also became a lucrative business, although this dwindled in the more peaceful eighteenth century.[40] The importance of trade

35 Priester, *Geschiedenis*, 475, 477, 480, 481, 483, 485, 486.

36 Brusse, "Bevolking," 118.

37 Middelburg had approximately 17,000 inhabitants until its collapse in the late 1790s. The town then lost a great number of inhabitants. Vlissingen appears the most resilient of the main towns after the Republic's dissolution, because it maintained its population of about 6,000 inhabitants from 1750 until after 1800: Brusse, *Gevallen stad*, 31, 33–37; Older estimates for Middelburg suggested a somewhat larger population: approximately 26,000–27,000 people in 1670–1700. But this is almost certainly too high. Lourens and Lucassen, *Inwoneraantallen*; The population of the other smaller towns was less prone to variation, although Veere's population structurally declined over the period: Van Cruyningen, "Bevolking," 105; Brusse, "Bevolking," 118–19.

38 Feenstra, "Between Shared."

39 e.g. Kluiver, *De souvereine en independente staat Zeeland*.

40 Arie Van Steensel, "De economie van het platteland," in *Geschiedenis van Zeeland. Dl. 1: Prehistorie-1550*, ed. Paul Brusse, Pieter Arij Henderikx, and Frans Beekman (Zwolle: WBOOKS, 2012), 265–76; Van Cruyningen, "Economie"; Brusse, "Economie"; Adrianus Paulus van Vliet, *Vissers in oorlogstijd: de Zeeuwse zeevisserij in de jaren 1568–1648*, Werken / uitg. door het Koninklijk Zeeuwsch Genootschap der Wetenschappen, ISSN

and commercial agriculture made Zeeland vulnerable to international competition and a decline in the demand for its agricultural products.

Zeeland had solid colonial connections. The province was a relatively big investor in the Dutch East India Company (VOC, founded in 1602) and West India Company (WIC, founded in 1621): 20 per cent of the money invested, or one-fifth, came from Zeeland, while its population was one-eighth of Holland's. This earned Zeeland places on the boards of directors, alongside Holland's delegations. This was not the case for the other provinces, or not to the same extent.[41] Later, Zeeland investors invested in other colonial companies such as the Guyana Company in 1771 and, most significantly, the *Middelburgse Commercie Compagnie* (MCC) in 1720, which became the Dutch Republic's largest slave trader.[42] Even though the profitability of these investments remains a matter of dispute, other sectors in the supply chain benefitted from the demand.[43] Colonial trade also provided direct employment. The VOC's shipyard was Zeeland's largest employer. The Zeeland port towns supplied the hinterlands of Flanders and Brabant in the Southern Low Countries with colonial goods and exported textiles from those regions. When the Austrian government in the Southern Low Countries began to protect its market,

0168–7182 14 (Middelburg: Koninklijk Zeeuwsch Genootschap der Wetenschappen, 2003), 85–89, 159.

41 Liesker and Fritschy, *Gewestelijke financiën: vol. 4. Holland*; 't Hart, *The Making of a Bourgeois State*; 't Hart, "De Nederlandse Republiek"; Gaastra, *Geschiedenis*, 20–21; Den Heijer, *De geschiedenis van de WIC*; Veenstra, *Tussen gewest en Generaliteit*; Van Cruyningen, "Economie," 88, 97; Van de Voort, *Westindische plantages*, 28; Den Heijer, *De geoctrooieerde compagnie*, 61.

42 Ruud Paesie, *Geschiedenis van de MCC: opkomst, bloei en ondergang* (Zutphen: Walburg Pers, 2014), 27; Neele, *De ontdekking van het Zeeuwse platteland*, 103; Van de Voort, *Westindische plantages*, 28–29, 125–26, 132–33; Brusse, *Gevallen stad*, 72; Brusse, "Economie," 98–100; Suze Zijlstra, *Anglo-Dutch Suriname: Ethnic Interaction and Colonial Transition in the Caribbean, 1651–1682* (unpublished PhD-thesis Universiteit van Amsterdam, 2015), 11–13.

43 Gerhard de Kok, "Cursed Capital: The Economic Impact of the Transatlantic Slave Trade on Walcheren around 1770," *Tijdschrift Voor Sociale En Economische Geschiedenis/ The Low Countries Journal of Social and Economic History* 13, no. 3 (September 16, 2016): 11, https://doi.org/10.5 117/TSEG2016.3.GKOK; The debate about the economic effects of the slave trade on the Dutch economy was reinvigorated by Van Rossum and Fatah-Black: Matthias Van Rossum and Karwan Jalal Fatah-Black, "Wat is winst? De economische impact van de Nederlandse trans-Atlantische slavenhandel," *Tijdschrift voor sociale en economische geschiedenis* 9, no. 1 (2012): 3–29.

Zierikzee's economy declined instantly.[44] Even if the colonial trade was not immensely profitable, it prevented an earlier collapse.

Agriculture was also highly commercialised by the end of the sixteenth century. The lease of land to tenants had become the norm in the sixteenth and early seventeenth centuries.[45] The rural areas were well connected to the urban markets. Commercialisation made this sector vulnerable to market price fluctuations, especially for wheat and to a lesser extent madder.[46] Until the 1660s, Zeeland's farmers benefitted from high agricultural prices in Europe. Wheat proved particularly important. Thirty-five to 40 per cent of the cultivated land was planted with this export crop. Wheat prices increased from around 1740 until the 1780s.[47] In response to faltering wheat prices in 1660–1740, farmers in Zeeland had turned to madder production, a red dyestuff. Urban elites supplied capital for building expensive madder ovens to process the madder root into powdered dye.[48]

The lull in agricultural prices also affected land prices and the use of land. Since the late Middle Ages, urban entrepreneurs had invested in land recla-

---

44 Van Cruyningen, "Economie," 74–75, 90–91, 100–101: the fishing industry underwent several transformations between the late sixteenth century and mid-eighteenth century. Declining profits in herring fishery, due to a deteriorating competitive position vis-à-vis the Hollanders, ousted the Zeeland fishers, who then turned to cod and – the more capital intensive – Iceland fisheries, although this sector nevertheless declined overall. Vliet, *Vissers in oorlogstijd*, 85–89, 159; Brusse, "Economie," 85–86, 102; Brusse, *Gevallen stad*, 61–63, 67–79; V. Enthoven, "'Veel vertier'. De Verenigde Oostindische Compagnie in Zeeland, een economische reus op Walcheren," *Archief: vroegere en latere mededeelingen voornamelijk in betrekking tot Zeeland*, 1989, 87–105 Enthoven argues that over its entire existence the VOC in Zeeland had paid more to employees than to investors (p. 96).

45 Piet Van Cruyningen, "From Disaster to Sustainability: Floods, Changing Property Relations and Water Management in the South-Western Netherlands, c.1500–1800," *Continuity and Change* 29, no. 02 (2014): 241–65, https://doi.org/10.1017/S0268416014000149.

46 Priester, *Geschiedenis*, 78–85, 305–10, 361, 364–65: characterised its rural economy probably as early as the fourteenth century; Van Cruyningen, "Economie," 64–68; Brusse, *Gevallen stad*, 118.

47 Van Cruyningen, "Economie," 57; Throughout the nineteenth century, prices for Middelburg and Dordrecht – a town relatively near Zeeland in the south of the province of Holland – show very high correlations. For Dordrecht a wheat prices series exists that is unavailable for Middelburg in the seventeenth and eighteenth centuries. Given the high correlation in the nineteenth century, I followed Priester's suggestion that the Dordrecht prices form a good indication for the developments in Zeeland. Priester, *Geschiedenis*, 79–85, 648–53, 676–83.

48 Van Cruyningen, "Economie," 65–66, 79.

mation, drainage projects and dyke repairs.[49] By the mid-seventeenth century, urban landowners possessed 50 to 60 per cent of all arable land, and an even higher proportion in newly drained polders.[50] Until the 1660s, high land rents had stimulated land reclamation. Even though land rents started to decrease in the 1640s, land reclamation only halted in the 1660s, and did not resume until the 1750s. The Zeeland urban elites purchased cheap arable land from the 1690s on which to build country houses with large pleasure gardens and woods. Between 1690 and 1750 their number increased vastly, especially on the island of Walcheren.[51] At the same time, urban merchants purchased manors (Dutch: *ambachtsheerlijkheid*) and manorial rights in the countryside, as investments in status.[52] Several city councils also purchased manors, yielding significant control over the countryside.[53] So the urban elites invested in various ways in the rural economy, where they also acquired political power. Agricultural price rises reversed this process from around 1750.[54] First, numerous country houses and gardens were returned to productive agricultural land. Then land reclamation projects increased once more.

Farmers and merchants actively responded to the changing conditions when economic growth declined after 1650. Markets and investments tied the members of the urban elite to the countryside. New initiatives could be used to raise the required capital, which appears to have been in relatively sufficient supply, especially in Middelburg. The money earned during the phase of fast economic growth in the sixteenth century and beginning of the seventeenth century did not suddenly disappear, but it did not generate additional growth in the following period.

---

49 Van Cruyningen, "From Disaster to Sustainability"; Cornelis Dekker and Roland Baetens, *Geld in het water: Antwerps en Mechels kapitaal in Zuid-Beveland na de stormvloeden in de 16e eeuw* (Hilversum: Verloren, 2010).

50 Van Cruyningen, "Economie," 60; Van Cruyningen, "From Disaster to Sustainability," 251–52, 259.

51 Brusse, *Gevallen stad*, 131–32; Paul Brusse, "Land en water," in *Geschiedenis van Zeeland Dl. III: 1700–1850*, ed. Paul Brusse and Jeannine Dekker (Zwolle: WBOOKS, 2013), 41–46; Piet Van Cruyningen, "Land en water," in *Geschiedenis van Zeeland. Dl. II: 1550–1700*, ed. Paul Brusse and Wijnand Mijnhardt (Zwolle: WBOOKS, 2012), 47–48.

52 Brusse and Mijnhardt, *Towards*, 44; Dekker, *Onderdanig en opstandig*, 46–48; Brusse, "Land," 41–46.

53 Van Cruyningen, "Economie," 133–35.

54 Brusse, *Gevallen stad*, 142.

2.3 *Wages*

The commercialisation of agriculture not only resulted in a division between landholders and tenants but also caused a division between the few large-scale commercial farmers and the large number of wage labourers.[55] Zeeland's labour market was consequently dynamic, with many short-term wage fluctuations.[56] Farmers willingly invested in maintaining soil fertility since the high labour costs involved in pulling out the weeds (for which seasonal labourers were contracted) could be earned back due to persistently high crop yields.[57] Those high labour costs were the consequence of both labour-intensive production and relatively high nominal wages.

Agricultural labourers could earn almost a guilder a day during the summer. This level had already been reached around 1600 and was retained until around 1850. However, day wages have not been researched in much detail. The few available observations confirm the level of a guilder per day. In 1761, a certain Matthijs Gerritsen kept guard over a lighter at the MCC wharf, for which he received 20 *stuivers*, or 1.0 guilder, per day, and half that amount per night. The nature of the activity suggests little schooling.[58] Similarly, dockers on the VOC wharf in Middelburg earned 18 *stuivers*, or 0.9 guilders a day, in 1790. Labourers working for the cooper earned 1.1 guilders.[59] Piecework rates show fluctuations in wage levels, with peaks around 1650 and 1700. Only in the third quarter of the eighteenth century did piecework wages rise above a guilder a day.

Wages in Zeeland appear to have been slightly higher than in Holland. The difference was around 10 per cent throughout the period.[60] Two early-nineteenth-century reports confirm the high wages in Zeeland. The wage level was 25 per cent to 40 per cent higher than in the eastern Netherlands, which made its wages the highest in the country.[61] Like the other parts of the econ-

---

55 Van Steensel, "Economie van het platteland," 275: Like other characteristics in Zeeland's economy, wage labour was already a widespread phenomenon in the late Middle Ages; Priester, *Geschiedenis*, 91.

56 Priester, *Geschiedenis*, 95–110, 668–74.

57 Van Cruyningen, "From Disaster to Sustainability," 243, 253, 255–56, 259–60.

58 ZA, MCC, inv.no. 1445, p. 8, p 12.

59 Enthoven, "'Veel vertier'. De Verenigde Oostindische Compagnie in Zeeland, een economische reus op Walcheren," 124–25.

60 De Vries and Van der Woude, *The First Modern Economy*, 610–11.

61 For an extensive analysis of day wages and conversion of piece rates into day wages, consult the appendix of : Feenstra, "Between Shared"; We focussed here on male summer wages, for the comparability with the other case. Female wages were also high. The estimates for 1818–1819 show that this wage level applied all over Zeeland, save for Zeeuws-Vlaanderen, the former Staats-Vlaanderen, where the wages were lower: 0.6

omy, wages appear to have been relatively high early on, and to have persisted at that level until the end of the eighteenth century, without structural growth.

2.4 *The Capital Market*

Remarkably little is known about Zeeland's capital market, considering its relatively advanced economy and substantial investments in chartered colonial companies. Part of the explanation is the loss of notarial archives for this period.[62] This study uses other archives to provide an impression of the functioning of the capital market in Zeeland. From the admittedly fragmentary evidence, it appears that Zeeland was capital-abundant, consequently enjoyed relatively low costs of capital and was well connected to other capital markets, inside and outside the Dutch Republic.

Zeeland's wealth is evident from a few observations in the eighteenth century. An extraordinary wealth tax (the Liberale Gift or Voluntary Gift) in 1747 yielded 1.7 million guilders of income. A conservative estimate based on the tax rate implies that Zeeland's richest inhabitants must have had assets worth at least 85 million guilders.[63] The amount was substantial, considering the wage rate of about a guilder per day, and the population of fewer than 80,000 people. If divided equally over all residents, each inhabitant would possess more than 1,100 guilders in assets. Within Zeeland, Middelburg, as the capital city, was probably the wealthiest place. In 1760, it had more than 360 individuals with an income of over 1,000 guilders.[64] These figures not only indicate the wealth of the population, but they also provide substance for the argument of the States of Groningen, when Zeeland pleaded for a reduction in its contribution to the Union.

Such an abundant stock of capital would exercise downward pressure on interest rates.[65] The first indication in the development of the price of capital is

---

guilders to 1.3 guilders: Priester, *Geschiedenis*, 96–99, 668, 674, 770; Van Cruyningen, *Behoudend maar buigzaam*, 76. The day wage in Staats-Vlaanderen was estimated at 0.75 guilders in 1713, and persisted at this level until about 1850.

62 The notarial archives prior to 1796 were lost when a fire ravaged the town of Middelburg in 17 May 1940, as a consequence of fighting in the Second World War. Zeeuws Archief, "Notariële Archieven Zeeland 1796–1842, 1796–1842 Okt. 15". Wietse Veenstra suggested that municipal archives in other towns may still have similar archival sources; this remains to be researched.

63 Veenstra, *Gewestelijke financiën: vol. 7. Zeeland*, 74–83, 194: 1.7 million / 2% = 85 million guilders.

64 Brusse, *Gevallen stad*, 64.

65 Dennis O. Flynn, "Big History, Geological Accumulations, Physical Economics, and Wealth," *Asian Review of World Histories* 7, no. 1–2 (January 23, 2019): 80–106, https://doi.org/10.1163/22879811-12340047.

derived from the interest paid on deposits by the Exchange Bank of Middelburg (*Wisselbank*). The more than 200 observations in 1620–1671 show a declining interest rate, from around 6 per cent to 4 per cent.[66] Unfortunately, such data is lacking for the eighteenth century. For the seventeenth century, it seems representative of the overall level of interest rates. Loans issued by the water board polder on the Island of Walcheren had a coupon of 5 per cent around 1650 that declined to 4 per cent by 1657. This was the same as the coupon of the Rijnland water board in Holland.[67] Similarly, a 4 per cent bond issued by the town of Veere, in 1665, matches the deposit interest rates from the *Wisselbank* for that year.[68] The decline in private interest rates continued into the eighteenth century, to 3 per cent. This was the rate on collateralised loans as well as private bonds, in the 1730s and later also for a drainage project in 1774.[69] Investments in land reclamation were part of diversified urban investment portfolios, which also included shipping, trade, shares in the chartered companies, privateering and dwellings.[70] The interest rate at which the MCC borrowed money was also generally at this level, and in the 1720s and 1730s even slightly below it.[71] The accumulated capital resulted in declining interest rates, to around 2 to 3.5 per cent in the eighteenth century (Graph 3.2).

Zeeland's capital market appears to have been well connected to other parts of the Dutch Republic and Britain. The very presence of an Exchange Bank signals the importance of cross-border transactions and their economic and financial sophistication. Again, Zeeland was the only Dutch province to possess such an institution besides Holland.[72] These connections allowed for both direct investments and access to capital markets outside of Zeeland. As a result, it is not always clear where a debt instrument was issued, or which part of a loan was issued within the province. For instance, the Admiralty of Zeeland issued a loan in 1716 in both Amsterdam and Zeeland at an interest rate of 3.5 per cent. Half a million guilders were issued in Zeeland and 100,000 guilders

66 Van Dillen, *Bronnen tot de geschiedenis der wisselbanken*, 1158–1203.

67 Milja Van Tielhof, "After the Flood. Mobilizing Money in Order to Limit Economic Loss (the Netherlands, Sixteenth-Eighteenth Centuries)," *Gestione Dell'acqua in Europa* (*XII–XVIII Secc.*). *Water Management in Europe* (*12th–18th Centuries*), Atti delle "Settimane di Studi" e altri Convegni, 49 (2018): 401.

68 ZA, (Hereafter ZA), Weeskamer Veere, inv.no. 151, unfol. (1665).

69 ZA, Archief van de Familie Schorer, 1547–1983 (1991) (hereafter: Schorer), inv.no. 462.

70 P. J. Van Cruyningen, "Profits and Risks in Drainage Projects in Staats-Vlaanderen, c.1590–1665," *Jaarboek Voor Ecologische Geschiedenis*, 123–142, 2006, 132–37; Van Cruyningen, "From Disaster to Sustainability," 257–58.

71 Paesie, *Geschiedenis van de MCC*, 119.

72 Van Dillen, *Bronnen tot de geschiedenis der wisselbanken.*

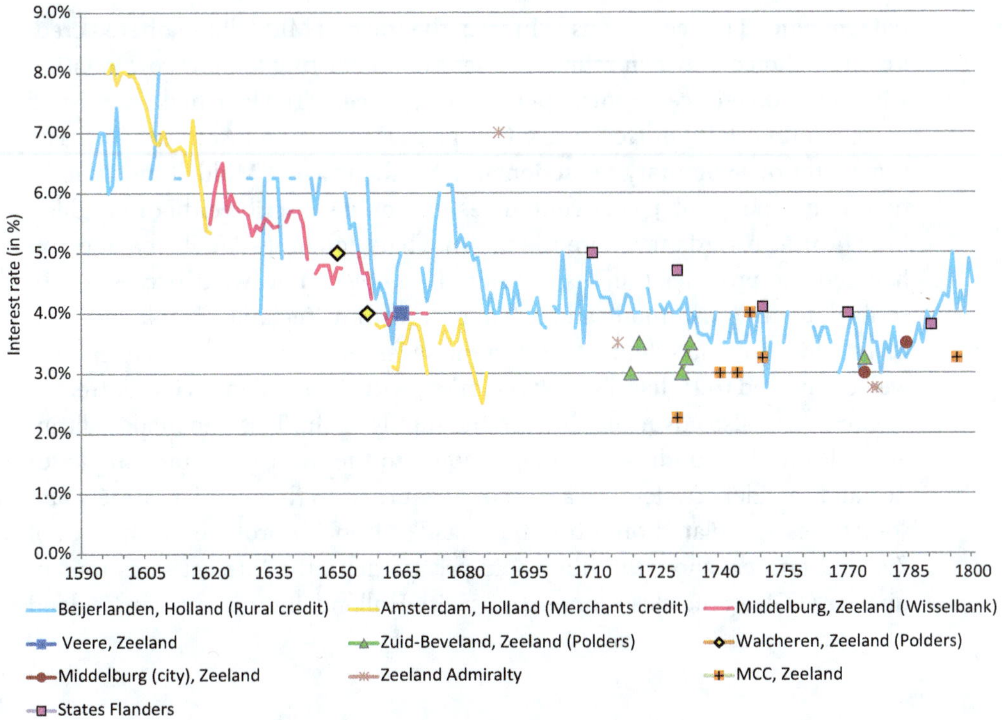

GRAPH 3.2 Private interest rates in Zeeland and Holland, 1590–1795.
SOURCES: ZEELAND: ZA, SCHRORER, INV.NO., INV.NO. 462, 899; Z.A. WEESKAMER VEERE, INV.NO. 151; VAN DILLEN, *BRONNEN TOT DE GESCHIEDENIS DER WISSELBANKEN*, P. 1158–1203; VAN TIELHOF, 'AFTER THE FLOOD' (2018), P. 401; PASIE, *GESCHIEDENIS VAN DE MCC*, P. 119; Z.A., MIDDELBURGSCHE COMMERCIE COMPAGNIE (MCC), INV.NO. 1727.3, P.6; VEENSTRA, 'GELD IS DE ZENUW', P. 108, VEENSTRA EN OTTE, 'FINANCIERING', P. 30, 32, 35; *LEYDSE COURANT*, 18 JULY 1774,; *MIDDELBURGSCHE COURANT*, 27 NOVEMBER 1784; HOLLAND: GELDERBLOM & JONKER (2004), GELDERBLOM, KOOL AND JONKER (2016), BAARS, *BEIJERLANDEN*, P. 118; STATES' FLANDERS (STAATS-VLAANDEREN): VAN CRUYNINGEN, *BEHOUDEND*, P. 300.

in Amsterdam. Remarkably, the interest rate was half a percentage point less than the 4 per cent rate that the Amsterdam Admiralty paid at that time.[73] For other loans, this is not so clear. In 1688, the Zeeland Admiralty borrowed at 7 per cent, and in 1776 and 1777 at 2.75 per cent, money which was used to

73 Wietse Veenstra, "Geld is de zenuw van de oorlog," *Archief: vroegere en latere mededeelingen voornamelijk in betrekking tot Zeeland*, 2008, 103; Wietse Veenstra and Arjan Otte, "Financiering van de oorlogvoering te water. De admiraliteit van Zeeland, 1597–1795," in *Overheidsfinanciën tijdens de Republiek en het Koninkrijk, 1600–1850*, ed. Hendrik Boels (Hilversum: Verloren, 2012), 32.

redeem older 4 per cent loans.[74] In 1774, the town of Middelburg offered creditors the choice between reimbursement of an existing loan or continuation with a coupon reduced from 3.5 per cent to 3 per cent. The loan had been issued via a certain Adolf Jan Heshuys & Comp., in Haarlem and Amsterdam.[75] Ten years after this voluntary reduction, in 1784, the town of Middelburg issued a new loan at a rate of 3.5 per cent. Investors could subscribe either in Middelburg or in Amsterdam, where the intermediary Johannes Menkema and Son handled the provincial affairs.[76] Again, it is not certain what part was subscribed to in Amsterdam and what part within Zeeland. Zeelanders also invested in Holland's debt, at least in the seventeenth century.[77] Zeeland was well connected to Holland's capital market, with Amsterdam as its centre.

Credit was also advanced through the supply chain. This tied madder farmers to Rotterdam traders in Holland, home to the most important staple for Zeeland madder. Traders advanced buyers' credit to the madder farmers and sometimes speculated on future harvests.[78] Although probate inventories of Zeeland farmers show that they held private debt, the interest rates remain unclear.[79] Given the close connections with Holland, interest rates in Zeeland

---

74 Veenstra and Otte, "Financiering," 30, 32, 35: Veenstra suspects that the 7 per cent rate may have included armortisation (kind remark by e-mail, 16 July 2023); Veenstra, "Geld is de zenuw," 108.

75 Advertentie. "Leydse courant". Te Leyden, 18-07-1774, p. 2. Accessed at Delper op 10-04-2023, https://resolver.kb.nl/resolve?urn=ddd:010912647:mpeg21:p002

76 Middelburgsche Courant, 27 November 1784; in Middelburg the cashier Jan van de Kruysse supervised the subscription. For Menkema, see the chapter on Friesland and Alberto Feenstra, 'More than Merchant Bankers: Second-Class Financial Intermediation in Eighteenth-Century Amsterdam', in *Credit Networks in The Preindustrial World: A Social Network Analysis Approach*, ed. Elise M. Dermineur and Matteo Pompermaier (Cham: Palgrave Macmillan / Springer Nature Switzerland, 2025), 145–200, https://doi.org/10.1007/978-3-031-67117-3_6.

77 *Notulen van de Edel Mogende Heeren Staten van Zeelandt; Notulen van de Staten van Zeelandt; Notulen Der Provisionele Repraesentanten van Het Volk van Zeeland; Notulen van de Vertegenwoordigers Des Volks van Zeeland; Notulen van Het Departementaal Bestuur van Zeeland; Notulen van Zeelant*, 1798, 78 (16 August 1679).

78 Cornelis Wiskerke, "De Geschiedenis van Het Meekrapbedrijf in Nederland," *Economisch-Historisch Jaarboek : Bijdragen Tot de Economische Geschiedenis van Nederland* 25 (1951): 74, 78–80.

79 Paul Brusse and Arno Neele, "Zeeuwse boedelinventarissen, 1755–1855. DANS," 2011, http://dx.doi.org/10.17026/dans-zf3-qfp4: The database also lacks interest rates. Whether these were only omitted when the database was set up or whether the sources did not contain the interest rates either is unclear from the database.

were probably connected to and relatively similar to those in Holland: slightly lower than in the adjacent rural region of Beijerlanden, but not as low as merchant credit in Amsterdam.[80]

Zeeland's financial connections with Holland went beyond these direct loans, not least concerning colonial enterprises. In addition to investments in the VOC, the WIC and the MCC, the colonies of Suriname, Berbice and Essequibo-Demerara were considered Zeeland's possessions in the seventeenth century. However Zeeland gradually lost control of these possessions, in part due to pressure from Amsterdam. In 1683 the Society for Suriname, which was part owned by the city of Amsterdam, assumed control of Suriname.[81] In 1720, a coalition of Amsterdam investors and the Zeeland regent Cornelis van Pere founded the Society of Berbice, which took over that territory from the Van Pere family.[82] In 1772, Zeeland lost its monopoly of the trade with Essequibo-Demerara, again under pressure from Amsterdam merchants.[83] Anticipating

80 Baars, *De geschiedenis van de landbouw in de Beijerlanden*: Baars' data largely concern mortgaged loans, with farms or farmland as collateral, even though this is not systematically indicated. In the adjecent region of Staats-Vlaanderen/Zeeuws-Vlaanderen, Van Cruyningen found the presence or absence of collateral made little difference in credit among farmers there. Van Cruyningen, *Behoudend maar buigzaam*; With special thanks to Oscar Gelderblom, Clemens Kool and Joost Jonker, who shared their data with me: Gelderblom, Jonker, and Kool, "Direct Finance"; Gelderblom and Jonker, "Completing a Financial Revolution"; The data that Dehing derived from the Bank of Amsterdam appear to contain some risk premium, since they differ from Gelderblom, Kool and Jonker's figures: Pit Dehing, *Geld in Amsterdam: wisselbank en wisselkoersen, 1650–1725* (Hilversum: Uitgeverij Verloren Amsterdam : Universiteit van Amsterdam, 2012); The same goes for the data series that Flandreau et al presented: Flandreau et al., "Bell Jar."

81 Zijlstra, *Anglo-Dutch Suriname*, 11–13; Van de Voort, *Westindische plantages*, 28–29, 125–26; Murk Van der Bijl, *Idee en interest: voorgeschiedenis, verloop en achtergronden van de politieke twisten in Zeeland en vooral in Middelburg tussen 1702 en 1715*, Historische studies 42 (Groningen: Wolters-Noordhoff/Bouma's Boekhuis, 1981), 216–17; Karwan Fatah-Black, *Sociëteit van Suriname 1683–1795: het bestuur van de kolonie in de achttiende eeuw* (Zutphen: WalburgPers, 2019), 14–25.

82 Van de Voort, *Westindische plantages*, 28–29: The Van Pere family had possessed this since 1627 and ruled it as a hereditary fief of the WIC since 1678. J.P. Van de Voort, "Dutch Capital in the West Indies during the Eighteenth Century," *Acta Historiae Neerlandicae : Studies on the History of the Netherlands* 14 (1981): 87: Investment in Berbice took off after 1732, when the States General opened the trade with the colony to individuals not related to the WIC.

83 Stadholder William V granted, by way of compromise, Zeeland's WIC Chamber the right to equip the first sixteen ships to sail to Essequibo each year. Neele, *De ontdekking van het Zeeuwse platteland*, 103: This decision was presumably part of the negotiations about a reduction in Zeeland's provincial contribution to the Union budgets, which will be discussed below. Brusse, "Economie," 98–100.

this event, Middelburg merchants raised 300,000 guilders within three weeks to establish the Society of Essequibo, to trade with Guyana.[84] Zeeland gradually lost its grip on colonies in South America, under pressure from and in favour of Amsterdam.

In the years before the lifting of Zeeland's monopoly, Middelburg investors had invested 3.4 million guilders in plantations in Essequibo-Demerara. That amount exceeded the combined investments in the VOC and WIC and was part of a boom in West Indies plantation loans that began in the 1760s and lasted until the financial crisis of 1773.[85] During the boom, Holland invested fifteen times as much as Zeeland, but for Essequibo-Demerara only one-and-a-half times as much as Middelburg.[86] Per capita, investments were fairly similar: 213 guilders per capita in Amsterdam and 201 in Middelburg.[87] Part of the capital in West Indies plantation loans registered in Middelburg was provided by investors in Holland and Utrecht. These payments would be made by the bankers Abraham and Simeon Boas in The Hague and the notaries Willem and Dirk Wernard van Vloten in Utrecht.[88] Also, by investing in the existing chartered companies, Holland investors gained more shares and influence at the expense of Zeeland, particularly in the Zeeland VOC chamber. Around 1700, less than half of the Zeeland VOC shares were held by people from Zeeland.[89] Hence, Zeeland investors remained rich and active, yet were overtaken over time by Amsterdam, both financially and politically, with regard to colonial investments.

In addition to these colonial investments, providers of more sophisticated financial products found investors in both provinces. The Middelburg regent Meynard van Visvliet invested in a mutual fund established in The Hague in 1772. The participants would receive 3 per cent of their investment by way of

84 Van de Voort, *Westindische plantages*, 132–33; Brusse, *Gevallen stad*, 72; Brusse, "Economie," 98–100.

85 Van de Voort, *Westindische plantages*, 100–105; The total capital invested in West Indies loans between 1766 and 1775 amounted to 57,845,657 guilders.

86 Although 3.4 million was still a considerable amount – considering the unskilled urban day wage of 0.9 guilders.

87 Brusse, *Gevallen stad*; Lourens and Lucassen, *Inwoneraantallen*.

88 *Middelburgsche Courant*, 13 November 1770, These notaries appear to have been involved in all kinds of financial transactions in Utrecht, including the auctions of public securities: Het Utrechts Archief (HUA), Notarissen Utrecht, inv.nos. U169a012 (akte 108), in 1748, U242a003 (akte 31), U247a002 (akte 145 & 150), U204a007 (akte 87), U188a023 (akte 136) in 1763.

89 Van der Bijl, *Idee en interest*, 206–8, 211, 213, 216, 218–20.

dividends and be reimbursed according to a complex lottery scheme.[90] A financial derivate, called 'society of survival' (*contract van overleving*) was set up in Vlissingen in 1776 and advertised in various towns in both Holland and Zeeland; this was a private tontine loan: a mutual fund based on life annuities.[91] The initial instalment had to be made in the form of an ordinary Zeeland bond with a value of 600 guilders, which implies that Holland residents possessed Zeeland bonds or at least were able to acquire these without much difficulty.[92]

Similarly, three advertisements in the *Middelburgsche Courant* newspaper of 18 August 1772 sought to attract capital from Zeeland. First, the banking house of Clifford and Sons announced a lottery draw in Amsterdam for Danish debt. Second, a Middelburg inhabitant had, when fleeing the town, taken life annuities with him that he had invested in Danish plantation loans, issued by the soon-to-be-bankrupt Amsterdam firm of Abraham ter Borgh. Third, a society of survival announced the availability of its prospectus in forty-one towns all over the Dutch Republic. Investors could participate with a minimum investment of ten guilders, which allowed less well-to-do people to participate too.[93]

Finally, other advertisements in the *Middelburgsche Courant* suggest that investments outside the Republic's territory had some significance as well. For instance, in 1772, the newspaper reported that the Austrian Empress – Maria Theresia – had issued a 4 per cent loan in Brussels, with a total value of

---

90 ZA, Schorer, inv.no. 613. Visvliet signed this contract as "a former pensionary of the town of Middelburg".

91 For a more detailed analysis of these societies of survival as predecessors of mutual funds, see: K. Geert Rouwenhorst, "The Origins of Mutual Funds," in *The Origins of Value: The Financial Innovations That Created Modern Capital Markets*, ed. William N. Goetzmann and K. Geert Rouwenhorst (Oxford etc.: Oxford University Press, 2005), 250–53; Herman Wagenvoort, *Tontines: een onderzoek naar de geschiedenis van de lijfrenten bij wijze van tontine en de contracten van overleving in de Republiek der Verenigde Nederlanden* (Utrecht, 1961).

92 Middelburgsche Courant, 27 June 1776, in Zeeland: Vlissingen, Middelburg, Zierikzee and Goes, in Holland: Amsterdam, Leiden, Rotterdam, Dordrecht, The Hague and Delft.

93 Middelburgsche Courant, 18 August 1772, The towns were: Amsterdam (H), Alkmaar (H), Arnhem (Gld), Bolsward (Fr.), Breda (Staats-Brabant), Kampen (O), Delft (H), Deventer (O), Dockum (Fr.), Dordrecht (H), Enkhuizen (H), Franeker (Fr.), Gorinchem (H), Gouda (H), Groningen (Gr), Haarlem (H), Den Haag (H), Harderwijk (Gld), Harlingen (Fr.), 's Hertogenbosch (Staats-Brabant), Hoorn (H), Leeuwarden (Fr.), Leiden (H), Meppel (D), Middelburg (Z), Naarden (H), Nijmegen (Gld), Purmerend (H), Rotterdam (H), Schiedam (H), Steenwijk (O), Utrecht (U), Vlissingen (Z), Weesp (H), Zaandam (H), Zierikzee (Z), Zutphen (Gld) and Zwolle (O); (D) is Drenthe, (Fr) is Friesland, (Gld) is Gelderland, (Gr) is Groningen, (H) is Holland, (O) is Overijssel (U) is Utrecht and (Z) is Zeeland.

3 million guilders.[94] Also, the London prices of English public and semi-public securities appear regularly in the *Middelburgsche Courant* as well, for example consols, Bank of England shares, East India Company and South Sea Company shares, as well as exchange rates.[95] The regular quotations of exchange rates and British funds are evidence of their relative importance to investors from Zeeland.

Capital was widely available in Zeeland and could be easily supplemented by imports, while the province exported capital too. This adds substance to the argument of sceptical provinces about Zeeland's claims of impoverishment after 1750. The large capital stock pushed coupon rates down to around 2 to 3.5 per cent from around 1720. Despite the availability of capital and considerable investments in the Caribbean colonies, Amsterdam investors gradually side-lined Zeeland investors, as they were even richer and they outnumbered the Zeelanders.

Zeeland's economy can be characterised as advanced, stable and rich. Wages were high, and the province was very urbanised and commercialised – even the rural economy. Zeeland's development was one of relative decline relative to Holland, to borrow a concept.[96] Zeeland's economy, therefore, appears to have formed a stable basis for taxation, yet without further growth after the early seventeenth century.

3 Public Finance

Zeeland's fiscal resources were important in sustaining the early stages of the Revolt. To raise the necessary sums, Zeeland introduced indirect taxes on daily necessities in 1574. The tax revenues from these indirect excise duties grew along with the expanding economy.[97] Nevertheless, the provincial government sold part of its former royal domains to cover its deficits, following

94 *Middelburgsche Courant*, 21 April 1772.

95 *Middelburgsche Courant*, *passim*, 1758–1800, e.g. 10 May, 7 & 24 June, 3 July, 8 August, 21 November 1758, 29 May 1759, 19 June, 4 September, 23 October, 1 & 27 November, 13 December 1759, 21 February 1761, 5 March 1763 (including the size of Britain's public debt and the amount of interest paid), 14 August 1784, 21 July 1785. The Zeeland regent Daniël Rademacher also possessed securities that predominantly consisted of English securities, as mentioned above, in around 1770 (Source: Courtesy of Gerhard de Kok by email).

96 De Vries, *Economische achteruitgang*, 177.

97 Fritschy, *Public Finance*, 23, 103–12, 142; Veenstra, *Gewestelijke financiën: vol. 7. Zeeland*, 15–16.

Holland's example, in this period.[98] The introduction of these 'common means' ended the relative under-taxation of the urban economy.[99] There was a tenfold increase in tax revenue from less than 100,000 guilders in the 1570s to over 1.2 million guilders in 1600. Hence, like Holland, Zeeland underwent a 'tax revolution' that increased the tax burden to well above that in other European states.[100]

Despite the importance of Zeeland's financial support, the other provinces accepted several decreases in its contribution to the shared expenses. In 1574, Zeeland's contribution was 29 per cent that of Holland's. This gradually decreased to 15.8 per cent of Holland's in 1616, or 9.1 per cent of the total.[101] Fritschy argues that this reflected Zeeland's decline and was not an attempt at free riding.[102] Afterwards, Zeeland's population declined relative to Holland's from one-eighth of Holland's population in 1616 to one-tenth in 1660. Yet the States of Zeeland did not request a reduction in its quota until after 1750. This suggests that until the mid-eighteenth century, Zeeland managed to maintain healthy public finances with its tax income.

To analyse how Zeeland's income and expenses developed, this section first examines the government budget balances to identify the timing and nature of any deficits. Secondly, expenditure will be scrutinised to explore the causes of the deficits. Thirdly, changes in the composition of tax revenues provide insight into attempts to remedy financial deficits. Together, this indicates why and when Zeeland had to resort to the capital market to fill the financial gaps and for what amounts.

3.1 *Government Budget Balances*

During the first three-quarters of the seventeenth century, Zeeland's income and expenditure remained largely balanced. The three naval wars with Britain (1652–1654, 1665–1667 and 1672–1674) caused temporary deficits, from which

98 Tracy, "Emigré," 255–66; Veenstra, *Gewestelijke financiën: vol. 7. Zeeland*; Fritschy, *Public Finance*, 130; 't Hart, *The Making of a Bourgeois State*, 80.

99 Veenstra, *Gewestelijke financiën: vol. 7. Zeeland*, 18–19. Around the same date the States of Holland approved these taxes there.

100 Fritschy, *Public Finance*, 23, 110, 112, 141, 373; Fritschy, "Financial Revolution"; Luciano Pezzolo, "Sovereign Debts, Political Structure, and Institutional Commitments in Italy, 1350–1700," in *Questioning Credible Commitment: Perspectives on the Rise of Financial Capitalism*, ed. D'Maris Coffman, Adrian Leonard, and Larry Neal, Macroeconomic Policy Making (Cambridge: Cambridge University Press, 2013), 180; Liesker, "Tot zinkens toe," 158–60.

101 Fritschy, *Public Finance*, 105, 109.

102 Fritschy, 112.

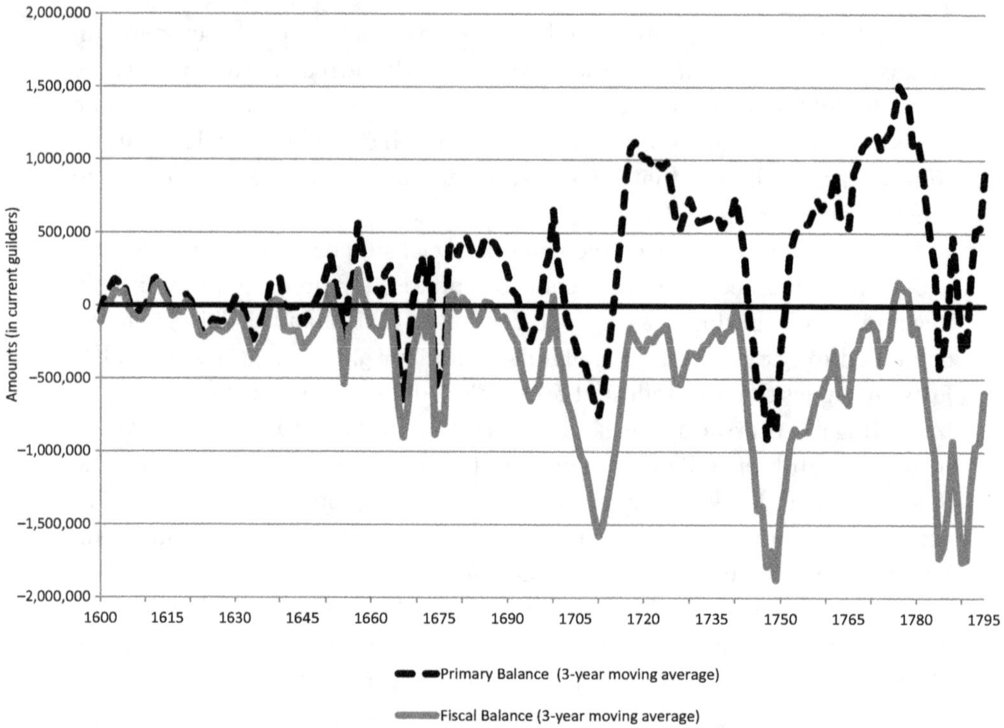

GRAPH 3.3 Primary and fiscal balances in Zeeland, 1600–1795.
SOURCES: VEENSTRA, *GEWESTELIJK FINANCIËN, VOL. 7: ZEELAND*; CORRECTIONS FOR TAX ON BONDS, AS IN THE TEXT.

Zeeland recovered quickly. After the last of the three wars, the fiscal expenditure was equal to tax revenue and the primary budget showed a surplus of around 0.5 million guilders. The latter amount included an estimated 100,000 guilders from a withholding tax on bonds, levied since 1673. This was recorded as revenue, not as a reduction in the interest payments – although that was the effect in practice.[103] However, after 1688, Zeeland's primary surplus was hardly ever sufficient to cover the interest payments, resulting in almost constant fiscal deficits (Graph 3.3).[104] Nevertheless, Zeeland achieved a balanced fiscal

103 Fritschy, 156–58; Veenstra, *Gewestelijke financiën: vol. 7. Zeeland*, 188–89. Calculated by applying the tax rate to the debt estimates in this chapter.

104 The records for the early period (1574–1598) are very fragmented. Therefore, the analysis starts in 1600. Veenstra, *Gewestelijke financiën: vol. 7. Zeeland*, 59–60. From the total income and expenses I subtracted the income and expenses related to Zeeland's rule, on behalf of the States General, of Staats-Vlaanderen. Only the losses or surpluses after the closing of the accounts were cleared. This was less than 3 per cent of the income and expenses.

budget on three occasions (1700, 1749, 1777–1780). This implies that the province was able to recover, albeit with difficulty.

Fiscal deficits imply that the States of Zeeland required additional loans to cover the interest payments. The reduction in the fiscal deficits in the long run also implies that the province was able to either reduce the burden of debt or increase the tax income accordingly. On the first occasion, in 1700, the fiscal budget was balanced shortly after the Nine Years' War (1688–1697). Zeeland took a long time to recover from the War of the Spanish Succession (1702–1713) however. Just when Zeeland had achieved a balanced fiscal budget, the War of the Austrian Succession (1740–1748) nullified the effects of this careful policy. Again, it was a long time before the finances recovered – not until the late 1770s. Then another war (the Fourth Anglo-Dutch War, 1780–1784) plunged the budget into deficit again. This time, Zeeland's public finances did not recover. The recurring fiscal deficits imply that Zeeland was constantly having to borrow throughout the eighteenth century.

The question is how Zeeland balanced its income and expenditure in the long run to eliminate the deficit. The purpose of the rest of this section is to explain how and why the fiscal deficit was reduced and to look at the differences between the periods before and after the War of the Austrian Succession. The simultaneous decline of the primary surplus and fiscal deficit between 1715 and 1740 is particularly interesting.

3.2 *Expenses*

Zeeland's expenditure rose over the course of the seventeenth and eighteenth centuries from around 1 million guilders to 3 million guilders per year. In the final decade, it peaked at almost 6 million. These extraordinary peaks mainly consisted of subsidies to the near-bankrupt VOC in Zeeland.[105] The structural increase in total expenses stemmed from the rise in interest payments. The Peace of Utrecht (1713) was the turning point in the make-up of the expenditure. Up to that point, war expenditure was the largest expense; after that it was interest payments.

The interest payments were for loans issued to cover deficits resulting from warfare, as reflected in government budgets. Warfare constituted three-quarters of Zeeland's primary expenses and over 90 per cent of Zeeland's Gen-

105 "Gewestelijke Financiën Ten Tijde van de Republiek Der Verenigde Nederlanden 1572–1795 (Web)," ING Project, March 4, 2015, http://resources.huygens.knaw.nl/gewestelijkefinancien post 0028.

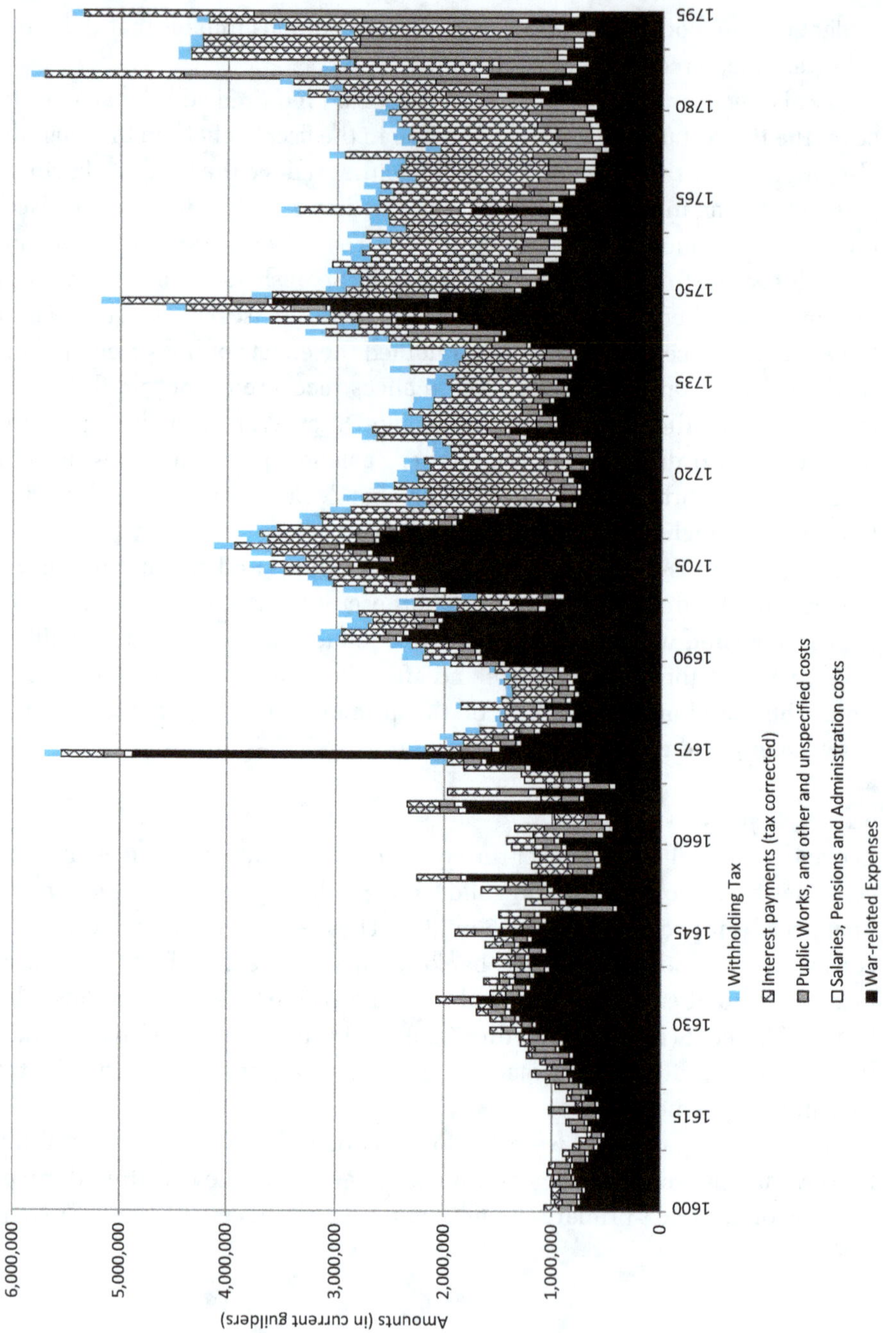

GRAPH 3.4 The composition of Zeeland's expenditure, 1600–1795
SOURCE: VEENSTRA, *GEESTELIJKE FINANCIËN, VOL. 7: ZEELAND*, P. 204–207, 250–257.

erality contributions.[106] This meant the States of Zeeland had only limited control over its main primary expense since foreign policy was the States General's responsibility.

The war-related expenses were relatively constant over the entire period, at an average of around 1.1 million guilders per year. Warfare was more frequent (in terms of the number of years at war) in the seventeenth century and more expensive in the eighteenth century. During the war years, Zeeland spent 1.3 million guilders a year in the seventeenth century and 1.9 million in the eighteenth century. War-related costs in peacetime remained relatively constant over the entire period at approximately 800,000 guilders annually. As a result, Zeeland spent around 1 million guilders per year in the seventeenth century, and 1.2 million in the eighteenth century.

The Republic's neutrality in the Seven Years' War helped to curb these expenses.[107] Zeeland spent less than 800,000 guilders per year after 1750. This was almost half the 1.5 million guilders spent during the first half of the eighteenth century, and less than the 900,000 guilders per year in the first half of the seventeenth century and 1.2 million in the second half.[108]

While war-related expenses decreased after a war ended and remained stable in the long term, interest payments increased almost continuously. Around 1600, the amount was almost negligible. During the Twelve Years' Truce (1609–1621) the annual amount even decreased from 50,000 guilders to around 22,000 guilders in 1616. But in the course of the seventeenth century, the trend was upwards. By the end of the Eighty Years' War, interest payments had risen to 200,000 guilders and they reached 0.5 million in 1690. The War of the Spanish Succession almost tripled that amount to 1.4 million guilders. Then a period of falling payments followed, until 1740. After the War of the Austrian Succession, the interest paid increased beyond the level of 1715. Thereafter the amount fluctuated, but increasing more than decreasing until 1795.

The falling interest payments between 1715 and 1740 did not result from the withholding tax on the bonds. The amount withheld as tax remained constant until the 1750s. That is not to say that the tax had no effect. Without this tax, the fiscal deficits would have been almost 200,000 guilders bigger, throughout the period. Yet the effect was a constant lowering of the interest paid. This was because the withholding tax was only levied on bonds issued before 1694. Later debt issues were as a rule exempt from the tax. Zeeland honoured this

106 't Hart, *The Dutch Wars of Independence*, 154–55; Veenstra, *Gewestelijke financiën: vol. 7. Zeeland*, 203–48.

107 Aalbers, *De Republiek*.

108 Veenstra, *Gewestelijke financiën: vol. 7. Zeeland*, 204–7.

commitment made in promises of tax exemption.[109] The temporary decrease in interest payments stemmed entirely from cheaper borrowing, as will be detailed below.

3.3 *Income*

The question is how the States of Zeeland covered its rising expenses, and ultimately, whether the reduction in its contribution in 1792 was justified. This part of the section analyses the taxes levied by the States of Zeeland: how much, what and when. Even after its tax revolution in the late sixteenth century, Zeeland continued to increase its public revenue, from approximately 1 million guilders in 1600 to 2.5 million guilders in the 1790s. Despite the substantial increase, the revenue proved insufficient to cover the 3 million guilders in expenses at the end of the 18th century (see Graph 3.5).

Zeeland's tax income can be divided into four categories. First, indirect taxes, or the common means, were levied on daily necessities and were thus dependent on the level of economic activity. Second, direct taxes on real estate burdened the proprietors of houses and land, including owners of windmills and orchards. Third, wealth taxes were levied on various financial transactions and visible expressions of wealth, such as domestic servants, carriages and coaches. This tax category also encompassed an inheritance tax, tax on the sale of movable and immovable property, and the withholding tax on bonds and other public financial assets. Graph 3.5 shows the tax on bonds separately because it was recorded as income, yet it functioned as an interest rate reduction. Finally, the miscellaneous taxes consisted, as the name suggests, of a wide array of smaller taxes, often with irregular revenue streams.[110]

Tax revenues followed expenditure. Until 1750, public revenue fluctuated between periods of war and peace. The States of Zeeland increased taxes to meet the demands of warfare, and revenues fell in peacetime: during the Twelve Years' Truce, after the end of the Eighty Years' War in 1648, after the Franco-Dutch War (1672–1678) and after the War of the Spanish Succession. But after the War of the Austrian Succession taxes did not fall, which was a clear break from the past.

The composition and size of the tax revenues in 1672 foreshadowed Zeeland's income structure from 1688 until the end of the Dutch Republic. The

109 Later issues always referred to the conditions of the 1694 loan issue, until 1704, as the ones that applied; *Notulen van Zeeland*, 1697; 120–21, 126–27; 1698: 80–83; 1701: 163–64; 1702: 346–347; ZA, Verzameling Verheye van Citters, inv.no. 125b: "sonder eenige kortinge, en vry van alle lasten, Schattingen en ongelden".

110 Veenstra, *Gewestelijke financiën: vol. 7. Zeeland*, 74–202.

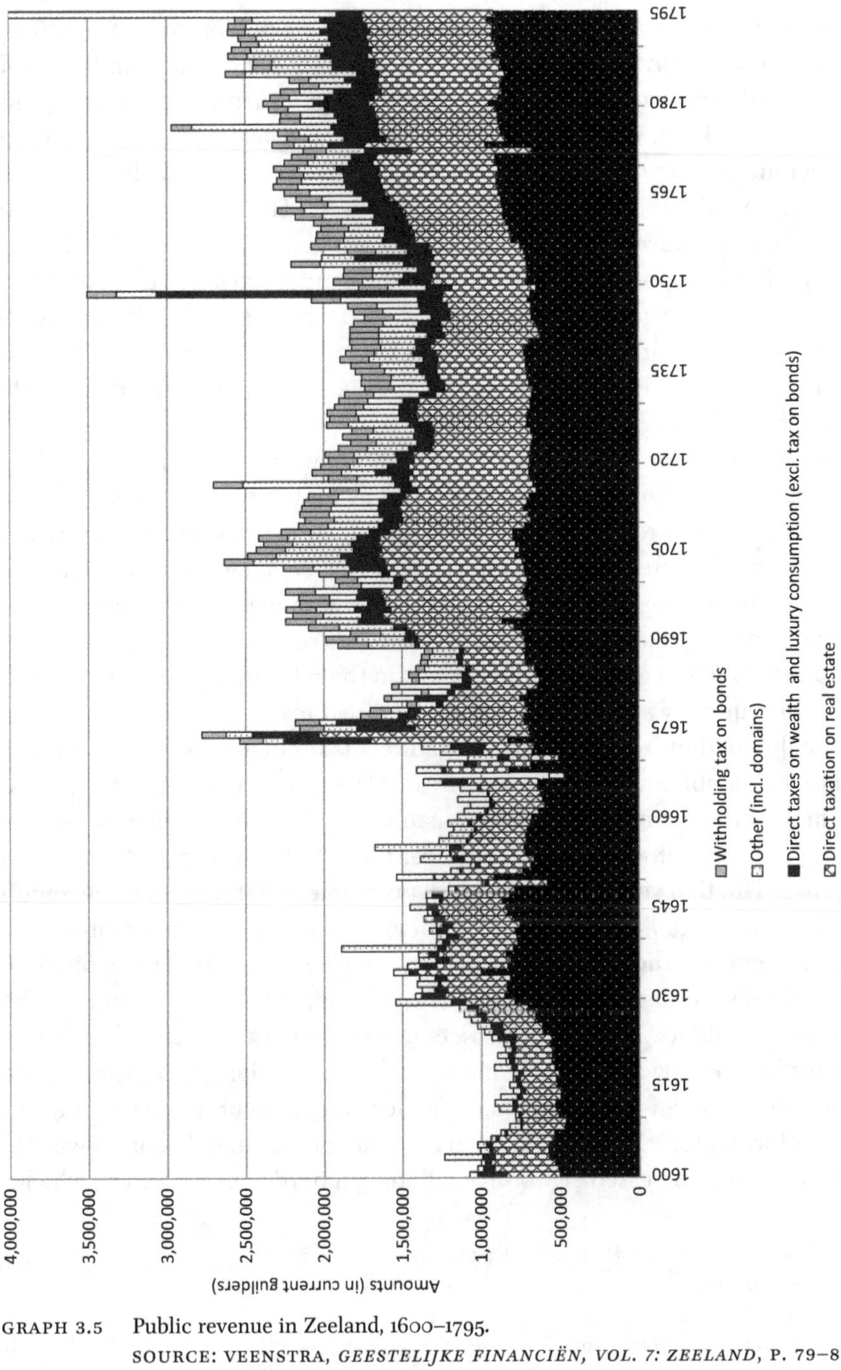

GRAPH 3.5 Public revenue in Zeeland, 1600–1795.
SOURCE: VEENSTRA, *GEESTELIJKE FINANCIËN, VOL. 7: ZEELAND*, P. 79–83.

States of Zeeland almost tripled its income, from 1 million in 1671 to almost 3 million guilders in 1674. Until then, income rarely surpassed 1.5 million guilders, even during wartime. The Franco-Dutch War also formed a turning point in the composition. The common means had so far yielded the lion's share of the income, about 65 per cent. The increase in revenue during this war largely resulted from direct taxes on wealth and property. The new taxes in common means and increased tax rates yielded around 100,000 guilders of extra income. More importantly, the States of Zeeland started to structurally tax public securities: shares in the VOC and WIC, the provincial debt, and the *Bank van Lening* (urban pawn shop, similar to mounts of piety).[111] After the war, the States of Zeeland temporarily abolished several taxes and reduced the tax rates of others.[112]

After 1688, direct taxes became Zeeland's main source of income and the preferred option was to increase taxes. To pay for the Nine Years' War (1688–1697), the Zeeland regents reintroduced several abolished taxes or increased existing ones.[113] After 1688, the direct taxes yielded some 1.3 million guilders per year. Meanwhile, the income from the common means remained stable at around 750,000 guilders. Only after 1750 did this revenue category increase to just under 1 million guilders. Adjustments in the relaxation of the tax incomes were consequently also to be found in the direct taxes.

The fluctuations in the income from direct taxes depended on the political will to tax inhabitants. This is most obvious from the tax on real estate, where the moderate decline in land prices cannot explain the decline in revenue during the first half of the eighteenth century.[114] The year 1747 stands out in this regard. In that year, a special wealth tax was levied throughout the Republic: the '*Liberale Gift*' or Voluntary Gift of 1747. Zeeland was under direct military threat due to the French capture of the fortified town of Bergen op Zoom on Zeeland's border with Brabant. The Voluntary Gift in Zeeland yielded 1.7 million guilders. Inhabitants' assets were taxed at the rates of 2 per cent for those possessing assets worth more than 2,000 guilders, 1 per cent for those possessing between 1,000 and 2,000 guilders, and a voluntary percentage for the less fortunate.[115] The 1.7 million in revenue implies that Zeeland's wealthiest inhabitants possessed eighty-five million guilders' worth of assets, which is

111 Veenstra, 68–69, 74–83, 102–17, 133, 181–97.

112 Veenstra, 65.

113 Veenstra, 65.

114 Priester, *Geschiedenis*, 654–66: Over the period 1715–1740, land prices declined by 8 per cent, revenues from real estate by 21 per cent; the difference is even larger when taking 1696 as the start and 1744 as the end.

115 Veenstra, *Gewestelijke financiën: vol. 7. Zeeland*, 194, 74–83.

more than forty times Zeeland's annual provincial budget.[116] Hence, assets formed an attractive object of taxation, but this required the elites to tax themselves.

Regarding taxes on assets, the tax on public securities is a special case. The part that concerned the VOC, the WIC and the *Bank van Lening* was a real tax. The other part, levied on Zeeland's provincial public debt, was in practice an interest rate reduction affecting the province's interest payments. The total income from wealth taxes averaged around 0.5 million guilders from 1688. Around one-third of that amount stemmed from the interest rate reduction. The rest was actual public revenue. After 1760, the share of the family tax, a poll tax per household, within the wealth taxes increased, whereas the income from the withholding tax on bonds declined.[117] The latter effect was due to the redemption of old 4 per cent bonds issued until 1674; this tax on bonds only applied to the first 96 bond issues since 1603. If the tax had been applied to all bonds, the revenues would have increased throughout the eighteenth century and the total revenues from the tax on public securities would have been higher (Table 3.1). Why the States of Zeeland reimbursed this low-cost part of the debt remains puzzling. Meanwhile, the withholding tax rate remained almost constantly at 2 per cent, save for six years, and was not changed at all after 1727.[118]

3.3.1 Tax Burden

Without economic and demographic growth, every tax increase would have implied an increasing tax burden for Zeeland's inhabitants. To test the States of Groningen's allegation that Zeeland undertaxed its population, the tax burden is compared to that in Holland, which was regarded as the most heavily taxed place of its time.[119] The analysis also considers the distribution of the tax burden over the population, again relative to Holland.

The tax pressure on ordinary people may explain why the States of Zeeland opted to increase direct taxes from the late seventeenth century onwards. The common means pressed relatively hard on the ordinary urban populace. A

116 1.7 million / 2% = 85 million guilders. The alternative was 1.7 / 1% = 170 million guilders.

117 The poll tax, the family tax (Dutch: *familiegeld*), which some of the literature deems very important, appears less so compared to the withholding tax. Brusse, *Gevallen stad*, 106–11; Veenstra, *Gewestelijke financiën: vol. 7. Zeeland*, 192–94; Remarkably, the revision of this tax in 1758 did not include adjustments of the tax rates, only of the classes, which increased from 19 in 1742 to 28 in 1758.

118 Veenstra, *Gewestelijke financiën: vol. 7. Zeeland*, 189.

119 Fritschy, "Overheidsfinanciën"; Fritschy, "Taxation," 65, 701988; Fritschy, *De patriotten*, 66–67; Fritschy, "Financial Revolution."

TABLE 3.1 Debt, interest and tax for the first 96 bond issues.

	4%-debt of 1st 96 issues	Interest	Tax rate	Total tax yield from public securities	Estimated tax yield from the 4% bonds	Estimated tax yield *if* applied to all bonds
1668	10,270,119	410.805	[none]	–		–
1675	10,190,489	407.620	1.50%	455,358	152,857	163.319
1682	9,996,538	399.862	0.45%	133,050	44,984	52.295
1703	9,344,801	373.792	2.00%	385,716	186,896	261.157
1709	9,343,601	373.744	2.00%	355,878	186,872	406.817
1710	9,343,601	373.744	2.00%	356,748	186,872	436.952
1713	9,343,601	373.744	2.00%	346,446	186,872	495.098
1716	9,343,601	373.744	2.00%	339,126	186,872	512.544
1722	9,295,823	371.833	2.00%	332,022	185,916	502.124
1727	9,293,423	371.737	2.00%	338,964	185,868	513.097
1730	9,293,423	371.737	2.00%	336,258	185,868	521.028
1733	9,293,423	371.737	2.00%	336,546	185,868	487.727
1737	9,293,423	371.737	2.00%	334,656	185,868	481.556
1744	9,293,423	371.737	2.00%	339,882	185,868	512.921
1745	9,293,423	371.737	2.00%	335,202	185,868	535.514
1746	9,293,423	371.737	2.00%	343,830	185,868	555.232
1747	9,293,423	371.737	2.00%	344,136	185,868	585.607
1748	9,293,423	371.737	2.00%	334,674	185,868	609.614
1751	9,293,422	371.737	2.00%	339,342	185,868	694.415
1760	8,759,194	350.368	2.00%	321,030	175,184	823.439
1779	6,248,685	255.416	2.00%	271,752	124,974	835.575
1780	6,248,685	242.393	2.00%	262,698	124,974	878.160
1781	6,248,685	249.947	2.00%	266,274	124,974	862.932
1782	6,248,685	249.947	2.00%	251,610	124,974	861.980
1785	6,248,685	249.947	2.00%	145,356	124,974	887.439
1793	5,699,090	237.392	2.00%	235,044	113,982	1.056.181
1795	5,517,427	220.697	2.00%	146,556	110,349	1.058.515
1797	5,478,987	219.874				

SOURCES: DEBT AND INTEREST: ZA, RKC, INV.NOS. 4510, 4580, 4630, 4840, 4900, 4910, 4940, 4970, 5030, 5080, 5110, 5140, 5180, 5250, 5260, 5270, 5280, 5290, 5340, 5520, 5850, 5860, 5910, 5970, 5990, 6010, TAX YIELD FROM PUBLIC SECURITIES: *GEWESTELIJKE FINANCIËN*, ONLINE DATABASE.

relatively large share of their income was taxed because indirect taxes were included in the prices of daily necessities. An increase in the public revenue from excises would consequently have increased the burden on the common people.

The high tax burden also fuelled social unrest. Discontent about the persistence of high taxes after the Peace of Münster in 1648 was one reason for the riots and factional struggle in Middelburg in 1651. The grain tax was reduced and another faction gained power.[120] A high tax burden was also dangerous for the ruling factions during the Wars of the Spanish and Austrian Succession. Following the death of Stadholder-King William III in 1702, revolutionary leaders in Middelburg and Goes explicitly blamed the Orangist factions for excessive taxation. The citizenry called for the reform of the city council and public finance. The towns of Vlissingen, Middelburg, Goes and Tholen admitted new regents to the city councils. After 1710, the old faction reconciled itself with the newcomers by drawing up 'contracts of correspondence' that divided offices among the regents' families.[121] The taxes, however, were not reduced. But the regents understood that further increases in the common means would only add to the unrest.

In 1748, new protests arose against the levying of the common means (*pachtersoproer*), while the political tables had turned in favour of the Orangist factions.[122] The protests led to the decision to end the practice of tax farming and use collection by state officials instead. Although gross income increased, the question remains whether this was more efficient, since the collection costs also increased.[123] Whereas indirect tax incomes had reached a social ceiling by the early eighteenth century, the pressure from direct taxes on the richer inhabitants hit a tax ceiling after 1750. Laurens van der Spiegel, the future Grand Pensionary of Zeeland, argued in 1772 that new taxes would completely ruin the province's public finances and accelerate Zeeland's depopulation due to the migration of wealthy families to Holland.[124]

Contemporaries' perception of the high tax burden was real enough. Until 1700, the tax burden in Zeeland was as high as in Holland. Like in Holland, Zeeland's per capita tax burden was already the equivalent of twelve days'

---

120 't Hart, "Autonoom," 55–56.

121 Dekker, "Politieke verhoudingen," 169–72.

122 Veenstra, *Gewestelijke financiën: vol. 7. Zeeland*, 29; Dekker, "Politieke verhoudingen," 181.

123 Veenstra, *Gewestelijke financiën: vol. 7. Zeeland*, 29–31; De Vries and Van der Woude, *The First Modern Economy*, 123–24; Israel, *The Dutch Republic*, 1072–74; Dormans, *Het tekort*, 98–99 This implies that tax farming had been relatively efficient.

124 Neele, *De ontdekking van het Zeeuwse platteland*, 102–3.

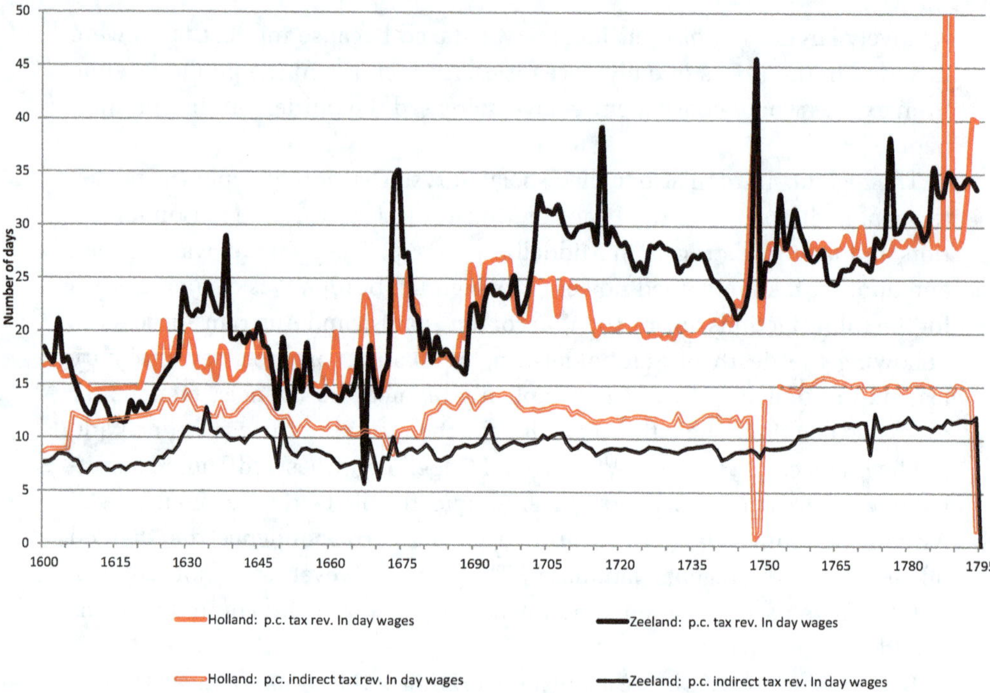

GRAPH 3.6 Tax burden expressed in day wages, in Holland and Zeeland, 1600–1795.
SOURCES: SEE TEXT AND FEENSTRA, *BETWEEN SHARED*, APPENDIX.

wages before 1600, a level that other European states only reached by the end of the eighteenth century.[125] After 1750, the total tax burden developed similarly to that in Holland: hovering between 25–30 days' wages until 1780 and increasing to 35 days' in 1780–1795. On top of that, Dutch wage levels were comparatively high internationally – and even slightly higher in Zeeland than in Holland. Both provinces extracted large amounts in taxes from their respective populations, and Zeeland often more than Holland.[126] The biggest difference between Holland and Zeeland was in the first half of the eighteenth century, when the tax burden in Zeeland exceeded Holland's. Zeeland subsequently experienced a gradual decrease in direct taxes, which caused reconvergence between the two provinces in the 1740s. Hence, the tax burden in Zeeland was at least as high as in Holland and sometimes even higher (graph 3.6).

125 Drelichman and Voth, *Lending to the Borrower from Hell*, 28; 't Hart, "Gewetenloze kapitalisten," 435–36.

126 De Vries and Van der Woude, *Nederland 1500–1815*, 707, 742; Allen, "The High Wage Economy and the Industrial Revolution."

However, the provinces differed in the composition of the tax burden. In Holland, the common means continued to form the backbone of taxation, much more so than in Zeeland. The divergence started around 1680 and was the result of Holland's limited economic growth from that point.[127] On the other hand, Zeeland's inability to increase tax income from the common means suggests it had exhausted the fiscal capacity of its economy and had little alternative than to turn to the taxation of property instead. Consequently, Zeeland's elites taxed themselves relatively heavily compared to the rest of the population and compared to Holland's elites.

Until the War of the Austrian Succession, the Zeeland elite accepted high wealth taxes for three reasons. Firstly, income from the common means had reached its social limits by 1700. Further increases would be difficult or even dangerous for the position of the elite. Secondly, wealth taxes were the lesser evil compared to a default on the public debt, since most of the debt was issued domestically in Zeeland, implying that a large proportion of that debt was held by that same elite. Thirdly, the economic slack meant lucrative investment opportunities were scarce while capital was relatively abundant and cheap. This allowed the States of Zeeland to borrow cheaply. Hence, the Zeeland elites were committed to the interests of the state, but only if there was light at the end of the tunnel. The departure of wealthier inhabitants illustrates that this was no longer the case after 1750, and their loyalty had its limits.

3.3.2 The Quest for a Reduction Zeeland's Contribution to the Union's Budget

In 1766, the States of Zeeland began lobbying for a reduction in their share of the Republic's common expenses.[128] First, they petitioned the new Stadholder, Prince William v of Orange, arguing that Zeeland could not pay its contribution.[129] Meanwhile, the States of Zeeland also hoped that the Generality would provide financial solace in two other cases: Zeeland's high expenditure during the War of the Austrian Succession and the right to tax marshes

127 Van Zanden and Van Leeuwen, "Persistent but Not Consistent."

128 NA, Provinciale Resoluties, inv.no. 309; This file consists of approximately 550 pages of resolutions, reports and other correspondence between the States General, the Stadholder, the States of Zeeland, other provincial States, and the town councils of Zeeland i.e. the constituent members of the States of Zeeland.

129 NA, Provinciale Resoluties, inv.no. 309; letter from the States of Zeeland to Stadholder William v, 31 December 1766.

and a polder (Dutch: *IJzendijkse schorren*) in the Scheldt estuary.[130] Zeeland argued that overspending in the war was the cause of the current financial trouble.

In its appeal to the solidarity of the other provinces, the States of Zeeland emphasised that the overspending was beneficial to all since it had been to protect all the Republic's territories.[131] The States claimed that the war had two related consequences: firstly, Zeeland had to bear war expenses out of proportion to its allotted share; secondly, this had led to an intolerable debt burden. The States of Zeeland also warned that if the province could no longer support itself, the Generality's debtholders and the army would go unpaid and the province would be useless to the Republic.[132] If the other provinces were susceptible to their argument, the knife would cut both ways: reducing the immediate costs of warfare and limiting the growth of the debt in any subsequent war.

Most other provinces remained unconvinced of the precariousness of Zeeland's financial situation.[133] The States of Utrecht argued that its inhabitants bore a heavier tax burden than those in Zeeland, while the States of Groningen

130 Dekker, "Politieke verhoudingen," 181–82; Neele, *De ontdekking van het Zeeuwse platteland*, 104.

131 NA, Provinciale resoluties, inv.no. 309, "Missive aan Zynde Doorluchtige Hoogheid, den Heere Prince van Orange etc., houdende een ampel naauwkeurig verslag der tegenwoordige situatie van 's Lands financiën", 31 December 1766: "De source van Ons ongeluk is niet ver te zoeken; de Troubles na den dood van Keizer Karel den VI onststaan, de daar uit volgende Invasie der Fransche Troepes in staatsch Vlaanderen en Braband, en de hulp ter bescherming door deze Provincie, toen de Frontieren van de Republicq aan die zyde zynde, aan de Bondgenooten, ver boven vermogen toegebracht, heeft alles trapsgewyze de Provincie van Zeeland in die calamiteit gebracht, waar in dezelve zig thans bevind!".

132 NA, Provinciale resoluties, inv.no. 309; letter form the States of Zeeland to Stadholder William V, 31 December 1766: "*Wy schrikken zo van de gevolgen, dat nogthans zekerlyk te wagten, zoo men deze Provincie, die nu 26 Jaaren tegens alle wederwaardigheden aan, zonder hulp gelaten is, nog verder voor zich zelv' zou willen laten zorgen: wanneer het Provinciaal Comptoir tot die engte gebragt wordt, dat het gesloten zal moeten gehouden worden: wanneer de verschuldigde Furnissementen ten Comptoire van de Unie niet meer zullen kunnen opgebragt worden, en ook dat Comptoir gesloten zal moeten blyven: wanneer Weduwen en Weezen die ter goeder trouwe hare Gelden aan de Provincie opgeschoten hebben, onbetaald zullen moeten gelaten worden: wanneer de Militie al mede onbetaald zal moeten blyven en Zeeland, die de eerste gronden van de Unie heeft helpen leggen, geäbandonneerd, ten eenemale nutteloos voor het Bondgenootschap zal zyn*!"

133 NA, Provinciale resoluties, inv.no. 309, provincial responses in late 1767 to a report by the Council of State and Stadholder.

doubted Zeeland's claims of impoverishment.[134] The States of Zeeland refuted the allegations of being insincere or unwilling to bear its fair share.[135]

The States of Zeeland opened its account books to show the allegations were false. However unusual this move given provincial fiscal autonomy, the States of Zeeland had nothing to hide and stood to gain nothing from the customary secrecy in public finance. The financial deterioration was real enough.[136] The States of Zeeland had the numbers right. It accurately estimated a deficit of approximately 500,000 guilders in 1765.[137] Zeeland was also able to show it was paying seventy times as much in interest as in 1616: 1.5 million guilders compared with 22,000 guilders.[138] A report of 1767 confirmed that Zeeland had not undertaxed its population since the tax rates were similar to Holland's.[139]

As a result, Zeeland received a temporary reduction of 200,000 guilders.[140] The States of Overijssel reluctantly submitted to the proposal but added that two years would be more than enough to reform Zeeland's finances.[141] The

134 NA, Provinciale resoluties, inv.no. 309, "Advis van Utrecht", 25 November1767. "... *dat de ingezetene dezer Provincie ongelyk zwaarder belast zyn, dan de ingezetene van Zeeland...*"; "Advis van Stad en Lande", 23 December 1767. "Dat boven dien overwegende de Rykdom der ingezetenen van Zeeland, in tegenoverstelling van die in deze provincie, alsmede de aanzienelijke scheepvaart en koophandel ..."

135 NA, Provinciale resoluties, inv.no. 309, "Instructie, waar naar de Heeren Gedeputeerden gaande naar Den Haag, zig zullen moeten reguleren.", November/December 1768: "Dat dit genoeg zou zyn om H: H: Mog: te overtuigen dat 'er geene redenen voor handen zyn, voor de beschuldigingen H: Ed: Mog: by deze Missive te laste gelegd, dat de zaak H: Ed: Mog: niet genoeg op het hart zoude wegen, en dat de redenen en motiven by het Rapport en Advis van Zyne Hoogdheid en den Raad van Staten vermeld, hun effect by H: Ed: Mog: niet hadden verkregen; waar by H: Ed: Mog: gelieven te voegen, te verwagten, dat by H: Ed: Mog: zig op eenen geheel anderen voet zullen gedragen, en niet langer willen dralen ook dadelyke en doorslaande preuves te geven, waardoor de Bondgenoten mogen zien en verzekerd zyn, dat H: Ed: Mog: niets begeren te verzuimen, wat in Zeeland tot eigen behoud behoord gedan en in 't werk gesteld te worden."

136 The opposite was true for Friesland, as we will see in the next chapter.

137 NA, Provinciale Resoluties, inv.no. 309; letter form the States of Zeeland to Stadholder William V, 31 December 1766.

138 Veenstra, *Gewestelijke financiën: vol. 7. Zeeland*, 250–57: The estimate is accurate for both instances.

139 NA, Provinciale resoluties, inv.no. 309, "Advis van Utrecht", 18 November 1767.

140 NA, Provinciale resoluties, inv.no. 309, "Missive", 30 December 1767.

141 NA, Provinciale resoluties, inv.no. 309, "Advis van Overyssel", 17 November 1767: "...*en zulks alleen, voor den tyd van twee Jaren, in die hoop en billyke verwagting, dat hooggemelde Heeren Staten met eenen ongeïnterrumpeerden iever handen aan het werk zullen slaan, om hunne Financiën in beteren staat, en daar aan het voldoende redres toe te brengen door het arresteren van daar toe bekwame Middelen, ten einde, zoo wel H: Ed.*

States of Zeeland disagreed and continued to strive for a permanent reduction because the existing distribution would only increase its debt.[142] Moreover, it argued that equality between provinces in the burden they bore had been the leading organising principle since the Union of Utrecht of 1579.[143]

The final report by a Generality committee, in 1769, endorsed Zeeland's argument that one of the leading principles of the Union was now being violated: the common expenses were no longer divided equally across the provinces. It added that in 1616 the distribution had been set provisionally and the constituent members should be accommodated if so required by the financial situation. The Generality committee sought to persuade the States General in late 1769 to accept their proposals to accommodate Zeeland financially.[144] Nothing changed.

Apparently, no one wanted to pay for Zeeland's relief; after all, rearranging the shares in the common budget was a zero-sum game. Therefore, in 1771, the States General again turned to the Stadholder, to act as a mediator. He proposed that Zeeland should receive the sum of 300,000 guilders from the

---

Mog: hinnen Heeren Principalen, als de andere provinciën hoop mogen scheppen, dat derzelver instantiën in dezen meerder vrugt mogen zyn, als in vele andere gelegenheden, tot hier toe, hebben moeten ondervinden."

142 NA, Provinciale resoluties, inv.no. 309, Extract uit het Register der Resolutiën van de Hoog Moogende Heeren Staten Generaal der Vereenigde Nederlanden: zynde het Rapport van Hoogstderzelver Gedeputeerden met Heeren Gedeputeerden wegens de Provincie Zeeland, over het Werk harer Financien hebbende gebesogneerd. Relatif tot het Rapport door laatstgemdel Heeren ter Tafel van H: E: Mog: de Heeren Staten dier Provincie deswegens uitgebragt, den 4 December 1769. p. 28; 3 november 1769: "… met geenen schyn van redelykheid van haar zoude kunnen vergen, of verwagten om in nieuwe extraodinaris Petitien, hoe nuttig, hoe noodzakelyk ook, op den ouden gedisproportioneerden voet, consent te dragen, veel min tot de dadelyke praestatie van dezelve consenten zig in nieuwe schulden te wikkelen!"

143 NA, Provinciale resoluties, inv.no. 309, "Extract uit het Register der Resolutiën van de Hoog Moogende Heeren Staten Generaal der Vereenigde Nederlanden: zynde het Rapport van Hoogstderzelver Gedeputeerden met Heeren Gedeputeerden wegens de Provincie Zeeland, over het Werk harer Financien hebbende gebesogneerd. Relatif tot het Rapport door laatstgemelde Heeren ter Tafel van H: E: Mog: de Heeren Staten dier Provincie deswegens uitgebragt, den 4 December 1769". p. 7, 15–17, 25–28; 3 november 1769.

144 NA, Provinciale resoluties, inv.no. 309, "Extract uit het Register der Resolutiën van de Hoog Moogende Heeren Staten Generaal der Vereenigde Nederlanden: zynde het Rapport van Hoogstderzelver Gedeputeerden met Heeren Gedeputeerden wegens de Provincie Zeeland, over het Werk harer Financien hebbende gebesogneerd. Relatif tot het Rapport door laatstgemelde Heeren ter Tafel van H: E: Mog: de Heeren Staten dier Provincie deswegens uitgebragt, den 4 December 1769". p. 7, 15–17, 25–28; 3 november 1769.

Union's income from 1772 to 1778.[145] The term of the arrangement would be prolonged to 1785 if Zeeland's financial situation had not improved.[146]

The Stadholder also mediated in the other two disputes between the States General and the States of Zeeland. Firstly, the matter of overspending during the War of the Austrian Succession remained unsolved as a separate issue.[147] Secondly, the right to tax the *IJzendijkse schorren* in the Scheldt estuary was settled by assigning 60 per cent to Zeeland and 40 per cent to the Generality.[148] The effect was minimal.

Only in 1792 was a structural solution found. Zeeland received a reduction of almost 60 per cent in its contribution, from a quota of 9.1 per cent to 4 per cent. The other provinces were finally convinced of Zeeland's relative decline.[149] A survey held in 1789 formed the basis for this decision. The survey compared the provincial tax surpluses after the deduction of the provincial expenses. Zeeland's residual amount was small since it paid so much interest. In this new distribution, Holland's share increased to 64.9 per cent, sixteen times as much as Zeeland's share.[150] This ratio is similar to that in the investment in plantation loans in the 1770s. For 1790, Fritschy compared the provincial fiscal surpluses. This shows that Zeeland's share amounted to 4.4 per cent of all provincial fiscal surpluses. Furthermore, a comparison of tax income in 1807 shows that Zeeland contributed more than 6 per cent to the total income.[151] By then the central government was levying taxes on an equal footing throughout the country. Table 3.2 provides an overview of all the provincial shares to put the 1792 revision of the contributions to the Union in per-

---

145 This amount was more or less equal to the amount in primary provincial expenses at that time and exactly equal to the amount of capital the *Societeyt ter Navigatie op Essequebo en annexe Rivieren* could raise in 1771.

146 NA, Gedeputeerde Haarlem, inv.no. 1272.

147 NA, Gedeputeerde Haarlem, inv.no. 1273: "… omtrent het Generaliteits Rapport van den 5 Juny (July(?)) te vooren (1777), op het eerste poinct hunner geproponeerde grieven met betrekking op het eerste tot de overbetaalingen, door hun in de troubles, met de vreede van Aaken in 1748 geëindigd, gedaan, als meede van sekere onvervankelyken consideratien van hunnentweegen in Mey 1775 ontworpen, op de in Maart te voorin het Generaliteits Besogne overlegde Reflexien, betrekkelyk hunne Pro Memoria van 1774, ten ende als breeder daar by vervat is, en hier na volgt geinsereert".

148 NA, Gedeputeerde Haarlem, inv.no. 1273; Dekker, "Politieke verhoudingen," 181–82; Neele, *De ontdekking van het Zeeuwse platteland*, 104.

149 Fritschy, "Schulden als leerschool?," 22; Dormans, *Het tekort*, 160–61 from 9.2% to 3.8%.

150 Dormans, *Het tekort*, 161.

151 Pfeil, *"Tot redding,"* 553.

TABLE 3.2 1792 revision of the quota of in context.

Description	Fixed share	Tax income residue for the Union (in % of the total)	Fiscal surplus (in % of the total)	Fixed share (incl. Generality)	Fixed share (excl. Generality)	Tax income, under the new taxation scheme
Year / Province	1616	1789	±1790	1792	1792	1807
Gelderland	5.6%	7.7%	10.4%	6.0%	6.3%	5.6%
Holland	57.8%	60.4%	47.1%	62.1%	64.9%	62.8%
Zeeland	9.2%	3.8%	4.4%	3.8%	4.0%	6.2%
Utrecht	5.8%	5.4%	7.8%	4.5%	4.7%	7.6%
Friesland	11.5%	12.1%	15.0%	9.4%	9.8%	11.2%
Overijssel	3.6%	3.7%	5.0%	3.5%	3.7%	1.1%
Groningen	5.7%	6.9%	9.1%	5.4%	5.6%	5.5%
Drenthe	1.0%		1.1%	1.0%	1.0%	
Generality				4.4%		
Total	100.0%	100.0%	100.0%	100.0%	100.0%	100.0%

SOURCES: FRITSCHY, *PATRIOTTEN*, 159; PFEIL, '*TOT REDDING*', 553; DORMANS, *HET TEKORT*, 161.

spective. It shows that the 1616 share for Zeeland was too large a burden by the end of the eighteenth century, and probably was from the start. Friesland is the odd one out. Its financial situation improved as measured by all the parameters, but its contribution decreased. Zeeland's complaints, however, proved justified. The zero-sum game and requests for unanimity resulted in institutional sclerosis, delaying necessary changes.[152]

Until 1740, the States of Zeeland balanced income and expenditure in two ways. Firstly, tax increases covered the rising expenses for most of the seventeenth century. Secondly, it was able to constantly reduce the interest payments and consequently the fiscal deficit in 1715–1740. After 1750, The States

152 Olson, *Rise and Decline of Nations*; Vries, "Does Wealth Entirely Depend on Inclusive Institutions and Pluralist Politics?," 90.

of Zeeland understood a more structural solution was required to maintain fiscal health.

During the seventeenth century, warfare formed Zeeland's most important category of expenditure. Until the War of the Spanish Succession, Zeeland was able to achieve a balanced budget as soon as peace was restored. But this war had been so costly that from that point on, interest payments formed Zeeland's main expense item. Reducing the costs of the debt, therefore, formed an important strategy to balance income and expenditure. Moreover, the States of Zeeland had only a shared say in matters of war and peace, while it remained autonomous concerning its own debt and interest payments.

Besides reducing expenses, Zeeland also increased tax income even further. Revenue increases could only be achieved by increasing direct taxes. Increasing income from indirect taxes was difficult as they were related to economic activity; Zeeland's economy had stopped growing and therefore so had the indirect tax income. The high tax burden made additional tax increases in excises problematic after 1690 because they could spark off riots. The direct taxes doubled Zeeland's income, meaning that its elite taxed itself intensively. The elite appeared financially committed to the public state, which offers support to Prak Van Zanden's claims about citizenship morale.

That commitment was not unlimited. When the fiscal deficits gradually decreased, the income from direct taxes declined too. This suggests that the States aligned income and expenditure and that the elites provided just enough support to prevent bankruptcy. That point of view was rejected after 1750. The huge fiscal deficits that resulted from the War of the Austrian Succession showed the Zeeland elites that fiscal sobriety would not restore the health of Zeeland's public finances as long as Zeeland remained obliged to pay its relatively large contribution to the Generality. Any new war would nullify efforts and result in new and larger debts.

Zeeland's difficulties in covering the debts were not the result of undertaxing the population. Rather, even after Zeeland's late sixteenth-century tax revolution, tax levels continued to increase. On various occasions, taxation in Zeeland exceeded Holland's. Neither had it attempted free riding on the back of Holland's financial strength. This is also what the various Generality committees and the Stadholder found. The prolonged opposition of the other provinces worsened the situation. To avoid a default, Zeeland could only increase its debt, since the constant deficits had brought the province to the verge of bankruptcy.

4 Public Debt Management

Fritschy argues that Zeeland's 'tax revolution' was not followed by a 'real financial revolution' between 1600 and 1609, as in Holland.[153] Debt service, as the States of Zeeland emphasised itself, had assumed vast proportions by the eighteenth century. The question is whether or when and how Zeeland experienced a 'real' financial revolution. To answer that question, this section analyses Zeeland's public debt development and the decision-making process behind it. It focuses on three main aspects: a shift from short-term to long-term debt, a substantial increase in the size of the public debt and decreasing interest rates.

4.1 *Zeeland's Debt Development*

In Zeeland, the transition from short-term to long-term debt appears to have taken place precisely in the first decade of the seventeenth century. Zeeland numbered all loans it issued from 1603 onwards. Although Zeeland paid interest before 1603, these pre-1603 loans were not numbered, nor do they show in later overviews of the debt. Some of the earlier loans were forced.[154] The loans issued since 1603 remained on the books until the end of the eighteenth century.[155] Hence, Zeeland established long-term debt in this period.

Zeeland's debt grew almost constantly over the entire period. The increase began gradually up to the end of the Eighty Years' War, to approximately 4 million guilders.[156] The three consecutive naval wars with Britain pushed the debt up further. In 1670, just before the Franco-Dutch War and the Third Anglo-Dutch War, Zeeland's debt had doubled to around 8 million guilders. The growth continued to almost 12 million guilders in 1682 and 13 million at the start of the War of the Spanish Succession. This war nearly doubled Zeeland's debt, to over 25 million guilders in 1716. In the period up to the War of the Austrian Succession, the size of the debt remained largely stable at around 25 million guilders. The War of the Austrian Succession caused a steep rise that continued until the end of the 1750s. By 1760 the debt amounted to over 41 million guilders, equal to about 535 guilders per capita. The Fourth Anglo-Dutch War led to the final increase in the debt. In the 1780s, the debt grew to

153 Fritschy, *Public Finance*, 23, 110, 112, 141, 373; Fritschy, "Financial Revolution."

154 Fritschy, *Public Finance*, 110.

155 ZA, Archief van de Rekenkamer C (hereafter: RkC), inv.no. 5850, f 5 (Account book 1779).

156 Veenstra, *Gewestelijke financiën: vol. 7. Zeeland*, 62, 202.

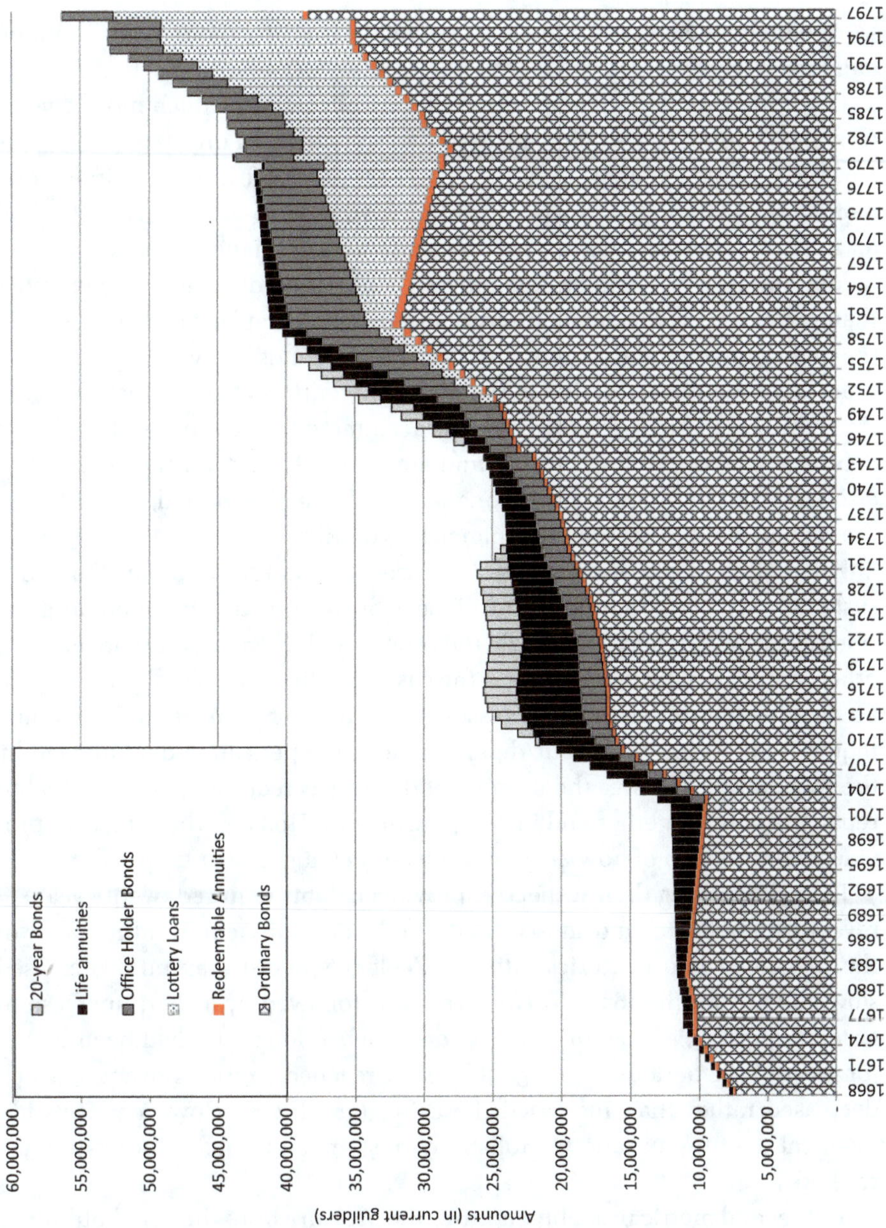

GRAPH 3.7 Zeeland's public debt size and composition, 1668–1797.

SOURCES: ZA, RKC, INV.NOS. 4510,4580, 4590, 4600, 4630, 4840, 4900, 4910, 4940, 4970, 5030, 5080, 5110, 5140, 5180, 5250, 5260, 5270, 5280, 5290, 5340, 5520, 5850, 5860, 5870, 5880, 5910, 5970, 5990, 5990, 6000, 6010.

50 million guilders. It was almost 53 million in 1795 and more than 56 million guilders in 1797.[157]

Over this period, the composition of the debt became much more diverse (graph 3.7). In 1668, the debt consisted almost entirely of ordinary bonds, plus 2 per cent in redeemable annuities and 4 per cent in life annuities. In the first half of the century, the province experimented with 20-year loans, which had an implicit amortisation. Around the same time, Zeeland introduced office-holder bonds, which gained some importance yet hardly ever made up more than 10 per cent of the debt. Lottery loans eventually replaced life annuities as the main supplementary instrument to ordinary bonds. They gained in importance after their introduction in the mid-eighteenth century, especially in the 1770s. By the end of the century, bonds accounted for two-thirds of Zeeland's debt, and the lottery loans for around a quarter of the debt. Hence, Zeeland also substantially increased its long-term debt in this period, which fulfils the second condition for a real financial revolution.

Zeeland's almost constant debt increases raise questions about the debt's sustainability. The common metric of the debt-to-GDP ratio undoubtedly deteriorated since the debt grew while the economy slackened. Alternatively, two other metrics can be used to assess the sustainability of Zeeland's public debt. Firstly, the debt-to-tax ratio expresses the number of years of public revenue required to redeem the public debt. Secondly, the per capita debt divided by the wage level expresses the number of day wages required per individual to repay the debt. Together and in comparison with Holland, these metrics provide an impression of how Zeeland's solvency changed over time.

In 1795, repaying their respective provincial debts required twenty years of revenue for both Holland and Zeeland. Yet the development over the course of the preceding two centuries differed. Zeeland's debt-to-tax ratio increased slowly to 5 from the 1650s to 1700. This was followed by a sharp increase to around 13 in 1715 and 20 in 1750. Holland's debt-to-tax ratio had been higher for most of the period up to 1750. In 1715, it reached a ratio of over 20, which decreased rather than increased thereafter (graph 3.8). However, Zeeland's identical debt-to-tax ratio to Holland corresponded to higher per capita tax revenues.

The second metric probably captures the pressure from the debt better. The two provinces show similar developments, with gradual increases until the 1690s, followed by large increases due to the Nine Years' War and the War of the Spanish Succession. In Zeeland, the number of days required per person amounted to over 370 days by the end of the latter war: more than a full year of

157 ZA, RkC, inv.nos. 5990, 6000, 6010.

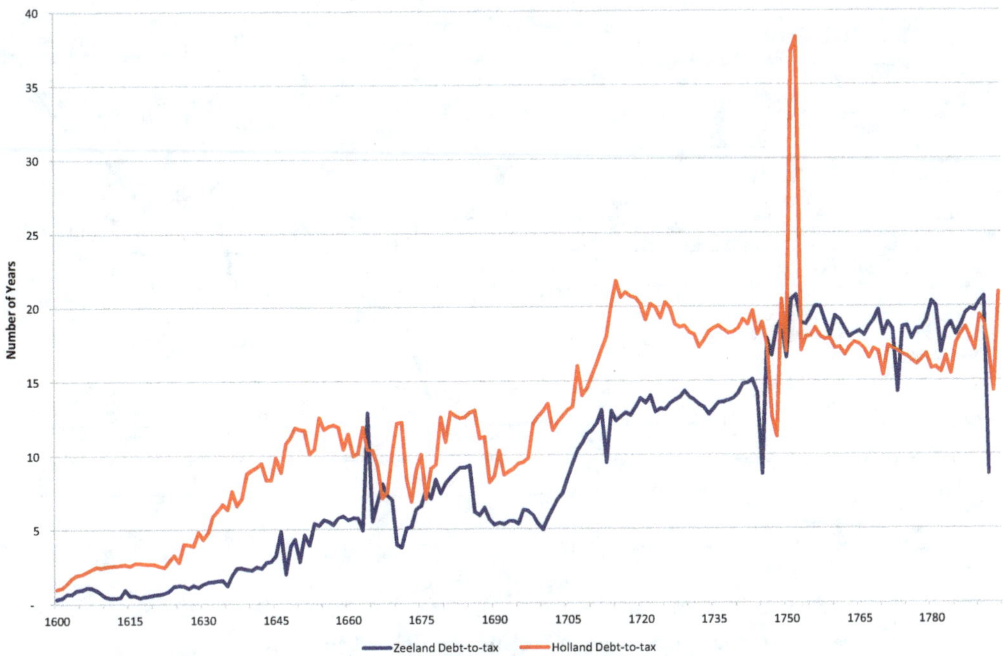

GRAPH 3.8 Debt to tax ratios in Zeeland and Holland, 1600–1795.
SOURCES: GRAPH 2.6; GRAPH 3.5; GRAPH 3.7.

labour. For Holland, this was even more, up to 400 days. Following the War of the Austrian Succession, Zeeland's debt equalled 600 days, whereas this figure in Holland amounted to 500 days. In Holland, the metric subsequently increased only marginally until 1795. Zeeland's debt-to-wage ratio increased to 680 day wages per person. Its debt burden exceeded Holland's already high debt, even after correction for the relatively high incomes.

4.2 *Issuance and Redemption Frequency*

Borrowing remained a relatively modest source of income for Zeeland until around 1700. On average the States of Zeeland borrowed 195,000 guilders annually between 1650 and 1700.[158] After the War of the Spanish Succession, two

158 Veenstra, *Gewestelijke financiën: vol. 7. Zeeland*, 202 Up until 1649, the various Tax Receivers General issued loans on their private account to supplement deficits for the province. These are not recorded in the source publication of Gewestelijk financiën. Therefore, the analysis starts in 1650, when the loans issued by the Receivers formally became part of the public administration.

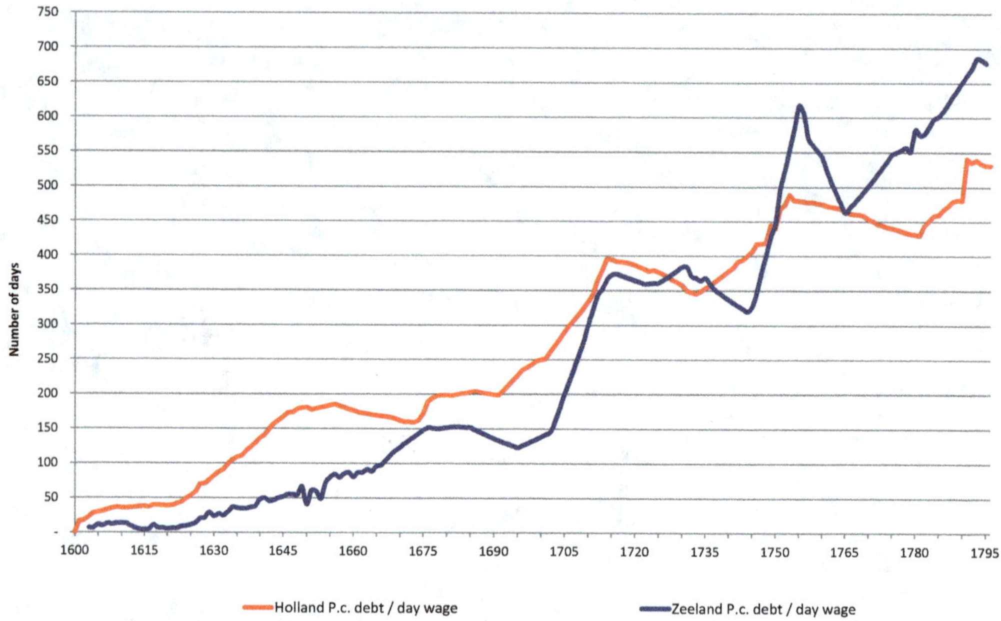

GRAPH 3.9 Debt per capita in day wages in Zeeland and Holland, 1600–1795.
SOURCES: SEE TEXT AND FEENSTRA, *BETWEEN SHARED*, APPENDIX.

things changed. Firstly, the direct relationship between borrowing and warfare disappeared. Secondly, the magnitude of the loans increased to almost 900,000 guilders per year between 1700 and 1795. Out of a total of 94.2 million in 1650–1795, Zeeland issued 84.2 million guilders in the eighteenth century.[159] Zeeland did thus not withdraw from the capital market after 1713, as De Vries and Van der Woude suspected.[160]

Borrowing became a structural part of Zeeland's fiscal policy. Previously, Zeeland borrowed during wartime and paid off debt during peacetime. After 1715, Zeeland issued debt in all but five years, even though it was involved in only three more wars with a total duration of fifteen years (graph 3.10).[161]

159 Veenstra, 74–83, 250–57.

160 De Vries and Van der Woude, *The First Modern Economy*, 121: De Vries and Vand er Woude's claim that "Zeeland the other major borrower was no longer able to borrow on a large scale" after 1713 can in no way be linked to the archival evidence presented here.

161 The War of the Austrian Succession, the Fourth Anglo-Dutch War and the French Revolutionary War (1792–1795).

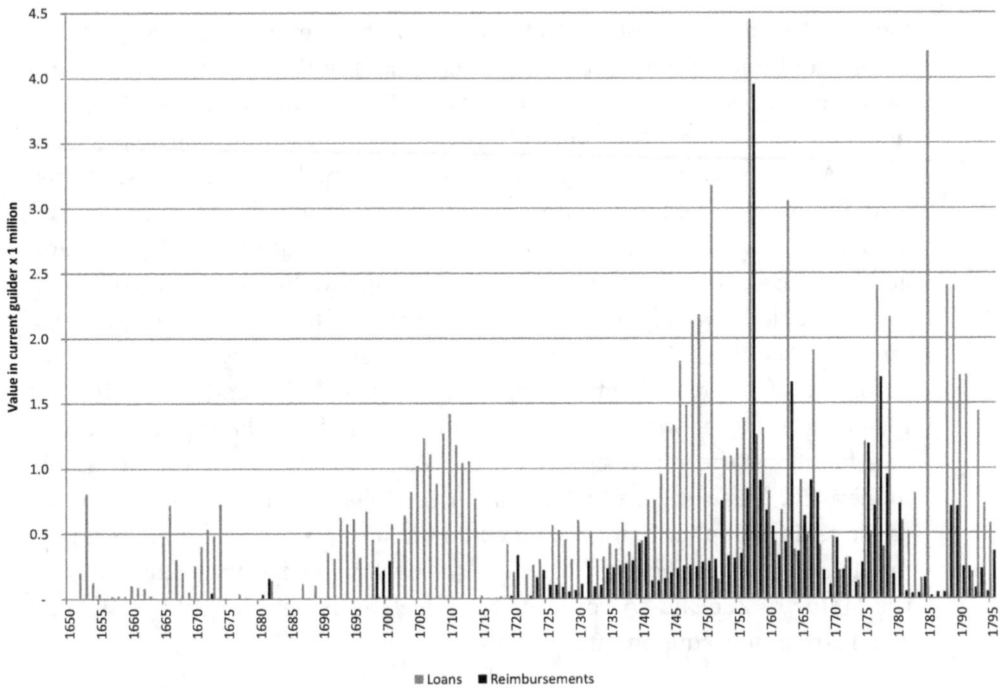

GRAPH 3.10 Zeeland public debt issues and repayments, 1650–1795.
SOURCE: VEENSTRA, *GEWESTELIJKE FINANCIËN. VOL. 7: ZEELAND*, 74–83, 250–257.

Moreover, Zeeland repaid debt each year without exception after 1719, with redemptions totalling 30 million guilders. The constant conversion operations were aimed at lowering the interest burden.

The interest payments and reimbursements created a self-sustaining demand for new loans. The money in the hands of investors increased, while economic stagnation reduced alternative commercial investment opportunities. Creditors could thus reinvest surplus money in the debt, at decreasing coupon rates.[162] This self-sustained debt financing was similar to Holland's situation.

Graph 3.11 displays the cumulative results to depict long-term trends for three scenarios. An upward slope implies that the States of Zeeland required additional financing and a downward slope indicates Zeeland's savings pool

162 The method and the reinvestment rates are copied from De Vries' and Van der Woude's analysis for Holland: De Vries and Van der Woude, *The First Modern Economy*, 120–21. Additional finance requirement = (borrowing – reimbursements) – (reinvestment rate x net interest payments). I also corrected for the withholding tax on the old 4 per cent bonds.

increased. I explore investors' preferences at reinvestment rates of 25 per cent, 40 per cent and 50 per cent. In each scenario, the Wars of the Spanish and Austrian Succession and the Fourth Anglo-Dutch War increased Zeeland's financing requirements beyond the reinvestment rates for several consecutive years. After the War of the Spanish Succession, the States of Zeeland transferred more to creditors than they reinvested, in all scenarios. In the 50 per cent scenario, the amounts in 1715 and 1750 both totalled 7.5 million guilders, suggesting that the loans issued during the War of the Austrian Succession could be wholly financed by the portion of the interest receipts since 1715 that creditors wished to reinvest. In the period 1750–1780 too, the reinvestment of interest payments exceeded the net demand for additional financing. In other words, after retaining savings from the interest receipts and financing the increasing debt, the Zeeland investors still had ample money left. Meanwhile, reimbursement of Holland's provincial debt added to the savings pool, which Zeeland could tap into.[163] Hence, the interest payments and reimbursements formed a self-sustaining system, which allowed the States of Zeeland to constantly service the increasing debt by issuing new loans at low coupon rates.

4.3 *Coupons and Instruments*

Zeeland also met the third condition for a real financial revolution, namely declining interest rates. However, Fritschy argues that the decline in interest rates in Holland and Zeeland resulted from an abundance of capital and forced measures, such as forced conversions and the tax on bonds, rather than credible commitment.[164] The coupon on Zeeland's main debt instrument, the bond, fell from 6.25 per cent in the 1630s to 2.5 per cent, a rate sustained for most of the eighteenth century (graph 3.12).[165] Zeeland rarely issued redeemable annuities. When it did, it did so as tokens of regard to the

163 Fritschy and Van der Voort, "From Fragmentation to Unification," 72–73; Dormans, Het tekort, 110–11; De Vries and Van der Woude, Nederland 1500–1815, 157–58, 189; Dehing and 't Hart, "Linking Fortunes," 57; Gelderblom and Jonker, "Public Finance"; Gelderblom, Jonker, and Kool, "Direct Finance"; Fritschy, De patriotten, 42, 72.

164 Fritschy, *Public Finance*, 110, 112, 202.

165 In the ledgers of the provincial administration, 1603 serves as the first year, when the series of loan issues starts with number 1 and the numbering continues through to 1797. Throughout the seventeenth and eighteenth centuries all records begin with bonds issued in that year, but not earlier. Three major gaps exist in the issuance of bonds: 1604–1619, 1675–1681, 1683–1693. Sources: ZA, RkC, *passim*, e.g., 6010, 3v/4r.

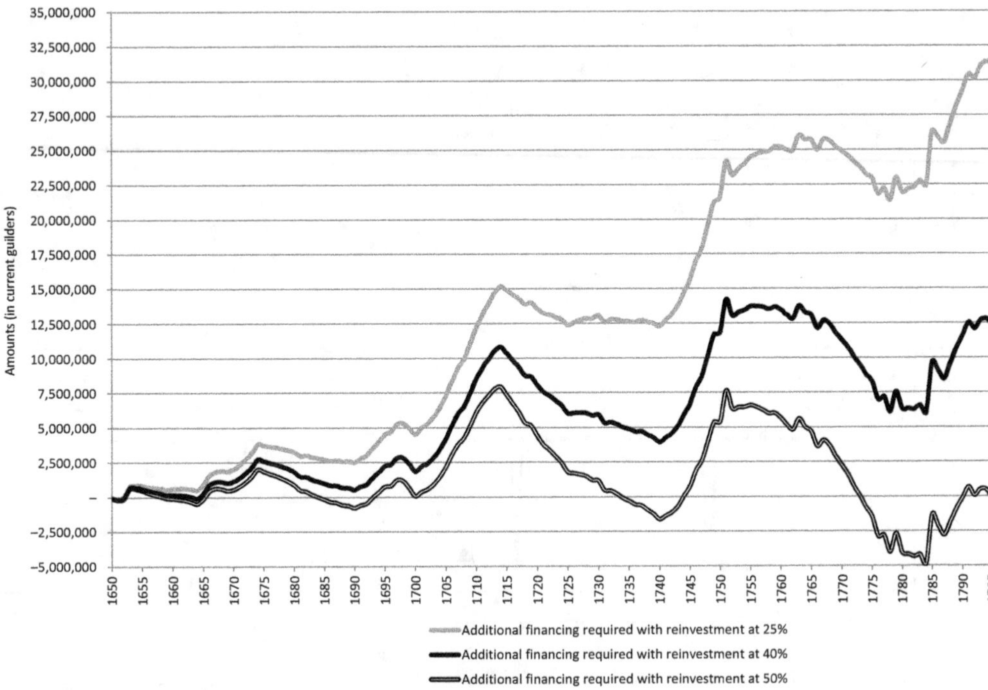

GRAPH 3.11 Zeeland's additional financing requirements, 1650–1795.
SOURCES: VEENSTRA, *GEWESTELIJKE FINANCIËN. VOL. 7: ZEELAND*, PP. 74–83, 250–257; TABLE 3.1.

Princes of Orange, for instance.[166] Creditors preferred bonds, which were not liable to transfer taxes and regulations. As a result, the States of Zeeland could issue bonds more cheaply than annuities.[167] For instance, in 1641, the Receiver-General Brouwer indicated that he could issue redeemable annuities at 6.25 per cent but bonds at 5 per cent.[168] Until 1673, interest reductions lowered the coupon; in 1668, all bonds issued since 1603 had an interest rate of 4 per cent. From 1673, the debt issued prior to then became liable to the withholding tax on bonds.

---

166 It also appears that this form of annuities was primarily used as a gift for the princes of Orange or the German Emperor, as a token of regard. ZA, RkC 5870, 'Van zijne Keyserlijke Majesteit', 'From his imperial majesty' and 'Zyne Hoogheyt', 'His Highness'. At some point in the 1760s or 1770s, Zeeland also issued some redeemable annuities for the general public; ZA, RkC, 5520, and 5850.

167 Veenstra, *Gewestelijke financiën: vol. 7. Zeeland*, 183; Gelderblom and Jonker, "Public Finance," 8.

168 *Notulen van Zeeland*, 237 16 August 1641 .

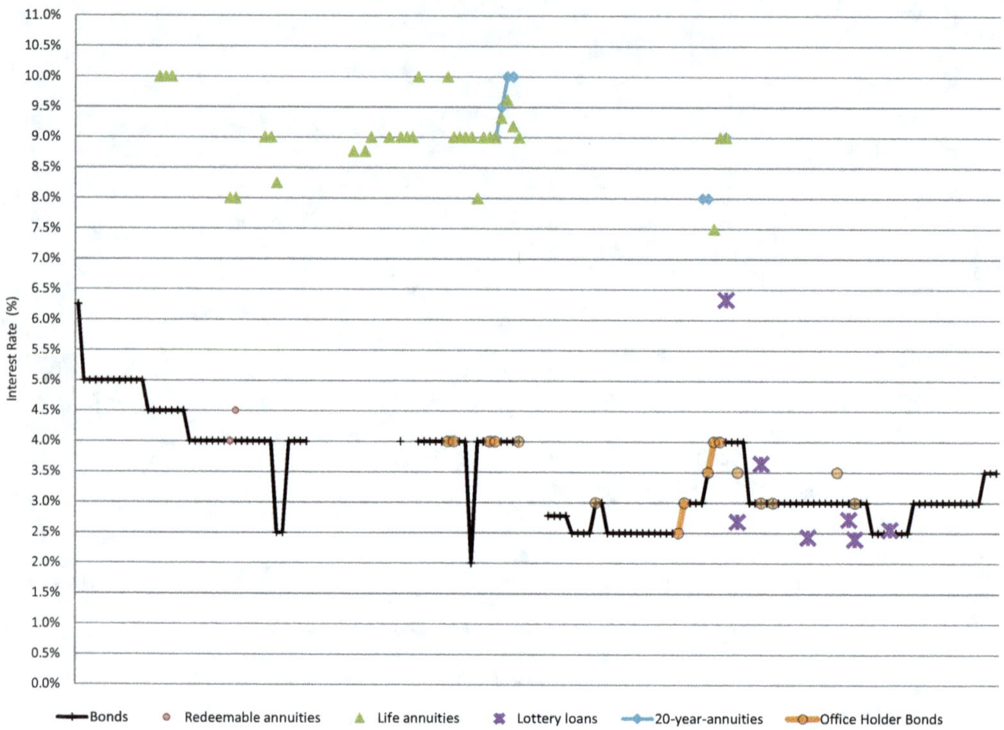

GRAPH 3.12 Zeeland's coupons per credit instrument at issuance, 1639–1795.
SOURCES: Z.A. RKC, INV.NOS.: 4510,4580, 4590, 4630, 4840, 4900, 4910, 4940, 4970, 5030, 5080, 5110, 5140, 5180, 5250, 5260, 5270, 5280, 5290, 5340, 5520, 5850, 5860, 5870, 5880, 5910, 5970, 5990, 6000, 6010; SCHORER, INV.NO. 159; VERZ. VERHEYE VAN CITTERS. INV. NO. 125B; *NOTULEN STATEN VAN ZEELAND*, 1640, P. 47; 1641, PP. 130, 237; VEENSTRA, *GEWSTELIJKE FINANCIËN VOL. 7*: ZEELAND, P. 189.

The 1690s marked the beginning of a decisive change in Zeeland's debt management policy. This was caused by the withholding tax on bonds and the tax exemption for new loans. There were some temporary exceptions to that rule. Reducing the interest payments was irrevocably connected to systematic refinancing and reimbursements, which began in 1719. Hence, the transformation in issuing and redemption frequency followed from the tax exemption that the creditors obtained when the province was in dire need of funds during the Nine Years' War and the ensuing War of the Spanish Succession.

Therefore the transformation that took place between the 1690s and 1719 requires additional scrutiny. Between 1674 and 1694, the States of Zeeland issued life annuities instead of bonds.[169] The absence of new bond issues

169 Z.A. RkC, inv.nos. 4840, 5870.

might be explained by investors' fear of the taxation of bonds. Whatever the reason, the new bond issue in 1694 explicitly tax-exempted the new bonds and established a sinking fund to guarantee reimbursement.[170] To provide the creditors with even more security, the States of Zeeland instructed the provincial Receiver-General in 1698 to prioritise interest payments over all other expenses.[171] Zeeland lived up to its contractual obligations. Indeed, later in the eighteenth century, the States of Zeeland argued that it had explicitly promised not to tax these new bonds.[172] The bonds issued between 1694 and 1705 disappeared from the account books soon after the War of the Spanish Succession, while earlier and later loan issues show up until the end of the eighteenth century.[173] This implies that Zeeland repaid these loans as promised and thus also lived up to this aspect of the agreement.

The promise of tax exemption was, however, temporarily suspended in 1706. The States ordered the issue of 'tax-exempt 4 per cent bonds to which a 2 per cent tax applied'.[174] Within a year, the States revoked the policy. Instead, it ordered the Receiver to issue the 'exempt' bonds at par, without any reduction.[175] In the last issue in this war period, the States offered 4 per cent for new tax-exempt bonds.[176] Hence, the tax exemption was real for all new bonds.

Decreases in interest payments resulted in voluntary conversions and reductions that began in 1719.[177] The States of Zeeland offered the bondholders

---

170 Later issues always referred to the conditions of the 1694 loan issue, until 1704, as the ones that applied; *Notulen van Zeeland*, 1697; 120–21, 126–27; 1698: 80–83; 1701: 163–64; 1702: 346–347; ZA, Verzameling Verheye van Citters, inv.no. 125b: "sonder eenige kortinge, en vry van alle lasten, Schattingen en ongelden".

171 *Notulen van Zeeland*, 17 April 1698, 83–84 "…alles oock met dien verstande en expresse begeerte, dat de Interesten, Erf en Lijf-Renten, altoos praeferabel sullen moeten zijn en blijven, en, voor de andere Huys en andere Lasten, eerst versorght en betaelt, sonder dat hier ontrent eenige de minste intermissie sal konnen of mogen werden gebruykt, alsoo de eer en het credijt van 't Lant, en het belangh der goede Ingesetenen van dien, de Provincie, op haer gegeven woort en belofte, gecrediteert hebbende, 't selve en geene deele en souden konnen lijden."

172 NA, Provinciale Resoluties, inv.no. 309; Rapport van de Heeren Extraordinaris Gedeputeerdens naar 's Hage, tot het geven van nadere ouvertures van de situatie der Financiën binnen deze Provincie van Zeeland, ingevolge Hunn' Ed: Mog: Resolutie van 21 November 1768, 11–12.

173 ZA, RkC, inv.no. 4840, 4900.

174 *Notulen van Zeeland*, 1702: 346–47; 1706: 336, 347: negotiatie op exempte obligatien, tegens vier per cento, tot Haer ed. Mog. naedere ordre, onder kortinge van twee per cento."".

175 *Notulen van Zeeland*, 121 (1707).

176 *Notulen van Zeeland*, 40–41 (1714).

177 *Notulen van Zeeland* resolution of 6 April 1719 and 20 December 1719.

the choice between redemption and a reduction in the rate to 3.5 per cent in April and 3 per cent in December for bonds originally issued at 4 per cent.[178] Meanwhile, it issued new debts at similar rates and even some bonds for short-term debt at 2 per cent.[179] By 1722, the States had reduced the interest rate of all other loans issued at 4 per cent to 3 per cent. From 1724 to 1741, Zeeland issued bonds at 2.5 per cent most years, except for 1727 and 1728, when it paid 3 per cent.[180] The 2.5 per cent rate was identical to the going rate in Holland at the time. From this new loan income, the province gradually paid off the loans issued between 1694 and 1705.[181] The holders of the old 4 per cent bonds – the first 96 bond issues until 1674 – must have lacked the option to demand redemption. Otherwise, they would have swapped the 2 per cent effective coupons for the new 2.5 per cent or 3 per cent tax-exempt bonds. The States of Zeeland benefitted from the abundant capital supply as this allowed it to achieve a significant reduction in the interest charges.

Zeeland's regents understood that the economic slowdown of the later seventeenth century reduced alternative investment opportunities. In 1679, the States of Zeeland encouraged the legal guardians of minors to purchase provincial bonds and annuities at market prices. The decree explicitly considered the diminishing value of real estate and the lack of new investment opportunities to cover the costs for the guardians.[182] An extension of the decree in 1695 widened the coverage to the securities of all public institutions within the province. Both edicts explicitly mention the secondary market trade within Zeeland and the use of these securities as collateral.[183] The States of Zeeland actively sought to benefit from the lack of alternatives which allowed it to borrow relatively cheaply from the late seventeenth century onwards.

The War of the Austrian Succession increased the demand for loans. To attract investments, the States promised creditors a 3 per cent coupon during the first ten years and 2.5 per cent after that.[184] This was not enough. Coupons

178 Z.A. 508 Rekenkamer C, inv.no. 5030, f. 57r, f. 61r.

179 Z.A. 508 Rekenkamer C, nv.nr. 5030, f. 57r, f 61r (the 2 per cent 1719 loan was to reimburse the most pressing debts ("*krijtende schulden*"), probably related to military expenses, ZA, RkC, inv.no. 5520).

180 ZA, RkC, inv.no.5030.

181 ZA RkC, inv.nos. 5030, 5180, 5340.

182 *Notulen van Zeeland*, 43–44; 31 May 1679: "een prijse soo als die bevonden sullen worden, ganckbaer te wesen."

183 ZA, Verzameling Verheye van Citters, inv.no. 125b.

184 ZA, RkC, 4280, f. 72r-74r.

increased to 4 per cent in 1746 and 1747.[185] After the war, the States tried to reduce the burden. In 1753, the States of Zeeland discussed the possibility of issuing a loan with conditions similar to the 1742 to 1745 issuances: the first eight years would yield 3 per cent, and 2.5 per cent after that.[186] This must have failed since these loans still paid 3 per cent in 1781. Overall, the coupons did not return to the pre-war level and loans were generally issued at 3 per cent until the 1770s.[187] This was the least the creditors accepted since the States depended entirely on the market's willingness to absorb the new debt.

The constant conversions required knowledge of capital market conditions to prevent cash from running out during a conversion. It is clear that the regents closely monitored investors' responses. In 1754, for instance, they feared that too long a timespan in issuing the loan could damage their credit. Therefore, they decided that it would be better to issue the loan at 3 per cent rather than to wait until a 2.5 per cent bond issue was fully subscribed.[188] Between 1751 and 1792, 3 per cent remained the going rate at issuance, save for the years 1774–1781. As soon as the regents saw an opportunity to reduce the interest rates, they tried to benefit from favourable circumstances by engineering conversions of existing loans. The States of Zeeland converted older bonds from 3.5 per cent to 3 per cent in 1763.[189] After successfully issuing a 2.5 per cent bond loan in Amsterdam in 1774, Zeeland again offered its creditors the choice between reimbursements or an interest reduction on older loans, namely in

185 ZA, RkC, 5270, 5280, 5290, 5340, borderel.
186 *Notulen van Zeeland*, 638 (1753)6 December 1753.
187 ZA, RkC, inv.no. 5870.
188 *Notulen van Zeeland*, 173, in 1754.
189 *Middelburgsche Courant*, 7 July 1763.

1774,[190] 1775[191] and 1777,[192] this time from 3 per cent to 2.5 per cent.[193] The province was constantly trying to convert older debt into new debt with a lower coupon, always on a voluntary basis. The States of Zeeland feared that the taxation of public bonds would jeopardise the provincial creditworthiness.[194] The regents in the States of Zeeland hence appear prudent administrators who followed the market closely.

In times of financial hardship, the receivers supplemented the bond issues with other debt instruments. Life annuities were the main public security Zeeland employed to this end, until 1748 when the lottery loans began to fulfil this

---

190 Familiebericht. "Oprechte Haerlemsche courant". Haerlem, 29–12-1774, p. 2. Accessed at Delper op 08–02-2022, https://resolver.kb.nl/resolve?urn=MMNHA02:164952326:mpeg21:p00002. Den Ontfanger Generaal van Zeeland, Johan Valentyn Sprenger, maakt bekend aan de Houders der obligatien, ten laste dier Provincie, croisserende thans ten Intereste van 3 per Cento, gesprooten uit de 110, 111 en 112 Lichtingen, vervallen in de Maand Maart, dat met en na de vervaldagen derzelver in Maart 1775, volgens Resolutie der Heeren Staaten van Zeeland, zullen worden gehouden voor gereduceert op do lnterest van 2 ½ per Cento: En dat zy die hunne Gelden tot dien verminderden Interest niet begeeren te laaten, hunne Kapitaalan ten voorschreeve vervaldage konnen terug ontfangen, mits zig aangeevende voor den eersten February 1775, aan het Comptoir Generaal, waartoe op de ordinaire dagen zal worden gevaceerd, en niet aangeevende, zullen die Kapitaalen voor gereduceert worden gehouden, terwyl aan hun die des begeerende, van de gereduceerde Kapitaalen zullen worden afgegeeven Duplicaten, omme den Intereft daarop by vervolg te konnen ontfangen.

Wordende voorts alle de Houders der Obligatien, ten lasten de Provincie van Zeeland, verzogt, de achterstalljge Interesten op dezelve vervallen, ten spoedigsten, ten Comptoir Generaal, alsmede van de Zeeuwsche-Loteryen van Anno 1751 en 1770, benevens van de Inwisselinge van de nog mankeerende Origineele Obligatien tegens de Duplicaten ten Comptoire van den Agendaris deezer Provincie Johannes Menkema t'Amsterdam af te haalen en te komen ontfangen.

191 Middelburgsche Courant, 18 August 1775: "Den ontfanger Generaal van Zeeland, Johan Valentyn Spenger, adverteerd aan de Houders der Effecten tot 3 pro Cento, die hunne Capitalen tegen February 1776 hebben opgeeischt, dat zy met en na den 8 January 1776 dezelve Dagelyks, op de Ordinaris Compoir Dagen, met het volle jaar Interest, kunnen afhalen, zonder na de preciese Verval Dagen te wagten." ["The Receiver-General of Zeeland, Johan Valentyn Spenger, advertises to the possessors of 3 per cent securities, who called their capital in February 1776, that they may collect this from January 8 onwards, every day during opening hours, plus the entire sum of interest of the year due, without waiting for the official maturity date."].

192 ZA, RkC, 5910, inv. f. 40v.

193 *Middelburgsche Courant*, 26 and 28, 30 December 1775, 28 January 1777.

194 NA, Provinciale Resoluties, inv.no. 309; Rapport van de Heeren Extraordinaris Gedeputeerdens naar 's Hage, tot het geven van nadere ouvertures van de situatie der Financiën binnen deze Provincie van Zeeland, ingevolge Hunn' Ed: Mog: Resolutie van 21 November 1768, 11–12.

function. Life annuities yielded between 8 and 10 per cent, which was markedly more than bonds. But life annuities did not require reimbursement because they only yielded a fixed sum for the lifetime of the nominee. The principal expired when the nominees died, which could take time due to the often young age of the nominees.[195] Prior to the late 1680s, Zeeland issued life annuities on only eight occasions, and only during periods of warfare.[196] Issues intensified during the Nine Years' War and the War of the Spanish Succession when the Receiver-General issued life annuities almost every year, but not during the interwar years from 1698 to 1702.[197] At the end of the latter war, Zeeland offered the investors the choice between 9 per cent life annuities that would always be exempt from interest reductions or taxes, and 10 per cent life annuities with a tax exemption for twenty years.[198]

Due to the ultimately higher costs, a report by the Provincial Court of Audit in 1713 deemed life annuities a 'lethal' instrument and advised against using them. Instead, the province should issue a lottery loan on conditions resembling those applicable in Holland.[199] The understanding that annuities involved a high cost was not new; Holland's Grand Pensionary Johan de Witt had already explained this in 1671.[200] This advice was not put into practice until the War of the Austrian Succession. Rather, in 1714 the province issued another 9 per cent life annuity. The next time the province issued life annuities, in 1746, it applied age classes ranging from 5 per cent to 10 per cent.[201]

195 Dormans, *Het tekort*, 58–61, 145 Therefore, these loans typically yielded twice as much as redeemable annuities or bonds. Gelderblom and Jonker assume an average annual extinction rate of 1.25 per cent; it therefore takes 80 years for the whole of the life annuities issue to expire. Gelderblom and Jonker, "Public Finance," 31; François R. Velde and David R. Weir, "The Financial Market and Government Debt Policy in France, 1746–1793," *The Journal of Economic History* 52, no. 1 (1992): 1–39; James E. Poterba, "Annuities in Early Modern Europe," in *The Origins of Value: The Financial Innovations That Created Modern Capital Markets*, ed. William N. Goetzmann and K. Geert Rouwenhorst (Oxford etc.: Oxford University Press, 2005), 207–24.

196 In 1616, 1653, 1654, 1655, 1665, 1666, 1671 and 1672.

197 ZA, RkC, inv.no. 4940.

198 ZA, RkC, inv.no. 4910 borderel, inv.no. 4940, borderel, inv.no. 5340, f. 84v-177r, inv.no. 5910, f. 45 v-74v.

199 ZA, Verzameling Verheye van Citters, inv.no. 125b, unfoliated.

200 Johan de Witt had already calculated the costs of life annuities versus redeemable annuities in 1671, in his Waerdye.. Houtzager, *Hollands lijf- en losrenterekeningen*, 92, 96–99, 105–6; Zuijderduijn, *Medieval Capital Markets*, 98.

201 In 1672, Amsterdam also issued life annuities to which it had applied age categories. Houtzager, *Hollands lijf- en losrenterekeningen*, 105–6; Poterba argued that this Amsterdam innovation in age differentation was not reproduced elsewhere. This example shows that Zeeland did this too, although it was somewhat belated. Poterba, "Annuities,"

TABLE 3.3 Nominee age classes for the 1746 and 1747 life annuities in Zeeland.

Age class	Coupon
1–10 years	5%
11–20 years	6%
21–30 years	7%
31–40 years	8%
41–50 years	9%
51 years and over	10%

SOURCE: ZA, RKC, INV.NO. 5290.

Also in 1747 – the year of the Voluntary Gift – it issued another 575,000 guilders' worth of life annuities with age classes.[202] Still in urgent need of money, the States once again offered a flat rate of 9 per cent in 1748 to attract investors. So, despite the high costs attached, the States tried to obtain more money from the general public by widening the scope and offering investment opportunities to individuals beyond the regular investors.

From 1749, lottery loans became the preferred instrument to supplement the bonds. The States of Zeeland made the first issue, in 1749, too attractive for potential investors. Over the years the costs of the loan differed in the ledgers. On average, it returned approximately 6.4 per cent to investors.[203] Later offers were less generous, which indicated the States learned from this experience.[204] The lottery issue of 1755 offered prizes in the form of 25-year loans

212. And so did the province of Groningen, also in 1672. Alberto Feenstra and Sabine Muller, "Wie wil wachten op het zoet? De laatste adem van Amsterdamse kopers van Groningse lijfrenten, 1660–1760," *Historisch Jaarboek Groningen*, 2016, 55–56.

202 ZA, RkC, inv.no. 5290.

203 ZA, RkC, inv.no. 5340, f. 83r, 5520, 5850, 5860, 5870, 5970, 5990.

204 Although the instrument was new for Zeeland's provincial public finances, it was widely used elsewhere. Lotteries were certainly not unknown as means to raise money. Apart from lotteries in England, Holland and those of the States General, a number of Zeeland towns, villages and institutions such as orphanages also used them in this period. Van Cruyningen, "Bevolking," 132–33; Donald Haks, *Vaderland en vrede, 1672–1713: publiciteit over de Nederlandse Republiek in oorlog* (Hilversum: Verloren, 2013), 262: Arendskerke 1698, Arnemuiden 1677, Domburg 1675, Middelburg, 1678 + 1694, Tholen 1698, Vlissingen 1695, Zierikzee 1694; Anne L. Murphy, "Lotteries in the 1690s: Investment or Gamble?," *Financial History Review* 12, no. 02 (2005): 227–46, https://doi.org/10.1017/S0968565005000119; Dormans, *Het tekort*, 77.

and tontines that cost the Provincial States 4 per cent of the borrowed capital.[205] More intriguing – and more profitable to the States of Zeeland – was the lottery loan of 1758. It paid 950 guilders in cash premiums and prize bonds of up to 15,000 guilders. The winners of prizes of 1,000 guilders or more received half of the prize immediately in cash and the other half as transferable scrip with a 3.5 per cent coupon, to be reimbursed the next year. In total, this lottery scheme yielded the States of Zeeland a net profit of 23,246 guilders.[206] After 1763, the prize bonds were divided into two categories: a smaller portion (11 per cent in 1763) yielded 2.5 per cent, and the rest (89 per cent in 1763) yielded 2 per cent.[207] Of course, additional prizes increased the potential yields, which made these loans more attractive than the ordinary 3 per cent bonds. For the States of Zeeland, however, this was a cheaper alternative.

From 1710, the province also began experimenting with fixed-term annuities, with a term to maturity of twenty years in Zeeland – around the same time that Holland issued similar annuities with 'double interest'.[208] Like lottery loans and life annuities, fixed-term annuities formed an additional instrument to supplement the ordinary bonds, and were probably intended to extend the group of participants. The use of this credit instrument was limited to seven years: 1710–1713, 1745–1746 and 1749, which not coincidentally coincided with the Wars of the Spanish and Austrian Succession.[209]

This credit instrument had a fixed term and a higher coupon than ordinary bonds. This higher coupon was compensation for the initial investment, which was not reimbursed when the loan reached maturity but expired at the end of the period. Consequently, the amounts transferred to creditors were recorded as interest payments alone and not as part reimbursement.[210] The proposed interest reduction on the twenty-year bonds, in 1724, was not realised.[211] For the duration of the loan, the ledgers show identical annual

205 ZA, RkC, inv.no. 5850, f.1v, these were recorded as expenses for the lottery loan, not as separate securities.

206 Middelburgsche Courant, 1 July 1758.

207 ZA, Rekenkamer C, inv.no. 5850: In 1770: 85% & 15%; in 1771 97% & 3%; 1777: 94% & 6%.

208 A similar loan was issued in Holland in 1710. Dormans, *Het tekort*, 77; Liesker and Fritschy, *Gewestelijke financiën: vol. 4. Holland*, 119, 383; And in Overijssel, in 1711 and 1712. Fritschy and Liesker, "Overheidsfinanciën, kapitaalmarkten," 177; Fritschy, *Public Finance*, 162 In this publication, she states that Holland started issuing this instrument in 1711.

209 ZA, RkC, inv.no. 5910, f. 43v. The 20-year bonds of the first series expired as scheduled in the 1730s. The bonds of the second series that were issued in the 1740s were converted into ordinary bonds in 1756 in the 158th bond issue, according to the ledgers.

210 For instance, ZA, RkC, inv.no. 5290.

211 *Notulen van Zeeland*, 188 (1724)17 August 1724.

TABLE 3.4 Yields of fixed-term-annuities in Zeeland, 1710–1749.

Issuer	Year of issuance	Coupon	Period (years)	Effective yields
Zeeland	1710	9.0%	20	6.39%
Zeeland	1711	9.5%	20	7.08%
Zeeland	1712	10.0%	20	7.75%
Zeeland	1712–1713	10.0%	20	7.75%
Zeeland	1745	8.0%	20	4.96%
Zeeland	1746	8.0%	20	4.96%
Zeeland	1749	9.0%	20	6.39%

SOURCES: ZA, RKC, INV.NOS. 4940, 1970, 5260, 5270, 5280, 5290, 5340.

instalments of 10 per cent, 9.5 per cent, and 9 per cent interest on the loans' nominal values. These instalments are similar to modern annuities that consist of part amortisation and part interest, for instance in mortgages. Like in Holland, the yields in Zeeland exceeded the going rates of the ordinary bonds. Yet the gap was much bigger in Zeeland. The yield of 7.75 per cent in 1712–1713 suggests that Zeeland had difficulties finding investors. The high coupon and implicit reimbursement widened the market of potential investors by another 2.4 million guilders.[212]

A consequence of the qualification as interest payments was that the honouring of the twenty-year loans was prioritised over other reimbursements. In 1754, the States of Zeeland ordered the receiver to halt all reimbursements in 1755, except those that were issued as 'double interest'.[213] This halt in reimbursements signals a slowdown in the process of constant redemptions and new loans rather than a default. The payments that continued concerned the twenty-year loans issued during the War of the Austrian Succession, which would be converted into ordinary bonds in 1756.[214] Those issued in 1745–1746 had an 8 per cent coupon; the one issued in 1749 paid 4 per cent nominally.[215] The States of Zeeland improved the conditions during wartime

212 ZA, RkC, inv.nos. 4970, 5030, 5110.

213 *Notulen van Zeeland*, 635 (1754) Den heer ontfanger Generaal gelast, met de aflossinge der Capitaalen, dewelke niet op een dubbele interest zyn genegotieert, inde aanstaande Jaare 1755 stil te staan." (20/12/1754)".

214 ZA, RkC, inv.no. 5910, f. 43v.

215 ZA, RkC, inv.no. 5340.

to enlarge the scope and attractiveness of the loan issues, but adjusted them again as soon as the political situation allowed.

Finally, from 1693 the States of Zeeland issued forced loans from officials, known as officeholder bonds (Dutch: *ambtobligaties*).[216] This was a combination of debt and tax. The province only paid interest on the bond. The officeholder received half the value of the bond as reimbursement from his successor, who, in turn, received no reimbursement. The next successor to the office has to buy a new bond from the States, and so on. Between 1702 and 1776, the States resorted sixteen times to this instrument.[217] The coupons on these officeholder bonds generally equalled the coupon on the ordinary bonds, which was thus a form of income for the officeholders.[218] It is not hard to see the resemblance between this system of forced loans and the practice of venal office purchases that existed elsewhere in early modern Europe.[219] The experience of a financial revolution did not forestall such practices of selling offices.

4.4 *Extending the Geographical Scope of the Market*

How and where Zeeland floated loans remains somewhat uncertain. Probably, the local district receivers in Zeeland fulfilled a similar function to those in Holland.[220] For instance, the participants in the lottery loan of 1758 could buy

216 This appears quite similar to practices in the Southern Netherlands during the eighteenth century. Oscar Gelderblom and Joost Jonker, "Alba's Irony. Urban Autonomy and Public Finance in the Low Countries (1384–1713)," *Utrecht University Working Papers*, 2011, 15.

217 Veenstra, *Gewestelijke financiën: vol. 7. Zeeland*, 191 d.d. 17 maart 1693 (1e 'furnissement'), 5 maart 1694 (2e), 7 april 1702 (3e), 22februari 1703 (4e), 4november 1709 (5e), 11 augustus 1710 (6e), 13augustus en 20 september 1714 (7e), 16januari 1727 (8e), 22 september 1741 (9e), 15januari 1742 (10e), 14juni 1746 (IIe), 11 juli 1747 (12e), 14oktober 1748 (13e), 13mei 1751 (14e), 1 september 1755 (15e), 25 april 1757 (16e), bijlagen anno 1768 (lijst van tauxen behorend bij het 17e furnissement, vastgesteld door Gecommitteerde Raden van Zeeland d.d. 11 januari 1768), 18 november 1771 (18e furnissement). Reading from the late eighteenth century archives, coupons were between 2.5 per cent and 4 per cent; ZA, RkC, 5970.

218 That is, in as far as this could be established from the sources: ZA, RkC, inv.no,. 5080, 5110, 5140, 5180, 5250, 5870, f 3r.; ZA, Schorer, inv.no. 159. A more detailed account is provided in Feenstra, *Between Shared*, appendix.

219 Stephen Miller, "Venal Offices, Provincial Assemblies and the French Revolution," *French History* 28, no. 3 (September 1, 2014): 343–65, https://doi.org/10.1093/fh/cru048; Rui Esteves, "Archomania. Venality and Private Finances on the Eve of the French Revolution," *Paper Prepared for the 2014 EHA Meeting in Columbus, OH*, 2014, http://eh.net/eha/wp-content/uploads/2014/05/Esteves.pdf.

220 Gelderblom and Jonker, "Public Finance," 4.

tickets at the office of the provincial Receiver-General or from district tax receivers.[221] Only during the Franco-Dutch War did the towns themselves serve as intermediaries.[222] Zeeland's towns appear, nevertheless, to be the most plausible locations for the issuance of debt. Zeeland only started issuing part of its debt in Holland during the second half of the eighteenth century.

The evidence that Zeeland did not issue debt in Holland before that is indirect and circumstantial. The records of the bonds only provide names, not the places. Nevertheless, after 1750 separate registers were held for Middelburg in Zeeland and Amsterdam in Holland. They were all for lottery loans, except for one ordinary bond loan, issued in 1774.[223]

Zeeland turned to Holland's capital market after 1750. The province issued lottery loans and paid interest in Amsterdam.[224] At least in 1750, it advertised in Holland with a notice about the interest payments on the 1749 lottery loan.[225] Equally, the Amsterdam intermediary Johannes Menkema advertised in 1752 that he collected interest on Zeeland's 1751 lottery loan.[226] The next year, he offered to collect lottery tickets to exchange them for bills and pay the interest due.[227] For some reason, his services must have been terminated or taken over. At least, in 1758, Zeeland's Receiver-General announced that, in response to a great many requests, creditors could henceforth permanently collect their interest at the cashier's office of Jacob van Thiel in Amsterdam. This was a policy change since the creditors could previously only collect their interest there during a particular fortnight in November.[228] Slightly later, Amsterdam brokers offered the opposite service, to collect lottery tickets in Amsterdam and then send them over to Zeeland in return for bonds.[229] In the

221 Middelburgsche Courant, 1 July 1758

222 Veenstra, *Gewestelijke financiën: vol. 7. Zeeland*, 18, 188.

223 On only one occasion, in 1774, did Zeeland issue an ordinary bond loan in Amsterdam, worth 503,000 guilders: ZA, RkC, inv.no. 5910, f. 40v.

224 On only one occasion, in 1774, did Zeeland issue an ordinary bond loan in Amsterdam, worth 503,000 guilders: ZA, RkC, inv.no. 5910, f. 40v.

225 Advertentie. "Leydse courant". Te Leyden, 19-01-1750, p. 2. Accessed at Delper op 26–10-2022, https://resolver.kb.nl/resolve?urn=ddd:010909665:mpeg21:p002.

226 Advertentie. "Amsterdamse courant". Amsterdam, 01-01-1752, p. 2. Accessed at Delper op 18–06-2022, https://resolver.kb.nl/resolve?urn=MMSAA06:165538157:mpeg21:p00002.

227 Advertentie. "Amsterdamse courant". Amsterdam, 09-08-1753, p. 2. Accessed at Delper op 19–06-2022, https://resolver.kb.nl/resolve?urn=MMSAA06:165538408:mpeg21:p00002.

228 Advertentie, *Middelburgsche Courant,* 9 November 1758, Accessed at Zeeuwse Kranten-database on 14-05-2014.

229 Advertentie. "Amsterdamse courant". Amsterdam, 20-12-1763, p. 2. Accessed at Delpher on 08-02-2022, https://resolver.kb.nl/resolve?urn=ddd:010710153:mpeg21:p002.

1770s, Zeeland extended its service even further by adding The Hague as a separate location.[230]

Zeeland probably turned to Holland after 1750 because money was in greater supply there, and coupons within Zeeland did not return to the pre-war level of 2.5 per cent. The States of Holland reimbursed part of its provincial public debt and paid 2.5 per cent on the rest. Turning to Holland may have given the States of Zeeland more leverage compared to Zeeland's domestic investors. The above analysis of the private capital market indicates that the availability of capital formed no impediment. Moreover, the reinvestment rates also suggested that investors could finance their investment in the debt from receipts from the debt service. Hence, the explanation for turning to the Holland market after the 1750s was most probably to benefit from Holland's public debt reductions. This yielded room for the States of Zeeland to get more favourable coupons.

Table 3.5 reveals how capital from Holland became increasingly important compared to Zeeland's domestic market, with a greater diversification in the location. Initially, the market in Middelburg remained the largest. It is not clear as yet what the situation was for the earlier loans. Nevertheless, newspaper advertisements about interest payments in 1774 on the 1751 loan make references to an Amsterdam register for that particular loan.[231] Within a decade, Holland's markets had become dominant for this type of loan. Even so, the shift within Holland is of interest. In the 1779 lottery loan, the political centre The Hague had become of equal importance to Amsterdam, Holland's economic centre. Moreover, this was the first instance of Zeeland explicitly recording interest payments outside of the province.

By the 1770s, the office of Johannes Menkema had permanently taken over Van Thiel's function as Zeeland's agent in Amsterdam. Since 1774, creditors could collect the interest from Zeeland lottery loans there.[232] In 1775, his office

230 ZA, RkC, inv.no. 5910, f 36r, 38v.

231 Advertentie. "Oprechte Haerlemsche courant". Haerlem, 28-07-1774, p. 2. Accessed at Delper op 08-02-2022, https://resolver.kb.nl/resolve?urn=ddd:010800369:mpeg21:p002; Advertentie. "Oprechte Haerlemsche courant". Haerlem, 04-08-1774, p. 2. Accessed at Delper op 08-02-2022, https://resolver.kb.nl/resolve?urn=ddd:010800372:mpeg21:p002.

232 Advertentie. "Oprechte Haerlemsche courant". Haerlem, 02-08-1774, p. 2. Accessed at Delper op 08-02-2022, https://resolver.kb.nl/resolve?urn=MMNHA02:164952261:mpeg21:p00002; Advertentie. "Oprechte Haerlemsche courant". Haerlem, 04-08-1774, p. 2. Accessed at Delper op 08-02-2022, https://resolver.kb.nl/resolve?urn=ddd:010800372:mpeg21:p002; "Advertentie". "*Leydse courant*". Te Leyden, 08-08-1774. Accessed at Delpher on 15–09-2016, http://resolver.kb.nl/resolve?urn=ddd:010912656:mpeg21:a0011.

TABLE 3.5 Geographical spread of interest paid to lottery loan creditors in 1785.

	1770	1771	1777	1779
Middelburg (Zeeland)	70%	100%	53%	39%
Amsterdam (Holland)	30%		24%	31%
The Hague (Holland)			23%	30%

SOURCE: ZA, RKC, INV.NO. 5910, F. 32R, 34V, 36R, 38V.

paid the interest on the 2.5 per cent loan from 1774.[233] Zeeland relied on his services to pay the interest on all bonds in the Amsterdam register payable until 1796.[234] In The Hague, Zeeland relied on the services of the bankers Abraham and Simeon Boas and additionally on a certain Wouter Jochems and Son.[235] The Hague quickly became as important as Amsterdam, the city the States of Zeeland had first turned to, while both gained in importance compared to Middelburg.

For a loan in 1789 as well, the bankers Boas serviced The Hague and Menkema and Son Amsterdam. The purpose of the loan was to support the Zeeland Chamber of the VOC. The States of Zeeland planned to issue 9 million guilders for the company, at 3 per cent. Subscribers had to pay at least half in cash. The rest was payable in provincial bonds, according to the following rates: the 3 per cent bonds were considered on par, the 2.5 per cent bonds at 83 per cent of their face value and the 2 per cent bonds at 66.7 per cent of their face value.[236] The yields all returned 3 per cent in this way. The States of Zee-

233 "Advertentie". "Amsterdamse courant". Amsterdam, 09-03-1775. Accessed at Delpher on 15-09-2016, http://resolver.kb.nl/resolve?urn=ddd:010711687:mpeg21:a0010.

234 "Advertentie". "*Oprechte Haarlemse courant*". Haarlem, 18-03-1797. Accessed at Delpher on 15-09-2016, http://resolver.kb.nl/resolve?urn=ddd:010728749:mpeg21:a0008 .

235 "Artykel I.". "Hollandsche historische courant". Delft, 06-05-1779. Accessed at Delpher on 15-09-2016, http://resolver.kb.nl/resolve?urn=ddd:010796948:mpeg21:a0013; "Advertentie". "*Oprechte Haerlemsche courant*". Haerlem, 04-09-1792. Accessed at Delpher on 15-09-2016, http://resolver.kb.nl/resolve?urn=ddd:010802870:mpeg21:a0010; Advertentie. "Middelburgsche courant". Middelburg, 28-06-1777, p. 2. Accessed at Delper op 26-10-2022, https://resolver.kb.nl/resolve?urn=ddd:010199089:mpeg21:p002.

236 Advertentie. "Amsterdamse courant". Amsterdam, 25-06-1789, p. 2. Accessed at Delper op 18-04-2023, https://resolver.kb.nl/resolve?urn=ddd:010716071:mpeg21:p002; NEDERLANDEN. 'S GRAVENHAGE, den 14 Augustus.. "Hof courant". 's-Gravenhage, 15-08-1789, p. 1. Accessed at Delper op 18-04-2023, https://resolver.kb.nl/resolve?urn=ddd:010719061:mpeg21:p001.

land deemed its own credit still good enough to carry the additional debt of the VOC, which was a doubtful assumption.

Zeeland hardly used the option of borrowing under the States General's guarantee, probably because it had few advantages. Zeeland did report some arrears in a Generality loan on '*double interest*' in 1709.[237] In 1715, the Union transformed Zeeland's 3 million guilders of overdue provincial contributions into a formal debt. The States General was a much more important source of debt for the provinces of Friesland and, especially, Groningen than for Zeeland, as we shall see in the following chapters. After a temporary suspension of interest payments by the Union's office in 1715, the States General paid 3 per cent interest on its debt throughout the eighteenth century.[238] This was as much or even more than Zeeland paid on its provincial debt, as the States of Zeeland argued in the discussions about its contribution to the Union.[239] Moreover, the Generality now had a history of defaulting, while Zeeland did not. Mediation by the Generality was not an attractive alternative for Zeeland.

4.5 *Secondary Market in Holland and Zeeland*

Towards the end of the eighteenth century, Zeeland's public debt yields increased. This was a period of intensive political turmoil and inflation. The political instability of the Dutch Republic in the 1780s – defeat in the Fourth Anglo-Dutch War, the Patriot Revolution and Orangist restoration of 1787 – pushed the market rates down. This and the coalition wars against revolutionary France formed a prelude to the end of the Dutch Republic in 1795. By 1788, the yield on Zeeland bonds had risen to 4.4 per cent in Amsterdam.[240] Similarly, in Utrecht the yield was 4.5 per cent in 1793.[241] Between 1792 and 1795, the yields on Zeeland's 2.5 per cent bonds rose from around 4 per cent to 5 per cent, and more dramatically to over 9 per cent in 1797. The yields for Zeeland went up further than those of other Dutch creditors, suggesting that the risk of default was greater.[242] The few other secondary market transactions

237 Veenstra, *Gewestelijke financiën: vol. 7. Zeeland*, 204–7; *Notulen van Zeeland*, 132 (1709).

238 Dormans, *Het tekort*, 148, 158.

239 NA, Provinciale Resoluties, inv.no. 309; Rapport van de Heeren Extraordinaris Gedeputeerdens naar 's Hage, tot het geven van nadere ouvertures van de situatie der Financiën binnen deze Provincie van Zeeland, ingevolge Hunn' Ed: Mog: Resolutie van 21 November 1768, 12–13.

240 Riley, *International Government Finance*, 50–51, 71–73, 275–76.

241 HUA, notarial deeds, U255a011 act 75.

242 Riley, *International Government Finance*, 50–51.

suggest the yield increases were recent and yields had been low before the 1780s.

Before 1750, hardly any secondary market prices are available for Zeeland.[243] The first observation concerns a purchase in Holland, in 1690, by one of the richest men in the Dutch Republic.[244] Pieter de Graeff, from Amsterdam, bought a 4 per cent bond from the Enkhuizen office of the VOC at 73 per cent of face value. He factored in the overdue interest and withholding tax, for seven and a half months.[245] The clean price equals a current yield of 2.74 per cent. Meanwhile, the effective coupon of new Zeeland bonds was 2 per cent (4 per cent minus 2 per cent withholding tax). Hence, the yield slightly exceeded the effective coupon, although both were low.

Cornelis van Tongerlo's price list of 1747 offers price quotations in Holland.[246] On average, Zeeland's bonds yielded 4.29 per cent in this year of severe crisis.[247] So even in a crisis year, the coupon rate of 4 per cent was relatively close to the yield the market was willing to pay. Furthermore, the quotations indicate that Zeeland's credit was not worse than that of the other Dutch provinces.

More observations exist for the period after 1750. First, auction data from Amsterdam informs us about the development of Zeeland's credit there.[248] The yields fluctuated between 2.75 per cent and 3.5 per cent between 1748 and 1765. This was as a rule slightly above the coupon rates. Second, several observations from Zeeland indicate that in the early 1760s the yields dropped slightly below the coupon rate of 3 per cent. Also, the decline in the coupon in

---

243 The notarial archives prior to 1796 were lost when a fire ravaged the town of Middelburg in 17 May 1940, as a consequence of fighting in the Second World War. Zeeuws Archief, "Notariële Archieven Zeeland 1796–1842, 1796–1842 Okt. 15."

244 Kees Zandvliet, *De 250 rijksten van de Gouden Eeuw: kapitaal, macht, familie en levensstijl*, ed. Paulien Retèl (Amsterdam: RijksmuseumAmsterdam : Nieuw Amsterdam, 2006), 93–97.

245 Stadsarchief Amsterdam (hereafter SAA), Archief van de Familie de Graeff, inv.no. 153A.

246 Van Dillen, "Effectenkoersen," 1–2, 4, 13–14.

247 Van Dillen, 4, 13.

248 Courtesy of Joost Jonker, Oscar Gelderblom and Christiaan van Bochove, who shared their findings in their auctions database with me. For Zeeland, this concerns thirty-seven observations, auctioned over the years 1748, 1754–1757, 1759–1760, 1762–1765, where the coupon was known in sixteen instances and could be estimated by me in two cases: these were issued in 1673 and I assumed an effective 2 per cent coupon, as a result of a 4 per cent nominal coupon and 2 per cent withholding tax. These auctions took place in 1748, 1754, 1756, 1759, 1760, 1762. Thereof seven bonds were part of lottery loans, which had different yields because of the prizes involved, and were therefore left out because otherwise this would have obscured the comparisons.

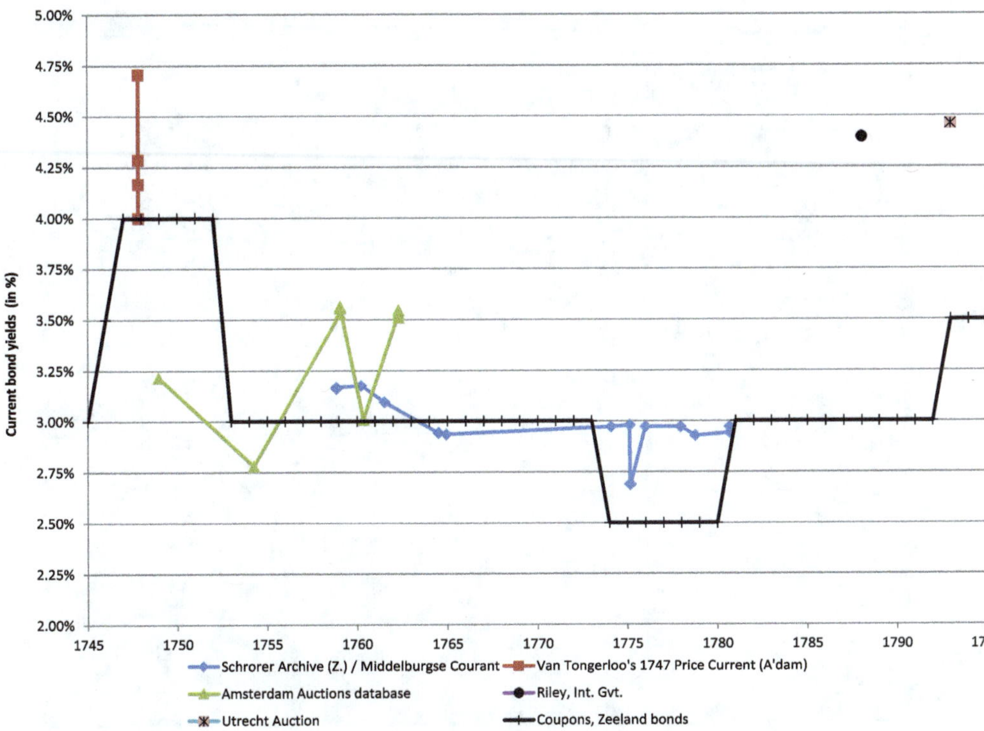

GRAPH 3.13 Current yields of Zeeland bonds, 1747–1781.
SOURCES: *MIDDELBURGSCHE COURANT*, 18 NOVEMBER 1758; ZA, SCHORER, INV.NO. 159; VAN DILLEN, 'EFFECTENKOERSEN', P. 13; AMSTERDAM AUCTIONS DATABASE, GELDERBLOM, JONKER AND VAN BOCHOVE [UPON REQUEST]; RILEY, *INTERNATIONAL*, P. 276, HUA, UTRECHT, NOTARIAL DEEDS, U255A011, ACT 75.

the 1770s coincided with a drop in the yields.[249] Finally, the high yields of the late 1780s and 1790s were not entirely mirrored by the coupons, which suggests that there were still investors accepting this lower coupon. Nevertheless, the yields and coupons kept in relatively close step with one another.

The pre-printed forms used for the limited number of transactions on which we have information indicates that transfers were common. Sophisticated preprinted standardised forms were used to execute the transactions in all but one case. Transfers were regular enough to justify the production of such forms. The forms offer spaces for the names of the buyers and sellers, dates, a description of the underlying asset, the name of the broker, and room to fill out the accrued interest since the last coupon payment and the market value – quoted as the clean price – both as a percentage and in currency (Figure 3.2).[250] The

249 ZA, Schorer, inv.no. 159.
250 ZA, Schorer, inv.no. 159.

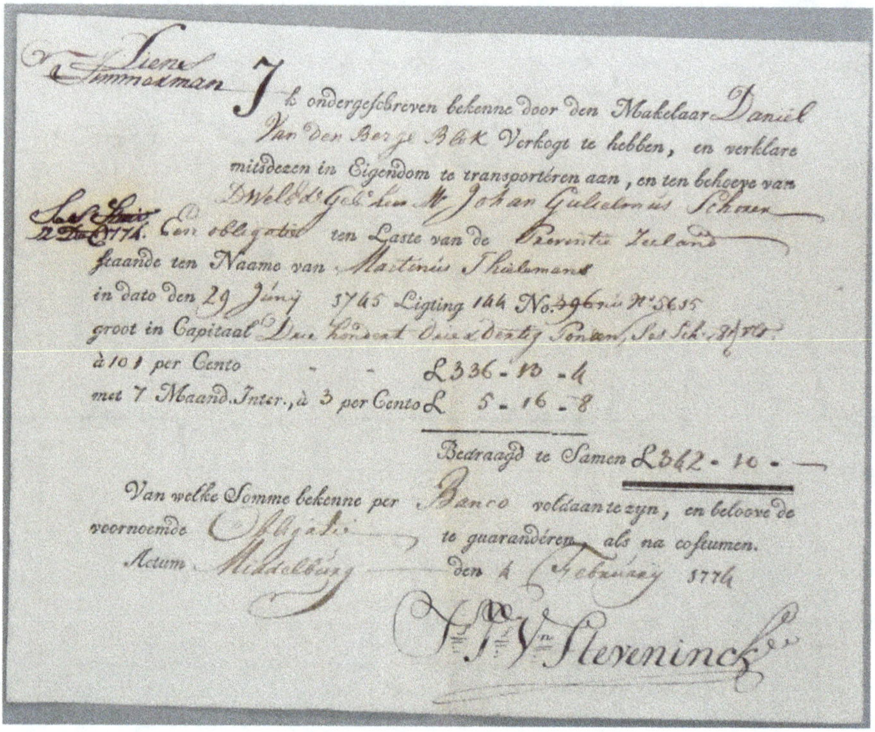
Tiens
Timmerman
Ik ondergeschreven bekenne door den Makelaar Daniël Van der Berge [illegible] Verkogt te hebben, en verklare mitsdeezen in Eigendom te transporteeren aan, en ten behoeve van D Weled. Gestr. heer Mr. Johan Gulielmus Schorer

[illegible] 1774. Een obligatie ten Laste van de Provintie Zeeland staande ten Naame van Martinus Thielemans in dato den 29 Junij 1745 Ligting 144 No. [illegible] No. 5655 groot in Capitaal Drie honderd drie en dertig Ponden, [illegible]

à 101 per Cento - - £336-10-4
met 7 Maand. Inter., à 3 per Cento £ 5-16-8
Bedraagd te Samen £342-10-–

Van welke Somme bekenne per Banco voldaan te zyn, en belove de voornoemde Obligatie te guaranderen, als na costumen.
Actum Middelburg den 4 February 1774
[illegible] Steveninck

FIGURE 3.2 Public security transfer by use of a pre-printed form, 4 February 1774.
ZA, SCHORER, INV. NO. 159.

sophistication of the pre-designed options indicates a well-developed secondary bond market in Zeeland.[251]

The regular announcements of public sales of securities in newspapers are another indication of a functioning secondary market. When advertising such sales the brokers announced what was offered for sale, but did not give the sales prices afterwards. For, instance the brokers Knouwen and Pagter announced the sale of various Zeeland bonds and redeemable annuities, together with a MCC share, on 6 March 1760, in the newspaper of 19 February.[252] Similarly, the broker Daniël van de Berge offered a batch of securities that contained tontines and 25-year bonds from the 1756 lottery loan, a prize bond of the 1749 lottery loan, a 2 per cent bond of the town of Veere and a

251 Neal, "How It All Began:" Neal argued that the political fragmentation of the Dutch Republic prevented the emergence of a liquid secondary market for public debt. This observation suggests otherwise.

252 *Middelburgsche Courant*, 19 February 1760.

share in the Oyster Company (Dutch: *Oester-Sociëteit*), also in Veere.[253] Another indication that there was a market for Zeeland bonds is the newspaper advertisements reporting stolen or lost bonds. The general public was warned not to purchase these assets, but to inform the newspaper if they were encountered and offered for sale.[254] Even though securities were publicly traded, price quotations for Zeeland public bonds were relatively scarce, but when they showed up, the prices seem quite close to par.

Until 1780, the market showed no signs of distrust. The market expected the States of Zeeland not to default. Whatever the reasons, we may assume that the coupon rates reflect the going market rates accurately.

At the same time, the clearest signal the creditors received regarding the provincial solvency or risk of default was the timeliness of the interest payments – financial overviews were only published after the Batavian Revolution of 1795 overthrew the Old Dutch Republic.[255] However, the punctuality of Zeeland's debt service was an issue towards the end of the century. From the late 1770s, arrears accrued. In 1785, no interest was paid on the loan of 1774, as mentioned previously. Rather, even the arrears for 1781 were not paid out.[256] It appears that this was not merely the consequence of the last war, but part of a more structural problem in the timely payment of creditors. In 1795, the province paid 75,000 guilders in overdue interest, accumulated since 1777, which still left a residual sum of 20,000 guilders. Most arrears concerned the most recent years (Graph 3.14).[257] The remaining 20,000 guilders equalled only 1.22 per cent of 1,680,697 guilders in Zeeland's annual interest payments. That a residue remained was worrying enough for investors.

The creditors understood these signals implied an increasing risk of default on Zeeland's provincial debt since the late 1780s. Even though its financial difficulties did not lead to an official repudiation of part of the debt – only to very late and irregular payments – the declining market prices suggest that creditors considered there to have been an increase in Zeeland's default risk.

The States of Zeeland managed to hold out for a long time. It kept the soaring debts after 1713 in check by constant conversions of massive new issuances into lower-yielding debt and reimbursement of existing debt. The constant conversion process marks a first shift in Zeeland's dependence on the creditors' goodwill. The newly issued debt since the 1690s was to be reim-

253 *Middelburgsche Courant*, 18 and 21 October 1766.

254 *Middelburgsche Courant*, 18 August 1772.

255 Riley, *International Government Finance*, 55.

256 ZA, RkC, 5910, inv. f. 40v.

257 ZA, RkC, inv.no. 5990, f.13r-19r.

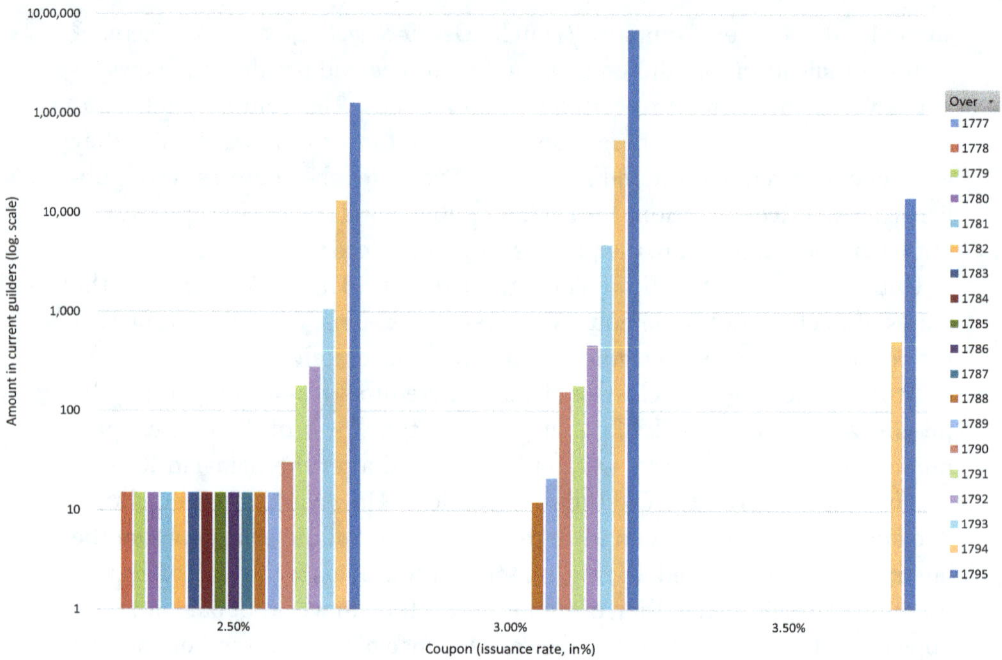

GRAPH 3.14 Interest paid on bonds in 1795, per year and coupon.
SOURCE: ZA, RKC, INV.NO. 5990, 13R-18V.

bursed on the creditors' demand and was exempt from the withholding tax on the bonds. So long as there was more capital offered than required, this worked to the States of Zeeland's advantage. After the War of the Austrian Succession, Zeeland's debt grew out of hand. The States stretched the limits of its credit by increasing the diversification of the debt and by enlarging the geographical scope of the market. On top of extensive borrowing in ordinary bonds, it issued various debt instruments to find new segments of creditors, tapping into Holland's capital surplus too. The policy yielded relatively low coupon rates compared to the private market and Holland's bonds. Creditors had only limited alternatives that seemed as secure Zeeland's public debt, as the financial crises of 1763 and 1772–1773 suggest. But by the late 1770s, Zeeland reached the limits of its credit. It could no longer pay its creditors fully and on time. The system of self-sustained reinvestment and abundant capital supply was finally exhausted.

5 Conclusion

After 1750, Zeeland could no longer sustain its debt independently. The deterioration of Zeeland's public finances was real and the request to reduce its allotted share in the Republic's common expenses was justified. This was also the conclusion of a States General committee in 1769. However, it took another twenty-two years to bring about a change in the 1616 quotas.

The worsening of Zeeland's financial health as a province had four related causes. Firstly, Zeeland's share in the common expenses was disproportionally large from the outset and the disproportion only became worse. It contributed one sixth of Holland's share, whereas its population was only one eighth that of Holland in 1616, and one tenth after 1660. Zeeland's slightly higher income level could not compensate for that difference and incomes did not grow.

Secondly, a direct cause was the expenses during the War of the Austrian Succession (1740–1748). Prudent fiscal policy since the Peace of Utrecht, in 1713, resulted in a balanced fiscal budget in 1740. The States of Zeeland gradually reduced the primary surplus and fiscal deficit at the same time. The former measure relieved the pressure on the heavily taxed population whenever possible. The latter restored the health of public finances. That policy rested on cheaper borrowing through conversions and high direct taxes. However, the new war increased the debt so much that any hope of further restoration of the public finances was destroyed.

Thirdly, Zeeland reached a tax ceiling. This first concerned the common means, where a ceiling was reached by the end of the seventeenth century. Since the late sixteenth-century tax revolution, the tax burden was as high as Holland's, or higher. A high tax burden is in line with Fritschy's argument about the urban system and Van Zanden and Prak's argument about urban tax morale. Zeeland was not fiscally free riding on Holland, as Van Zanden and Van Riel suggest. However, without economic growth, income from excises could not increase indefinitely. Direct taxes were necessary. This increasingly burdened the rich. Migration by wealthy Zeeland families to Holland suggests at least some of the elite voted with their feet after 1750.

Finally, Zeeland could hardly borrow any more cheaply than it did. With its reliance on voluntary conversions, the States of Zeeland exposed itself to the whims of the capital market. De Vries and Van der Woude's assumption that Zeeland had little need for borrowing should be revised. Continued borrowing was the only option as long as the other provinces refused to accommodate the province's request. Their sloth and inflexibility worsened the situation, and the province began running up arrears in the 1770s. The defective payments are symptomatic of the States of Zeeland's difficulties in footing the bill.

By 1750, it was out of options. A further increase in direct taxes would chase away the wealthy, an increase in indirect taxes was likely to lead to popular protests or riots, as had happened in 1702 and 1748, and even cheaper borrowing by voluntary conversions was almost impossible.

The first sign that Zeeland had reached its fiscal limits was when the Receiver-General turned to Holland's capital market after 1750. Until then, Zeeland's domestic savings had furnished sufficient capital for the States of Zeeland. The analysis of the reinvestment rates shows that Zeeland paid back more to investors than it required for additional loans. As a result, Zeeland's debt could grow, while the capital in the hands of investors accumulated. This increased the already large stock of capital within Zeeland. The expansion to encompass Holland's capital market, where capital was even more abundant than in Zeeland, helped Zeeland continue its debt management through constant reimbursements and by issuing new loans. The low coupons until the 1780s suggest that investors trusted the States of Zeeland's commitment to prioritise interest payments, even though Zeeland's per capita debt rapidly outgrew Holland's. The low coupon rates reflect trust in Zeeland's 'credible commitment' and not just capital abundance and forced measures by the tax on bonds, as Fritschy states.

Zeeland's commitment to the debt was remarkable. This stalwart behaviour, following Tomz's typology, forestalled defective payments for a long time and hid fiscal problems behind regular interest payments. The growing capital supply was helpful, as alternative investments became scarce and rather than leaving the money idle, investors accepted low returns. Even when the debt grew out of hand, Zeeland paid interest. A default would have hit the population hard, especially the urban elites who controlled the representative assembly, the States of Zeeland. This is in line with Stasavage's distributive view of the credible commitment thesis.

Yet urban political power and credible commitment could not sustain the debt. The absence of economic growth, and even deurbanisation, eroded the basis for taxation that funded the debt. The Republic's inflexibility, when it came to adjusting the fiscal burden in line with changes in the relative economic, demographic and fiscal capacity of the provinces, reinforced the deterioration in Zeeland's public finances, gradually at first from the start in 1616 and in a more pronounced way after 1750. The reluctance to make adjustments lends credence to the institutional impotence thesis of the Dutch Republic, albeit at the expense of Zeeland, not Holland. Despite Zeeland's tax revolution, classic financial revolution and credible commitment to the public debt, economic growth came to a halt. This suggests that economic growth is a precondition to sustain a financial revolution and that the causal direction is from growth to finance.

The next chapter examines debt management and commitment in Friesland, where the urban representatives formed a minority in the Provincial States.

CHAPTER 4

Friesland's Limited Commitment

Friesland's fiscal self-image was quite the opposite of its image among the other provinces: Friesland considered itself overburdened in its contribution to the shared expenses of the Dutch Republic, while the others considered it the most uncooperative member state and a difficult contributor to the Generality. In 1616, Friesland was assigned the second-largest contribution of 11.5 per cent in the common expenses. Frieland's delegates disputed its share from the beginning of the Revolt until the end of the eighteenth century. They argued on the one hand that the inland provinces of Overijssel and Gelderland contributed too little. On the other hand, they emphasised that Friesland was not as rich as Holland and Zeeland, lacking their thriving international ports and trade.[1] Although Friesland was also considered one of the maritime provinces, like Holland and Zeeland, it differed in its economic structure and institutional developments before and during the Dutch Revolt.[2] This chapter analyses which of the two opposing discourses holds water and what effects Friesland's contribution to the Generality had on its public finances and debt management.

There are arguments for both positions. On the one hand, Prak deemed Friesland's share too large, accepting the position of the nineteenth-century Frisian historiographer Van den Berg.[3] Spanninga also tentatively concludes that Friesland was disproportionately burdened. He points to economic differ-

1 Cor Trompetter, *Gewestelijke financiën ten tijde van de Republiek der Verenigde Nederlanden. Deel VI. Friesland (1587–1795)*, 221 (Den Haag: Instituut voor Nederlandse Geschiedenis, 2007), 12–24; Marijke Bruggeman, *Nassau en de macht van Oranje: de strijd van de Friese Nassau's voor de erkenning van hun rechten, 1702–1747* (s.n.], 2005), 133; Hotso Spanninga, *Gulden vrijheid?: politieke cultuur en staatsvorming in Friesland, 1600–1640* (Hilversum: Verloren, 2012), 37, 125; J. C. Van den Berg, "Friesland's Belastingen in de vorige eeuw," *De economist : tijdschrift voor alle standen, tot bevordering van volkswelvaart, door verspreiding van eenvoudige beginselen van staatshuishoudkunde* 39 (1890): 364–67; Hotso Spanninga, "Friesland in de nadagen van het Ancien Régime," in *Geschiedenis van Friesland 1750–1995*, ed. Jouke Arend Frieswijk, Fryske Akademy 853 (Amsterdam etc.: BoomLeeuwarden : Fryske Akademy, 1998), 28, 35–36.

2 Spanninga, *Gulden vrijheid?*, 35–36; Fritschy, *Public Finance*, 46; 't Hart, *The Dutch Wars of Independence*, 176–77; 't Hart, *The Making of a Bourgeois State*, 134.

3 Van den Berg, "Friesland's Belastingen"; Maarten R. Prak, *Gezeten burgers: de elite in een Hollandse stad* (Amsterdam: De Bataafsche Leeuw, 1985), 122.

 DOI:10.1163/9789004745254_005

ences compared with Holland and Zeeland to underpin this interpretation.[4] Trompetter considers Friesland's claims justified because Friesland's relative share in the Republic's total population declined from the mid-seventeenth century. On the other hand, he also remarks that when the quota distribution was rearranged in 1792, the ratio between the populations was identical to the ratio of the quota distribution of 1616.[5] He thus suggests that Friesland was overburdened until the situation improved in the late eighteenth century. However, Friesland's per capita contribution in 1616 was almost equal to Holland's and almost double that of Gelderland and Overijssel. Van Zanden and Van Riel, and Van Zanden and Prak argue that the other provinces were free riding on Holland's account, and Friesland in particular did so.[6] The question is whether these economic, demographic and political factors caused such big differences compared with the other coastal provinces – Holland and Zeeland – that it justified Friesland's lamentations. These three factors are the subjects of the first sections of this chapter. The second part of the chapter analyses the effects on public finance and debt management.

1 Provincial State Formation and Institutional Context

Friesland's political system under the Republic was characterised by broad representation and rural dominance. The wide-ranging representation made Frisian decision-making complex, notoriously slow and laborious. The explanation lies in the relative underdevelopment of provincial institutions before the Revolt. Local noblemen and freehold farmers held power in the villages and towns, without sovereign or central institutions and with little internal coherence. This 'Frisian Freedom' ended in 1498. Duke Albrecht of Saxony intervened in a conflict at the invitation of one of the Frisian factions. In 1515, Emperor Charles v succeeded him as Friesland's new overlord. He created centralised provincial institutions in which he was to appoint all the important officials. Daily authority rested with a Stadholder and the Court of Friesland. They appointed the heads of the local districts in the countryside (*grietmannen*) and magistrates in the towns. Representatives of the clergy, nobility and freeholders (*eigenerfden*) formed the States of Friesland but

4 Spanninga, *Gulden vrijheid?*, 35–36, 412.

5 Trompetter, *Gewestelijke financiën: vol 6. Friesland*, 12–13.

6 Van Zanden and Van Riel, *Nederland 1780–1914*, 52–53; Prak and Van Zanden, *Pioneers of Capitalism*, 150.

held no legislative power.[7] Hence, when Friesland joined the Revolt in 1576–1577, the provincial institutions were in their infancy and contested, without urban representation.

The Revolt offered the opportunity to regain the lost 'Frisian Freedom', without higher authorities and with local self-rule or broad 'democratic' representation.[8] These two aspects of the Frisian Freedom became the organising principles of the provincial institutions from the beginning of the Revolt. The States of Friesland assumed sovereignty over all provincial matters, including taxation. It now consisted of three rural Quarters and an urban Quarter. Each

---

7 J.J. Woltjer, "In de Leerschool Der Monarchie," in *Geschiedenis van Friesland*, ed. Jacob Jetzes Kalma, Johan Jacob Spahr van der Hoek, and Klaas de Vries, Fryske Akademy, ISSN 2352-6947 325 (Drachten: Laverman, 1968), 259–68; Johann Samuel Theissen, *Centraal gezag en Friesche vrijheid: Friesland onder Karel V* (Groningen: M. De Waal, 1907); Cornelis Jan Guibal, *Democratie en oligarchie in Friesland tijdens de Republiek*, Van Gorcum's historische bibliotheek 9 (Assen: Van Gorcum, 1934), 9, 19; Spanninga, *Gulden vrijheid?*, 37–42, 52–53, 80–81; Wim Blockmans, "Van private naar publieke macht in de vijftiende en zestiende eeuw," in *Fryslân, staat en macht 1450–1650 : bijdragen aan het historisch congres te Leeuwarden van 3 tot 5 juni 1998*, ed. J. Frieswijk et al., FA 875 (Hilversum: VerlorenLeeuwarden : Fryske Akademy, 1999), 20–25; Oebele Vries, "Staatsvorming in Zwitserland en Friesland in de vijftiende en zestiende eeuw," in *Fryslân, staat en macht 1450–1650 : bijdragen aan het historisch congres te Leeuwarden van 3 tot 5 juni 1998*, ed. J. Frieswijk et al., FA 875 (Hilversum: VerlorenLeeuwarden : Fryske Akademy, 1999), 37–42. The only central institution in Friesland before the sixteenth century was a council that consisted of the judges in the local courts, to which was later added the abbots of the monastries. It was reorganised, and in 1424 their meetings were referred to as Diets, (Dutch: *Landdagen*). J.A. Mol, "Hoofdelingen en huurlingen. Militaire innovatie en de aanloop tot 1498," in *Fryslân, staat en macht 1450–1650 : bijdragen aan het historisch congres te Leeuwarden van 3 tot 5 juni 1998*, ed. J. Frieswijk et al., FA 875 (Hilversum: VerlorenLeeuwarden : Fryske Akademy, 1999), 81–82: The fragmentation of Friesland implied that the fiscal basis of the local noblemen was only small. The rising costs of warfare exceeded the financial capacity of these local warlords, which fostered anarchy, pillaging and plunder by unpaid soldiers. Paul Baks, "Saksische heerschappij in Friesland, 1498–1515: dynastieke doelstellingen en politieke realiteit.," in *Fryslân, staat en macht 1450–1650 : bijdragen aan het historisch congres te Leeuwarden van 3 tot 5 juni 1998*, ed. J. Frieswijk et al., FA 875 (Hilversum: VerlorenLeeuwarden : Fryske Akademy, 1999), 85–86: More centralised taxation was a delicate part of the state formation in Friesland. The first attempts failed, as they met with too much resistance from the Diet. Rather, the Saxon dukes decided to implement decentralised taxes within the whole of Friesland. Trompetter, *Gewestelijke financiën: vol 6. Friesland*, 9; 't Hart, *The Making of a Bourgeois State*, 5; Prak, *The Dutch Republic*, 10–12; Hempenius-van Dijk, *Hof van Friesland*, 11–12. In 1524, when Friesland formally accepted the Habsburg rule, it acquired the "ius de non appellando". This meant that no appeal was possible against rulings by the Court of Friesland, thus giving it supreme authority. This was a deviation from the legislative system in the other Habsburg lands, which granted access to the Great Council of Malines.

8 Spanninga, *Gulden vrijheid?*, 40–41, 55–59.

Quarter had one vote.[9] Their independent membership of the States improved the towns' position compared to the situation before the Revolt when they were part of the rural Quarters.[10] Decisions on most matters were taken by majority vote, while some required unanimity, including fiscal matters.[11]

Members of the States of Friesland were elected by a large proportion of the Frisian population in multi-stage annual elections, rather than being appointed by the Court.[12] Each town and district sent two delegates to the meetings of the States of Friesland, the Frisian Diet. Each of the thirty rural districts elected one nobleman and one freeholder to one of three rural Quarters. The eleven city councils and magistrates elected the urban representatives.[13] Because elections were held annually, the eighty-two delegates could be held accountable more easily than elsewhere, where representatives were often co-opted for life.[14] Sovereignty thus truly rested with the urban magistrate and rural electorate.[15] The rural electorate dominated this bottom-up institutional structure.

Friesland remained an oligarchy of nobility, landowners and urban patricians nonetheless. Rural ballot rights were concentrated in the hands of several wealthy families in the late seventeenth century. This granted them various rights in the villages, such as the appointment of Protestant ministers, judges and other officials.[16] At the provincial level, the States of Friesland appointed the Court of Friesland, the Stadholder and, annually, the Executive Committee (*Gedeputeerde Staten*) to run Friesland's daily affairs. Finally, two representatives from each Quarter formed the *Mindergetal* committee to pre-

---

9 Spanninga, 52, 82; Trompetter, *Gewestelijke financiën: vol 6. Friesland*, 9.

10 Spanninga, *Gulden vrijheid?*, 102–4: In exchange for admission to the Frisian Diet, the towns had to raise one ninth of the provincial contribution to the Generality. Guibal, *Democratie en oligarchie*, 11.

11 Spanninga, *Gulden vrijheid?*, 49–50, 96, 305–9; Trompetter, *Gewestelijke financiën: vol 6. Friesland*, 10.

12 Guibal, *Democratie en oligarchie*, 11; Spanninga, *Gulden vrijheid?*, 46.

13 Spanninga, *Gulden vrijheid?*, 43, 57–58.

14 Spanninga, 50.

15 Guibal, *Democratie en oligarchie*, 19, 86.

16 In theory, about one in three adult males could cast a vote in Friesland's rural areas. In total, about 10,000 voters annually elected the rural representatives. If we assume an average rural population size of approximately 100,000 people, 10,000 voters implies 10 per cent of the population. If we also assume that half the population was female, this figure rises to 20 per cent of male inhabitants. Given the high child mortality and the limited population growth over the period 1650–1800, we may assume that about 20 per cent of the population was under-aged. In that case, we arrive at the figure of on in three adult males who could cast a vote in Friesland. Spanninga, *Gulden vrijheid?*, 46–49; Spanninga, "Friesland in de nadagen," 21.

pare and facilitate decision-making. This was often slow as representatives frequently went back to their towns or districts for consultation (*ruggespraak*). Matters on which no decision was taken were postponed until the next six-week session of the Diet.[17] From their ranks, the representatives also nominated representatives for Republic's central institutions: the States General, the Council of State, the Board of Admiralties and the Generality Court of Audit.[18] A shrinking group of families divided those offices among themselves to safeguard their income and position.[19]

The position of the Stadholder in Friesland was ambivalent. On the one hand, the Revolt had robbed him of his dominant position. He was now a servant of the province, appointed by the States and subjected to tight constraints. For instance, he could not own real estate in the province because this was linked to rural ballot rights and hence political influence. On the other hand, Friesland formed the power base of the family of Orange-Nassau in the eighteenth century. Friesland held on to a Stadholder of the House of Nassau-Dietz when the other provinces entered the Second Stadholderless Period (1711–1747).[20]

Again, the concept of Frisian Freedom helps to understand the relationship. As an expression of its autonomy, Friesland had appointed different Stadholders to Holland since the death of William of Orange in 1584. This ended in 1747 when the Frisian Stadholder William IV was promoted to Stadholder of all the provinces.[21] The Frisian delegates had supported his case for doing this for some time.[22] Furthermore, the Frisians hoped that a Stadholder of their own would protect Frisian interests in the face of Holland's dominance in the States General.[23]

A similar symbiosis of shared interests led to a complex sharing of authority within the province. For instance, in consultation with the Executive Committee, the Stadholder nominated the members of the legal Court of Friesland and appointed military officers on Friesland's payroll; on the other hand, as army commander, he required the Executive Committee's approval to move

17 Guibal, *Democratie en oligarchie*, 14, 17–18, 20–21; Spanninga, *Gulden vrijheid?*, 42–51, 60, 96–97, 351.

18 Guibal, *Democratie en oligarchie*, 52.

19 Guibal, 88.

20 Guibal, 23; Israel, *The Dutch Republic*, 224, 302–4, 1071; Spanninga, *Gulden vrijheid?*, 42, 98–99, 383; Fruin, *Geschiedenis der Staatsinstellingen*, 205–7.

21 Spanninga, *Gulden vrijheid?*, 41–42.

22 Bruggeman, *Nassau en de macht van Oranje*, 133, 246.

23 Bruggeman, 133; Spanninga, *Gulden vrijheid?*, 41–42, 58, 125.

troops.[24] He also presided over the *Mindergetal* committee. This increased his influence over financial matters because Friesland's approval of the Republic's annual budget depended on the Committee's assessment.[25] He could appoint towns' magistrates, together with the Court.[26] The position of the Stadholder remained restricted but gradually improved, culminating in the Reform Statute (*Reglement Reformatoir*) of 1748. After the subsequent tax farming riots (*pachtersoproer*), and riots of the civic militia movement (*doelistenbeweging*) calling for reform of the oligarchy, he emerged as the victor from the struggle between the oligarchy and the forces of democracy.[27] At the end of the eighteenth century, Frisian Patriots invoked the Frisian Freedom to overthrow the Stadholder's patronage system (*Stadhoudelijk stelsel*) and the oligarchy of the 'Ancient Regime'.[28] Each province cherished its autonomy, but Friesland arguably most of all.

1.1 *Friesland's Reluctance to Contribute to the Republic's Budget*

Friesland's reluctance to contribute to the Republic's shared expenses illustrates its desire for autonomy. Friesland did everything to keep its contribution as low as possible, before and after the fixation of its share at 11.5 per cent

24 Guibal, *Democratie en oligarchie*, 24; Spanninga, *Gulden vrijheid?*, 132–33; Fruin, *Geschiedenis der Staatsinstellingen*, 205.

25 Trompetter, *Gewestelijke financiën: vol 6. Friesland*, 10–11.

26 Guibal, *Democratie en oligarchie*, 25, 102–3, 115–16, 202–3; Spanninga, *Gulden vrijheid?*, 52, 97–102; Hempenius-van Dijk, *Hof van Friesland*, 12; The Court was not without influence, however. In 1649, the Leeuwarden burgomaster Alle van Burum still deemed it wise to maintain good relations with the Councillors, for they could provide the necessary legal protection. Van Buren described to the Stadholder William Frederick the arbitrariness with which the Councillors rendered justice. Janssen, *Creaturen van de macht*, 21, 60–61; Yme Kuiper and Annemarie Zijlstra, "'Een yeder hadt te doen met poten, planten en andere dingen'. Het buitenleven van rijke en voorname Friezen in de Gouden Eeuw.," in *Buitenplaatsen in de Gouden Eeuw: de rijkdom van het buitenleven in de Republiek*, ed. Yme Kuiper and Ben Olde Meierink, Adelsgeschiedenis ; XIV (Hilversum: Verloren, 2015), 103: The Court must also have involved itself in political matters, because in 1663 it was warned that it should refrain from interfering in such affairs.

27 Guibal, *Democratie en oligarchie*, 188–89; Israel, *The Dutch Republic*, 1072–73.

28 Jelte Olthof, "Oer 'Fryske Frijheid': Fries En Vrij in Revolutietijd," *It Beaken. Tydskrift Fan de Fryske Akademy* 81, no. 1/2 (2019): 15–30; Spanninga, "Friesland in de nadagen"; Hempenius-van Dijk, *Hof van Friesland*, 11–12. In 1524, when Friesland formally accepted the Habsburg rule, it acquired the "ius de non appellando". This meant that no appeal was possible against rulings by the Court of Friesland, which thus gave it supreme authority. This was a deviation from the legislative system in the other Habsburg lands, which granted access to the Great Council of Malines.

in 1616.[29] Friesland opposed the States General introducing the excises of the common means until 1602. Internal discord caused a temporary split of the Diet into two separate meetings, with one recruiting soldiers of its own, in 1600. Even the armed intervention by Stadholder William Louis of Nassau did not solve this. In 1602, the States General forced Friesland to introduce the common means because it was in arrears with its payments according to the quota.[30]

Control over the military became the recurring issue in the quarrels about Friesland's contribution to the Generality. At regular intervals, Friesland used erratic troop payments as leverage. For instance, in 1610, it singlehandedly dismissed nine companies on its payroll, each stationed far enough outside of the province.[31] When embassies sent by the Generality failed to achieve any results, the Council of State sent the dismissed troops up to Friesland to collect their overdue wages in 1612. Under the pretext of safeguarding the Republic's internal harmony, Friesland now paid the overdue soldiers' wages.[32]

Regardless of ideological arguments, Friesland could afford this poor payment behaviour because of its favourable strategic geographical position. It was hardly endangered during wars. After 1594, Groningen served as a buffer state to its east, whereas the moors in Drenthe to the southeast were hard to cross.[33] It maintained a garrison in the fortified town of Steenwijk, in the province of Overijssel, which was the main gateway to its southeast.[34] At sea, the interests of Holland and Zeeland exceeded Friesland's, so those two provinces therefore maintained the navy.[35] From that comfortable position, there was little trouble with unpaid soldiers unless they were allowed to collect their money in person, as in 1612.

29 Trompetter, *Gewestelijke financiën: vol 6. Friesland*, 11.

30 Trompetter, 18–24; Bruggeman, *Nassau en de macht van Oranje*, 257; Spanninga, *Gulden vrijheid?*, 108–17; 't Hart, *The Making of a Bourgeois State*, 121–23, 135, 146–48.

31 Spanninga, *Gulden vrijheid?*, 124.

32 A. Th. van Deursen, "De plaats van het gewest Friesland in de Republiek," in *Fryslân, staat en macht 1450–1650: bijdragen aan het historisch congres te Leeuwarden van 3 tot 5 juni 1998*, ed. Jouke Arend Frieswijk et al., FA 875 (Hilversum: VerlorenLeeuwarden : Fryske Akademy, 1999), 229–30.

33 Spanninga, *Gulden vrijheid?*, 33; This was not unlike the provinces Overijssel and Gelderland for Holland and Zeeland: 't Hart, *The Dutch Wars of Independence*, 173, 195–96.

34 Israel, *The Dutch Republic*, 245–47, 303: This was much to the chagrin of the States of Overijssel, who deemed this a violation of its provincial autonomy; Spanninga, *Gulden vrijheid?*, 124.

35 Veenstra, *Tussen gewest en Generaliteit.*

After the expiry of the Truce in 1621, Friesland regularly refused to pay troops or other military expenses, which caused unpaid soldiers to defect.[36] Even with the threat of an invasion from East Friesland in Germany, in 1628, the States of Friesland refused to pay for improvements of fortifications.[37] Rather, in 1630–1631 Friesland again dismissed troops in an attempt to reduce its fixed share in the Generality budget.[38] Arrears in soldiers' wages in 1634 preceded a renewed request for a discount in 1635.[39] Delegates from other provinces, however, argued that taxation in Friesland was comparatively low.[40] The Council of State feared that Friesland's beggar-thy-neighbour policy would incite other provinces to withhold payments as well.[41] Intervention in Friesland's politics was urgently needed.[42]

Internal disagreements over taxation were indeed one reason for the arrears. Therefore the States General threatened Friesland with execution in 1625: it warned that if fiscal reforms were not made, it would seize goods and take hostages. However, a rioting crowd chased away a Council of State's embassy in 1626.[43] In 1632, 2,000 soldiers guarded the Council of State. As soon as these troops left the province, the States of Friesland reversed the fiscal measures.[44] An intervention in 1634 also failed because the Frisian Stadholder Henry Casimir took control of the Generality troops.[45] By the end of 1635, the envoys of the States General concluded that without military assistance there would be no lasting fiscal reforms in Friesland.[46] Assured of military backup, the Council of State returned to Friesland in 1637. There, it supported a counter-coup against the original coup of 1635.[47] Only the increase in the number of soldiers in October 1637 pushed the Diet to finally adopt the

36 't Hart, *The Making of a Bourgeois State*, 170–71; Spanninga, *Gulden vrijheid?*, 134–35, 141, 411. At the time, in 1622, the commissioners were sent to Gelderland, Zeeland, Overijssel and Groningen as well, in order to increase tax revenues from there.

37 Spanninga, *Gulden vrijheid?*, 174.

38 Spanninga, 179; P. J. D. van Slooten, "Frieslands financiën in 1709 en 1770," *Friesche Volksalmanak*, 1885, 365.

39 Spanninga, *Gulden vrijheid?*, 156, 193–209, 232, 334; 't Hart, *The Making of a Bourgeois State*, 147.

40 Deursen, "De plaats van de noordelijke gewesten," 20.

41 Spanninga, *Gulden vrijheid?*, 35, 217–63, 268–69, 272, 287, 294.

42 Spanninga, 272; 't Hart, *The Making of a Bourgeois State*, 146–48.

43 Spanninga, *Gulden vrijheid?*, 152–56, 181.

44 Spanninga, 182–83.

45 Spanninga, 193–209, 232, 334.

46 Spanninga, 256.

47 Spanninga, 35, 217–63, 268–69, 272, 287, 294.

fiscal reforms.[48] The Council of State emerged as the winner in the power struggle over the control over troops and funds.

The real challenge was to *maintain* the fiscal reforms because the electorate pressured the representatives to reverse them as soon as the soldiers were out of sight.[49] This had happened in 1626, 1632 and 1634. From 1638, all delegates had to swear to maintain all existing taxes until the end of the war. Candidates for the Diet were forbidden to win over voters by promises of tax reductions.[50] The fact that elections were held annually made this form of populism a real danger.

Therefore, the adoption of the fiscal reforms was assured literally at gunpoint. To prevent the abolition of the new taxes, Friesland's Executive Committee instructed the Council of State to attend the next session of the Diet, in June 1638. There, the Council of State took the entire Diet hostage and soldiers collected absent delegates from their homes. Armed guards prevented the delegates from leaving the conference room until a resolution was accepted that satisfied the Generality.[51] Ultimately military force secured the Generality's income from Friesland – and not persuasion.[52]

However victorious, this was also the last occasion on which the Generality enforced payments by military means. Rather, the States of Friesland appear to have made it a policy to withhold soldiers' wages to blackmail the Generality into a reduction in the shared expenses. Already in 1642, Friesland reduced the payments to the companies on their payroll by 25 per cent.[53] For the States General, this posed less of a problem than Holland's simultaneous resistance to the size of the army, which may explain why no further action was taken against Friesland.[54] Again, during the Franco-Dutch War (1672–1678) Friesland requested a reduction, followed by the unilateral dismissal of troops in 1679. The States of Friesland justified its action by referring to a 1651 resolution that determined the recruitment and dismissal of troops as a provincial matter. Despite their objections, Stadholder William III and the Generality accepted this course of affairs.[55]

48 Spanninga, 312–17.

49 Spanninga, 172.

50 Spanninga, 328, 334, 343–45, 371.

51 Spanninga, 328, 334, 343–45, 371.

52 Aalbers, *De Republiek*, 61, 66, 117.

53 Spanninga, *Gulden vrijheid?*, 359.

54 Israel, *The Dutch Republic*, 541–45.

55 Jan Wagenaar, *Vaderlandsche historie, vervattende de geschiedenissen der nu Vereenigde Nederlanden, inzonderheid die van Holland, van de vroegste tyden af: Vyftiende deel, beginnende met het jaar 1679, en eindigende met de verheffing van den prinse en prinsesse*

Without means of coercion, the Generality relied on embassies to urge Friesland either to approve or to pay its contribution to the common budget. To this end, no fewer than fifteen embassies travelled to Friesland between 1667 and 1748.[56] One such embassy, in 1730, concerned arrears for Generality-guaranteed debts that amounted to almost 2.5 million guilders. For a change, the States of Friesland claimed impotence and financial deterioration and did not dispute the validity of the claim. Only after repeated requests did the States of Friesland produce a projection for 1730 that showed a deficit of 7,363 guilders. A closer examination reveals that these calculations included 8,000 guilders to reimburse annuities and projected the full payments of its liabilities with respect to the Generality.[57] Hence, to substantiate the claim of financial hardship Friesland had to manipulate the figures.

Despite the promising projections of full payments, the embassy was left empty-handed. Rather, after weeks of meetings, the *Mindergetal* committee kindly thanked the gentlemen ambassadors for their concern and informed them that the dissolution of that year's Diet prevented decision-making. The issue was to be discussed in the next Diet session.[58] To make matters worse, the States of Friesland secretly agreed to withhold their approval to the Generality budgets above the desired 9 per cent share as leverage to obtain a reduction. This happened literally behind the embassy's back.[59]

In 1770, Friesland again required manipulated financial statements to underpin its claim of financial impotence. It claimed a deficit of 189,000 guilders. However, correcting for 144,500 guilders to repay the public debt leaves a deficit of only 44,500 guilders. Furthermore, cattle stock mortality was assumed to reduce the projected income from the cattle tax by 70,000 guilders compared to previous years.[60] Without these manipulations, Friesland would dispose of a fiscal surplus of 25,000 guilders.

---

van Oranje, tot koning en koningin van Groot-Britanje, in 't jaar 1689 (Te Amsterdam,: by Johannes Allart, 1794), 24–35; Brandon, *Masters of War*, 43; Slooten, "Frieslands financiën," 365.

56 NA, Archief Staten-Generaal, inv.nos. 8898, 8899, 8904, 8909, 8919, 8924, 8925, 8930, 8931, 8933, 8936, 8941, 8949, 8951, 8955

57 Tresoar, Gewestelijke bestuursinstellingen van Friesland 1580–1795 (hereafter: SvF), inv. no. 267, f. 232v, 15 March 1730.

58 NA, Staten-Generaal, inv.no. 8951. The embassy lasted from 2 March to 22 March 1730, of which a day-to-day report has survived. The amounts are derived from the appendices no. 3 and 4 within the archival files; the arrears amounted to 2,488,907 guilders on 31 December 1729.

59 Tresoar, Gewestelijke bestuursinstellingen van Friesland 1580–1795 (hereafter: SvF), inv. no. 267, f. 232v, 15 March 1730.

60 NA, Provinciale resoluties, inv.no. 484.

The manipulation of these financial statements makes the claims of financial impotence more a habitual complaint than a realistic assessment. Nevertheless, the province again unilaterally reduced its contribution to 9 per cent in 1783.[61] This time, however, the other provinces gave in. In 1783, a Generality committee advised that Friesland would pay less towards the fortifications outside its provincial borders. This solution was similar to that for Zeeland a few years before.[62] The discount appears the result of two centuries of complaining rather than genuine financial hardship.

2 Economic Developments

Friesland's economy was characterised by commercial agriculture and the absence of a strict separation between urban and rural economic activities. The development of the Frisian economy follows the broad trend in northwest European: growth in the sixteenth to mid-seventeenth centuries, followed by stagnation and decline until the mid-eighteenth century, after which growth picked up again. Prak and Van Zanden, however, argue that the Frisian Freedom slowed growth in the late Middle Ages compared to other parts of the Netherlands.[63] This section analyses the main economic developments in order to assess the basis of Friesland's fiscal capacity. This helps to answer the question of whether the fiscal distribution of 1616 overburdened Friesland, and if so when.

2.1 *Demographic Developments*

In 1616, the per capita contributions of Holland and Friesland to the Generality were almost identical. Both provinces had shared in the sixteenth-century upswing. For Friesland, this meant a doubling of the population compared to 1511, from approximately 75,000 to 130,000 inhabitants. Population growth

61 Dorothea Josephine Antoinette Roodhuyzen-van Breda Vriesman, "Onfrisse Friese zaken. Een admiraliteit in opspraak," in *In het kielzog: maritiem-historische studies aangeboden aan Jaap R. Bruijn bij zijn vertrek als hoogleraar zeegeschiedenis aan de Universiteit Leiden*, ed. Jacobus Ruurd Bruijn and Leonardus Maria Akveld (Amsterdam: De Bataafse Leeuw, 2003), 99: It now paid ƒ 8:13:2 for each ƒ 100 instead of the former ƒ 11:13:2.

62 NA, Raad van State, (1574) 1581–1795 (1801), inv.no. 2116.

63 Johannes Alle Faber, *Drie eeuwen Friesland: economische en sociale ontwikkelingen van 1500 tot 1800*, vol. I, A.A.G. bijdragen 17 (Wageningen: Landbouwhogeschool, Afd. Agrarische Geschiedenis, 1972), 391–93; Prak and Van Zanden, *Pioneers of Capitalism*, 34–36.

continued to about 165,000 in the 1660s, and was concentrated in the towns.[64] As a result, the degree of urbanisation increased from approximately 22 per cent in 1511 to 33 per cent in 1689.[65] Still, urbanisation was less than in Holland and Zeeland. After the 1660s, the total population declined to around 135,000 people by the mid-eighteenth century. The decline was probably abrupt. The number of beds and amount of bed linen in Frisian households decreased after 1650, as did household size and fertility.[66] Renewed growth after 1740 was concentrated in the countryside. The population recovered almost to the level of the 1660s by 1795, but urban population growth lagged behind, causing a fall in the degree of urbanisation to approximately 25 per cent.[67] Friesland's tax base thus expanded until the 1660s and again after 1740, first in the towns, and subsequently in the countryside (see: graph 4.1).

This raises the question of how its demographic development affected the requested contribution to the common expenses, relative to the other provinces. In 1616, both Friesland's quota and its population were one-fifth of Holland's. Around 1700, Friesland's population was less than one-sixth of Holland. Friesland's population growth compared favourably relative to Zeeland, however. In 1616, Zeeland's population amounted to almost 60 per cent of Friesland's, but from the 1660s to 1795 it was barely half. By 1700, demographic developments had increased Friesland's relative burden by 25 per cent relative to Holland but the relative burden decreased by 17 per cent compared to Zeeland. Friesland's demographic growth after 1750 restored its relative position compared to Holland by 1795. These mixed results do not provide a definitive answer on whether Friesland became overburdened.

64 Faber, *Drie eeuwen Friesland*, 1972, I:90–91; Faber, *Drie eeuwen Friesland*, 1972, II:412–13; H. P. H. Nusteling and Ph. van der Weegen, "Dopen en trouwen en de bevolkingsomvang van Friesland in de periode 1655–1794," *It beaken : meidielingen fan de Fryske Akademy* 46 (1984): 106, 123, 131. In 1655, for instance, they estimate the population to have amounted to about 165,000 people, which is 10,000 more than Faber. Prak, *The Dutch Republic*, 251; Spanninga, *Gulden vrijheid?*, 36–37.

65 Faber, *Drie eeuwen Friesland*, 1972, II:413.

66 Jan De Vries, "Peasant Demand Patterns and Economic Development, Friesland 1550–1750," in *European Peasants and Their Markets: Essays in Agrarian Economic History*, ed. William Nelson Parker and Eric Lionel Jones (Princeton, N.J. etc.: Princeton University Press, 1975), 219; Faber, *Drie eeuwen Friesland*, 1972, I:90.

67 Faber, *Drie eeuwen Friesland*, 1972, I:90–91; Faber, *Drie eeuwen Friesland*, 1972, II:412–13; Spanninga, *Gulden vrijheid?*, 104. It has been argued that the failure of the Frisian towns to acquire staple rights over the countryside caused their stunting in the long run.

GRAPH 4.1 Friesland's population trends, 1575–1795.
SOURCES: FEENSTRA, *BETWEEN SHARED*, APPENDIX.

2.2 *Economic Trends in Friesland*

With about two-thirds of the population living in the countryside, Friesland was more rural than Holland and Zeeland. The question is whether this meant a different type of economy, one that reduced Friesland's fiscal capacity, as claimed by Friesland's representatives. The degree of urbanisation is a difficult proxy for economic growth in the case of Friesland because the separation between towns and villages in economic activities was less strict than in Holland. In Holland the towns dominated and craft activities were forbidden in the countryside. In Friesland, the rural quarters dominated and trade and crafts were not restricted to the towns.[68] In 1601, some occupations were forbidden in the countryside, in exchange for a higher fiscal contribution.[69] Still, some villages were larger than other urban centres with official town status and they performed urban services and functions.[70] This reduced the need to move to

68 Faber, *Drie eeuwen Friesland*, 1972, I:124 In Holland the "Order op de Buitennering" forbade crafts in the countryside in 1531. Spanninga, *Gulden vrijheid?*, 102.

69 Trompetter, *Gewestelijke financiën: vol 6. Friesland*, 24.

70 Spanninga, *Gulden vrijheid?*, 36–37.

towns. Because the distinction between urban and rural economies was less clear than elsewhere, it makes more sense to distinguish between agricultural and non-agricultural activities rather than rural and urban activities.

Urban growth was, nevertheless, an expression of the economic transformation in the sixteenth century. In 1511, over 80 per cent of the rural population worked in agriculture. By the mid-seventeenth century, this had decreased to around 60 per cent of the rural population, plus a handful of urban dwellers. Consequently, agriculture accounted for over 40 per cent of the workforce, and other sectors for over 50 per cent. This occupational structure was presumably the same between 1650 and 1750.[71] Hence, only looking at the degree of urbanisation leads to an overestimation of the agricultural sector by approximately 50 per cent.[72]

Moreover, the rural economy developed from predominantly self-sufficient in the early sixteenth century to market-oriented in the seventeenth century.[73] Depending on the economic prospects, farmers alternated between arable farming and livestock farming. Livestock farming became more important in the seventeenth century, while farmers switched back to arable farming at the beginning of the eighteenth century. The rinderpest epizootic of 1744 led in turn to more cattle breeding.[74] The cattle plague of 1769 was also

71 Faber, *Drie eeuwen Friesland*, 1972, I:99–105, 108, 111; Faber, *Drie eeuwen Friesland*, 1972, II:440–41: About 57.5 per cent of the labour force worked outside the agricultural sector. De Vries assumed that Friesland's occupational structure did not change significantly between 1650 and 1750, which would mean the 1749 assessment register reflects the mid-seventeenth-century situation as well. Jan De Vries, "De economische ontwikkeling van Friesland na het einde van de Friese vrijheid," in *Fryslân, staat en macht 1450–1650 : bijdragen aan het historisch congres te Leeuwarden van 3 tot 5 juni 1998*, ed. J. Frieswijk et al., FA 875 (Hilversum: VerlorenLeeuwarden : Fryske Akademy, 1999), 149. De Vries, however, argues that a much larger share of the population must have been involved in peat digging than reported in the census of 1749. A considerable proportion of the common labourers, whose activities were not specified, probably earned a living from this sector : De Vries, "Peasant Demand," 262–63; A. T. Schuitema Meijer, "Sociaal-economische aspecten van de stad," in *Historie van Groningen: stad en land*, ed. Wiebe Jannes Formsma (Groningen: Tjeenk Willink, 1976), 355. In the adjacent province of Groningen, the city possessed the staple rights. Although the City Council deemed this a favourable institution for both countryside and city, others argued that the situation in neighbouring Friesland was much better, for it was not hindered by this right. Spanninga, *Gulden vrijheid?*, 102.

72 Two thirds, or 67 per cent, lived in rural areas; around 42.5 per cent were occupied in agriculture: 67%/42.5% = 157%.

73 De Vries, "Economische ontwikkeling," 150–54.

74 De Vries, 150–54; De Vries, "Peasant Demand," 213–16; Faber, *Drie eeuwen Friesland*, 1972, II:583–97; Kees Kuiken, *Het Bildt is geen eiland: capita cultuurgeschiedenis van een vroegmoderne polder in Friesland*, Historia agriculturae 45 (Groningen: Nederlands Agrono-

serious, but took place during an economic upturn. Other setbacks for agriculture were floods such as the Christmas Flood of 1717. After this disaster, the dykes were raised substantially. After 1731, shipworms (*paalwormen*) weakened the wooden dykes. Restoration with expensive stones resulted in stronger dykes and lower maintenance costs. This prevented major floods until 1825, which contributed to the recovery of agriculture.[75]

From the mid-sixteenth century, Amsterdam was the main market for Frisian grain. A grain merchant from the adjacent province of Groningen was more likely to purchase Frisian barley through the Amsterdam market than directly in Friesland.[76] Therefore, the town of Leeuwarden had a permanent agent in Amsterdam from 1638 onwards, who reported grain prices every week.[77] Frisians exported wheat to Holland and imported rye for their own consumption.[78] Contemporaries considered the seventeenth-century Frisian farmers to be wealthy, their soils rich and taxes low.[79]

Until around 1650, rising agricultural prices caused land leases to triple. From around 1660, agricultural prices fell until about 1735.[80] Land rents, however, hardly declined at all, except for a few temporary drops in the 1680s-1690s, 1730s and 1740s. The price rise that began in the 1770s caused land rents to triple again by 1800.[81]

---

misch Historisch Instituut, 2013), 162. Some farmers even turned their back on farming. For instance, Arjen Gijsberts invested his gains from grain cultivation in a Harlingen brewery in 1652, which he sold in the 1660s, just before the Frisian brewing industry declined.

75 Faber, *Drie eeuwen Friesland*, 1972, I:147–48, 150, 154, 221.

76 Lesger, *The Rise of the Amsterdam Market and Information Exchange*; Kuiken, *Het Bildt*, 77.

77 Kuiken, *Het Bildt*, 80.

78 de Vries, *The Price of Bread*, 157; De Vries, "Economische ontwikkeling," 150.

79 Kuiken, *Het Bildt*, 2: From the Spanish military commander Fransisco Verdugu in 1586 to the Frisian historiographer Christaan Schotanus in 1664. Spanninga, *Gulden vrijheid?*, 353.

80 Merijn T. Knibbe, *Lokkich Fryslân: een studie naar de ontwikkeling van de productiviteit van de Friese landbouw 1505–1830*, Historia agriculturae, ISSN 0439–2027 38 (Groningen etc.: Nederlands Agronomisch Historisch Instituut, 2006), 118–20. The land rents were expressed in "florenen", guilders of 28 *stuivers*. The derivative "floreen" tax was one of the most important taxes in Friesland and was levied until the end of the eighteenth century. De Vries, "Economische ontwikkeling," 141; Faber, *Drie eeuwen Friesland*, 1972, I:132, 134; Faber, *Drie eeuwen Friesland*, 1972, II:574; Johannes Alle Faber, "De Oligarchisering van Friesland in de Tweede Helft van de Zeventiende Eeuw.," A.A.G. *Bijdragen* 15 (1970): 59: The lower land prices prompted members of the elite to seek more income from public offices and withdraw from the rest of society.

81 Knibbe, *Lokkich Fryslân*, 90, 91, 93, 135, 138.

Although agriculture remained the largest sector, the majority of Friesland's population worked outside agriculture. Crafts and industry formed the second largest sector, employing more than a quarter of the population. Trade and transportation offered a living to almost 20 per cent of the working population. Less than 10 per cent worked in professions such as Protestant ministers, schoolmasters, or officials in legal or administrative services and the military. Urban wage labour, peat digging, fisheries and hunting together accounted for less than 5 per cent of the population. The few workers combining multiple occupations is further evidence of the far-reaching occupational specialisation.[82]

Production was largely for the local market, with little produced for export. The brick, tile and pottery industries were exceptions. The specialised producers served the growing local market in the countryside as well. Even farmers and peasants purchased bread rather than making it themselves. Specialised production and consumption remained local, in both urban and rural areas. These included goldsmiths and silversmiths who served the increasingly wealthy farmers in the eighteenth century.[83]

The majority of the traders and transporters lived in villages. The network of inland waterways facilitated the domestic redistribution of goods. Increasing demand for peat first prompted improvements in canal construction in the period up to 1650. The demand for this fuel subsequently stagnated until around 1750, when it increased again.[84] Exports also consisted primarily of agricultural produce and peat, mostly destined for Holland.[85] Further trade and transportation focused on Holland, Scandinavia and the Baltic. Frisian skippers acquired a prominent position in the transport of Norwegian wood. After 1650, they compensated for the loss of the Norwegian timber trade by sailing across the Baltic Sea. The Baltic trade grew after 1720; between 1740 and 1770, half of the Dutch ships in the Baltic sailed under Frisian skippers. They often worked for Holland traders and shipowners on Holland ships, mostly from Amsterdam. The Frisian town of Harlingen in particular developed an

82 Faber, *Drie eeuwen Friesland*, 1972, I:100–105, 125; Faber, *Drie eeuwen Friesland*, 1972, II:440–41.

83 De Vries, "Peasant Demand."

84 Faber, *Drie eeuwen Friesland*, 1972, I:295–96.

85 Michiel A. W. Gerding, *Vier eeuwen turfwinning: de verveningen in Groningen, Friesland, Drenthe en Overijssel tussen 1550 en 1950*, AAG bijdragen, ISSN 0511–0726 35 (Wageningen: Afdeling Agrarische Geschiedenis, Landbouwuniversiteit, 1995), 296; Faber, *Drie eeuwen Friesland*, 1972, I:291–93.

intensive trade relationship with Amsterdam.[86] Unlike Holland and Zeeland, Friesland had no major international ports.[87] It did not have a seat on the general boards of the VOC or WIC.[88] Accordingly, the province also lacked an Exchange Bank.

From the sixteenth century, the number of wage workers increased. These workers were primarily agricultural, accounting for around 15 per cent of the population.[89] But the job opportunities deteriorated between 1660 and 1735. This is best expressed in the increasing number of Frisians enlisting in the VOC, because it was considered the worst imaginable job. Before 1660 and after 1740, the VOC recruited more 'foreigners' than personnel from Holland and Friesland.[90] After 1750, the total demand for labour in Friesland exceeded Friesland's labour supply, as shown by the growing number of non-Frisians on Frisian ships.[91] These labour market developments are consistent with the general economic and demographic trends.

2.3 *Wages*

Wages in Friesland followed the general economic and demographic trends. Wages rose dramatically in the late sixteenth and early seventeenth centuries and remained largely stagnant thereafter until the end of the eighteenth century.[92] Hod carriers earned around 3 *stuivers* or 0.15 guilders per day in the 1530s and 0.60–65 guilders in the 1620s. This was only slightly less than their wage of 0.7 guilders in 1782–1783.[93] Similarly, the wages of hay mowers doubled from 0.35–0.40 guilders in the late sixteenth century to 0.75 guilders in

86 Kuiken, *Het Bildt*, 85–88; These relations often extended beyond business relations and also included marriages between families on both sides of the Zuiderzee. Faber, *Drie eeuwen Friesland*, 1972, I:274.

87 Faber, *Drie eeuwen Friesland*, 1972, I:272; Faber, *Drie eeuwen Friesland*, 1972, II:602–3, 646–47; Cornelis Trompetter, *Eén grote familie: doopsgezinde elites in de Friese Zuidwesthoek 1600–1850*, Doperse documentaire reeks ; nr. 4; Fryske Akademy 998 (Hilversum: Verloren, 2007), 68.

88 Femme S. Gaastra, "Friesland en de VOC," in *Negen eeuwen Friesland-Holland: geschiedenis van een haat-liefdeverhouding*, ed. Philippus H. Breuker and Antheunis Janse, FA 846 (Ljouwert/Leeuwarden: Fryske AkademyZutphen : Walburg Pers, 1997), 184–96; Gaastra, *Geschiedenis*; Den Heijer, *De geschiedenis van de WIC*.

89 Faber, *Drie eeuwen Friesland*, 1972, I:100; Faber, *Drie eeuwen Friesland*, 1972, II:440–41.

90 Jan Lucassen, *Migrant Labour in Europe, 1600–1900: The Drift to the North Sea*, ed. Donald A. Bloch (London etc.: Croom Helm, 1987), 156–58; Gaastra, "Friesland en de VOC," 190–91.

91 Trompetter, *Eén grote familie*, 76.

92 Nijboer, *Fatsoenering*, 75.

93 Nijboer, 131–32.

the early seventeenth century.[94] Peat diggers received 0.7 guilders a day in the mid-seventeenth century.[95] There is one exceptional observation of 0.9 guilders for hay harvesting in eighteenth-century Friesland, without a specific time, place or circumstance.[96] Only in the early nineteenth century did wages for harvesting rise to about 1–1.25 guilders.[97] All other unskilled day wages mentioned in the second half of the eighteenth century were 0.7 guilders (Graph 4.2).[98] The day wage of 0.7 guilders was about 25 to 30 per cent less than equivalent wages in Holland and Zeeland.

The comparison with other types of wages shows a similar development, indicating that the data for unskilled male wages are representative. First, skilled wages for masons and carpenters more than doubled from 0.25–0.3 guilders per day in the sixteenth century to 0.6 guilders in the 1590s and 0.75 guilders in the 1620s. Master masons and carpenters earned a guilder in the eighteenth century.[99] Second, male summer day wages for painters amounted to 0.9 guilders from at least 1712 and rose to 1.0 guilder in the nineteenth century. Second, female unskilled day wages for cleaners show a similar stability and increased by the end of the eighteenth century from 0.5 guilders to 0.6 guilders. Annual wages of farm hands and farm maids also remained largely stable during the eighteenth century, with a brief dip in the first decades.[100] Hence the deterioration in job prospects that drove wage workers to enlist in the VOC did not result in lower wages.

2.4 *The Private Capital Market*

Little is known about capital markets before 1500. The first known example is the financing of the reclamation of the Bildt polder in 1505, with money from

94 Nijboer, 133: Nijboer provides minimum and maximum wages in the eighteenth century, until 1780, that were between 10 and 16 *stuivers*. The difference between the upper and lower estimates partly depended on non-monetary rewards such as board and lodging.

95 Gerding, *Vier eeuwen turfwinning*, 305.

96 De Vries, "An Inquiry into the Behaviour of Wages in the Dutch Republic and the Southern Netherlands, 1580–1800," 83.

97 Nijboer, *Fatsoenering*, 133: Nijboer provides minimum and maximum wages in the eighteenth century, until 1780, that were between 10 and 16 *stuivers*. The difference between the upper and lower estimates partly depended on non-monetary rewards such as board and lodging.

98 De Vries, "An Inquiry into the Behaviour of Wages in the Dutch Republic and the Southern Netherlands, 1580–1800," 95: 14 stuivers, 1760–1774, (Sneek); 14 stuivers, 1773–1781 (Drachten); 10 stuivers, 1793 (Drachten), 14 stuivers, 1801–1810, (Drachten).

99 Nijboer, *Fatsoenering*, 131–32: 1715, 1760, 1777, 1782, 1783: 20 stuivers.

100 Knibbe, *Lokkich Fryslân*, 106–10: I thank Merijn Knibbe for sharing his underlying data with me.

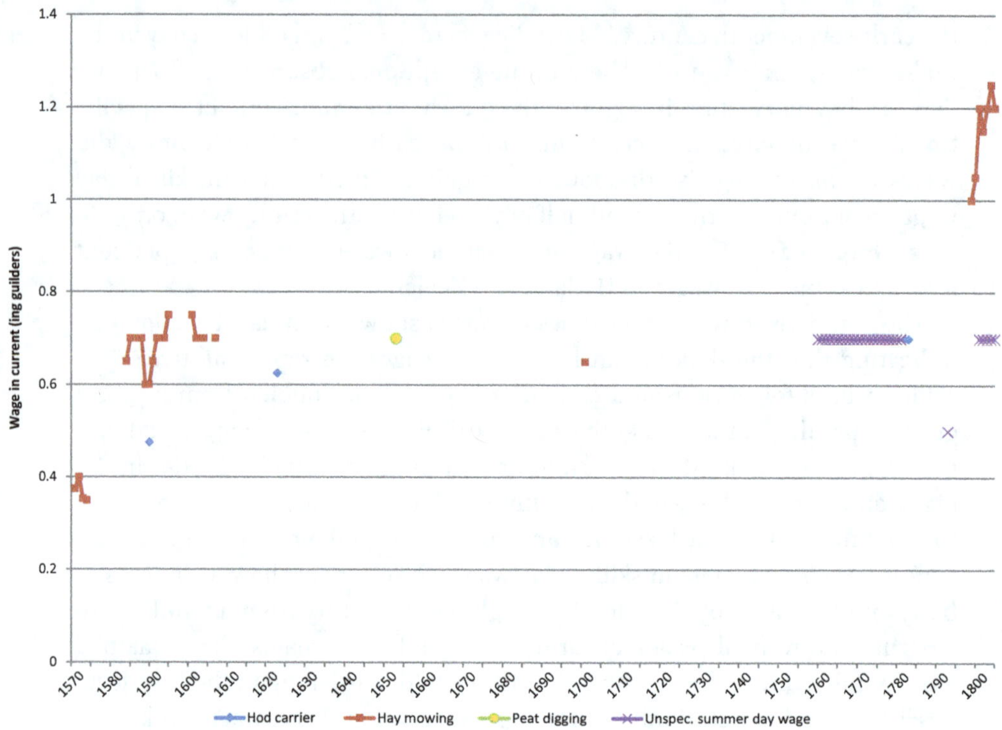

GRAPH 4.2 Unskilled day wages in Friesland, 1570–1805.
SOURCES: NIJBOER, *FATSOENERING*, P.131–132; GERDING, *VIER EEUWEN*, P. 305; DE VRIES, 'INQUIRY', P. 95.

Holland. Lease income from this polder served as collateral for a loan from Charles V in 1531. It was not until 1536–1538 that Frisian nobles and an Overijssel merchant bought these *Bildtrenten*. The increase in the interest rate to 6.25 per cent in 1558 attracted investors from Amsterdam and Flanders and the Augsburg bankers Fugger.[101]

With the arrival of the Habsburgs, the registration of debts also started. Lenders and borrowers could either register the transaction upon conclusion of the transaction or later. Collateral was not systematically included in the contract; the recording of the debt in the register served as additional security for the creditor. From the 1530s onwards, such registers emerged in the *grietenijen*, the lower courts. Such a register from the *grietenij* Henneradeel shows

101 H. Sannes, "De Bildtrenten," *De vrije Fries : mengelingen* 39 (1948): 91–118; Kuiken, *Het Bildt*, 72–73, 86–87.

an increase in interest from around 5.5 per cent to 6.3 per cent for the period 1537–1555.[102]

In the Frisian capital Leeuwarden, the registration of debts began in 1588.[103] The presence of collateral made no difference to the interest rates, which dropped from around 7 per cent in the 1590s to less than 3 per cent in the 1760s. Only the War of the Spanish Succession caused a temporary increase from around 4 per cent in 1704 to 5.6 per cent in 1713.[104] Other wars did not lead to crowding out. The introduction of a wealth tax (*reëele goedschatting*) in 1711 had no visible influence on the downward trend in the Friesland interest rates.[105] The tax was mentioned in the contracts and factored in.[106] The decline in interest rates continued to approximately 3 per cent in the 1760s. Interest rates increased in the 1780s to 4 per cent by the end of the eighteenth century.[107]

102 Merijn T. Knibbe and Paul Borghaerts, "A Capital Market without Banks. Lending and Borrowing in Hennaarderadeel, Friesland, 1537–1555," in *Financial Development, Economic Crises and Emerging Market Economies.*, ed. Faruk Ülgen (New York: Routledge, 2017), 126–41; Nijboer, *Fatsoenering*, 72–74.

103 Nijboer, *Fatsoenering*, 73: Until then, the towns fell under the jurisdictions of the *grietenijen.*

104 Nijboer, 73, 129; The going rate at the time, 1716, was 5 per cent not only in Leeuwarden, but also in Harlingen. Source: Tresoar Frysk Histoarysk en Letterkundich Sintrum (hereafter: Tresoar), Toegang 269, Doopsgezinde gemeente Harlingen, inv.no. 452, unfol.

105 Trompetter, *Gewestelijke financiën: vol 6. Friesland*, 108–11, 164–65.

106 Historisch Centrum Leeuwarden (hereafter: HLC), Toegang 1001, Archief van de stad Leeuwarden, 1426–1811, inv.no. 3882, f. 11r: "met de interesse van dien tot vier en een vierde Cargls: van yder hondert Cargls: 's Jaars onder kortinge van een guld: voor de Reele Penn: en alzo zuiver drie en een vierde gulds: heden aanvang nemende.": Translation HAF: "with the interest of four and an quarter Caroli guilders for every hundred Caroli guilders per year, under the discount of one guilder for the Real Penny; and thus net three and a quarter guilders." If this was not factored in, this was also explicitly stated. For instance, Michiel Gijzen and his wife Catharina Bernardus promised in 1781 to pay:"the interest of three Caroli guilders for every hundred, net, without the discount for the Real Penny": HCL, Toegang 1001, Archief van de stad Leeuwarden, 1426–1811, inv. nos. 3887, f. 55r: " de renten dies tot drie Cargls: van yder hondert zuiver zonder kortinge van de Reële Penn."

107 For the period 1720–1757, I thank Harm Nijboer for sharing his unpublished raw data (sources: HCL, Oudrechterlijk archief, GG110 t/m f. 101r., GG116 t/m f. 50v., GG120 t/m f. 61r., GG125 t/m f. 50v., GG130 t/m f. 76r., GG135 t/m f. 65r.); For the period 1737–1771, I collected additional archival materials from, HCL, Toegang 1001, Archief van de stad Leeuwarden, 1426–1811, inv.nos. 3872, 3877, 3882, 3887, 3892, 3897. This is a similar type of source, but this was rearranged and renamed in the time between my collection and Nijboer's.

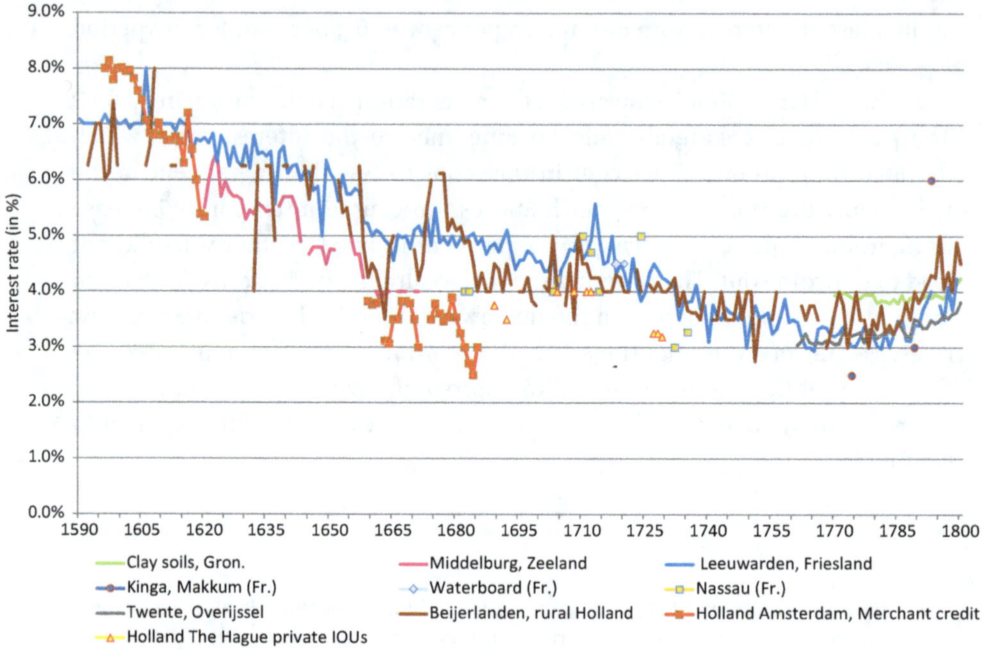

GRAPH 4.3 Private interest rates in Friesland, 1590–1800.

SOURCES: FRIESLAND: HCL, OUDRECHTERLIJK ARCHIEF, GG110 T/M F. 101R., GG116 T/M F. 50V., GG120 T/M F. 61R., GG125 T/M F. 50V., GG130 T/M F. 76R., GG135 T/M F. 65R.; ARCHIEF VAN DE STAD LEEUWARDEN, 1426–1811, INV.NOS. 3872, 3877, 3882, 3887, 3892, 3897; TRESOAR, FA. M.H. KINGMA TE MAKKUM, INV.NO. 442, F. 37, INV.NO. 616, INV.NO. 623; (WATERBOARD, FR.) FABER, *DRIE EEUWEN FRIESLAND*, VOL. I, P. 146–47; BRUGGEMAN, *NASSAU*, P. 44–47; OVERIJSSEL: TROMPETTER, 'BURGERS EN BOEREN-GELD EN GROND', P. 35; GRONINGEN: PAPING, *HANDVOL*, P. 360–361; ZEELAND: VAN DILLEN, *BRONNEN TOT DE GESCHIEDENIS DER WISSELBANKEN*, P. 1158–1203; HOLLAND (AMSTERDAM): GELDERBLOM & JONKER, 'COMPLETING', GELDERBLOM, KOOL AND JONKER, 'DIRECT FINANCE'; HOLLAND (BEIJERLANDEN) BAARS, BEIJERLANDEN, P. 118; (DEN HAAG) DE MUINCK, *REGENTENHUISHOUDING*.

Some comparisons give an impression of the extent to which Leeuwarden's development was representative (Graph 4.3). First, within Friesland, a water board paid an identical interest rate of 4.5 per cent in 1718 and 1720.[108] Second, the Kingma family firm in Makkum normally lent and borrowed money at around 2.5 per cent in the 1770s.[109] This was below the going rate in Leeuwarden. Thirdly, the Frisian Nassau family borrowed within their network in the Stadholder's Court in Leeuwarden. These rates deviated from Leeuwarden's

108 Faber, *Drie eeuwen Friesland*, 1972, 1:146–47.

109 Tresoar, Fa. M.H. Kingma te Makkum, inv.no. 442, f. 37, inv.no. 616, inv.no. 623.

rates in both directions.[110] This indicates that the Leeuwarden series reflects Friesland's development.

Interest rate developments in Friesland lagged behind those in Amsterdam, Middelburg and The Hague. The faster decline in interest rates in the latter locations caused substantial interest rate differentials. In the period 1665–1690, Amsterdam interest rates could be half of Leeuwarden's 5 per cent.[111] On the other hand, interest rates in rural Holland remained well above the level in Amsterdam.

The Leeuwarden and Beijerlanden interest rates correlate better with one another than either do with Amsterdam.[112] The correlation coefficient for these series over the entire period 1590–1800 is 80.5 per cent. This is even though they are located in different provinces and Amsterdam was geographically closer to both locations.

Friesland may therefore be better compared with other rural areas. There are data series for the late eighteenth century for two areas. The series for the region of Twente in the eastern province of Overijssel starts in 1761; the Groningen data are available from 1770.[113] In the period until 1800, the Twente and Friesland interest rates both increased from 3 per cent to 4 per cent. In Groningen, the increase was smaller, from just under 4 per cent to just above. This is remarkable because Groningen was geographically closer than Twente. Nevertheless, Leeuwarden's interest rates resemble those in rural parts of the Dutch Republic more than those in Amsterdam and Middelburg.

Leeuwarden's higher interest rates suggest that capital imports from Amsterdam would be an attractive option. However, the decline in interest rates in Leeuwarden presumably reduced the need for capital imports. The local capital supply increased and the declining interest rate differential limited the possibility for arbitrage.

110 Bruggeman, *Nassau en de macht van Oranje*, 44–47.

111 This casts some doubt on Nijboer's suggestion that private wealth in Friesland was quite similar to that in Holland around 1650: Nijboer, *Fatsoenering*, 143, note 16.

112 Baars, *De geschiedenis van de landbouw in de Beijerlanden*, 118; Gelderblom, Jonker, and Kool, "Direct Finance:" Among wealthy Amsterdam merchants, interest charges differed per transaction, due to the variation in the risk assessment per creditor, debtor or transaction. Gelderblom and Jonker, "Public Finance," 7 Oscar Gelderblom kindly shared the data of the Weesmeesterkennissen, VOC bonds and private merchant credit, for which I am grateful. Liesker and Fritschy, *Gewestelijke financiën: vol. 4. Holland.*

113 Trompetter, "Burgers en boeren," 26, 27–28, 30, 35: Trompetter attributes the low interest rates in Twente to a large capital supply, compared to Groningen where capital was more expensive. We cannot rule out that the additional security of mortgages may have had a similar effect. Paping, *"Voor een handvol stuivers,"* 360–61.

This appears to have been the case for the peat-digging enterprise Dekema, Cuyck & Foeyts. In 1551, the Frisian nobleman Peter van Dekema established the company with the Utrecht patricians Jan van Cuyck and Floris Foeyts. Peat digging was one of the sectors that attracted capital from outside the province. Non-Frisian investors dominated the initial funding. By the second half of the eighteenth century, half of the shareholders came from Friesland.[114]

In the eighteenth century, shipbuilders raised capital in both Friesland and Amsterdam.[115] For instance, Wieger Annes Visser sent the skipper Age Obbes to Amsterdam in 1778 – not to raise the entire amount, only to add to the required sum. The money was sought within the network of suppliers. In return for an investment, a sailmaker received the promise that he would be able to supply the sails for the ship. That promise may have been more attractive than the profit from the investment, as returns were low.[116] Hence, Amsterdam investors supplemented the capital that was raised within Friesland.

From early on, capital flows were not just one-way traffic. For instance, in 1530 a Frisian tenant purchased a piece of land near the town of Delft in Holland.[117] A Frisian widow invested in a life annuity from the Holland town of Leiden in 1550.[118] The Dordrecht patrician family Van Wijngaarden borrowed money from a Harlingen merchant in 1615.[119] On a smaller scale, in 1623 a store in Franeker owed half its debt to suppliers in Amsterdam. The claim that a

---

114 In addition to the cases discussed, Hollanders also invested in peat in Drenthe: Gerding, *Vier eeuwen turfwinning*, 12–132, 136–37, 139, 140–41, 203, 483–84; Also see: Johannes Stienstra and Gerrit Groenhuis, "De Veenhuizer venen in de gouden eeuw: een mislukte Hollandse investering," *Nieuwe Drentse volksalmanak* 101 (1984): 69–83.

115 In Friesland, joint ownership of ships (*partenrederij*) existed at least from the mid-sixteenth century: Kuiken, *Het Bildt*, 3, 85–86, 89; This practice was new, nor was it limited to the Dutch: Gelderblom, *Cities of Commerce*, 188–89; In Holland this approach was also used to finance mills and other enterprises that required substantial amounts of capital: Gelderblom and Jonker, "Completing a Financial Revolution."

116 Wegener Sleeswijk overestimated the average return at 10 per cent by considering a loss to be a 0 per cent return, rather than a negative return. My recalculation of the averge return (5 per cent) and Net Present Value (-1 per cent) gives lower numbers, although a discount rate is lacking: R. S. Wegener Sleeswijk, "Rendement van 36 Friese partenrederijen (1740–1830)," *Jaarboek Fries Scheepvaart Museum en Oudheidkamer*, 1986, 67, 70, 77, 80, 84; Trompetter, *Eén grote familie*, 77–79.

117 Kuiken, *Het Bildt*, 73: Tenants benefitted from the fixed land leases, since 1525, and rising grain prices, from around 1530.

118 Kuiken, 1, 86, 145.

119 Kuiken, 84.

small drapery store in Kollum had with respect to an Amsterdam resident probably related to grain delivered in 1629.[120]

In the mid-seventeenth century, the Frisian capital supply was large enough to establish a peat company with Frisian money.[121] In addition, Frisians financed peat companies in the neighbouring province of Drenthe. In the sixteenth century, that money had come from Holland and Utrecht.[122] In 1793, Frisians financed a fishing boat in the nearby Holland island of Vlieland. The financing schedule involved joint ownership (*partenrederij*) and a 6 per cent loan.[123] This interest rate probably reflects the high risk. Normally, one of the main investors, the firm of Kingma, borrowed and lent money at 2.5 per cent.[124] That was below even the going rate in Leeuwarden. Hence, Frisian capital supply increased over time and replaced imported money from Holland, all within personal networks.

Local financing was also preferred over interprovincial transactions because of the difficulty of enforcing contracts. Four cases illustrate why. First, in 1689, the Frisian messenger Aelber Meyert set off for Rotterdam with money for Brandenburg troops. But he did not get that far. Upon disembarking in Holland, inhabitants from Monnickendam ambushed him. The town's under-bailiff secured the seized 43,000 guilders.[125] The bailiff argued that the money in his custody was unsound. The States of Holland, however, ordered the money to be sent to Brussels for the troop payment.[126] Meyert's case was no isolated event. That same year the military broker Overschie requested a

120 Obe Postma, "Slechte betalers in de Gouden Eeuw," *De vrije Fries* 45 (1962): 155–60: Postma interpreted the large debts as indications of bad financial behaviour. Although some ran up significant arrears, it can also be understood as a high-confidence society in which credit functioned reasonably well.

121 Gerding, *Vier eeuwen turfwinning*, 142–45, 148–49, 151: After the company's activities had bogged down, it recapitalised for 20,000 guilders in 1716. Even though this did not produce an immediate effect, the company made a profit in every single year between 1737 and 1780, which enabled dividend payments of 50,000 guilders in total. After 1779, the returns ran dry; dividend payments were not resumed until the nineteenth century.

122 From the first half of the seventeenth century, Friesians also participated in peat companies in the adjacent province of Drenthe: Gerding, 151–54, 203 In Drenthe a similar shift from the import of Holland capital to local capital was visible in the first half of the seventeenth century. Also see: Stienstra and Groenhuis, "De Veenhuizer venen in de gouden eeuw."

123 Tresoar, Fa. M.H. Kingma te Makkum, inv.no. 623, unfol.

124 Tresoar, Fa. M.H. Kingma te Makkum, inv.no. 442, f. 37.

125 Brandon, *Masters of War*, 241.

126 NA, Staten van Holland, inv.no. 5121, p. 412–413, 428–430.

safeguard for money from the provinces of Utrecht and Overijssel. He feared that urban officers within Holland would otherwise seize it.[127]

Second, the heirs of the Frisian Stadholder Henry Casimir II of Nassau-Dietz ran into trouble when Friesland stopped paying interest in Holland in 1711. Since 1682, the States of Friesland had guaranteed and paid for his loan. Creditors from three notable Amsterdam families, Pels, Pellicorne and Valckenier, threatened to either seize the Stadholder's yacht or organise a forced court auction sale of the manor *Kruidberg* in Holland. This implicit appeal to the Law of Reprisal was a real threat. Under strict confidentiality, the banker Reus resumed payments on behalf of the Nassau family. In 1735, the loan was repaid, after a missed instalment. The Nassau family wanted to avoid a lawsuit before the Court of Holland.[128] Filing a lawsuit was a credible threat because the Stadholder's assets in Holland fell under that jurisdiction and it could harm his reputation.

Third, Yme Jansz., a Frisian navigator sailing to the West Indies, was imprisoned for debt in Amsterdam. In 1789, his wife, family and friends requested the aid of the Kingma merchant family in Makkum. The widow of his creditor was willing to release Jansz. if the costs of living over the last year were repaid. The widow Hijlke Jansz. Kingma, and some other Frisians advanced the 130 guilders necessary for his release. In 1794 he repaid his rescuers the 3 per cent bond that had been issued for this purpose.[129] This shows he had fewer difficulties arranging the local financing of his release than he experienced in Amsterdam.

Fourth, the Friesland Admiralty owed its main timber supplier, the Amsterdam widow of Jan Frederiks, almost 1 million guilders. In 1784, she asked the States of Holland to back her claim of unpaid bills incurred during the Fourth Anglo-Dutch War.[130] To illustrate the relative size of the claim, Friesland Admiralty's annual income was barely 0.5 million guilders and it had a debt of 2 million guilders.[131] To summarise, cross-border contract enforcement

127 NA, Staten van Holland, inv.no. 5121, p. 607–608.

128 Bruggeman, *Nassau en de macht van Oranje*, 45–46.

129 Tresoar, Fa. M.H. Kingma te Makkum, inv.no. 616, unfol.

130 Brandon, *Masters of War*, 160, 162: Brandon deems these troubles of the Friesland Admiralty Board as exceptional for Dutch institutions in general and the Admiralties in particular.

131 The Friesland admiralty collected only 2–3 per cent of the Dutch Navy's total income in the period 1680–1795, which was too small to finance its current expenses and overhead costs, let alone to fit out ships, or to fund a debt, because creditors appeared too reluctant to lend it any money. During the War of Austrian Succession, the Rotterdam Admiralty had to take care of the activities first allocated to the Friesland Admiralty Board:

between the two provinces was difficult, which must have hampered capital flows from and to Friesland.

Capital supply within Friesland increased during the seventeenth and eighteenth centuries. The registration of private loans was an institutional innovation that potentially fostered trust in the Frisian capital market. In any case, interest rates decreased and Frisians increasingly financed enterprises with domestic capital. Domestic capital replaced capital imports. Sometimes capital was exported to adjacent regions. These are signs of accumulated wealth in Friesland. The complex nature of cross-border contract enforcement shows provincial borders continued to matter. Market integration was not a given.

The image this gives of Friesland's economy is mixed. Friesland had lower wages, a lower degree of urbanisation, lower demographic growth, higher interest rates and less foreign trade than Holland and Zeeland and it lacked international ports. On the other hand, Friesland's domestic market redistributed goods in a closed economic system. The economy was also differentiated, market-oriented and commercial, including in agriculture. The labour market was also more dynamic than the stability of the nominal wages suggests. It had a high degree of occupational specialisation. The increasing material prosperity and falling interest rates imply an increasing supply of capital. The simultaneous wage stability and wealth accumulation suggests that inequality increased. This has consequences for the internal tax distribution over the population, but not necessarily for the fiscal capacity. The question remains whether the economic differences with Holland and Zeeland justified a lower contribution to the States General.

3 Friesland's Provincial Public Finances

It is difficult to determine whether Friesland was overburdened for most of the seventeenth century. Only snippets of information have survived about Fri-

Veenstra, *Tussen gewest en Generaliteit*, 11, 103–5, 110, 112–13, 121, 123, 135, 123, 135, 173, 275; Consequently, the Friesland Admiralty was totally unprepared to participate in the shipbuilding programme for the Fourth Anglo-Dutch War. Of the twelve ships that were eventually built, the largest two vessels could not leave the shipyard because the passages proved too narrow: Brandon, *Masters of War*, 169; The debt of more than 2 million guilders was assessed in 1785 by a committee of the Council of State that examined the state of the Admiralty's finances and the reasons for its errant performance: Roodhuyzen-van Breda Vriesman, "Onfrisse Friese zaken," 102.

sian government finances before 1679.[132] Yet the States General's intervention of 1637 appears to have paid off. Around 1680, interest payments were small, indicating a small debt. This implies that government deficits had also been limited until then. In short, tax revenues were enough to cover most expenses, and borrowing was limited.

But, as explained, maintaining reforms was a bigger problem than imposing them. The democratic nature of the Frisian political organisation tended to lessen the burden on its electorate. Did the States General's superimposed fiscal reform last long enough to solve internal disputes? Did the imposed reform also lead to a tax revolution, as in Holland and Zeeland? After all, the intervention aimed to secure the Frisian contribution to the joint war effort. Or did the Frisians balance their budgets by paying too little? This was not unthinkable, since even after 1637 the Frisians often paid less than their share, or threatened to do so. However, the economic tide was favourable and the population grew until the mid-seventeenth century. This may have increased Friesland's fiscal capacity.

To evaluate Friesland's claims about its inability to pay its share, this section first analyses the government budget balances. Secondly, it examines expenditures to determine what burdened Friesland's pubic finances the most. Thirdly, a scrutiny of the revenues indicates how and to what extent Friesland covered these expenses. This includes the development of the tax burden on the population. This allows us to evaluate how real Friesland's claim of overburdening was and whether the other provinces were correct in concluding Frisians were taxed too lightly.[133]

3.1 *Government Budget Balances*

Before 1679, the total income and expenditure are only known for 1619–1625 and 1651. In the 1620s, surpluses became deficits for the primary and fiscal balances. In 1651, Friesland had primary and fiscal surpluses of 200,000 and 75,000 guilders respectively.[134] In 1637, the Council of State estimated expenditure on warfare at 2 million guilders and income at slightly less. Friesland therefore already had a small primary deficit. But provincial expenditure came on top of that. It is unknown how much this was. In the 1620s and 1651, it averaged 280,000 guilders. This makes an estimated primary budget deficit of approximately 300,000 guilders seem realistic. On top of that were interest

132 Trompetter, *Gewestelijke financiën: vol 6. Friesland*, 53, 73–74.

133 Deursen, "De plaats van de noordelijke gewesten," 20.

134 Trompetter, *Gewestelijke financiën: vol 6. Friesland*, 69–70, 230–35, 244–47, 262–67.

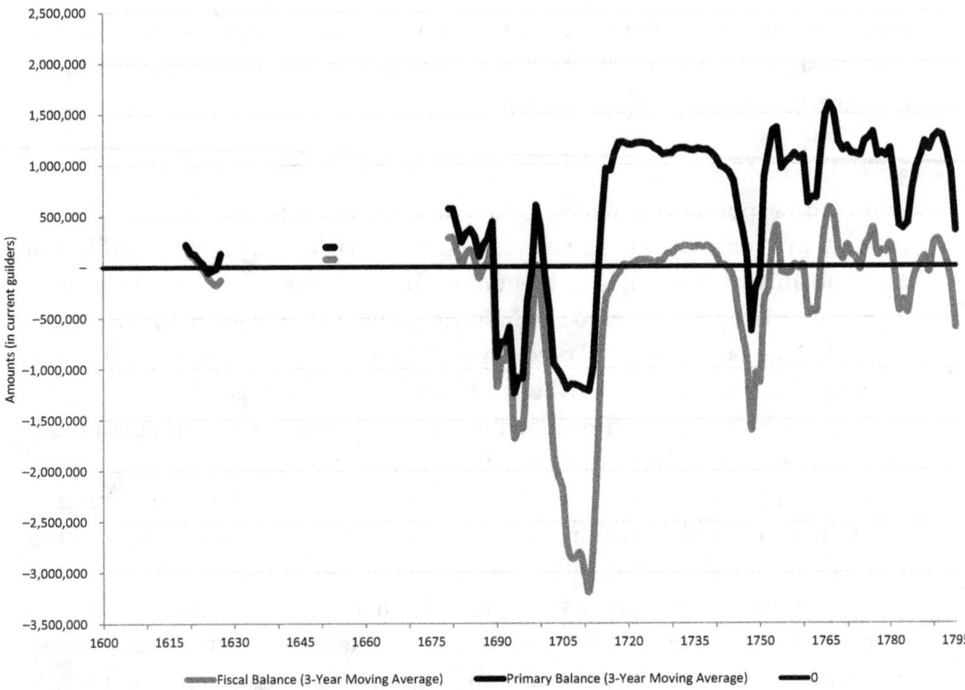

GRAPH 4.4 Primary and fiscal balances in Friesland, 1600–1795.
SOURCE: TROMPETTER, *GEWESTELIJKE FINANCIËN. VOL. 6 FRIESLAND.*

costs of 0.5 million guilders.[135] This results in a fiscal deficit of 800,000 guilders. The urgency of tax reforms is therefore clear. But Friesland's public revenue in 1651, of 1.4 million guilders, was lower than in 1637.

In the 1680s, Friesland enjoyed budget surpluses. These were, however, small and declining. The Nine Years' War and the War of the Spanish Succession changed this. The deficits increased the debt burden and interest payments. As a result, a difference emerged of around 1 million guilders between the primary and fiscal balances. Friesland had an almost constant primary surplus, apart from during the War of the Austrian Succession. It balanced its fiscal income and expenditure with a few exceptions (Graph 4.4). This indicates that Friesland balanced its income and expenses in the long run and its debt burden remained under control in proportion to its income.

The picture of Friesland's government budget balances looks remarkably similar to eighteenth-century Holland. This province too enjoyed an almost constant primary surplus, from which it balanced total expenses. This con-

135 Spanninga, *Gulden vrijheid?*, 323, 422–23.

trasts with Zeeland, where interest payments grew out of hand after the 1740s. The question of how Friesland achieved its balanced income and expenditure is analysed in the rest of the section.

3.2 *Expenses*

Friesland's expenditure increased more in the eighteenth century than in the seventeenth century. In the 1620s, expenditure rose from 1.3 million guilders to 2 million. In 1637, it was at least 2.5 million and probably 2.8 million. But in 1651, expenditure dropped again to 1.3 million guilders. This was equal to the level at the end of the Twelve Years' Truce in 1621. Expenditure increased slightly up to the early 1680s, to 1.7 million when the Nine Years' War began in 1688.

From then on, expenditure increased further. Wars caused sharp temporary increases, but expenditure also remained higher in peacetime. Annual expenditure averaged 2.5 million guilders between the Wars of the Spanish and Austrian Succession, After the War of the Austrian Succession, expenditure amounted to almost 3 million guilders per year (Graph 4.5).

Warfare and other military expenses formed Friesland's main expenses item. On average Friesland spent 1.6 million guilders for this purpose between 1679 and 1795. This was equal to almost 80 per cent of its primary expenses.[136] In peacetime, war-related expenses still amounted to 1 million guilders in the first half of the eighteenth century and 1.3 million in the second half. In wartime, military expenses doubled or tripled, which caused deficits. The War of the Spanish Succession cost 3.5 million guilders per year, while in 1687 the military expenses amounted to 1.2 million. This prolonged drain on its public finances made the Frisian regents repeatedly beg for peace in their correspondence with the States General from 1707 onwards.[137] Together with Zeeland, Groningen and Utrecht, Friesland wished to reduce the size of the army because of the deplorable state of their provincial public finances. But Friesland claimed to be worst off of these four provinces.[138] Given the large share of military expenses and the impact on its fiscal health, reducing its share in the common expenses was a sensible policy.

---

136 In this regard Friesland was no different from the other provinces: 't Hart, *The Dutch Wars of Independence*, 154–55.

137 Tresoar, SvF, inv.no. 267, p. 72–80 [secret resolutions, 1707–1709].

138 Jan Wagenaar, *Vaderlandsche historie, vervattende de geschiedenissen der nu Vereenigde Nederlanden, inzonderheid die van Holland, van de vroegste tyden af: Agttiende deel, beginnende met het jaar 1713, en eindigende met het sluiten van het Verdrag van Seville, in 't jaar 1729* (Te Amsterdam,: by Johannes Allart, 1795), 132–33.

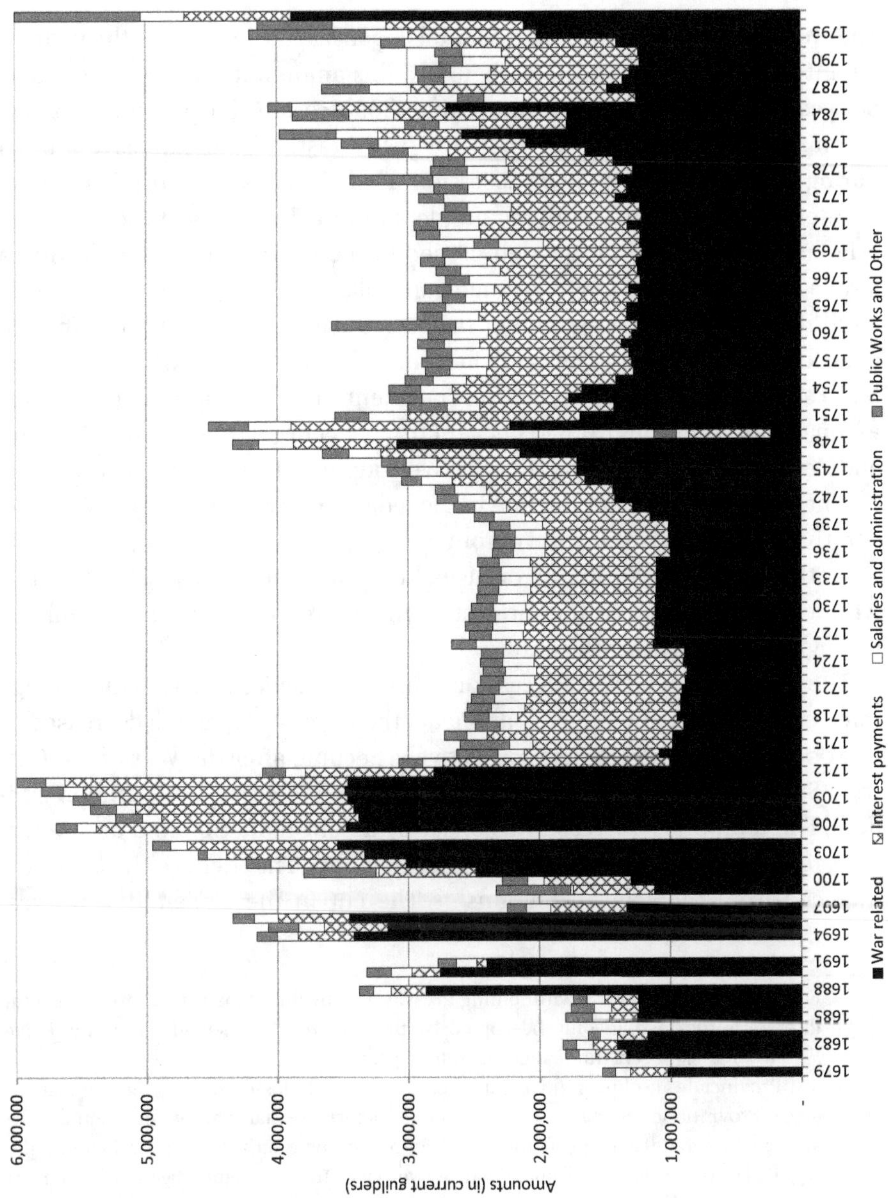

GRAPH 4.5 Friesland's public expenditure, 1679–1795.
SOURCES: TROMPETTER, *GEWESTELIJKE FINANCIËN. VOL. 6 FRIESLAND*, PP. 193–270.

The structural growth in Friesland's total expenses stemmed from the increasing interest payments. In the early 1680s, this amounted to 230,000 guilders per year. The Nine Years' War more than doubled interest payments to over 0.5 million guilders per year. That was just a taste of the explosive growth during the War of the Spanish Succession. That war caused a fourfold increase in interest payments to 2 million guilders in 1711. That proved too much for Friesland. It defaulted on the debt issued in the province of Holland. After a few years, Friesland resumed payments in Holland. Copying Holland and Zeeland, it introduced a withholding tax to reduce payments on all bonds to 2 per cent.[139] Both the external default and the subsequent withholding tax had a similar effect of halving interest payments. Friesland also reduced interest on the life annuities from 10 per cent to 7 per cent.[140] In contrast to Holland and Zeeland, Friesland recorded effective coupons of 2 per cent. Not registering the withholding tax as income in the ledgers was merely a form of administrative efficiency. This is shown from newspaper advertisements, which consistently refer to an 'ordinary' or 'usual' cut of the interest paid out.[141] The withholding tax lowered the interest payments to around 1 million guilders throughout the eighteenth century.[142]

The War of the Austrian Succession caused two deviations from the average interest payments. First, in 1748 and 1749, the interest payments decreased to 800,000 and 600,000 guilders respectively. Second, after the War of the Austrian Succession, interest payments temporarily increased to 1.7 million guilders. The temporary increase was offset by a debt reduction and an interest rate reduction on Friesland's Generality debt. The debt reduction was financed from the sale of domains.[143] The cut in the Generality's interest

139 Fritschy assumes that the withholding tax was a "convenient instrument to contain the interest burden would only be copied by the province of Zeeland.": Fritschy, *Public Finance*, 156–59; Feenstra, "Lange Schaduw," 97.

140 NA, Provinciale resoluties, inv.no. 484, p. 11: ""... dat de losse en lyfrenten, tot last van deeze Provintie loopende, zoo zeer hebben moeten bezwaar worden, dat men dezelve als 't ware gereduceerd heeft tot 2 pr. Cento van Losse en tot 7 van de Lyfrenten,..." (1770): Tresoar, SvF, inv.no. 569, Balance over 1730 ""N.B. de betaelinge der lijffrenthen staat boven wel uitgedrukt teegens 7 per cent; dogh is eigentlijk uitgerekent na afkortinge van 3/10 penn. Dogh de betaelinge geschiedt teegen 7 per cent volgens U Ed. Mogh. Ordres"

141 Advertentie. *Haerlemse courante*. Haerlem, 22-11-1768. Accessed at Delpher 15-09-2016, http://resolver.kb.nl/resolve?urn=ddd:010799795:mpeg21:a0008; Advertentie. Oprechte Haerlemsche courant. Haerlem, 26-01-1769. Accessed at Delpher 29-04-2016, http://resolver.kb.nl/resolve?urn=ddd:010799511:mpeg21:a0003

142 Trompetter, *Gewestelijke financiën: vol 6. Friesland*, 223–24, 258–60.

143 Trompetter, 182.

rate, from 4 per cent to 3 per cent, followed a default in 1754 due to incomplete provincial payments.[144]

Other expenses concerned administration costs and other salaries, for instance for Protestant ministers, university professors and schoolmasters. This amounted to 200,000 guilders in the first half of the eighteenth century and 300,000 guilders in the second half. Other provincial expenses added up to similar or slightly smaller amounts.[145] These formed relatively minor expenses with little impact on the total. The question is whether Frieland could have afforded a credible commitment to the debt, which would have required another 1 million guilders per year in tax revenues.

3.3 *Income*

The fiscal reforms imposed by the Generality did not last. To begin with, in 1638 the Frisian delegates only promised to maintain taxes for the duration of the war. When peace was imminent in 1648, the Diet cut the most important tax rates – and singlehandedly reduced troop numbers.[146] Tax income declined to 1.4 million guilders in 1651, a level similar to the 1620s. In the 1680s, revenues were less than the 2 million in revenues collected in 1637. The imposition of the common means did not cause a tax revolution in Friesland.[147]

Taxes increased dramatically, however, in the 1690s – by more than a quarter, from less than 2 million guilders in the 1680s to over 2.5 million in 1699. Public revenue suddenly increased again following the uprisings of 1747–1748, this time to 3 million guilders. Due to the tax increases in the 1690s and in 1748, tax revenue in 1750 was double that in 1650 (Graph 4.6).

Friesland achieved this by increasing all three main tax types, namely the common means, a property tax, and wealth and income taxes. That increase was unevenly distributed. In the 1680s, the common means yielded almost 800,000 guilders, or approximately 45 per cent of the total. This was already an increase compared to the income of 450,000 guilders in 1637 and 670,000 guilders in 1651. Revenue from these taxes rose further to 900,000 guilders in the years 1690–1750 and 1.2 million after 1750. Despite this 50 per cent increase compared to the 1680s, the share in total revenues decreased to 36 per cent.

144 Tresoar, SvF, inv.no. 159, f. 209, 9 November 1752

145 Trompetter, *Gewestelijke financiën: vol 6. Friesland*, 37 After the abolition of tax farming, in 1748, the collection costs amounted to approximately 6.25 per cent, which partly explains the rise in other expenses after 1750.

146 Spanninga, *Gulden vrijheid?*, 368.

147 Fritschy, *Public Finance*, 120.

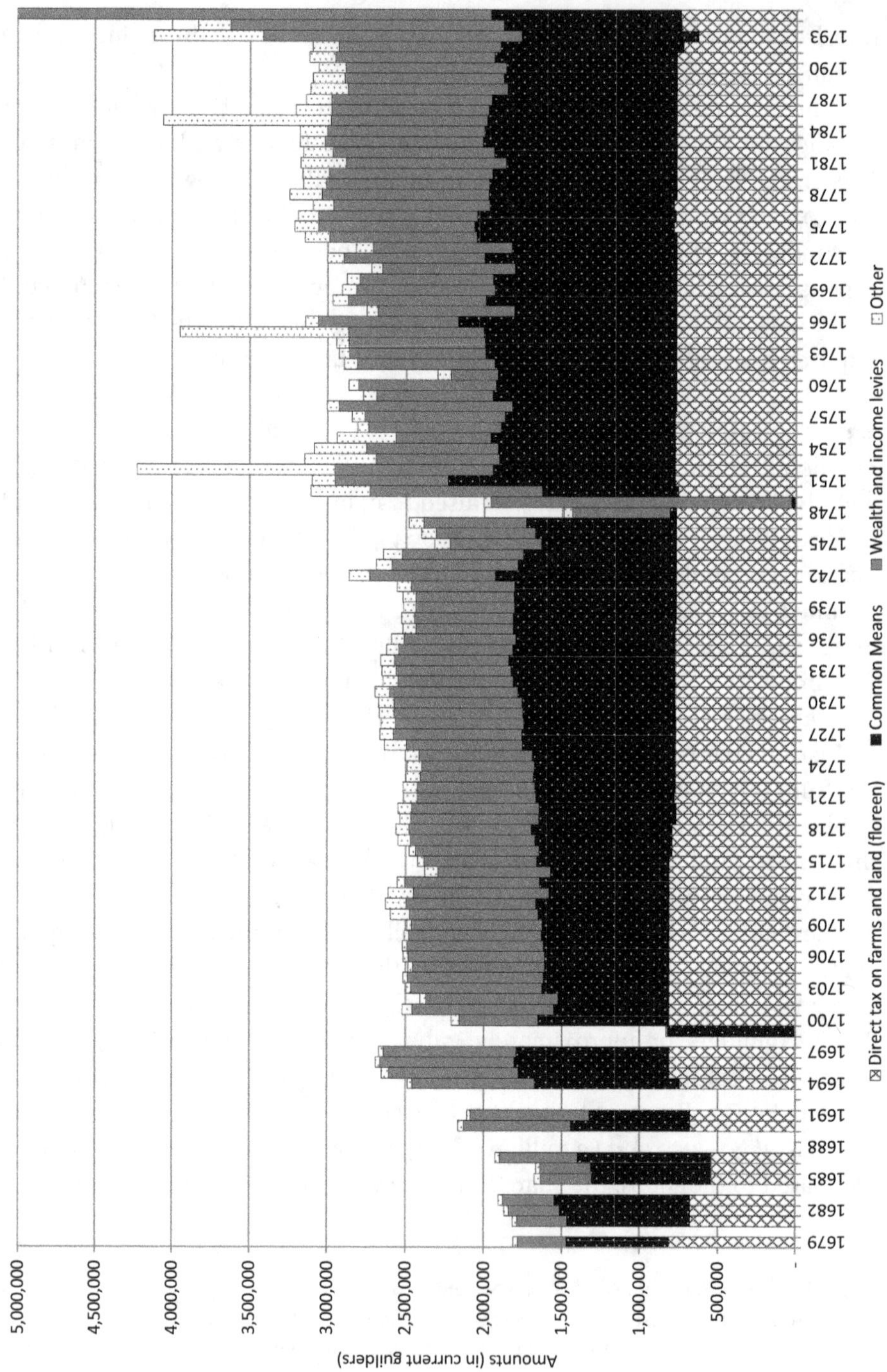

GRAPH 4.6 Composition of Friesland's public revenues, 1679–1795.

SOURCE: TROMPETTER, *GEWESTELIJKE FINANCIËN. VOL. 6 FRIESLAND*, PP. 83–86.

The second most important type of tax in the 1680s was the *floreenrente*, a real estate tax levied on the rental value of the land and farmhouses.[148] Between 1637 and the 1680s, the revenue from this tax decreased from 800,000 to 640,000 guilders.[149] In the 1690s, the tax income increased by almost 20 per cent to over 800,000 guilders. However, in the course of the eighteenth century, income from this property tax declined slightly and its relative importance sharply.

The explanation for this counterintuitive development is political. Until 1695, the tax rate fluctuated annually. In 1696, the States of Friesland fixed the tax rate at 37.5 per cent of the land rent.[150] In addition, a new register in 1700 replaced that of 1511, which had until then formed the basis for the tax. This register should be revised every ten years from 1708 onwards.[151] These measures should have generated higher tax revenues given that land rents increased, especially after 1770. The fact that this did not happen was presumably due to the organisation of the revisions of the assessment registers. The electoral registers were updated at the same time.[152] It is not hard to imagine that prospective delegates lowered the estimated land rents in return for votes at the next election. As a result, the share of the land tax declined from over one-third of all tax income to less than a quarter after 1750. The stability of the land taxes and the increasing rural population meant that the rural elites were paying less tax over time.

The third form of tax, taxes on wealth and income, accounted for most of the increase in public revenues. In the 1680s, this category accounted for less than 20 per cent of total tax income. The yield subsequently increased by a factor of two and a half from 325,000 guilders in the 1680s to over 800,000 guilders around 1700. After 1714 it decreased to 730,000 guilders until the 1740s. Between 1750 and 1795, the revenue amounted to 950,000 guilders per year, or one-third of the total tax revenue.

The increase is explained by three changes. The first was when the tax rate was fixed in 1696 at a relatively high rate. This concerned the oldest component of these taxes, the Five Species (*Vijf Speciën*): the hearth tax, poll tax, horse tax, sown lands tax and cattle tax. These five taxes had been collected

148 Trompetter, *Gewestelijke financiën: vol 6. Friesland*, 147: Per florin of 28 *stuivers* that the owner received as land rent, he paid a fixed amount as tax.

149 Spanninga, *Gulden vrijheid?*, 323; Trompetter, *Gewestelijke financiën: vol 6. Friesland*, 153.

150 Trompetter, *Gewestelijke financiën: vol 6. Friesland*, 149, 153: Actually, 21 stuivers per two-month period, so 10.5 stuivers per month for every 28 stuivers of land rent.

151 Trompetter, *Eén grote familie*, 148.

152 Trompetter, *Gewestelijke financiën: vol 6. Friesland*, 102–5.

and accounted for as a group since the 1630s.[153] The second change was the introduction of the wealth tax (*reële goedschatting*) in 1711, although predated by ad hoc levies of a similar kind in the 1690s. The tax applied to all kinds of property, including financial assets, but not farmland belonging to a farm. This also made it partly a withholding tax for public securities. But unlike Holland and Zeeland, it was not recorded as income, except for personal pensions and military ordinances.[154] The third change took place in 1742. A tax rate increase in the wealth tax immediately led to an increase in revenue from 300,000 to 400,000 guilders. After the uprisings of 1748, revenue gradually rose to over 500,000 guilders at the end of the eighteenth century.

The riots of 1748 did not lead to a fundamental reform of the tax system. Mobs smashed the windows of the tax farmers because they suspected that high taxes were due to abuses. Therefore, the Stadholder encouraged experimenting with a tax assessment in 1749. That yielded less than before, just as the States of Friesland had predicted. As a result, it was reversed. In the meantime, the *Liberale Gift* or Voluntary Gift in Friesland yielded only 230,000 guilders. What did change was the abolition of the tax farming system and the extension of controlling mechanisms.[155]

Finally, the confiscated former royal domains and former church properties played a role in the conflict of the 1630s. The towns demanded that these be sold before introducing common means. In Friesland, the domains still had some value, unlike in the other provinces. The Council of State wished to use these funds for soldiers and other Generality expenses. However, the Frisian fiscal problems had also led to debt arrears. Merchants, especially from Harlingen, feared being arrested for this in Holland. That is why, in 1637, the Frisians preferred using the money from the domains for the settlement of overdue interest payments and debt arrears. Ultimately, most of the domains were sold in 1644, which made it possible to pay off almost the entire debt of 6 million guilders. Similarly, the remaining domains were sold in 1752 to enable debt reduction, but the proceeds were only 750,000 guilders.[156]

153 Trompetter, 167–74: The horse tax was, for instance, lowered in 1649, while the poll tax was even abolished altogether that year. Both taxes were reintroduced or increased in 1653, in response to the outbreak of the First Anglo-Dutch War (1652–1654). Only the taxes on cattle and sown land tax increased constantly until 1696.

154 Trompetter, 108–11, 164–67.

155 Trompetter, 32–39, 110, 162–63: considering the tax rate of 2 per cent of the total wealth and property the sum of 230,000 guilders was indeed meagre, especially when compared to Zeeland's 1.7 million guilders.

156 Trompetter, 180–84; Fritschy, *Public Finance*, 130–31; Spanninga, *Gulden vrijheid?*, 276–77, 309, 317–18, 319–20, 336, 340, 363–64; Sannes, "De Bildtrenten," 104.

Hence, save for the debt reduction in the 1640s, the domains were of minor importance.

Therefore the growth in revenue since the 1690s stemmed from the common means and wealth and property taxes, excluding farms and farmlands. The contribution by the land-holding elite fell slightly in monetary value and considerably in relative importance. This means that urban dwellers and the ordinary people bore the bulk of the increase in taxes. The urban elites contributed through the Five Species and the other wealth taxes, the common people through excises of the common means, because subsistence farming had disappeared and occupational specialisation meant that even the farmers bought their bread.

3.3.1 Tax Burden

The question is what effects those tax increases had on the tax burden in Friesland and whether this supports Friesland's claims of overburdening compared to the other provinces. To make a fair comparison with Holland, the present analysis adjusts the tax income in three respects. Firstly, it corrects for the different registration of the withholding tax.[157] It therefore excludes the withholding tax from Holland's tax income, as was the practice in Friesland. Secondly, it corrects for the population size, to arrive at an estimate of the per capita taxes in current guilders. Thirdly, it corrects for the difference in wage levels, as a gauge for overall welfare levels. The quantitative analysis necessarily concentrates on the period 1679–1795 because earlier data for Friesland are fragmentary. Correspondence between the States of Friesland and taxpayers and tax farmers adds more perspective on how the tax burden was felt.

In guilders, Holland's inhabitants paid consistently more than those in Friesland. Over the whole of the period, Friesland paid a little over 80 per cent of Holland's contribution. Due to the inadequate seventeenth-century data, this finding mainly concerns the eighteenth century. In the 1620s, the per capita tax in Friesland amounted to 86 per cent that of Holland. By then, each Frisian paid 10 guilders a year in taxes, compared to 11.75 guilders in Holland. In the 1680s, the per capita tax in Friesland had increased to almost 12 guilders. Relative to Holland, the ratio had decreased to 72 per cent of Holland's 16 guilders. The tax increases of the 1690s narrowed the gap to less than 10 per cent. In 1714–1740, the per capita tax in Friesland amounted to 92 per cent that of Holland. In the early 1740s, per capita taxation in Friesland

157 Tresoar, SvF, inv.nos. 453, 491, 523, 541, 569, 586, 601, 604, 638, 683, 718, 766, 847, 880 and 933.

exceeded that in Holland. After 1750, Friesland's contribution per capita fell again to 75 per cent that of Holland's immediately before the revision of 1792. Friesland's lower per capita monetary contribution thus suggests that its lamentations were not justified.

However, the Frisian economy was less advanced than Holland and wages were lower. Expressed in day wages, the tax burden in Friesland and Holland hardly differed, and was if anything higher in Friesland than in Holland (Graph 4.7). In the 1620s, a Frisian already had to work a comparable number of days to someone in Holland to pay their taxes. In Holland, this was almost fifteen days, in Friesland almost sixteen. The difference was even smaller in the 1680s: 17.5 days in Friesland and 17.9 days in Holland. After the War of the Spanish Succession, the tax burden in Friesland exceeded that in Holland. In 1714–1740, Frisians had to work over twenty-five days to pay their taxes, while people in Holland had to work more than twenty days. After 1750, the tax burden increased in both provinces, but to a greater extent in Holland than in Friesland. The differences remained small until the revision of the distribution key in 1792. In Friesland, the tax burden rose to more than twenty-eight days, and in Holland to more than thirty days. This means that every Frisian paid 98 per cent of what a Holland resident paid. Yet taxation in Friesland was not as burdensome as in Zeeland, which consistently paid more per capita than Holland. Hence, as far as the data permit, the Frisian tax burden appears very similar to Holland's in the seventeenth century and after 1750; it exceeded Holland's in the first half of the eighteenth century.

The correction for the wage level thus alters the perspective on Friesland's contribution and efforts to pay for the common cause. It does not justify its constant complaints about its contribution to the Generality. Only in the first half of the eighteenth century could Friesland argue that it paid too much compared to Holland. Before and after, Friesland's contribution appears fair.

Still, in the revised distribution of 1792 Friesland's share declined to just under 10 per cent.[158] This followed the temporary reduction of 1783.[159] After the Stadholder's restoration, in 1787, the provinces provided an overview of their surpluses after deducting the provincial expenses. Friesland's share in the total surpluses amounted to 12 per cent.[160] If the survey of 1789 had been adopted as the sole basis for a readjustment of the shares, Frieland's contribu-

158 Fritschy, *De patriotten*, 159. The set-up of the renewed common budget differed slightly from the one in 1616. To provide a fair comparison, I compared Friesland's share relative to the set-up of 1616.

159 NA, Raad van State, (1574) 1581–1795 (1801), inv.no. 2116.

160 Dormans, *Het tekort*, 160–61.

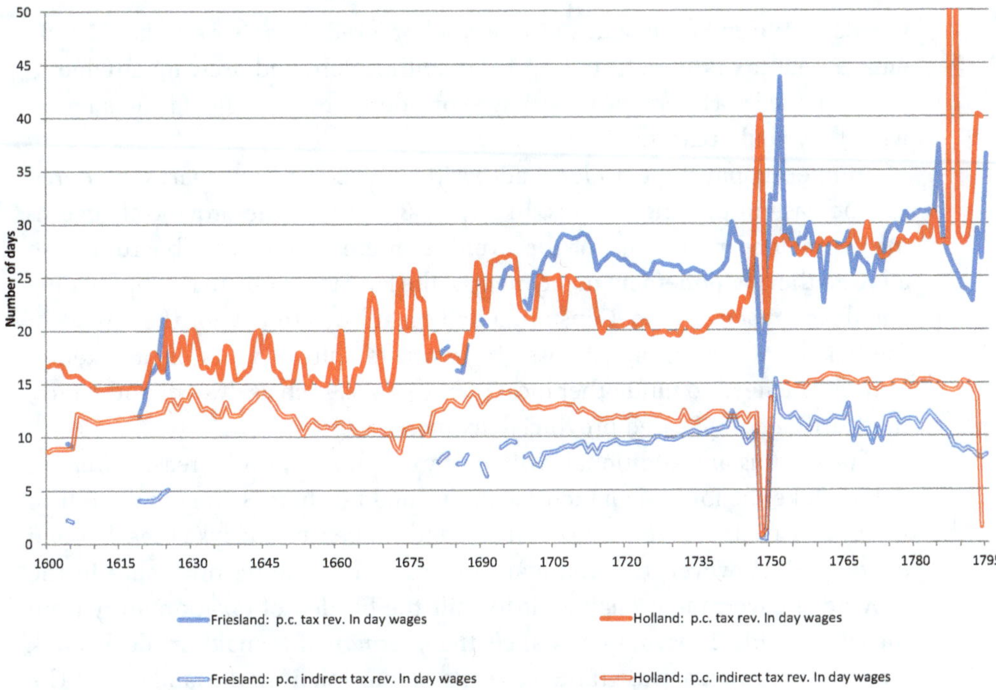

GRAPH 4.7 Tax burden expressed in day wages in Holland and Friesland, 1600–1795.
SOURCES: SEE TEXT AND FEENSTRA, *BETWEEN SHARED*, APPENDIX.

tion would have increased. Fortunately for Friesland, this did not happen. So the complaints that had continued for almost two centuries resulted in a minor and unjustified decrease.[161]

The next question is how the Frisians coped with that high tax burden and what effects it had. Already in 1633, several tax farmers were considered insolvent and received extended payment terms.[162] From around 1700, the States of Friesland regularly granted tax farmers tax exemptions and postponement of payment. For example, the tax farmer Sijbe Sijmons Ramkema was granted a respite of four months in March 1712.[163] Similarly, in 1715 and 1716, Jan and Oebele Doeckes were granted extended payment terms as tax farmers for

161 W. Fritschy, *Gewestelijke financiën ten tijde van de Republiek der Verenigde Nederlanden. Deel 1. Overijssel (1604–1795)*, vol. 1, Rijks geschiedkundige publicatiën. Kleine serie 86 (Den Haag: Instituut voor Nederlandse Geschiedenis, 1996), 10; Fritschy, *De patriotten*, 159. Friesland's share was reduced from 11.6 per cent to 9.8 per cent of the total, calculated based on the Seven Provinces plus Drenthe.

162 Spanninga, *Gulden vrijheid?*, 191.

163 Tresoar, SvF, inv.no. 119, 38v.

tobacco.[164] In 1716, the States of Friesland ordered the release of Jan Henckema, a peat tax farmer, from imprisonment for debt and drew up a redemption scheme.[165] The States must have considered that the tax farmers levied what they could reasonably extract.

Competing payments to local authorities, such as water boards, hindered the increase in provincial taxes. In 1717, 1718 and 1721, the provincial government provided remissions of the overdue interest to a water board. It also allowed the postponement of payment of the land taxes due to recent flooding and dyke breaches. Also, Constantia de Lespaul was to pay for the repairs of the dyke, a watermill and houses in return for fifteen years of tax exemption.[166] The need to fund other local public goods, such as dyke maintenance, thus further complicated provincial tax increases.[167]

The flooding and additional levies partly explain why tax increases after 1711 did not take the form of an increase in the land tax. In 1718, the inhabitants of six rural districts were exempt from the land tax because of dyke breaches and flooding.[168] However, the dominance of the land-holding rural elite in the provincial government enabled it to shift the burden of taxation away from the countryside. In 1727, for instance, the *grietman* of Menaldumadeel, Sjuuk Tjaad van Burmania, was granted a year's exemption from the land tax.[169] The 1748 tax riots, add to the image of a social ceiling for the tax burden, as felt by the urban population and the ordinary people. Consequently, they bore the brunt of the increase in taxes.

164 Tresoar, SvF, inv.no. 122, f. 23v; idem, inv.no. 123, f. 8v.

165 Tresoar, SvF, inv.no. 123, 71v.

166 Tresoar, SvF, inv.no. 124, 39v, 13 March 1717, the water board of 'Zeven Grietenijen' and the town of Sloten, concerning a loan for dyke repairs, provided by the Provincial States in 1701 and 1703; Tresoar, SvF, inv.no. 125, 68r, 17-3-1718, Ferwerderadeel, Westdongeradeel, Oostdongeradeel, Kollumerland, Achtkarspelen en Dantumadeel; Tresoar, SvF, inv. no. 267, 25r, 11-3-1721 in Ferwoudermeer.

167 This was in contrast to the inhabitants of neighbouring Groningen. There the inhabitants resisted forced dyke maintanance after the Christmas flooding of 1717, while it had been more severely hit than Friesland, because dyke maintanance was better in the latter province. Henk Boels and Hidde Feenstra, "Regentenheerschappij en economische recessie 1660–1749," in *Geschiedenis van Groningen II. Nieuwe Tijd*, ed. M. G. J. Duijvendak et al. (Zwolle: Waanders, 2008), 247; Knibbe, *Lokkich Fryslân*, 231: After 1717, a new design for dyke building from Friesland – broader, yet flatter dykes that prevented breaches in the dykes more effectively – was implemented in Groningen.

168 Tresoar, SvF., inv.no. 125, f. 68, it concerned the *Grietenijen*: Ferwerderadeel, Westdongeradeel, Oostdongeradeel, Kollumerland, Achtkarspelen and Dantumadeel and a committee was to assess similar claims for Leeuwarderadeel, Tietjerksteradeel and Idaarderadeel.

169 Tresoar, SvF., inv.no. 134, f. 43v.

Taxation in Friesland thus appears adequate relative to its expenses and the carrying capacity of its population and economy. The tax burden was hardly any lower than in Holland. The structurally higher taxes in the eighteenth century were necessary to cover interest payments. This was a break with the seventeenth-century tax policy when the debt was low and taxes fluctuated depending on whether the province was at war or peace. The debt was also low because of its near elimination in the 1640s following the sale of the domains. This was arguably the most lasting effect of the Generality's intervention of 1637–1638. The States General's intervention did not increase the tax burden to Holland's level. Rather, tax rates were lowered towards the end of the Eighty Years' War. Friesland underwent a tax revolution of its own making from around 1700.

Taxes increased in the 1690s and after 1750. Interest payments required constant primary surpluses and were the reason for the higher taxes. Interest payments and debt levels had been limited until the 1690s. The tax increases of the 1690s were not enough to pay all the interest. The Nine Years' War followed by the War of the Spanish Succession had placed so many demands on Friesland that it could no longer pay the interest. A selective default on the debt in Holland followed. From 1716, a withholding tax on bonds reduced effective interest rates to a sustainable level for Friesland. Expenses were brought in line with the increased income. Without a default, Friesland would have paid 1 million guilders extra in interest payments. This would have required an unrealistic increase of 40 per cent in the tax burden; the tax burden had already risen above Holland's level. Yet the landholding rural elite paid a declining share in these rising taxes. Its dominance in the provincial government enabled it to shift the burden of taxation to the towns and the ordinary people. This meant that the Frisian population was caught in a vice between increasing taxes and a slackening economy in the first half of the eighteenth century. The States of Friesland extracted as much as they could. After 1750, however, Friesland's repeated clamouring for a reduction in its contribution to the Generality was no longer justified.

4 Public Debt Management

It remains to be determined how Friesland made ends meet. Furthermore, it is possible that the repeated claims of overburdening affected the province's creditworthiness. Interest rates on Friesland's debt decreased during the seventeenth and eighteenth centuries. Therefore Fritschy assumes that Friesland experienced a financial revolution. However, the default of 1711 implies that decreasing coupon rates did not reflect lower risk or 'credible commitment'. The question is whether, when and how Friesland experienced a 'real' financial revolution.

This section analyses Friesland's public debt management. It focuses on three key elements of a financial revolution: a shift from short-term to long-term debt, a substantial increase in the size of the public debt, and decreasing coupon rates. It also looks at what caused the lower interest rates: forced measures, capital abundance or lower risk? The history of Frisian public debt can be divided into four periods. The first period covers the first debt creation and lasted until the redemption of the debt in the 1640s. The second period ended with the Nine Years' War, in 1688. The Frisian debt rose incrementally. The third period ended with the War of the Austrian Succession, and is marked by the dramatic debt increase and the selective external default in 1711. In the fourth period, from the 1750s to 1795, domestic debt increased and external credit was restored.

4.1 *Friesland's Debt Development*

The redemption of the 1640s interrupted the development of long-term debt in Friesland. After that and until 1688, Frisian debt remained lower than in 1637. Thereafter, the debt rose rapidly and dramatically. If Friesland ever experienced a financial revolution, it would have been in the 1690s. The total amount of debt never again fell below the level of the 1680s. This suggests that a transition to long-term debt took place. But whether that was part of a financial revolution is questionable given the subsequent default in 1711.

Friesland's debt developed as follows. In 1637, Friesland's debt amounted to almost 6 million guilders. By 1648, the debt had been redeemed except for 1.5 million guilders in life annuities, which could not be repaid.[170] On top, Friesland owed the Generality and other creditors 2.6 to 6.5 million guilders; these were not loans but unpaid arrears.[171] It remains uncertain how much the States issued during the First (1652–1654) and Second Anglo-Dutch Wars (1665–1667). In 1670, the debt amounted to 3.4 million guilders.[172] The Franco-Dutch War (1672–1678) increased the debt to almost 5 million guilders in 1680, but it declined again to 4 million in 1682.[173] The Nine Years' War more than

170 Spanninga, *Gulden vrijheid?*, 355–68.

171 Spanninga, 357, 362, 366, 368.

172 H. Oldenhof, "Skraebjen om jild," in *Friesland in het rampjaar 1672 : it jier fan de miste kânsen*, ed. Jacob Jetzes Kalma and Klaas de Vries, Fryske Akademy 421 (Ljouwert, 1972), 186–222.

173 Tresoar, SvF, inv.no. 1788, f. 46.

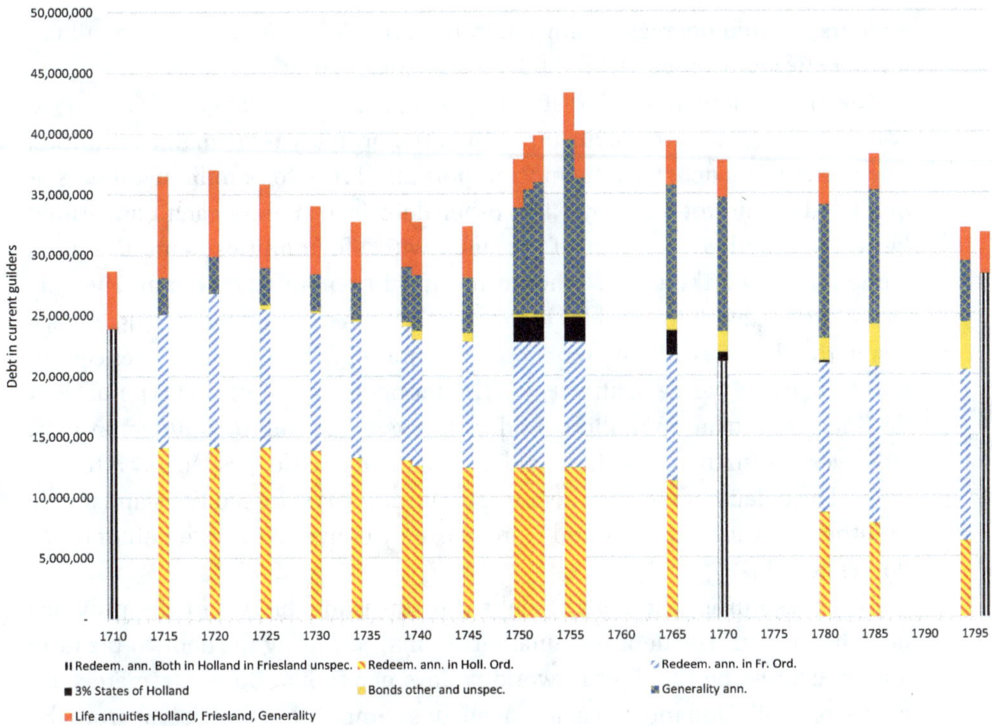

GRAPH 4.8 Friesland's public debt composition, 1710–1795.
SOURCES: TRESOAR, SVF, INV.NOS. 453, 491, 523, 541, 569, 586, 601, 604, 638, 683, 718, 766, 847, 880 AND 933; NA, RAAD VAN STATE, INV.NO. 2115; NA, PROVINCIALE RESOLUTIES, INV.NO. 484, P. 31–33; NA, ARCHIEF GOLDBERG, INV.NO. 11.

doubled the debt from almost 5 million to 11 million guilders in 1698.[174] The War of the Spanish Succession tripled the Frisian debt to over 33 million in 1715. The debt continued to rise after the war to 37 million guilders in 1720. That growth was partly because the Generality converted overdue payments into debt. The debt fell to 32 million guilders in 1740. During the War of the Austrian Succession, the debt rose again to 43 million guilders. The debt declined after 1750, a trend that was only interrupted by the Fourth Anglo-Dutch War. The increase during that war was modest, from 36 to 38 million

174 Trompetter, *Gewestelijke financiën: vol 6. Friesland*, 258: For 1687, the table reports 109,000 guilders, but this amount must be flawed for unknown reasons, as this volatility is impossible for life annuities. Instead, I took the average between the years 1686 and 1688 of 56,311 and 62,125 guilders respectively.

guilders. A rapid decrease followed. In 1795, the debt amounted to 32 million guilders.[175] On balance, the debt decreased after 1715.

The Frisian debt diversified after 1715 (Graph 4.8). All debt growth after 1720 consisted of debt instruments other than the ordinary redeemable annuities. The Generality's debt was the most important. It rose to 14 million guilders or one-third of the total in 1755. The other debt instruments each constituted between 15 and 20 per cent of the debt, with life annuities being the main component until the 1760s. Other forms of debt remained marginal. The only exception is a 2 million guilder loan from the States of Holland in 1745.[176] As a result, the share of ordinary redeemable annuities fell from over 80 per cent in 1710 to over 50 per cent after 1750. The monetary value of this type of debt declined from over 26 million guilders to a good 20 million guilders in 1795. However, the share of the debt paid in Holland decreased, especially after the 1760s. The default of 1711 and the interest rate cut of 1716 forced Friesland to rely on other debt instruments and it increasingly converted the remainder into domestic debt.

The question is whether the debt was unsustainable when the province defaulted in 1711. The debt sustainability is analysed using the debt-to-tax ratio and by expressing the debt in working days per capita. Both parameters are compared with Holland. For a homogeneous comparison, the income from the tax on bonds is excluded from Holland's income, as was the practice in Friesland.

Friesland consistently needed fewer years of tax revenue to pay off its debt than Holland (Graph 4.9). This ratio showed a similar development between 1650 and 1760. Between 1637 and 1650, the debt-to-tax ratio declined from three to one in Friesland, while in Holland, it increased from seven to twelve. The ratio then stabilised in both provinces until 1688. Between 1688 and 1720 this indicator rose from three to fifteen in Friesland and from eight to twenty-two in Holland. In short, the debt-to-tax ratio was not only lower in Friesland, it also increased by less than in Holland. Relatively, however, Frieland's increase in the debt-to-tax ratio was larger: It doubled from around one-third of Holland's ratio to two-thirds. In 1711, however, Friesland defaulted even though the debt-to-tax ratio was lower than Holland's.

During the rest of the eighteenth century, the debt-to-tax ratio declined in both provinces. In Friesland, the War of the Austrian Succession interrupted this trend. It led to Friesland's highest debt-to-tax ratio during the period of the Dutch Republic. In Holland, no clear trend breaks show, apart from the

175 Tresoar, SvF, inv.nos. 523, 541, 569, 586, 601, 638, 683, 718, 766, 847; NA, Raad van State, (1574) 1581–1795 (1801), inv.no. 2116, NA, Archief Goldberg, Inv.no. 11.

176 Fritschy, *Public Finance*, 160.

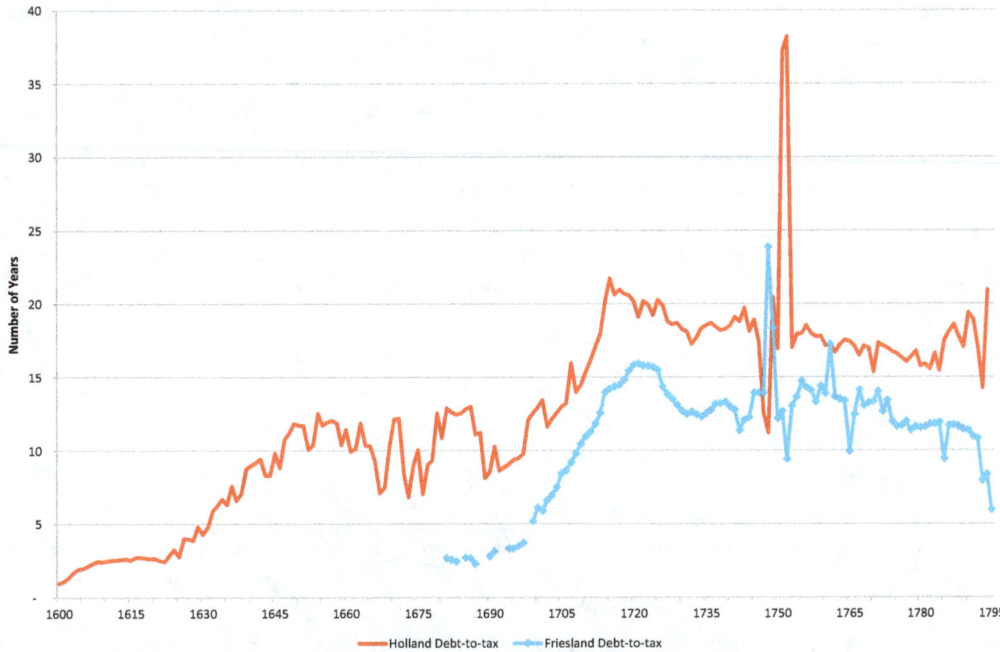

GRAPH 4.9 Debt-to-tax ratios in Holland and Friesland, 1600–1795.
SOURCES: SEE TEXT AND FEENSTRA, *BETWEEN SHARED*, APPENDIX.

disruptions caused by the uprisings of 1748. After the 1760s, the debt-to-tax ratio in Friesland fell faster and further than in Holland. Moreover, the Fourth Anglo-Dutch War caused an increase in Holland but not in Friesland. These developments in the debt-to-tax ratio do not give a reason to expect a default in Friesland.

The second gauge shows the number of day wages required per capita to repay the debt. As an alternative to the debt-to-GDP ratio, this better reflects the pressure from the debt on society. Even with this gauge, the debt burdened Friesland consistently less than Holland (Graph 4.10). However, the increase in Friesland's debt from the 1690s almost completely closed the gap with Holland. In both provinces, debt repayment required over a year of wages per person. Friesland's sevenfold increase was relatively larger, from fifty days to over 360 days, whereas this indicator doubled in Holland from 200 days to 400 days. The suddenness and magnitude of the increase in Friesland imply that Friesland's default risk increased abruptly.

Expressed in daily wages, the difference in public debt between Holland and Friesland remained equally small until the 1750s. In Friesland, the debt

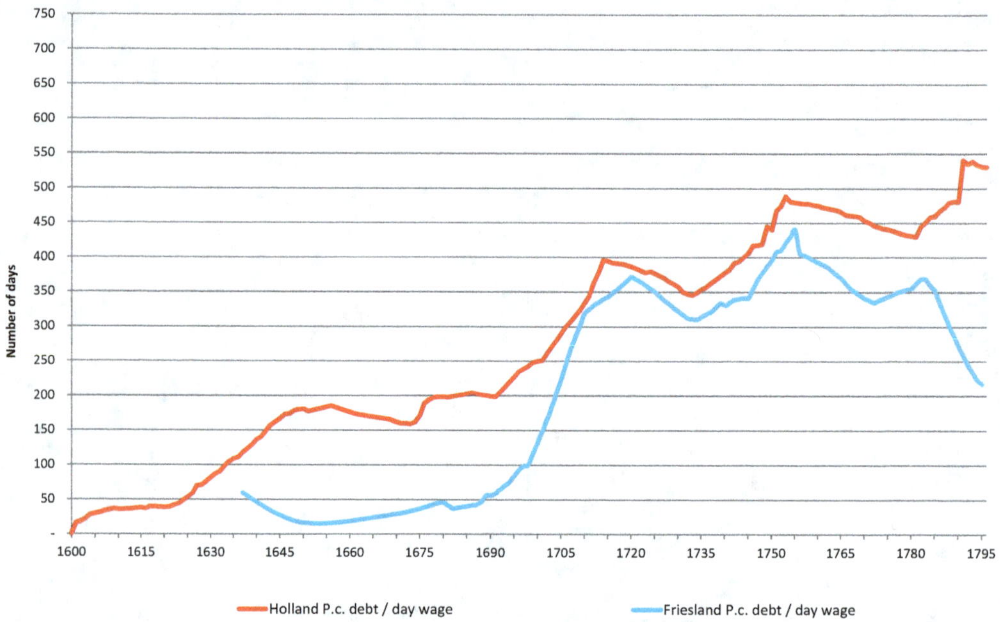

GRAPH 4.10 Debt per capita in day wages in Holland and Friesland, 1600–1795.
SOURCES: SEE TEXT AND FEENSTRA, BETWEEN SHARED, APPENDIX

burden peaked at 440 days. In Holland, the burden was slightly more at 480 days. Then developments diverged. After a period of decline, the debt burden increased in Holland. In the 1790s, it rose to well over 500 days. In contrast, a declining debt and growing population reduced per capita debt in Friesland. By 1795, Friesland's debt burden was not even half that of Holland.

4.2 *Coupons and Instruments*

Coupon rates on provincial loans fell in the seventeenth and eighteenth centuries. This led Fritschy to suspect a financial revolution in Friesland.[177] But the official coupon rates obscure the underlying problems. If Friesland could not borrow at the desired rates, it resorted to alternative measures. For instance, it resorted to forced loans or forced interest rate cuts, it sought to raise loans outside Friesland or it defaulted. So interest rates alone are not a reliable indicator for creditworthiness.

177 Fritschy, 160–61.

Until the 1660s, coupon rates for the redeemable annuities remained above the going rates on the private market. This *landschapsobligatie*, as it was called in Friesland, Friesland's main borrowing instrument. It had characteristics of both redeemable annuities and bonds. On the one hand, the instrument could be made out to bearers.[178] On the other hand, it was regularly described as redeemable annuities and redemption was at the discretion of the issuer. Despite the gradual decrease in coupons, Friesland had difficulty finding investors. The first known coupon concerns a 6 per cent forced loan in 1622.[179] In this period, Friesland offered redeemable annuities at 7 per cent and life annuities at 12 per cent to 14 per cent (Graph 4.11). The States of Friesland proposed more loans than were actually issued, which makes the actual interest rate uncertain.[180]

In the 1660s, finding investors remained difficult. A loan issue in 1665 at 4 per cent failed.[181] And a proposed interest rate reduction in 1669 from 5 per cent to 4 per cent probably failed as well.[182] Similarly, a voluntary 4 per cent loan issue failed in 1672. Only 80,000 guilders were subscribed on the eve of the Third Anglo-Dutch War and the Franco-Dutch War.[183] Instead, Friesland relied on forced loans from the rural districts and the Mennonites, a religious minority, to supplement voluntary loans. In that year, the province issued a forced 4 per cent loan from the Mennonites.[184] Hence the decline in coupons to 4 per cent or 5 per cent masks the underlying difficulties in attracting investors.

Only in 1680 was a voluntary interest rate reduction successful.[185] The interest rate was lowered to 4 per cent for redeemable annuities and 9 per cent for

178 Tresoar, SvF, inv.no. 497, 7-4-1716.

179 Martijn Van der Burg and Marjolein 't Hart, "Renteniers and the recovery of Amsterdams credit (1578–1605)," in *Urban public debts: urban government and the market for annuities in Western Europe (14th-18th centuries)*, ed. Marc Boone, Karel Davids, and Paul J. J. G. Janssens, Studies in European urban history (1100–1800) 3 (Turnhout: Brepols, 2003), 204–6; Spanninga, *Gulden vrijheid?*, 134–35. This was levied at a tax rate of 0.05 per cent on inhabitants' wealth that amounted at least 5,000 guilders.

180 Spanninga, *Gulden vrijheid?*, 180, 216, 356–57; Trompetter, *Gewestelijke financiën: vol 6. Friesland*, 185–91.

181 Tresoar, SvF, inv.no. 1788, f. 101, 12 October 1665, 22 februari 1666.

182 Tresoar, SvF, inv.no. 1788, f. 71.

183 Tresoar, SvF, inv.no. 1788, f. 101, 12 January 1672.

184 Trompetter, *Eén grote familie*, 40, 186: these loans served as a means to buy off military service, for the Mennonites, as confirmed pacifists, repudiated violence; Trompetter, *Gewestelijke financiën: vol 6. Friesland*, 186.

185 Tresoar, SvF, inv.no. 1788, f. 71.: "de Interessen gereduceerd op vier procento; dog konden de Crediteuren haren Capitalen opeischen op grote Landsdag". [The interest reduced to 4 per cent. The creditors were allowed to call in their capital at the Diet meeting].

life annuities.[186] Simultaneously, the States of Friesland declared redeemable annuities legal tender, turning them into interest-bearing paper money.[187] This was not the first time that debt securities could be used as a means of payment. In the 1640s, the domains could be paid for with debt securities and arrears of interest.[188] Like in the 1640s, the debt was reduced.[189]

During the Nine Years' War, Friesland usually borrowed at 4 per cent by way of redeemable annuities. Towards the end of the war, the rate increased to 4.5 per cent. The War of the Spanish Succession caused a further rise in the interest rate, to 6 per cent.[190] The States of Friesland repaid this loan in 1708, at least partly in Amsterdam.[191] The coupon rate of 5 per cent was still above the level of the 1680s.[192] The interruption of the downward trend had a knock-on effect on the private market. This implies that the War of the Spanish Succession caused crowding out.

Friesland's loss of credit prevented new ordinary redeemable annuities issues until the 1750s. Forced interest rate cuts on existing loans further eroded its credit. First, the tax on bonds (*reële goedschatting*) of 1711 reduced the effective interest rate by one percentage point, to 4 per cent.[193] Second, in July 1716, a forced interest rate cut limited the interest rate to 2.5 per cent.[194] The only exception was in 1725, when the States of Friesland borrowed 50,000 guilders to finance sluices near the town of Dokkum (*Dokkumer Nieuwe Zijlen*) at 5 per cent.[195] But between 1725 and 1730, the interest on old annuities was further reduced to 2 per cent.[196] Propositions in 1730 and 1763 to increase the interest to 3 per cent failed.[197] This made new loan issues impossible. Rather, in 1744, Friesland even found it too difficult to arrange forced loans from the towns and rural districts.[198] In 1759, Friesland issued redeemable

186 Trompetter, *Gewestelijke financiën: vol 6. Friesland*, 185–91.
187 Nijboer, *Fatsoenering*, 72.
188 Spanninga, *Gulden vrijheid?*, 344.
189 Tresoar, SvF, inv.no. 1788, f. 46.
190 Trompetter, *Gewestelijke financiën: vol 6. Friesland*, 187–89.
191 Advertentie. "Amsterdamse courant". Amsterdam, 07-02-1708, p. 2. Accessed on Delpher op 19-06-2022, https://resolver.kb.nl/resolve?urn=MMSAA06:166466016:mpeg21:p00002.
192 Tresoar, SvF, inv.nos. 267, p. 53–54.
193 Trompetter, *Gewestelijke financiën: vol 6. Friesland*, 164.
194 Tresoar, SvF, inv.no. 123, f. 137v: 25-7-1716.
195 Tresoar, SvF, inv.no. 267, pp. 215, 217, 13-7-1726 & 10-8-1726, [secrete resolutions]; inv.no, 541 (balance for 1725, mentions a 5 per cent loan within Friesland).
196 Tresoar, SvF, inv.nos. 541, 569.
197 Tresoar, SvF, inv.no. 1788, f. 72, 14 March 1730, proposal by the Friesland towns; Tresoar, 326 Familie thoe Schwartzenberg en Hohenlansberg, inv.no. 3512.
198 Trompetter, *Gewestelijke financiën: vol 6. Friesland*, 190.

GRAPH 4.11 Friesland's coupons per credit instrument at issuance, 1600–1795.
SOURCES: TROMPETTER, *GEWESTELIJKE FINANCIËN VOL. 6: FRIESLAND*, PP. 185–191, TRESOAR, SVF, INV.NOS. 267 (F.215–217), 453, 491, 523, 541, 569, 586, 601, 604, 638, 683, 718, 766, 847, 880, 933 AND 1788, F. 101; NA, RAAD VAN STATE, INV.NO. 2115; NA, PROVINCIALE RESOLUTIES, INV.NO. 484, P. 31–33

annuities again, this time at 3.5 per cent. From the 1760s until the 1790s, Friesland usually borrowed at 3 per cent. It issued several loans with the specific purpose of repaying the loan to the States of Holland. In 1778 and 1781, the coupon was as low as 2.75 per cent.[199] Friesland's public interest rate therefore followed the private market interest rate after 1750.

The default of 1711 also had consequences for the functioning of the redeemable annuities as legal tender. The price dropped to two-thirds of their original value in 1716 . A report for the Diet of April 1716 attributed this to the default on 'foreign creditors' ('*uijtheemse crediteuren*'). It further indicated that dishonest debtors had paid off their debts by buying cheap redeemable annuities and forcing them on their creditors at par. The report concluded that this harmed the daily economy for ordinary people.[200] As a consequence, newly registered

199 Tresoar, SvF, inv.nos. 766, 847, 880 and 933.

200 Tresoar, SvF, inv.no. 497, 7-4-1716.

private bonds contained the provision that interest payments and repayments should be in hard cash and not in Friesland's redeemable annuities.[201]

Also in 1716, two new taxes were made explicitly payable with redeemable annuities at face value: the inheritance tax (*collaterale successie*) and tax on the acquisition of military and administrative offices (*equivalent*). Ninety per cent of these taxes were paid in redeemable annuities. The States reduced this lucrative arrangement in 1742 to 75 per cent of the nominal value, unless the taxpayer proved that they had paid more.[202] The tax yields of 35,000 to 40,000 guilders per year would have reduced the debt to almost a million guilders by 1742.[203]

These tax payments form a quarter of the reduction of the debt in redeemable annuities. Another part can be attributed to a repurchase in 1732 at two-thirds of the nominal value. The States remarked that all interest should be paid on Friesland-registered annuities and with respect to the Holland-registered annuities only the interest that had been due for more than five years. At least 390,000 guilders were repurchased. The resolution was withdrawn five months later, however.[204] Between 1730 and 1734, this debt component decreased by almost 700,000 guilders.[205] The States thus benefitted from the fact that the redeemable annuities circulated below par.

Life annuities formed the second most important debt instrument in the seventeenth century. Its importance decreased in the eighteenth century because Friesland found other sources to supplement the redeemable annuities. The coupons on the life annuities decreased as well, in this case from 12–14 per cent in the 1620s and 1630s to 10–11 per cent in the 1660s and 8 per cent around 1690. The Nine Years' War in 1688 halted the decline in the coupons on the life annuities as well. During the War of the Spanish Succession, Friesland issued them at 9–10 per cent and even 12 per cent in 1713. This reflects the lack of money.

In 1726, the States of Friesland ordered the issue of life annuities for the waterworks in Dokkum. This was to supplement the issue of the redeemable annuities after Knock's failed loan issue in Amsterdam.[206] But this also failed.[207] Only after the War of the Austrian Succession did Friesland issue

201 HCL, 1001 Archief van de stad Leeuwarden, 1426–1811, inv.nos., 3872, 3877. In Dutch: "in klinkenden munte, sonder 's Landschapsobligatien of toonder deses".

202 Trompetter, *Gewestelijke financiën: vol 6. Friesland*, 159, 174–75.

203 Trompetter, 106, 109–10.

204 Tresoar, SvF, inv.no. 267, f. 238–239 (4 March 1732), f.243, (12 August 1732).

205 Tresoar, SvF, inv.nos. 569, 586.

206 Tresoar, SvF, inv.no. 267, pp. 215, 217, 13-7-1726 & 10-8-1726, [secrete resolutions].

207 The amount of annuities decreased between 1725 and 1730.

TABLE 4.1 Yields of fixed-term annuities in Friesland, 1725–1741.

Issuance year	Coupon	Term	Yields
1725	12.00%	13 years	7.05%
1734	12.00%	13 years	7.05%
1736	7.00%	15 years	0.62%
1739	12.00%	10 years	3.46%
1741	10.50%	15 years	6.30%

SOURCES: TRESOAR, SVF, INV.NOS. 569, 586,601, 604, 638, 683; NA, RAAD VAN STATE, INV.NO. 2115; TROMPETTER, *GEWESTELIJKE FINANCIËN. VOL. 6, FRIESLAND*, PP. 185–191.

life annuities.[208] Even then, the increase in life annuities in the 1750s remained limited to 300,000 guilders.

It was therefore no coincidence that Friesland began to issue fixed-term annuities from 1725. At the end of the term, the principal expired. The higher coupons compensated investors for the lack of reimbursement of the principal.[209] These instruments never accounted for more than a few hundred thousand guilders, despite the lucrative conditions (see: table 4.1).

Friesland depended on the Generality for substantial loans until the 1750s. In 1715–1720, coupon rates were lacking because the Generality converted Friesland's arrears into interest-bearing debt. The first loan the Generality issued for Friesland dates from 1739, and was for 1.5 million guilders.[210] These loans had an interest rate of 3 per cent.[211] This increased during the War of the Austrian Succession, to 3.5 per cent in 1746 and 4 per cent in 1747–1753.[212] Following the Generality's default of 1754, the interest rate was reduced to 3 per cent.[213] The exception to the Generality loans was a 2 million guilders loan from the States of Holland, also at 3 per cent, in 1745.[214] The Generality loans remained more important, amounting to 11 million guilders in 1755.

208 Trompetter, *Gewestelijke financiën: vol 6. Friesland*, 191.

209 Tresoar, SvF, inv.nos. 569, 586, 601, unfol. 'Balances over 1730, 1734 & 1739'; the low yield in 1736 is due to the conversion of a life annuity into a fixed-term annuity for which creditors had already received interest.

210 Tresoar, SvF, inv.no. 601.

211 Dormans, *Het tekort*, 147–48.

212 Trompetter, *Gewestelijke financiën: vol 6. Friesland*, 190–91; Tresoar, SvF, inv.no. 683, p. 13.

213 Dormans, *Het tekort*, 156; 't Hart, "United Provinces," 313; Fritschy, *De patriotten*, 39–41.

214 Trompetter, *Gewestelijke financiën: vol 6. Friesland*, 191.

Interest rates do not reflect Friesland's loss of credit and its dependence on the Generality. The price drop of the redeemable annuities, in 1716, to two-thirds of the nominal value equals a current yield of 6 per cent. At 5 per cent in 1725, not enough money could be raised in Friesland and none in Holland. Similarly, in 1732, the purchase value was two-thirds, equal to a yield of 3 per cent. At the same time, it was impossible to borrow at that rate. The 75 per cent of the nominal value in 1742 must also have been an absolute upper limit. The 6–7 per cent yields of the fixed-term annuities best reflect the compensation Friesland had to offer. This was similar to the 1620s and 1630s.

4.3 *Geographical Scope of the Market*

From the beginning, Friesland depended on capital imports. In 1600, the city of Amsterdam granted a small loan to the States of Friesland at an unknown interest rate.[215] In the 1620s and 1630s, creditors from Holland invested in Friesland's public debt. They must have understood that this was not without risk. Friesland's constant complaining that it could not pay the Generality contributions cannot have done its perceived creditworthiness any good.

In the 1630s, Friesland did indeed fail to pay its creditors inside and outside the province. Urban creditors within Friesland suffered from the former. The latter, however, was also potentially dangerous for Frisians. Merchants from Harlingen feared being arrested in Holland for Friesland's public debts.[216] Under the Law of Reprisal, citizens could be held accountable for their government's unpaid debt. Therefore, the States of Friesland decided to prioritise interest payments. The invocation of the Law of Reprisal was a real danger and consequently a credible threat. Friesland invoked the Law of Reprisal at least three times in this period. First, in 1585, this involved the arrest of people and goods from the town of Emden, in Germany. Second, in 1602, it targeted the inhabitants of the province of Overijssel. Third, in 1652, inhabitants in neighbouring Groningen fell victim.[217] The Law of Reprisal proved an effective judicial option for provincial cross-border contract enforcement.[218] In Fries-

215 Van der Burg and 't Hart, "Renteniers," 204–6.

216 Spanninga, *Gulden vrijheid?*, 319–20.

217 Georg Frederik baron Thoe Schwartzenberg en Hohenlansberg, ed., *Register van verbonden, zoenen, accoorden, privilegien, handvesten ... en missiven: zullende dienen, volgens de resolutie der Ed. Mog. Heeren Staaten van Vriesland de dato den 31 Augusti 1764. tot d'uitgave van een groot placaat- en charter-boek.: Aanvang neemende met de eerste en oudste gedenkstukken, en eyndigende met het jaar 1748.* (Te Leeuwarden,: gedrukt by Willem Coulon ..., 1765), 236, 394, 418.

218 Mitchener and Weidenmier, "Supersanctions and Sovereign Debt Repayment."

land, the Law had a similar disciplinary effect as in Holland in the sixteenth and seventeenth centuries, because the threat was credible.

But the Council of State wanted to prioritise troop payments, rather than interest payments. In the next phase of the conflict that evolved in the 1620s and 1630s, this contradiction emerged again. The States of Friesland wanted to accept redeemable annuities and overdue interest as payments for the domains. The Council of State preferred hard cash to pay the troops.[219] Eventually, one-third was payable in cash and the rest in redeemable annuities and overdue interest payments.[220] Wise buyers of the provincial domains presumably first tried to purchase the provincial redeemable annuities from debtholders before paying for the lands.[221] Meanwhile, the Court of Friesland ruled that the States had to pay the debtholders the overdue interest. As a result, the debt was redeemed in 1648, whereas the arrears with respect to the Generality remained unpaid.[222]

Holland and Amsterdam remained important sources of capital in the second half of the seventeenth century. Because the States was unable to borrow the amount it wanted within Friesland in 1665, it turned to Amsterdam. That issue, in 1666, was successful. However, Friesland had to offer a 5 per cent coupon, payable in Amsterdam.[223] In 1669, almost 1 million guilders were held in Holland, out of a total of 3.4 million.[224] It is uncertain how much Friesland borrowed in Holland during the Third Anglo-Dutch War or Franco-Dutch War. Just before the war, in 1671, it paid a fee to an Amsterdam broker. During the Nine Years' War, Friesland issued at least a quarter of its 6 million guilders in new loans in Holland.[225]

The War of the Spanish Succession drove Friesland again to Amsterdam. In 1702, the province failed to obtain a loan at 4 per cent from the Amsterdam magistrate.[226] A loan at 6 per cent *was* successful, however. Over the next few

219 Trompetter, *Gewestelijke financiën: vol 6. Friesland*, 118; Spanninga, *Gulden vrijheid?*, 180, 319–20, 362–68: The total debt incurred between 1627 and 1636 equalled the provincial outstanding debt in 1637.

220 Spanninga, *Gulden vrijheid?*, 344.

221 Spanninga, 322, 355.

222 Spanninga, 355–68.

223 Tresoar, SvF, inv.no. 1788, f. 101, 12 October 1665, 22 februari 1666.

224 Tresoar, SvF, inv.no. 1788, f. 45.

225 Trompetter, *Gewestelijke financiën: vol 6. Friesland*, 185–91; Fritschy, *Public Finance*, 161: Fritschy considers Amsterdam and Holland of minor importance, because she arrived at an estimate of 10 per cent during the Nine Years' War.

226 Tresoar Frysk Histoarysk en Letterkundich Sintrum (hereafter Tresoar), SvF, p. 40, 2 December 1702.

years, loans worth millions followed at 5 per cent.[227] The previous 6 per cent loan was also redeemed in 1708. The Amsterdam broker Jonas de Voogt repaid the creditors with interest.[228] But in 1710 the end of Frisian credit was in sight. The receiver Knock informed the States of Friesland that he could not pay the interest because his expenses exceeded his income. New bond issues were difficult because the 5 per cent bonds traded below par on the Amsterdam Exchange. A memorandum with daily market prices from broker Voogt supported Knock's claim.[229] Knock further restricted interest payments to matured instalments.[230]

In February 1711, the *Mindergetal* committee ordered the suspension of interest payments in Holland. The Diet confirmed this in October.[231] It halved interest payments, from almost 2 million guilders to less than 1 million guilders.[232] Friesland creditors only suffered a reduction in the rate of one percentage point to 4 per cent.[233] The States of Friesland anticipated the potential undermining effect in the response of the secondary market to this unequal treatment.[234] Holland creditors could sell their bonds to Frisians, who did receive interest. Therefore the resolution prohibited interest payments on Holland-issued annuities in Friesland unless the owner could

227 Tresoar, SvF, inv.no. 267 (Secrete Resoluties 1700–1748), p. 44–45, 17 December 1703; p.50, 12 April 1704; p. 53, 27 September 1704; p.54 12 December 1704; p. 57, 5 December 1705; p. 58, 13 February 1705.

228 Advertentie. "Amsterdamse courant". Amsterdam, 07-02-1708, p. 2. Geraadpleegd op Delpher op 19-06-2022, https://resolver.kb.nl/resolve?urn=MMSAA06:166466016:mpeg21:p00002.

229 Tresoar, SvF, inv.no. 453, 4 February 1710: "Verklaere ick ondergeschreve, Beedigden makelaar, binen de stadt Amsterdam, waer en warachtigh te weese, dat d'obligaties a vijff per cento losrente, lopen tot laste van de provintie van Vrieslant, alhier ter bursse dagelijckz worden gelaaten en verhandelt, tot 97: 97 1/2 en uijterlijck 98 per cento, tot welke verklaringhe van den heer ontfanger generaal der losrent, Johan Knock, versoecht sijnde hebben gepasseert, om te strecken na behooren, in Amsterdam, den 21 Januarij 1710, J.s. Voogt 1710 Makelaare".

230 Advertentie. "Amsterdamse courant". Amsterdam, 18-03-1710, p. 2. Geraadpleegd op Delpher op 20-06-2022, https://resolver.kb.nl/resolve?urn=MMSAA06:166470033:mpeg21:p00002.

231 Tresoar, Gewestelijke bestuursinstellingen van Friesland 1580–1795, Staten van Friesland (hereafter SvF), inv.no. 267 (Secrete Resoluties 1700–1748), p. 92.

232 Trompetter, *Gewestelijke financiën: vol 6. Friesland,* 222–25, 258–61.

233 Trompetter, 164.

234 Fernando Broner, Alberto Martin, and Jaume Ventura, "Sovereign Risk and Secondary Markets," *The American Economic Review* 100, no. 4 (2010): 1523–56.

prove that he or she had owned them before 10 February 1711.[235] The inclusion of this clause suggests that this was a real danger. Holland-issued debt could only be altered upon request to the States of Friesland.[236] Hence, Friesland used the distinction between domestic and non-domestic debt to discriminate against Holland creditors.

The default provoked protests from creditors and the States of Holland. In 1713, the States of Friesland argued that military expenditure prevented the resumption of foreign interest payments.[237] The States of Friesland allowed some Holland and Zeeland creditors to be considered residents, so that they could offset land taxes against the unpaid interest.[238] In 1714, the receiver of the life annuities paid one year of interest, due in 1711. He emphasised that the applied interest rate cut was similar to that in Friesland.[239] But these were exceptional cases. Rather, in 1716 the States of Friesland informed the States of Holland that resuming interest payments was beyond its financial capabilities. However, it made a gesture by proposing to resume interest payments at a rate of 2 per cent. This was the result of a reduction in the nominal interest rate to 4 per cent and a withholding tax of 2 per cent.[240] The States of Holland disagreed because this continued the unequal treatment of non-Frisian creditors. But the Frisians claimed higher interest payments were impossible.[241]

The States of Friesland probably paid interest in Holland in 1717: in February 1718, it announced the resumption of interest payments in Holland after a temporary suspension due to the Christmas Flood of 1717.[242] Meanwhile, it failed to pay the Generality.[243] This worsened the problems afflicting the Gen-

235 Tresoar, Gewestelijke bestuursinstellingen van Friesland 1580–1795, Staten van Friesland (hereafter SvF), inv.no. 267 (Secrete Resoluties 1700–1748), p. 92.

236 Trompetter, *Gewestelijke financiën: vol 6. Friesland*, 40.

237 Tresoar, SvF, inv.no. 120, f. 89r-v, 23 September 1713: "dog dat Haer E. Mog. enstige intentie is, om alles wat haer mogelijk en doenlijk sal wesen, in 't werk te stellen, om de supplianten, en andere hare Buijtenlandse creditoren aen betaelinge van los en lijfrenthen te verhelpen".

238 Tresoar, SvF, inv.no. 122, f. 29r; Tresoar, SvF, inv.no. 127, f. 78v.

239 "Advertentie". "Oprechte Haerlemsche courant". Haerlem, 01-05-1714. Accessed at Delpher 14-01-2017, http://resolver.kb.nl/resolve?urn=ddd:011220621:mpeg21:a0005

240 Tresoar, SvF, inv.no. 1713, point 6 at the agenda; These requests are repeated on 25 February and 24 March 1716: Tresoar, SvF, inv.no. 123, f. 54v; Tresoar, SvF, inv.no. 123, f. 54v – f. 56v: 'de betaelinge der buijtenlanse los en lijfrenthen'; Tresoar, SvF, inv.no. 123, f. 78v-80v.

241 Tresoar, SvF, inv.no. 123, f. 141, f. 151v, (30 May 1716 and 24 October 1716). f. 151v, 24-11-1716.

242 Tresoar, SvF, inv.no. 125, f. 12, 28-2-1718.

243 Prak, *The Dutch Republic*, 167.

erality, which had already suspended interest payments in 1715 and subsequently converted the Frisian arrears into interest-bearing loans. Friesland appears to have prioritised provincial debt service over its Generality obligations.

In 1719, Friesland resumed the interest payments in Amsterdam with a time lag that persisted until the end of the eighteenth century. The time lag differed for life annuities and redeemable annuities: the standard overdue term for redeemable annuities was five years, and four years for life annuities (Graph 4.12). This only applied to Holland-registered annuities; the Friesland-registered ones were paid.[244] Each year, the respective receiver of the life or redeemable annuities advertised the interest payment in Amsterdam.[245] From 1767, the Frisian agent in Amsterdam, Johannes Menkema, also paid interest in Haarlem. This consistent practice was only interrupted in 1748–1750.

Despite the consistency and predictability, Friesland suffered from credit rationing in Holland until the 1770s. The first confrontation with this was the failed attempt by the receiver Knock to issue a loan in Amsterdam in 1725. The offer of the same conditions as in Friesland, including 5 per cent interest, was not enough to persuade creditors.[246]

The resumption of interest payments did not mean the end of Friesland's payment problems. The province owed the States of Holland money, which the latter had advanced for troop recruitment. Because Friesland failed to repay, the States of Holland withheld the subsidy to the Frisian Admiralty in Harlingen in 1728.[247] At the same time, Friesland had arrears of 2.5 million guilders on the Generality debt. Friesland prioritised interest payments to private debt holders at the expense of public creditors.

Friesland was not very creditworthy during the War of the Austrian Succession. Just before the war, in 1739, Friesland's Generality debt increased from 3 million to 4.5 million guilders.[248] This was the last occasion on which Fries-

244 Tresoar, SvF, inv.no. 267, f. 238–239 (4 March 1732).

245 This is consistent with the recent analysis of the returns of the Utrecht merchant-investor Van der Muelen. He had inherited Friesland debt from Amsterdam relatives and consistently denoted a 2 per cent return on these assets over the period 1740–1799. Only after 1776 did some minor variations occur. Jeff Fynn-Paul, "Investment Behaviour in the Netherlands during the Long Eighteenth Century: An Analysis Based on the The Van Der Muelen Family Portfolio, 1738–1814," in *Publieke Financiën in de Lage Landen (1300–1800)*, ed. Jaco Zuijderduijn and Dries Raeymaekers, Publicaties van de Vlaams-Nederlandse Vereniging Voor Nieuwe Geschiedenis 14 (Maastricht: Shaker Publishing, 2015), 119, 130–31.

246 Tresoar, SvF, inv.no. 267, pp. 215, 217, 13-7-1726 & 10-8-1726, [secrete resolutions]; inv.no, 541 (balance for 1725, mentions a 5 per cent loan within Friesland).

247 Tresoar, SvF, inv.no. 135, f. 83v; 94r.

248 Tresoar, SvF, inv.no. 601, 604.

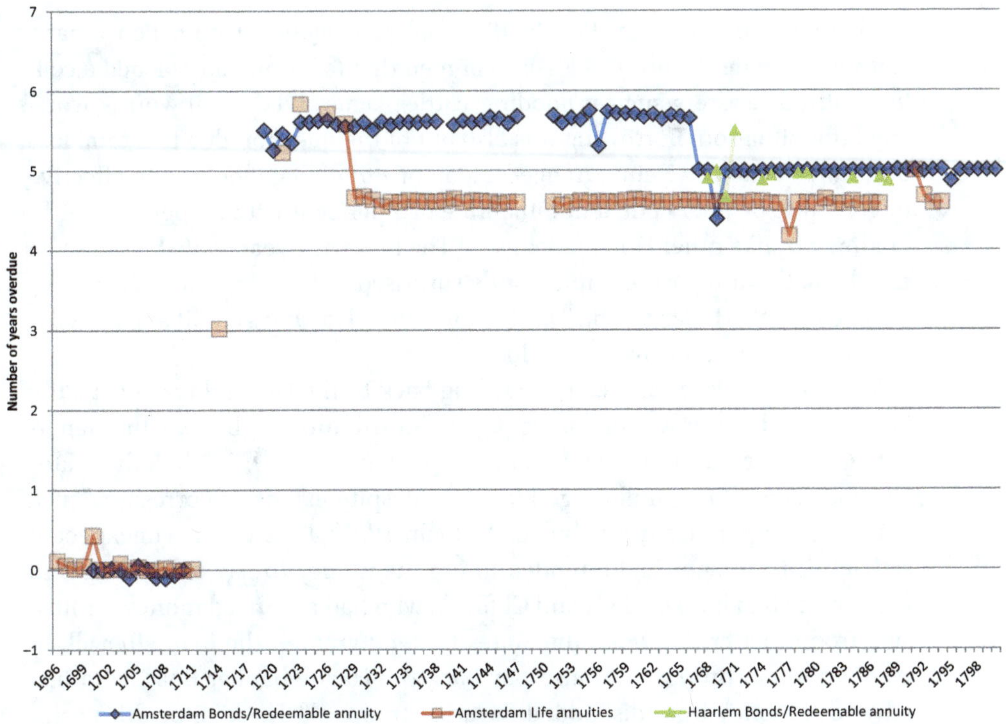

GRAPH 4.12 Timing of Friesland's debt service in Holland.
SOURCES: DATABASE, FRIESLAND NEWSPAPER 347 ADVERTISEMENTS, BASED ON DELPHER.NL, AS IN APPENDIX.

land obtained this type of loan for some time. In 1744, a forced loan from the towns and rural districts failed.[249] That same year, Friesland withheld its contributions to the Generality, until the Frisian Stadholder William IV was appointed General in the States Army.[250] This increased the irritation among the other provinces with Friesland as an errant contributor.[251] It certainly did not generate sympathy for Friesland. In 1745, Friesland could not issue a loan even with a guarantee from the Generality.[252]

249 Trompetter, *Gewestelijke financiën: vol 6. Friesland*, 191: The loan does not appear in the sources about the debt.

250 Bruggeman, *Nassau en de macht van Oranje*, 246; Israel, *The Dutch Republic*, 996. The Dutch Republic was not actively involved until 1744, although the war began in 1740.

251 Bruggeman, *Nassau en de macht van Oranje*, 133; Spanninga, *Gulden vrijheid?*, 125.

252 Tresoar, Verzameling Fries genootschap (hereafter: VFG), inv.no. 254, unfol. "*het totaal verval van credit, in zoo verre selvs, dat de Provincie, ook onder Garantie van Haar Hoog Mog. Geen gelden op interest kan bekoomen.*"

Therefore the States of Friesland turned to Holland's Grand Pensionary, Anthonie van der Heim. The Frisians argued that taxation had reached a ceiling. Natural disasters, such as flooding, cattle plague and the shipworms, worsened this situation. Borrowing was also out of the question due to a total loss of credit.[253] Van der Heim arranged a loan of 2 million guilders at an effective interest rate of 3 per cent: a nominal rate of 4 per cent with a 1 per cent withholding tax, like other Holland loans.[254] The following year, 1746, he refused a new loan. Creditors were unpleasantly surprised to find they had not to have invested in safe Holland debt. This compromised Holland's credit and forced it to issue a more expensive lottery loan.[255]

The States of Friesland came crawling back to the Generality. In 1745, the States argued that it was unable to pay its contribution.[256] In 1746, the Generality guaranteed a 1 million guilder loan at 3.5 per cent.[257] In 1747, the States General refused a 1.5 million guilder loan, despite extensive correspondence with and support from Stadholder William IV.[258] That was an unexpected setback. The Frisians had intended to use the money to pay off the debts to the Amsterdam bankers Pels and Clifford , who had advanced money for Russian troops. Later that year, the States General granted the loan after all. In 1749, Friesland proposed to also pay back the Hague banker Boas, who had advanced money from disbanded Bavarian troops.[259] These difficulties coincided with a fall in interest payments and a paucity of newspaper advertisements in Amsterdam. Until 1752, the Generality-guaranteed loans increased to about 9 million guilder.[260]

As was the case for Holland, the Generality's loan facilities granted to Friesland backfired. First, in 1752, a certain Mosis Moresco engineered an interest rate reduction from 4 per cent to 3 per cent on a 2 million guilder Generality

253 Tresoar, Verzameling Fries genootschap (hereafter: VFG), inv.no. 254, unfol. "*het totaal verval van credit, in zoo verre selvs, dat de Provincie, ook onder Garantie van Haar Hoog Mog. Geen gelden op interest kan bekoomen.*"

254 NA, Anthonie van der Heim, (1710) 1737–1746 (hereafter: Van der Heim), inv.no. 440, unfol. with notes of 22 July 1745; Tresoar, VFG, inv.no. 54: extract Secrete resolutie aan de Provintie van Vrieslant, op 14 May 1745.

255 NA, Van der Heim, inv.no. 295, 379; Tresoar, SvF, inv.no. 267, p. 306, 9 March 1746 (secret resolutions).

256 Tresoar, SvF, inv.no. 267, f. 280, 26 March 1745.

257 Trompetter, *Gewestelijke financiën: vol 6. Friesland*, 190; Tresoar, SvF, inv.no. 683, p. 13.

258 Tresoar, SvF inv.no. 267, f. 346, 4 March 1747, f. 352, 18 March 1747, f. 367, 7 July 1747; ibidem, inv.no. 153, f.92–93, 21 September 1747.

259 Tresoar, SvF, inv.no. 156 f.54, f. 140–142.

260 Tresoar, SvF, inv.no. 683; NA, Raad van State, inv.no. 2115.

loan to Friesland.[261] Then, in 1754, defective provincial contributions caused a Generality default. Friesland's share was considerable, with loans of 11 million guilders out of a total of 55 million guilders.[262] Hence, Friesland's financial difficulties had repercussions across the Republic's institutional structure.

After the Generality's default of 1754, Friesland no longer used Generality loans. Rather, it reduced its debt and increasingly converted non-domestic debt into domestic debt. From 1767, Friesland issued various loans to repay the loan to the States of Holland identical to the loans it issued at a rate of 3 per cent; it redeemed the loan in the early 1780s.[263] Cheaper borrowing was thus not the motive for this conversion. Friesland preferred domestic debt.

It remains puzzling what caused the shift within the ordinary annuities. The portion of debt that was Holland-registered decreased, while the Friesland-registered debt increased. This is different from the effect Van Bochove describes. He finds that public securities were traded back to the place of issue and interest payments.[264] Friesland had issued the debt in Amsterdam and paid the interest there. Moreover, the rate of 2 per cent was below the coupon rate of 3 per cent. A conversion into Friesland-registered debt for tax payments would not have caused an increase in that part of the debt.

The involvement of Johannes Menkema from 1767 changed three things: the redeemable annuities overdue term was shortened by six months, interest payments were introduced in Haarlem and, most importantly, Friesland's return to the Amsterdam capital market. From 1770, Friesland issued loans at 3 per cent through his office in Amsterdam.[265] The coupon was free from

261 Tresoar, SvF, inv.no. 159, f. 199v, f. 209.

262 E. H. M. Dormans, "De economie en de openbare financiën van de Republiek," in *Van tresorier tot thesaurier-generaal: zes eeuwen financieel beleid in handen van een hoge Nederlandse ambtsdrager*, ed. JTh de Smidt and R. M. Sprenger (Hilversum: Verloren, 1996), 104; Tresoar, SvF, 718.

263 Tresoar, SvF, inv.nos. 683, 718, 766 and 847, unfol. 'balance over 1780', p. 6–7.

264 Van Bochove, "Configuring Financial Markets."

265 Feenstra, 'More than Merchant Bankers'; "Advertentie". "Oprechte Haerlemsche courant". Haerlem, 18-07-1771. Geraadpleegd op Delpher op 30-01-2017, http://resolver.kb.nl/resolve?urn=ddd:010799898:mpeg21:a0007; "Advertentie". "Amsterdamse courant". Amsterdam, 25-07-1771. Geraadpleegd op Delpher op 30-01-2017, http://resolver.kb.nl/resolve?urn=ddd:010713599:mpeg21:a0013; Amsterdamse courant. Amsterdam, 28-07-1772, p. 1. Geraadpleegd op Delpher op 30-04-2016, http://resolver.kb.nl/resolve?urn=ddd:010714060:mpeg21:p002; Amsterdamse courant. Amsterdam, 28-07-1772, p. 1. Geraadpleegd op Delpher op 30-04-2016, http://resolver.kb.nl/resolve?urn=ddd:010714060:mpeg21:p002; Advertentie. Amsterdamse courant. Amsterdam, 19-07-1774. Geraadpleegd op Delpher op 15-09-2016, http://resolver.kb.nl/resolve?urn=ddd:010714369:mpeg21:a0011; Advertentie. Amsterdamse courant. Amsterdam, 26-07-1774. Geraadpleegd op Delpher op 30-04-2016, http://resolver.kb.nl/resolve?urn=ddd:010714372:mpeg21:a0014;

any discounts.[266] By the 1780s, his office gained a commanding position for Friesland. Investors in a 1-million-guilder loan in 1782 could only subscribe at the office of Menkema and Son. The advertisement did not mention any option for subscribing to the loan within Friesland.[267] Rather, the Leeuwarden stockjobber R. Storm sold the bonds Menkema issued in Amsterdam below par in Friesland.[268] Amsterdam was thus the prime market for issuing Friesland debt, including for Frisian investors.

In fact, Friesland had remained dependent on capital imports from Holland. After 1711, the Generality opened the back door to that market. Meanwhile, the consistent interest payments since 1719 may have increased trust. Furthermore, Friesland prioritised interest payments over debt service to Holland and the Generality in the 1720s. Even after the interruption of 1748–1750, investors again received the interest with the standard delay of four or five years in 1751.[269] Again, Friesland prioritised interest payments on its provincial debts over those owed to the Generality, which subsequently defaulted in 1754.

The question is whether investors benefitted from lending to Friesland and what this meant for the net flows of money. By 1770, investors had recouped their principal in interest; calculated as fifty-one years at 2 per cent interest

---

Advertentie. "Oprechte Haerlemsche courant". Haerlem, 28-07-1774, p. 2. Geraadpleegd op Delpher op 10-04-2023, https://resolver.kb.nl/resolve?urn=MMNHA02:164952259:mpeg21:p00002; "Advertentie". "Haarlemse Courant". Haarlem, 1775/07/25 00:00:00, p. 2. Geraadpleegd op Delpher op 28-11-2019, http://resolver.kb.nl/resolve?urn=ddd:010799119:mpeg21:p002.

266 "Advertentie". "*Amsterdamse courant*". Amsterdam, 29-04-1783. Accessed at Delpher 15-09-2016, http://resolver.kb.nl/resolve?urn=ddd:010716676:mpeg21:a0008

267 NEDERLANDEN. "Amsterdamse courant". Amsterdam, 13-04-1782, p. 1. Geraadpleegd op Delpher op 13-04-2023, https://resolver.kb.nl/resolve?urn=ddd:010714484:mpeg21:p001.

268 "Advertentie". "Leeuwarder courant". Leeuwarden, 1782/05/18 00:00:00, p. 5. Geraadpleegd op Delpher op 13-02-2020, http://resolver.kb.nl/resolve?urn=ddd:010576224:mpeg21:p005; Flandreau and Flores, "Bonds and Brands:" Storm thus benefitted from a run-up profit for professional investors – a technique used in London, some forty years later.

269 Advertentie. "Amsterdamse courant". Amsterdam, 31-07-1751, p. 2. Geraadpleegd op Delpher op 15-06-2022, https://resolver.kb.nl/resolve?urn=MMSAA06:165538091:mpeg21:p00002; Advertentie. "Amsterdamse courant". Amsterdam, 03-08-1751, p. 2. Geraadpleegd op Delpher op 19-06-2022, https://resolver.kb.nl/resolve?urn=MMSAA06:165538092:mpeg21:p00002; Advertentie. "Amsterdamse courant". Amsterdam, 05-08-1751, p. 2. Geraadpleegd op Delpher op 19-06-2022, https://resolver.kb.nl/resolve?urn=MMSAA06:165538093:mpeg21:p00002; Advertentie. "Amsterdamse courant". Amsterdam, 04-09-1751, p. 2. Geraadpleegd op Delpher op 15-06-2022, https://resolver.kb.nl/resolve?urn=MMSAA06:165538106:mpeg21:p00002.

since 1719. Friesland continued the interest payments until 1800. The additional twenty-five years yielded investors another 50 per cent of the principal. Hence, on balance capital flowed from Friesland to Holland, even without reimbursement of the principal. In addition, Friesland serviced and reimbursed its loan from the States of Holland. Until 1767, the principal remained untouched. Friesland paid 3 per cent during twenty-two years, equal to 66 per cent of the principal. In the next fifteen years, it repaid the debt. The interest and repayments exceeded the initial investment by almost 90 per cent. Again, there was a net capital flow from Friesland to Holland. On top of this were the interest payments on the Generality loans. As a result, lending to Friesland was also a self-sustaining investment that increased Holland investors' wealth, albeit in the very long run.

4.4 *The Secondary Market*

Those who did not wished to wait that long, turned to the secondary capital market. Even without price lists, the secondary market was important in providing investors with liquidity.[270] We have already seen that market prices were usually below par. The States of Friesland tried to make use of this fact. On the one hand, it did this by purchasing securities below par or accepting them as tax payment. On the other hand, it understood its potentially undermining effect, and blocked retrading to Friesland in the default of 1711. A systematic analysis of the secondary market provides better insight into the development of risk perception in the long run.

Market prices followed the same trend, despite geographical differences and different registers (Graph 4.13). Most observations stem from auctions in Amsterdam from 1712 to 1765, of both Amsterdam-registered and Leeuwarden-registered debt.[271] There was a big increase in yields after 1711, from just over

270 Neal, "How It All Began:" Neal argued that the political fragmentation of the Dutch Republic prevented the emergence of a liquid secondary market for public debt. This observation suggests otherwise.

271 Courtesy of Joost Jonker, Oscar Gelderblom and Christiaan van Bochove, who shared their findings in their auctions database with me. In this period, 574 transactions in Friesland redeemable annuities were recorded. Of these transactions only seven mention a coupon: two in 1712 reported a 5 per cent coupon and five others in 1753 a 2 per cent coupon. The other 567 auction sales did not report a coupon. Only two of these transactions, in 1724, indicated that this concerned the register of Leeuwarden, which means that these had a 2.5 per cent coupon. I presumed that for the remaining 565 redeemable annuities the standard 2 per cent coupon applied, similar to the five aforementioned 1753 sales. I made this assumption because the first transactions in this type of asset after 1712 occurred in 1720 – in between those years no transactions were reported.

5 per cent in 1710 to 7.5 per cent in 1712. This is in line with the report to the Frisian Diet of April 1716. The two-thirds price drop for 5 per cent annuities resulted in a current yield of 7.5 per cent.[272] A sharp decrease followed the resumption of interest payments in 1719, to 3–3.5 per cent. After 1735, yields fell below 3 per cent. This barely differed from the rates that Friesland accepted for tax payments. The War of the Austrian Succession raised yields to 4 per cent and briefly above 4.5 per cent. The 7 per cent from Van Tongerlo's price list in 1747 is not representative. After 1750, current yields declined, to 2.5 per cent in the late 1770s.

The trend corresponds to the development of the coupons. But Friesland hardly issued any debt between 1711 and 1759. There are exceptions to this. The coupon of 5 per cent in 1725 was higher than the market yield of 3.6 per cent in Amsterdam. The 5 per cent rate was too low to attract new investments, while creditors did trust that Friesland would pay the existing debt. Perhaps this also happened during the War of the Austrian Succession. Market yields largely remained below 4 per cent. That was the same as the interest on the Generality loans. It suggests that Friesland could also have borrowed at 4 per cent on its own credit. However, Friesland was still unable to issue loans on its own credit. Credit rationing thus remained a problem for new loans, despite falling market prices.

After 1754, yields also rose temporarily, from 3 per cent to 3.5 per cent. The fact that after 1754 the Generality bonds yielded only 3 per cent helped Friesland to issue loans at 3.5 per cent in 1759. In the following years, the new coupons fell to just above the market yields, which were also falling. Conversely, market yields rose to just below coupon rates in the early 1770s. After 1780, coupons and market yields rose again.[273] In 1793, Friesland could only borrow a small amount at 3 per cent, because this rate was below the market yields. On the other hand, the market prices for the debt of other provinces were similar or worse.[274] In 1793, Holland bonds had current yields of 3.38 per cent and 3.36 per cent and Zeeland bonds 4.4 per cent.[275] So, the coupons reflect the restoration of Friesland's credit, which allowed a return to the Amsterdam capital market.

272 Tresoar, SvF, inv.no. 497, 7-4-1716.

273 *Nieuwe Nederlandsche jaerboeken of vervolg der merkwaardigste: geschiedenissen die voorgevallen zyn in de Vereenigde Provincien de generaliteitslanden ende volksplantingen van de staat 1766–1792*, vol. 2, 23 (Amsterdam / Leiden, 1788), 1509–10.

274 Riley, *International Government Finance*, 276.

275 HUA, inv.no. U255a011, notarial deed 75, 24-8-1793.

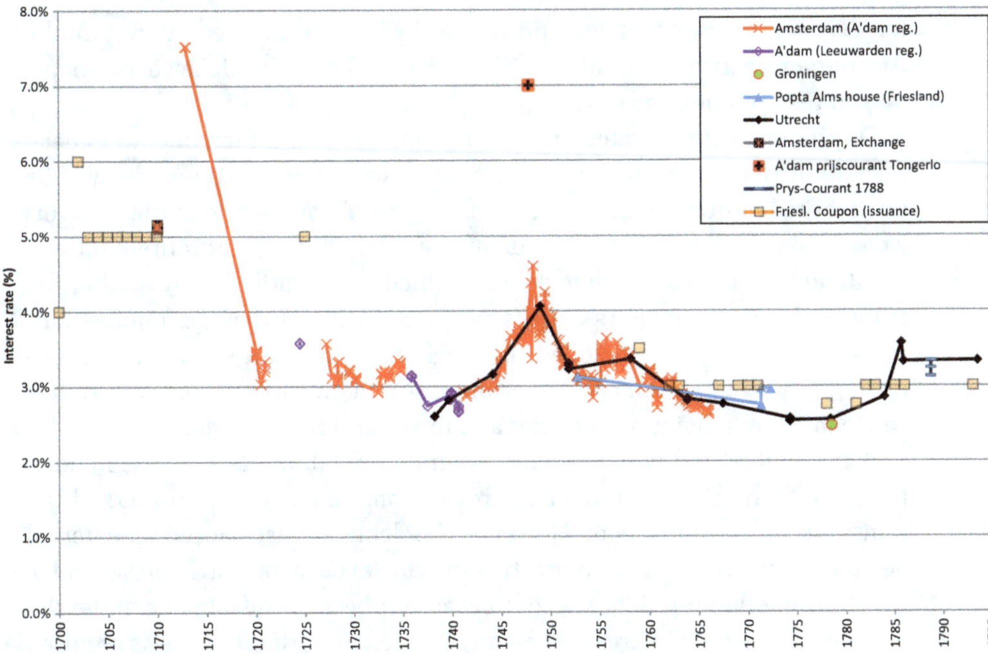

GRAPH 4.13 Market bond yields compared to coupon rates in Friesland, 1710–1780.
SOURCES: AUCTIONS DATABASE, JOOST JONKER, OSCAR GELDERBLOM AND CHRISTIAAN VAN BOCHOVE; HUA, NOTARIAL DEEDS, INV. NO. U169A013, ACT 109, 6 NOVEMBER 1751; INV. NO. U234A001, ACT 52, 18 FEBRUARY 1758; INV. NO. U188A026, ACT 53, 13 JUNE 1767; INV.NO. U247A017, ACT 53, 30 MAY 1778; RHC-GRA, FAMILIE VAN SWINDEREN EN DE MAREES VAN SWINDEREN, 1370–1982, INV.NO. 708708; *NIEUWE NEDERLANDSCHE JAERBOEKEN* 1766–1792, VOL. 23 (2), 1788, PP. 1509–1510; HUA, INV.NO. U255A011, NOTARIAL DEED 75, 24-8-1793.

Some remarks in the sources deepen the insight into the valuation of Frisian debt and its debt policy. First, the market became accustomed to Friesland's systematically belated payments. Sellers only received compensation for overdue interest that exceeded the five-year term. For instance, in Utrecht in 1767, the buyer paid the interest over 1761 but not over 1762 to 1766.[276] Second, even in neighbouring Groningen Frisian debt was categorised as 'foreign' debt, like Holland's and the Generality's.[277] This shows that provincial borders mat-

276 HUA, Notarial deeds, inv.no. U188a026, act 35, 13 June 1767.

277 Regionaal Historisch Centrum: Groninger Archieven (hereafter: RHC-GrA), Familie Van Swinderen en De Marees van Swinderen, 1370–1982, inv.no. 708708: It concerns the heritage of Maria Trip, a member of a prominent Amsterdam family. The inventory, for instance, also contains a share in the famous Trippenhuis in Amsterdam. So these

tered. However, creditors dealt pragmatically with the delayed interest on the Amsterdam-registered annuities. The consistency of the delayed payments helped restore Friesland's credit.

Do the low coupon rates mean that Friesland had undergone a financial revolution? First, the shift to long-term debt was interrupted and delayed by the debt redemption of the 1640s. The proceeds from the sale of the domains were used to redeem Friesland's debt. Even though the debt retirement was unintended, Friesland's public debt remained small until the 1690s. After the 1640s, Friesland coped with deficits by failing to fulfil its payment obligations to the Generality. This included the single-handed dismissal of troops. Borrowing proved more difficult. Friesland resorted on various occasions to forced loans from religious minorities and towns and rural districts.

Between 1688 and 1710, Friesland experienced a dramatic increase in debt, the second criterion for a financial revolution. This period also marked the transition to long-term debt. However, the debt increase caused an external default, in 1711. This implies firstly that provincial borders mattered. Secondly, the shift to long-term debt was not because it became sustainable, quite the opposite. To resume interest payments, a forced interest rate cut was required by way of a withholding tax on bonds. If Friesland had not taken this measure to halve the interest payments, it would have run up enormous and constant deficits, causing the debt to grow continually. Now the debt remained in proportion to tax income and the economic carrying capacity.

As a consequence of the default, Friesland suffered from credit rationing. This was because Friesland distinguished between domestic and non-provincial creditors. Until 1725, the tax on Friesland-registered annuities was less than on Holland-registered bonds. And throughout the eighteenth century, the interest on Holland-registered debt was paid with a five-year delay, while the interest on the Friesland-registered debt was paid promptly. The unequal treatment may explain why Friesland succeeded in issuing some debt within the province but not in Holland, despite offering identical conditions. Friesland did not repudiate the debt yet it unilaterally reduced the interest payments, which allowed it to maintain the debt and pay interest. This rather than favourable market conditions explains the transition to long-term debt.

This relates to the third element, the coupon rates. The decline in interest rates was slow, difficult and marginal until after 1750. The yields on the fixed-

redeemable annuities are probably Amsterdam-issued Friesland redeemable annuities, which thus yielded 2 per cent effective interest.

term annuities in 1725–1741 were similar to the ones on the redeemable annuities in the 1620s and 1630s. In the 1660s and 1670s, difficulties remained in raising sufficient amounts at the proposed rates. Superficially, the coupon rates declined, yet this hides the underlying problems. At times, Friesland resorted to alternatives such as forced loans. The debt increases of 1688–1710 were also accompanied by increasing interest rates. The decrease that followed was again a forced one, this time obtained by imposing a withholding tax on bonds. Except for the voluntary reduction of 1680, Friesland experienced difficulties in reducing interest rates. The cause of the decline until the 1750s was a combination of forced measures and limited demand.

After 1750, the local capital supply increased. This allowed Friesland to issue domestic debt to replace the loan from the States of Holland. The market for public debt followed the private market. Further decreases in the coupon followed in the 1770s and 1780s. This debt was, however, issued at least in part in Amsterdam. Hence, the low coupons reflect Holland's abundant capital and the effect of capital imports.

This then relates to the question about the origin of the money. Throughout the period, Holland was an important source of capital. Already in the 1620s and 1630s, money from Holland was being invested in Frisian public debt. It is unclear how much money flowed to Friesland. Nevertheless, all the money flowed back with interest in the 1640s. In 1669, almost a third of Friesland's provincial public debt was outstanding in Holland. In 1711 this proportion was half. By the 1780s, Amsterdam was the central place for Friesland's debt issues.

Between 1711 and 1770, Friesland found back doors to Holland's capital market. First and foremost it relied on the Generality's credit. This central institution had first converted arrears into interest-bearing debt. Later it issued debt for Friesland under its guarantee. When this temporarily failed, the States of Friesland persuaded Holland to grant a loan to Friesland. Earlier as well, in the 1720s, Holland had advanced money to Friesland. However, the Frisians paid these political intermediaries too little or too late. They preferred to prioritise continuous debt service. This suggests that Friesland deemed its reputation on the capital market more important than maintaining good political relations within the federation.

Similarly, in the 1630s and 1640s it put the interests of the creditors above those of the Generality. At the same time, creditors befitted from the Generality's forceful intervention, although poor debt service was not the reason for the intervention. Rather, friction arose as to whether the military or the creditors should benefit from the sale of the domains. This is in line with Tomz's understanding of gunboat diplomacy. Unpaid debts to private creditors are insufficient for military intervention.[278] On the other hand, pressure from Harlingen merchants suggests that the Law of Reprisal had a disciplining effect. In sum, Friesland did not undergo a classic financial revolution.

5 Conclusion

Politically and economically, Friesland was a distinct case. The economy was closed yet prosperous. Although well connected, it saw itself as having a separate history. Based on the concept of Frisian Freedom, it claimed more autonomy than the other member provinces. The almost constant complaints about its share in the common expenses caused increasing irritation among the other provinces about the Frisians. They considered Friesland the most reluctant contributor. There are arguments for and against Friesland's position. For most of the period, there is more evidence in support of Friesland's rhetoric, but these arguments lose power towards the end of the eighteenth century.

First, Friesland's contribution per capita equalled Holland's in 1616. After 1616, Holland's population outgrew that of Friesland, as seen in the development of the demographic ratio. As a consequence, the requested per capita contribution increased compared to Holland. In 1616, Friesland's population equalled one-fifth that of Holland, like Friesland's share in the Generality's budget. By 1700, it was less than one-sixth, a 20 per cent decline. By 1795, the population had almost returned to its original ratio with Holland. Yet Friesland's demographic development compared favourably to Zeeland. Moreover, wage levels in Friesland were consistently lower than in Holland and Zeeland. Each guilder in tax revenue required 30 per cent more labour in Friesland. As a result, Friesland's financial obligation per head increased to one and a half times that of Holland. After 1750, it fell again to more or less equal proportions in 1792.

Second, the tax burden matched or exceeded that of Holland. This was already the case in the 1620s. This implies that Friesland underwent a tax revolution. Nevertheless, Friesland regularly left troops unpaid, and inadequate payments caused an armed conflict with the Generality in the 1620s and 1630s. At gunpoint, the Council of State enforced fiscal reforms, which increased the tax burden even further. Friesland soon dismissed troops again and paid the Generality erratically. Still, the tax burden was on a par with that in Holland in the 1680s. Tax increases in the 1690s ensured that the tax

278 Tomz, *Reputation and International Cooperation.*

burden in Friesland kept pace with Holland. In 1700–1750, it exceeded Holland's level and subsequently was maintained at similar levels until 1795. Friesland was by no means a free rider on Holland's account, yet it frequently failed to pay the Generality what it owed. This is because, expressed in per capita wages, a higher contribution was demanded from Friesland than from Holland.

Third, borrowing required the assistance of the Generality and Holland after Friesland's default in 1711. Both advanced money and issued loans for Friesland, which gave Friesland a back door to Holland's capital market. Friesland's local capital supply was too limited to replace these capital imports. The Frisians had difficulty paying their bills and debts to Holland and the Generality. Holland forced Friesland to pay by withholding other subsidies. The Generality was never a priority. Rather, defective provincial contributions, by Friesland and others, caused the Generality to default in 1715 and 1754.

Fourth, claims of overburdening proved hard to substantiate given the fiscal surpluses. On the rare occasions when the books were opened to examination, Friesland needed to manipulate the figures in order to substantiate those claims. Moreover, the province reduced its debt. Hence, Friesland's financial situation improved, in particular after 1750. It nevertheless obtained a discount on its Generality contributions, temporarily in 1783 and permanently in 1792. Ironically, by this time the discount was no longer justified.

As a result, the case of Friesland provides insights into the functioning of the Dutch Republic's political economy. First, the default of 1711 was unavoidable to balance the books. Friesland's options were exhausted. Taxation had reached a social ceiling. The economic stagnation eroded the tax base and urbanisation decreased after the 1660s. Still, the high tax burden was insufficient to fully service the debt; the counterfactual of full debt service would have required another 40 per cent increase in taxes. Friesland's default severely limited its borrowing options. In Holland, Friesland suffered from credit rationing. In Friesland, there was too little capital, despite falling private interest rates. High taxes and a forced interest rate reduction through a withholding tax on bonds were necessary to achieve a healthy government balance sheet. Friesland could not afford the luxury of credible commitment.

Second, targeting the part of the debt issued outside the province was a deliberate act designed to benefit from provincial autonomy and hide behind its provincial borders. Friesland held separate registers for debt issued outside of the province, enabling a selective external default based on domicile. This underlines the importance of the Dutch Republic's fragmentation in hindering contract enforcement. Without an overarching legal framework, disadvantaged parties could only invoke the Law of Reprisal. Creditors from Holland threatened Harlingen merchants in the 1630s to do just that. This continued at least until the 1650s. The requests for safeguards during the Nine Years' War suggest that such problems persisted beyond then too. The Republic's provincial borders became relevant as soon as financial problems arose. After the default of 1711, however, the States of Holland protested but took no further action. Perhaps the implicit threat was sufficient to resume payments. The Dutch Republic's legal fragmentation hampered contract enforcement, and consequently capital flows and interest rate convergence.

Third, the reduced and consistently belated payments on the interest on the debt became a priority after the resumption of payments in 1719. The consistency signalled a credible commitment to its public debt and allowed Friesland to return to Holland's capital market in the 1770s. In the 1780s, the Amsterdam capital market was central to Friesland for issuing debt. This was as much an expression of Friesland's commitment as of Holland's capital surplus. The latter masks more fundamental problems with raising sufficient capital within Friesland, where the local capital supply remained limited.

Fourth, the eventual commitment to the debt was not the result of the democratic advantage of representative institutions but driven by self-interest and the wish to borrow more cheaply. The Diet did not protect the debtholders' interests. Non-Frisian debtholders' suffered from inadequate interest payments in the 1630s and 1711. The question remains what would have happened if the States General had not intervened in 1637. Friesland's highly representative electoral system served taxpayers' interests, which offered room for populism. In 1638, the Council of Stated forbade Diet candidates to promise tax reductions. After 1740, the dominant rural quarters shifted the tax burden from the countryside to the towns. Yet the main factor was that debtholders who lived outside the province were not represented in the Frisian Diet and therefore they were not able to protect their interests. External debtholders only received priority if sanctions were looming and if Friesland lacked alternatives, such as non-payment of the Generality. In Tomz's typology, Friesland would qualify as a fair-weather type. Yet serving its debt in full was more of an unattainable luxury than a realistic choice.

Finally, the tax revolution was not followed by a financial revolution. When the Dutch Revolt began, Friesland's provincial institutions had only just begun to develop. It lacked Holland's medieval experience in fiscal intermediation. In Holland, defaults on loans issued for the overlord formed learning experiences that Holland took on board in the sixteenth and seventeenth centuries. Friesland had to learn this lesson during the period of the Republic and it did so the hard way.

As a result, Friesland acted somewhat as a serial defaulter, in the 1630s, in 1711 and in 1748–1750.[279] This list only takes the bondholders into account, as on top of that there was the incomplete debt service with respect to the Generality. The most striking example is the treatment of the Generality embassy of 1730. Instead of paying its arrears to the Generality, Friesland lowered its contribution. This is the third form of defaulting. The lack of central power after 1651 facilitated such free riding. Perhaps the real question is why Friesland still taxed its population so heavily.

In the final chapter, we study the adjacent province of Groningen. It was less urbanised, and a province where urban and rural powers were balanced and the States General had great influence. Like Friesland, it lacked the medieval experience of fiscal intermediation. The question is how this affected Groningen's public finance, interest rates and risk of defaulting.

---

279 Mauricio Drelichman and Hans-Joachim Voth, "Serial Defaults, Serial Profits: Returns to Sovereign Lending in Habsburg Spain, 1566–1600," *Explorations in Economic History* 48, no. 1 (January 2011): 1–19, https://doi.org/10.1016/j.eeh.2010.08.002.

CHAPTER 5

Federal Power in Groningen

The case of Groningen serves as a counterfactual to the provincial autonomy in the other provinces. In Groningen, the States General maintained unprecedented rights to intervene in provincial politics. This institutional exceptionalism offered solutions that would be unthinkable elsewhere within the Dutch Republic. The study of Groningen thus provides the opportunity to assess the effects of the Dutch federal structure.[1]

The effects of the federalism are debated. On the one hand, the lack of centralisation is considered inefficient and to have enabled free riding, which eventually led to the Republic's downfall.[2] On the other hand, it is assumed to have fostered high tax morale and commitment to public debt, leading to lower borrowing costs.[3] The Generality's involvement had two possible, opposing effects on debt management and creditworthiness. On the one hand, it might have led to Groningen prioritising the Generality's expenditure at the expense of interest payments to creditors. On the other hand, it might have resulted in higher taxes and third-party control, which would provide creditors with more certainty.[4] This chapter examines when and how federal interference influenced public finance and debt handling.

The chapter thus is about the effects of coercion and control. The focus is on the level of taxation, commitment to the debt versus commitment to the common expenses, and defences. It starts by explaining the strategic importance of the city of Groningen to the Republic's defences, which was the Generality's responsibility. But regardless of who makes the decision, there is still the question of how much burden the economy can bear. The analysis of the

1 Hovy, "Institutioneel onvermogen"; Van Zanden and Van Riel, *The Strictures of Inheritance*; Fritschy, "Overheidsfinanciën."

2 Epstein, *Freedom and Growth*, 18, 24, 31, 33–34; Hovy, "Institutioneel onvermogen."

3 Stasavage, "What We Can Learn from the Early History of Sovereign Debt," 7–8; Stasavage, *States of Credit*; Prak and Van Zanden, "Tax Morale"; Van Zanden and Prak, "Towards"; 't Hart, *The Making of a Bourgeois State*, 174–79.

4 From the historiography the case of Greece is known, which issued a new loan in 1833 even though its 1826 default remained unsettled, Yet England, France and Russia acted as guarantors to the new loan and pledged all Greece's revenues to secure it. Tomz, *Reputation and International Cooperation*, 53–55: So the investors in the new loan were favoured over the creditors of the old debt, at their expense, by the external intervention of these three great powers.

 | DOI:10.1163/9789004745254_006

Groningen economy follows, intending to determine the province's fiscal carrying capacity. Then we assess whether the Generality's involvement caused a tax revolution or a classic financial revolution in Groningen.[5] In conclusion, the case of Groningen allows an evaluation of the effects of a more centralised Dutch Republic.

1 Groningen's Unique Institutional Position

In 1594, the Treaty of Reduction merged the City and rural Hinterlands (*Ommelanden*) of Groningen to form one province. This followed the Republic's conquest of the city of Groningen. After Stadholder Rennenberg's defection in 1580, Spanish troops raided the countryside from the city.[6,7] The countryside had remained loyal to the Revolt.[8] The city of Groningen proved of strategic value in controlling the north of the Dutch Republic.[9] To keep the city of Groningen on the side of the Revolt, the States General had to make concessions. Therefore, it restored the City to its claimed rights and forcefully united the City and rural Hinterlands of Groningen as equals into one province.

The forced union and equal power sharing was much to the chagrin of the Hinterlands. Its inhabitants had hoped to regain their independence from the City by joining the Revolt. Until 1536, the hinterlands had no worldly overlord, not unlike the situation with the Frisian Freedom in Friesland. As Frisians, the inhabitants of Groningen's hinterlands felt themselves superior to the city, which was of Lower-Saxon and Drenthe origin.[10] Hopes that they would be

5 Tracy, *A Financial Revolution in the Habsburg Netherlands*; Fritschy, "Financial Revolution."

6 Fruin, *Geschiedenis der Staatsinstellingen*, 178; Meindert Schroor and Otto S. Knottnerus, "De Opstand 1568–1594," in *Geschiedenis van Groningen II. Nieuwe Tijd*, ed. M. G. J. Duijvendak et al. (Zwolle: Waanders, 2008), 115–24.

7 Israel, *The Dutch Republic*, 206; Schroor and Knottnerus, "De Opstand," 124–25: this became known as Rennenberg's defection (Dutch: "Het verraad van Rennenberg").

8 L. Van der Ent and V. Enthoven, *Gewestelijke financiën ten tijde van de Republiek der Verenigde Nederlanden. Deel III. Groningen (1594–1795)*, 94 (Den Haag: Instituut voor Nederlandse Geschiedenis, 2001), 14, 17.

9 Schroor and Knottnerus, "De Opstand," 143; Israel, *The Dutch Republic*, 208, 247–48; J.J. Woltjer, "Van Katholiek tot Protestant," in *Historie van Groningen: stad en land*, ed. Wiebe Jannes Formsma (Groningen: Tjeenk Willink, 1976), 205. The Holland Grand Pensionary Van Oldenbarneveldt had knowledge of these negotiations.

10 Schroor and Knottnerus, "De Opstand," 108–12, 117; The Ommelanders argued in 1594 that it would be monstrous to put a Drenthe head upon a Frisian body (Drentsch hoofft up een Vriesche lichaem te setten). Meindert Schroor, "Heroriëntatie op de Unie en op

rewarded for their loyalty were dashed, however, because of the city's strategic importance as the gateway to the north of the Republic.

Decision-making ran the risk of stalemate because the Hinterlands and City each held one vote.[11] The more so, because the Hinterlands feared the City's dominance. Anticipating future deadlocks, the Treaty of Reduction granted the States General far-reaching powers, including settling disputes.[12] As a consequence, Groningen was less autonomous than the other constituent member provinces.[13]

The States General soon exercised this right. It enforced several fiscal reforms between 1597 and 1628.[14] Such interventions continued until 1749, when the Generality lost these rights to the Stadholder. After the Orangist revolution of 1747, the Reform Statute (*Reglement Reformatoir*) of 1749 came into effect.[15] Up to then, the States General had sent at least thirty-six embassies to solve internal conflicts or obtain overdue payments.[16]

The Reform Statute also restructured and professionalised the provincial legal system. The High Chamber of Justice (*Hoge Justitiekamer*) replaced the Chieftains Chamber (*Hoofdmannenkamer*). The new court extended its jurisdiction to all residents. The old court had settled conflicts between townspeo-

---

Holland," in *Geschiedenis van Groningen II. Nieuwe Tijd*, ed. M. G. J. Duijvendak et al. (Zwolle: Waanders, 2008), 155; Schroor quotes something similar: the head of a Drenthe bull upon a Frisian cow's rump ("de cop van een Drentsche bulle, op de romp van een Friesche koe)". Meindert Schroor, *Rurale metropool: bevolking, migratie en financiën van de stad Groningen ten tijde van de Republiek (1595–1795)*, Historia agriculturae, ISSN 0439–2027 46 (Groningen: Nederlands Agronomisch Historisch Instituut, 2014), 7; Meindert Schroor and Otto S. Knottnerus, "Stad en Lande, het Duitse Rijk en d Nederlanden 1498–1536," in *Geschiedenis van Groningen II. Nieuwe Tijd*, ed. M. G. J. Duijvendak et al. (Zwolle: Waanders, 2008), 35–49; Wiebe Jannes Formsma, "De landsheerlijke periode," in *Historie van Groningen: stad en land*, ed. Wiebe Jannes Formsma (Groningen: Tjeenk Willink, 1976), 173–206; Fruin, *Geschiedenis der Staatsinstellingen*, 18–19; Israel, *The Dutch Republic*, 64; Meindert Schroor and Otto S. Knottnerus, "Verharding en verscherping 1536–1568," in *Geschiedenis van Groningen II. Nieuwe Tijd*, ed. M. G. J. Duijvendak et al. (Zwolle: Waanders, 2008), 73, 92; Otto S. Knottnerus, "Het primaat van Rome aangevochten," in *Geschiedenis van Groningen II. Nieuwe Tijd*, ed. M. G. J. Duijvendak et al. (Zwolle: Waanders, 2008), 55–56.

11 Fruin, *Geschiedenis der Staatsinstellingen*, 98, 248–49.

12 Meindert Schroor, "Een Vlucht Voorwaarts," *Historisch Jaarboek Groningen*, 2003, 39; Schroor, "Heroriëntatie," 153–58.

13 E.H. Waterbolk, "Staatkundige geschiedenis," in *Historie van Groningen: stad en land*, ed. Wiebe Jannes Formsma (Groningen: Tjeenk Willink, 1976), 235.

14 Van der Ent and Enthoven, *Gewestelijke financiën: vol. 3 Groningen*, 14–16.

15 Fruin, *Geschiedenis der Staatsinstellingen*, 324; Israel, *The Dutch Republic*, 1077.

16 Boels and Feenstra, "Regentenheerschappij," 267.

ple and hinterlanders and among hinterlanders; the city had its own urban court. The States of Groningen could also be summoned to the new court. Furthermore, judges were forbidden to hold political functions, and were required to have a legal degree and take an oath upon appointment. Their independence was further increased because the Stadholder could appoint them without nomination.[17]

The intervention of the Reform Statute meant a break in Groningen's history under the Republic. The Generality favoured and supported the city council rather than the Hinterlands, believing this was best for the defence of the Republic. That had two reasons. The first was the protection of the northern flank of the Republic, where the city was the crucial stronghold. The second was to secure income from Groningen to pay for the army and navy. The staple right concentrated trade in the city. This made taxation easier and improved provincial public finances.

2 The Rural Engine of Groningen's Economy

Groningen's economy was primarily rural. The urban economy depended on the countryside rather than being a growth engine in its own right. To benefit from the rural economy, the City exercised political control, doing so in two ways. First, it held jurisdiction over some territories under its direct control: the Gorecht, the Oldambt, the peat colonies and Westerwolde. Groningen leased Westerwolde from the Generality, which made the tax receiver accountable to the Receiver-General of the Union.[18] It exploited these areas,

17 Wiebe Jannes Formsma, "Staatsinstellingen," in *Historie van Groningen: stad en land*, ed. Wiebe Jannes Formsma (Groningen: Tjeenk Willink, 1976), 286–87; Paulus Brood and Engbert Schut, *Hoofdmannenkamer, sinds 1749 Hoge Justitiekamer van Stad en Lande van Groningen: de civiele procesgang ten tijde van de Republiek der Verenigde Nederlanden*, Procesgidsen 4 (Hilversum: Verloren, 2006); J. E. Heeres, "Holland Contra Groningen," *Groningse Volksalmanak : Historisch Jaarboek Voor Groningen*, 1890, 177: Art. 19 read: "Voor dit Hoff zullen ter eerste instantie konnen werden ingesteld alle personele Actien, waar mede de Heeren Staaten van de Stad Groningen en Ommelanden conjunctim vel divisim of ook eenige gantsche Quartieren van de Ommelanden zouden mogen geconvenieert en met regte besproken worden." "(Translation HAF: To this court can brought, in the first instance, all personal questions that concern the Lords States of the City of Groningen and Ommelanden, individually or collectively, or entire Quarters of the Ommelanden as well were allowed to be convened and justice be done.); Schroor, *Rurale metropool*, 5.

18 Van der Ent and Enthoven, *Gewestelijke financiën: vol. 3 Groningen*, 19–21: Since 1619, the city leased it as a fief from the Generality. Meindert Schroor, "Interne staatkundige verhoudingen in Stad en Lande," in *Geschiedenis van Groningen II. Nieuwe Tijd*, ed. M. G. J.

for instance for peat production. Second, the staple right mandated the sale of agricultural produce in the city. But the Hinterlands objected. The States General intervened because the staple right made taxation easier. It confirmed the union of the City and Hinterlands, and the urban staple right, and designated excises to pay for the contribution to Generality.[19] The City therefore got a hold within the agricultural economy because this helped the Generality to secure its income.

The city lived off the countryside.[20] At best, the urban activities provided a service, for instance creating a marketplace.[21] The Hinterlands' representatives (correctly) argued that the staple right hampered economic development.[22] After the abolition of the staple right, after 1795, the city was bypassed for exports of agricultural products.[23] Contemporaries knew that the city depended economically on the countryside, as the Groningen city regent Bernhard Alting concluded in 1648. This included the staple right and a beer brewing monopoly; only the small town of Appingedam was exempted from that monopoly.[24] Only the sale of beer from the city was allowed in the hinter-

---

Duijvendak et al. (Zwolle: Waanders, 2008), 217–18; 't Hart, "Merits," 26; L.S. Meihuizen, "Sociaal-economische geschiedenis van Groningerland," in *Historie van Groningen: stad en land*, ed. Wiebe Jannes Formsma (Groningen: Tjeenk Willink, 1976), 310.

19 Van der Ent and Enthoven, *Gewestelijke financiën: vol. 3 Groningen*, 14–15; Schroor, *Rurale metropool*, 6–7; J. De Bruijn, *Plakkaten van stad en lande: overzicht van Groningse rechtsvoorschriften in de periode 1594–1795*, Historia Agriculturae 14 (Groningen: Nederlands Agronomisch-historisch Instituut, 1983), 7, 45; Meihuizen, "Sociaal-economische geschiedenis," 301; Schroor, "Een Vlucht Voorwaarts," 39.

20 Richard Paping, "Parasiteren op het platteland? De stad Groningen en de Ommelanden in de tweede helft van de achttiende eeuw," in *Stad en regio: opstellen aangeboden aan prof. dr. Pim Kooij bij zijn afscheid als hoogleraar economische en sociale geschiedenis aan de Rijksuniversiteit Groningen*, ed. Geurt A. Collenteur et al., Groninger historische reeks 40 (Assen: Koninklijke Van Gorcum, 2010), 57–70.

21 Schroor, *Rurale metropool*, 200–202; Paping, "Parasiteren"; Schuitema Meijer, "Sociaal-economische aspecten," 355: Upon the request of urban grain traders, the city erected a grain exchange in 1774.

22 Schroor, *Rurale metropool*, 5, 117, 201; Paping, "Parasiteren," 62, 64–65; Paping, *"Voor een handvol stuivers,"* 36; Henk Boels and Hidde Feenstra, "Redres, revolutie en economische groei, 1749–1795," in *Geschiedenis van Groningen II. Nieuwe Tijd*, ed. M. G. J. Duijvendak et al. (Zwolle: Waanders, 2008), 376–78; Schroor and Knottnerus, "Verharding," 79; Schuitema Meijer, "Sociaal-economische aspecten," 355; Schroor, "Een Vlucht Voorwaarts," 41.

23 Paping, "Parasiteren," 62–63; Paping convincingly rejects older visions that judged the staple right more positively. E.g.: Meihuizen, "Sociaal-economische geschiedenis," 302.

24 Schroor, *Rurale metropool*, 5; Paping, "Parasiteren," 63: this small town possessed some urban privileges, yet was represented by the Hinterlands and had no independent access to the States of Groningen.

lands.[25] Consequently, the City had disproportionate control over the rural economy on which it depended.

2.1 *Demographic Developments*

Groningen's population increased from around 57,000 in 1550 to 75,000–80,000 by 1606.[26,27] Growth stagnated in the mid-seventeenth century at around 80,000–90,000 people.[28] The population shrank to 77,000 inhabitants in 1700 and 70,000 in the 1740s.[29] A period of growth followed. By 1795, Groningen's population had increased to 106,400 people (Graph 5.1).[30]

Groningen's demographic development resembled Friesland's rather than that of Holland or Zeeland. As a result, Groningen's population was roughly equal to Zeeland's in the seventeenth century, but was one-third larger by the end of the eighteenth century. Holland's population was eight times as large in 1600 and 1800, but around 1740, Holland's population was more than twelve times as large as Groningen's. This meant a deterioration in the population ratio of 50 per cent.

Groningen's demographic development followed that of the coastal provinces to a lesser degree. It shared in the sixteenth-century expansion and increasing urbanisation.[31] The city's population more than doubled between

25 Schroor and Knottnerus, "Verharding," 79; Schroor, "Een Vlucht Voorwaarts," 41; Schroor, *Rurale metropool*, 5.

26 Meindert Schroor, "Mens en land in de zestiende eeuw," in *Geschiedenis van Groningen II. Nieuwe Tijd*, ed. M. G. J. Duijvendak et al. (Zwolle: Waanders, 2008), 26. This calculation excludes the region Westerwolde, as this later became a Generality land: a territory formally under the authority of the States General and not the province of Groningen.

27 I. B. M. Matthey, "Op fiscaal kompas. Een bijdrage tot de economische geschiedenis van het gewest Groningen in de 17e en 18e eeuw, met toespitsingen op de dorpen in de huidige gemeente Stedum.," in *Westeremden: het verleden van een Gronings terpdorp*, ed. I. B. M. Matthey, Studies / uitg. door de Kring Vrienden van het Rijksarchief in Groningen (Groningen, 1975), 251; Schroor, *Rurale metropool*, 54; Richard Paping, "Groei of stagnatie," *Gronings historisch jaarboek*, 2000, 43;: For a discussion of the estimates, see the appendix. Feenstra, "Between Shared."

28 Boels and Feenstra, "Regentenheerschappij," 278: these authors suggest that it continued until the 1660s, with an estimated population of 85,000 people. .

29 Van der Ent and Enthoven, *Gewestelijke financiën: vol. 3 Groningen*, 161–65, 246. The calcluations are based on the period from 1706 to 1795 as the tax rate was stable and reported without differentiation. Matthey, "Fiscaal kompas," 250–51. Matthey's suggestion is that the number people per hearth was about 3.5 in 1670 and 4.5 in the 1790s. Until 1750, I kept this figure stable at 3.5. Thereafer, it gradually increases to 4.5 in 1795 in my calculations.

30 Matthey, "Fiscaal kompas," 231 This figure also excludes Westerwolde, which was a Generality land.

31 Prak, *The Dutch Republic*, 251; Price, *Dutch Society*, 112, 158.

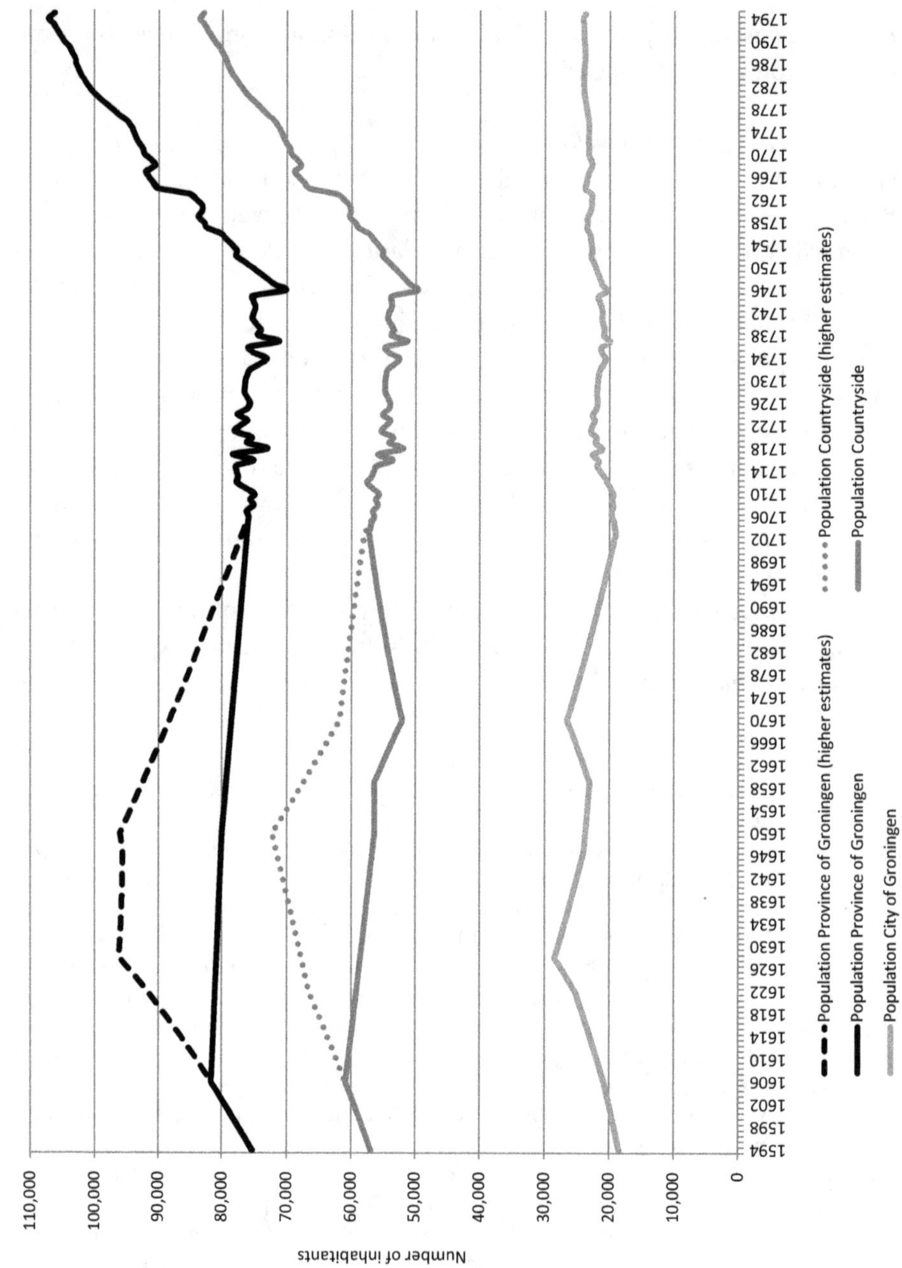

GRAPH 5.1 Population trends in Groningen, 1594–1795.
SOURCES: FEENSTRA, *BETWEEN SHARED*, APPENDIX.

1555 and 1628, to almost 30,000 inhabitants.[32] Until the end of the eighteenth century, the urban population fluctuated between 20,000 and 25,000. In 1795, Groningen numbered 23,770 urban dwellers.[33]

Population growth was concentrated in the countryside. As a result, the degree of urbanisation gradually declined. At its peak around 1630, it was about one-third. It gradually declined to 25 per cent around 1700 and 20 per cent by the end of the eighteenth century. Within the rural areas, growth was concentrated in the areas under urban jurisdiction. The share of the hinterlands declined in the total population. In 1606, more than 60 per cent of the population lived in the hinterlands, 16 per cent in rural areas in the city's jurisdiction, and 23 per cent in the city.[34] By the end of the eighteenth century, the share of the hinterlands had declined to 40 per cent. Still, 22 per cent lived within the city walls and more than one-third lived in the city's rural jurisdictions.[35] This resulted from growth in these districts and the depopulation of the hinterlands.[36] Hence, Groningen's population growth was concentrated in the city's rural jurisdictions.

2.2 *Wages*

Wages in Groningen were lower than in Friesland, Holland and Zeeland. The historiography reports day wages of 0.6 guilders from the 1770s onwards. In the final decade of the eighteenth century, wages started to rise.[37] In the 1680s, hod carriers and other labourers earned 0.6 guilders or 12 *stuivers* per day.[38] Matthey estimated the unskilled day wages at 0.6 guilders between 1741 and 1778.[39]

32 Schroor and Knottnerus, "Verharding," 75. Schroor and Knottnerus, 75.

33 For the estimates of the urban population, this study benefits from Schroor's recent *tour de force* to reconstruct these figures for the seventeenth and eighteenth centuries. Schroor, *Rurale metropool*, 27–82, especially 45–55. Schroor, 27–82, especially 45–55.

34 I. B. M. Matthey, ed., *Westeremden: het verleden van een Gronings terpdorp*, Studies / uitg. door de Kring Vrienden van het Rijksarchief in Groningen (Groningen, 1975), 251.

35 Paping, "Parasiteren," 58–59.

36 Matthey, "Fiscaal kompas," 245–46, 249–51.

37 Paping, *"Voor een handvol stuivers,"* 342–49, especially 345. De Vries's estimate of 0.75 guilders (15 stuivers) is not reached until the 1850s. Day wages during the winter were even lower. Paping relies on multiple observations per year for ninety consecutive years, until 1860; De Vries, "An Inquiry into the Behaviour of Wages in the Dutch Republic and the Southern Netherlands, 1580–1800," 95: The reported wages in *stuivers* of 15 (1635) 14–16 (1690) 14–18 (1750), 16 (1810) must be skilled wages, despite his description of "common outdoor labour".

38 I thank Richard Paping for sharing his unpublished archival notes.

39 Matthey, "Fiscaal kompas," 309–10.

Other wages, annual and skilled, indicate stable wage levels between 1740 and 1770; masons, carpenters and painters earned around 0.8 guilders.[40]

This was less in the early seventeenth century. Wages appear to have risen until the 1630s. The first indication is the payment of a mason and two helpers, in 1615, who worked on the city fortifications. Together, they received 16.1 *stuivers* per day. Per person, this equalled 5.4 *stuivers* or 0.27 guilders, for the work of one skilled and two unskilled workers. In 1619, the wages were higher: workmen earned seven *stuivers* or 0.35 guilders per day.[41]

Ecclesiastical sources for 1630 and 1631 include skilled and unskilled summer daily wages. In 1630, a dog-whipper earned 0.5 guilders (10 *stuivers*) per day. He received this money as a daily wage helping the carpenters. Carpenters and masons consistently earned 0.8 guilders a day in the summer. In winter this was 0.7 or 0.75 guilders for these skilled workers. A stonemason earned 0.9 guilders, both in summer and in winter.[42] In 1631, a gravedigger earned 0.6 guilders (12 *stuivers*) per day. This source also contains some annual wages; including the dog-whipper, who doubled as a guard and bell ringer.[43] This suggests he could supplement his annual wage with smaller jobs around the church.[44] Hence, unskilled wages in Groningen amounted to some 0.5–0.6 guilders from around 1630–1631 until the late eighteenth century. This was the lowest of the four provinces under consideration: some 40 per cent lower than in Holland and Zeeland and 20 per cent less than in neighbouring Friesland.

2.3 *The Centrality of the Rural Economy*

The rural economy was central to Groningen's economy. It expanded during the sixteenth and early seventeenth centuries. While the population doubled between 1555 and 1632, the area of farmland hardly changed.[45] Land rents doubled or tripled in the first half of the seventeenth century.[46] So did con-

---

40 Paping, *"Voor een handvol stuivers,"* 145, 340–42, 345–50.

41 Elwin Alexander Koster, *Stadsmorfologie: een proeve van vormgericht onderzoek ten behoeve van stedenbouwhistorisch onderzoek* (s.n., 2001), 255–56, 330.

42 RHC-Groninger Archieven, 1605 Stadsbestuur van Groningen (2) 1594–1815, inv.no 11265.

43 RHC-Groninger Archieven, 1605 Stadsbestuur van Groningen (2) 1594–1815, inv.no 11303. Other annual salaries: a schoolmaster received 75 guilders a year, an organist 112.5 guilders, a sacristan 56–90 guilders, a tower keeper 250 guilders, and a carillonneur 66–100 guilders. These wages imply low day wages, save for the tower keeper.

44 This article offers a critical systematic assessment of day wages compared to annual wages. This source suggests that day wages and annual wages could be earned by the same persons: Humphries and Weisdorf, "Unreal Wages?"

45 Schroor and Knottnerus, "Verharding," 75. Schroor and Knottnerus, 75.

46 Meihuizen, "Sociaal-economische geschiedenis," 304.

sumer prices and prosperity, until the 1640s.[47] After 1670, a series of flooding, cattle plagues and other disasters hit the rural economy.[48] Tenants suffered from plummeting incomes, while the peculiarities of Groningen's land laws (*Groninger beklemrecht*) hampered the adjustment of land rents.[49] At times, country-dwellers received tax reductions or exemptions. In 1718, peasants rioted in protest against being forced to work on dyke repairs after the Christmas Flood of 1717.[50] Between 1670 and 1750, land leases became increasingly fixed. This happened at a low level due to the stagnating economy.[51]

After 1750, the agricultural sector was the driver of economic growth. The demographic acceleration from the 1740s coincided with rising agricultural prices.[52] Tenants profited from price rises in agricultural products after 1750. Landowners could only benefit by selling the land.[53]

The agricultural production was market-oriented. Farmers relied on mixed farming and shifted their production capacity to what was most profitable.[54] In the sixteenth and seventeenth centuries, around 70 to 80 per cent of the land was used for husbandry. Grain production was insufficient to feed the city, which required grain imports.[55] This changed during the eighteenth century. Grasslands were converted into arable land for grain production. Around 1800, less than half of the countryside consisted of grasslands.[56] The cattle plagues of 1714–1717 and 1744–1749 accelerated the shift towards arable farm-

47 Meihuizen, 305–6.

48 Meihuizen, 313–14; Paping, *"Voor een handvol stuivers,"* 44; Boels and Feenstra, "Regentenheerschappij," 292, 300–302; Wagenaar, *Vaderlandsche historie, 15*, 335–36. For instance, the 1686 Sint-Maartensvloed caused the death of 1,200 eople and 5,000 pieces of cattle.

49 Meihuizen, "Sociaal-economische geschiedenis," 316; Boels and Feenstra, "Regentenheerschappij," 303–4.

50 Meihuizen, "Sociaal-economische geschiedenis," 314–15; Boels and Feenstra, "Regentenheerschappij," 246–47, 303–4.

51 Meihuizen, "Sociaal-economische geschiedenis," 318.

52 Meihuizen, 302.

53 Hidde Feenstra, *De bloeitijd en het verval van de Ommelander adel, (1600–1800)* (s.n.], 1981), 31; Meihuizen, "Sociaal-economische geschiedenis," 318–23; Boels and Feenstra, "Regentenheerschappij," 304; Boels and Feenstra, "Redres," 371–74: Not unlike in Zeeland, the number of "borgen" – the country houses of the nobility – decreased.

54 Schroor and Knottnerus, "De Opstand," 132.

55 Meihuizen, "Sociaal-economische geschiedenis," 302; Boels and Feenstra, "Redres," 348; Schroor and Knottnerus, "Verharding," 76–79; Boels and Feenstra, "Regentenheerschappij," 302.

56 Meihuizen, "Sociaal-economische geschiedenis," 302; Boels and Feenstra, "Redres," 348; Schroor and Knottnerus, "Verharding," 76–79; Boels and Feenstra, "Regentenheerschappij," 302.

ing after 1740.[57] The cattle plague of 1769 had less impact because the livestock population was smaller by then.[58] Groningen farmers also benefitted from rising international grain prices, which had fallen in the century before. They exported grain mainly to Britain. By the end of the century, prices had regained the level of the 1640s.[59] The price fluctuations within each year show a dynamic grain market (Graph 5.2). The long-term trend indicates that there was no structural inflation. The shift illustrates the commercial character of Groningen's agricultural sector.

In addition to the staple right, the city benefitted from the exploitation of territories under its jurisdiction.[60] Peat production was central. In the early seventeenth century, the city invested in peat production with Utrecht investors.[61] Production increased until the 1680s and then declined steadily until 1800.[62] Once the peat had been excavated, the city obliged the peat diggers to turn the subsoil into cultivatable land, for which it supplied urban waste as fertiliser.[63] Peat extraction also stimulated alt, brick and limekiln production,

---

57 Paping, *"Voor een handvol stuivers,"* 44–45; At least 50 per cent of the livestock was killed in this last epidemic: Meihuizen, "Sociaal-economische geschiedenis," 315.

58 Meihuizen, "Sociaal-economische geschiedenis," 320–21; Boels and Feenstra, "Redres," 345–48: Meanwhile the Enlightened farmer Geert Reinders worked together with the city's university professors Petrus Camper and Wouter van Doeveren who experimented with inoculations to reduce the number of cattle deaths.

59 Wigbolt Tijms, *Groninger graanprijzen: de prijzen van agrarische producten tussen 1546 en 1990*, Historia agriculturae, ISSN 0439-2027 31 (Groningen etc.: Nederlands Agronomisch Historisch Instituut, 2000) Table 55.

60 Schuitema Meijer, "Sociaal-economische aspecten," 355: Upon the request of urban grain traders, the city erected a grain exchange in 1774.

61 Schroor, "Een Vlucht Voorwaarts," 42; Schroor, "Heroriëntatie," 187; Gerding, *Vier eeuwen turfwinning*, 51, 71–73 In the 1570s, the local lord and noblemen Wigbold van Ewsum had found investors in Cologne to finance his peat entreprise in his lands in Nienoord, an area to the west of the city.

62 Gerding, *Vier eeuwen turfwinning*, 43–45, 78. In 1615, Johan Sems proposed a straight line through the Bourtange Moor as the border between Groningen and Drenthe: the Semslinie. This was only finally settled as the border in 1817. The production was concentrated in the north-western end of the Bourtanger Moor, a large peat bog. This swamp consisted of two legs: one stretched from the city, along the border with the province of Drenthe, to the border with the Holy Roman Empire in the southeast, the other from the border upwards to the Dollard estuary in the north. At this junction of the bog's legs, the fortress of Bourtange was built. The eastern branch of the swamp formed Groningen's – and thus the Republic's – eastern border area with the Prince-Bishopric of Münster. This part was not cultivated but was kept wet for its military (defensive) function.

63 Schroor, "Een Vlucht Voorwaarts," 47; Schroor, *Rurale metropool*, 220–22; Meihuizen, "Sociaal-economische geschiedenis," 311–12.

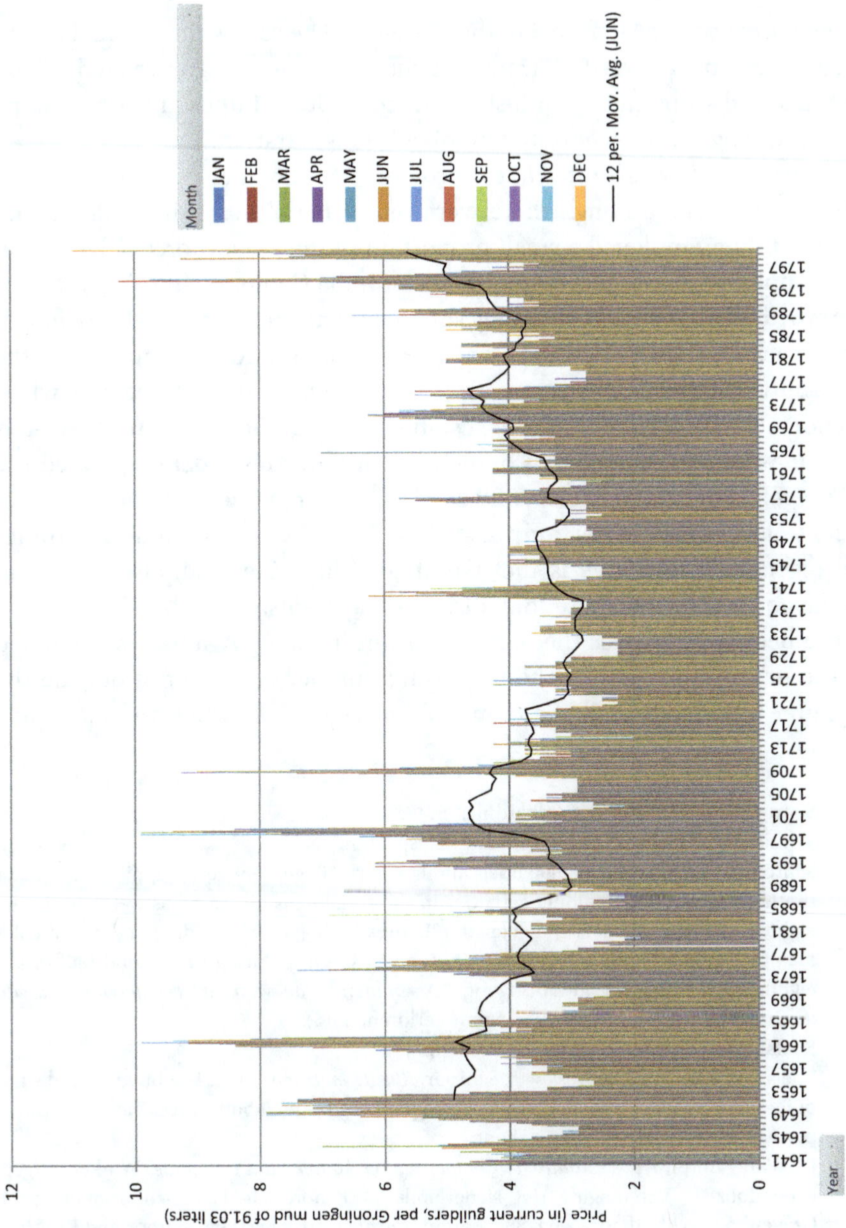

GRAPH 5.2 Monthly rye prices in Groningen, 1641–1800.
SOURCE: TIJMS, *GRONINGER GRAANPRIJZEN*, TABLE 55.

through the use of peat as fuel in these areas.[64] The canals the city had dug to carry off the peat served to transport these products.[65] The related inland shipping and shipbuilding industry formed another important urban activity.[66] Shipping was concentrated in inland transportation.

Overseas trade was limited as the province of Groningen did not possess an actual port town, although there were minor harbours.[67] Shipbuilding and transportation employed a small proportion of the labour force.[68] Nevertheless, Groningen acquired a seat in the West India Company (WIC) in 1621, but this provided little benefit. Seagoing ships could not enter the city harbour and wharf because the access waterway was too shallow and winding.[69] After the bankruptcy of the first WIC in 1674, private merchants rented the wharf intended for the WIC.[70,71] After the establishment of the second WIC, Amsterdam side-lined the Groningen branch. From 1711, Amsterdam equipped the Groningen ships, which also offloaded their cargo there.[72] The only real benefit of the WIC connection was that it offered career options to Groningen regents.[73] Illustrative is that Groningen, like Friesland, also lacked an Exchange Bank to facilitate long-distance payments.

The beer industry was the only significant industry. Again, this depended on the urban monopoly.[74] The increasing number of breweries outside the city after the abolition of the monopoly in 1795 implies that the monopoly

---

64 Schroor and Knottnerus, "Verharding," 81–82.

65 Schuitema Meijer, "Sociaal-economische aspecten," 352.

66 Schroor, *Rurale metropool*, 185; Boels and Feenstra, "Regentenheerschappij," 282–85: For the same reason shipbuilding activities in the rural areas increased as well later in the eighteenth century. Boels and Feenstra, "Redres," 354–55. Shipbuilding in the peat colonies probably became an even activity than in the city during the second half of the eighteenth century. Ingrid Wormgoor, *Turfschuiten en kustvaarders: een geschiedenis van de Groninger scheepsbouw* (Hilversum: Verloren, 2016).

67 Boels and Feenstra, "Regentenheerschappij," 282.

68 Boels and Feenstra, "Redres," 355; Schroor, *Rurale metropool*, 194: The builders and shipbuilders together constituted about 2 to 6 per cent of the labour force, the entire transportation sector less than 7 per cent.

69 P.J. Van Winter, *De Westindische Compagnie ter kamer Stad en Lande*, Werken uitgegeven door de Vereeniging Het Nederlandsch Economisch-Historisch Archief 15 ('s-Gravenhage: Nijhoff, 1978), 63, 88; Schroor, *Rurale metropool*, 185; Schroor and Knottnerus, "De Opstand," 135.

70 Van Winter, *De Westindische Compagnie ter kamer Stad en Lande*, 63.

71 Boels and Feenstra, "Regentenheerschappij," 285–87.

72 Boels and Feenstra, 285–87.

73 Feenstra, *De bloeitijd en het verval van de Ommelander adel, (1600–1800)*, 43–44; Van Winter, *De Westindische Compagnie ter kamer Stad en Lande*.

74 Schroor, *Rurale metropool*, 165.

had stifled the market before.[75] Attempts to start textile industries failed.[76] The stocking knitting industry was the only export-oriented textile activity in the eighteenth century. Yet again, this involved rural knitters.[77] The exploitation of its rural possessions improved the city's finances, which paid for the new fortifications between 1615 and 1630.[78]

Hence, Groningen benefitted less from the sixteenth-century upswing than Holland, Zeeland and Friesland. After the mid-seventeenth century, the economy declined until the 1740s. From 1750, the economy expanded significantly. The rural economy drove these developments, with the urban economy following and living off the backs of the rural businesses. Wages in Groningen lagged even further behind wages in Holland and Zeeland than the Frisian wages. Economic expansion mainly reflected demographic expansion rather than rising incomes.

2.4 *Private Capital Market*

The development of the capital market also appears to have lagged behind. Around 1780, private interest rates were higher than in Amsterdam a century before. They hovered around 4 per cent in 1770–1800, for farmers in the clay soil areas.[79] The decline in rates since the sixteenth century was limited. In the sixteenth century, freeholders lent and borrowed at 6 per cent. Freeholders (*eigenerfde*) formed a rural class of farmers owning land that granted them certain legal and administrative rights in the sixteenth century.[80] From the 1560s the interest rate differential increased. The average interest rate increased as well, to 7 per cent (Graph 5.3).[81] This development was similar to

75 Paping, "Parasiteren," 63.

76 Schuitema Meijer, "Sociaal-economische aspecten," 332–33, 349–51: Soon after the Reduction in 1594, it invited Flemish bombazine workers – and used the low costs of living as an argument to convince them to move to Groningen. This and later attempts all failed. Why Flemish migrants choose to branch out and settle in Holland and not elsewhere remains to be researched, but this is beyond the scope of the present study. In this regard, recent work by Gelderblom offers a potentially promising new direction for making future comparisons: Gelderblom, *Cities of Commerce*; See also: Gelderblom, *Zuid-Nederlandse kooplieden en de opkomst van de Amsterdamse stapelmarkt* (1578–1630).

77 Paping, "Parasiteren," 59; Schroor, *Rurale metropool*, 177.

78 Schroor, "Een Vlucht Voorwaarts"; Schroor, "Heroriëntatie," 189–90.

79 Paping, *"Voor een handvol stuivers,"* 355-360-61.

80 Hidde Feenstra and H. H. Oudman, *Een vergeten plattelandselite: eigenerfden in het Groninger Westerkwartier van de vijftiende tot de zeventiende eeuw*, Fryske Akademy 948 (Ljouwert/Leeuwarden: Fryske Akademy, 2004), 14–15.

81 According to Feenstra and Oudman this followed the Northern German trends: Feenstra and Oudman, 27–28, 52: This is not unexpected, given the orientation of Groningen's, and

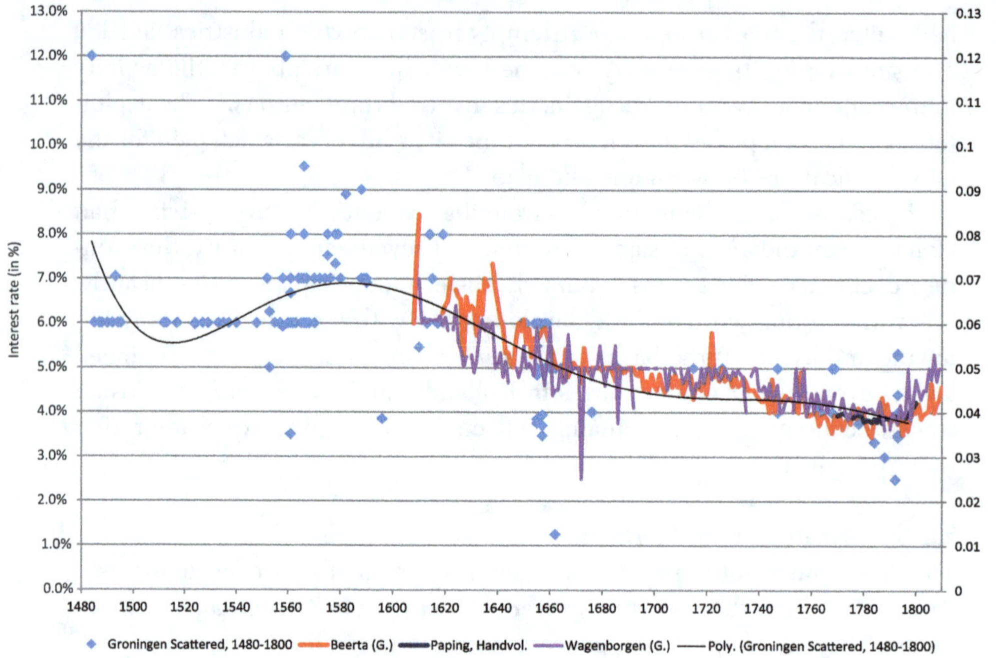

GRAPH 5.3 Private interest rates in Groningen, 1480–1811.
SOURCES: SEE FEENSTRA, *BETWEEN SHARED*, APPENDIX, AND RHC-GRA, GERECHTEN IN HET OLDAMBT, 1596–1811, INV.NO. 7072–7088 (BEERTA) AND 7326–7335 (WAGENBORGEN); PAPING, *"VOOR EEN HANDVOL STUIVERS"*.

Friesland.[82] The last observations of this type, in the 1610s, show interest rates of about 7 per cent.[83] The increase in the late sixteenth and early seventeenth centuries suggests that the Revolt increased risk and uncertainty.

The analysis of interest rates from 1608 onwards relies on transactions in the rural districts (*nedergerecht*) of Beerta and Wagenborgen, in the northeast of the province.[84] These transactions were concluded before the rural elites of the *jonkers* (landed gentry / untitled nobles), who functioned as notaries in

especially the Ommelanden, towards the German lands of Münster and Osnabrück, and much less to Holland, in contrast to Zeeland and Friesland; Knottnerus, "Primaat," 60.

82 Knibbe and Borghaerts, "Capital Market without Banks."

83 Feenstra and Oudman, *Vergeten plattelandselite*, 52, 144, 145, 146, 151, 153, 155, 156, 159, 168, 204, 209, 241, 252, 266, 268, 290, 306, 316, 348, 350, 354, 364, 377, 378, 390, 391, 404, 419, 422, 446, 459, 463, 465, 466, 471, 488, 521, 522, 525, 526, 528.

84 RHC-GrA, Gerechten in het Oldambt, 1596–1811, inv.no. 7072–7088 (Beerta) and 7326–7335 (Wagenborgen). For the creation of the dataset I relied on the transcription of Sebo Abels, (2000), available through his website: http://doopsgezinden.nl/pdf.html and upon request at the University Library of the University of Amsterdam, accessible

Groningen.[85] The transactions from the Beerta and Wagenborgen districts consist of private loans. The presence of collateral did not affect the interest rates. Additional loans from urban inventories and some scattered transactions show a similar development to those in the rural districts. Also, Paping's series based on probate inventories fits the results from the Beerta and Wagenborgen districts. The development is as follows. The going interest rate dropped from 6 per cent to 5 per cent around 1650. From around 1695 the rate further decreased to below the 5 per cent level. In the 1730s and 1740s, rates dropped further to 4 per cent, dipping slightly below that level in the 1760s. Towards the end of the century, the trend was upward.[86]

Interest rates decreased everywhere in the seventeenth and eighteenth centuries, but the decline in Groningen was smallest (Graph 5.4). Rates in Holland declined most. Insofar as the data overlap, the differences were largest with respect to Holland and Zeeland. By the 1680s, private interest rates in Groningen were double those of Amsterdam and Middelburg. Even in the equally remote area of Twente in Overijssel, the interest rate was a percentage point lower than in Groningen in the 1760s. After the 1720s, interest rates in Friesland declined faster and further than in Groningen. The difference increased to a percentage point in the 1750s and 1760s. Capital was thus consistently expensive from an internal Dutch perspective.

The more distant from Amsterdam, the higher the interest rate. Therefore, States' Flanders and Groningen had the highest interest rates. The persistent interest rate differential made capital imports potentially attractive. But this was not a given. In 1768, a Groningen water board advertised a 3.25 per cent

---

via Wilma Goossens, whom I cordially thank for arranging Sebo Abels' transcription and to Richard Paping (RuG) who kindly pointed out the existence of the transcriptions.

85 Richardus F.J. Paping and Paulus Brood, "De protocollen van verzegelingen in de Groningse oud-rechterlijke archieven," in *Broncommentaren 4: Bronnen betreffende de registratie van onroerend goed in Middeleeuwen en Ancien Régime.*, ed. G.A.M. Van Synghel (Den Haag: Instituut voor Nederlandse Geschiedenis, 2001), 61: Only after 1811 official notaryship was established in Groningen. Hidde Feenstra, *Spinnen in het web: Groningse regenten in relatie tot het omringende platteland tijdens de Republiek*, Groninger historische reeks 36 (Assen: Koninklijke Van Gorcum, 2007), 144; These *jonkers* merely functioned as officials to conclude the transactions, not as intermediaries or brokers, as was the case in eighteenth-century Paris: Philip T. Hoffman, Gilles Postel-Vinay, and Jean-Laurent Rosenthal, *Priceless Markets: The Political Economy of Credit in Paris, 1660–1870* (Chicago etc.: The University of Chicago Press, 2000).

86 Paping, *"Voor een handvol stuivers,"* 355, 360–61. The similarity in the trends suggests that the results from Beerta are consistent with other parts of the province and therefore representative.

loan in Holland. However, to examine the conditions, investors had to travel to Groningen.[87] Such practical barriers raised transaction costs in a way that limited or even prevented market integration.

Integration was difficult even at small distances. The correlation between the interest rates in Beerta and Wagenborgen was less than the correlation of each with the rates in Leeuwarden in Friesland. Interest rates in Beerta and Wagenborgen had a correlation coefficient of 0.74 per cent, Beerta and Leeuwarden of 0.89 per cent, and Wagenborgen and Leeuwarden of 0.78 per cent. This was counterintuitive because the Groningen districts were geographically closer to each other than to Leeuwarden and were within the same province, while Leeuwarden was in Friesland. This suggests that correlation patterns reflect coincidence rather than market integration. Capital markets remained primarily local, even in two districts so near to each other and within one province.

Insofar as Groningen elites possessed public debt, they primarily held provincial and urban Groningen debt. This formed 15 to 20 per cent of their portfolios. Other Dutch public debt securities were held in smaller amounts or were absent. Moreover, the other forms of Dutch debt were classified as 'foreign', like loans to the East Frisian town of Emden, English securities or French 'Billets de Canada'.[88] The opposite was also true. About 90 per cent of Groningen's urban debt was in the hands of its inhabitants. That was a relatively new phenomenon because in the sixteenth century Westphalian creditors owned that debt.[89] However, the shift to domestically-held debt depended on forced measures.

---

87 "Advertentie". "*Haerlemse courante*". Haerlem, 22-11-1768. Accessed at Delpher 15-09-2016, http://resolver.kb.nl/resolve?urn=ddd:010799795:mpeg21:a0008: "In het aanstaende Voorjaar in de Maanden Maart, April, Mai en Juny, eene Somme van plusminus 100000 Guldens, tot het leggen van eenen Nieuwen Dyk, achter Oost- en Finsterwolden den Oldambte, benoodigt zullende zyn, zo adverteeren de Gevolmagtigden tot gemelde indykinge by deezen, dat iemand genegen zynde, daartoe, by capitaalen van 1000 of 1500 Guldens naar 3 en een vierde ten hondert op te schieten, zig van nu tot den eersten January naast komende, kan vervoegen by den Boekverkooper J. Bolt te Groningen, by wien de Conditien te zien zyn."

88 RHC-GrA, Fam. Wolthers, inv.no. 20 and 124; Familie Van Swinderen en De Marees van Swinderen, 1370–1982, inv.no. 120 and 708.

89 Schoor noticed this strong regional focus in the distribution of Groningen urban debt; in 1620–1623, about 10 per cent of the debt was held outside the provinces of Groningen and Drenthe: Schroor, *Rurale metropool*, 232, 269–71; the debt that was held by creditors living outside these areas was called "*buitenrenten*" (external annuities). All debt held within Groningen and Drenthe was described as "*binnenrenten*" (internal annuities). Zuijderduijn, "Foreign Investment," 6, 10: Zuijderduijn also sees the German lands as a

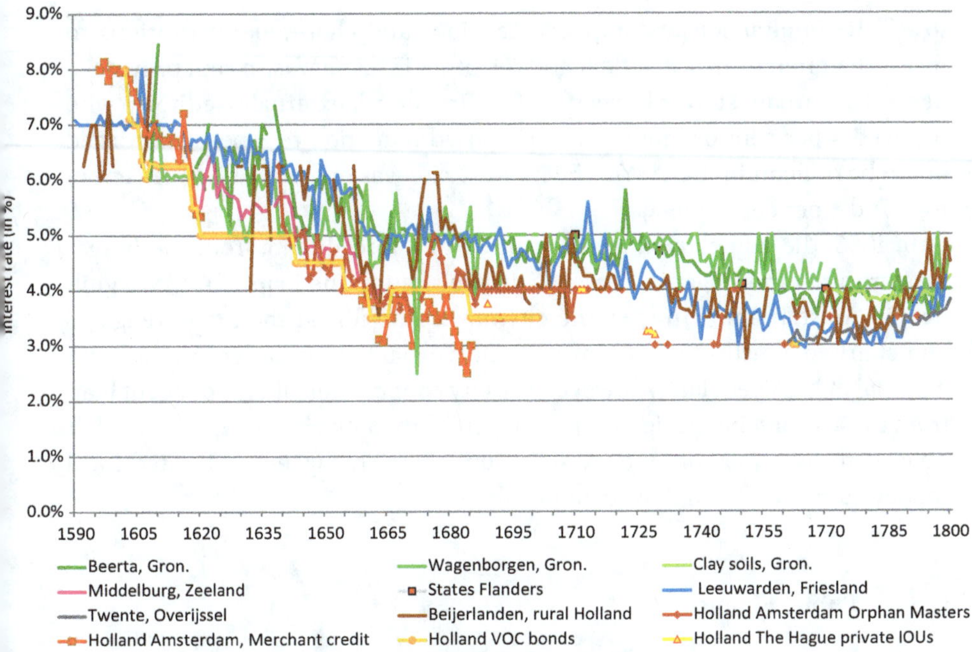

GRAPH 5.4 Private interest rates in the Dutch Republic, 1590–1800.
SOURCES: SEE TEXT, FEENSTRA, *BETWEEN SHARED*, APPENDIX, AND GELDERBLOM, KOOL AND JONKER, FOR HOLLAND ORPHAN MASTERS, MERCHANT CREDIT AND VOC BONDS (PART).

Forced loans, forced interest rate reductions and imports allowed the city of Groningen to borrow at or below market rates. In 1618, the magistrate supplemented a voluntary 7 per cent loan with a 4 per cent forced loan from the leasers of urban lands (*stadsmeiers*).[90] In 1626, the city magistrate reduced the interest rate from 7 per cent to 6 per cent, and again to 5 per cent in

source of capital for urban debts for cities at the eastern border of what would later become the Dutch Republic. He analysed Nijmegen's debt in the years 1535–1536 and 1548. Interest was also paid out in the cities of Cologne, Kampen and Hamburg. Tracy, *A Financial Revolution in the Habsburg Netherlands*, 28–29, 115, 117, 223–51: Also, Holland issued part of its public debt in the sixteenth century in Flanders, Zeeland, Utrecht and Brabant. Zuijderduijn, *Medieval Capital Markets*, 157, 178–81.

90 Schroor, "Een Vlucht Voorwaarts," 46, 51 The loan size was 31,675 guilders. Schroor, *Rurale metropool*, 214–15 This loan had an intended size of 24,000 guilders. P. J. van Herwerden, "Geschiedenis van het Sint Geertruids- of Pepergasthuis te Groningen," *Economisch-historisch jaarboek: bijdragen tot de economische geschiedenis van Nederland* 28, no. 1960 (1960 1958): 159, 166–67.

1634.[91] It simultaneously compelled religious and charitable institutions to invest their money in urban debt and sell other investments, except provincial debt. The urban steward meanwhile reimbursed external creditors, who received 5 per cent or more.[92] The proposed reduction to 4 per cent turned out to be difficult in 1652.[93] Yet the interest rate was reduced to 4.5 per cent in 1658 and 4 per cent in 1659.

In 1666, the city council again resorted to a forced loan, from the burgomasters and other regents.[94] In 1672, it issued a tontine loan of 100,000 guilders in Amsterdam.[95] In 1722, the city magistrate forced the urban religious and charitable institutions to invest in provincial debt in order to reimburse external debt. A year later, however, the city council took out a 4 per cent loan from these urban institutions.[96] Groningen's urban magistrate apparently felt obliged to use coercion and external funds, which suggests a limited local money supply and a shallow capital market.

3 Public Finance

After the conquest of the city of Groningen and the Treaty of Reduction in 1594, Groningen had to contribute to the common war efforts. In a rare display of unity, the City and Hinterlands objected to all proposals, arguing that the province was too poor. Pending the outcome of the negotiations, the States of Groningen paid not a penny. After five years of negotiations, the States General and Groningen agreed on a 7 per cent share in the contribution. At that point, only Holland, Zeeland, Utrecht and Friesland contributed to the Generality's budget, for the other provinces were still suffering from Spanish occupation or warfare.[97] Eventually, Groningen's share was fixed at one-tenth of Holland's, or 5.8 per cent of the total, in 1616.[98]

Agreeing on the share in the common budget was one thing, setting taxes to raise the money was another. The City and the Hinterlands could not agree. The City feared overburdening if the common means were introduced, as

91 Schroor, *Rurale metropool*, 271.
92 Schroor, 222.
93 Schroor, 224.
94 Schroor, 225, 271–72.
95 Schroor, 268: This suggests the changed orientation from the German lands in the east to Holland in the west. Wagenvoort, *Tontines*, 12.
96 Schroor, *Rurale metropool*, 229–30.
97 Van der Ent and Enthoven, *Gewestelijke financiën: vol. 3 Groningen*, 17–18.
98 't Hart, "Merits," 15–16.

intended in the Treaty of Reduction. Strapped for cash, the States General decreed the levy of the common means in 1597. In response, the city magistrate imprisoned some tax farmers who had obeyed the States General's order.[99]

This provoked a strong response from the States General. In 1600, it sent an embassy and troops, but to no avail. In response, the States General erected a coercive castle (*dwangburcht*), next to a city gate to force Groningen to pay. This new castle must have brought back memories of the Duke of Alva's castle a few decades earlier.[100] In addition, the States General took three members of the Groningen city magistrate hostage in The Hague.[101] Having raised tax rates and obtained promises of better behaviour, the States General withdrew its troops and allowed the City to dismantle the stronghold in 1607.[102]

But this was not enough. The resumption of warfare in 1621 necessitated more funds. The Generality imposed another tax reform, between 1622 and 1628, which doubled Groningen's tax revenue to 1 million guilders.[103] Groningen delegates now argued that the Generality-imposed fiscal reforms increased the tax burden disproportionally with respect to the other provinces. Therefore, they advocated tax increases elsewhere as well, especially in Friesland.[104]

What effect did these superimposed tax increases have in Groningen? Did they overburden Groningen, as it claimed? Or did these reforms merely raise Groningen's tax levels to those in Holland and Zeeland? And did this lead to a tax revolution, similar to that in Holland, Zeeland and eventually Friesland?

---

99 Van der Ent and Enthoven, *Gewestelijke financiën: vol. 3 Groningen*, 14–15; L. Van der Ent et al., "Public Finance in the United Provinces of the Netherlands in the Seventeenth and Eighteenth Centuries," in *Crises Revolutions and Self-Sustained Growth: Essays in European Fiscal History, 1130–1830*, ed. William Mark Ormrod, Margaret Bonney, and Richard Bonney (Stamford: Shaun Tyas, 1999), 252; Fritschy, "Financial Revolution," 63; Schroor, "Heroriëntatie," 159–60; Waterbolk, "Staatkundige geschiedenis," 237.

100 Schroor, "Heroriëntatie," 159–60; Schroor and Knottnerus, "Verharding," 96–100; Schroor and Knottnerus, "De Opstand," 109, 118: Alva's fortress was dismantled in 1577, after the Pacification of Ghent in 1576. Van der Ent and Enthoven, *Gewestelijke financiën: vol. 3 Groningen*, 14–18; Schroor, "Een Vlucht Voorwaarts," 40; Fritschy, *Public Finance*, 119.

101 Schroor, "Heroriëntatie," 159–60; Only one of them, Joachim Alting, returned to power in 1608. The others were excluded from any offices for the rest of their lives. Schroor, "Een Vlucht Voorwaarts," 39; Van der Ent and Enthoven, *Gewestelijke financiën: vol. 3 Groningen*, 15.

102 Van der Ent and Enthoven, *Gewestelijke financiën: vol. 3 Groningen*, 18; Schroor, "Een Vlucht Voorwaarts," 40.

103 't Hart, *The Making of a Bourgeois State*, 170.

104 Deursen, "De plaats van de noordelijke gewesten," 20.

These questions concern Groningen's allotted share in the common expenses, but also whether this resulted in a disproportionate tax burden following the Generality's intervention. After all, the provinces did not always pay what they were obliged to. For example, around 1650, the Generality threatened to billet troops or force the sale of the domains if Groningen failed to pay its arrears.[105] Moreover, Holland threatened to withhold its contribution and to increase Groningen's to 8 per cent structurally.[106] This threat echos the accusation of free riding on Holland's account. To assess whether Groningen paid its fair share, this section analyses how Groningen footed the bill and how this determined the constraints for debt management policies. It pays special attention to the tax burden in Holland and Groningen to assess the relative commitment to the Generality's expenses.

3.1 *Government Budget Balances*

The attempts to increase tax revenues are understandable because Groningen had difficulties balancing income and expenditure from an early stage. It suffered from deficits during the Twelve Years' Truce and after the resumption of warfare in 1621. Only in the mid-1630s did income match expenditure. This was the result of Generality-imposed fiscal reforms. New deficits arose after the end of the Eighty Years' War, in 1648. This is puzzling considering that war expenses decreased. After some fluctuations, the two wars with Münster (1665–1667, 1672–1674) caused substantial deficits. This was the first time that the fiscal and primary balances diverged notably. Groningen's public finances recovered, with apparent ease in view of the surpluses in the 1680s. Then the Nine Years' War temporarily turned the fiscal surpluses into deficits. Between this war and the War of the Spanish Succession, Groningen again created a fiscal surplus. The latter war, however, caused unprecedented deficits. As a result, Groningen had to spend much more on interest payments than before. Income was high enough that the War of the Austrian Succession did not lead to primary deficits and the Fourth Anglo-Dutch War only resulted in small primary deficits. Hence, except for three major wars, after 1650 Groningen was well able to cover its current expenses from its income (Graph 5.5).

For most of the eighteenth century, Groningen also enjoyed fiscal surpluses.[107] It used this to reduce the debt burden. This is evident from the

105 Waterbolk, "Staatkundige geschiedenis," 244–45; About Friesland, see the previous chapter.

106 Waterbolk, 244–45.

107 The interest estimations are based on my debt reconstruction, the available coupons and incidental reports of interest paid. Groningen's fiscal balance is an approximation, rather

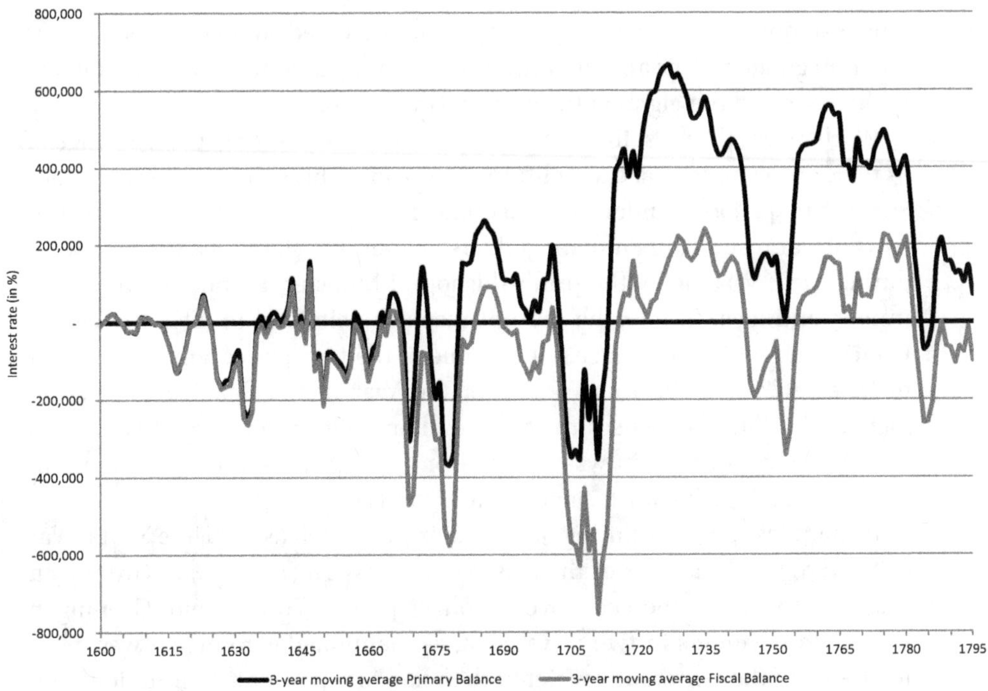

GRAPH 5.5 Groningen's government budget balances, 1600–1795.
SOURCES: VAN DER ENT AND ENTHOVEN, *GEWESTELIJKE FINANCIËN, VOL. 3 GRONINGEN*; AND APPENDIX TO THIS BOOK

decreasing difference between the fiscal and primary balances.[108] In other words, Groningen balanced income and expenses in the long run.

3.2 *Expenses*

Groningen's expenses grew from around 0.5 million guilders in the early seventeenth century to over 1.5 million guilders by the end of the eighteenth century. It peaked at almost 2.5 million guilders during the War of the Spanish Succession. However, the most significant growth came as early as the 1620s.

---

than a precise account. Provincial accounts grouped reimbursements and interest payments into one expense item. The distinction was only made for individual transactions. Solving this problem by working from archival materials on individual transactions would require us to enter every payment made to each creditor, since even totals per loan or year are often lacking.

108 Own calculations based upon: Van der Ent and Enthoven, *Gewestelijke financiën: vol. 3 Groningen*, 91–95, 128, 110–19, 189–93, 359–62.

The resumption of the Eighty Years' War increased annual costs to over 1 million guilders. This amount only gradually increased to 1.5 million guilders in the course of the eighteenth century (Graph 5.6).

Warfare was the most important expense item, accounting for an average of 55 to 60 per cent of total expenditure. In wartime, this expenditure was about 800,000 to 900,000 guilders. In peacetime, it was about half that amount. The costs of war rose above 1 million guilders on four occasions. The first two were during the invasions by the prince-bishop of Münster, Bernhard von Galen, in 1665 and 1672. In 1665, he did not reach the city and in 1672, the city of Groningen repulsed the siege – it was one of the few rays of hope in the Year of Disaster.[109] On the third occasion, the War of the Spanish Succession increased military expenses to over 1 million guilders for several years in a row. The fourth occasion was when Groningen surpassed this threshold in one year during the Fourth Anglo-Dutch War (1780–1784).

It spent less per year during other major wars, such as the Nine Years' War (1688–1697) and the War of the Austrian Succession (1740–1748). Groningen was able to spread the costs over a longer period. To that end, Groningen smoothed payments in two ways. First, as mentioned, Groningen was often in arrears to the Generality, which it then had to repay after negotiations and embassies. Second, it took considerable time for Groningen to pay the military solicitors the money advanced for troop payments. These were deferred war expenditures. For instance, it took twenty to twenty-five years to pay them after the Wars of the Spanish and Austrian Succession.[110] Moreover, the amounts involved were considerable. In 1752, deferred troop payments totalled 300,000 guilders. This provided a financial breathing space and made the financial impact of the wars less acute. Postponing and spreading the payments also increased peacetime war-related expenditure, most notably after 1750.

Interest payments became the second most important expense item between the 1670s and 1770s. The two wars with Münster increased Groningen's debt, which had been small until then. The debt service expanded accordingly to over 20 per cent of total costs. Debt and interest payments continued to grow until 1725. Groningen was far behind in all kinds of Generality expenditure, including interest. The Generality had issued loans for Gronin-

109 Boels and Feenstra, "Regentenheerschappij," 256–57; A.T. Schuitema Meijer, "De Stad Groningen tijdens het beleg," in *Groningen constant: Groningen-Munster 1672*, ed. Abraham Westers (Groningen: Wolters-Noordhoff, 1972), 80; Münster troops retreated in late August 1672.

110 RHC-GrA. SvSL, inv.no. 515: *f* 1,064,315-3-8; NA, Staten-Generaal, inv.no. 8952.

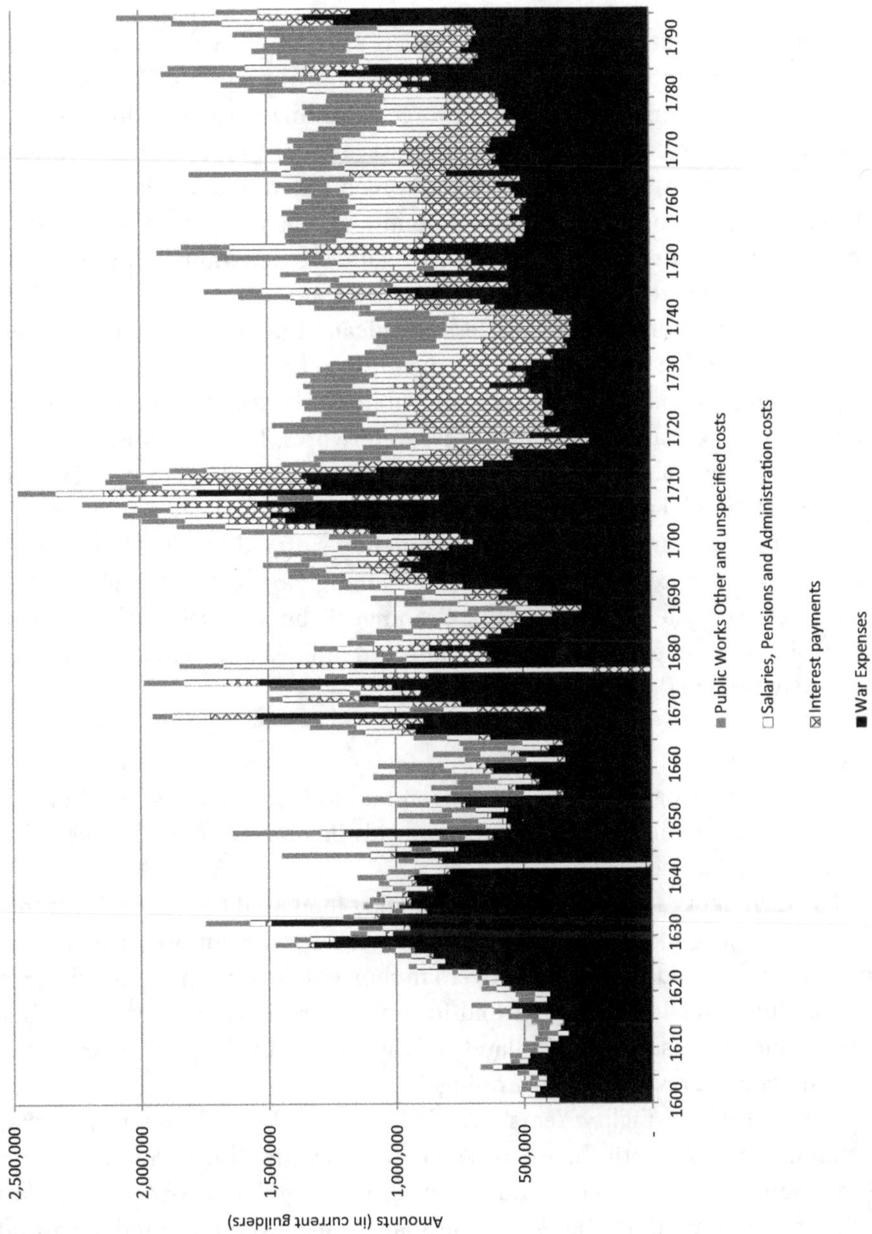

GRAPH 5.6 Groningen's expenditure, 1600–1795.
SOURCE: VAN DER ENT AND ENTHOVEN, *GEWESTELIJKE FINANCIËN, VOL. 3 GRONINGEN*, PP. 294–374.

gen, under its guarantee. But Groningen failed to pay both the military expenses that the Generality had advanced and the interest. Therefore the Generality intervened once again. It forced Groningen to pay a lump sum of 390,000 guilders per year to cover interest and debt repayments.[111] Interest payments decreased as a result of the forced redemptions. The War of the Austrian Succession pushed these amounts up again but to a lesser extent than the War of the Spanish Succession. Again, the Generality imposed forced repayments, lowering interest payments after 1754.

Other expenditure items were less significant. Public administration amounted to around 13 per cent of total expenditure. This increased when tax collection replaced tax farming after 1749. Public works accounted for 8 per cent, mainly for dyke maintenance and other waterworks. The budget was raised in response to several floods, most notably the Christmas Flood of 1717. The purpose was to model water defences on Friesland, where dyke maintenance was better organised and which had consequently suffered less.[112] Finally, many smaller expense items consumed the remaining 7 per cent of the budget. In conclusion, only a small portion of Groningen's budget was under its direct control. The main expense items, warfare and interest payments, were subject to the Generality's authority.

3.3 *Income*

To cover the rising expenses, Groningen had to increase revenues. Immediately after the conquest of 1594, Groningen's income amounted to less than 300,000 guilders per year.

The Generality's intervention in 1600–1607 increased Groningen's revenue to 0.5 million guilders per year. The next fiscal intervention, in 1622–1628, more than doubled its income to over 1 million guilders, mainly through direct taxes. Thus taxes increased fourfold in thirty years. This was not as much as the tenfold increase seen in Holland and Zeeland, but still spectacular enough to suspect a tax revolution in Groningen.

The end of the Eighty Years' War led to an easing in taxes to less than a million guilders, until the 1660s. The two wars with Münster required more funds, and taxes increased to more than a million guilders. After a temporary relaxation around 1690, the War of the Spanish Succession resulted in new tax increases, with taxes reached the level of 1.5 million guilders. Tax revenue fluctuated in the period up to 1750, and then stabilised around the level of 1.5 million guilders (Graph 5.7).

111 RHC-GrA, SvSL (1), inv.no. 515.

112 Boels and Feenstra, "Regentenheerschappij," 247.

The indirect taxes from the common means formed a stable basis for income. Tax revenue was increased mainly through increases in direct taxes. The tax reform of the 1620s doubled the income from the common means to 600,000 guilders, a level that was sustained until the 1680s. As a result, the common means yielded 60 per cent of the total revenue in this period. Disastrous floods in the 1680s decreased receipts by a quarter by 1690.[113] As a result, the relative contribution of the common means to Groningen's revenue declined from around 60 per cent in the 1680s to 35–40 per cent. Income from the excises did not recover until after 1750.

After 1750, income from the general means increased, in both absolute and relative terms, accounting for 40–45 per cent of total tax income. There are two reasons for the increase. Firstly, tax collection replaced tax farming after the tax riots and the Orangist revolution of 1747.[114] This effect was limited: gross receipts increased, but so did collection costs. The net increase in revenue amounted to 16,000 guilders.[115] Secondly and more importantly, economic growth led to a more structural increase in the general means after 1750. Until then, revenue increases had to be found through direct taxes.

Direct taxes were adjusted according to the fiscal needs. The Generality's intervention in 1622–1628 tripled these revenues – income other than the general means – from 200,000 guilders to 550,000 guilders. The Peace of Münster in 1648 reduced the requirement for taxation, and several direct taxes were either abolished or relaxed. This was done to such an extent that it resulted in deficits. To pay for the wars with Münster in 1665–1667 and 1672–1674, tariffs were raised and previously abolished taxes reintroduced.[116] From the 1690s, direct taxes consistently yielded most of the revenue, accounting for about 60 per cent of fiscal income in the eighteenth century.

Real estate taxes became the most important direct taxes. Groningen increased real estate taxes in the 1690s in response to the declining income

113 Meihuizen, "Sociaal-economische geschiedenis," 313; Wagenaar, *Vaderlandsche historie, 15*, 335–36: Wagenaar reports a large number of victims of the Sint-Maarten flooding of 1686: 1,200 people and 5,000 heads of cattle in Groningen. Boels and Feenstra, "Regentenheerschappij," 292.

114 Van der Ent and Enthoven, *Gewestelijke financiën: vol. 3 Groningen*, 41–43.

115 Van der Ent and Enthoven, 328–32. Calculated as follows: to distinguish to what extent the increasing revenues stemmed from economic growth or more efficient tax collection, I compared the income just before and after the turbulent years 1747–1748. The gross receipts increased by 48,000 guilders; from 595,000 guilders in 1744–1746 to 643,000 guilders in 1750–1759. Collection costs increased by 32,000 guilders. The replacement of the tax farmers resulted in a net revenue increase of 16,000 guilders.

116 Van der Ent and Enthoven, 110–19, 250–51.

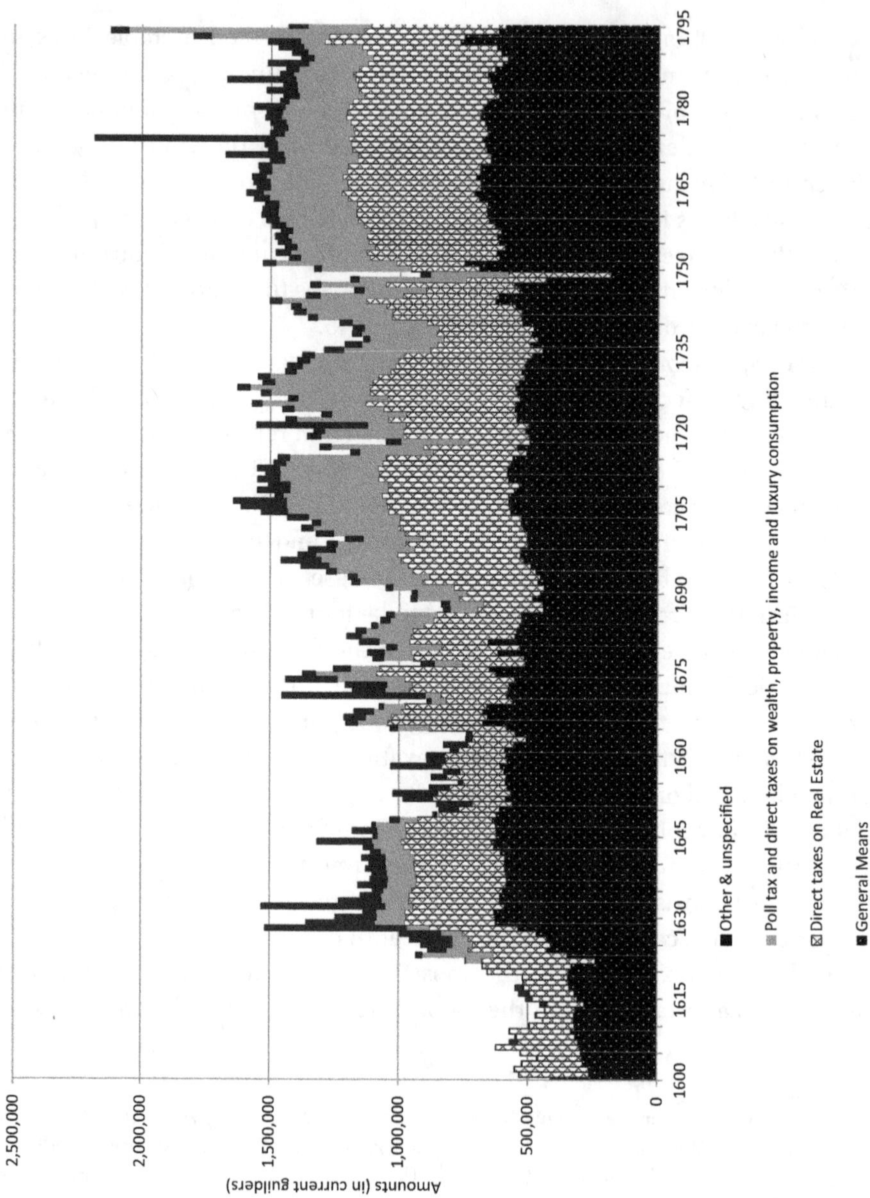

GRAPH 5.7 Groningen's public revenue, 1600–1795.
SOURCE: VAN DER ENT AND ENTHOVEN, *GEWESTELIJKE FINANCIËN, VOL. 3 GRONINGEN*, PP. 102–292.

from excises. These taxes yielded almost 500,000 guilders, or one-third of the fiscal revenue. They consisted of a land tax and a hearth tax on houses.[117] Until 1680, more than 80 per cent of the revenue from real estate taxes came from the land tax. After the floods of the 1680s, the hearth taxes increased in importance, accounting for almost a quarter of the revenue in this category until 1795.[118] Strangely enough, the increase followed the abolition of the progressive tax rate for each additional hearth.[119] This suggests either stricter control in the eighteenth century or tax evasion before the 1690s. It is nevertheless clear that the hinterlands paid the lion's share of the real estate tax.

Groningen also taxed other kinds of wealth and luxury. The poll tax formed the direct tax. The revenues were highest during the Wars of the Spanish and Austrian Succession.[120] This underlines the use of the direct taxes as an emergency measure. Moreover, the tax base was determined by self-assessment. In 1751, wealthy taxpayers resisted declaring the correct value under oath. The taxation of securities, jewellery and cash in particular proved arduous and susceptible to tax evasion.[121] In the early eighteenth century, Groningen began taxing luxury consumption, such as coffee, tea, chocolate and sugar wares. Although intended as temporary taxes when introduced in 1718, they were maintained throughout the eighteenth century.[122] The increasing importance of direct taxes demonstrates that the economy could no longer keep pace with the province's expenses, and it therefore felt it needed to target the richer inhabitants.

These increases were insufficient: Groningen failed to meet its obligations to the Generality. The arrears increased on the loans that the Generality had issued for Groningen. The result was a new fiscal intervention by the States General in 1726. The new temporary luxury taxes expired in 1725. The City and Hinterlands could not agree on alternatives. A States General embassy advised the sale of provincial domains, mostly former monastery lands bequeathed

117 Van der Ent and Enthoven, 235–43.
118 Van der Ent and Enthoven, 161–65, 246.
119 Van der Ent and Enthoven, 244.
120 Van der Ent and Enthoven, 173–175, 258–263: For instance, in 1693, Groningen levied the tax three times, equaling a 0.75 per cent tax rate: which increased the tax revenue from 98,000 guilders in 1692 to 146,000 guilders in 1693. For the rest of the period, we do not possess the tax incidence and therefore we do not know the effective tax rate.
121 Van der Ent and Enthoven, 262.
122 Van der Ent and Enthoven, 177–78, 265–70.

during the Revolt.[123] The States of Groningen refused and found alternative means. In addition to new taxes and increased tax rates, it reduced the interest on the provincial debt and agreed on the general means for twenty-five years.[124] The fiscal reform bore fruit, which the States of Groningen spelt out half a century later when discussing Zeeland's financial difficulties. It emphasised how great the effort had been, how much it had been praised and how well Groningen had managed to reduce the Generality debt.[125]

The Generality's proposal to sell the former ecclesiastical lands was the second such proposal within a few years: in 1720, an internal provincial committee had already recommended selling the lands, considering the income from rents to be too low.[126] The States of Groningen ignored the recommendations of both the 1720 and 1726 committees. The Reform Statute (*Reglement Reformatoir*) of 1749 repeated the advice. This time, the States of Groningen accepted.[127] It took until 1764 before Groningen actually started selling the domains. Low, fixed land rents prevented landowners from benefiting from the price increases and economic growth after 1750, and therefore sale of the domains was the only way of benefitting from the rising land prices. Sales yielded almost 3.5 million guilders between 1764 and 1774. This was enough to redeem the debts of the domain's steward and reduce the Generality's

123 Van der Ent and Enthoven, 28–29, 271–272 375–381; Meihuizen, "Sociaal-economische geschiedenis," 302–3: About a quarter of the province had been in the hands of ecclesiastical instititutions at the time of the Reduction in 1594.

124 Van der Ent and Enthoven, *Gewestelijke financiën: vol. 3 Groningen*, 271–72.

125 NA, Provinciale resoluties, inv.no. 309, "Advis van Stad en Lande", 23 December 1767. "Dat zulks alles egter nog niet voldoende zynde, hebben H: Ho: Mog: in den Jare 1726 Gecomitteerden herwaarts gezonden, welke den staat dezer Provincie in loco naauwkeurig hebben geëxamineerd, en betuigd, dat van die efforts de ongemeene cordaatheid niet genoeg kon worden geprezen, en waar van het gevolg is geweest, dat in alle des tyds bepaalde Middelen voor den tyd van 25 Jaren is geconsenteerd, en vele daar van geässigneerd voor de betaling der schulden aan de Generaliteit verpligt, onder zulk een sterk verband der Regering, waar van geen exempel zal kunnen worden gevonden."

126 E.H. Roelfsema, *De klooster- en proosdijgoederen in de provincie Groningen* (Groningen etc.: Wolters, 1928), 93–94.

127 Meihuizen, "Sociaal-economische geschiedenis," 302; Boels and Feenstra, "Redres," 363–69; Van der Ent and Enthoven, *Gewestelijke financiën: vol. 3 Groningen*, 28–30, 287–88, 375–81: The refusal to sell the former ecclesiastical land in the 1720s might have been informed by the land rents it yielded to the province. Income from the former ecclesiastical land was to a large extent earmarked and administered by a special provincial steward (*rentmeester*). He paid part of the salaries of the poorer Protestant ministers and schoolmasters, supported deaconries and contributed to the university. Roelfsema, *Klooster- en proosdijgoederen*, 95–96.

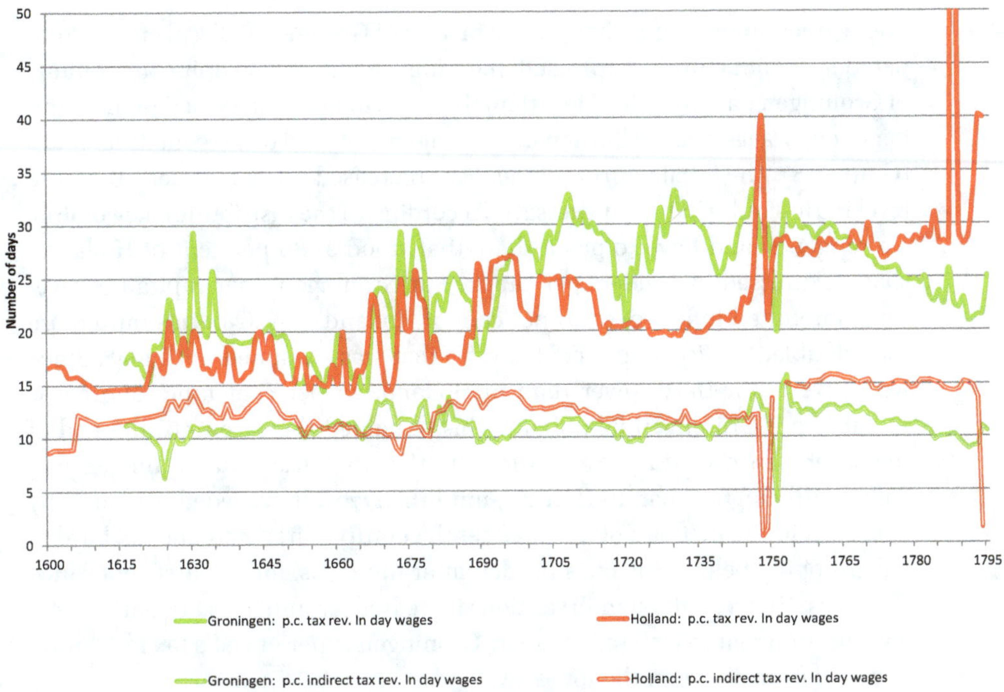

GRAPH 5.8 Tax burden in Holland and Groningen, 1600–1795.
SOURCES: SEE TEXT AND FEENSTRA, *BETWEEN SHARED*, APPENDIX.

debts.[128] Hence, thanks to the States' initial refusal to sell, the province enjoyed a more lucrative deal half a century later because the prices had risen.

3.3.1 Tax Burden

The next question is what effects the interventions had on the tax burden. Groningen liked to emphasise the appreciation of its fiscal efforts after 1726. Around 1616, Groningen argued that its share in the common expenses was too high because it was poorer than the other provinces. This argument makes sense, considering that wages were lowest in Groningen. The question is whether this justified the lower contribution per capita, as analysed in Chapter One. People in Groningen paid 20 per cent less per capita than the inhabitants of Holland and Friesland and 40 per cent less than the Zeelanders in 1616. The analysis of the tax burden given here relates the per capita taxes to local wage levels in Holland and Groningen, expressing per capita taxes in the equivalent number of unskilled male summer day wages.

128 Van der Ent and Enthoven, *Gewestelijke financiën: vol. 3 Groningen*, 287–88, 375–81; Roelfsema, *Klooster- en proosdijgoederen*, 96–102.

The correction for wages changes the picture of Groningen's fiscal efforts compared to nominal taxes. Expressed in nominal guilders per capita, inhabitants of Groningen paid one-third less than those in Holland. Expressed in the number of day wages, the tax burden in Groningen matched or exceeded Holland's (Graph 5.8). The fiscal reforms of the 1620s increased the tax burden above the level in Holland. That was necessary. According to the distribution key of 1616, Groningen would have to pay a share that stood at 80 per cent of Holland's share, expressed in guilders per capita. But Groningen's per capita tax revenues amounted to just over 40 per cent of Holland's. In 1630, this ratio more than doubled, to 80–90 per cent, a ratio that was sustained until 1648. Since wages were one-third lower than in Holland, 20 per cent more effort was required per Groningen inhabitant. This remained the case until the end of the seventeenth century. From then on, the tax burden in Groningen was consistently higher than in Holland, until the 1770s. It exceeded Holland's by one-third in the first half of the eighteenth century. After 1750, the tax burden fell, dropping below Holland's burden after the 1770s, for the first time since the 1620s. Hence, federal interventions increased Groningen's tax burden to a level beyond that in Holland. As such, Groningen experienced a tax revolution imposed from above in the 1620s.

Groningen's higher tax burden resulted from the direct taxes. Income from the common means yielded similar amounts per capita when corrected for wage differentials. In both provinces, the tax burden on the common people hovered around eleven to twelve day wages until 1750. Acceptance of tax increases reached a social ceiling in the early eighteenth century. Social unrest flared up in 1709, before the rinderpest epidemic of 1714–1715 and the Christmas Flood of 1717, and again in 1740.[129] In 1749 there were tax riots.[130] After 1750, the tax burden from the common means in Groningen and Holland diverged, declining to less than ten day wages in Groningen at the end of the century and hovering around fifteen day wages in Holland. The lower share of indirect taxes in the total tax burden in Groningen implies direct taxes were more important in raising tax revenue. In other words, Groningen demanded much more from wealth-owners than Holland did. Groningen was definitely not free riding on Holland's account.

The Generality exercised substantial control over Groningen's public finances under the Treaty of Reduction. From the outset, it enforced tax increases. As a result, the tax burden in Groningen was similar to or higher than in

129 Meihuizen, "Sociaal-economische geschiedenis," 314.

130 Van der Ent and Enthoven, *Gewestelijke financiën: vol. 3 Groningen*, 41, 84, 157.

Holland. Hence, it was the Generality that imposed a tax revolution in Groningen. After the War of the Spanish Succession, the Generality also controlled the debt charges. It again increased taxes and imposed debt reductions in 1726. These exceptional powers gave the Generality both income and control over Groningen's finances. Groningen benefitted because this helped to keep its interest payments in check.

4 Public Debt Management

What effect did the Generality's interference had on Groningen's public debt management? Did it also produce a 'real' or classic financial revolution, after the enforced tax revolution? To answer these questions, this section considers the three key characteristics of a financial revolution: a shift from short-term to long-term debt, a substantial increase in the size of the public debt and decreasing coupon rates. Moreover, it assesses the commitment to the debt.

Fritschy suggests that Groningen followed Holland's financial developments, albeit with a time lag. To this end, she points to the decline in interest rates in Groningen.[131] However, it is too simple to assume a financial revolution based on this alone. The historical reality was more complex. For instance, the interest rate of 2.5 per cent she mentions was part of a debt restructuring process and not a coupon rate.[132] Rather, this marked the end of a period of credit rationing.

The history of Groningen's debt management can be divided into four periods. The first is until 1665 when the First Münster War caused the first serious increase in the debt. The second is between 1665 and the 1680s when Groningen issued loans on its provincial account in Holland and Groningen. The third period is one of dependence on Generality loans, from the 1680s until the 1750s. In the fourth period, Groningen's provincial credit was restored.

4.1 *Groningen's Debt Development*

The shift from short-term and unfunded to long-term and funded debt occurred around 1625. Until 1624, income from loans was not recorded as

131 Fritschy, *Public Finance*, 160–61.

132 Feenstra, "Hiding"; Feenstra and Muller, "Wie wil wachten?"; Heeres, "Holland Contra Groningen," 196.

such.[133] Later records all refer only to loans issued since 1626.[134] Until the 1660s, this consisted entirely of redeemable annuities, a long-term instrument.

Until the First War with Münster, in 1665, Groningen's debt remained small and homogeneous (Graph 5.9). Around 1626, the debt amounted to almost 200,000 guilders. In the late 1620s, Groningen issued several substantial loans. As a result, the debt fluctuated around 300,000 guilders until 1650.[135] It then tripled to 900,000 guilders in 1664, on the eve of the First Münster War.[136]

The First Münster War led to an increase and diversification in Groningen's debt. In 1669, after this war and the simultaneous war with Britain ended, its debt amounted to almost 3 million guilders. Life annuities supplemented the redeemable annuities. In the years between the First and Second Münster Wars (1672–1674), Groningen reduced its debt to 2.2 million guilders. The Second Münster War and the simultaneous wars with France and Britain increased the debt to 3.6 million guilders in 1678, and life annuities now formed one-third of the debt. The second period ended in the 1680s, when Groningen increasingly failed to pay life annuities issued in Holland.[137]

From the start of the Nine Years' War, in 1688, debt increases consisted of Generality-guaranteed debt. This war increased the debt slightly. The subsequent War of the Spanish Succession led to an increase in the debt by a factor of more than three to 11 million guilders. This debt largely consisted of Generality-guaranteed loans, totalling almost 8 million guilders.[138]

After peaking in 1715, Groningen's debt declined to 6 million guilders in 1741. This was the result of the Generality's imposed financial austerity and forced reductions. Consequently, the debt owed to the Generality had halved to 3.6 million guilders and total debt had been reduced by 45 per cent.

The War of the Austrian Succession led to a need for new loans. The Generality again functioned as an intermediary for issuing debt, and Groningen's debt increased to some 8.5 million guilders in 1750.

The debt declined in the period up to the Fourth Anglo-Dutch War, to 5.5 million guilders. The decline was only interrupted by the settlement of the 'old' unpaid Holland debt in 1761. In that year, the arrears from the unpaid

133 Van der Ent and Enthoven, *Gewestelijke financiën: vol. 3 Groningen*, 46–47.

134 E.g. RHC-GrA, SvSL, inv.no. 513, 2801, 2802.

135 RHC-GrA, SvSL, inv.no. 1873, f. 86r-136v.

136 RHC-GrA, SvSL, inv.no. 1887, f. 107r-200v, the interest amounted to fl. 37,764, all at 4 per cent interest. The largest individual amounts were checked to rule out possible reimbursements that distorted the estimate.

137 Feenstra, "Hiding"; Feenstra and Muller, "Wie wil wachten?"

138 Dormans, *Het tekort*, 148; NA, Van der Heim, inv.no. 524.

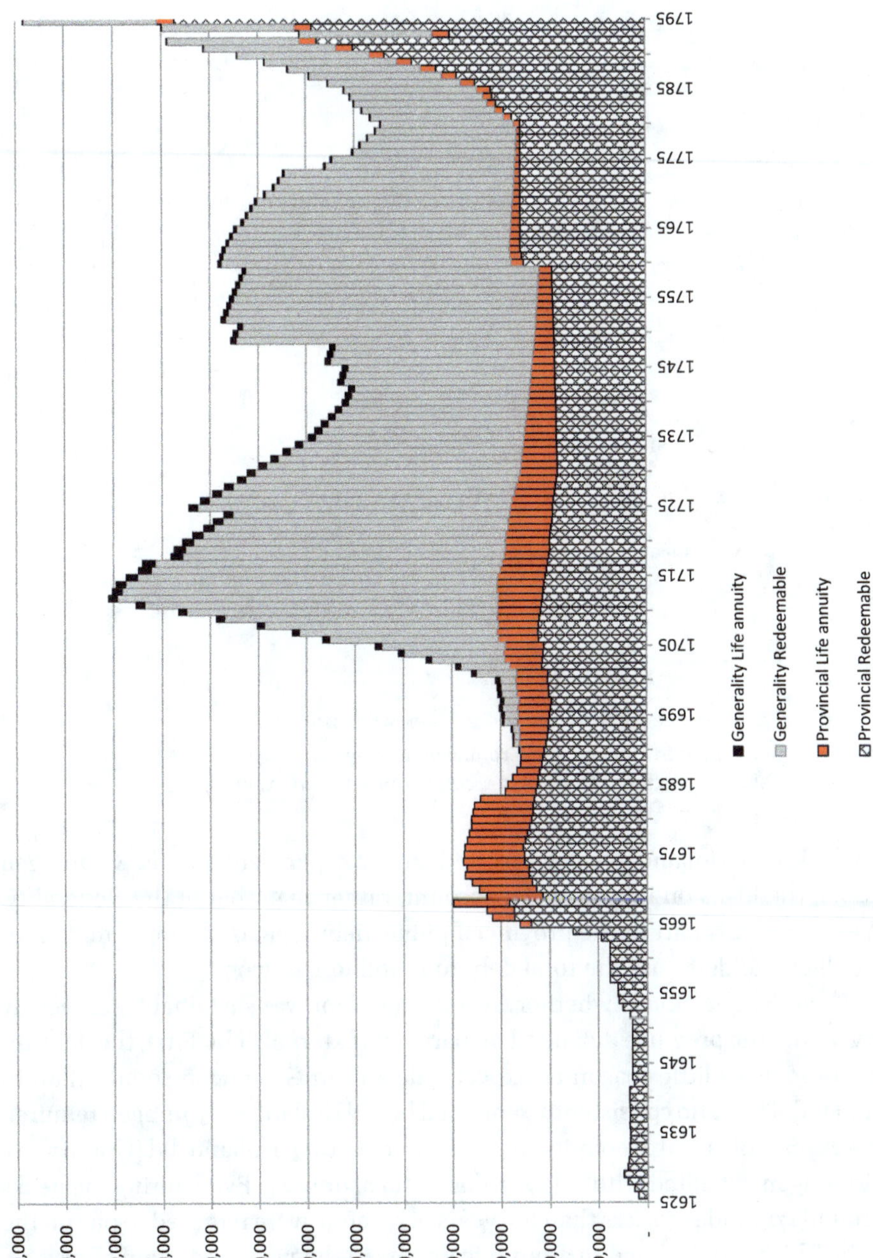

GRAPH 5.9 Groningen's public debt composition, 1625–1795.
SOURCES: FEENSTRA, *BETWEEN SHARED*, APPENDIX AND APPENDIX TO THIS BOOK.

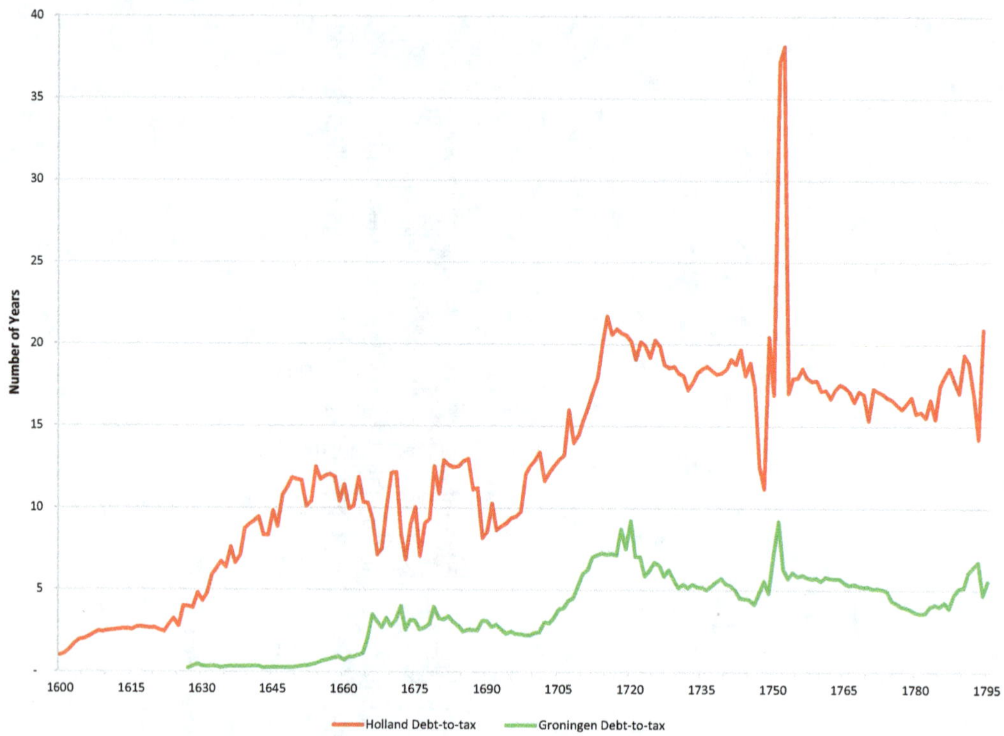

GRAPH 5.10 Debt-to-tax ratio in Holland and Groningen, 1600–1795.
SOURCES: SEE TEXT AND FEENSTRA, *BETWEEN SHARED*, APPENDIX.

annuities in Holland were converted into 2.5 per cent bonds. Groningen issued the loans on its provincial account, rather than that of the Generality. As a result, this part of the provincial public debt increased from 2 million to 7 million guilders, and the total debt to 10 million, in 1795.

The next question is whether Groningen's debt was sustainable, especially given that the province defaulted on part of its external debt. First, the debt-to-tax ratio gives little reason to expect a default in Groningen sooner than in Holland. This ratio consistently remained below Holland's: Groningen required fewer years of taxes to repay its entire public debt than Holland did (Graph 5.10). Groningen defaulted with a debt-to-tax ratio of only 2.5. Even during the peaks around 1715 and 1750, less than ten years of revenue were required to pay off the debt. This ratio declined to around five years in the 1730s and again after 1750. Holland's debt-to-tax ratio, on the other hand, increased to twenty-two years in 1715. Like in Groningen, debt redemptions caused the debt-to-tax ratio to fall in the eighteenth century. As a result, the difference between the two provinces in debt-to-tax ratios did not change much. Relative to Holland, Groningen's debt remained comfortably in proportion to its income.

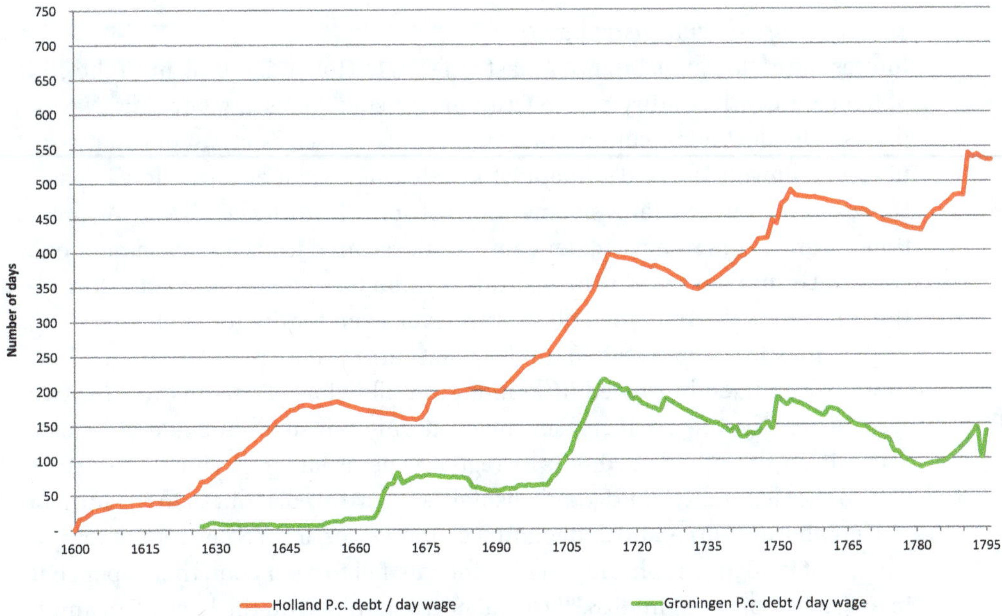

GRAPH 5.11 Debt per capita in day wages in Holland and Groningen, 1600–1795.
SOURCES: FEENSTRA, *BETWEEN SHARED*, APPENDIX.

The second method for assessing the sustainability of the debt also indicates that Groningen's debt compared favourably to Holland's (Graph 5.11). Expressed in the number of day wages, the pressure of Groningen's debt at its peak in 1715 was about half that of Holland. Groningen's per capita debt equalled 216 day wages at this point. In Holland, this figure had risen to 400. More importantly, this level was an all-time high in Groningen, whereas in Holland the debt continued to increase further. By 1750, Groningen's debt equalled less than 200 day wages versus 480 in Holland, and in 1795, this figure was 150 in Groningen and 530 in Holland. Consequently, the debt burden was less in Groningen.

Both indicators show that Groningen's debt remained comparatively small. The Generality's interventions had two effects. On the one hand, they led to higher taxes. On the other hand, the imposed repayments resulted in a small debt. Given the agricultural expansion in the second half of the eighteenth century, the debt did not unduly burden Groningen. It is questionable whether the increases in debt in the late seventeenth and early eighteenth centuries were large enough to be considered a financial revolution.

4.2 *Coupons and Instruments*

Interest rates declined, but not as fast or far as in Holland. It took until the end of the eighteenth century before Groningen issued loans at 3 per cent. Nevertheless, the decline in coupon rates underpins Fritschy's argument that Groningen followed Holland's financial developments, albeit at a slower pace. However, the interest rates she mentions obscure historical reality.[139] As mentioned earlier, the rate of 2.5 per cent in 1761 resulted from the settlement of a default. Groningen never achieved this coupon for a voluntary loan subscription. Interest rates remained above this level, even for the forced loans.

The question is how, when, under what terms and where Groningen borrowed. Groningen borrowed little money at all before 1665. This was for two reasons. Firstly, the tax increases meant it only ran small budgetary deficits. Secondly, it smoothed payments by regularly being late in paying its contribution to the Generality's budget.[140] Insofar as it borrowed, it did so in the form of redeemable annuities and at declining coupon rates, from 8 per cent in 1627 to 4 per cent in 1659 (Graph 5.12). In 1628 the rate fell to 7 per cent, then 6 per cent in 1629 and 5 per cent in 1638.[141] Dorsal notes scribbled on the back of an annuity show that the coupon was reduced from 5 per cent to 4 per cent in 1659, but was raised again to 4.5 per cent in 1666.[142] Until the 1780s, interest rates did not decline further; they fluctuated between 4 per cent and 5 per cent, sometimes within one year.[143] In 1726, the Generality proposed an interest rate reduction for the provincial 5 per cent annuities to 4 per cent and a 10 per cent reduction for the life annuities.[144] In 1746, it issued a 4 per cent loan that was only fully

139 Fritschy, *Public Finance*, 160–61: Unfortunately, annotation is lacking for the reference to Groningen. It is presumably based upon the Gewestelijke Financiën of Groningen.; This publication mentions the 2.5 per cent and 3 per cent rates of the 1780s and 1790s, yet does not contain references to interest rates of 3–3.5 per cent in 1744: Van der Ent and Enthoven, *Gewestelijke financiën: vol. 3 Groningen*, 285–86.

140 Van der Ent and Enthoven, *Gewestelijke financiën: vol. 3 Groningen*, 291,404. These unpaid/residual sums (Dutch: *restanten*) were common, and were probably mere slow payments as the province prioritised other expenses. Waterbolk, "Staatkundige geschiedenis," 244–45.

141 Van der Ent and Enthoven, *Gewestelijke financiën: vol. 3 Groningen*, 285.

142 RHC-GrA. SvSL, inv.no. 2694, unfol. Around the same time, the Groningen city council also struggled to reduce the interest rate to 4 per cent, in which it succeeded in doing in 1659 as well.

143 RHC-GrA, SvSL, inv.no. 2802, f. 212r-226v.

144 NA, Van der Heim, inv.no. 524, p. 1–4. When this was implemented remains uncertain. In 1731, Groningen's debt still contained parts at 4.5 per cent and 5 per cent. (RHC-GrA, SvSL, inv.no. 2802); RHC-GrA, SvSL, inv.no. 515. Inv.no. A reference in 1794 describes the debt as the ordinary debt issued between 1726 and 1748 at 4% "Capitalen na 4 Pro cento genegotieerd van de Jaare 1626 tot 1748)".

subscribed in 1752. Loan issues in the 1750s were also at 4 per cent.[145] In the 1780s and 1790s, Groningen issued loans at 3 to 3.5 per cent.

The two Münster Wars forced Groningen to employ additional debt instruments and turn to the Holland capital market. It issued life and redeemable annuities in Groningen and Holland. On top of that, it resorted to two types of forced loans. Firstly, it forced a group of pacifist dissenters, the Mennonites, to lend money at 3 per cent.[146] Secondly, it imposed a 5 per cent loan upon wealth-owners in 1672.[147] In 1728, Groningen once more demanded a forced loan from the Mennonites, this time at 4 per cent.[148] It was not until after the fall of the Dutch Republic, in 1795, that Groningen resorted again to forced loans.[149]

From 1666, life annuities supplemented the redeemable annuities. Coupons were typically double that of redeemable annuities.[150] Groningen issued life annuities in Holland and Groningen. Initially, the coupons in the two provinces were identical. Yet in 1669, the annuities were issued at the lower rate of 9 per cent in Amsterdam, compared with 10 per cent in Groningen.[151] From a risk perspective, a lower coupon outside the province is counterintuitive.[152]

---

145 J.E. Heeres, "Stad en Lande tijdens het erfstadhouderschap van Willem IV," *Bijdragen voor vaderlandsche geschiedenis en oudheidkunde*, 1888, 280; Van der Ent and Enthoven, *Gewestelijke financiën: vol. 3 Groningen*, 285–86.

146 Van der Ent and Enthoven, *Gewestelijke financiën: vol. 3 Groningen*, 285; Trompetter, *Gewestelijke financiën: vol 6. Friesland*, 40, 186; Trompetter, *Eén grote familie*, 212 Although it was not specifically stated in the case of Groningen, in Friesland these loans served as a means to buy off military service. In any case, the Groningen Mennonites were as opposed to violence as the Frisian Mennonites. Marcel Ronald Kremer, *Huwelijk en vermogen: een (rechts)historische case study naar de verzorging van de langstlevende echtgenoot in de stad Groningen onder doopsgezinden (1699–1809)*, Ars notariatus 155 (Deventer: KluwerAmsterdam : Universiteit van Amsterdam, 2013), 39, 230–34, 239, 372.

147 Van der Ent and Enthoven, *Gewestelijke financiën: vol. 3 Groningen*, 287.

148 RHC-GrA, SvSL, inv.no. 2802.

149 Van der Ent and Enthoven, *Gewestelijke financiën: vol. 3 Groningen*, 264.

150 Van der Ent and Enthoven, 285.

151 RHC-GrA, SvSL, inv.no. 96, f. 28v, 14 May 1669; inv.no. 2801.

152 Carmen M. Reinhart and Kenneth S. Rogoff, *This Time Is Different: Eight Centuries of Financial Folly* (Princeton, NJ etc.: Princeton University Press, 2009), 80–81; Tomz, *Reputation and International Cooperation*, e.g. 177; Van Bochove, "External Debt and Commitment Mechanisms"; Stasavage, *States of Credit*; Murphy, "Demanding 'Credible Commitment'"; Marc Flandreau et al., "Monetary Geography before the Industrial Revolution," *Cambridge Journal of Regions, Economy and Society* 2, no. 2 (July 1, 2009): 149–71, https://doi.org/10.1093/cjres/rsp009; Zuijderduijn, "Foreign Investment."

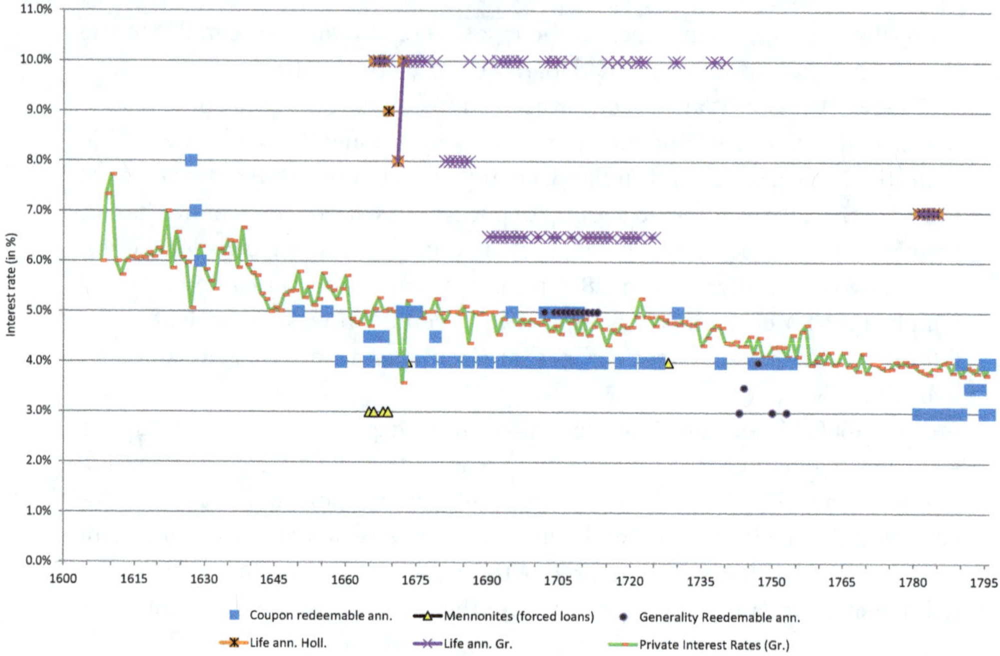

GRAPH 5.12 Coupons per credit instrument in Groningen, 1600–1795.
SOURCES: GRONINGEN: RHC-GRA, SVSL, INV.NOS. 96, 513, 515, 516, 1888–1894, 2018, 2277, 2694, 2801, 2802; NA, VAN DER HEIM, INV.NO. 524; *GEWESTELIJK FINANCIËN*, DOWNLOAD: 'LENINGEN (SUBPOSTEN)' [FOR THE LIFE ANNUITIES]; FOR THE PRIVATE INTEREST RATES, SEE: GRAPH 5.4, AVERAGE OF PAPING'S CLAY SOILS, BEERTA AND WAGENBORGEN.

The explanation is that Groningen took advantage of Holland's large capital supply to borrow more cheaply. This is also evident from the comparison with the other provinces. Zeeland and Overijssel offered higher coupons and Holland a lower one (Table 5.1). Perhaps this created domestic leverage to borrow more cheaply; in 1671, Groningen issued life annuities at 8 per cent in both Holland and Groningen. Hence, Groningen benefitted from Holland's abundant capital supply.

This advantage disappeared in 1672 when the demand for capital was high. Groningen issued age-specific life annuities, whereby the coupons differed depending on the age. Groningen raised double the amount compared to the flat rate in the first months of that year. The downside of that success was an average coupon of 27 per cent.

Issuing loans in Holland turned out to be a temporary solution. Groningen defaulted on the Holland-registered debt in the 1670s and 1680s. This had different outcomes for life annuities and redeemable annuities. Groningen settled with the holders of redeemable annuities, but not with the life annuity

TABLE 5.1 Coupons on life annuities issued by Groningen, Zeeland, Holland and Overijsel, 1666–1671.

Year	Groningen (in Groningen)	Groningen (in Holland)	Overijssel	Holland	Zeeland
1666	10%	10%	10%	8.3%	8.3%
1667	10%	10%	10%	8.3%	
1668	10%	10%		8.3%	
1669	10%	9%		7.1%	
1671	8%	8%	12%	7.1%	9%
1672-Jan-April		10%			
1672-Sept-Oct		27%			
1672	10%				
1673–1677	10%				

SOURCES: GRONINGEN: RHC-GRA, SVSL, INV.NOS. 1888–1894; 2801; HOLLAND: GF DL 4 HOLLAND, P. 382; GF DL 1 OVERIJSSEL: P. 216; ZEELAND: ZA, RKC, INV.NO. 4510, F.393–414 AND ZA, 87 VERZAMELING VERHEYE V CITTERS, INV.NO. 125B.

holders.[153] The consequence of the unpaid debt was that the door to the Amsterdam capital market was shut.

After the default of the 1680s, Groningen issued two types of life annuities. One, with a coupon of 6.5 per cent, was to redeem Holland-issued debt. The other had a 10 per cent coupon for other purposes.[154] Their value remained limited, however, to 1 million guilders between 1683 and 1725.[155]

The Generality's credit formed Groningen's financial lifeline after the default on Holland-issued debt. On the one hand, Groningen suffered from credit rationing in Holland, and on the other hand the domestic supply of capital was limited. The advantage of the Generality was that it offered access to substantial loans, primarily during the Wars of the Spanish and Austrian Succession.

Comparing the coupons demonstrates that volume was the reason for Generality loans. During the War of the Spanish Succession, the Generality-

153 Feenstra, "Hiding," 81.

154 RHC-GrA, SvSL, inv.no. 2018, f. 636r-638r.

155 "Gewestelijke Financiën (on-Line)" Postnrs: b005, b019. This level of detail is not available in the printed version of the Gewestelijke Financiën-series, only in the online database.

guaranteed loans had a coupon of 5 per cent. Within the province, the States of Groningen issued both 4 per cent and 5 per cent loans, but only in limited amounts.[156]

The War of the Austrian Succession increased the coupons on the Generality-guaranteed loans from 3 per cent to 3.5 per cent in 1744 and 4 per cent in 1747.[157] The latter coupon was identical to what Groningen offered, without a Generality guarantee, in 1746. However, the 100,000 guilders of this loan were not fully subscribed until after the war.[158] The Generality loans, on the other hand, totalled 1 million guilders.[159] Additional loans at 3 per cent in 1750 and 1753 amounted to another 2.5 million guilders. Still, the Generality loans were not necessarily cheaper than unguaranteed loans, but they did offer access to substantial amounts of capital.

After the 1750s, Groningen no longer required the Generality's assistance. Firstly, it did not need to borrow because of its fiscal surpluses, until the 1780s. Secondly, after settling the default in 1761, Groningen was able to return to the Amsterdam capital market without the Generality's guarantees. In the 1780s, Groningen issued loans at 3 per cent in both Holland and Groningen, without requiring force or guarantees.

Interest rates thus declined during two periods when the debt was either hardly growing or falling. The decline in coupon rates was greatest in 1626–1659, from 8 per cent to 4 per cent. Then rates increased rather than decreased, until the 1740s. The low coupons of 1715–1744 applied only to the Generality-guaranteed loans. Still, Groningen issued debt below the going rates on the private market. This and the difficulties in raising substantial amounts suggest that the capital market was shallow. The lack of credible commitment to the debt prevented capital imports that might have driven down the price of capital. The slow and limited decline in interest rates provides little ground for concluding a classic financial revolution took place in Groningen.

4.3 *Geographical Scope of the Market*

The larger capital supply drew Groningen to Amsterdam to cover the deficits of the First Münster War. This led to lower coupon rates, as was evident from

156 RHC-GrA., SvSL, inv.no. 2802.
157 RHC-GrA, SvSL, inv.no. 513.
158 Heeres, "Stad en Lande," 280.
159 RHC-GrA, SvSL, inv.no. 513.

the coupons for life annuities in 1669. In 1671, the States of Groningen tried to benefit from this difference. It ordered the Receiver-General to issue 50,000 guilders in redeemable or life annuities. Within Groningen, he was to offer 4 per cent and 8 per cent coupons and in Holland 3.5–4 per cent and 7–8 per cent, depending on what the market would accept.[160] Turning to Amsterdam was a policy aimed at borrowing at a lower cost.

The province soon experienced difficulties servicing the external debt in Holland. Groningen ran up arrears in 1671, despite promises of prompt payments in Amsterdam.[161] An auditing committee was installed to handle the unpaid interest in Holland.[162] After a failed life annuity issue at 8 per cent, Groningen increased the offer to 9 per cent or 10 per cent, depending on what the creditors accepted.[163] Groningen was competing with the other provinces for cash to finance the imminent war.[164]

Groningen now offered a novel instrument, the age-specific life annuity. The Holland Grand Pensionary Johan De Witt had only recently published an analysis stating that flat rates made life annuities expensive. With flat rates, the age of the nominees was skewed towards children. Therefore, he proposed lowering the coupon for younger nominees.[165] But cash-strapped Groningen did the opposite: it increased the coupon for older nominees, up to 33.3 per cent for nominees aged above seventy-five.[166] This made the loan even more expensive for the borrower and even more attractive for investors. The Amsterdam magistrate offered an identical loan and coupons but prohibited the nomination of people older than fifty.[167] The identical conditions

160 RHC-GrA, SvSL, inv.no. 96, f. 40r, 23 December 1671.

161 RHC-GrA, SvSL, inv.no. 96, f. 41v, 15 April 1671

162 RHC-GrA, SvSL, inv.no. 96, f. 41v, 26 August 1671

163 RHC-GrA, SvSL, inv.no. 96, f. 41v, 9/19 January 1672, and 18 January 1672

164 Gelderblom and Jonker, "Public Finance," 18.

165 Houtzager, *Hollands lijf- en losrenterekeningen*, 96–99, 105; Poterba, "Annuities," 211–12: Poterba assumed that the practice of issuing age-specific annuities was not widely copied. This makes usage by the relatively remote province of Groningen all the more intriguing. The city of Rotterdam also applied these new insights by De Witt: Martijn Van der Burg, "Burgers En Bestuurders : Rotterdamse Stadsfinanciën in de Tweede Helft van Den Zeventiende Eeuw.," *Rotterdams Jaarboekje*, 2003, 110–11; During the eighteenth century, it became common knowledge that the lifelong payment made it attractive to nominate children because of the higher life expectancy: Christophe Chamley, "Interest Reductions in the Politico-Financial Nexus of Eighteenth-Century England," *The Journal of Economic History* 71, no. 03 (September 2011): 555–89, https://doi.org/10.1017/S0022050711001847; Velde and Weir, "Financial Market and Government Debt Policy in France."

166 RHC-GrA, SvSL, inv.no. 1896, f. 682r.

167 Houtzager, *Hollands lijf- en losrenterekeningen*, 105–6.

emphasise that the high compensation was due mainly to the scarcity of capital rather than risk considerations.[168]

The case of Jan Du Try provides a telling example of how this encouraged speculation. In 1669 and 1672, he and his wife Geertruit Tourquois purchased 4,000 guilders' worth of life annuities on the lives of their children, Maria, Jan and Cornelis, aged nine, six and three.[169,170] Yet in September 1672, he purchased seven annuities, amounting to 7,500 guilders, on the lives of unrelated persons aged over seventy. The subsequent annual instalment amounted to 2,100 guilders.[171] His investment behaviour was representative of what happened with this loan: the ages of the nominees were skewed towards older people and the amounts paid out and coupons were triple that of the previous years.

Groningen found it increasingly difficult to pay all the bills. In 1673, it prioritised military expenses over creditor payments.[172] Borrowing was difficult. Between 1673 and 1677, the province raised less than 100,000 guilders in redeemable annuities in Holland and Groningen.[173] In need of money, the States of Groningen turned to the Generality. In 1675, the Council of State approved a Generality-guaranteed loan to pay subsidies to German allies.[174] Although it is uncertain whether the loan was ever realised, Groningen had now discovered the Generality loans as a suitable alternative.[175]

Still, Groningen increasingly fell behind in fulfilling its debt obligations in Holland. In 1677, the States General urged the States of Groningen to pay at least one instalment.[176] By 1680, about half of the outstanding debt was in Amsterdam, as was more than half of the annual interest (Table 5.2).[177] The States of Groningen expressed its willingness to accommodate the 'foreign cor-

168 Feenstra, "Hiding," 96–99; Feenstra and Muller, "Wie wil wachten?," 56; Velde and Weir, "Financial Market and Government Debt Policy in France"; Drelichman and Voth, "Serial Defaults, Serial Profits."

169 RHC-GrA, SvSL, inv.no. 1892, f. 38r.

170 RHC-GrA, SvSL, inv.no. 1896, f. 672r-v.

171 RHC-GrA, SvSL, inv.no. 1896, 683r-v, 684v.

172 RHC-GrA, SvSL, inv.no. 96, f. 55r, 7 March 1673.

173 RHC-GrA, SvSL, inv.no. 2801 (60,000 guilders in Holland and 30,000 in Groningen).

174 RHC-GrA, SvSL, inv.no. 96, f. 69r, 5 June 1675.

175 In the summary of 1677–1678, the loan does not show: RHC-GrA, SvSL, inv.no. 2801.

176 NA, Raad van State: Extra Aanwinsten 1904 XII, 17–18, 1 June 1677.

177 RHC-GrA, SvSL, inv.no. 2801, this figure amounted to 126,000 guilders of the Holland-held external or foreign debt. Groningen was also liable to 95,000 guilders within the province.

TABLE 5.2 Groningen's debt composition per type and location, in 1677.

		Holland	Groningen	Total
Debt	Redeemable annuities	896,541	1,638,538	2,535,079
Debt	Life annuities	894,522	301,250	1,195,772
Debt	**Total**	**1,791,063**	**1,939,788**	**3,730,851**
Interest	Redeemable annuities	38,705	68,969	107,675
Interest	Life annuities	87,404	30,105	117,509
Interest	**Total**	**126,109**	**99,074**	**225,084**

SOURCE: RHC-GRA, SVSL, INV.NO. 2801.

respondents' (*buitenlantsche correspondenten*) in Holland.[178] However, in 1680 creditors had received only a year and a half of the overdue interest since 1672.[179]

Creditors' complaints were mainly conveyed through the agent in Amsterdam, a certain Christoffer Indisraven. He arranged the debt issuance and interest payments. The life annuities contracts stated specifically that instalments were payable in Amsterdam.[180] In 1680, the States of Groningen summoned him to collect and transport money to Amsterdam.[181] Since little is known about him, he was probably a minor player in the Amsterdam capital market.

Indisraven regularly reported complaints from dissatisfied creditors, as Groningen increasingly failed to pay what it owed.[182] Without formal repudiation, an increasing number of Holland creditors received little or nothing, particularly in the mid-1680s.[183] Following Indisraven's unsolicited advice, the States of Groningen opened negotiations with the creditors. Meanwhile, he ignored the States' instruction to pay interest in Amsterdam. This frus-

178 RHC-GrA, SvSL, inv.no. 96, f. 75v, 2 March 1678, 25 April 1678 ('buitenlantsche correspondenten van de provintie nae de provintie van Hollandt en Frieslandt'), f. 76r, 27 April 1678.

179 RHC-GrA, SvSL, inv.no. 1457, f. 605r-605v, 7th / 17th August 1680.

180 RHC-GrA, SvSL, inv.no. 2698. We do not have any other information about this merchant or his family. His name also appears with different spellings in the sources, for example Indischraven or Indise Raven and also as Christoffer.

181 RHC-GrA, SvSL, inv.no. 96, f. 114v, 21 August 1680; f. 115r, 21 August 1680.

182 RHC-GrA, SvSL, inv.no. 96, f. 156v 6 January 1683; f. 157v, 28 February 1683; f. 158r 1 March 1683;

183 Feenstra and Muller, "Wie wil wachten?," 50, 60–61.

trated the States, who used it as leverage with respect to the creditors. In 1686, the holders of redeemable annuities in Holland accepted an interest rate cut to 4 per cent.[184] Negotiations with life annuity holders failed. After 1690, 90 per cent of these creditors in Holland received nothing.[185] This selective external default saved Groningen around 80,000 guilders in interest per year.[186]

As a result of the default, Groningen suffered from credit rationing in Amsterdam.[187] To overcome this problem, the States of Groningen turned to the Generality. In November 1687, Groningen declared that maintenance of fortifications required an injection of money from outside the province. To reinforce its argument, it temporarily withheld its contribution to the Generality.[188] In exchange for a 4 million guilder loan, the States of Groningen would agree to the construction of new warships.[189] A Generality embassy travelled to Groningen to discuss this matter.[190] Emphasising the province's strategic position was a convincing argument after the invasions of 1665 and 1672.

During the Nine Years' War, the Generality issued loans for Groningen under its guarantee. Yet again, Groningen failed to meet its debt obligations. In the autumn of 1698, a Generality embassy was necessary to enforce interest payments.[191] In December of the same year, the States General transformed the provincial share in the common budget into a loan.[192] Groningen depended on the Generality's credit, yet still failed to pay.

Meanwhile, Groningen issued provincial debt within the province. This was not to cover deficits, but rather to convert Holland-issued debt into domestic

184 RHC-GrA SvSL, inv.no. 96, f. 197v; f. 199r, 25–26 February 1686: the resolutions mentioned on the one hand a 25 per cent reduction and on the other payments at 4 per cent; later reports consistently mention a 4 per cent interest rate on this part of the debt, e.g. RHC-GrA SvSL, inv.no. 2802.

185 RHC-GrA., SvSL, inv.no. 2802, f. 245r, 247v.

186 RHC-GrA., SvSL, inv.no. 2801.

187 The one notable execption to this rule was Greece, which issued a loan in 1833 even though its 1826 default remained unsettled. Yet England, France and Russia guaranteed the loan and pledged all Greece's revenues to secure it. Tomz, *Reputation and International Cooperation*, 53–55; Mitchener and Weidenmier, "Supersanctions and Sovereign Debt Repayment."

188 RHC-GrA, SvSL, inv.no. 96, f. 233v, 18th November 1687.

189 RHC-GrA, SvSL, inv.no. 96, f. 242v-243r, 26th June 1688.

190 RHC-GrA, SvSL, inv.no. 96, f. 243r, 27th July 1688; NA, Archief Staten-Generaal, inv.no. 8919.

191 Van der Ent and Enthoven, *Gewestelijke financiën: vol. 3 Groningen*, 287–88.

192 RHC-GrA, SvSL, inv.no. 96, p. 51, 14th December 1699.

debt. It started to issue loans for that specific purpose in the mid-1670s.[193] Between 1676 and 1747, it issued 4 per cent loans with that end in mind. Other loans had a 5 per cent interest rate in the first twenty-five years and 4 per cent later. Moreover, in 1689–1697 and 1710–1718, the States of Groningen exclusively issued loans for the conversion to domestic debt, despite the budgetary deficits.[194]

This conversion operation also involved life annuities.[195] In March 1680, the States set the coupon of life annuities designed to achieve this conversion at 6.5 per cent. Instead of repurchasing the debt directly, it encouraged its inhabitants to do so, who could reinvest this through a nominee living in Groningen.[196] Some of these annuities were still being paid in 1795; the oldest was issued in 1704.[197]

The States of Groningen actively supported its inhabitants in purchasing Holland-issued debt. For instance, in 1700 it rewarded the merchant Jan Boelens for transferring money to redeem Holland-issued debt.[198] The effect of the conversion was a more than 80 per cent reduction in Holland-registered debt, from almost 900,000 guilders in 1677 to 166,000 in 1731.[199]

To stimulate this conversion to domestically-held debt, the States of Groningen obliged creditors to collect the interest in Groningen. In 1698, it withheld payments of instalments to its agent Indisraven in Amsterdam.[200] The Amsterdam magistrate complained. In response, the States of Groningen issued bills of exchange for the debts that Indisraven had personally guaranteed, but nothing more.[201] The termination of interest payments in Amsterdam coincided with the Generality's conversion of unpaid contributions into debt. Ironically, the Generality created the opportunity for Groningen to use its limited borrowing capacity to realise a conversion rather than paying external creditors, including the Generality itself.

193 RHC-GrA, SvSL, 516, p. 11: The overviews that the new regime compiled in 1796 explicitly mention part of the debt as intended to reimburse Holland debt, and the year 1676 as the moment this conversion operation began: "Van 1676 tot 1700 genegotieerd tegen afgeloste Hollandsche Capitalen, f 258,683-12-6".

194 RHC-GrA, SvSL, 2018, 397r-497r.

195 "Gewestelijke Financiën (on-Line)" Postnrs: b005, b019. This level of detail is not available in the printed version of the Gewestelijke Financiën-series, only in the online database.

196 RHC-GrA, SvSL, inv.no. 96, f. 237r, 2 March 1688.

197 RHC-GrA, SvSL, inv.no. 2018, f. 628r-235r.

198 RHC-GrA, SvSL, inv.no. 96, p. 102, 7 August 1698

199 RHC-GrA, SvSL, inv.no. 2801, 2802.

200 RHC-GrA, SvSL, inv.no. 96, f. 231r, 7 August 1698.

201 RHC-GrA, SvSL, inv.no. 96, p. 56, 3 March 1699.

Groningen's incomplete interest payments contributed to the Generality's default in 1715.[202] The States General's embassy of 1726 explicitly blamed Groningen for having caused this default.[203] The unintended consequence was an interest rate reduction from 4 per cent to 3 per cent on Groningen's debt owed to the Generality.[204] Still Groningen failed to pay. Between 1715 and 1725, Groningen's overdue interest increased to more than 1 million guilders.[205] Meanwhile, Groningen also ran up arrears of 3 million guilders in military expenses.[206] The failure to pay its main creditor, the Generality, was Groningen's second default. This second default also spared its domestic creditors.

In 1726, the Generality intervened. The States of Groningen claimed incomplete payments were due to 'notorious impotence', not unwillingness.[207] It emphasised declining tax incomes due to natural disasters and expensive dyke maintenance and repairs.[208] It also argued that Groningen's remoteness from Holland made money scarce.[209] The States General admitted that the province was affected by these disasters, but argued that it was internal disagreements about the means to fund the debt that prevented sound payments.[210]

An internal report from 1720 served as a blueprint for the Generality's intervention in 1726.[211] This involved a sinking fund to service and repay the Generality's debt and reduce the outstanding provincial debt to 4 per cent.[212] The Generality indeed demanded interest rate reductions to 4 per cent for the redeemable annuities and a 10 per cent cut for the life annuities.[213] To service

---

202 Dormans, *Het tekort*, 145–47.

203 Heeres, "Stad en Lande," 281.

204 Dormans, *Het tekort*, 148; 't Hart, "United Provinces," 313; Fritschy, *De patriotten*, 39–41; Van der Ent et al., "Public Finance," 265; The financial troubles were not limited to the Dutch Republic. Britain faced similar troubles in footing the bill and consequently also suspended payments for months and discounted short-term public bonds. Murphy, "Demanding 'Credible Commitment,'" 181–82.

205 RHC-GrA. SvSL, inv.no. 515: *f* 1,064,315-3-8; NA, Staten-Generaal, inv.no. 8952, recorded the higher figure of *f* 1.168.072-9-0 concerning unpaid interest from 1712 to 1726.

206 NA, Staten-Generaal, inv.no. 8952.

207 NA, Van der Heim, inv.no. 524, p. 21: „... dat het niet en is een gebrek van goede wille, dat daerop geene betaelinge is gedaen, maer een notoire onmagt, ..."

208 NA, Van der Heim, inv.no. 524, p. 17.

209 NA, Van der Heim, inv.no. 524, p. 21: "... ende dat in een afgelegene en afgesonderde Provincie daar het geld altyd seer schaars is en weinig rouleert."

210 NA, Van der Heim, inv.no. 524, p. 1.

211 NA, Van der Heim, inv.no. 525, p. 6.

212 NA, Van der Heim, inv.no. 524, p. 18.

213 NA, Van der Heim, inv.no. 524, p. 1, 4.

TABLE 5.3 Generality payments and primary and fiscal balances, 1731.

Description	Amount (in gld.)
Primary surplus	540,000
Generality interest payments	–182,000
Prov. Life annuities	–145,000
Prov. Redeemable ann.	–76,000
Fiscal surplus	137,000
Generality reimbursement	–208,000
Liquidity shortage	–71,000

SOURCES: GRAPH 5.5 AND NA, VAN DER HEIM, INV. NO. 524.

and repay the Generality debt, the States General claimed 390,000 guilders of income from Groningen's most important sources of revenue – the land tax, the hearth taxes and excises on grain milling.[214] It offered financial assistance if reimbursements of bondholders refusing the reduction proved too large an amount for the provincial coffers.[215] This time the conversion was advantageous, as the provincial debt would cost 4 per cent and the Generality's debt 3 per cent. The Generality thus funded its debt and prioritised interest payments over this part of the debt.[216]

The Generality's forced debt redemption hampered the service of Groningen's provincial debt (Table 5.3). The Generality claimed an annual lump sum; over time, the ratio between interest and redemption payments shifted as the

214 NA, Van der Heim, inv.no. 524, p. 4–5.

215 NA, Van der Heim, inv.no. 525, p. 4: „Dat ingevalle des niet te min de houders van voorsz. Obligatien en Ordonnantien gants onvermoedelyk als nog swarigheyd soude make de voorsz. moduique reductie te ondergaan, als dan aan die gene, welke hare Capitalen souden mogen wederom eysschen, deselve sullen worden gerestitueert, en in sulken overhoopten cas, het appuy en de hulpe van Haar Ho. Mog. Sal worden versogt, indien de Penningen daar toe nodig binnen dese Provincie niet souden konnen worden bekomen."

216 NA, Van der Heim, inv.no. 524, p. 21: „Dat den Ontfanger Generael van de Provincie soude werden gelast ten eersten te voldoen de agterstallige interessen op den voorsz. Voet, soo haast Haar Hoog Mog. d'Ontfanger Generael van de Unie maer gelieven te authoriseren de penningen te ontfangen, en d'interessen te betalen tegen 3 ten 100, als vooren."

debt decreased. The fiscal surplus around 1730 implies that Groningen had money to spare after paying all its expenses, including the interest to Generality and provincial creditors. But the obligatory redemptions exceeded Groningen's fiscal surplus by 71,000 guilders. Consequently, the obligatory Generality debt reduction caused liquidity shortages, which forced the province to borrow locally.

Meanwhile, the Generality shielded Groningen from claims made by Holland creditors, who demanded a settlement of the default of the 1680s. The States of Groningen ignored or brushed aside creditors' requests and warnings by the States of Holland.[217] It argued that in 1726 the States General declared Groningen powerless to make payments other than to the Generality.[218]

Still, in May 1739 the States of Holland delivered an ultimatum for an understanding to be reached before May 1740.[219] The outbreak of the War of the Austrian Succession prevented this ultimatum from being enforced.[220] The States of Groningen nevertheless converted part of the arrears to Holland creditors into 4 per cent redeemable annuities in 1739 and 1748.[221] Mediation by the new Stadholder William IV, in 1751, confirmed that Groningen should only be concerned about the Generality debt.[222]

Groningen improved its fiscal position after the War of the Austrian Succession, following another Generality intervention. The war increased Gronin-

217 Petrus Adriaanszoon Loosjes and Jan Wagenaar, *Vaderlandsche historie, vervattende de geschiedenissen der Vereenigde Nederlanden, uit de geloofwaardigste schrijvers en egte gedenkstukken zamengest.: ten onmiddelyken vervolge van Wagenaars Vaderlandsche historie door Jan Wagenaar. Drie-en-twintigste deel. Beginnende met den jaare 1759 en eindigende met den jaare 1765, bevattende het tydperk der minderjaarigheid des erfstadhouders Willem den V*, vol. 23 (Amsterdam: by Johannes Allart, 1789), 139–41; Heeres, "Holland Contra Groningen," 175–76.

218 NA, Raad van State: Extra Aanwinsten 1904 XII, inv.no. 23c, excerpt from the Resolutions Book of the province of Stad and Lande, 10 December 1759: "Waar van ook haar Hoog Mog. Gecommitteerden eenige instantien op de betaaling deeser Lyfrenten doende, ten volle overreed zyn geworden, en genoodsaakt te declareeren dat, aan cordate Bondgenooten boven de toenmaals gedaane offerts niets meer konde werden gevergt".

219 NA, Raad van State: Extra Aanwinsten 1904 XII, inv.no. 23c, excerpt from the Book of Resolutions of Holland and West-Friesland, 11 November 1739.

220 Loosjes and Wagenaar, *Vaderlandsche historie*, 23:140.

221 RHC-GrA. SvSL, inv.no. 2018, f. 694r-695r.

222 NA, Raad van State: Extra Aanwinsten 1904 XII, inv.no. 23c, excerpt from the Resolutions Book of the province of Stad and Lande, 10 December 1759: "weshalven ook door sijn Doorlugtige Hoogheid, glorieuser gedagtenisse, in die tyden niet geschroomt heeft aan de Gecommitteerden van Stad en Lande te declareeren, dat de Provincie met de betaaling van verdere schulden niet soude werden gemoeit."; Heeres, "Holland Contra Groningen," 183, 192.

gen's debt to the Generality.[223] But Groningen did not keep up with its payments after 1746, as the Council of State and the Stadholder pointed out.[224] This was one factor causing the default by the Generality in 1754. Like in 1715, the Generality lowered the interest rate from 4 per cent to 3 per cent.[225] After 1754, Groningen repaid the Generality debt from the sale of the former ecclesiastical lands, following Stadholder William IV's advice.[226] Like in 1726, the Generality designated specific taxes, without requiring increases in tax rates or number of taxes.[227] This reflects the weakening of the Generality's position compared to that of the Stadholder. Groningen did not require any new loans until 1781.[228]

Until the 1780s, Groningen's debt only increased in 1761 when it settled the default from the 1680s. The States of Groningen ignored creditors' requests in 1753 and 1754, or referred them to a special committee.[229] Expectations for a favourable settlement were low, judging from the market prices. Life annuities traded at 8–10 per cent of face value in the mid-1750s.[230] In 1755, creditors sued the States of Groningen before the High Chamber of Justice (*Hoge Justitiekamer*). When the States objected, the court reminded it of the judges' oath to protect and uphold the law.[231] Meanwhile, the Amsterdam merchant Jacob Roeters Sr mobilised as many creditors as possible to support the claim.[232] Because little progress was made, in 1758 the creditors turned to the States of Holland.

223 RHC-GrA. SvSL, inv.no. 513: 272,500 (March 1744), 327,500 (September 1744), 153,500 (March 1747), 246,500 (July 1747).

224 Karsien Hildebrand, *Het reglement reformatoir in Stad en Lande in de praktijk, (1749–1780)* (Groningen etc.: Wolters, 1932), 134.

225 't Hart, "United Provinces," 313; Fritschy, *De patriotten*, 39–41; Dormans, *Het tekort*, 165; RHC-GrA. SvSL, inv.no. 513, unfol.

226 Roelfsema, *Klooster- en proosdijgoederen*, 95–96.

227 NA, Raad van State: Extra Aanwinsten 1904 XII, inv.no. 23c, excerpt from the Resolutions Book of the province of Stad and Lande, 10 December 1759.

228 Van der Ent and Enthoven, *Gewestelijke financiën: vol. 3 Groningen*, 119. Van der Ent and Enthoven, 119.

229 Heeres, "Holland Contra Groningen," 176–79.

230 Heeres, 186–89.

231 Loosjes and Wagenaar, *Vaderlandsche historie*, 23:140; Heeres, "Holland Contra Groningen," 177–78.

232 "Advertentie". "Leydse courant". Te Leyden, 08-12-1755. Accessed at Delpher 25-08-2017, http://resolver.kb.nl/resolve?urn=ddd:010910185:mpeg21:a0006; "Advertentie". "Leydse courant". Te Leyden, 10-12-1755. Accessed at Delpher 25-08-2017, http://resolver.kb.nl/resolve?urn=ddd:010910187:mpeg21:a0009; "Advertentie". "Amsterdamse courant". Amsterdam, 02-10-1760. Accessed at Delpher 25-08-2017, http://resolver.kb.nl/resolve?urn=ddd:010708213:mpeg21:a0008.

In May 1759, the States of Holland gave Jacob Roeters Jr – his father had died – the right to exercise the Law of Reprisal in October of that year. The implementation was delayed to allow Groningen to resolve this issue.[233] Groningen opted for retaliation, with disastrous consequences for Groningen's trade.[234] Even ferries ended up chained.[235]

Holland's permission to invoke the Law of Reprisal changed the legal status of the conflict from a disagreement between private persons to a dispute between two provinces. This gave the States General the right to mediate under the Union of Utrecht.[236] Meanwhile, the Generality safeguarded the money Groningen sent to Holland for Generality debt redemption and interest payments.[237] The States of Groningen, of course, claimed impotence due to Münster's invasions, flooding in 1686 and 1717 and the burden of interest payments after the War of the Spanish Succession. It also pointed to the increased

233 NA, Raad van State: Extra Aanwinsten 1904 XII, inv.no. 23c, excerpt from the Resolutions Book of the province of Holland and West-Friesland, 9 May 1759: "Edele Groot Mog. Protective en sterke hand, als het eenigste overig zynde middle om de Geinteresseerdens aan betaalinge te helpen en klagteloos te stellen, in gevolge de Missieve dienaangaande by haar Edele Groot Moge. op den 11 November 1739 aan den Heeren Staaten van de Provincie van Stad en Lande geschreeven" (…), "dog waar van Haar Edele Groot Mog., volgens al het gunt deesen gedaan hebben, sig volkoomen vry kennen en onschuldig houden, en die alleen te wyten sullen zyn aan de eige conduites van de Heeren Staten van Stad en Lande, die al het selve door dees laatste vriendelijke passe van Haar Edele Groot Mog. alsnog kunnen voorkoomen, indien by deselve maar een waare geneegentheid is, om op deese of geene genoegdoende wyse een reëele en billik genoegen te willen geeven aan de meenigwerf herhaalde versoeken daar toe aan de Heeren Staaten van Stad en lande selve gedaan,".

234 NA, Raad van State: Extra Aanwinsten 1904 XII, inv.no. 23c, excerpt from the Resolutions Book of the province of Stad and Lande, 18 September 1759: "Heeren Staaten van Stad en Lande niet konden verbergen hare surprise over de verschreeve haar Edele Groot Mog. Resolutie."; Heeres, "Holland Contra Groningen," 185; Debt imprisonment remained a contract enfoorcement mechanism, mostly applied to non-residential or foreign debtors. In Groningen, this was used at least until 1780, when an Albanian-Venetian fraud was arrested because of accumulated debts. Koen Stapelbroek and Antonio Trampus, "Commercial Reform against the Tide: Reapproaching the Eighteenth-Century Decline of the Republics of Venice and the United Provinces," *History of European Ideas* 36, no. 2 (June 1, 2010): 200, https://doi.org/10.1016/j.histeuroideas.2009.11.001.

235 Jacobus Kok, *Vaderlandsch Woordenboek: met kaarten, plaaten en pourtraitten*, ed. Jan Fokke, vol. XVIII (Te Amsterdam,: bij Johannes Allart, 1785), 678.

236 Fruin, *Geschiedenis der Staatsinstellingen*, 385–86.

237 Loosjes and Wagenaar, *Vaderlandsche historie*, 23:142–43; Zuijerduijn pointed out that use of safeguards undermined the ability of creditors to enforce their threat to seize goods in the late Middle Ages. Zuijderduijn, *Medieval Capital Markets*, 130: something similar applied here well into in the eighteenth century, too. Also, in Friesland in 1689, such an issue of a safeguard was requested by the military-broker Overschie.

taxes and reminded Holland that the States General and Stadholder had declared Groningen to be overburdened in 1726 and 1751 respectively.[238] After mediation, Groningen paid 60 per cent of the arrears, 10 per cent in cash and 50 per cent as debt at 2.5 per cent.[239] The subsequent increase in the debt by 598,193 guilders remained on the books until 1796.[240] In March 1761, the States of Holland lifted the restraints on the Groningen property.[241]

The settlement reopened the opportunity to borrow in Holland on Groningen's provincial account. However, Groningen's domestic capital market had become more important by then. In the 1780s, nearly 90 per cent of the new loans were issued domestically.[242] The Receiver-General Van Iddekinge paid the interest on the non-Groningen annuities in Amsterdam from the office of the cashiers Van de Brink and Van Rossen, albeit with some delay; in 1785 he announced payment of the interest over the years 1781–1783.[243] The large share of domestically issued debt and low coupon rate indicate that Groningen's local capital supply had increased.

4.4 *The Secondary Market*

Secondary market prices are rare for Groningen. So far, only a merchant guild account book in the city of Groningen has been found that mentions prices, for 1741 and 1742. Redeemable annuities traded at 6–10 per cent above par, averaging a current yield of 3.72 per cent.[244] This suggests that the coupon rate of 4 per cent between 1746 and 1754 reflects the local market price for Groningen debt in the form of redeemable annuities.[245] Groningen creditors did not consider the provincial securities to be risky assets.

Prices outside the province are also scarce and are limited to the eighteenth century. Groningen's unsettled default affected the prices there. This left the Generality-guaranteed loans as the sole option for issuing debt. An Amster-

238 NA, Raad van State: Extra Aanwinsten 1904 XII, inv.no. 23c, excerpt from the Resolutions Book of the province of Stad and Lande, 10 December 1759.

239 NA, Provinciale Resoluties, inv.no. 715, pp. 1279–1285.

240 RHC-GrA. SvSL, inv.no. 2276., inv.no. 513, and inv.no. 2803, inv.no. 516, p. 13.

241 "NEDERLANDEN". "Amsterdamse courant". Amsterdam, 14-03-1761. Accessed at Delpher 25-08-2017, http://resolver.kb.nl/resolve?urn=ddd:010708280:mpeg21:a0003.

242 RHC-GrA. SvSL, inv.no. 513, 2018 f. 696r-715r; The share of the debt that Groningen issued outside of the province was again described as 'foreign' (*buitenlands*), a description that was used in the account book of 1770 (RHC-GrA. SvSL, inv.no. 1993).

243 "Advertentie". "*Amsterdamse courant*". Amsterdam, 29-10-1785. Accessed at Delpher 15-09-2016, http://resolver.kb.nl/resolve?urn=ddd:010715969:mpeg21:a0011

244 RHC-GrA., Gilden 1317–1883 (1325), inv.no. 32a, f. 286r, 287v.

245 RHC-GrA., SvSL, inv.no. 2018, 490r-500r.

dam auction in 1711 shows that trust was low, even with the Generality's guarantee. A batch of thirty redeemable bonds sold at 25 per cent below par.[246] This resulted in a current yield of 6.7 per cent. History proved the investors right in their low level of confidence, as the States General defaulted in 1715.

As a consequence of Groningen's forced prioritisation of the Generality expenses, the debts issued under the latter's guarantee were traded at reasonable prices in Holland. In 1726, a 3 per cent Generality-guaranteed annuity yielded 3.2 per cent in Holland.[247] Similar rates applied in Amsterdam between the wars of the Spanish and Austrian Succession. Only in 1747 did prices drop. A 3 per cent guaranteed annuity sold at 29 per cent under par in Amsterdam: a current yield of 4.23 per cent.[248] In November of that same year, 3 per cent and 3.5 per cent annuities sold under par with current yields of 4.4–4.5 per cent. However, 1747 was a turbulent year because of the French invasion and the restoration of the Stadholderate. This pushed the market prices for all provincial bonds below par.[249] Given this uncertainty, a 4.5 per cent yield was not too bad.

Prices after 1750 indicate that Groningen's reputation improved. In 1764, a 2.5 per cent converted life annuity bond sold at 20 per cent below par. Although below par, the yield of 3.11 per cent was low. Groningen's Generality-guaranteed loans yielded less: 2.94 per cent.[250] At an auction in Utrecht in 1778, a Generality-guaranteed loan and a converted life annuity bond yielded almost identical rates of 2.93 per cent and 2.92 per cent respectively.[251] Although the yield of the converted bond declined, it was still above the offi-

246 Courtesy of Joost Jonker, Oscar Gelderblom and Christiaan van Bochove, who shared their work-in-progress on the Amsterdam auctions database with me.

247 A quotation of 93.375 per cent, to be precise: De Muinck, *Een regentenhuishouding omstreeks 1700*, 97: No such bonds were issued by Groningen at its own account. Hence, this must have been a Generality-guaranteed loan.

248 Courtesy of Joost Jonker, Oscar Gelderblom and Christiaan van Bochove, who shared their work-in-progress on the Amsterdam auctions database with me.

249 De Muinck probably follows Van Dillen, although there is no reference in the text. The figure match perfectly, however. De Muinck, *Een regentenhuishouding omstreeks 1700*, 97; In Van Dillen's representation of Van Tongerlo's price current, it was stated that these bonds were guaranteed by the Generality. Van Dillen, "Effectenkoersen," 13.

250 Courtesy of Joost Jonker, Oscar Gelderblom and Christiaan van Bochove, who shared their work-in-progress on the Amsterdam auctions database with me. There was no coupon in the data, so I based this upon the information about the coupons for the converted life annuities and the Generality loans as discussed above. The subsequent calculation is based on that assumption.

251 Het Utrechts Archief (hereafter HUA), inv.no. U247a017, notarial deed 53, 19 September 1778.

cial coupon of 2.5 per cent. Nevertheless, by the late 1770s, buyers deemed them as safe as the Generality-guaranteed loans. The few yields, however, confirm that Groningen's credit was restored. The level of less than 3 per cent was low by any early-modern standards and similar to those of Friesland and Zeeland.[252]

Groningen's external default turned out to be a blessing in disguise. Now that it was shut out from the Amsterdam capital market, it depended on the Generality for substantial loans. The Generality functioned as a buffer between Groningen and the Holland capital market. On the one hand, it offered Groningen the opportunity to tap into Holland's wealth through the back door. On the other hand, Groningen did not need to reach a settlement with the market. The States General and Stadholder fended off potential threats from creditors.

It was probably no coincidence that Holland invoked the Law of Reprisal when central powers were weakened. The Reform Statute eroded the Generality's power in 1749 and the Stadholder died in 1754. The Reform Statute also removed the legal provincial line of defence against external creditors; judges considered themselves independent of the political powerholders, the States of Groningen in this case. Bound by an oath, they would rule impartially, which would probably have favoured the Holland creditors.

For the Generality, Groningen's dependence came at the price of increased risk. If Groningen failed to pay, the Generality first had to tackle the problems itself. In this regard, the Generality defaults of 1715 and 1754 stand out. Meanwhile, Groningen used what was left of its domestic credit for the conversion of Holland-issued debt into domestically-held debt. This was what the limited capital supply of the domestic market could bear. For large loans, it relied on the Generality.

This came at a price. Groningen's say in its public finance became even more limited than it already was. But like the default, this turned out a blessing in disguise. The Generality forced Groningen to reimburse the debt, in combination with high taxes. The consequence was the lowest debt per capita of the four provinces discussed in this book. After 1750, the coupon rates dropped to levels similar to those in the other provinces.

Yet Groningen did not experience a classic financial revolution. The only condition it met of the criteria for a financial revolution was a transition to long-term debt in the 1620s. It was not credibly committed to the debt. The

252 Homer and Sylla, *History*; Epstein, *Freedom and Growth*, 20–22; Sussman and Yafeh, "Institutional Reforms, Financial Development and Sovereign Debt"; Velde and Weir, "Financial Market and Government Debt Policy in France."

debt remained consistently the smallest in size of the four provinces, including after correcting for population and income levels. Interest rates declined slowly, due to the limited local money supply. This made Groningen dependent on capital imports. Only after 1750 did the local capital supply increase and interest rates decline. Until then, Groningen depended on the Generality's authority, a dependence that proved beneficial in the long run.

5 Conclusion

The case of Groningen shows that centralisation had a positive effect on public finance. Taxes in Groningen equalled or exceeded those in Holland. This was the result of various interventions by the States General. The tax revolution imposed from above made borrowing largely redundant until 1665. From 1726, further tax increases were accompanied by a forced reduction in the debt of 45 per cent in about fifteen years. After 1750, the Generality again forced Groningen to reduce its debt, which it did, this time by some 35 per cent. As a result of the interventions, Groningen had a low debt-to-tax ratio, with high taxes and low debt. Groningen's per capita debt was the lowest of the four provinces analysed, even after correcting for income levels.

This is all the more remarkable because Groningen was the least economically developed of the four provinces. It had the lowest degree of urbanisation, it had no seaports or exporting industries and wage levels were 30 per cent lower than in Holland and Zeeland. Insofar as there was a capital market, it served local purposes well enough. Yet as the States of Groningen complained, money was scarce. This severely limited its options for domestic borrowing. The agricultural sector was the economic engine, and this sector only expanded after 1750. Long before this expansion began, Groningen was able to combine significant tax revenues with a low debt.

This was not thanks to its own merits; it was the result of central control. The City and Hinterlands notoriously disagreed with one another. With only one city, there was no urban system of control. Rather, the Hinterlands feared and resisted urban dominance. This also applied to taxation. The only thing they agreed on was their objection to payments for the common cause, be it contributions or interest payments. On such occasions, the States of Groningen emphasised backwardness, poverty and scarcity of money. The Generality then coerced the province into obedience and made it pay.

There was no classic financial revolution in Groningen. It was not committed to the debt. In Tomz's typology, Groningen would qualify as a lemon. Despite the low levels of debt, it still defaulted. The debt increases were not accompanied by declining coupon rates. Only after 1750 did the increasing local capital supply push down public interest rates. This again suggests that economic growth is necessary to form a savings pool for a financial revolution and that the causal direction is from growth to finance.

For creditors, the effects were mixed. It mattered, following Stasavage, who controlled the debt. They can be divided into three groups: domestic creditors, private external creditors, and the investors in Generality-guaranteed loans. Domestic debt formed a small portion of the total debt. These creditors received payments most consistently. The States of Groningen protected the domestic creditors' property rights. External private creditors suffered the most. First, they were hit by the default in the 1680s. Then the Generality and Stadholder protected Groningen against creditors' sanctions. Only a weakening of the central powers created space for a solution, after invoking the antiquated Law of Reprisal. Although the Generality subordinated the private creditors' interests, this was not enough to avoid problems. The States of Groningen prioritised the conversion of Holland-held debt into domestic debt over debt obligations with respect to the Generality. This second default by Groningen partly caused the Generality's default of 1715. The central control temporarily improved the debt service. However, the Generality fell victim yet again to incomplete payments by Groningen, leading to the Generality's second default in 1754. Again, creditors who had invested in Generality-guaranteed loans suffered from deficiencies in the debt service. Higher taxes coupled with external control created more certainty towards the end of the eighteenth century. Hence, the short-term effect was negative, and the long-term effect was ultimately positive.

The case demonstrates that internal borders mattered. The capital market was fragmented and primarily local. De Vries' and Van der Woude's assumption of one integrated Dutch economy does not hold, neither does Van Zanden and Van Riel's argument about free riding. In this case, the Generality prevented Groningen from doing just that. Still, this case confirms that stricter central control may have benefitted the Dutch Republic's finances as a whole.

CHAPTER 6

Conclusion

The Dutch Republic remains a fascinating case of a comparatively small and loose association of autonomous units that won its independence and became wealthy. Its Golden Age was finite and so was the independence of the Dutch Republic. The financial sector played a role in both its rise and fall, but less so than has been suggested. Until the Truce (1609–1621), loans were less important for financing the Dutch Revolt than tax revenues. The importance of a classical financial revolution is therefore smaller than sometimes suggested. Likewise, it was not a lack of enterprise that caused the decline, but a lack of domestic investment opportunities that drove eighteenth-century investors to risky foreign investments. In a similar way, the Dutch Republic's decentralised structure is considered vital in explaining both its rise and decline. This book shows, on the one hand, that fiscal decentralisation did not lead to low taxes. On the other hand, it argues that the decentralised structure did hamper capital flows within the Dutch Republic, varying over time. This book has explored how decentralisation affected public debt management, interest rates and capital flows over two centuries.

The capital flows from Holland to other parts of the country were limited and varied over time and per province. Until the late seventeenth century, there was limited need for other provinces to borrow in Holland. Zeeland raised money in its domestic market. Friesland and Groningen had small deficits and debts and regularly ran up arrears in their contributions to the Union. The wars of the late seventeenth century prompted Groningen and Friesland to turn to Holland for loans. Both defaulted on these loans. Creditors responded with credit rationing, refusing to lend money to defaulters, as the Friesland tax receiver Knock experienced in 1726. After 1750, rural economic growth increased the domestic capital supply in Friesland and Groningen. These provinces also returned to Holland's capital market but to a limited extent. A local savings pool was the main source of loans for Friesland and Groningen after 1760 and 1780 respectively. In this period, Zeeland increasingly turned to Holland's capital market. It did so because capital was even more abundant than in its domestic market. Hence, the need for borrowing in Holland depended largely on the local capital supply, which in turn depended on economic growth and previous capital accumulation.

Hence, the Dutch Republic's decentralised organisation shaped markets for public debt in two related ways, which explain the persistent interest rate

 | DOI:10.1163/9789004745254_007

differentials. First, the fiscal fragmentation resulted in differences in default risks. Second, the lack of integration of capital markets prevented the efficient distribution of funds. The latter was partly the economic effect of legal fragmentation – within provinces, private-market interest rate differentials persisted as well. As regards the public market, the fiscal and legal fragmentation were related. Investors could differentiate between debtors, ex-ante. Debtors could distinguish between creditors, ex-post. The former was the result of fiscal fragmentation. The latter was the consequence of legal fragmentation. This is in line with Chilosi's highlighting of legal fragmentation, rather than fiscal fragmentation. More importantly, the Dutch economy was not a single, uniform capital market, as De Vries and Van der Woude suspected.

The persistent differences in risk were reinforced with the strengthening of provincial autonomy after 1650–1651. The Great Assembly of 1651 eroded the power of central institutions to force unwilling member provinces to stay in line, if necessary. Although the States General had not exercised its powers often, it did when it considered action inevitable, for instance in Friesland in the 1630s. The disappearance of a credible threat to discipline individual provinces encouraged free riding and inadequate contributions to the common expenses.

However, the greater fiscal autonomy did not lead to lower tax burdens in the provinces outside of Holland. Rather, each province demanded similar contributions, or more, from their populations than Holland. Considering that the tax burden in Holland was high in an international perspective, this also applies to the other three provinces. Each province underwent a tax revolution, or first financial revolution, as Fritschy found in Holland. All four provinces hit tax ceilings in the late seventeenth and eighteenth centuries. From a tax perspective, there was no free riding to benefit from Holland's fiscal strength and no institutional impotence, contrary to Van Zanden and Van Riel's expectations.

The risk of default instead depended on population and economic growth, the variation in income levels and the provincial expenses. All these elements come together in the impact of the fixed distribution key of 1616. For every 100 guilders in Generality costs, each province contributed a fixed percentage. The aim was to allocate the contributions according to capacity. While that division remained fixed until 1792, the carrying capacity of the provinces changed.

This is first evident from the per capita contribution. Zeeland contributed the most per capita in 1616; Holland and Friesland the same and Groningen 80 per cent that of Holland. Different demographic growth rates changed these proportions. Holland's population grew most and for longest. As a result, the requested relative (per capita) contribution decreased compared to the other provinces. Zeeland stagnated first and for longest. The unfavourable starting position therefore only worsened. Until 1750, Friesland and Groningen too experienced increasing per capita contributions. But from the mid-eighteenth century their populations grew, while Holland's stagnated and shrank. As a result, the populations of Groningen, Friesland and Holland had returned to the relative proportions of 1616 by the end of the eighteenth century. In the meantime, Groningen and Friesland had consistently been required to pay a higher per capita contribution than Holland.

Wages were less dynamic but also indicated differences in economic power and fiscal carrying capacity. In each province, the growth of daily wages stagnated sometime between 1600 and 1640, so the differences persisted. Wages in Zeeland slightly exceeded those in Holland. In Friesland and Groningen, wage levels were 30 to 40 per cent less. Hence, to produce the same amount in tax revenues, people in Friesland and Groningen had to work longer.

The qualitative assessment of economic developments largely follows the demographic trends. In Holland, growth stagnated between the 1670s and 1760s but peaked in the late eighteenth century, although without renewed population growth. Friesland and Zeeland also experienced stagnation between the mid-seventeenth and mid-eighteenth centuries. Groningen suffered considerably from natural disasters such as floods. This probably caused the biggest economic contraction in that province, which was already the least commercialised of the four provinces. After 1750, the rural economy expanded in all provinces, though most significantly in Groningen and Friesland, which had the largest rural sectors.

Similarly, the degree of urbanisation stagnated or declined everywhere, indicating an economic slowdown. In Holland and Zeeland, more than half the population lived in towns. In Friesland and Groningen, this proportion was only one-third or a quarter. As a proxy for economic growth, urbanisation suggests a stark division between Holland and Zeeland on the one hand and Groningen and Friesland on the other. It also indicates little economic growth after the mid-seventeenth century. In Zeeland, colonial and other overseas connections prevented urban decline for most of the eighteenth century. The maritime sector and finance probably benefitted the most. The financial sector had a moderating effect on the economic decline; the Zeeland elite earned money through overseas investments, which was necessary to keep public finances in order through direct taxes. In Holland too, finance was a growth sector, although it is questionable whether it had a knock-on effect on other sectors of the domestic economy. Throughout the period, Holland's economy was the strongest and most resilient; after a dip, it peaked in the late eighteenth century. Holland's prolonged economic strength ensured this province could levy more easily than the other provinces.

Increasing the already high tax levels proved difficult without economic or demographic growth. This first affected income from the excises. As long as the economy expanded, these indirect taxes did as well. When economic growth slowed around the mid-seventeenth century, the excises hit a tax ceiling and direct taxes became more important. The relative importance of direct taxes differed between provinces. Direct taxes were most important in Zeeland and from an earlier stage than in the other provinces. In Holland, indirect taxes continued as the main source of income, which was made possible by continued economic strength. Zeeland and Holland could not increase direct taxes endlessly; financial capital was a moveable asset and capital flight was a real threat. In Friesland and Groningen, wealth taxes depended more on land and other fixed assets. Moreover, the expanding rural economy after 1750 made these taxes easier to bear, whereas Holland and Zeeland reached a second tax ceiling for wealth taxes. The relatively favourable economic and demographic developments made the per capita fiscal burden easier to bear for Holland's population than for the other provinces.

Failure to adjust contributions to the changing fiscal capacity increased inequality between provinces. This rigidity created an enormous public debt and interest burden in Zeeland, which it ultimately could not bear. Similarly, Friesland could no longer bear the interest burden in 1711. In both cases, the requested contributions to the war expenses were the problem, not an excessively low tax burden. The lack of adaptability to economic reality was a form of institutional sclerosis or institutional impotence.

Borrowing was the alternative to taxes to cover rising expenses. The question was whether this was a viable alternative for provinces other than Holland and whether they underwent a classic financial revolution like Holland did, as Fritschy suspected. Of the three other provinces discussed here, only Zeeland did. It was credibly committed to the debt and enjoyed decreasing coupon rates on a growing long-term debt. Groningen and Friesland did not experience a financial revolution. Most importantly, they were not credibly committed to the debt. They did not meet this precondition for decreasing interest rates, which would have allowed debt to increase at stable costs. Both provinces defaulted multiple times. Friesland did so in the 1630s, 1711 and around 1750; Groningen in the 1680s and 1715–1726.

More importantly, when defaulting Friesland and Groningen targeted creditors outside their provinces. They distinguished between creditors based on domicile and prioritised the domestic ones; these were external defaults. In both cases, the repeated designation of 'foreign' creditors also revealed their perception of that part of the debt. The unequal treatment based on this distinction was precisely the accusation that the States of Holland made against the States of Friesland. An administrative delay in interest payments to non-domestic creditors – but not domestic creditors – remained in place until the end of the eighteenth century. The distinction between creditors was only possible due to the fiscal and legal decentralisation within the Dutch Republic.

But Friesland and Groningen were not alone in prioritising their domestic creditors; each province, including Holland, disadvantaged creditors lending to the Generality. All prioritised their domestic provincial creditors. The Generality depended on provincial contributions for 80 per cent of its income. Moreover, after 1651 it lacked the means to enforce contributions. Without a central tax base or means of coercion, the Generality could not adequately service the debt. In 1715 and 1754, this caused a default by the Generality. By prioritising provincial domestic debt service, the provincial particularism violated the property rights of the Generality and its creditors. Without a solid tax basis, the central government's borrowing was vulnerable and risky.

This also shows the limitation of Holland's credible commitment to the debt. It could service its provincial debt more easily by outsourcing part of the debt to the States General. In this way, it increased its debt by 10 per cent during the War of the Spanish Succession without risking its reputation. This was the period when Holland gave greater priority to its debt and creditors and switched completely to voluntary loans. Until then, the debt management was not unproblematic. Earlier defaults in 1572, 1653 and 1672-1678 disadvantaged the domestic creditors, who did not receive repayments or received less interest. The diversification of the debt composition also indicates Holland's dependence on the market in this period. Hence, Holland's credible commitment relied on the additional credit of the Generality, which ultimately caused the latter to default.

Credible commitment depended not only on willingness to service and sustain the debt but also on the ability to do so. The four provinces' debts developed differently. Holland and Zeeland consistently had the highest per capita debts. More importantly, developments diverged in the eighteenth century. On balance, debts decreased in Groningen and Friesland and increased in Holland and Zeeland. In Groningen, debts peaked after the War of the Spanish Succession. In Friesland, the debt was highest after the War of the Austrian Succession. The debt in both provinces was lower in 1795 than in 1715. However, the public debt in Zeeland and Holland continued to rise, despite repayments after the Spanish and Austrian Wars of Succession. To reduce the burden of interest payments, Holland, Zeeland and Friesland used a withholding tax to cut effective coupons. Yet for Zeeland, this only applied to part of the debt; new issues were exempt and Zeeland depended entirely on the market. These three provinces also diversified their debts, using fixed-term annuities as well, whereas Groningen depended on Generality loans. The policies to manage the debt thus show similarities in debt and tax instruments, yet with varying outcomes.

Zeeland remained committed, even though its debt grew out of hand; the debt burden exceeded Holland's in terms of per capita wages and, after 1750, also in terms of the debt-to-tax ratio. Friesland's debt-to-tax ratio, however, was lower than Holland's when it defaulted in 1711. Groningen defaulted at even lower debt-to-tax ratios and with smaller debt levels measured in day wages. The Generality loans offered an escape without needing to come to terms with the market. But in Friesland's case, the default appears to have been out of necessity. The tax burden exceeded Holland's. The fixed share in the war expenses left Friesland insufficient room to sustain the debt. This was also the case for Zeeland. Yet unlike Friesland, Zeeland remained credibly committed to the debt.

The difference in commitment must be attributed to the difference in the representation of the debtholders in the respective representative assemblies. As such, the Frisian case sheds light on the assumed democratic advantage that supposedly reduces the default risk. Friesland was the most democratic province, having the most widely spread ballot rights. It was also a serial defaulter. The creditors who were not represented, the external ones, suffered first and most. The rural representatives managed to keep land taxes low despite rising land prices in the eighteenth century. Hence in the opposition between taxpayers and creditors, it mattered who was represented in the assembly, as Stasavage's distributive interpretation of the credible commitment thesis presumed. There was no impartial democratic advantage of a representative assembly for commitment to the debt.

The composition of the assembly mattered for the level of commitment, more than urbanisation. Commitment increased with the members' interest in the debt. Assemblies protected only the interests of their members and their constituencies, mainly the domestic investors. Urban elites in Holland and Zeeland dominated their provincial assemblies and were the largest holders of the domestic debt. In Groningen, the city was relatively overrepresented with half of the votes, whereas it only accounted for 20 to 30 per cent of the population and the economy. The Frisian towns had only a quarter of the votes and housed a comparable proportion of the population. Yet the agricultural sector formed about 40 per cent of the economy because the non-agricultural activities were not limited to official towns. Friesland and Groningen defaulted with respect to external creditors; those who were not represented in their assemblies suffered. Zeeland even remained committed to an unsustainable debt. The economic structure was similar to Friesland, where the rural economy accounted for less than half of the economy. However, as in Holland, the domestic capital market in Zeeland was deeper than in Friesland and Groningen. Consequently, domestic interests in servicing the debt were greater, as the debt was largely domestically held; the urban elites had their skin in the game. Representation of creditors in the assemblies thus strengthened the commitment to the debt. This protection did not go as far as Oosterlinck describes, with the power of the debtholders preventing a reduction in the coupon. So, a strong representation of the urban financial sector in assemblies increases credible commitment, reduces the risk of default and leads to lower interest rates.

The provincial States dealt with the capital market fragmentation and used this to their advantage whenever possible. Firstly, if the domestic market could not supply sufficient capital, or was too expensive, the provincial States turned to Holland's capital market. Each province held separate registers for external debt issues. Groningen started in the 1660s, Friesland in the 1690s and Zeeland in the 1750s. The separate registers for external debt are not watertight proof of the location of the debtholder. For instance, in the late eighteenth century, Amsterdam-issued Frisian debt was offered in Leeuwarden. Inheritances or marriages also blurred the distinction. Secondly, the separate registers eased selective defaults – and were indeed soon followed by such defaults in the cases of Friesland and Groningen. Thirdly, defaulters hid behind provincial borders, as external creditors had few options to enforce payments. Moreover, Friesland even forestalled retrading after the 1711 default. Fourthly, as soon as the provincial public finances allowed, a province would swap externally held debt for domestic debt, as Friesland and Groningen did after 1750 – the latter expressed the domestic provincial savings growth.

The prime motive for turning to Holland's capital market was thus the relative capital abundance and the low interest rates. In Groningen and Friesland, the private capital markets were functioning yet shallow. They provided sufficient capital to finance the local economy, but the demands from the provincial States exceeded that supply. Zeeland's capital supply was sufficient to finance the provincial public debt; the constant interest payments and reimbursements created a self-sustaining system that increased investors' wealth. This was similar to the situation in Holland. In the 1750s, Zeeland also turned to Holland, mainly by issuing lottery loans. This was intended to create leverage in the domestic market in order to lower interest rates rather than due to a lack of local supply.

However, investors only supplied capital as long as the debt was serviced. Defaulting provinces suffered from credit rationing, which they could circumvent with Generality loans or loans from Holland. The Dutch Republic's decentralised structure thus offered a political opt-out. It was beneficial for defaulters, but not for investors. The capital supply determined the issuance location, but the success of loan issues also depended on the issuers' reputation, especially the history of defaults.

Provincial public borrowing by the other provinces in Holland does not prove capital market integration. This is evident from the private market, where interest rate differentials persisted, even within provinces. The lowest rates were found in Holland and Zeeland; Groningen lagged behind. The further from Amsterdam, the higher the interest rates. Local domestic savings formed the source for private capital market transactions; this probably depended on local and personal networks. Insofar as markets were connected, this involved major trading centres such as Amsterdam and Middelburg, both of which were also connected to London. Moreover, cross-border credit was risky but not necessarily more expensive. There were legal and institutional problems with contract enforcement, as shown by the private Frisian case and the military solicitors' need for safeguards. Hence, not only did border effects hamper capital market integration, but so did the legal and financial infrastructure (as Van Zanden and Van Riel suspected).

Decentralisation also shaped secondary capital markets. As Neal suspects, there was not one central capital market. However, contrary to his expectation, the Republic's fragmentation did not prevent the emergence of a liquid secondary market for public debt. The problem was that the provincial States understood and frustrated its functioning when they encountered difficulties, as did Friesland in 1711. In all cases, the coupons and yields developed in parallel. On the one hand, this was because the provincial States depended on voluntary loans. On the other hand, creditors easily adapted to changes, most obviously seen from the influence of the withholding tax on bonds. The level of sophistication differed. In Holland and Zeeland, secondary market transactions appear to have been common. The importance for Friesland and Groningen remains unclear. Furthermore, the yields at different locations were roughly similar. For example, yields in Utrecht largely resembled those in Amsterdam and those in the issuing province. So the secondary market functioned well enough for the provinces to want to obstruct it deliberately for cross-border transactions.

Still, questions remain about the secondary market. First and foremost, why did the secondary market persist in Holland after 1672 and did the Holland district tax receivers still offer liquidity? Second, how was information transmitted given the scarcity of price lists, and why did they eventually emerge? Third, how common were auctions, and how representative of market prices? Fourth, who facilitated these market transactions and how?

The study of the provincial public finances and economies implies that Holland's development was exceptional. In the first place, long-term economic growth was unmatched, although the short-term pace of growth fluctuated. Economic growth expanded the savings pool, bolstering the financial sector and making borrowing cheaper in the sixteenth and seventeenth centuries. Later in the seventeenth century, the economic slowdown reinforced the downward trend interest rates. In the eighteenth century, Holland's financial sector was a growth sector. It facilitated a large provincial debt at low costs, especially in the eighteenth century. The supply of private capital was unprecedented, generated first from economic growth, later from returns on previously accumulated capital, including government debt. This income included returns on investments in foreign and other provincial debts, which yielded net profits despite defaults. Holland's urban centres remained central, although the importance of agriculture increased again after 1750. As a result, indirect taxes yielded relatively high revenues and the direct taxes were less of a burden on the many rich people in Holland. The Dutch elite preferred to finance the state in the eighteenth century in the form of loans rather than extra direct taxes. This was in contrast to Great Britain, around 1800, where taxes were increased with a similarly high debt-to-GDP ratio. Loans were of course more attractive to the ruling urban elites than higher direct taxes, because this provided them with interest income. The rich in Holland were not taxed to the maximum, because of the real risk of capital flight. This was possible again due to the continued growth in all periods. This was not the case in Zeeland, Friesland and Groningen. In each of these three cases, economic growth slowed down and each province encountered fiscal difficulties; Friesland and Groningen actually defaulted, and Zeeland only narrowly escaped a default. Holland's persistently strong economy enabled it to weather fiscal crises more easily and protect the interests of its ruling elites and its financiers. The abundance of capital helped to quickly resolve disruptions such as those in 1653 and 1672, including the structural interest rate reductions through the tax on bonds. This was a delicate balancing act designed to lower the effective interest rate without ruining its credit. The large domestic savings pool and persistent economic growth helped Holland, which means its development is unrepresentative for the Dutch Republic as a whole.

Finally, the counterfactual case of Groningen offers the opportunity to assess whether the lack of centralisation was a missed opportunity. It focuses on a comparison with Friesland, which was closest in various respects, not only geographically. Unlike in Holland and Zeeland, the urban centres did not dominate the provincial States. The degree of urbanisation was also substantially lower. Neither province experienced a financial revolution, nor could they build on medieval experiences or fiscal institutions. Even without a classic financial revolution, debts increased in Friesland and Groningen. The selective defaults limited their debt expansion in the eighteenth century: Friesland and Groningen suffered from credit rationing in Holland. However, the Generality loans offered creditors a back door to Holland's capital market in each case. This provides two lessons about the potential benefit of centralisation, one about long-term fiscal health and the other about contract enforcement. First, central surveillance resulted in healthy public finances; a high tax burden and forced reimbursements ensured Groningen had the smallest per capita debt. Second, Groningen did not need to come to terms with the market because of the active protection by central institutions after its default. Creditors received satisfaction when that protection was lost and the law was impartially enforced. Although the outcomes for Groningen were slightly more favourable, the differences with Friesland were marginal; economic growth improved the fiscal situation after 1750 in each case, with a reduced tax burden and a declining debt burden. Centralisation does not seem to have been a remedy that could have prevented the downfall of the Republic.

Economic growth was the driver of fiscal improvements in Friesland and Groningen after 1750, as it had in Holland and Zeeland in the late Middle Ages and the sixteenth and early seventeenth centuries. Economic growth expanded the tax base and the private savings pools. During or before the expansion, capital imports covered part of the fiscal deficits, with the provinces benefitting from capital abundance elsewhere. These imports at best accelerated rudimentary growth; a sophisticated financial sector was not a precondition for growth. The capital imports had a downside. Inadequate external debt service caused difficulties, as Holland, Groningen and Friesland experienced. The most positive impact of capital imports is perhaps an indirect learning effect in the disciplinary consequences of previous external defaults. This encouraged a focus on the local capital market. It highlights the importance of the domestic capital supply and the Republic's internal borders. Still, a large domestic savings pool had to be replenished to prevent draining. Without economic growth, public debt could not be increased indefinitely, as Zeeland discovered. In Friesland and Groningen, economic growth enabled the public debt to be reduced after 1750; in Holland, limited economic growth sustained the debt expansion, although public debt growth outpaced economic growth after 1670. Hence, the sustainability of the debt depended largely on persistent economic growth, something which only Holland experienced. Regarding the finance-growth nexus, finance followed growth.

A strong financial sector nevertheless had positive effects. In Holland and Zeeland, the financial revolution catalysed the initial growth and the financial sector reinforced the economy later. In Holland, it was one of the drivers of economic growth in the eighteenth century. In Zeeland, it dampened economic decline yet could not engineer renewed growth. The positive effects of a well-developed financial sector remained during the eighteenth century.

A financial revolution and commitment to the debt were insufficient to prevent economic stagnation or a default. Strong urban representation increased commitment to the domestic debt. However, even if the representative assembly served the interests of the debtholders, the full service of the debt depended on the state of the economy. Without economic growth, debt growth was finite, regardless of the assembly's commitment.

The state of the economy also determined the effect and visibility of the Republic's internal legal and political borders. They became less visible and had less impact when the economic tide was high and resurfaced at economic low tide. Economic growth was not driven by capital imports, but was emerging domestically within the local context and institutions. Eventually, capital imports led to long-lasting selective defaults rather than growth. Imports and defaults are also related to the economic cycle. First, economic growth increased Holland's capital surplus. Because of that abundance, internal borders did not seem to be an obstacle to capital exports. Then the economic slowdown further stimulated capital movement; a lack of domestic demand meant excess capital sought an outlet, to other provinces and abroad in sovereign loans and colonial projects like the VOC. At the same time, economic stagnation made servicing that growing debt more difficult and increased the risk of defaults. Then internal borders resurfaced and became relevant obstacles for contract enforcement. When the economy picked up after 1750, capital exports started again. Thus, capital flows followed the economic cycle.

To summarise, borders mattered. The introduction promised to show how, when and why. Borders restricted capital flows, which caused an incomplete integration of capital markets. This was most evident during the economic stagnation between the 1670s and 1750s. Legal borders resulted in a lack of contract enforcement. This limited power to enforce payment across borders applied to both private parties and the provincial States. As a result, the geographical limitations of legal and political competencies formed the frontiers to economic and financial integration, limiting financial institutions' scope. The Republic's borders were not administrative remnants but formed an economic reality separating markets. Consequently, the Republic's internal borders functioned as frontiers of finance.

Appendix: Reconstruction of Groningen's Debt, Interest and Reimbursements

Groningen's bookkeeping practice of grouping interest payments and reimbursements made it difficult to reconstruct Groningen's debt and interest payments.[1] The two components could only be distinguished at the level of the individual transactions. The core problem is that these are different kinds of payments. Interest is a cost, repayment is not; if the province were a company, debt would be considered a liability in the balance sheet, and interest payments would be considered a cost in the income statement. Similarly, loans are income but not revenue, and repayments are payments, not costs. Repayment reduces the public debt and reduces the claim of creditors on the debtor. This has consequences for three related aspects of the analysis of Groningen's public finances: debt reconstruction, government budget balances and ultimately debt sustainability.

The grouping of interest payments and reimbursements had different consequences for analysing the three aspects of Groningen's public finance. First, it makes estimates of the debt more difficult. On the one hand, this prevents debt estimates by dividing the payment by the coupon. On the other hand, it makes it unclear how large the repayment is, and therefore by how much the debt is reduced. Second, it creates uncertainty about the financial health. If rising payments consist largely of repayment, the debt decreases, which points to a surplus on the government budget balance. If rising payments consist largely of interest, this indicates a rising debt, assuming a stable coupon. In that case, this points to deficits in government budget balances. The same amount in the combined expense item thus can easily imply opposite effects in Groningen's fiscal health and debt sustainability.

In my PhD dissertation, I remedied this for 1650–1795 by interpolating point estimates of the debt from contemporary reports. In this book, I have improved these estimates and extended the period covered to the earliest possible moment, 1624–1626. The present reconstruction also offers an estimate of the

1 Van der Ent and Enthoven, *Gewestelijke financiën: vol. 3 Groningen*, 77, 91–95; Only on the level of individual transactions was this distinction made. Solving this problem by working from archival materials would require us to enter every single payment made to each creditor, since even totals per loan or per year are lacking. This was considered too laborious for the purpose of this thesis.

 | DOI:10.1163/9789004745254_008

annual interest payments. This allows me to reconstruct the fiscal balances and total expenses, which had until now been missing this expense item.

To estimate the interest payments, I relied on two methods depending on the period. For each period, I took the debt estimates as the point of departure. In the period up to the 1660s, the debt uniformly consisted of provincial redeemable annuities. For the first period, until 1677, I took the debt estimates of 1650 as the starting point. A detailed overview of the debt in 1677 provided a solid indication of the composition of the debt. For the second period, after 1677, I combined and distinguished between the main components; the Generality became Groningen's main creditor, which yielded a clear overview for most of the eighteenth century. The smaller, provincial, part of the debt proved harder to estimate, as explained below. The total amounts paid to creditors formed the upper boundary, even if the estimated interest due exceeded it.

Only from 1626 onwards are new loans explicitly and systematically included in the accounts of the Receiver-General, as income. Although interest payments were mentioned from 1617 onwards, this was inconsistent and possibly included repayments.[2] In later overviews, there is often a category of "old interest", the series of which begins in 1626.[3]

In 1650, Groningen paid 14,821 guilders in interest. This is the first year for which I retrieved data on debt and interest from the archive. The debt consisted entirely of redeemable annuities. The corresponding debt amounted to 305,464 guilders. According to the source publications of the Provincial Finances of the Dutch Republic 1572–1795 (*Gewestelijke Financiën*), Groningen issued a total of 438,619 guilders in debt in the period 1624–1650. This means that at least 133,000 guilders were repaid in this period. In order to obtain a well-substantiated indication of the debt history, I worked backwards from 1650. To this end, I compared two alternative methods. First, I multiplied the amounts paid by the applicable coupon interest. Second, I analysed whether deviations compared to the surrounding years were explained by loans or repayments. I then corrected the estimated debt for these amounts. I then assumed that the remaining deviations represented repayments. I determined the amount of the repayment by considering the amounts in the surrounding years, the year before and the year after, as interest payments. I then took the difference with respect to the intervening year as the repayment. I subtracted that estimated repayment amount from the debt estimated at that time. Such corrections often coincided with new loans, which indicates conversions.

2 Van der Ent and Enthoven, 285.

3 E.g.: RHC-GrA, inv. 513, 2801, 2802

Similarly, I interpolated to the next reference year, 1664. That was the last year before the First Münster War (1665–1667). In 1664 the debt amounted to 944,103 guilders, with interest of 37,764 guilders. That equals a debt growth of almost 640,000 guilders. According to the *Gewestelijke Financiën*, Groningen issued 455,000 guilders in new debt between 1650 and 1664. That is an underestimation of the actual borrowed amounts of 185,000 guilders. Therefore I have taken the course of the total payments as debt service as the starting point for the debt development.

The 1660s and 1670s formed a transition period. The debt diversified and expanded substantially. In the years 1665–1669, Groningen borrowed 1,871,843 guilders. As a result, the debt rose to 2,815,946 guilders. Of that new debt in 1665–1669, 962,000 guilders remained in 1677 and of the debts up to and including 1664, 852,000; a total of 1,814,000 guilders. This means that approximately[4] one million guilders had to be repaid between 1670 and 1677.

The repayments must have largely been made in 1670. From 1672 onwards, Groningen had to borrow money to pay the war costs due to the Second Münster War. In 1670, Groningen paid 982,532 guilders in interest and repayments combined. Groningen also borrowed 58,500 guilders at 4 per cent in 1669 or 1670, depending on the source used (1670 according to GF, 1669 according to Archive overview 1677–1678). This must have been used to repay the more expensive loans at 4.5 per cent in 1666–1669. However, with the newly incurred debts, the interest obligations on the annuities also rose to 120,000 guilders. In the years 1665–1669, Groningen paid less interest than due, each year. Before repayment could be made, the arrears had to be paid first. Correcting for the arrears in repayments and annuity payments, 717,000 guilders remained for repayment. In 1671, too, the actual payment of interest and repayment exceeded the interest due by more than 100,000 guilders. The amount in loans registered in 1669 is incomplete. In 1677, a higher amount was registered for this date.[5] Therefore I accept the amount from the 1677 report as the most accurate estimate of the debt in 1669.

Between the First and Second Münster Wars, Groningen reimbursed part of the debt incurred. But first, it had to pay the overdue interest. Based on the actual debt service paid, I calculated the arrears in the period 1665–1672. Table 1 summarises the development of the cumulative arrears and room for reimbursements.

4 RHC-GrA, inv. 2801.

5 RHC, inv. 2801

TABLE 1 Cumulative arrears and reimbursements (Groningen), 1665–1672.

	Interest payable	Paid	Overdue interest (cumulative)	Reimbursement
1665	60,886	45,765	15,121	
1666	99,326	52,651	61,796	
1667	114,620	45,926	130,490	
1668	114,867	231,834	13,523	
1669	118,815	105,938	26,401	
1670	121,155	864,309	–	–716,753
1671	78,954	182,744	–	–103,791
1672	82,534	82,197	337	

SOURCES: RHC-GRA, INV. 1887, 2801; VAN DER ENT AND ENTHOVEN, *GEWESTELIJK FINANCIËN VOL. 3 GRONINGEN*, P. 360.

From the 1690s, most of Groningen's debt consisted of Generality debt. A specified overview of the debt development, from 1726 to 1795, offered valuable insights into the composition of the debt service. First, it enabled a distinction between interest payments and reimbursements of this major part of the debt. Second, a smaller residue was left for the provincial debt service after subtracting the interest payments and mandatory reimbursements from the total debt service. This concerned life annuities and redeemable annuities. Both consisted of domestic and Holland-issued debt.

The payments of the Holland-issued life annuities were largely halted in the 1680s. An overview from 1731 provides information on these interest payments. The interest paid on the domestically-issued life annuities proved harder to estimate. This depended on the individual nature of the contract, based on the deaths of the individual nominees. Therefore, I applied interpolations of the average percentage of the actual interest paid over the life annuities. To that end, I divided the amount of interest paid by the life annuities in a known year. I did the same for the next year for which data was available. Then I interpolated these percentages and multiplied them by the debt estimates to arrive at the amounts of interest paid in the intermediate years.

Finally, there were but small margins to service the provincial redeemable annuities until the 1740s. When applying the going rates of interest to the estimated debt, the debt charges met or even exceeded the available residues from the total actual payments. This implies that Groningen had to borrow additional sums to cover all interest expenses, which it did. In 1731, the interest was given for each loan separately. From 1739, Groningen borrowed domestically at 4per cent, and at 3 per cent in the 1780s.[6] To estimate the interest payments for most of the eighteenth century, I multiplied the estimated debt by the coupon.

TABLE 2 Groningen's debt estimates, total and per capita

Year	Total debt	Per capita debt	Interest
1627	193,313	2	15,465
1628	273,313	3	19,132
1629	408,663	5	24,520
1630	490,404	6	29,424
1631	410,999	5	24,660
1632	384,968	5	23,098
1633	363,435	4	21,806
1634	363,435	4	21,806
1635	355,352	4	21,321
1636	355,352	4	21,321
1637	361,114	4	21,667
1638	358,074	4	21,484
1639	358,074	4	21,484
1640	362,624	4	21,757
1641	369,424	5	22,165
1642	366,652	4	21,999
1643	270,650	3	16,239
1644	310,219	4	18,613
1645	302,264	4	18,136
1646	302,264	4	18,136
1647	302,264	4	18,136
1648	305,464	4	18,328
1649	305,464	4	18,328
1650	305,464	4	15,273
1651	305,464	4	15,273
1652	305,464	4	15,195
1653	355,464	4	17,695
1654	500,464	6	24,945

6 RHC-GrA, inv.no. 513 and 1984.

TABLE 2 Groningen's debt estimates, total and per capita (*cont.*)

Year	Total debt	Per capita debt	Interest
1655	577,464	7	28,795
1656	600,464	7	29,945
1657	600,464	7	29,945
1658	760,464	9	37,910
1659	760,464	9	30,328
1660	760,464	9	30,298
1661	760,464	9	30,298
1662	760,464	9	30,298
1663	760,464	9	30,298
1664	944,103	11	37,764
1665	1,522,153	18	60,886
1666	2,607,437	32	106,936
1667	3,166,924	38	122,231
1668	3,284,303	40	122,579
1669	3,972,175	48	112,907
1670	3,285,922	40	85,521
1671	3,437,881	42	90,557
1672	3,579,305	43	94,138
1673	3,728,414	45	121,111
1674	3,691,677	45	122,611
1675	3,765,577	46	124,084
1676	3,745,211	46	100,007
1677	3,730,851	46	107,675
1678	3,683,128	45	101,523
1679	3,640,116	45	112,070
1680	3,596,345	44	112,340
1681	3,594,622	44	102,457
1682	3,564,530	44	101,968
1683	3,535,100	44	100,438
1684	3,411,302	43	100,778
1685	2,901,375	36	99,730
1686	2,851,611	36	97,957
1687	2,745,131	34	96,021
1688	2,659,761	33	96,319
1689	2,592,587	33	96,707
1690	2,596,217	33	99,040

TABLE 2 Groningen's debt estimates, total and per capita (*cont.*)

Year	Total debt	Per capita debt	Interest
1691	2,627,147	33	98,419
1692	2,746,377	35	100,551
1693	2,758,711	35	100,007
1694	2,791,607	36	97,943
1695	2,975,243	38	125,515
1696	2,976,883	38	100,995
1697	3,026,381	39	100,884
1698	3,004,833	39	100,517
1699	3,056,433	39	100,050
1700	3,078,773	40	97,889
1701	3,109,162	40	92,841
1702	3,598,044	47	122,420
1703	3,926,642	51	119,879
1704	4,541,085	59	143,195
1705	5,114,521	67	161,661
1706	5,592,731	73	179,972
1707	6,675,309	88	197,088
1708	7,301,095	96	239,836
1709	8,037,067	106	219,591
1710	8,881,772	118	235,633
1711	9,673,471	128	87,000
1712	10,539,677	138	86,233
1713	11,108,728	144	85,147
1714	11,021,889	142	84,718
1715	10,954,121	141	83,994
1716	10,740,845	140	82,986
1717	10,490,826	136	81,945
1718	10,406,071	142	80,914
1719	9,823,082	138	79,974
1720	9,756,290	143	79,157
1721	9,579,176	140	79,568
1722	9,375,241	140	78,988
1723	9,139,419	140	78,005
1724	8,948,343	140	77,064
1725	8,733,076	141	76,590

TABLE 2 Groningen's debt estimates, total and per capita (*cont.*)

Year	Total debt	Per capita debt	Interest
1726	9,451,476	151	76,712
1727	9,212,225	144	76,037
1728	8,959,460	136	75,146
1729	8,714,469	129	74,339
1730	8,437,451	122	91,765
1731	8,240,018	117	76,017
1732	7,996,056	111	90,951
1733	7,746,773	105	91,147
1734	7,488,173	100	91,345
1735	7,228,096	98	91,544
1736	6,960,046	95	91,745
1737	6,826,960	95	91,947
1738	6,694,628	92	92,151
1739	6,547,728	89	73,565
1740	6,406,074	86	73,730
1741	6,261,657	84	73,897
1742	6,194,429	86	74,064
1743	6,127,285	90	74,233
1744	6,352,528	97	74,403
1745	6,309,549	100	74,574
1746	6,261,624	106	74,747
1747	6,616,297	117	74,920
1748	6,563,365	121	74,775
1749	6,517,112	118	74,951
1750	8,570,923	144	75,128
1751	8,524,427	141	75,306
1752	8,427,840	138	75,486
1753	8,780,598	140	75,667
1754	8,720,939	138	75,849
1755	8,661,095	137	76,032
1756	8,600,686	134	76,216
1757	8,535,775	131	76,402
1758	8,469,093	128	76,589
1759	8,405,670	125	76,777
1760	8,337,087	124	76,966
1761	8,839,742	130	100,034

TABLE 2 Groningen's debt estimates, total and per capita (*cont.*)

Year	Total debt	Per capita debt	Interest
1762	8,800,007	129	101,487
1763	8,754,192	127	102,776
1764	8,674,887	122	102,776
1765	8,593,197	117	102,776
1766	8,509,467	113	102,776
1767	8,357,006	110	102,776
1768	8,266,641	109	102,776
1769	8,173,928	107	102,776
1770	8,078,970	105	102,776
1771	7,893,175	102	102,776
1772	7,702,506	99	102,776
1773	7,595,582	94	102,776
1774	7,487,989	84	102,776
1775	6,632,441	71	102,776
1776	6,496,459	69	102,776
1777	6,055,839	64	102,744
1778	5,902,352	61	102,712
1779	5,744,216	59	102,681
1780	5,580,769	57	102,650
1781	5,473,705	55	76,965
1782	5,685,921	57	82,122
1783	5,856,743	58	87,064
1784	6,019,756	59	91,747
1785	6,103,282	60	94,158
1786	6,226,393	61	95,095
1787	6,557,584	64	104,930
1788	6,947,072	67	116,210
1789	7,388,594	71	129,146
1790	7,881,776	76	143,980
1791	8,446,233	81	160,992
1792	9,138,918	87	210,584
1793	9,893,144	93	236,686
1794	7,144,355	67	140,552
1795	9,998,099	94	206,083
1796	12,851,670	120	291,693

SOURCE: FEENSTRA, BETWEEN SHARED, APPENDIX.

TABLE 3 List of newspapers in the database

Name of the newspaper	Number of advertisements per newspaper, per date
Amsterdamse Courant	288
1696-9-4	1
1696-9-8	1
1697-5-18	1
1697-5-21	1
1697-9-21	1
1697-9-26	1
1698-5-3	1
1699-5-14	1
1699-5-16	1
1700-5-29	1
1700-6-3	1
1700-6-5	1
1700-10-26	1
1700-10-28	1
1700-12-14	1
1701-4-23	1
1701-5-17	1
1701-9-10	1
1701-9-13	1
1701-9-22	1
1702-4-4	1
1702-4-20	1
1702-4-22	1
1702-8-5	1
1702-9-5	1
1703-6-23	1
1703-8-30	1
1704-5-10	1
1704-5-13	1
1704-8-30	1
1704-10-7	1
1704-11-25	1
1704-11-27	1
1705-3-24	1

TABLE 3 List of newspapers in the database (*cont.*)

Name of the newspaper	Number of advertisements per newspaper, per date
1705-4-18	1
1705-8-6	1
1705-8-29	1
1706-1-21	1
1706-4-13	1
1706-6-24	1
1706-8-17	1
1707-4-21	1
1707-9-3	1
1708-1-14	1
1708-5-1	1
1708-5-31	1
1708-8-21	1
1709-3-28	1
1709-3-30	1
1709-4-20	1
1709-8-22	1
1709-9-17	1
1709-12-28	1
1709-12-31	1
1710-3-18	1
1710-3-25	1
1710-4-19	1
1710-8-21	1
1711-5-2	1
1714-5-1	1
1714-5-3	1
1719-4-11	1
1719-4-15	1
1720-3-12	1
1720-3-14	1
1721-6-3	1
1721-7-3	1
1721-7-5	1
1721-8-26	1

TABLE 3 List of newspapers in the database (*cont.*)

Name of the newspaper	Number of advertisements per newspaper, per date
1722-4-25	1
1723-6-29	1
1723-7-1	1
1723-10-14	1
1723-10-16	1
1724-8-8	1
1724-8-10	1
1725-8-7	1
1725-8-9	1
1726-7-2	1
1726-7-4	1
1726-9-7	1
1727-7-24	1
1728-7-13	1
1728-7-15	1
1728-7-20	1
1728-7-22	1
1729-7-5	1
1729-7-9	1
1729-8-18	1
1730-7-18	1
1730-7-20	1
1730-8-22	1
1731-6-19	1
1731-6-21	1
1731-8-11	1
1732-7-8	1
1732-7-10	1
1732-8-5	1
1732-8-7	1
1733-7-16	1
1733-8-1	1
1734-7-27	2
1734-7-29	2
1735-8-2	1

TABLE 3 List of newspapers in the database (*cont.*)

Name of the newspaper	Number of advertisements per newspaper, per date
1735-8-4	1
1735-8-6	1
1735-8-9	1
1736-7-31	1
1736-8-4	1
1736-8-7	1
1736-8-9	1
1737-7-30	1
1737-8-1	1
1737-8-8	1
1738-7-31	1
1738-8-2	1
1738-8-5	1
1739-8-8	1
1739-8-11	1
1740-7-23	1
1740-8-13	1
1741-8-3	1
1741-8-10	1
1742-7-28	1
1742-8-4	1
1742-8-7	1
1743-8-1	1
1743-8-3	1
1743-8-8	1
1744-7-30	1
1744-8-1	1
1744-8-22	1
1745-7-27	1
1745-8-21	1
1746-7-28	1
1746-7-30	1
1746-8-2	1
1747-7-27	1
1747-7-29	1

TABLE 3 List of newspapers in the database (*cont.*)

Name of the newspaper	Number of advertisements per newspaper, per date
1747-9-2	1
1751-7-31	1
1751-8-3	1
1751-8-5	1
1751-9-4	1
1752-7-15	1
1752-7-18	1
1752-7-20	1
1752-8-1	1
1753-3-28	1
1753-7-24	1
1753-7-26	1
1753-7-28	1
1754-7-30	1
1754-8-3	1
1754-8-6	1
1754-8-15	1
1755-7-26	1
1755-7-29	1
1755-9-25	1
1756-7-22	1
1756-7-24	1
1756-7-27	1
1756-9-18	1
1757-7-21	1
1757-7-23	2
1757-9-22	1
1758-7-25	1
1758-7-27	1
1758-8-1	1
1758-9-14	1
1759-7-24	1
1759-7-28	1
1759-8-2	1
1759-9-13	1

TABLE 3 List of newspapers in the database (*cont.*)

Name of the newspaper	Number of advertisements per newspaper, per date
1760-8-14	1
1760-9-11	1
1761-8-6	1
1761-8-8	1
1761-8-27	1
1762-7-29	1
1762-8-3	1
1762-9-9	1
1763-7-28	1
1763-8-2	1
1763-8-18	1
1764-7-26	1
1764-7-31	1
1764-8-2	1
1764-9-6	1
1765-7-27	1
1765-8-1	1
1765-8-8	1
1765-8-29	1
1766-8-2	1
1766-8-7	1
1766-8-19	1
1767-7-30	1
1767-8-1	1
1767-7-1	1
1767-8-4	1
1767-8-7	1
1768-2-18	1
1768-7-21	1
1768-7-26	1
1768-7-28	1
1768-8-4	1
1769-7-18	1
1769-7-25	1
1769-8-1	1

TABLE 3 List of newspapers in the database (*cont.*)

Name of the newspaper	Number of advertisements per newspaper, per date
1770-7-26	1
1770-7-28	1
1770-7-31	1
1770-8-4	1
1771-7-18	1
1771-7-25	1
1771-7-27	1
1771-8-1	1
1772-7-23	1
1772-7-25	1
1772-7-28	2
1773-7-22	1
1773-7-27	1
1773-7-31	1
1774-7-19	1
1774-7-21	1
1774-7-26	2
1775-7-13	1
1775-7-22	1
1775-7-25	2
1776-7-27	2
1777-7-17	1
1777-7-19	1
1777-7-23	1
1777-7-29	1
1778-7-23	1
1778-7-28	1
1779-7-13	1
1779-7-22	1
1779-7-29	1
1779-7-31	1
1780-7-18	1
1780-7-29	1
1781-7-17	1
1781-8-2	1

TABLE 3 List of newspapers in the database (*cont.*)

Name of the newspaper	Number of advertisements per newspaper, per date
1781-9-6	1
1782-7-23	1
1782-7-27	2
1783-7-19	1
1783-7-22	1
1783-7-24	1
1783-8-2	1
1784-8-3	1
1784-8-5	1
1785-7-23	1
1785-7-26	1
1785-7-28	1
1786-7-27	1
1786-7-29	1
1786-8-5	1
1787-7-28	2
1788-7-26	1
1789-7-30	1
1790-7-31	1
1791-7-30	2
1792-7-28	1
1792-9-1	1
1793-7-30	2
1794-7-31	2
1795-4-11	1
1795-4-16	1
1795-8-1	1
1797-7-27	1
1797-7-29	1
1798-8-4	1
1799-8-1	1
1800-8-2	1
Haarlemse Courant	**4**
1776-7-30	1
1795-4-11	1

TABLE 3 List of newspapers in the database (*cont.*)

Name of the newspaper	Number of advertisements per newspaper, per date
1795-4-14	1
1799-8-3	1
Haerlemse Courante	**5**
1768-10-21	1
1768-11-22	1
1775-12-5	1
1778-12-1	1
1779-12-14	1
Leydse courant	**1**
1769-1-30	1
Oprechte Haerlemsche courant	**47**
1700-12-14	1
1705-8-19	1
1705-8-29	1
1706-4-15	1
1706-8-19	1
1707-4-21	1
1707-7-23	1
1707-9-3	1
1708-8-23	1
1709-4-18	1
1709-8-22	1
1710-4-19	1
1711-5-2	1
1711-5-5	1
1714-5-1	1
1714-8-25	1
1721-8-26	1
1769-1-26	1
1769-6-6	1
1770-5-29	1
1770-11-27	1
1771-5-28	1
1771-11-26	1
1774-7-28	1

TABLE 3 List of newspapers in the database (*cont.*)

Name of the newspaper	Number of advertisements per newspaper, per date
1774-11-12	1
1777-8-2	1
1778-7-28	1
1780-8-1	1
1782-7-30	1
1784-7-31	1
1784-11-23	1
1787-7-31	1
1787-11-27	1
1788-7-29	1
1788-11-11	1
1789-8-1	1
1790-7-31	1
1791-7-30	2
1792-7-31	1
1792-9-4	2
1794-8-2	2
1795-8-4	1
1796-7-30	1
1800-8-2	1
Oprechte Leydse courant	2
1705-8-29	1
1710-4-19	1
Grand total	**347**

SOURCE: DELPHER: www.delpher.nl/.

Bibliography

Primary Sources

www.delpher.nl, newspaper database (*insofar as not in the appendix*)

Amsterdamse courant, 07-02-1708.
Amsterdamse courant, 18-03-1710.
Amsterdamse courant, 31-07-1751.
Amsterdamse courant, 03-08-1751.
Amsterdamse courant, 05-08-1751.
Amsterdamse courant, 04-09-1751.
Amsterdamse courant, 01-01-1752.
Amsterdamse courant, 09-08-1753.
Amsterdamse courant, 20-12-1763.
Amsterdamse courant, 28-07-1772.
Amsterdamse courant, 09-03-1775.
Amsterdamse courant, 19-03-1782.
Amsterdamse courant, 30-03-1782.
Amsterdamse courant, 13-04-1782.
Amsterdamse courant. 25-06-1789.
Amsterdamse courant, 27-07-1782.
Amsterdamse courant, 29-04-1783.
Amsterdamse courant, 01-08-1795.
Haerlemse courante, 18-02-1768.
Haerlemse courante, 22-11-1768.
Haarlemse Courant, 25-07-1775.
Hof courant, 15-08-1789.
Hollandsche historische courant, 06-05-1779.
Hollandsche historische courant, 11-04-1782.
Leeuwarder courant, 18-05-1782.
Leydse courant, 19-01-1750.
Leydse courant, 18-07-1774.
Leydse courant, 08-08-1774.
Middelburgsche courant, 28-06-1777.
Oprechte Haerlemsche courant, 01-05-1714.
Oprechte Haerlemsche courant, 26-01-1769.
Oprechte Haerlemsche courant, 28-07-1774.
Oprechte Haerlemsche courant, 02-08-1774.
Oprechte Haerlemsche courant, 04-08-1774.

Oprechte Haerlemsche courant, 29-12-1774.
Oprechte Haerlemsche courant, 11-04-1782.
Oprechte Haerlemsche courant, 04-09-1792.
Oprechte Haarlemse courant, 18-03-1797.
Opregte Leydse courant, 21-04-1710.

Het Utrechts Archief (*HUA*)

Notarissen in de stad Utrecht 1560–1905 (34–4)

Historisch Centrum Leeuwarden (*HLC*)

Archief van de stad Leeuwarden, 1426–1811, (1001)

Krantendatabank Zeeland

http://www.krantenbankzeeland.nl/periodicals/mco
Middelburgsche Courant, d.d.
10 May, 7 June, 24 June, 1 and 3 July, 8 August, 9, 18 and 21 November 1758
29 May, 19 June, 4 September, 23 October, 1 and 27 November, 13 December 1759
19 February 1760, 21 February, 21 April 1761
7 July 1763
18 and 21 October 1766
13 November 1770
21 April, 18 August 1772
18 August, 26 and 28, 30 December 1775
27 June 1776
28 January 1777
5 March, 14 August, 27 November 1784
21 July 1785

Nationaal archief, Den Haag (*NL-NA*)

Anthonie van der Heim, (1710) 1737–1746 (3.01.22)
Gedeputeerde Haarlem (3.01.09)
jhr. J. Goldberg [levensjaren 1763–1828], (1482) 1795–1827 (2.21.006.51)
Provinciale Resoluties (1.12.01)
Raad van State, (1574) 1581–1795 (1801) (1.01.19)
Raad van State: Extra Aanwinsten 1904 XII (1.01.19.02)
Staten-Generaal (1431) 1576–1796 (1.01.02)
Staten van Holland na 1572 (3.01.01.01)

Regionaal Historisch Centrum: Groninger Archieven (*RHC-GrA*)

Familie Van Swinderen en De Marees van Swinderen, 1370–1982 (552)
Gilden, 1317–1883 (1325)

Gerechten in het Oldambt, 1596 – 1811 (731)
Staten van Stad en Lande, 1594–1798 (1)
Stadsbestuur van Groningen (2) 1594–1815

Stadsarchief Amsterdam (SAA)

Familie De Graeff (76)

Tresoar Frysk Histoarysk en Letterkundich Sintrum (*Tresoar*)

Doopsgezinde gemeente Harlingen (269)
Fa. M.H. Kingma te Makkum (98)
Familie thoe Schwartzenberg en Hohenlansberg (326) Verzameling Fries Genootschap (344)
Gewestelijke Bestuursinstellingen van Friesland 1580–1795 (5)
Poptagasthuis in Marssum (131)

Zeeuws Archief (ZA)

Familie Schorer (157)
Middelburgsche Commercie Compagnie (MCC, 1445)
Rekenkamer C (508)
Verzameling Verheye van Citters (87)
Weeskamer Veere (2030)

Literature

Aalbers, J. *De Republiek en de vrede van Europa: de buitenlandse politiek van de Republiek der verenigde Nederlanden na de vrede van Utrecht (1713), voornamelijk gedurende de jaren 1720–1733. Dl. 1. Achtergronden en algemene aspecten*. Historische studies 39. Groningen: Wolters-Noordhoff enz, 1980.

Acemoglu, Daron, and James A. Robinson. *Why Nations Fail: The Origins of Power, Prosperity, and Poverty*. London etc.: Profile Books, 2012.

Adams, Julia. *The Familial State: Ruling Families and Merchant Capitalism in Early Modern Europe*. The Wilder House Series in Politics, History, and Culture. Ithaca, NY etc.: Cornell University Press, 2005.

Ahn, Doohwan. "From 'jealous Emulation' to 'Cautious Politics': British Foreign Policy and Public Discourse in the Mirror of Ancient Athens (ca. 1730–ca. 1750)." In *Ideology and Foreign Policy in Early Modern Europe (1650–1750)*, edited by David Onnekink and Gijs Rommelse, 93–130. Politics and Culture in Europe. Farnham, Surrey: Ashgate, 2011.

Alesina, Alberto F. *The Size of Nations*. Cambridge, Mass., [etc.]: The MIT Press, 2003.

Allen, Robert C. "The Great Divergence in European Wages and Prices from the Middle Ages to the First World War." *Explorations in Economic History* 38, no. 4 (October 2001): 411–47. https://doi.org/10.1006/exeh.2001.0775.

Allen, Robert C. "The High Wage Economy and the Industrial Revolution: A Restatement." *The Economic History Review* 68, no. 1 (2015): 1–22. https://doi.org/10.1111/ehr.12079.

Allen, Robert C., Jean-Pascal Bassino, Debin Ma, Christine Moll-Murata, and Jan Luiten Van Zanden. "Wages, Prices, and Living Standards in China, 1738–1925: In Comparison with Europe, Japan, and India." *The Economic History Review* 64 (February 1, 2011): 8–38. https://doi.org/10.1111/j.1468-0289.2010.00515.x.

Álvarez-Nogal, Carlos, and Christophe Chamley. "Debt Policy under Constraints: Philip II, the Cortes, and Genoese Bankers." *The Economic History Review* 67, no. 1 (2014): 192–213. https://doi.org/10.1111/1468-0289.12010.

Baars, Cornelis. *De geschiedenis van de landbouw in de Beijerlanden*. Wageningen: Centrum voor landbouwpublikaties en landbouwdocumentaties Pudoc, 1973.

Baks, Paul. "Saksische heerschappij in Friesland, 1498–1515: dynastieke doelstellinge en politieke realiteit." In *Fryslân, staat en macht 1450–1650 : bijdragen aan het historisch congres te Leeuwarden van 3 tot 5 juni 1998*, edited by J. Frieswijk, A.H. Huussen jr., Y.B. Kuiper, and J.A. Mol, 85–106. FA 875. Hilversum: VerlorenLeeuwarden : Fryske Akademy, 1999.

Bavel, Bas van. *The Invisible Hand? How Market Economies have Emerged and Declined Since AD 500*. Oxford University Press, 2016.

Blockmans, Wim. "Van private naar publieke macht in de vijftiende en zestiende eeuw." In *Fryslân, staat en macht 1450–1650 : bijdragen aan het historisch congres te Leeuwarden van 3 tot 5 juni 1998*, edited by J. Frieswijk, A.H. Huussen jr., Y.B. Kuiper, and J.A. Mol, 11–25. FA 875. Hilversum: VerlorenLeeuwarden : Fryske Akademy, 1999.

Blom, Hans. "Decay and the Political Gestalt of Decline in Bernard Mandeville and His Dutch Contemporaries." *History of European Ideas* 36, no. 2 (June 1, 2010): 153–66. https://doi.org/10.1016/j.histeuroideas.2010.01.002.

Boels, Henk, and Hidde Feenstra. "Redres, revolutie en economische groei, 1749–1795." In *Geschiedenis van Groningen II. Nieuwe Tijd*, edited by M. G. J. Duijvendak, H. Feenstra, M. Hillenga, and C.G. Santing, 345–92. Zwolle: Waanders, 2008.

Boels, Henk, and Hidde Feenstra. "Regentenheerschappij en economische recessie 1660–1749." In *Geschiedenis van Groningen II. Nieuwe Tijd*, edited by M. G. J. Duijvendak, H. Feenstra, M. Hillenga, and C.G. Santing, 245–344. Zwolle: Waanders, 2008.

Boerner, Lars, and Albrecht Ritschl. "Individual Enforcement of Collective Liability in Premodern Europe: Comment." *Journal of Institutional and Theoretical Economics (JITE) / Zeitschrift Für Die Gesamte Staatswissenschaft* 158, no. 1 (March 1, 2002): 205–13. https://doi.org/10.2307/40753064.

Bogart, Dan, Mauricio Drelichman, Oscar Gelderblom, and Jean-Laurent Rosenthal. "State and Private Institutions." In *The Cambridge Economic History of Modern Europe*, edited by S. N. Broadberry and Kevin H. O'Rourke, 1: 1700–1870:70–95. Cambridge: Cambridge University Press, 2010.

Bonney, Richard, ed. *The Rise of the Fiscal State in Europe, c.1200–1815*. Oxford etc.: Oxford University Press, 1999.

Boone, Marc, Carolus Augustinus Davids, and Paul J. J. G. Janssens, eds. *Urban Public Debts: Urban Government and the Market for Annuities in Western Europe (14th-18th Centuries)*. Studies in European Urban History (1100–1800) 3. Turnhout: Brepols, 2003.

Brandon, Pepijn. *Masters of War: State, Capital, and Military Enterprise in the Dutch Cycle of Accumulation (1600–1795)*. Amsterdam: [s.n.], 2013.

Brandon, Pepijn. "'The Whole Art of War Is Reduced to Money': Remittances, Short-Term Credit and Financial Intermediation in Anglo-Dutch Military Finance, 1688–1713." *Financial History Review* 25, no. 1 (April 2018): 19–41. https://doi.org/10.1017/S0968565017000282.

Brewer, John. *The Sinews of Power: War, Money and the English State, 1688–1783*. London etc.: Hyman, 1989.

Broner, Fernando, Alberto Martin, and Jaume Ventura. "Sovereign Risk and Secondary Markets." *The American Economic Review* 100, no. 4 (2010): 1523–56.

Brood, Paulus, and Engbert Schut. *Hoofdmannenkamer, sinds 1749 Hoge Justitiekamer van Stad en Lande van Groningen: de civiele procesgang ten tijde van de Republiek der Verenigde Nederlanden*. Procesgidsen 4. Hilversum: Verloren, 2006.

Bruggeman, Marijke. *Nassau en de macht van Oranje: de strijd van de Friese Nassau's voor de erkenning van hun rechten, 1702–1747*. s.n.], 2005.

Bruin, G. de. "O. van Nimwegen, De Republiek Der Verenigde Nederlanden Als Grote Mogendheid. Buitenlandse Politiek En Oorlogvoering in de Eerste Helft van de Achttiende Eeuw En in Het Bijzonder Tijdens de Oostenrijkse Successieoorlog (1740–1748)." BMGN – Low Countries Historical Review 118, no. 3 (January 1, 2003): 390–92. https://doi.org/10.18352/bmgn-lchr.5905.

Brusse, Paul. "Bevolking en sociale verhoudingen." In *Geschiedenis van Zeeland Dl. III: 1700–1850*, edited by Paul Brusse and Jeannine Dekker, 117–67. Zwolle: WBOOKS, 2013.

Brusse, Paul. "Economie." In *Geschiedenis van Zeeland Dl. III: 1700–1850*, edited by Paul Brusse and Jeannine Dekker, 49–115. Zwolle: WBOOKS, 2013.

Brusse, Paul. *Gevallen stad: stedelijke netwerken en het platteland, Zeeland 1750–1850*. Balans tussen stad en platteland 1. Zwolle: Waanders : Universiteit Utrecht, 2011.

Brusse, Paul. "Land en water." In *Geschiedenis van Zeeland Dl. III: 1700–1850*, edited by Paul Brusse and Jeannine Dekker, 15–47. Zwolle: WBOOKS, 2013.

Brusse, Paul, and Willem van den Broeke. *Provincie in de periferie: de economische geschiedenis van Zeeland*, 1800–2000. Utrecht: Matrijs, 2005.

Brusse, Paul, and Jeannine Dekker, eds. *Geschiedenis van Zeeland Dl. III: 1700–1850*. Zwolle: WBOOKS, 2013.

Brusse, Paul, and Wijnand Mijnhardt, eds. *Geschiedenis van Zeeland. Dl. II: 1550–1700*. Zwolle: WBOOKS, 2012.

Brusse, Paul, and Wijnand Mijnhardt, eds. *Towards a New Template for Dutch History: De-Urbanization and the Balance between City and Countryside*. Translated by Beverley R. Jackson. Zwolle: Waanders : Universiteit Utrecht, 2011.

Brusse, Paul, and Arno Neele. "Zeeuwse boedelinventarissen, 1755–1855. DANS," 2011. http://dx.doi.org/10.17026/dans-zf3-qfp4.

Buchinsky, Moshe, and Ben Polak. "The Emergence of a National Capital Market in England, 1710–1880." *The Journal of Economic History* 53, no. 1 (1993): 1–24.

Buist, Marten Gerbertus. *At Spes Non Fracta : Hope and Co. 1770–1815, Merchant Bankers and Diplomats at Work*. Den Haag: Nijhoff, 1974.

Carlos, Ann M., and Larry Neal. "Amsterdam and London as Financial Centers in the Eighteenth Century." *Financial History Review* 18, no. 1 (April 2011): 21–46. https://doi.org/10.1017/S0968565010000338.

Carlos, Ann M., and Larry Neal. "The Micro-Foundations of the Early London Capital Market: Bank of England Shareholders during and after the South Sea Bubble, 1720–251." *The Economic History Review* 59, no. 3 (August 1, 2006): 498–538. https://doi.org/10.1111/j.1468-0289.2005.00332.x.

Carter, Alice Clare. *Getting, Spending and Investing in Early Modern Times: Essays on Dutch, English and Huguenot Economic History*. Aspects of Economic History: The Low Countries 1. Assen: Van Gorcum, 1975.

Cassis, Youssef. *Capitals of Capital: A History of International Financial Centres, 1780–2005*. Edited by Jacqueline Collier Jespersen. Cambridge etc.: Cambridge University Press, 2006.

Chamley, Christophe. "Interest Reductions in the Politico-Financial Nexus of Eighteenth-Century England." *The Journal of Economic History* 71, no. 03 (September 2011): 555–89. https://doi.org/10.1017/S0022050711001847.

Chilosi, David. "Risky Institutions: Political Regimes and the Cost of Public Borrowing in Early Modern Italy." *The Journal of Economic History* 74, no. 03 (2014): 887–915. https://doi.org/10.1017/S0022050714000631.

Clark, Gregory. "Debt, Deficits, and Crowding out: England, 1727–1840." *European Review of Economic History* 5, no. 3 (2001): 403.

Coffman, D'Maris, Adrian Leonard, and Larry Neal, eds. *Questioning Credible Commitment: Perspectives on the Rise of Financial Capitalism*. Macroeconomic Policy Making. Cambridge: Cambridge University Press, 2013.

De Bruijn, J. *Plakkaten van stad en lande: overzicht van Groningse rechtsvoorschriften in de periode 1594–1795*. Historia Agriculturae 14. Groningen: Nederlands Agronomisch-historisch Instituut, 1983.

De Muinck, B.E. *Een regentenhuishouding omstreeks 1700: gegevens uit de privéboekhouding van Mr. Cornelis de Jonge van Ellemeet, ontvanger-generaal der Verenigde Nederlanden (1646–1721)*. 's-Gravenhage: Martinus Nijhoff, 1965.

De Vries, J. "An Inquiry into the Behaviour of Wages in the Dutch Republic and the Southern Netherlands, 1580–1800." *Acta Historiae Neerlandicae : Studies on the History of the Netherlands* 10 (1978): 79–97.

De Vries, Jan. "De economische ontwikkeling van Friesland na het einde van de Friese vrijheid." In *Fryslân, staat en macht 1450–1650 : bijdragen aan het historisch congres te Leeuwarden van 3 tot 5 juni 1998*, edited by J. Frieswijk, A.H. Huussen jr., Y.B. Kuiper, and J.A. Mol, 140–57. FA 875. Hilversum: VerlorenLeeuwarden : Fryske Akademy, 1999.

De Vries, Jan. "Peasant Demand Patterns and Economic Development, Friesland 1550–1750." In *European Peasants and Their Markets: Essays in Agrarian Economic History*, edited by William Nelson Parker and Eric Lionel Jones. Princeton, N.J. etc.: Princeton University Press, 1975.

De Vries, Jan. *The Dutch Rural Economy in the Golden Age, 1500–1700*. Yale Series in Economic History. London: Yale University Press, 1974.

De Vries, Jan. "The Political Economy of Bread in the Dutch Republic." In *The Political Economy of the Dutch Republic*, edited by O.C. Gelderblom, 85–114. Farnham etc.: Ashgate, 2009.

De Vries, Jan. *The Price of Bread: Regulating the Market in the Dutch Republic*. Cambridge Studies in Economic History – Second Series. Cambridge: Cambridge University Press, 2019. https://doi.org/10.1017/9781108639590.

De Vries, Jan, and Ad Van der Woude. *Nederland 1500–1815: de eerste ronde van moderne economische groei*. Amsterdam: Balans, 1995.

De Vries, Jan, and Ad Van der Woude. *The First Modern Economy: Success, Failure, and Perseverance of the Dutch Economy, 1500–1815*. Cambridge etc.: Cambridge University Press, 1997.

De Vries, Johannes. *De economische achteruitgang der Republiek in de achttiende eeuw*. Leiden: Stenfert Kroese, 1968.

Dehing, Pit. *Geld in Amsterdam: wisselbank en wisselkoersen, 1650–1725*. Hilversum: Uitgeverij Verloren Amsterdam : Universiteit van Amsterdam, 2012.

Dehing, Pit, and Marjolein 't Hart. "Linking the Fortunes: Currency and Banking, 1550–1800." In *A Financial History of The Netherlands*, edited by Marjolein 't Hart, Joost Jonker, and Jan Luiten Van Zanden, 37–63. Cambridge: Cambridge University Press, 1997.

Dekker, Cornelis, and Roland Baetens. *Geld in het water: Antwerps en Mechels kapitaal in Zuid-Beveland na de stormvloeden in de 16e eeuw*. Hilversum: Verloren, 2010.

Dekker, Jeannine. *Onderdanig en opstandig: desurbanisatie en de politieke verhoudingen op het platteland in Zeeland, 1750–1850*. Balans tussen stad en platteland 2. Zwolle: Waanders : Universiteit Utrecht, 2011.

Dekker, Jeannine. "Politieke verhoudingen." In *Geschiedenis van Zeeland Dl. III: 1700–1850*, edited by Paul Brusse and Jeannine Dekker, 169–219. Zwolle: WBOOKS, 2013.

Dekker, Rudolf. *Holland in beroering: oproeren in de 17de en 18de eeuw*. Baarn: Ambo, 1982.

Den Heijer, Henk. *De geoctrooieerde compagnie: de VOC en de WIC als voorlopers van de naamloze vennootschap*. Amsterdam: Stichting tot Bevordering der Notariële Wetenschap Deventer : Kluwer, 2005.

Den Heijer, Henk. *De geschiedenis van de WIC*. Zutphen: Walburg Pers, 2002.

Deursen, A. Th. van. "De plaats van de noordelijke gewesten in de Republiek." In *Nederland en het Noorden. Opstellen aangeboden aan prof.dr. M.G. Buist ter gelegenheid van zijn afscheid als hoogleraar in de Moderne Geschiedenis van Financiën en Bestuur en in de Contemporaine Geschiedenis aan de Rijksuniversiteit te Groningen op 25 september 1990*, edited by K. van Berkel, H. Boels, and M. G. Buist, 19–26. Assen etc: Van Gorcum, 1991.

Deursen, A. Th. van. "De plaats van het gewest Friesland in de Republiek." In *Fryslân, staat en macht 1450–1650: bijdragen aan het historisch congres te Leeuwarden van 3 tot 5 juni 1998*, edited by Jouke Arend Frieswijk, A.H. Huussen jr., Y.B. Kuiper, and J.A. Mol, 218–31. FA 875. Hilversum: Verloren Leeuwarden : Fryske Akademy, 1999.

Dickson, P.G.M. *Finance and Government under Maria Theresia 1740–1780*. Oxford: Clarendon Press, 1987.

Dickson, P.G.M. *The Financial Revolution in England: A Study in the Development of Public Credit, 1688–1756*. London etc.: MacMillan, 1967.

Dincecco, Mark. "Fiscal Centralization, Limited Government, and Public Revenues in Europe, 1650–1913." *The Journal of Economic History* 69, no. 1 (2009): 48–103.

Dincecco, Mark. "Political Regimes and Sovereign Credit Risk in Europe, 1750–1913." *European Review of Economic History* 13, no. 1 (2009): 31–64.

Dormans, E. H. M. "De economie en de openbare financiën van de Republiek." In *Van tresorier tot thesaurier-generaal: zes eeuwen financieel beleid in handen van een hoge Nederlandse ambtsdrager*, edited by J. Th. de Smidt and R. M. Sprenger, 89–110. Hilversum: Verloren, 1996.

Dormans, E. H. M. *Het tekort: staatsschuld in de tijd der Republiek*. NEHA-series III 14. Amsterdam: NEHA, 1991.

Drelichman, Mauricio, and Hans-Joachim Voth. *Lending to the Borrower from Hell: Debt, Taxes, and Default in the Age of Philip II*. The Princeton Economic History of the Western World. Princeton: Princeton University Press, 2014.

Drelichman, Mauricio, and Hans-Joachim Voth. "Serial Defaults, Serial Profits: Returns to Sovereign Lending in Habsburg Spain, 1566–1600." *Explorations in Eco-*

nomic History 48, no. 1 (January 2011): 1–19. https://doi.org/10.1016/j.eeh.2010.08.002.

Eaton, Jonathan, and Mark Gersovitz. "Debt with Potential Repudiation: Theoretical and Empirical Analysis." *Review of Economic Studies* 48, no. 2 (1981): 289–309.

Eijnatten, Joris van. *Liberty and Concord in the United Provinces: Religious Toleration and the Public in the Eighteenth-Century Netherlands*. Brill's Studies in Intellectual History, ISSN 0920-8607 111. Leiden etc.: Brill, 2003.

Enthoven, Victor. "'Veel vertier'. De Verenigde Oostindische Compagnie in Zeeland, een economische reus op Walcheren." *Archief: vroegere en latere mededeelingen voornamelijk in betrekking tot Zeeland*, 1989, 49–127.

Enthoven, Victor. "Een symbiose tussen koopman en regent." In *Ondernemers & bestuurders: economie en politiek in de Noordelijke Nederlanden in de late Middeleeuwen en vroegmoderne tijd*, edited by Clé Lesger and Leo Noordegraaf, 203–36. Neha-series III. Amsterdam: NEHA, 1999.

Enthoven, Victor. *Zeeland en de opkomst van de Republiek: handel en strijd in de Scheldedelta, c. 1550–1621*. s.n., 1996.

Epstein, Stephan R. *Freedom and Growth: The Rise of States and Markets in Europe, 1300–1750*. Routledge Explorations in Economic History 17. London etc.: Routledge, 2000.

Esteves, Rui. "Archomania. Venality and Private Finances on the Eve of the French Revolution." *Paper Prepared for the 2014 EHA Meeting in Columbus, OH*, 2014. http://eh.net/eha/wp-content/uploads/2014/05/Esteves.pdf.

Faber, Johannes Alle. "De Oligarchisering van Friesland in de Tweede Helft van de Zeventiende Eeuw." *A.A.G.Bijdragen* 15 (1970): 39–65.

Faber, Johannes Alle. *Drie eeuwen Friesland: economische en sociale ontwikkelingen van 1500 tot 1800. Vol. II. A.A.G. bijdragen* 17. Wageningen: Landbouwhogeschool, Afd. Agrarische Geschiedenis, 1972.

Faber, Johannes Alle. *Drie eeuwen Friesland: economische en sociale ontwikkelingen van 1500 tot 1800. Vol. I. A.A.G. bijdragen* 17. Wageningen: Landbouwhogeschool, Afd. Agrarische Geschiedenis, 1972.

Fatah-Black, Karwan. *Sociëteit van Suriname 1683–1795: het bestuur van de kolonie in de achttiende eeuw*. Zutphen: WalburgPers, 2019.

Feenstra, Alberto. "De Lange Schaduw van de Spaanse Successieoorlog (1701–1713) in Friesland." In *Nederland in Last. Vijfhonderd Jaar Overheidsfinanciën in de Lage Landen, 1500–2000*, by Victor Enthoven, 89–109. Leiden: Primavera Pers, 2021.

Feenstra, Alberto. "Hiding in a Twilight Zone: Credible Commitment in the Dutch Republic and Groningen's 1680s Default." *Histoire & Mesure* XXX, no. 2 (2015): 79–116.

Feenstra, Alberto. "More than Merchant Bankers: Second-Class Financial Intermediation in Eighteenth-Century Amsterdam". In *Credit Networks in The Preindustrial*

World: A Social Network Analysis Approach, edited by Elise M. Dermineur and Matteo Pompermaier, 145–200. Cham: Palgrave Macmillan / Springer Nature Switzerland, 2025. https://doi.org/10.1007/978-3-031-67117-3_6.

Feenstra, Alberto, and Sabine Muller. "Wie wil wachten op het zoet? De laatste adem van Amsterdamse kopers van Groningse lijfrenten, 1660–1760." *Historisch Jaarboek Groningen*, 2016, 46–65.

Feenstra, H.A. *Between Shared and Conflicting Interests. The Political Economy of the Markets for Public Debt in the Dutch Republic, 1600–1795*. Unpublished PhD-thesis Universiteit van Amsterdam, 2018.

Feenstra, Hidde. *De bloeitijd en het verval van de Ommelander adel, (1600–1800)*. [s.n.], 1981.

Feenstra, Hidde. *Spinnen in het web: Groningse regenten in relatie tot het omringende platteland tijdens de Republiek*. Groninger historische reeks 36. Assen: Koninklijke Van Gorcum, 2007.

Feenstra, Hidde, and H. H. Oudman. *Een vergeten plattelandselite: eigenerfden in het Groninger Westerkwartier van de vijftiende tot de zeventiende eeuw*. Fryske Akademy 948. Ljouwert/Leeuwarden: Fryske Akademy, 2004.

Feldstein, Martin, and Charles Horioka. "Domestic Saving and International Capital Flows." *The Economic Journal* 90, no. 358 (June 1, 1980): 314–29. https://doi.org/10.2307/2231790.

Felloni, G. "Italy." In *An Introduction to the Sources of European Economic History, 1500–1800*, edited by Charles Henry Wilson and Geoffrey Parker, 1–36. World Economic History. London: Weidenfeld and Nicolson, 1977.

Flandreau, Marc, and Juan H. Flores. "Bonds and Brands." *The Journal of Economic History* 69, no. 3 (2009): 646–84.

Flandreau, Marc, Christophe Galimard, Clemens Jobst, and Pilar Nogués-Marco. "Monetary Geography before the Industrial Revolution." *Cambridge Journal of Regions, Economy and Society* 2, no. 2 (July 1, 2009): 149–71. https://doi.org/10.1093/cjres/rsp009.

Flandreau, Marc, Christophe Galimard, Clemens Jobst, and Pilar Nogués-Marco. "The Bell Jar: Commercial Interest Rates between Two Revolutions, 1688–1789." In *The Origins and Development of Financial Markets and Institutions: From the Seventeenth Century to the Present*, edited by Jeremy Atack and Larry Neal, 161–208. Cambridge etc.: Cambridge University Press, 2009.

Flynn, Dennis O. "Big History, Geological Accumulations, Physical Economics, and Wealth." *Asian Review of World Histories* 7, no. 1–2 (January 23, 2019): 80–106. https://doi.org/10.1163/22879811-12340047.

Formsma, Wiebe Jannes. "De landsheerlijke periode." In *Historie van Groningen: stad en land*, edited by Wiebe Jannes Formsma, 173–206. Groningen: Tjeenk Willink, 1976.

Formsma, Wiebe Jannes. "Staatsinstellingen." In *Historie van Groningen: stad en land*, edited by Wiebe Jannes Formsma, 277–92. Groningen: Tjeenk Willink, 1976.

Fritschy, Wantje. "Binnenlandse Constituties of Buitenlandse Omstandigheden?" *BMGN – Low Countries Historical Review* 117, no. 3 (January 1, 2002): 344–51. https://doi.org/10.18352/bmgn-lchr.5713.

Fritschy, Wantje. *Gewestelijke financiën ten tijde van de Republiek der Verenigde Nederlanden. Deel I. Overijssel (1604–1795)*. Vol. 1. Rijks geschiedkundige publicatiën. Kleine serie 86. Den Haag: Instituut voor Nederlandse Geschiedenis, 1996.

Fritschy, Wantje, ed. *Gewestelijke financiën ten tijde van de Republiek der Verenigde Nederlanden. Deel I. Overijssel (1604–1795), (Den Haag 1996); Deel II. Drenthe (1602-1795) (1998); Deel III. Groningen (1594-1795) (2001); Deel IV. Holland (1572–1795) (2004); Deel V. Utrecht (1579–1798) (2006); Deel VI. Friesland (1587–1795) (2007); Deel VII. Zeeland (1573–1795) (2009)*. Rijks geschiedkundige publicatiën. Kleine serie. Den Haag: Instituut voor Nederlandse Geschiedenis, 1996.

Fritschy, Wantje. "A 'financial Revolution' Reconsidered: Public Finance in Holland during the Dutch Revolt, 1568–1648." *The Economic History Review* 56, no. 1 (2003): 57–89.

Fritschy, Wantje. *De patriotten en de financiën van de Bataafse Republiek: Hollands krediet en de smalle marges voor een nieuw beleid (1795–1801)*. 's-Gravenhage: Stichting Hollandse Historische Reeks, 1988.

Fritschy, Wantje. "Geld en oorlog : financieel beleid in Holland en Overijssel vergeleken met Groot-Brittanië en Oostenrijk (1740–1785)." In *De Republiek tussen zee en vasteland: buitenlandse invloeden op cultuur, economie en politiek in Nederland 1580–1800*, edited by Carolus Augustinus Davids, 207–25. Leuven/Apeldoorn: Garant, 1995.

Fritschy, Wantje. "Overheidsfinanciën als uiting van het 'institutioneel onvermogen' van de achttiende eeuwse Republiek?" *Economisch- en sociaal-historisch jaarboek* 48 (1985): 19–47.

Fritschy, Wantje. *Public Finance of the Dutch Republic in Comparative Perspective: The Viability of an Early Modern Federal State (1570s–1795)*. Library of Economic History, ISSN 1877-3206 9. Leiden: Brill, 2017.

Fritschy, Wantje. "Schulden als leerschool?: de Unie der Zeven Verenigde Provinciën en de Europese Unie." *Tijdschrift voor Sociale en Economische Geschiedenis* 9, no. 2 (2012): 3–28.

Fritschy, Wantje. "Taxation in Britain, France and the Netherlands in the Eighteenth Century." *Economic and Social History in the Netherlands* 2 (1990): 57–79.

Fritschy, Wantje. "The Poor, the Rich and the Taxes in Heinsius' Times." In *Anthonie Heinsius and the Dutch Republic 1688–1720: Politics, War, and Finance*, edited by Jan Arie Frederik de Jongste and Augustus Johannes, Veenendaal jr, 242–58. ING-Workshop Series; RGP. The Hague: Institute of Netherlands History, 2002.

Fritschy, W., and R. Liesker. "Overheidsfinanciën, kapitaalmarkten en 'institutionele context' in Holland en Overijssel tijdens en na de Spaanse Successie-oorlog." In *Kapitaal, ondernemerschap en beleid: studies over economie en politiek in Nederland, Europa en Azië van 1500 tot heden*, edited by C. A. Davids, W. Fritschy, and L.A. Van der Valk, 165–96. NEHA-series III 25. Amsterdam: NEHA, 1996.

Fritschy, Wantje, Marjolein 't Hart, and Edwin Horlings. "Long-Term Trends in the Fiscal History of the Netherlands, 1515–1913." In *The Rise of Fiscal States: A Global History, 1500–1914*, edited by Bartolomé Yun-Casalilla and Patrick Karl O'Brien, 39–66. Cambridge etc.: Cambridge University Press, 2012.

Fritschy, Wantje, and René Van der Voort. "From Fragmentation to Unification: Public Finance, 1700–1914." In *A Financial History of the Netherlands*, edited by Marjolein 't Hart, Joost Jonker, and Jan Luiten Van Zanden, 64–93. Cambridge: Cambridge University Press, 1997.

Fruin, Robert J. *Geschiedenis der staatsinstellingen in Nederland tot den val der Republiek*. Edited by H. Th. Colenbrander. 's-Gravenhage: Nijhoff, 1901.

Fynn-Paul, Jeff. "Investment Behaviour in the Netherlands during the Long Eighteenth Century: An Analysis Based on the Van Der Muelen Family Portfolio, 1738–1814." In *Publieke Financiën in de Lage Landen (1300–1800)*, edited by Jaco Zuijderduijn and Dries Raeymaekers, 111–37. Publicaties van de Vlaams-Nederlandse Vereniging Voor Nieuwe Geschiedenis 14. Maastricht: Shaker Publishing, 2015.

Gaastra, Femme S. *De geschiedenis van de VOC*. Zutphen: Walburg Pers, 2007.

Gaastra, Femme S. "Friesland en de VOC." In *Negen eeuwen Friesland-Holland: geschiedenis van een haat-liefdeverhouding*, edited by Philippus H. Breuker and Antheunis Janse, 184–96. FA 846. Ljouwert/Leeuwarden: Fryske Akademy Zutphen : Walburg Pers, 1997.

Gabriëls, Adrianus Johannes Cornelis Maria. *De Heren Als Dienaren En de Dienaar Als Heer: Het Stadhouderlijk Stelsel in de Tweede Helft van de Achttiende Eeuw*. Hollandse Historische Reeks 14. 's-Gravenhage: Stichting Hollandse Historische Reeks, 1990.

Gelderblom, O. C. "Introduction." In *The Political Economy of the Dutch Republic*, edited by O.C. Gelderblom, 1–18. Farnham etc.: Ashgate, 2009.

Gelderblom, O. C., ed. *The Political Economy of the Dutch Republic*. Farnham etc.: Ashgate, 2009.

Gelderblom, O. C. . *Zuid-Nederlandse kooplieden en de opkomst van de Amsterdamse stapelmarkt (1578–1630)*. Hilversum: Verloren, 2000.

Gelderblom, Oscar. *Cities of Commerce: The Institutional Foundations of International Trade in the Low Countries, 1250–1650*. The Princeton Economic History of the Western World. [s.n.], 2013.

Gelderblom, Oscar, Mark Hup, and Joost Jonker. "Public Functions, Private Markets: Credit Registration by Aldermen and Notaries in the Low Countries, 1500–1800."

In *Financing in Europe: Evolution, Coexistence and Complementarity of Lending Practices from the Middle Ages to Modern Times*, edited by Marcella Lorenzini, Cinzia Lorandini, and D'Maris Coffman, 163–94. Palgrave Studies in the History of Finance. Cham: Springer International Publishing, 2018. https://doi.org/10.1007/978-3-319-58493-5_7.

Gelderblom, Oscar, and Joost Jonker. "Alba's Irony. Urban Autonomy and Public Finance in the Low Countries (1384–1713)." *Utrecht University Working Papers*, 2011.

Gelderblom, Oscar, and Joost Jonker. "Completing a Financial Revolution: The Finance of the Dutch East India Trade and the Rise of the Amsterdam Capital Market, 1595–1612." *The Journal of Economic History* 64, no. 3 (2004): 641–72.

Gelderblom, Oscar, and Joost Jonker. "Mirroring Different Follies. The Character of the 1720 Bubble in the Dutch Republic." In *The Great Mirror of Folly: Finance, Culture, and the Crash of 1720*, edited by William N. Goetzmann, Catherine Labio, K. Geert Rouwenhorst, and Timothy G. Young, 121–39. Yale Series in Economic and Financial History. New Haven: Yale University Press, 2013.

Gelderblom, Oscar, and Joost Jonker. "Public Finance and Economic Growth." *The Journal of Economic History* 71, no. 1 (2011): 1–40.

Gelderblom, Oscar, Joost Jonker, and Clemens Kool. "Direct Finance in the Dutch Golden Age." *The Economic History Review* 69, no. 4 (November 2016): 1178–98. https://doi.org/10.1111/ehr.12285.

Gerding, Michiel A. W. *Vier eeuwen turfwinning: de verveningen in Groningen, Friesland, Drenthe en Overijssel tussen 1550 en 1950. AAG bijdragen.* Wageningen: Afdeling Agrarische Geschiedenis, Landbouwuniversiteit, 1995.

"Gewestelijke Financiën Ten Tijde van de Republiek Der Verenigde Nederlanden 1572–1795 (Web)." *ING Project*, March 4, 2015. http://resources.huygens.knaw.nl/gewestelijkefinancien.

Glete, Jan. *War and the State in Early Modern Europe: Spain, the Dutch Republic and Sweden as Fiscal-Military States, 1500–1660*. Warfare and History. London etc.: Routledge, 2002.

Goetzmann, William N., Catherine Labio, K. Geert Rouwenhorst, and Timothy G. Young, eds. *The Great Mirror of Folly: Finance, Culture, and the Crash of 1720*. Yale Series in Economic and Financial History. New Haven: Yale University Press, 2013.

Grafe, Regina. *Distant Tyranny: Markets, Power, and Backwardness in Spain, 1650–1800*. The Princeton Economic History of the Western World. Princeton, N.J, 2012.

Greif, Avner. "Institutions and Impersonal Exchange: From Communal to Individual Responsibility." *Journal of Institutional and Theoretical Economics (JITE) / Zeitschrift Für Die Gesamte Staatswissenschaft* 158, no. 1 (2002): 168–204.

Greif, Avner. *Institutions and the Path to the Modern Economy: Lessons from Medieval Trade. Political Economy of Institutions and Decisions.* Cambridge etc.: Cambridge University Press, 2006.

Greif, Avner. "The Fundamental Problem of Exchange: A Research Agenda in Historical Institutional Analysis." *European Review of Economic History* 4, no. 3 (January 12, 2000): 251–84. https://doi.org/10.1017/S1361491600000071.

Groenveld4, Simon. "Politieke verhoudingen." In *Geschiedenis van Zeeland. Dl. II: 1550–1700*, edited by Paul Brusse and Wijnand Mijnhardt, 147–97. Zwolle: WBOOKS, 2012.

Guibal, Cornelis Jan. *Democratie en oligarchie in Friesland tijdens de Republiek.* Van Gorcum's historische bibliotheek 9. Assen: Van Gorcum, 1934.

Haks, Donald. *Vaderland en vrede, 1672–1713: publiciteit over de Nederlandse Republiek in oorlog*. Hilversum: Verloren, 2013.

Hanus, Jord. "Een efficiënte pre-industriële kapitaalmarkt? Het vroeg zestiende-eeuwse 's-Hertogenbosch als voorbeeld." *Tijdschrift voor Sociale en Economische Geschiedenis* 6, no. 3 (2009): 82–113.

Hart 't, Marjolein C. . "Autonoom maar kwetsbaar. De Middelburgse regenten en de opstand van 1651." *De zeventiende eeuw* 9 (1993): 51–62.

Hart, Marjolein C. "'The Devil or the Dutch'. Holland's Impact on the Financial Revolution in England, 1643–1694." *Parliaments, Estates & Representation = Parlements, États & Représentation* 11 (1991): 39–52.

Hart, Marjolein C. "Coercion and Capital Revisited. Recent Trends in the Historiography of State-Formation." In *Economies, Public Finances, and the Impact of Institutional Changes in Interregional Perspective: The Low Countries and Neighbouring German Territories (14th-17th Centuries)*, edited by Remi Schaïk, 23–32. Studies in European Urban History (1100–1800) (SEUH) 36. Turnhout: Brepols, 2015.

Hart, Marjolein C. "De Nederlandse Republiek en de betekenis van de steden." *In Een wonder weerspiegeld : de Nederlandse Republiek in Europees perspectief*, edited by Karel Davids and Jan Lucassen, 53–89. Amsterdam: Aksant, 2005.

Hart, Marjolein C. "Gewetenloze kapitalisten, handige fiscalisten, strategische huisvaders of gedisciplineerde calvinisten? De Nederlandse Republiek als casestudy." *BMGN – Low Countries Historical Review* 121, no. 3 (January 1, 2006): 418. https://doi.org/10.18352/bmgn-lchr.6450.

Hart, Marjolein C. "How Did States Further the Rise of the Great Divergence?" *TSEG – The Low Countries Journal of Social and Economic History* 12, no. 2 (June 15, 2015): 51–62. https://doi.org/10.18352/tseg.56.

Hart, Marjolein C. "Mobilising Resources for War. The Dutch and British Financial Revolutions Compared." In *War, State and Development: Fiscal-Military States in the Eighteenth Century*, edited by Rafael Torres Sánchez, 189–200. Pamplona: Ediciones Universidad de Navarra, 2007.

Hart, Marjolein C. "Mutual Advantages: State Bankers as Brokers between the City of Amsterdam and the Dutch Republic." In *The Political Economy of the Dutch Republic*, edited by O.C. Gelderblom, 115–42. Farnham etc.: Ashgate, 2009.

Hart, Marjolein C. *Oorlog en ongelijkheid: een inclusieve geschiedenis van de Gouden Eeuw*. Amsterdam: Boom, 2022.

Hart, Marjolein C. "Public Loans and Moneylenders in the Seventeenth Century Netherlands." *Economic and Social History in the Netherlands* 1 (1989): 119–39.

Hart, Marjolein C. *The Dutch Wars of Independence: Warfare and Commerce in the Netherlands 1570–1680*. Modern Wars in Perspective. London: Routledge, 2014.

Hart, Marjolein C. *The Making of a Bourgeois State: War, Politics and Finance during the Dutch Revolt*. Manchester etc.: Manchester University Press, 1993.

Hart, Marjolein C. "The Merits of a Financial Revolution: Public Finance, 1550–1700." In *A Financial History of the Netherlands*, edited by Marjolein 't Hart, Joost Jonker, and Jan Luiten Van Zanden, 11–34. Cambridge: Cambridge University Press, 1997.

Hart, Marjolein C. "The United Provinces, 1579–1806." In *The Rise of the Fiscal State in Europe*, c.1200–1815, edited by Richard Bonney, 309–25. Oxford etc.: Oxford University Press, 1999.

Hart, Marjolein C. *Waarom belastingen goed zijn voor democratie: staatsvorming en politieke cultuur in wereldhistorisch perspectief*. Vrije Universiteit, Amsterdam. Faculteit der Letteren: VU, Vrije Universiteit Amsterdam, Faculteit der Letteren, 2014.

Hart, Marjolein 't, Joost Jonker, and Jan Luiten Van Zanden. "Introduction." In *A Financial History of the Netherlands*, edited by Marjolein 't Hart, Joost Jonker, and Jan Luiten Van Zanden, 1–10. Cambridge: Cambridge University Press, 1997.

Heeres, J. E. "Holland Contra Groningen." *Groningse Volksalmanak : Historisch Jaarboek Voor Groningen*, 1890, 175–97.

Heeres, J. E. "Stad en Lande tijdens het erfstadhouderschap van Willem IV." *Bijdragen voor vaderlandsche geschiedenis en oudheidkunde*, 1888, 252–344.

Helliwell, John F. *How Much Do National Borders Matter? Integrating National Economies*. Washington, D.C: Brookings Institution, 1998.

Hempenius-van Dijk, Barendina Sijtje. *Hof van Friesland: de hoofdlijnen van het procederen in civiele zaken voor het Hof van Friesland zowel in eerste instantie als in appel*. Procesgidsen 2. Hilversum: Verloren, 2004.

Herwerden, P. J. van. "Geschiedenis van het Sint Geertruids- of Pepergasthuis te Groningen." *Economisch-historisch jaarboek : bijdragen tot de economische geschiedenis van Nederland* 28, no. 1960 (1960 1958): 149–217.

Hildebrand, Karsien. *Het reglement reformatoir in Stad en Lande in de praktijk, (1749–1780)*. Groningen etc.: Wolters, 1932.

Hirshleifer, David, and Guo Ying Luo. "On the Survival of Overconfident Traders in a Competitive Securities Market." *Journal of Financial Markets* 4, no. 1 (January 1, 2001): 73–84. https://doi.org/10.1016/S1386-4181(00)00014-8.

Hoffman, Philip T. *Why Did Europe Conquer the World? The Princeton Economic History of the Western World*. Princeton: University Press, 2015.

Hoffman, Philip T., and Kathryn Norberg. "Conclusion." In *Fiscal Crises, Liberty, and Representative Government, 1450–1789*, edited by Philip T. Hoffman and Kathryn Norberg, 299–310. The Making of Modern Freedom. Stanford, Calif.: Stanford University Press, 1994.

Hoffman, Philip T., Gilles Postel-Vinay, and Jean-Laurent Rosenthal. *Priceless Markets: The Political Economy of Credit in Paris, 1660–1870*. Chicago etc.: The University of Chicago Press, 2000.

Homer, Sidney, and Richard Eugene Sylla. *A History of Interest Rates*. 4th edition, 1st edition 1963. Hoboken, NJ: Wiley, 2005.

Hoppit, Julian. "The Myths of the South Sea Bubble." *Transactions of the Royal Historical Society* 12 (2002): 141–65.

Houtzager, Dirk. *Hollands lijf- en losrenteleningen vóór 1672*. Schiedam: HAV Bank, 1950.

Hovy, Johannes. "Institutioneel onvermogen in de 18de eeuw." In *Algemene geschiedenis der Nederlanden. Nieuwe tijd : politieke- en religiegeschiedenis 18de eeuw, sociocultурele geschiedenis 1500–1800, overzeese geschiedenis 17de en 18de eeuw*, edited by D.P. Blok, W. Prevenier, D.J. Roorda, A.M. Van der Woude, J.A. Van Houtte, H.F.J.M. Van den Eerenbeemt, Th. Van Tijn, and H. Balthazar, 9:126–38. Algemene geschiedenis der Nederlanden. Haarlem, 1980.

Humphries, Jane, and Jacob Weisdorf. "Unreal Wages? Real Income and Economic Growth in England, 1260–1850." *The Economic Journal* 129, no. 623 (October 1, 2019): 2867–87. https://doi.org/10.1093/ej/uez017.

Irigoin, Alejandra, and Regina Grafe. "Bounded Leviathan: Fiscal Constraints and Financial Development in the Early Modern Hispanic World." In *Questioning Credible Commitment: Perspectives on the Rise of Financial Capitalism*, edited by D'Maris Coffman, Adrian Leonard, and Larry Neal, 199–227. Macroeconomic Policy Making. Cambridge: Cambridge University Press, 2013.

Israel, Jonathan I. *The Dutch Republic: Its Rise, Greatness, and Fall 1477–1806*. The Oxford History of Early Modern Europe. Oxford: Clarendon Press, 1995.

Janssen, Geert H. *Creaturen van de macht: patronage bij Willem Frederik van Nassau (1613–1664)*. Amsterdam: Amsterdam University Press, 2005.

Jedwab, Remi, and Dietrich Vollrath. "Urbanization without Growth in Historical Perspective." *Explorations in Economic History* 58 (October 1, 2015): 1–21. https://doi.org/10.1016/j.eeh.2015.09.002.

Jonker, Joost. "Lachspiegel van de Vooruitgang. Het Historiografisch Beeld van de Nederlandse Industriefinanciering in de Negentiende Eeuw." *NEHA-Bulletin: Orgaan Ten Behoeve van de Economische Geschiedenis in Nederland* 5 (1991): 5–23.

Jonker, Joost. *Merchants, Bankers, Middlemen: The Amsterdam Money Market during the First Half of the 19th Century*. NEHA-Series III 24. Amsterdam: NEHA, 1996.

Kleer, Richard. "'The Folly of Particulars': The Political Economy of the South Sea Bubble." *Financial History Review* 19, no. 02 (August 2012): 175–97. https://doi.org/10.1017/S0968565012000078.

Klein, Peter Wolfgang. "Kapitaal en stagnatie tijdens het Hollands vroegkapitalisme." In *Kapitaal, ondernemerschap en beleid: studies over economie en politiek in Nederland, Europa en Azië van 1500 tot heden*, edited by C.A. Davids, W. Fritschy, and L.A. Van der Valk, 37–54. NEHA-series III 25. Amsterdam: NEHA, 1996.

Kluiver, Jan Hendrik. *De souvereine en independente staat Zeeland: de politiek van de provincie Zeeland inzake vredesonderhandelingen met Spanje tijdens de Tachtigjarige Oorlog tegen de achtergrond van de positie van Zeeland in de Republiek*. Middelburg: De Zwarte Arend, 1998.

Knibbe, Merijn T. *Lokkich Fryslân: een studie naar de ontwikkeling van de productiviteit van de Friese landbouw 1505–1830*. Historia agriculturae, ISSN 0439-2027 38. Groningen etc.: Nederlands Agronomisch Historisch Instituut, 2006.

Knibbe, Merijn T., and Paul Borghaerts. "A Capital Market without Banks. Lending and Borrowing in Hennaarderadeel, Friesland, 1537–1555." In *Financial Development, Economic Crises and Emerging Market Economies.*, edited by Faruk Ülgen, 126–41. New York: Routledge, 2017.

Knottnerus, Otto S. "Het primaat van Rome aangevochten." In *Geschiedenis van Groningen II. Nieuwe Tijd*, edited by M. G. J. Duijvendak, H. Feenstra, M. Hillenga, and C.G. Santing, 51–70. Zwolle: Waanders, 2008.

Kok, Gerhard de. "Cursed Capital: The Economic Impact of the Transatlantic Slave Trade on Walcheren around 1770." *Tijdschrift Voor Sociale En Economische Geschiedenis/ The Low Countries Journal of Social and Economic History* 13, no. 3 (September 16, 2016).

Kok, Jacobus. *Vaderlandsch Woordenboek: met kaarten, plaaten en pourtraitten*. Edited by Jan Fokke. Vol. XVIII. Te Amsterdam: bij Johannes Allart, 1785.

Koster, Elwin Alexander. *Stadsmorfologie: een proeve van vormgericht onderzoek ten behoeve van stedenbouwhistorisch onderzoek*. s.n., 2001.

Kremer, Marcel Ronald. *Huwelijk en vermogen: een (rechts)historische case study naar de verzorging van de langstlevende echtgenoot in de stad Groningen onder doopsgezinden (1699–1809)*. Ars notariatus 155. Deventer: KluwerAmsterdam: Universiteit van Amsterdam, 2013.

Kuiken, Kees. *Het Bildt is geen eiland: capita cultuurgeschiedenis van een vroegmoderne polder in Friesland*. Historia agriculturae 45. Groningen: Nederlands Agronomisch Historisch Instituut, 2013.

Kuiper, Yme, and Annemarie Zijlstra. "'Een yeder hadt te doen met poten, planten en andere dingen'. Het buitenleven van rijke en voorname Friezen in de Gouden Eeuw." In *Buitenplaatsen in de Gouden Eeuw: de rijkdom van het buitenleven in de*

Republiek, edited by Yme Kuiper and Ben Olde Meierink, 96–127. Adelsgeschiedenis ; XIV. Hilversum: Verloren, 2015.

Le Bris, David. "Wars, Inflation and Stock Market Returns in France, 1870–1945." *Financial History Review* 19, no. 03 (December 2012): 337–61. https://doi.org/10.1017/S0968565012000170.

Lee, R. D., and R. S. Schofield. "British Population in the Eighteenth Century." In *Economic History of Britain Since 1700, Vol. 1: 1700–1860*, edited by Roderick Floud and Donald McCloskey, 17–35. Cambridge: Cambridge University Press, 1981.

Leeb, Isidore Leonard. *The Ideological Origins of the Batavian Revolution: History and Politics in the Dutch Republic 1747–1800*. The Hague: Nijhoff, 1973.

Lemmink, Fredericus Hermanus Jacobus. *Het ontstaan van de Staten van Zeeland en hun geschiedenis tot het jaar 1555*. Roosendaal: Van Poll Suykerbuyk, 1951.

Leonard, Adrian. "Contingent Commitment: The Development of English Marine Insurance in the Context of New Institutional Economics, 1577–1720." In *Questioning Credible Commitment: Perspectives on the Rise of Financial Capitalism*, edited by D'Maris Coffman, Adrian Leonard, and Larry Neal, 48–75. Macroeconomic Policy Making. Cambridge: Cambridge University Press, 2013.

Lesger, Clé. *Handel in Amsterdam ten tijde van de Opstand: kooplieden, commerciële expansie en verandering in de ruimtelijke economie van de Nederlanden ca. 1550-ca. 1630*. Amsterdamse historische reeks : Grote serie dl. 27. Hilversum: Verloren, 2001.

Lesger, Clé. "Intraregional Trade and the Port System in Holland, 1400–1700." Edited by Karel Davids and Leo Noordegraaf. Dutch *Economy in the Golden Age, Economic and Social history in the Netherlands*, 1993, 186–217.

Lesger, Clé. *The Rise of the Amsterdam Market and Information Exchange: Merchants, Commercial Expansion and Change in the Spatial Economy of the Low Countries, c.1550–1630*. Translated by John Christopher Grayson. Aldershot etc.: Ashgate, 2006.

Liesker, R. "Tot zinkens toe bezwaard. De schuldenlast van het Zuiderkwartier van Holland 1672–1794." In *Bestuurders en geleerden: opstellen over onderwerpen uit de Nederlandse geschiedenis van de zestiende, zeventiende en achttiende eeuw, aangeboden aan Prof. Dr. J.J. Woltjer bij zijn afscheid als hoogleraar van de Rijksuniversiteit te Leiden*, edited by Jan Juliaan Woltjer, Simon Groenveld, and Marianne Elisabeth Henriette Nicolette Mout, 151–60. Amsterdam etc.: De Bataafsche Leeuw, 1985.

Liesker, R., and W. Fritschy. *Gewestelijke financiën ten tijde van de Republiek der Verenigde Nederlanden. Deel IV. Holland (1572–1795)*. Rijks geschiedkundige publicatiën. Kleine serie, ISSN 0921-9064 100. Den Haag: Instituut voor Nederlandse Geschiedenis, 2004.

Loosjes, Petrus Adriaanszoon, and Jan Wagenaar. *Vaderlandsche historie, vervattende de geschiedenissen der Vereenigde Nederlanden, uit de geloofwaardigste schrijvers en egte gedenkstukken zamengest.: ten onmiddelyken vervolge van Wagenaars Vaderlandsche historie door Jan Wagenaar. Drie-en-twintigste deel. Beginnende met den jaare 1759 en eindigende met den jaare 1765, bevattende het tydperk der minderjaarigheid des erfstadhouders Willem den V.* Vol. 23. Amsterdam: by Johannes Allart, 1789.

Lourens, Piet, and Jan Lucassen. *Inwoneraantallen van Nederlandse steden ca. 1300–1800*. Amsterdam: NEHA, 1997.

Lucassen, Jan. *Migrant Labour in Europe, 1600–1900: The Drift to the North Sea*. Edited by Donald A. Bloch. London etc.: Croom Helm, 1987.

Matthey, I. B. M. "Op fiscaal kompas. Een bijdrage tot de economische geschiedenis van het gewest Groningen in de 17e en 18e eeuw, met toespitsingen op de dorpen in de huidige gemeente Stedum." In *Westeremden: het verleden van een Gronings terpdorp*, edited by I. B. M. Matthey, 195–360. Studies / uitg. door de Kring Vrienden van het Rijksarchief in Groningen. Groningen, 1975.

Matthey, I. B. M, ed. *Westeremden: het verleden van een Gronings terpdorp*. Studies / uitg. door de Kring Vrienden van het Rijksarchief in Groningen. Groningen, 1975.

Meerendonk, Suzanne van de, Margriet van Eikema Hommes, Ester Vink, and Ad van Drunen. "Striving for Unity: The Significance and Original Context of Political Allegories by Theodoor van Thulden for 's-Hertogenbosch Town Hall." *Early Modern Low Countries* 1, no. 2 (December 22, 2017): 231–72. https://doi.org/10.18352/emlc.26.

Meihuizen, L.S. "Sociaal-economische geschiedenis van Groningerland." In *Historie van Groningen: stad en land*, edited by Wiebe Jannes Formsma, 293–330. Groningen: Tjeenk Willink, 1976.

Miller, Stephen. "Venal Offices, Provincial Assemblies and the French Revolution." *French History* 28, no. 3 (September 1, 2014): 343–65. https://doi.org/10.1093/fh/cru048.

Mitchell, B. R. *British Historical Statistics*. CUP Archive, 1988.

Mitchener, Kris James, and Marc D. Weidenmier. "Supersanctions and Sovereign Debt Repayment." *Journal of International Money and Finance* 29, no. 1 (February 2010): 19–36. https://doi.org/10.1016/j.jimonfin.2008.12.011.

Mokyr, Joel. *Industrialization in the Low Countries, 1795–1850*. Yale Series in Economic History. New Haven, Conn., etc.: Yale University Press, 1976.

Mol, J.A. "Hoofdelingen en huurlingen. Militaire innovatie en de aanloop tot 1498." In *Fryslân, staat en macht 1450–1650 : bijdragen aan het historisch congres te Leeuwarden van 3 tot 5 juni 1998*, edited by J. Frieswijk, A.H. Huussen jr., Y.B. Kuiper, and J.A. Mol, 64–84. FA 875. Hilversum: VerlorenLeeuwarden : Fryske Akademy, 1999.

Murphy, Anne L. "Demanding 'Credible Commitment' : Public Reactions to the Failures of the Early Financial Revolution." *The Economic History Review* 66, no. 1 (2013): 178–97.

Murphy, Anne L. . "Lotteries in the 1690s: Investment or Gamble?" *Financial History Review* 12, no. 02 (2005): 227–46. https://doi.org/10.1017/S0968565005000119.

Murphy, Anne L. . *The Origins of English Financial Markets: Investment and Speculation before the South Sea Bubble.* Cambridge Studies in Economic History . Second Series. Cambridge etc.: Cambridge University Press, 2009.

Neal, Larry. "How It All Began: The Monetary and Financial Architecture of Europe during the First Global Capital Markets, 1648–1815." *Financial History Review* 7, no. 2 (2000): 117–40.

Neele, Arno. *De ontdekking van het Zeeuwse platteland: culturele verhoudingen tussen stad en platteland in Zeeland 1750–1850.* Balans tussen stad en platteland 3. Zwolle: Waanders : Universiteit Utrecht, 2011.

Niessen, Willy. *De Nijmeegse onroerend goedmarkt 1570–1630: een onderzoek naar de bewegingen op en de deelnemers aan de Nijmeegse onroerend goed- en kredietmarkt.* [s.n.], 2005.

Nieuwe Nederlandsche jaerboeken of vervolg der merkwaardigste: geschiedenissen die voorgevallen zyn in de Vereenigde Provincien de generaliteitslanden ende volksplantingen van de staat 1766–1792. Vol. 23–2. 23. Amsterdam / Leiden, 1788.

Nieuwland, Pieter. *Friezen gezocht: gids voor stamboomonderzoek in Friesland.* Leeuwarden: Tresoar Den Haag : Centraal Bureau voor Genealogie, 2005.

Nijboer, Harm Tjeerd. *De fatsoenering van het bestaan: consumptie in Leeuwarden tijdens de Gouden Eeuw.* [s.n.], 2007.

Nijenhuis, Ida J.A. "'Shining Comet, Falling Meteor': Reflections on the Dutch Republic as a Commercial Power during the Second Stadholderless Era." In *Anthonie Heinsius and the Dutch Republic 1688–1720: Politics, War, and Finance*, edited by Jan Arie Frederik de Jongste and Augustus Johannes, Veenendaal jr, 115–29. ING Workshop Series; RGP. The Hague: Institute of Netherlands History, 2002.

Nimwegen, O. van. "The Dutch Barrier: Its Origins, Creation, and Importance for the Dutch Republic, 1697–1718." In *Anthonie Heinsius and the Dutch Republic 1688–1720: Politics, War, and Finance*, edited by Jan Arie Frederik de Jongste and Augustus Johannes, Veenendaal jr, 147–76. ING-Workshop Series; RGP. The Hague: Institute of Netherlands History, 2002.

Nobel, Arjen. *Besturen op het Hollandse platteland. Cromstrijen 1550–1780*. Zutphen: Walburg Pers, 2012.

Noordegraaf, Leo, and Jan Luiten Van Zanden. "Vroegmoderne economische groei en levensstandaard in de Gouden Eeuw." In *Een wonder weerspiegeld: de Nederlandse Republiek in Europees perspectief*, edited by Karel Davids and Jan Lucassen, 381–408. Amsterdam: Aksant, 2005.

North, Douglass C., and Barry R. Weingast. "Constitutions and Commitment: The Evolution of Institutions Governing Public Choice in Seventeenth-Century England." *The Journal of Economic History* 49, no. 4 (1989): 803–32.

Notulen van de Edel Mogende Heeren Staten van Zeelandt; Notulen van de Staten van Zeelandt; Notulen Der Provisionele Repraesentanten van Het Volk van Zeeland; *Notulen van de Vertegenwoordigers Des Volks van Zeeland; Notulen van Het Departementaal Bestuur van Zeeland; Notulen van Zeelant*, 1798.

Nusteling, H. P. H., and Ph van der Weegen. "Dopen en trouwen en de bevolkingsomvang van Friesland in de periode 1655–1794." *It beaken : meidielingen fan de Fryske Akademy* 46 (1984): 105–38.

Occhino, Filippo, Kim Oosterlinck, and Eugene N. White. "How Much Can a Victor Force the Vanquished to Pay? France under the Nazi Boot." *The Journal of Economic History* 68, no. 01 (March 2008): 1–45. https://doi.org/10.1017/S0022050708000016.

Oddens, Joris, Mart Rutjes, and Arthur Westeijn, eds. *Discourses of Decline: Essays on Republicanism in the Honor of Wyger R.E. Velema*. Leiden: Brill, 2021. https://doi.org/10.1163/9789004470651_006.

Oldenhof, H. "Skraebjen om jild." In *Friesland in het rampjaar 1672 : it jier fan de miste kânsen*, edited by Jacob Jetzes Kalma and Klaas de Vries, 186–222. Fryske Akademy 421. Ljouwert, 1972.

Olson, Mancur. *Rise and Decline of Nations: Economic Growth, Stagflation, and Social Rigidities*. Yale University Press, 2008.

Olthof, Jelte. "Oer 'Fryske Frijheid': Fries En Vrij in Revolutietijd." *It Beaken. Tydskrift Fan de Fryske Akademy* 81, no. 1/2 (2019): 15–30.

Onnekink, David. *Reinterpreting the Dutch Forty Years War, 1672–1713*. London: Palgrave Macmillan, 2016.

Oosterlinck, Kim, Loredana Ureche-Rangau, and Jacques-Marie Vaslin. "Aristocratic Privilege. Exploiting 'Good' Institutions'." *CEPR Discussion Paper Series DP* 140771 (v.2) (October 2019).

Oosterlinck, Kim, Loredana Ureche-Rangau, and Jacques-Marie Vaslin. "Baring, Wellington and the Resurrection of French Public Finances Following Waterloo." *The Journal of Economic History* 74, no. 04 (December 2014): 1072–1102. https://doi.org/10.1017/S0022050714000862.

Oppers, Stefan E. "The Interest Rate Effect of Dutch Money in Eighteenth-Century Britain." *The Journal of Economic History* 53, no. 1 (1993): 25–43.

Ormrod, William Mark, Margaret Bonney, and Richard Bonney, eds. *Crises Revolutions and Self-Sustained Growth: Essays in European Fiscal History, 1130–1830*. Stamford: Shaun Tyas, 1999.

Paesie, Ruud. *Geschiedenis van de MCC: opkomst, bloei en ondergang*. Zutphen: Walburg Pers, 2014.

Panizza, Ugo. "4 Is Domestic Debt the Answer to Debt Crises?" In *Overcoming Developing Country Debt Crises*, edited by Barry Herman, José Antonio Ocampo, and

Shari Spiegel, 91–108. Oxford University Press, 2010. https://doi.org/10.1093/acprof:oso/9780199578788.003.0004.

Paping, Richard. "General Dutch Population Development 1400–1850: Cities and Countryside." *Paper Presented at 1st ESHD Conference*, Alghero, Italy., 2014.

Paping, Richard. "Groei of stagnatie." *Gronings historisch jaarboek*, 2000, 41–58.

Paping, Richard. "Parasiteren op het platteland? De stad Groningen en de Ommelanden in de tweede helft van de achttiende eeuw." In *Stad en regio: opstellen aangeboden aan prof. dr. Pim Kooij bij zijn afscheid als hoogleraar economische en sociale geschiedenis aan de Rijksuniversiteit Groningen*, edited by Geurt A. Collenteur, Maarten Duijvendak, Richard Paping, and Hanneke Vries de, 57–70. Groninger historische reeks 40. Assen: Koninklijke Van Gorcum, 2010.

Paping, Richard. *"Voor een handvol stuivers": werken, verdienen en besteden*. Groningen: Nederlands Agronomisch-Historisch Instituut, 1995.

Paping, Richardus F.J., and Paulus Brood. "De protocollen van verzegelingen in de Groningse oud-rechterlijke archieven." In *Broncommentaren 4: Bronnen betreffende de registratie van onroerend goed in Middeleeuwen en Ancien Régime*, edited by G.A.M. Van Synghel, 55–82. Den Haag: Instituut voor Nederlandse Geschiedenis, 2001.

Petram, Lodewijk. *The World's First Stock Exchange: How the Amsterdam Market for Dutch East India Company Shares Became a Modern Securities Market, 1602–1700*. Amsterdam: Unpublished PhD-thesis Universiteit van Amsterdam, 2011.

Petram, Lodewijk Otto. *De bakermat van de beurs: hoe in zeventiende-eeuws Amsterdam de moderne aandelenhandel ontstond*. Amsterdam etc.: Atlas, 2011.

Pezzolo, Luciano. "Sovereign Debts, Political Structure, and Institutional Commitments in Italy, 1350–1700." In *Questioning Credible Commitment: Perspectives on the Rise of Financial Capitalism*, edited by D'Maris Coffman, Adrian Leonard, and Larry Neal, 169–98. Macroeconomic Policy Making. Cambridge: Cambridge University Press, 2013.

Pfeil, Tom. *"Tot redding van het vaderland": het primaat van de Nederlandse overheidsfinanciën in de Bataafs-Franse tijd 1795–1810*. NEHA-series III 28. Amsterdam: NEHA, 1998.

Poell, Thomas. "Local Particularism Challenged, 1795–1813." In *The Political Economy of the Dutch Republic*, edited by O.C. Gelderblom, 223–54. Farnham etc.: Ashgate, 2009.

Postma, Obe. "Slechte betalers in de Gouden Eeuw." *De vrije Fries* 45 (1962): 155–60.

Poterba, James E. "Annuities in Early Modern Europe." In *The Origins of Value: The Financial Innovations That Created Modern Capital Markets*, edited by William N. Goetzmann and K. Geert Rouwenhorst, 207–24. Oxford etc.: Oxford University Press, 2005.

Prak, Maarten. "Republiek En Vorst. De Stadhouders En Het Staatsvormingsproces in de Noordelijke Nederlanden, 16e-18e Eeuw." *Amsterdams Sociologisch Tijdschrift* 16 (1989): 28–52.

Prak, Maarten. *Gezeten burgers: de elite in een Hollandse stad.* Amsterdam: De Bataafsche Leeuw, 1985.

Prak, Maarten. *The Dutch Republic in the Seventeenth Century: The Golden Age*. Translated by Diane L. Webb. Cambridge etc.: Cambridge University Press, 2005.

Prak, Maarten, and Jan Luiten Van Zanden. "Tax Morale and Citizenship in the Dutch Republic." In *The Political Economy of the Dutch Republic*, edited by O.C. Gelderblom, 143–66. Farnham etc.: Ashgate, 2009.

Prak, Maarten, and Jan Luiten van Van Zanden. *Pioneers of Capitalism the Netherlands 1000–1800*. Princeton: Princeton University Press, 2022.

Price, John Leslie. *Dutch Society, 1588–1713*. Harlow etc.: Longman, 2000.

Priester, Peter R. *Geschiedenis van de Zeeuwse landbouw, circa 1600–1910. A.A.G. bijdragen*, 37. Wageningen: Afdeling Agrarische Geschiedenis, Landbouwuniversiteit, 1998.

Prins, Izak. *Het faillissement der Hollandsche steden: Amsterdam, Dordrecht, Leiden en Haarlem in het jaar 1494, uit de wordingsgeschiedenis van den Nederlandschen Staat.* Amsterdam: Van Looy, 1922.

Reinhart, Carmen M., and Kenneth S. Rogoff. "Growth in a Time of Debt." *The American Economic Review* 100, no. 2 (May 1, 2010): 573–78.

Reinhart, Carmen M., and Kenneth S. Rogoff. *This Time Is Different: Eight Centuries of Financial Folly*. Princeton, NJ etc.: Princeton University Press, 2009.

Riley, James C. *International Government Finance and the Amsterdam Capital Market, 1740–1815*. Cambridge etc.: Cambridge University Press, 1980.

Rodger, N. A. M. "From the 'Military Revolution' to the 'Fiscal-Naval State.'" *Journal for Maritime Research* 13, no. 2 (November 1, 2011): 119–28. https://doi.org/10.1080/21533369.2011.622886.

Roelfsema, E.H. *De klooster- en proosdijgoederen in de provincie Groningen.* Groningen etc.: Wolters, 1928.

Roodhuyzen-van Breda Vriesman, Dorothea Josephine Antoinette. "Onfrisse Friese zaken. Een admiraliteit in opspraak." In *In het kielzog: maritiem-historische studies aangeboden aan Jaap R. Bruijn bij zijn vertrek als hoogleraar zeegeschiedenis aan de Universiteit Leiden*, edited by Jacobus Ruurd Bruijn and Leonardus Maria Akveld, 98–110. Amsterdam: De Bataafse Leeuw, 2003.

Roseveare, Henry. *The Financial Revolution, 1660–1760*. Seminar Studies in History. London [etc]: Longman, 1991.

Rousseau, Peter L., and Richard Sylla. "Emerging Financial Markets and Early US Growth." *Explorations in Economic History* 42, no. 1 (2005): 1–26.

Rousseau, Peter L., and Richard Sylla. "Financial Revolutions and Economic Growth: Introducing This EEH Symposium." *Explorations in Economic History* 43, no. 1 (January 2006): 1–12. https://doi.org/10.1016/j.eeh.2005.10.002.

Rousseau, Peter L., and Richard Sylla. "Financial Systems, Economic Growth, and Globalization." In *Globalization in Historical Perspective*, edited by Michael D. Bordo, Alan M. Taylor, and Jeffrey G. Williamson, 373–415. National Bureau of Economic Research Conference Report. Chicago, IL etc.: University of Chicago Press, 2003.

Rouwenhorst, K. Geert. "The Origins of Mutual Funds." In *The Origins of Value: The Financial Innovations That Created Modern Capital Markets*, edited by William N. Goetzmann and K. Geert Rouwenhorst, 249–69. Oxford etc.: Oxford University Press, 2005.

Sannes, H. "De Bildtrenten." *De vrije Fries : mengelingen* 39 (1948): 91–118.

Schroor, Meindert. "Een Vlucht Voorwaarts." *Historisch Jaarboek Groningen*, 2003, 37–57.

Schroor, Meindert. "Heroriëntatie op de Unie en op Holland." In Geschiedenis van Groningen II. Nieuwe Tijd, edited by M. G. J. Duijvendak, H. Feenstra, M. Hillenga, and C.G. Santing, 153–210. Zwolle: Waanders, 2008.

Schroor, Meindert. "Interne staatkundige verhoudingen in Stad en Lande." In *Geschiedenis van Groningen II. Nieuwe Tijd*, edited by M. G. J. Duijvendak, H. Feenstra, M. Hillenga, and C.G. Santing, 211–30. Zwolle: Waanders, 2008.

Schroor, Meindert. "Mens en land in de zestiende eeuw." In *Geschiedenis van Groningen II. Nieuwe Tijd*, edited by M. G. J. Duijvendak, H. Feenstra, M. Hillenga, and C.G. Santing, 11–34. Zwolle: Waanders, 2008.

Schroor, Meindert. *Rurale metropool: bevolking, migratie en financiën van de stad Groningen ten tijde van de Republiek (1595–1795)*. Historia agriculturae, ISSN 0439-2027 46. Groningen: Nederlands Agronomisch Historisch Instituut, 2014.

Schroor, Meindert, and Otto S. Knottnerus. "De Opstand 1568–1594." In *Geschiedenis van Groningen II. Nieuwe Tijd*, edited by M. G. J. Duijvendak, H. Feenstra, M. Hillenga, and C.G. Santing, 107–52. Zwolle: Waanders, 2008.

Schroor, Meindert, and Otto S. Knottnerus. "Stad en Lande, het Duitse Rijk en de Nederlanden 1498–1536." In *Geschiedenis van Groningen II. Nieuwe Tijd*, edited by M. G. J. Duijvendak, H. Feenstra, M. Hillenga, and C.G. Santing, 35–49. Zwolle: Waanders, 2008.

Schroor, Meindert, and Otto S. Knottnerus. "Verharding en verscherping 1536–1568." In *Geschiedenis van Groningen II. Nieuwe Tijd*, edited by M. G. J. Duijvendak, H. Feenstra, M. Hillenga, and C.G. Santing, 71–106. Zwolle: Waanders, 2008.

Schuitema Meijer, A. T. "Sociaal-economische aspecten van de stad." In *Historie van Groningen: stad en land*, edited by Wiebe Jannes Formsma, 331–60. Groningen: Tjeenk Willink, 1976.

Schuitema Meijer, A.T. "De Stad Groningen tijdens het beleg." In *Groningen constant: Groningen-Munster 1672*, edited by Abraham Westers, 55–80. Groningen: Wolters-Noordhoff, 1972.

Schultz, Kenneth A., and Barry R. Weingast. "The Democratic Advantage: Institutional Foundations of Financial Power in International Competition." *International Organization* 57, no. 1 (January 2003): 3–42. https://doi.org/10.1017/S0020818303571065.

Schultz, Kenneth A., and Barry R. Weingast. *The Democratic Advantage: The Institutional Sources of State Power in International Competition*. Essays in Public Policy. Stanford, Calif.: Hoover Institution on War, Revolution, and Peace, Stanford University, 1996.

Sicking, Louis. "Politieke geschiedenis, gewestelijke en bovengewestelijke bestuursinstellingen." In *Geschiedenis van Zeeland. Dl. 1: Prehistorie-1550*, edited by Paul Brusse, Pieter Arij Henderikx, and Frans Beekman, 226–42. Zwolle: WBOOKS, 2012.

Slooten, P. J. D. van. "Frieslands financiën in 1709 en 1770." *Friesche Volksalmanak*, 1885, 1–16.

Spanninga, Hotso. "Friesland in de nadagen van het Ancien Régime." In *Geschiedenis van Friesland 1750–1995*, edited by Jouke Arend Frieswijk, 18–39. Fryske Akademy 853. Amsterdam etc.: Boom Leeuwarden : Fryske Akademy, 1998.

Spanninga, Hotso. *Gulden vrijheid?: politieke cultuur en staatsvorming in Friesland, 1600–1640*. Hilversum: Verloren, 2012.

Stapelbroek, Koen, and Antonio Trampus. "Commercial Reform against the Tide: Reapproaching the Eighteenth-Century Decline of the Republics of Venice and the United Provinces." *History of European Ideas* 36, no. 2 (June 1, 2010): 192–202. https://doi.org/10.1016/j.histeuroideas.2009.11.001.

Stasavage, David. *States of Credit: Size, Power, and the Development of European Polities*. The Princeton Economic History of the Western World. Princeton, NJ etc.: Princeton University Press, 2011.

Stasavage, David. "What We Can Learn from the Early History of Sovereign Debt." *Explorations in Economic History* 59 (January 2016): 1–16. https://doi.org/10.1016/j.eeh.2015.09.005.

Stienstra, Johannes, and Gerrit Groenhuis. "De Veenhuizer venen in de gouden eeuw: een mislukte Hollandse investering." *Nieuwe Drentse volksalmanak* 101 (1984): 69–83.

Sussman, Nathan, and Yishay Yafeh. "Institutional Reforms, Financial Development and Sovereign Debt: Britain 1690–1790." *The Journal of Economic History* 66, no. 04 (2006): 906–35. https://doi.org/10.1017/S0022050706000374.

Sylla, Richard. "Financial Systems and Economic Modernization." *The Journal of Economic History* 62, no. 02 (2002): 277–92. https://doi.org/10.1017/S0022050702000505.

Temin, Peter, and Hans-Joachim Voth. "Credit Rationing and Crowding out during the Industrial Revolution: Evidence from Hoare's Bank, 1702–1862." *Explorations in Economic History* 42, no. 3 (2005): 325–48. https://doi.org/10.1016/j.eeh.2004.10.004.

Theissen, Johann Samuel. *Centraal gezag en Friesche vrijheid: Friesland onder Karel V.* Groningen: M. De Waal, 1907.

Thoe Schwartzenberg en Hohenlansberg, Georg Frederik baron, ed. *Register van verbonden, zoenen, accoorden, privilegien, handvesten ... en missiven: zullende dienen, volgens de resolutie der Ed. Mog. Heeren Staaten van Vriesland de dato den 31 Augusti 1764. tot d'uitgave van een groot placaat- en charter-boek.: Aanvang neemende met de eerste en oudste gedenkstukken, en eyndigende met het jaar 1748.* Te Leeuwarden,: gedrukt by Willem Coulon ..., 1765.

Tijms, Wigbolt. *Groninger graanprijzen: de prijzen van agrarische producten tussen 1546 en 1990.* Historia agriculturae, ISSN 0439-2027 31. Groningen etc.: Nederlands Agronomisch Historisch Instituut, 2000.

Tilly, Charles. *Coercion, Capital, and European States, AD 990–1992. Studies in Social Discontinuity.* Cambridge, MA etc.: Blackwell, 1992.

Tomz, Michael. *Reputation and International Cooperation: Sovereign Debt across Three Centuries.* Princeton, NJ etc.: Princeton University Press, 2007.

Torres Sánchez, Rafael. "Absolutism and Fiscal Transparency in Eighteenth-Century Spain." *Histoire & Mesure* XXX, no. 2 (2015): 189–214.

TorresSánchez, Rafael, ed. *War, State and Development: Fiscal-Military States in the Eighteenth Century.* Pamplona: Ediciones Universidad de Navarra, 2007.

Tracy, James. "The Age of Fiscal Intermediation in Europe, 1300–1800." In *Publieke financiën in de Lage Landen (1300–1800)*, edited by Jaco Zuijderduijn and Dries Raeymaekers, 13–26. Publicaties van de Vlaams-Nederlandse Vereniging Voor Nieuwe Geschiedenis 14. Maastricht: Shaker Publishing, 2015.

Tracy, James D. *A Financial Revolution in the Habsburg Netherlands: "Renten" and "Renteniers" in the County of Holland, 1515–1565.* Berkeley etc.: University of California Press, 1985.

Tracy, James D. "Emigré and Ecclesiastical Property as the Sheet-Anchor of Holland's Finance, 1572- 1584." In *Reformation, Revolt and Civil War in France and the Netherlands 1555–1585*, edited by Philip Benedict, Guido Marnef, and Henk van Nierop, 255–66. Verhandelingen Der Koninklijke Nederlandse Akademie van Wetenschappen. Afd. Letterkunde: Nieuwe Reeks 176. Amsterdam: Royal Netherlands Academy of Arts and Sciences, 1999.

Tracy, James D. "Holland's New Fiscal Regime, 1572–1576." In *The Political Economy of the Dutch Republic*, edited by O.C. Gelderblom, 41–54. Farnham etc.: Ashgate, 2009.

Trompetter, Cor. *Gewestelijke financiën ten tijde van de Republiek der Verenigde Nederlanden. Deel VI. Friesland (1587–1795).* 221. Den Haag: Instituut voor Nederlandse Geschiedenis, 2007.

Trompetter, Cornelis. "Burgers en boeren – geld en grond." *NEHA-jaarboek voor economische, bedrijfs- en techniekgeschiedenis* 60 (1997): 7–35.

Trompetter, Cornelis. *Eén grote familie: doopsgezinde elites in de Friese Zuidwesthoek 1600–1850*. Doperse documentaire reeks ; nr. 4; Fryske Akademy 998. Hilversum: Verloren, 2007.

Unger, Richard W. "Beer and Taxes: The Fiscal Significance for Holland and England in the Seventeenth and Eighteenth Centuries." *TSEG – The Low Countries Journal of Social and Economic History* 19, no. 1 (April 20, 2022): 61–86. https://doi.org/10.52024/tseg.11492.

Van Bavel, Bas, Tine De Moor, and Jan Luiten Van Zanden. "Introduction." *Continuity and Change* 24, no. 1 (2009): 9–22.

Van Bavel, Bas, and Jan Luiten Van Zanden. "The Jump-Start of the Holland Economy during the Late-Medieval Crisis, c.1350-c.1500." *The Economic History Review* 57, no. 3 (2004): 503–32.

Van Bochove, Christiaan. "Configuring Financial Markets in Preindustrial Europe." *The Journal of Economic History* 73, no. 1 (2013): 247–78.

Van Bochove, Christiaan. "External Debt and Commitment Mechanisms: Danish Borrowing in Holland, 1763–1825." *The Economic History Review* 67, no. 3 (August 1, 2014): 652–77. https://doi.org/10.1111/1468-0289.12050.

Van Bochove, Christiaan, and Heleen Kole. "Uncovering Private Credit Markets: Amsterdam, 1660–1809." *Tijdschrift Voor Sociale En Economische Geschiedenis* 11, no. 3 (2014): 39–72.

Van Bochove, Christiaan, and Ton van Velzen. "Loans to Salaried Employees: The Case of the Dutch East India Company, 1602–1794." *European Review of Economic History* 18 (2014): 19–38. https://doi.org/10.1093/ereh/het021.

Van Bochove, C.J. *The Economic Consequences of the Dutch: Economic Integration around the North Sea, 1500–1800*. Amsterdam: Aksant, 2008.

Van Cruyningen, P. J. Behoudend maar buigzaam: boeren in West-Zeeuws-Vlaanderen, 1650–1850. s.n.], 2000.

Van Cruyningen, P. J. "Economie." In *Geschiedenis van Zeeland. Dl. II: 1550–1700*, edited by Paul Brusse and Wijnand Mijnhardt, 51–101. Zwolle: WBOOKS, 2012.

Van Cruyningen, P. J. "Profits and Risks in Drainage Projects in Staats-Vlaanderen, c. 1590–1665." *Jaarboek Voor Ecologische Geschiedenis*, 123–142, 2006.

Van Cruyningen, Piet. "Bevolking en sociale verhoudingen." In *Geschiedenis van Zeeland. Dl. II: 1550–1700*, edited by Paul Brusse and Wijnand Mijnhardt, 103–45. Zwolle: WBOOKS, 2012.

Van Cruyningen, Piet. "Credit and Agriculture in the Netherlands, Eighteenth-Nineteenth Centuries." In *Credit and the Rural Economy in North-Western Europe, c.1200-c.1850*, edited by Phillipp R. Schofield and Thijs Lambrecht, 99–107. Corn Publication Series 12. Turnhout: Brepols, 2009.

Van Cruyningen, Piet. "From Disaster to Sustainability: Floods, Changing Property Relations and Water Management in the South-Western Netherlands, c.1500–1800." *Continuity and Change* 29, no. 02 (2014): 241–65. https://doi.org/10.1017/S0268416014000149.

Van Cruyningen, Piet. "Land en water." In *Geschiedenis van Zeeland. Dl. II: 1550–1700*, edited by Paul Brusse and Wijnand Mijnhardt, 15–49. Zwolle: WBOOKS, 2012.

Van de Voort, Jan. *De Westindische plantages van 1720–1795 : financiën en handel* / Johannes Petrus van de Voort. Sl: sn Eindhoven:, 1973.

Van de Voort, J.P. "Dutch Capital in the West Indies during the Eighteenth Century." *Acta Historiae Neerlandicae : Studies on the History of the Netherlands* 14 (1981): 85–105.

Van den Berg, J. C. "Friesland's Belastingen in de vorige eeuw." *De economist : tijdschrift voor alle standen, tot bevordering van volkswelvaart, door verspreiding van eenvoudige beginselen van staatshuishoudkunde* 39 (1890): 364–67.

Van der Bijl, Murk. *Idee en interest: voorgeschiedenis, verloop en achtergronden van de politieke twisten in Zeeland en vooral in Middelburg tussen 1702 en 1715*. Historische studies 42. Groningen: Wolters-Noordhoff/Bouma's Boekhuis, 1981.

Van der Burg, Martijn. "Burgers En Bestuurders : Rotterdamse Stadsfinanciën in de Tweede Helft van Den Zeventiende Eeuw." *Rotterdams Jaarboekje*, 2003, 106–30.

Van der Burg, Martijn, and Marjolein 't Hart. "Renteniers and the Recovery of Amsterdams Credit (1578–1605)." In *Urban public debts: urban government and the market for annuities in Western Europe (14th-18th centuries)*, edited by Marc Boone, Karel Davids, and Paul J. J. G. Janssens, 197–218. Studies in European Urban History (1100–1800) 3. Turnhout: Brepols, 2003.

Van der Ent, L., and V. Enthoven. *Gewestelijke financiën ten tijde van de Republick der Verenigde Nederlanden. Deel III. Groningen (1594–1795)*. 94. Den Haag: Instituut voor Nederlandse Geschiedenis, 2001.

Van der Ent, L., W. Fritschy, E. Horlings, and R. Liesker. "Public Finance in the United Provinces of the Netherlands in the Seventeenth and Eighteenth Centuries." In *Crises Revolutions and Self-Sustained Growth: Essays in European Fiscal History, 1130–1830*, edited by William Mark Ormrod, Margaret Bonney, and Richard Bonney, 249–93. Stamford: Shaun Tyas, 1999.

Van der Heijden, Manon. *Geldschieters van de stad: financiële relaties tussen stad, burgers en overheden 1550–1650*. Amsterdam: Bakker, 2006.

Van Dillen, J. G. "Effectenkoersen aan de Amsterdamsche Beurs 1723–1794." *Economisch-Historisch Jaarboek. Bijdragen tot de Economische Geschiedenis van Nederland* 17 (1931): 1–46.

Van Dillen, J.G., ed. *Bronnen tot de geschiedenis der wisselbanken.* (Amsterdam, Middelburg, Delft, Rotterdam). Rijks geschiedkundige publicatiën 60. 's-Gravenhage: Nijhoff, 1925.

Van Nimwegen, Olaf. *De Nederlandse burgeroorlog, 1748–1815*. Amsterdam: Prometheus, 2017.

Van Rossum, Matthias, and Karwan Jalal Fatah-Black. "Wat is winst? De economische impact van de Nederlandse trans-Atlantische slavenhandel." *Tijdschrift voor sociale en economische geschiedenis* 9, no. 1 (2012): 3–29.

Van Steensel, Arie. "De economie van het platteland." In *Geschiedenis van Zeeland. Dl. 1: Prehistorie-1550*, edited by Paul Brusse, Pieter Arij Henderikx, and Frans Beekman, 265–76. Zwolle: WBOOKS, 2012.

Van Tielhof, Milja. "After the Flood. Mobilizing Money in Order to Limit Economic Loss (the Netherlands, Sixteenth-Eighteenth Centuries)." *Gestione Dell'acqua in Europa (XII–XVIII Secc.). Water Management in Europe (12th-18th Centuries), Atti delle "Settimane di Studi" e altri Convegni*, 49 (2018): 393–411.

Van Winter, P.J. *De Westindische Compagnie ter kamer Stad en Lande*. Werken uitgegeven door de Vereeniging Het Nederlandsch Economisch-Historisch Archief 15. 's-Gravenhage: Nijhoff, 1978.

Van Zanden, J. L., and Arthur Van Riel. "Economische Geschiedenis Met Een Menselijk Gezicht." *BMGN – Low Countries Historical Review* 117, no. 3 (January 1, 2002): 364–69. https://doi.org/10.18352/bmgn-lchr.5715.

Van Zanden, Jan Luiten. "De demografische ontwikkeling van Overijssel 1475–1795." *Overijsselse historische bijdragen : verslagen en mededelingen van de Vereeniging tot Beoefening van Overijsselsch Regt en Geschiedenis* 109 (1994): 39–49.

Van Zanden, Jan Luiten. "Kosten van levensonderhoud en loonvorming in Holland en Oost-Nederland 1600–1850. De voorbeelden van Kampen en Alkmaar." *Tijdschrift voor sociale geschiedenis* 11 (1985): 309–23.

Van Zanden, Jan Luiten, and Maarten Prak. "Towards an Economic Interpretation of Citizenship." *European Review of Economic History* 10, no. 2 (2006): 111–46.

Van Zanden, Jan Luiten, and Bas Van Leeuwen. "Persistent but Not Consistent: The Growth of National Income in Holland 1347–1807." *Explorations in Economic History* 49, no. 2 (2012): 119–31. https://doi.org/10.1016/j.eeh.2011.11.002.

Van Zanden, Jan Luiten, and Arthur Van Riel. *Nederland 1780–1914: staat, instituties en economische ontwikkeling*. Amsterdam: Balans, 2000.

Van Zanden, Jan Luiten, and Arthur Van Riel. The *Strictures of Inheritance: The Dutch Economy in the Nineteenth Century*. The Princeton Economic History of the Western World. Princeton, NJ etc.: Princeton University Press, 2004.

Van Zanden, Jan Luiten, Jaco Zuijderduijn, and Tine De Moor. "Small Is Beautiful: The Efficiency of Credit Markets in the Late Medieval Holland." *European Review of Economic History* 16, no. 1 (January 2, 2012): 3–22. https://doi.org/10.1093/ereh/her007.

Veenendaal jr, Augustus J. "Fiscal Crises and Constitutional Freedom in the Netherlands, 1450–1795." In *Fiscal Crises, Liberty, and Representative Government, 1450–*

1789, edited by Philip T. Hoffman and Kathryn Norberg, 96–139. The Making of Modern Freedom. Stanford, Calif.: Stanford University Press, 1994.

Veenstra, Wietse. "Geld is de zenuw van de oorlog." *Archief: vroegere en latere mededeelingen voornamelijk in betrekking tot Zeeland*, 2008, 91–120.

Veenstra, Wietse. *Gewestelijke financiën ten tijde van de Republiek der Verenigde Nederlanden. Deel VII. Zeeland (1573–1795)*. Rijks geschiedkundige publicatiën. Kleine serie 110. Den Haag: Instituut voor Nederlandse Geschiedenis, 2009.

Veenstra, Wietse. *Tussen gewest en Generaliteit: staatsvorming en financiering van de oorlog te water in de Republiek der Verenigde Nederlanden, in het bijzonder Zeeland* (1586–1795). Nederland, 2014.

Veenstra, Wietse, and Arjan Otte. "Financiering van de oorlogvoering te water. De admiraliteit van Zeeland, 1597–1795." In *Overheidsfinanciën tijdens de Republiek en het Koninkrijk, 1600–1850*, edited by Hendrik Boels, 9–38. Hilversum: Verloren, 2012.

Velde, François R., and David R. Weir. "The Financial Market and Government Debt Policy in France, 1746–1793." *The Journal of Economic History* 52, no. 1 (1992): 1–39.

Velema, Wyger R. E. *Republicans: Essays on Eighteenth-Century Dutch Political Thought*. Brill's Studies in Intellectual History, ISSN 0920-8607 155. Leiden etc.: Brill, 2007.

Verhas, Christel M.O. *De beginjaren van de Hoge Raad van Holland, Zeeland en West-Friesland: ... tot onderhoudinge van de Politique ordre ende staet der Landen van Hollandt, Zeelandt, Vrieslant ...* 5. Den Haag: Algemeen Rijksarchief, 1997.

Verstegen, S.W. *Gewestelijke financiën ten tijde van de Republiek der Verenigde Nederlanden. Deel V. Utrecht (1579–1798)*. Rijks geschiedkundige publicatiën. Kleine serie 105. Den Haag: Instituut voor Nederlandse Geschiedenis, 2006.

Vliet, Adrianus Paulus van. *Vissers in oorlogstijd: de Zeeuwse zeevisserij in de jaren 1568–1648*. Werken / uitg. door het Koninklijk Zeeuwsch Genootschap der Wetenschappen, ISSN 0168-7182 14. Middelburg: Koninklijk Zeeuwsch Genootschap der Wetenschappen, 2003.

Vries, Oebele. "Staatsvorming in Zwitserland en Frieland in de vijftiende en zestiende eeuw." In *Fryslân, staat en macht 1450–1650 : bijdragen aan het historisch congres te Leeuwarden van 3 tot 5 juni 1998*, edited by J. Frieswijk, A.H. Huussen jr., Y.B. Kuiper, and J.A. Mol, 26–42. FA 875. Hilversum: VerlorenLeeuwarden : Fryske Akademy, 1999.

Vries, P. H. H. State, *Economy and the Great Divergence Great Britain and China, 1680s-1850s*. London etc.: Bloomsbury, 2015.

Vries, Peer. "Does Wealth Entirely Depend on Inclusive Institutions and Pluralist Politics? A Review of Daron Acemoglu and James A. Robinson, Why Nations Fail. The Origins of Power, Prosperity and Poverty." *TSEG – The Low Countries Journal of Social and Economic History* 9, no. 3 (September 15, 2012): 74–93. https://doi.org/10.18352/tseg.278.

Vries, Peer. "Inevitable Decline? A Review of Bas van Bavel, The Invisible Hand? How Market Economies Have Emerged and Declined since Ad 500 (Oxford, 2016)." *International Review of Social History* 62, no. 1 (April 2017): 131–47. https://doi.org/10.1017/S0020859017000025.

Wagenaar, Frederik Pieter. "Achttiende-eeuwse overheidsfinanciën: kleine veranderingen met grote gevolgen." In *Overheidsfinanciën tijdens de Republiek en het Koninkrijk, 1600–1850*, edited by Hendrik Boels, 119–35. Hilversum: Verloren, 2012.

Wagenaar, Jan. *Vaderlandsche historie, vervattende de geschiedenissen der nu Vereenigde Nederlanden, inzonderheid die van Holland, van de vroegste tyden af: Agttiende deel, beginnende met het jaar 1713, en eindigende met het sluiten van het Verdrag van Seville, in 't jaar 1729*. Te Amsterdam,: by Johannes Allart, 1795.

Wagenaar, Jan. *Vaderlandsche historie, vervattende de geschiedenissen der nu Vereenigde Nederlanden, inzonderheid die van Holland, van de vroegste tyden af: Vyftiende deel, beginnende met het jaar 1679, en eindigende met de verheffing van den prinse en prinsesse van Oranje, tot koning en koningin van Groot-Britanje, in 't jaar 1689*. Te Amsterdam,: by Johannes Allart, 1794.

Wagenvoort, Herman. *Tontines: een onderzoek naar de geschiedenis van de lijfrenten bij wijze van tontine en de contracten van overleving in de Republiek der Verenigde Nederlanden*. Utrecht, 1961.

Waterbolk, E.H. "Staatkundige geschiedenis." In *Historie van Groningen: stad en land*, edited by Wiebe Jannes Formsma, 235–76. Groningen: Tjeenk Willink, 1976.

Wegener Sleeswijk, R. S. "Rendement van 36 Friese partenrederijen (1740–1830)." *Jaarboek Fries Scheepvaart Museum en Oudheidkamer*, 1986, 66–89.

Weingast, Barry R. "Second Generation Fiscal Federalism: The Implications of Fiscal Incentives." *Journal of Urban Economics* 65, no. 3 (May 1, 2009): 279–93. https://doi.org/10.1016/j.jue.2008.12.005.

Weststeijn, Arthur. *Commercial Republicanism in the Dutch Golden Age: The Political Thought of Johan & Pieter De La Court*. Leiden: BRILL, 2011.

Wilson, Ch. *Anglo-Dutch Commerce and Finance in the Eighteenth Century*. Cambridge Studies in Economic History 84261320X. Cambridge [etc.]: Cambridge University Press, 1941.

Wiskerke, Cornelis. "De Geschiedenis van Het Meekrapbedrijf in Nederland." *Economisch-Historisch Jaarboek : Bijdragen Tot de Economische Geschiedenis van Nederland* 25 (1951): 1–144.

Woltjer, J.J. "In de Leerschool Der Monarchie." In *Geschiedenis van Friesland*, edited by Jacob Jetzes Kalma, Johan Jacob Spahr van der Hoek, and Klaas de Vries, 259–83. Fryske Akademy, ISSN 2352-6947 325. Drachten: Laverman, 1968.

Woltjer, J.J. "Van Katholiek tot Protestant." In *Historie van Groningen: stad en land*, edited by Wiebe Jannes Formsma, 207–34. Groningen: Tjeenk Willink, 1976.

Wormgoor, Ingrid. *Turfschuiten en kustvaarders: een geschiedenis van de Groninger scheepsbouw*. Hilversum: Verloren, 2016.

Yun-Casalilla, Bartolomé, Patrick Karl O'Brien, and Francisco Comín Comín, eds. *The Rise of Fiscal States: A Global History, 1500–1914*. Cambridge etc.: Cambridge University Press, 2012.

Zandvliet, Kees. *De 250 rijksten van de Gouden Eeuw: kapitaal, macht, familie en levensstijl*. Edited by Paulien Retèl. Amsterdam: Rijksmuseum Amsterdam: Nieuw Amsterdam, 2006.

Zeeuws Archief. "Notariële Archieven Zeeland 1796–1842, 1796–1842 Okt. 15." Accessed July 27, 2015. http://www.archieven.nl/nl/zoeken?mivast=0&mizig=210&miadt=239&micode=13.1&milang=nl&miview=inv2.

Zijlstra, Suze. *Anglo-Dutch Suriname: Ethnic Interaction and Colonial Transition in the Caribbean, 1651–1682*. unpublished PhD-thesis Universiteit van Amsterdam, 2015.

Zuijderduijn, C. Jaco. "De laatmiddeleeuwse crisis van de overheidsfinanciën en de financiële revolutie in Holland." *Bijdragen en mededelingen betreffende de geschiedenis der Nederlanden* 125, no. 4 (2010): 3–24.

Zuijderduijn, C. Jaco. "Foreign Investment in Public Debt. Investors in Urban Public Debt in the Northern Low Countries, Fifteenth to Sixteenth Centuries." *Academia – Working Paper*, June 13, 2016.

Zuijderduijn, C.J. *Medieval Capital Markets: Markets for Renten, State Formation and Private Investment in Holland (1300–1550)*. Leiden etc.: Brill, 2009.

Zuijderduijn, Jaco. "The Emergence of Provincial Debt in the County of Holland (Thirteenth–Sixteenth Centuries)." *European Review of Economic History* 14, no. 3 (January 12, 2010): 335–59. https://doi.org/10.1017/S1361491610000055.

Zuijderduijn, Jaco. "Wining and dining of water en brood? Het fundamental problem of exchange in middeleeuws Dordrecht (ca. 1300)." In *Publieke financiën in de Lage Landen (1300–1800)*, edited by Jaco Zuijderduijn and Dries Raeymaekers, 27–48. Publicaties van de Vlaams-Nederlandse Vereniging Voor Nieuwe Geschiedenis 14. Maastricht: Shaker Publishing, 2015.

Zwitzer, Hans. L. "Het quotenstelsel onder de Republiek der Verenigde Nederlanden alsmede enkele beschouwingen over de generale petitie, de staat van oorlog en de repartitie." *Mededelingen van de Sectie Militaire Geschiedenis, Landmachtstaf* 5 (1982): 5–57.

Index